The Economic Development of the EEC

The Economic Development of Modern Europe since 1870

Series Editor: Charles Feinstein
Chichele Professor of Economic History
All Souls College, Oxford

The Economic Development of the EEC

Edited by

Richard T. Griffiths

Professor of Economic and Social History, Rijksuniversiteit Leiden, The Netherlands

THE ECONOMIC DEVELOPMENT OF MODERN EUROPE SINCE 1870

An Elgar Reference Collection
Cheltenham, UK • Lyme, US

Published by
Edward Elgar Publishing Limited
8 Lansdown Place
Cheltenham
Glos GL50 2HU
UK

Edward Elgar Publishing, Inc.
1 Pinnacle Hill Road
Lyme
NH 03768
US

A catalogue record for this book is available from the British Library.

Library of Congress Cataloguing in Publication Data
The economic development of the E.E.C. / edited by Richard T.
   Griffiths.
        (The Economic development of modern Europe since
   1870; 12)
      Includes bibliographical references.
        1. European Economic Community—History. 2. Europe—Economic
integration—History. 3. European Economic Community countries-
-Economic policy—History. I. Griffiths, Richard T. II. Title:
Economic development of the EEC. III. Series.
HC241.2.E29248   1997
337.1'42—DC21   97–25025
                                                        CIP

ISBN 1 85278 782 1

Printed and bound in Great Britain by Bookcraft (Bath) Ltd

Contents

Acknowledgements

The editor and publishers wish to thank the authors and the following publishers who have kindly given permission for the use of copyright material.

Berg Publishers for excerpt: Werner Bührer (1995), 'German Industry and European Integration in the 1950s', in Clemens Wurm (ed.), *Western Europe and Germany. The Beginnings of European Integration 1945–1960*, 87–114.

Blackwell Publishers Ltd for articles: David G. Mayes (1978), 'The Effects of Economic Integration on Trade', *Journal of Common Market Studies* **XVII** (1), September, 1–25; Dimitrios G. Demekas, Kasper Bartholdy, Sanjeev Gupta, Leslie Lipschitz and Thomas Mayer (1988), 'The Effects of the Common Agricultural Policy of the European Community: A Survey of the Literature', *Journal of Common Market Studies*, **XXVII** (2), December, 113–45; Charles Young (1972), 'Association with the EEC: Economic Aspects of the Trade Relationship', *Journal of Common Market Studies*, **XI** (2), 120–35.

C.A.B. International for excerpt: Lionel Hubbard and Christopher Ritson (1991), 'The Reform of the CAP', in Christopher Ritson and David Harvey (eds), *The Common Agricultural Policy and the World Economy. Essays in Honour of John Ashton*, Chapter 16, 295–310.

F. Fauri for her own article: *Italy and the EEC Negotiations: An Economic Perspective*, EUI PhD, Chapter 6, 177–225.

Kogan Page Ltd for excerpt: Martin Bangemann (1992), 'The Best Example of Industrial Policy: The Single Market', *Meeting the Global Challenge: Establishing a Successful European Industrial Policy*, Chapter 3, 36–51.

Lothian Foundation Press for excerpt: W. Asbeek Brusse (1997), 'Regional Plans for European Trade, 1945–1957', in R.T. Griffiths (ed.), *Economic and Monetary Unions in the Past: From Continental System to Common Market*, forthcoming.

Methuen & Co. for excerpt: Alan S. Milward (1984), 'The Schuman Plan', *The Reconstruction of Western Europe 1945–51*, Chapter XII, 362–420.

M.I.T. Press for excerpt: J. Bradford De Long and Barry Eichengreen (1993), 'The Marshall Plan: History's Most Successful Structural Adjustment Program', in Rudiger Dornbush, Wilhelm Nölling and Richard Layard (eds), *Postwar Economic Reconstruction and Lessons for the East Today*, Chapter 8, 189–230.

Nederlandsch Economisch-Historisch Archief (NEHA) for excerpts: Richard T. Griffiths (1990), 'The Beyen Plan', in Richard T. Griffiths (ed.), *The Netherlands and the Integration of Europe 1945–1957*, Chapter VIII, 165–82; Richard T. Griffiths (1990), 'The Common Market', in Richard T. Griffiths (ed.), *The Netherlands and the Integration of Europe 1945–1957*, Chapter IX, 183–208.

Oxford University Press for excerpts: Michael Davenport (1982), 'The Economic Impact of the EEC', in Andrea Boltho (ed.), *The European Economy. Growth and Crisis*, Chapter 8, 225–58; Loukas Tsoukalis (1993), 'Regional Policies and Redistribution', *The New European Economy. The Politics and Economics of Integration*, Chapter 8, Second Revised Edition, 228–77, references.

Pinter Publishers, a Cassell imprint, and St. Martin's Press, Inc. for excerpt: Andrew Scott (1992), 'Internal Market Policy', in Simon Bulmer, Stephen George and Andrew Scott (eds), *The United Kingdom and EC Membership Evaluated*, Chapter 3, 16–28.

Pinter Publishers, a Cassell imprint, in association with the Royal Institute of International Affairs for excerpts: Elke Thiel (1990), 'Changing Patterns of Monetary Interdependence', in William Wallace (ed.), *The Dynamics of European Integration*, Chapter 4, 69–86; Margaret Sharp (1990), 'Technology and the Dynamics of Integration', in William Wallace (ed.), *The Dynamics of European Integration*, Chapter 3, 50–68.

Routledge for excerpts: Kevin Featherstone (1990), 'The Economic Implications of "1992"', *European Internal Market Policy*, 23–37; Frances M.B. Lynch (1993), 'Restoring France: The Road to Integration', in Alan S. Milward, Frances M.B. Lynch, Fuggero Ranieri, Federico Romero and Vibeke Sørensen (eds), *The Frontier of National Sovereignty. History and Theory 1945–1992*, Chapter 3, 59–87, notes.

Royal Institute of International Affairs for excerpt: Wynne Godley (1980), 'The United Kingdom and the Community Budget' plus 'Comment' by Stephen Milligan, in William Wallace (ed.), *Britain in Europe*, Chapter 4, 72–90; published by Heinemann for the N.I.E.S.R., P.S.I. and R.I.I.A. in the Joint Studies in Public Policy Series.

Sage Publications Ltd for excerpt: Andrew Britton and David Mayes (1992), 'The Road to Monetary Union', *Achieving Monetary Union in Europe*, Chapter 1, 1–21, references.

St. Martin's Press, Inc. and Macmillan Press Ltd for excerpt: Federico Romero (1996), 'U.S. Attitudes towards Integration and Interdependence: The 1950s', in Frances H. Heller and John R. Gillingham (eds), *The United States and the Integration of Europe: Legacies of the Postwar Era*, Chapter 5, 103–21.

In addition the publishers wish to thank the Library of the London School of Economics and Political Science and the Marshall Library of Economics, Cambridge University for their assistance in obtaining these articles.

Introduction

Richard T. Griffiths

Standing amid the rubble of bombed-out cities in the early summer of 1945 and reflecting upon a Europe dislocated by five years of war and destruction, few would have been optimistic about the prospects for future peace and prosperity. Even fewer would have expected that over the next six decades the two old enemies, France and Germany, would have formed the driving force of a series of initiatives that were to become the focus of the economic and political ambitions of an entire continent. From the Treaty of Rome (1957) to the Treaty of Maastricht (1992) that subsumed it into the European Union, these initiatives were dominated by the European Economic Community (EEC). This literature collection is not an economic history of Western Europe or of its constituent economies. Rather it attempts to follow the economic history of the creation and development of the EEC as an institution and to assess the impact on the policy areas under its control.

Towards the EEC 1945–55

The Marshall Plan has been assessed and reassessed from several perspectives. Its motivation has been variously ascribed (in approximate chronological order) to American altruism, American Cold War strategy and American enlightened self-interest. The evaluation of its macroeconomic impact has likewise swung from a critical contribution to European recovery to a more prosaic judgement that it merely facilitated an investment boom already underway. This down-playing of the quantitative aspect of the European Recovery Program (ERP) has generally been accepted by historians, but it has produced a reaction by some who emphasize, instead, the institutional dimensions. In this version, the ERP contributed to European recovery by consolidating a domestic consensus around growth and prosperity, and by creating an international framework that reduced 'transaction costs' and boosted business confidence. In this second dimension, the Marshall Plan becomes a useful starting point for an analysis of European 'integration' in the old-fashioned sense of the word (growing together). In Chapter 1, Brad De Long and Barry Eichengreen examine the impact of ERP in an implicit counterfactual that juxtaposes the European experience after World War I with that of Argentina after World War II. They conclude that its operation justifies the label of 'history's most successful structural adjustment programme through its contribution to financial stability, the reassertion of market forces and the creation of a "social contract" conducive to "supergrowth"'.[1]

This analysis represented the first major institutionalist contribution to the revisionism of the Marshall Plan and Eichengreen, especially, was to go on to develop the argument more strongly and more in the direction of the international framework that it inspired. Because of the focus of this volume, we have been unable to do this full justice but the argument hinges on the contribution of the trade liberalization and payments schemes initiated in 1950 that provided the context for the trade, and industrial, boom of the following decade. It was against this backdrop that a more limited group of countries – comprising initially France, Germany, Italy and the three Benelux countries – undertook a series of initiatives that were to lead to the formation of the European Economic Community (EEC). It also, thereby, initiated what is often referred to as the 'process of European integration', the term 'integration' referring now to a collectivity of decision-making and a surrender of national sovereignty.

The recent historical literature devoted to explaining early European integration falls largely into two categories. The more dominant political and federalist approach is to concentrate on the *form* of international organization and thus to trace a line from the 'European' ideas formulated in the wartime resistance, through the European movement and the Council of Europe to the supranational experiments launched by the European Coal and Steel Community (ECSC) and culminating in 1957 in the European Economic Community. In this type of account, the *object* plays, at best, a subsidiary role in the explanation. The economic approach pays far more attention to the nature of the problems to which new institutional frameworks were addressed. It claims to provide a better explanation for the *timing* and the *content* of new agreements than the more traditional approach. Whereas the two approaches are often juxtaposed, and indeed are often antipathetical towards each other, they are not necessarily incompatible. Jean Monnet, the architect of the ECSC, believed what was important was not the problem that had to be solved but the way in which it was done; but at least he acknowledged that it did have to be solved.

Wendy Asbeek Brusse in Chapter 2 demonstrates the persistence of the trade question in post-war Europe and places both the ECSC and the EEC within the context of a continuous search for a multilateral commercial agreement that resulted in a stream of initiatives launched in different international fora and addressed to different combinations of countries. She picks up the story with the Marshall Plan and the creation in the OEEC of a Study Group for a European Customs Union. However, the opposition of the United Kingdom and uncertainty over the future of West Germany after occupation led to the abandonment of the attempt in 1950. By that time a far more successful programme had been initiated that targeted the quantitative restrictions (quotas and licences) on European imports. Deficiencies in the programme and the 'unfair' workings for smaller economies prompted new initiatives, some of which tried to liberate particular sectors (including the ECSC) and others that attempted to obtain satisfactory treatment of tariffs. It was the failure of the latter in the Organization for European Economic Cooperation (OEEC), the General Agreement on Tariffs and Trade (GATT) and the Council of Europe, that prompted the search for an agreement among a smaller group of countries and that led to the EEC's creation.[2]

For those authors who describe the process of European integration in terms of supranational aspirations and supranational institutions, the Schuman plan that launched the ECSC is the first example of integration in practice. In Chapter 3, however, Alan Milward demonstrates why the sectors selected were coal and steel, why a new institutional structure was required in 1950 and why, in his eyes, it took the form it did. In each case the answer is found less in the tradition of federalist thought than in the conjuncture of real economic problems. He illustrates how the lifting of controls on German industry threatened to undermine the principles of French post-war planning and how this was aggravated by the danger of a slackening demand for steel. At the same time, the political legitimacy of the existing tripartite control over German economic and foreign policy was reduced by the recognition of the new German state whilst the effectiveness of that control was diminished by the differing policy priorities of the three Western allies. For these reasons French planners needed a new control over German heavy industry and, if necessary to attain it, they were willing to subject their own industry to the same regime. That such an outcome could count on the support of federalist groups in Europe, and coincided with ill-defined American desires for greater European integration, only increased the attractiveness of the solution.[3]

If French politicians had been wary of German reindustrialization they were even more horrified, a few months after the announcement of the Schuman Plan, when the Americans demanded German rearmament. Again the solution was sought in supranationality and the Pleven plan was announced for a European army. By 1952 the negotiations had progressed sufficiently for the six ECSC partners to sign the treaty creating a European Defence Community (EDC). At this point the Italians suggested that the treaty provisions for a new institutional structure should not wait until ratification, but that the process envisaged in the treaty be commenced immediately. The Dutch, who had only reluctantly participated in the EDC and who were cool towards the Italian proposal, made their acceptance conditional on the inclusion of economic tasks under the responsibilities of any new political arrangements. In this way, the Six soon found themselves discussing the Beyen plan for the creation of a customs union. My own contribution in Chapter 4 traces the range of opinion towards this initiative and demonstrates how the self-same linkages that brought it into the political agenda also served to bring about its demise. The rejection of the EDC by the French parliament killed off the Beyen plan as well. Yet, less than a year later, it was back on the agenda when the foreign ministers of the Six met at Messina.[4]

The Creation of the EEC

For all the symbolic baggage that the Messina meeting subsequently acquired for 'relaunching' Europe and starting the process that would lead to the Treaty of Rome and the creation of the European Economic Community (EEC) it was far from clear at the time that it would lead to a common market. The French, who had earlier resisted the Beyen plan, arrived at Messina determined to launch negotiations for an atomic energy community. The Germans, realizing that nothing could be achieved over the back of French opposition, arrived armed with fairly negative instructions on the issue. The Messina resolution avoided failure by including both the common market and the atomic community in a list of proposals (which included an extension of the ECSC to other classical energy forms and a transport community) referred to a study group under the leadership of the Belgian foreign minister Paul-Henri Spaak.

Frances Lynch in Chapter 5 ascribes French membership of the EEC to a search to secure national interests in the face of a competitive disadvantage inherited from before the war. If the common market could be constructed not only to alleviate some of the competitive problems, but also to relieve the colonial burden and to find a vent for agrarian surpluses, it could be an attractive proposition to policy makers. Lynch dates this realization to mid-1956 and attributes it to the threat posed by vague British free trade alternatives that would penalize the economy without offering any countervailing benefits. It is worth noting that this interpretation is at odds with that of historians who place the decisive change either earlier (with the arrival of a new government in January 1956) or later (in the aftermath of the Suez crisis in November 1956). Certainly France attained sufficient 'side-payments' during the Rome treaty negotiations to ensure its parliamentary acceptance, and these were not available through the existing OEEC or GATT structures.[5]

The main fear perceived by French policy makers was of German competition. This had already prompted the Schuman plan and underlay French strategy in the Messina negotiations. In Chapter 6, Werner Bührer examines the position as perceived by German industrialists. Against those who argue that the leading industrial interest group (the BDI) was dominated by Ruhr heavy industry, he suggests that the evidence from both the organizational structure and the support for European integration demonstrate that this was far from the case. Although the BDI complained about its lack of opportunity for detailed intervention in the ECSC and EEC negotiations, it was broadly in favour of both initiatives, but in a narrowly pragmatic way. It was cool towards the political aspirations attached to both initiatives and concerned that European commitments did not interfere with wider commercial relations.[6]

My own chapter (Chapter 7) on the attitudes of the Dutch government towards the common market attempts to resolve the question why the country that had so persistently pursued the policy was the least enamoured of the result. It suggests that the structure of Dutch imports diverged from that of the other members and that, as a result, the government felt disadvantaged by the incidence of the proposed common external tariff. Moreover, having secured their prime aim of a durable customs union, the Dutch were unable to resist other elements added to the package such as the French demands for social equalization and arrangements for overseas territories. On the other hand it suggests that, as the Dutch were squeezed out by bilateral bargaining during the closing phases of the negotiations, they became increasingly enamoured of the supranational options built into the treaty.[7]

In her article, Francesca Fauri (Chapter 8) demonstrates that the Italian presence at the Messina negotiations was the outcome of a long search for a commercial accommodation with important trading partners. This was reinforced by the trade boom of the early 1950s that reduced the resistance of industrialists to measures of trade liberalization and that so shifted the geographical pattern of trade as to make the 'Six' logical partners. Once in the negotiations, the Italian presence shaped the outcome. Although such aspects as the free movement of agricultural products and the free movement of labour were essential if the aim were to create a common market, the Italian economy was certain to benefit. Equally, the investment bank and the re-adaption fund may have been open to all, but they were also designed as side-payments to Italian negotiators. Fauri's contribution, moreover, draws out the link between domestic politics (in this case employment plans and development schemes for the South) and the demands in the international arena.[8]

Always in the background, as the Six struggled with one initiative after another, was the United States of America. Ever since Marshall Aid, both the Truman and the Eisenhower administrations had supported efforts at closer integration, partly from security motives and partly as a solution to the dollar shortage. In Chapter 9, Federico Romero describes how, from the mid-1950s, the economic rationale for support for European integration was increasingly questioned but, at this stage, without triggering a switch in policy, and the EEC was formed under benign American patronage. A sudden and sharp deterioration in the US balance of payments in 1958, however, acted as a catalyst for a reorientation of attitudes, which led to only luke warm support for the British plans for a pan-European free trade area and a determination to reactivate multilateral trade negotiations in the GATT. Romero suggests that 'had it come about one or two years later the EEC certainly would have received a different treatment in Washington'.[9]

The Economic Development of the EEC, 1957–92

During the first decade of its existence, the EEC's main accomplishments in economic policy were the creation of the customs union and the realization of a common agricultural policy. Chapter 10 provides a useful survey of these early achievements. In it, Michael Davenport reviews the economic theory underpinning any analysis of potential effects of such initiatives as well as the assessments of their impact on the economies of the member states. Despite the apparent sophistication of the methods employed by economists and the 'exactness' of their estimates, Davenport concludes that it is difficult to say whether the economic effects were negative or positive. This was partly because it is difficult to isolate effects deriving from other changes that were influencing the European economies at the same time, and because the likely positive effects on industrial trade were offset by the protectionist direction of the policy towards agriculture.[10]

In Chapter 11, David Mayes takes a more detailed look at the empirical work assessing the impact of economic integration on trade, both for the EEC and for the seven-country European Free Trade Association (EFTA) formed in 1960. Besides assessing the various methodologies, Mayes presents the results of almost twenty scientific studies. In contrast with Davenport he suggests, looking at the 'static' effects for the EEC where most work had been done, that the net impact on trade growth was positive. However, individual studies varied widely on the exact impact, so that the probable range, by 1970, lay anywhere between $8 bn. and $15 bn. He concludes that the difficulty in obtaining more accurate assessments lies partly in the problems of data but largely in the failure of the models to capture the full complexity of the economic reality.[11]

The new community attempted not only to regulate trade among its members but to provide a framework of preferential trading relationships through associate membership for its colonies and ex-colonies. Until Britain's accession to the EEC in 1973, these relations were with French, Belgian and Dutch (ex-)colonial territories. The nature of these arrangements is examined in Chapter 12 by Charles Young. He suggests, through a static analysis, that in the 1960s EEC exports to the associated states were probably 20 per cent higher than they would have been in the absence of the EEC's arrangements and that this imposed a 'cost' to the associates equivalent to, at most, 2 per cent of their import bill. A similar calculation for the static gain to the associate states for their exports to the EEC suggests that they may have been equivalent to 2 per cent of their exports. Young concludes that biases in the calculations may alter the picture so as to produce an overall positive gain for the associated states, but that it would certainly not have been a large one.[12]

Although the EEC was primarily defined by the formation of the customs union, its major policy achievement lay in agriculture. At its peak, the common agricultural policy (CAP) absorbed over three quarters of the Community budget, and this for a sector employing less than 10 per cent of the EEC workforce and contributing even less to its combined GDP. Chapter 13 traces the increasing strength of the agrarian lobby from the end of the nineteenth century and its institutionalization in the aftermath of World War II. Yet, as national regimes of agricultural protection began generating domestic surpluses, the common regulation of European markets assumed greater importance. It was no surprise that, if and when such a regulation could be agreed, it would be restrictive rather than liberal in approach. This chapter suggests that CAP's construction owed much to the perceived weakness, rather than strength, of the agricultural lobby and the failure of other checks and balances to operate as anticipated.[13] The theory behind market regulation in general, and agricultural regulation in particular, is explained by Dimitrious Demekas *et al.* in Chapter 14. They also review the empirical studies into the costs of the CAP, all of which show that the 'budgetary cost' of the CAP represented only a small part of the burden of the policy and that a far greater element in the transfer of resources to agriculture was represented by the 'consumer cost' in the form of higher prices. For the nine-member EEC, the overall 'deadweight' loss to EEC economies imposed by the CAP amounted to one per cent of GNP, a sizable transfer given the relative size of the agricultural sector. Moreover, internationally, they review studies that demonstrate the negative impact of the CAP on international commodity trade and prices.[14] The fact that the CAP was both costly and inefficient generated a healthy literature suggesting how it could be reformed. The debate on the options for reform is reviewed by Lionel Hubbard and Christopher Ritson in Chapter 15. They argue that there was a remarkable consistency in analysis, and in the policy alternatives advanced, over almost a quarter century of discussion. They distinguish between those measures designed to increase revenue and those directed at reducing expenditure. However, until relatively recently, in neither case was there any real determination to implement any of them.[15]

The creation of the customs union and the realization of the CAP (however flawed) represented the main achievements of the EEC in the first decade of its existence. In the 'Eurospeak' so often adopted to describe these things, they both represented a 'deepening' of the common market. At the end of the 1960s, the EEC embarked on negotiations that were to lead to a 'widening' of the market to embrace three new members – the United Kingdom, Denmark and Ireland. In Chapter 16 Andrew Scott surveys the UK's experience of EEC membership. He emphasizes that in Britain's case, the early prognoses of the static benefits of EEC membership were not particularly rosy but that there was an assumption that there would be positive dynamic gains. He suggests that these dynamic gains might also have been overestimated and that, anyway, they appeared to have been falsified by the British growth experience in the first decade after membership, even if the real explanation for the relatively poor performance lay elsewhere. In his judgement, it was 'ironic' that, having possibly gained least from EEC membership in this respect, the UK should have been in the vanguard of those in the early 1980s demanding measures to 'complete' the common market.[16]

The poor economic performance of the UK in the aftermath of the oil crisis and its association in the public mind, at least in part with EEC membership dampened whatever popular enthusiasm had existed for the project. The context of the debate, however, was determined by the rising net contribution to the EEC budget. Chapter 17 was written in the middle of the British budgetary crisis, which held the EEC in its grip virtually from the moment of the British accession until it was finally resolved in the mid-1980s. As Wynne Godley demonstrates, the origins of the budget crisis lay, on the one hand, in the income sources of the EEC's budget and, on the other, in the preponderance of agriculture in its expenditures (combined with the fact that the UK had a small agricultural sector). The impact of the 'transfer problem' was compounded by the consumer cost of switching food imports from low-cost World producers to high-cost Community suppliers. Combining the two elements, Godley contends that one of the poorer economies among the then nine member states became one of the largest net contributors to Community transfers. Whilst the focus of the chapter is on the British case, the statistics clearly illuminate the national cost-benefits of the CAP mechanism at the time of its major excesses.[17] The budget issue dominated British attitudes for the first decade of its membership, prompting the Labour government's (largely cosmetic) renegotiation of the Treaty of Accession and driving the party (in opposition) to fighting the 1982 election on a platform of withdrawal. It also fuelled the resentment of the Conservatives and provided much of the ammunition for the assault of the Thatcher government on the Community's institutions.

The first extension of EEC membership also coincided with the collapse of the regime of (relatively) stable exchange rates that had characterized the two decades since the last major currency alignment of September 1949. Only late in the day had the EEC grasped the question of economic and monetary union (EMU), prompted by the dislocation caused to the common agricultural policy by the devaluation of the French franc and the revaluation of the Deutschmark in the Autumn of 1969. The Werner plan had recommended that EMU be attained by 1980, but this goal was lost in the turmoil on exchange markets that followed the Smithsonian agreement sanctioning the currency realignment of 1971 and the final collapse of the entire system of fixed currencies eighteen months later. In Chapter 18, Elke Thiel examines the fate of European arrangements such as the 'snake' (1973–9) and the European Monetary System (1979–) that were introduced in the wake of these developments. Having abandoned the goal of EMU, the EEC then found itself with the far more difficult task of trying to maintain some stability in members' mutual exchange rates but it had few means of influencing the domestic monetary and fiscal policy of member states and a world characterized by increasingly large and volatile currency movements. The costs of failure, however, kept the issue of EMU on the political agenda.[18]

As the EEC was learning to cope with the 'British problem' and with currency disequilibria, it was confronted with yet another challenge. Until 1973 the EEC had been made up of relatively rich countries. Aside from some pockets of deprivation elsewhere, the main regional problem had been represented by Southern Italy. The expansion of 1973 had added Ireland and some areas of urban decline in the United Kingdom to the list of problem areas and had prompted the Community to develop its own regional policy. The expansion of the Community to include Greece (1981), Spain and Portugal (1986) added to the Community nearly 60 million inhabitants whose per capita incomes varied between 55 and 75 per cent of the EEC average. In Chapter 19, Loukas Tsoukalis examines the structural weaknesses of the EEC's poorer members and the effectiveness of the measures adopted to ameliorate these income disparities. He concludes that the amounts transferred were inadequate, and that the transfers lacked any overall internal direction or cohesion. An awareness of this failure, coupled with a need to compensate poorer countries for the dislocation associated with parallel initiatives to 'complete' the common market contributed, in 1988, to an increase in scale and purpose in EEC activities. Further development, he observes, is impeded by the limits on Community income, the priority of agriculture in Community expenditure and the distortions inherent in the CAP itself.[19]

The stagnation and inflation accompanying the oil crisis of 1973 was initially interpreted as a failure in demand management but as growth rates failed to return to earlier levels and as unemployment remained high, the diagnosis was increasingly sought in competitive failure. This explanation, in its turn, acquired two dimensions. Competitive failure was seen either as a consequence of supply-side distortions or as a result of failures in technological management. In Chapter 20, Margaret Sharp confirms the evidence for a widening technological gap between Western Europe and the USA and Japan, although the intensity varied between industrial sectors and nations. Part of that fault she attributes to a deficiency in the research and development effort in terms both of scale and of purpose. The fragmentation of the European effort prompted a search for more collaborative strategies. This stimulated integration at the firm level, through a network of technology cooperation agreements and created a role for the European Commission in the form of its 'Esprit' and 'Eureka' programmes.[20] Another approach to the problem of faltering international competitiveness was to increase competition within the Community and, at the same time, to extend the 'internal' market for European producers.

Martin Bangemann had been the minister of Economic Affairs in West Germany before becoming a Vice-President in the second Delors Commission. In Chapter 21, in a somewhat propagandist piece, he spells out the benefits for industry to be obtained from the creation of a single European market. The future European market would no longer be the featherbedded cushion for European industries but, shorn of its subsidies and regulations, it would become the competitive training ground for success in world markets.[21] The entire purpose of the exercise was to assist industrial restructuring, and to enhance economic growth and employment. Whilst most commentators agreed that this would probably be the case, there was less consensus about how great the impact would be. In Chapter 22 Keith Featherstone surveys the range of estimates made on the effects of the '1992' programme (a shorthand for the single-market package, referring to the date by which all the necessary measures would have needed to be implemented). The Commission's own estimates were by far the most optimistic. The measures themselves would add between 4.4 and 5.3 per cent to gross domestic product but, should governments ease their fiscal policies to take advantage of the improved climate, the addition to GDP could rise to 7 per cent, in the process creating five million new jobs. Most other estimates were considerably more cautious.[22]

The success of the single-market package encouraged the Commission to adopt a more forceful stance towards 'deepening' the Community, extending its responsibilities into foreign and security policy as well as social policy whilst, at the same time, relaxing the unanimity rule in decision-making. In Chapter 23, Andrew Britton and David Mayes survey the developments leading to these decisions. The preparation of these policies coincided with a relatively stable exchange rate regime among (most of) the EEC member states. The ill-fated 'snake' had been abandoned in 1979 and replaced by the European Monetary System (EMS) which, despite some adjustment shocks, appeared to be working very well. It was decided, therefore, to add the goal of economic and monetary union to the package.[23] All these measures, with various opt-out clauses, were included in a new treaty signed by the EEC member states at Maastricht in March 1992. This signalled the end of the European

Economic Community and its rebirth as the European Union. For us, it also marks the end of the period covered in this volume.

It is unfair, and not a little misleading, to leave the story at this precise juncture. The Maastricht treaty, for all the carping, hesitation and reserve that accompanied its creation, marked a high-point in the aspirations for European integration. Its lack of a proper foundation in popular appeal was rapidly demonstrated by its narrow rejection in the Danish referendum of June 1992 and its equally narrow acceptance by the French electorate. It was dealt a further blow, however, by the transparency of its ambitions for economic and monetary union (EMU). The EMS had been relatively successful, but it had required periodic currency realignment. Because there was no regularized provision for such adjustment, these realignments usually took place in a 'crisis' environment. Despite this glaring omission, the EMS had been chosen as the catalyst towards achieving EMU. In September 1992 tidal waves of speculation, accompanied by panic reactions among central banks, swept away the image of a gradual progress to EMU. By the time the speculation had subsided the pound and the lira had been forced to abandon their efforts to maintain their currencies within the system altogether, and Spain and Portugal were allowed to manage their currencies against central rates within wider bands. Within the following five months four further currency adjustments were made within the EMS. In August 1993 a renewed surge of speculation, targeted mainly on the French franc forced the EMS to adjust its bands to 15 per cent (!) either side of the central rate in order to maintain the fiction of a common currency regime.

As these events unfurled many commentators seemed to regard them as dealing a mortal blow to the pretensions for further integration. Yet the crisis had emphasized the difficulties in maintaining *national* currency rates in the face of privately-held foreign currency balances capable of overwhelming any official *national* reserves. The currency crisis may have punctured the illusion that further progress was somehow going to be easy or automatic, but equally it punctured the pretence that any *national* alternative was possible or even desirable.

Notes

1. J.B. De Long and B. Eichengreen, 'The Marshall Plan: History's Most Successful Structural Adjustment Program', in: R. Dornbush, R. Layard and W. Nolling (eds), *Postwar Reconstruction 1945–1949: Implications for Eastern Europe*, Cambridge (Mass.), London, 1991, 189–230.
2. W. Asbeek Brusse, 'Regional Plans for European Trade, 1945–1957' in R.T. Griffiths (ed.) *Economic and Monetary Unions in the Past: from Continental System to Common Market*, Lothian Foundation Press, London, 1997.
3. A.S. Milward, *The Reconstruction of Western Europe, 1945–1951*, Methuen, London, 1984, 362–420.
4. R.T. Griffiths, 'The Beyen Plan' in R.T. Griffiths (ed.), *The Netherlands and the Integration of Europe 1945–1957*, NEHA, Amsterdam, 1990, pp 165–182.
5. F.M.B. Lynch, 'France: the road to integration' in A.S. Milward *et al.*, *The Frontier of National Sovereignty. History and Theory 1945–1992*, Routledge, London, 1993, 59–87.
6. W. Bührer, 'German Industry and European Integration in the 1950s' in C. Wurm (ed.) *Germany and European Integration. The Beginnings of European Integration*, Oxford, 1995, 87–114.

7. R.T. Griffiths, 'The Common Market' in R.T. Griffiths (ed.), *The Netherlands and the Integra-tion of Europe 1945–1957*, NEHA, Amsterdam, 1990, pp. 183–208.

8. F. Fauri, *Negotiating for Industrialization: Italy's Commercial Strategy and Industrial Expan-sion in the Context of the Attempts to Further European Integration*, EUI PhD, 1994, Chapter 6, 177–225.

9. F. Romero, 'U.S. Attitudes towards Integration and Interdependence: The 1950s' in J. Heller and J.R. Gillingham *The United States and the Integration of Europe: Legacies of the Postwar Era*, St. Martins Press, New York, 1996, 103–21.

10. M. Davenport, 'The Economic Impact of the EEC' in M. Boltho, *The European Economy, Growth and Crisis*, Oxford UP, 1982, pp. 225–58.

11. D.G. Mayes, 'The Effects of Economic Integration on Trade' in *Journal of Common Market Studies*, **17**, 1978, 1–25.

12. C. Young, 'Association with the EEC: Economic Aspects of the Trade Relationship' in *Journal of Common Market Studies*, **17**, No 1, 1978, 120–35.

13. R.T. Griffiths 'Agricultural Development and Agricultural Trade, 1945–1973' (original in Portu-guese in *Portugal e a Europa, 50 anos de integraçao*, Lisbon, 1996.

14. D. Demekas *et al.*, 'The Effects of the Common Agricultural Policy of the European Commu-nity: A Survey of the Literature' in *Journal of Common Market Studies*, **27** (2), 1988, 113–45.

15. L. Hubbard and C. Ritson, 'The Reform of the CAP' in C. Ritson and D. Harvey, *The Common Agricultural Policy and the World Economy. Essays in Honour of John Ashton*, CAB Interna-tional, Wallingford, 1991, 295–310.

16. A. Scott, 'Internal Market Policy' in S. Bulmer, S. George and A. Scott (eds), *The United Kingdom and EC Membership Evaluated*, London: Pinter, 1992, 16–28.

17. W. Godley, 'The United Kingdom and the Community Budget' in W. Wallace (ed.) *Britain and Europe*, Heinemann, London, 1980, 72–86.

18. E. Thiel, 'Changing Patterns of Monetary Interdependence' in W. Wallace (ed.), *The Dynamics of European Integration*, Pinter, London, New York, 69–86.

19. L. Tsoukalis, *The New European Economy. The Politics and Economics of Integration*, Oxford, 1993, 228–77.

20. M. Sharp, 'Technology and the Dynamics of Integration', in W. Wallace (ed.), *The Dynamics of European Integration*, Pinter, London, New York, 1990, 50–68.

21. M. Bangemann, *Meeting the Global Challenge: Establishing a Successful European Industrial Policy*, London: Kogan Page, 1992, 36–51.

22. K. Featherstone, *European International Market Policy*, London, Routledge, 1990, 23–37.

23. A. Britton and D. Mayes, *Achieving Monetary Union in Europe*, London: Sage, 1992, 1–21.

Part I
Towards the EEC

[1]

8

**The Marshall Plan:
History's Most Successful
Structural Adjustment
Program**

J. Bradford De Long and
Barry Eichengreen

*[T]he world of suffering people looks to us for leadership. Their thoughts,
however, are not concentrated alone on this problem. They have more immediate
and terribly pressing concerns where the mouthful of food will come from, where
they will find shelter tonight, and where they will find warmth. Along with the
great problem of maintaining the peace we must solve the problem of the
pittance of food, of clothing and coal and homes. Neither of these problems can
be solved alone.*
—George C. Marshall, November 1945

*Can you imagine [the plan's] chances of passage in an election year in a
Republican congress if it is named for Truman and not Marshall?*
—Harry S. Truman, October 1947

1 Introduction

The post–World War II reconstruction of the economies and polities of
Western Europe was an extraordinary success. Growth was fast, distributional conflicts in large part finessed, world trade booming. The stability of
representative democracies in Western Europe made its political institutions the envy of much of the world. The politicians who in the post–
World War II years laid the foundations of the postwar order had good
warrant to be proud. They were, as Truman's Secretary of State Dean
Acheson put it in the title of his memoirs, *Present at the Creation* of an
extraordinarily successful set of political and economic institutions.

Perhaps the greatest success of the post–World War II period was the
establishment of representative institutions and "mixed economies" in that
half of Europe not occupied by the Red Army. A similar opportunity is
open today in Eastern Europe, with the possibility of replacing Stalinist
systems with market-oriented industrial democracies. The future will judge

politicians today as extraordinarily farsighted if they are only half as successful as Acheson and his peers.

Many argue that the West should seize this opportunity by extending aid to the nations of Eastern Europe in exchange for a commitment to reform. Advocates evoke as a precedent the Marshall Plan—the program that transferred $13 billion in aid from the United States to Western Europe in the years from 1948 to 1951. They argue that we should emulate the steps taken by the founders of the postwar order half a century ago by extending aid to Eastern Europe.

Any such argument by analogy hinges on two links. First, that the Marshall Plan in fact played a key role in inaugurating the postwar era of prosperity and political stability in Western Europe. Second, that the lessons of the postwar era translate to present-day Eastern Europe. In this chapter we examine both propositions. The bulk of this chapter evaluates the Marshall Plan. The conclusion steps back and weighs the extent to which the lessons of the post–World War II period can be applied to Eastern Europe including the regions of the Soviet Union today.

Summary of Conclusions

Our central conclusion is that the Marshall Plan did matter. But it did not matter in the way that the folk wisdom of international relations assumes. Milward (1984) is correct in arguing that Marshall Plan aid was simply not large enough to significantly stimulate Western European growth by accelerating the replacement and expansion of its capital stock. Nor did the Marshall Plan matter by financing the reconstruction of devastated infrastructure, for as we show, reconstruction was largely complete before the program came on stream.[1]

The Marshall Plan did play a role in alleviating resource shortages. But this channel was not strong enough to justify the regard in which the program is held. By 1948 and the beginning of Marshall Plan aid, bottlenecks were scarce, and markets were good at alleviating their impact.

Rather, the Marshall Plan significantly sped Western European growth by altering the environment in which economic policy was made. In the immediate aftermath of World War II, politicians who recalled the disasters of the Great Depression were ill-disposed to "trust the market," and eager to embrace regulation and government control. Had European political economy taken a different turn, post–World War II European recovery might have been hobbled by clumsy allocative bureaucracies that rationed scarce foreign exchange and placed ceiling prices on exportables to protect the consumption of urban working classes.

Yet in fact the Marshall Plan era saw a rapid dismantling of controls over product and factor markets in Western Europe. It saw the restoration of price and exchange rate stability. To some degree this came about because underlying political-economic conditions were favorable (and no one in Europe wanted a repeat of interwar experience). To some degree it came about because the governments in power believed that the "mixed economies" they were building should have a strong promarket orientation. Marshall Plan aid gave them room to maneuver in order to carry out their intentions: without such aid, they would have soon faced a harsh choice between contraction to balance their international payments and severe controls on admissible imports. To some degree it came about because Marshall Plan administrators pressured European governments to decontrol and liberalize even when they wished to otherwise.

In post–World War II Western Europe the conditions imposed, formally and informally, for the receipt of U.S. aid encouraged the reductions in spending needed for financial stability, the relaxation of controls that prevented markets from allocating resources, and the opening of economies to trade. Marshall Plan "conditionality" pushed governments toward versions of the mixed economy that had more market orientation and less directive planning in the mix. While post–World War II European welfare states and governments are among the most extensive in proportion to economic life in history, they are built on top of, and do not supplant or bypass, the market allocation of goods and factors of production. The Marshall Plan should thus be thought of as a large and highly successful structural adjustment program.[2]

The experience of the Marshall Plan therefore suggests lessons for the role the West can play today. It suggests that the yield of a Marshall Plan for Eastern Europe and the Soviet Union could be high, but the benefits are not direct increases in productive capacity made possible by aid. Aid to Eastern Europe will accelerate growth in the manner of the Marshall Plan if it leads to policies that accelerate the move toward market organization, free trade, and financial stability. Aid can help as an incentive and as a cushion to make reform possible. But aid cannot substitute for reform. The key remains the successful execution of structural adjustment.

Organization of the Chapter

After this introduction, section 2 of the chapter develops the "folk image" and contrasts it with the reality of the Marshall Plan. It is followed by a series of sections that consider in turn alternative channels through which the Marshall Plan could have accelerated economic recovery. First, Marshall Plan aid might have quickened the pace of private investment. Second, it might have supported public investment in infrastructure. Third, it might have eliminated bottlenecks. Fourth, it might have facilitated the negotiation of a progrowth "social contract" that provided the political stability and climate necessary to support the postwar boom. We argue that the first two were of negligible importance, that the third had some but not overwhelming significance during the years of the Marshall Plan, and that the fourth was vital but is difficult to quantify.

Throughout the chapter we use two sets of comparisons to structure and discipline the argument. The first comparison is with Europe after World War I. In contrast to the post–World War II era, after World War I European reconstruction had been a failure. Alternating inflation and deflation retarded recovery. Growth had been slow, distributional conflicts had been bitter, and the network of trade fragile and stagnant. Representative government had been tried and rejected by all save a handful of European nations.[3] The critical question from our perspective is to what degree the Marshall Plan was responsible for the different outcomes of the two postwar periods. The comparison addresses this issue and highlights features of the international environment besides the Marshall Plan that must figure in an adequate analysis.

The second comparison is with the experience of Argentina. Before the war, Argentina had been as rich as Continental Europe. In 1913 Buenos Aires was among the top twenty cities of the world in telephones per capita. In 1929 Argentina had been perhaps fourth in density of motor vehicles per capita, with approximately the same number of vehicles per person as France or Germany. Argentina from 1870–1950 was a country in the same class as Canada or Australia.

Yet after World War II, Argentina grew very much more slowly than France or Germany, rapidly falling from the ranks of the First World to the Third (see figure 8.1). Features of the international economic environment affecting Argentina as well as Europe—the rapid growth of world trade under the Bretton Woods system, for example—are not sufficient therefore to explain the latter's singular stability and rapid growth. Again the comparison points to factors aside from the direct effects of foreign aid that mattered, and factors in conjunction with which foreign aid must work in order to unleash a period of rapid growth.

The concluding section of the chapter summarizes our argument and applies our analysis of the Marshall Plan to options for dealing with Eastern Europe.

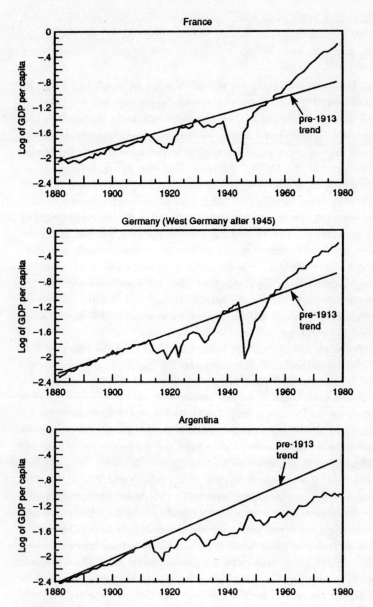

Figure 8.1
Very long run economic growth, 1880–1980
Sources: Angus Maddison, *Phases of Capitalist Development*; Robert Summers and Alan
Heston, *Penn World Table V*; Carlos Diaz Alejandro, *Essays on the Economic History of the
Argentine Republic*

2   The Marshall Plan: Image and Reality

The Folk Image

Western Europe's recovery from World War II had ground to a halt by the end of 1947.[4] The first phase of postwar expansion and recovery had come to an end. Reserves of foreign assets had been depleted. Export earnings were insufficient to finance purchases of raw materials and equipment from the only remaining functioning industrial economy, the United States. Bankers in the United States recalled the dismal returns on investments in Europe after World War I. Observing Communist electoral strength, they were unwilling to loan capital to Europe on any terms.[5] Incomes were too low to provide savings needed to finance reconstruction. Taxes were inadequate to balance government budgets. Inflation and financial chaos eroded Western Europe's ability to reconstruct and reorganize its economy. Internal U.S. State Department memoranda spoke of an approaching breakdown of the division of labor between town and country, and between resource extraction, manufacturing, and distribution sectors. Many feared an economic collapse in Europe as soon as U.S. humanitarian aid ceased to prop it up.

Such is the picture of Western Europe on the eve of the Marshall Plan painted by biographers of statesmen and by historians of international relations.[6] The Marshall Plan, they allege, solved these problems at a stroke. It provided funds to finance investment and public expenditure. It allowed countries to import from the United States. It eliminated bottlenecks that had obstructed economic growth. It set the stage for prosperity. European growth was very rapid after 1948 and the beginning of Marshall Plan aid, as figure 8.2 charts.

At the time, it was not even clear that post–World War II Western Europe would utilize market mechanisms to coordinate economic activity. Belief in the ability of the market to coordinate economic activity and support economic growth had been severely shaken by the Great Depression. Wartime controls and plans, while implemented as extraordinary measures for extraordinary times, had created a governmental habit of control and regulation. Seduced by the very high economic growth rates reported by Stalin's Soviet Union and awed by its war effort, many expected centrally planned economies to reconstruct faster and grow more rapidly than market economies. Memory of the Great Depression was fresh, and countries relying on the market were seen as likely to lapse into a period of underemployment and stagnation. Communists predicted that post–World War

The Marshall Plan

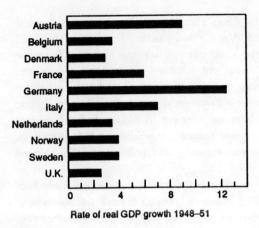

Rate of real GDP growth 1948-51

Figure 8.2
Economic growth in European nations during the Marshall Plan years

II reconstruction would dramatically reveal the superiority of central planning. Europe's East would pull ahead of whatever regions in the West remained attached to market organization and private property.[7]

Moreover, it seemed at least an even bet that the United States would withdraw from Western Europe. The U.S. government had done so after World War I, when the cycles of U.S. politics had led to the erosion of the internationalist Wilson administration and the rise to dominance of a Republican isolationist Congress. The same pattern appeared likely after World War II: Republican Congressional leader Robert Taft, the dominant figure in the Senate after the election of 1946, was extremely isolationist in temperament.

By all indications, the American commitment to relief and reconstruction was limited. The end of hostilities against Japan had led to the immediate cessation of lend-lease to Britain. Humanitarian aid under the auspices of the United Nations was seen as limited and transitional. The Truman administration was viewed as internationalist, but weak. Congressional critics called for balanced budgets. The 1946 congressional elections were a disaster for the Democratic party.

Considerable economic aid had been extended to Europe from the United States after World War I, first by the Herbert Hoover-led relief and reconstruction effort and then by private capital speculating on a restoration of monetary stability and pre–World War I exchange rates. The very magnitude of U.S. private capital flows after World War I militated against their repetition. Post–World War I reconstruction loans had been sold as sound private investments. They did not turn out to be so. Seymour Harris (1948) calculated that in present value terms nearly half of American private investments in Europe between the wars had been lost. Once burned, twice shy.[8] With strong Communist parties in Italy and France, a nationalization-minded Labour government in Britain, and a Germany once again pressed for reparations transfers, capital flows from American investors gambling on European recovery and political stability seemed unlikely.

Nevertheless, within two years after the end of the war it became U.S. government policy to build up Western Europe politically, economically, and militarily. The first milestone was the Truman Doctrine: President Truman asked Congress to provide aid to Greece to fill the gap left by the retreating British. The Truman Doctrine inaugurated the policy of containment. Included in the doctrine was a declaration that containment required steps to quickly regenerate economic prosperity in Western Europe. This policy extended beyond Greece and Turkey to the rest of Western Europe as well. As columnist Richard Strout summarized the informal conversations, leaks, and trial balloons emanating from the government in early 1947, "State Department strategists have now come around—to the point a good many 'visionaries' have been urging all along—that one way of combating Communism is to give western Europe a full dinner pail."[9]

Employing Secretary of State George C. Marshall's reputation as the architect of military victory of World War II, conservative fears of the further extension of Stalin's empire, and a political alliance with influential Republican Senator Arthur Vandenberg, Truman and his administration outflanked isolationist and antispending opposition and maneuvered the Marshall Plan through Congress. In the first two post–World War II years, the United States contributed about $4 billion a year to relief and reconstruction through United Nations Relief and Recovery Administration (UNRRA) and other programs.[10] The Marshall Plan continued these flows at comparable rates. But a significant difference was that UNRRA aid could be, and was expected to be, cut off at any time. Each additional quarter it was continued was a windfall. Its continuation was not something upon which Europe could count.

By contrast, the Marshall Plan was a multiyear commitment. From 1948 to 1951, the United States contributed $13.2 billion to European recovery: $3.2 billion went to the United Kingdom, $2.7 billion to France, $1.5 billion to Italy, and $1.4 billion to the Western-occupied zones of Germany that would become the post–World War II *Bundesrepublik*.

In its first year, half of all Marshall aid was devoted to food. Overall, 60 percent was spent on primary products and intermediate inputs: food, feed, fertilizers, industrial materials, and semifinished products, divided evenly between agricultural goods and industrial inputs. One-sixth was for fuel. One-sixth was spent on machinery, vehicles, and other commodities.[11]

The received image of the Marshall Plan sees it as the catalyst for Western European recovery. Before Marshall aid began to arrive, all was stagnation and fear of collapse. After, all was growth and optimism. Charles Mee's (1984) narrative is one of the most enthusiastic: "The ink was not dry before the first ships set sail—[with] 19,000 tons of wheat—followed by the SS *Godrun Maersk* with tractors, synthetic resin, and cellulose acetate; the SS *Gibbes Lykes* with 3,500 tons of sulfur; the SS *Rhondda* with farm machines, chemicals, and oil; the SS *Geirulo*, and SS *Delmundo*, and the SS *Lapland* with cotton. When shipments of carbon black began to reach Birmingham—Europe's largest tire plant was put back into production and 10,000 workers returned to their jobs."

The Reality: The European Economy following the Two Wars

Such is the folk image of the Marshall Plan. We now seek to contrast that image with historical reality. In this section we reassess the state of Europe's economy, turning in subsequent sections to our reassessment of the Marshall Plan. This section brings out four points. (1) World War II was more destructive than World War I. (2) Economic recovery was significantly faster after World War II. (3) There is no necessary relationship between the two preceding points. Rapid growth after World War II was not mainly a "rubber band effect" (the reversal of wartime output losses); rather, it was a sustained acceleration. (4) Nor did rapid postwar growth simply reflect a favorable international economic environment. Not all countries experienced comparable accelerations despite all being exposed to the same favorable international economic climate.

1. World War II was more destructive. When World War II ended, more than 40 million people in Europe were dead by violence or starvation. More than half of the dead were inhabitants of the Soviet Union. Even west of the post–World War II Soviet border, perhaps one in twenty were killed—close to one in twelve in Central Europe. In World War I the

J. Bradford De Long and Barry Eichengreen   198

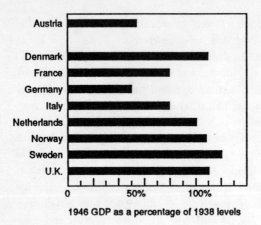

1946 GDP as a percentage of 1938 levels

Figure 8.3
Production immediately after World War II

overwhelming proportion of those killed had been soldiers. During World War II fewer than half of those killed were in the military.[12]

Material damage in World War II was spread over a wider area than in World War I. Destruction in the First World War was by and large confined to a narrow belt around a static trenchline. Although material destruction along the trenchline was overwhelming, it extended over only a small proportion of the European continent. World War II's battle sites were scattered more widely. Weapons were a generation more advanced and more destructive. World War II also saw the first large-scale strategic bombing campaigns.[13] Figure 8.3 plots relative levels of national product in the year immediately after World War II, relative to a prewar 1938 base.

Thus the aftermath of World War II saw many of Western Europe's people dead, its capital stock damaged, and the web of market relationships torn. Relief alone called for much more substantial government expenditures than reduced tax bases could finance. The post–World War I cycle of hyperinflation and depression seemed poised to repeat itself. Prices rose in Italy to thirty-five times their prewar level. France knocked four zeroes off the franc.

Industrial production recovered somewhat more rapidly than agricultural output after 1945. But two years after the end of the war, coal production in Western Europe was still below levels reached before or during the war. German coal production in 1947 proceeded at little more than half of the pre–World War II pace. Dutch and Belgian production was 20 percent below, and British 10 percent below, pre–World War II 1938 levels.[14] Demands for coal for heating reduced the continent's capacity to produce energy for industry. During the cold winter of 1946–47 coal earmarked for industrial uses had to be diverted to heating. Coal shortages led to the shutdown of perhaps a fifth of Britain's coal-burning and electricity-using industry in February 1947. Western European industrial production in 1946 was only 60 percent, and in 1947 only 70 percent, of the pre–World War II norm.[15]

Problems of agriculture were, if anything, more serious. Denmark's 1945–46 crops were 93 percent of prewar averages, but those in France, Belgium, Germany, and Italy were barely half. The harvest of 1947 was a disaster. Fertilizer and machinery remained in short supply. A fierce winter and a dry spring froze and withered trees and crops. Financial chaos meant that a large part of the harvest was not marketed. Farmers hoarded crops for barter and home consumption. Western Europe in 1946–47 had four-fifths its 1938 supply of foods. Its population had increased by twenty million—more than a tenth—even after accounting for military and civilian deaths.

Europe's ability to draw resources and import commodities from the rest of the world was heavily compromised by World War II. Traditionally, Western Europe had exported industrial goods and imported agricultural goods from Eastern Europe, the Far East, and the Americas. Now there was little prospect of rapidly restoring this international division of labor. Eastern European nations adopted Russian-style central planning and looked to the Soviet Union for economic links. Industry in the United States and Latin American had expanded during the war to fill the void created by the cessation of Europe's exports. Imports of food and consumer goods for relief diverted hard currency from purchases of capital goods needed for long-term reconstruction.

Changes in net overseas asset positions reduced Western Europe's annual earnings from net investments abroad. Britain had liquidated almost its entire overseas portfolio in order to finance imports during the war. The reduction in invisible earnings reduced Western Europe's capacity to import by approximately 30 percent of 1938 imports. The movement of the terms of trade against Western Europe gave it in 1947–48 32 percent fewer imports for export volumes themselves running 10 percent below pre–World War II levels; higher export volumes might worsen the terms of trade further. The net effect of the inward shift in demand for exports

J. Bradford De Long and Barry Eichengreen   200

Table 8.1
European balance of payments position, 1946–47 and 1919–20 (billions of 1946–47
dollars at annual rates)

	1946–47	1919–20
European imports	11.2	11.8
European exports	5.2	4.6
Trade account	− 6.0	− 7.2
Net income from investments	0.4	1.1
Other current account	− 1.1	1.3
Total current account	− 6.7	− 4.8
Reduction in European assets	− 1.8	− 2.0
Total loans and grants from U.S.	4.9	2.8

Source: Authors' calculations based on United Nations (1948) and United Nations (various
years).

and the collapse of the net investment positions was to give Europe in
1947–48 only 40 percent of the capacity to import that it had possessed in
1938.

By contrast, after World War I Europe's external position had appeared
more favorable. Europe emerged from the Great War with its overseas
investments still large.[16] European shipping still generated substantial net
revenues. Invisible receipts financed more than 20 percent of European
imports in the years immediately after World War I. The shift in terms
of trade against Europe was smaller after World War I than after World
War II.

More important, virtually every European nation quickly regained access to the international capital markets after World War I. This was true
even of reparations-burdened Germany until the spring of 1921, when the
stage for hyperinflation was set.[17] American private investors were eager
after World War I to make loans for European recovery. In the decade after
World War I, they loaned more than $1 billion a year overseas, primarily
to European nations. Government restrictions on foreign loans were rare
and by and large limited to cases in which countries had unsettled war
debts owing to the United States.[18]

Table 8.1 summarizes Europe's balance-of-payments position after the two
wars. Even though United States-provided UNRRA and other government-
provided assistance in the pre–Marshall Plan years was much larger in real
terms than all sources of financing—public and private loans and public
and private grants—had been in the equivalent period after World War I,

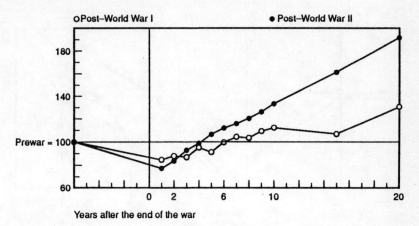

Figure 8.4
Post–World War I and Post–World War II recoveries of GDP per capita, average of
Britain, France, and Germany*
Sources: Angus Maddison, *Phases of Capitalist Development*; Robert Summers and Alan
Heston, *Penn World Table V*

the higher volume of financing did not allow Europe to import more from
the rest of the world. Real imports were in fact a shade higher after World
War I than after World War II because of the substantial deterioration in
Europe's invisible balance in the latter instance.

Thus Europe after World War II was in at least as bad economic shape
as it had been after World War I. Rapid reconstruction and a return to
prosperity did not seen inevitable. Another episode of financial and political chaos like that which had plagued the Continent following World War
I appeared likely. U.S. State Department officials wondered whether Europe
might be dying—like a wounded soldier who bleeds to death after the
fighting. State Department memoranda in 1946–47 presented an apocalyp-
tic vision of a complete breakdown in Europe of the division of labor—
between city and country, industry and agriculture, and between different
industries themselves.[19] In the aftermath a Communist triumph was seen as
a distinct possibility.

2. Recovery from World War II was faster. In 1946, the year after the end
of World War II, national product per capita in the three largest Western
European economies had fallen at least 25 percent below its 1938 level.
This was half again as much as production per capita in 1919 had fallen

J. Bradford De Long and Barry Eichengreen   202

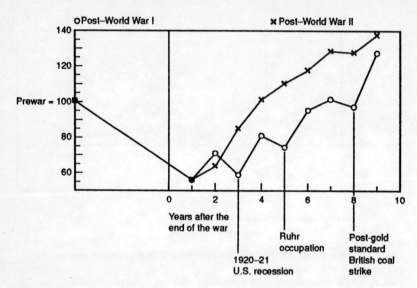

Figure 8.5
Post—World War I and Post—World War II recoveries of Western European steel
production
Sources: B. R. Mitchell, *European Historical Statistics*; U.N. Economic Commission for
Europe, *Economic Survey of Europe since the War*; Ingmar Svennilson, *Growth and Stagnation
in the European Economy*

below its prewar (1913) level. Yet the pace of post—World War II recovery
soon surpassed that which followed World War I. As figure 8.4 shows, by
1949 national income per capita in Britain, France, and Germany had recovered to within a hair of prewar levels.

Recovery at that date was some two years ahead of its post—World War
I pace. By 1951, six years after the war and at the effective end of the
Marshall Plan, national incomes per capita were more than 10 percent
above prewar levels. Measured by the yardstick of the admittedly imperfect national product estimates, the three major economies of Western
Europe had achieved a degree of recovery that post—World War I Europe
had not reached in the eleven years separating World War I from the
Great Depression. Post—World War II Europe accomplished in six years
what took post—World War I Europe sixteen.

Post—World War II recovery dominated post—World War I recovery by
other economic indicators as well. Figures 8.5 though 8.7 plot the comparative pace of post—World War I and post—World War II recoveries of

The Marshall Plan   203

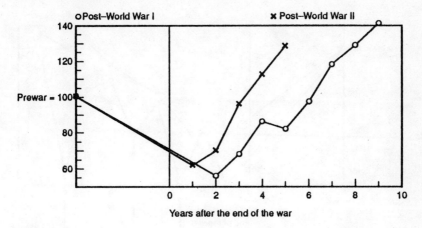

Figure 8.6
Post–World War I and Post–World War II recoveries of Western European cement
production*
Sources: B. R. Mitchell, *European Historical Statistics*; U.N. Economic Commission for
Europe, *Economic Survey of Europe since the War*; Ingmar Svennilson, *Growth and Stagnation
in the European Economy*

Western European steel, cement, and coal production. Since all three are
measured in physical units, these indices are not vulnerable to the potential
sources of error afflicting national income and product accounts. Figure 8.5
shows that by 1950—five years after the end of the Second World War—
Western European steel production had surpassed its prewar level. After
World War I, in contrast, steel production did not exceed its 1913 level
until nine years after the fighting ended. Figure 8.6 shows that the relative
recovery of cement production after World War II ran three years ahead of
its post–World War I pace.

The recovery of coal production after World War II also outran its
post–World War I pace by a substantial margin, as figure 8.7 shows, even
though coal was seen as in notoriously short supply in the post–World
War II years. By contrast, the recovery of coal production after World War
I was erratic. Coal production declined from 1920 to 1921—falling from
83 percent of pre–World War I levels in 1920 to 72 percent in 1921—as
a result of the deflation imposed on the European economy by central
banks that sought the restoration of pre–World War I gold standard
parities, accepted the burden of deflation, and allowed the 1921 recession
in the United States to be transmitted to their own countries. After World

J. Bradford De Long and Barry Eichengreen   204

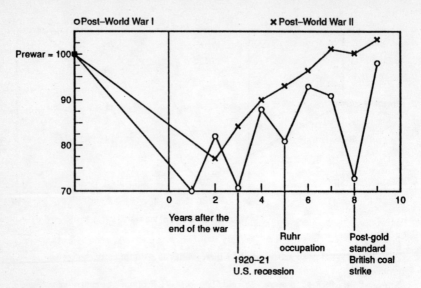

Figure 8.7
Post–World War I and Post–World War II recoveries of Western European coal
production*
Sources: B. R. Mitchell, *European Historical Statistics*; U.N. Economic Commission for
Europe, *Economic Survey of Europe since the War*; Ingmar Svennilson, *Growth and Stagnation
in the European Economy*

War II, no central bank or government pursued monetary orthodoxy so
aggressively in order to roll back price and wage increases and preserve the
real wealth of rentiers.

Coal production fell again in 1922–23. The breakdown of negotiations
over German reparations led the French to occupy the Ruhr. Their occupation did not lead to significantly increased transfers from Germany to
France. But it did begin the German hyperinflation.

Coal production fell for yet a third time in 1926. Attempts to reduce
wages in the aftermath of Britain's deflationary return to gold triggered a
walkout by British coal miners, accompanied by a short-lived general strike.
The twenties in Britain saw stubborn attachment by successive governments to a policy of a high real exchange rate and deflation, and an extraordinary degree of downward nominal wage inflexibility as well.

The course of coal production shows that to a large extent the slow
post–World War I recovery was inflicted by Europeans on themselves.

The major factors hindering a rapid post–World War I recovery were not strictly economic but social and political. One interpretation is that post–World War I Europe saw the recovery of output repeatedly interrupted by political and economic "wars of attrition," in the language of Alesina and Drazen (1991), that produced instability in European finance, politics, and labor relations.

In the aftermath of World War I, the distribution of wealth both within and between nations, the question of who would bear the burden of post-war adjustment, and the degree to which government would act to secure the property of the rentier were all unresolved issues. Social classes, political factions, and nation-states saw that they had much to lose if they did not aggressively promote their claims for favorable redistribution. Much of the social and economic history of interwar Europe can be seen in terms of such "wars of attrition," in which fiscal, financial, monetary, and labor relations instability—and concomitant slow economic growth—are trials of strength over who would succeed in obtaining a favorable redistribution of wealth.

After World War II such "wars of attrition" were less virulent. Memories of the disastrous consequences of the aggressive pursuit of redistributional goals during the interwar period made moderation appear more attractive to all. The availability of Marshall Plan aid to nations that had accomplished stabilization provided a very strong incentive to compromise such distributional conflicts early and gave European countries a pool of resources that could be used to cushion the wealth losses sustained in restructuring.[20]

3. *This was "supergrowth" and not simply a "rubber band effect."* More-over, post–World War II reconstruction did more than return Western Europe to its previous growth path. As figure 8.1 showed, French and West German growth during the post–World War II boom raised national product per capita at rates that far exceeded pre–World War II, pre-1929, or even pre-1913 trends.

This was not merely a process of making up ground lost during the war. In fact, there is no strong connection between the fall in levels of production across the wartime period and the pace of the subsequent recovery, contrary to what would be expected if fast post–World War II growth was primarily a process of catch-up to prewar trends. The bivariate relationship is statistically significant at standard confidence levels (see Dumke 1990), but when one controls for other characteristics of countries like openness and the investment rate, the significance of the relationship evaporates and even its sign becomes uncertain (see Eichengreen and Uzan 1991).

The reconstruction of Western Europe in the aftermath of World War II appears to have created economies capable of dynamic economic growth an order magnitude stronger than had previously been seen in Europe. Postwar Europe's "supergrowth," as Charles Kindleberger has termed it, was much more than catch-up and reattainment of a prewar neoclassical growth path.

4. "Supergrowth" reflected more than a favorable environment. Yet such rapid growth and recovery as Western Europe saw after World War II was not inevitable. It was not a natural consequence of a favorable international regime. The post–World War II expansion of world trade under Bretton Woods was a great aid to European recovery, but Western European growth reflected more than a rising tide of international trade lifting all boats.

As figure 8.1 showed, a Latin American country like Argentina, as rich in the years before and immediately after World War II as industrial Western Europe, grew slowly even under the post–World War II expansionary Bretton Woods regime. Fast post–World War II growth and catch-up to American standards of productivity were to a large degree specific to Western Europe, and thus to the countries that received Marshall Plan aid.

3   The Marshall Plan and Private Investment

Investment is an obvious channel through which the Marshall Plan might have accelerated economic growth in post–World War II Western Europe. Postwar Europe was poor and capital scarce. Maintaining living standards at levels the citizenry regarded as minimally tolerable consumed a large share of total product, leaving little for the replacement of railroads, buildings, and machines damaged by war. The Marshall Plan could have relaxed this constraint.

It is difficult to ascribe large effects to this channel. Viewed relative to total investment in the recipient countries, the Marshall Plan was not large. Marshall Plan grants were provided at a pace that was not much greater in flow terms than previous UNRRA aid and amounted to less than 3 percent of the combined national incomes of the recipient countries between 1948 and 1951. They equalled less than a fifth of gross investment in recipient countries. Only 17 percent of Marshall Plan dollars were spent on "machinery and vehicles" and "miscellaneous." The rest were devoted to imports of industrial materials, semi-finished products, and agricultural commodities. The commodities bought directly with Marshall Plan dollars were not additions to the fixed capital stock of Western Europe that would have boosted output permanently.

Marshall Plan dollars did significantly affect the level of investment: countries that received large amounts of Marshall Plan aid invested more. Eichengreen and Uzan (1991) calculate that out of each dollar of Marshall Plan aid some 65 cents went to increased production and 35 cents to increased investment. The returns to new investment were high. Eichengreen and Uzan's analysis suggests that social returns may have been as high as 50 percent a year: an extra dollar of investment raised national product by 50 cents in the subsequent year.

Even with such strong links between the Marshall Plan and investment and between investment and growth, the investment effects of Marshall Plan aid were simply too small to trigger an economic miracle. U.S. aid in the amount of 3 percent of West European output per year raised the share of private investment in national income by one percentage point. An increase of one percentage point in the ratio of investment to national income would increase economic growth by one-half of one percentage point.

Over the four years of the Marshall Plan, this increase in growth cumulates to 2 percent of national product. Eichengreen and Uzan's estimates of the strength of this investment channel suggest thus that it led to Western European national income levels after 1951 that were some 2 percent higher than would have been the case otherwise. While this was a valuable addition, it is hardly the sort of dramatic change trumpeted by champions of the Marshall Plan. It was too little to make the difference between prosperity and stagnation. It was not enough to make the Marshall Plan a decisive factor in the long boom of the post–World War II period.

4   The Marshall Plan and Public Investment

A second channel through which the Marshall Plan could have stimulated growth was by financing public spending on infrastructure. Western European roads, bridges, railroads, ports, and other infrastructure had been severely damaged by the war. They were prime targets of the Allied strategic bombing campaign. Their destruction had been the first priority of retreating Nazis. The social rate of return to their repair and reconstruction was very high. This task was one of the principal objectives of postwar governments. Those same governments had limited resources out of which to finance infrastructure repair. National tax systems were in disarray. The tax base had been eroded by the war. Social programs competed for scarce

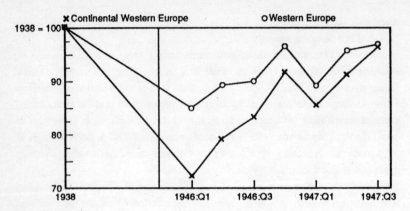

Figure 8.8
Post–World War II recovery of Western European rail traffic*
Source: U.N. Economic Commission for Europe, *Economic Survey of Europe 1948*

public revenues. Inflationary finance was at odds with the imperative of financial stabilization.

The question is how tightly the fiscal constraint limited public spending on infrastructure repair. In fact, the damage to European infrastructure was not that thorough or that long lasting. Although Allied generals had learned during World War II that strategic bombing could destroy bridges, paralyze rail yards, and disrupt the movement of goods and troops, they had also learned that bridges could be quickly rebuilt and tracks quickly relaid.

Europe's transportation infrastructure was in fact quickly repaired. As figure 8.8 shows, by the last quarter of 1946 almost as much freight was loaded onto railways in Western Europe as had been transported in 1938. Including British railways, total goods loaded and shipped in the last quarter of 1946 amounted to 97 percent of prewar traffic. Weighted by the distance traveled—measured in units not of tons carried but multiplying each ton carried by the number of kilometers traveled—1947 railroad traffic was a quarter higher than pre–World War II traffic. European recovery was not significantly delayed by the lack of track and rolling stock.[21]

5   Bottlenecks and Foreign Exchange Constraints

Another channel through which the Marshall Plan might have stimulated growth was by relaxing foreign exchange constraints. Marshall Plan funds were hard currency in a dollar-scarce world. They might have allowed Europe to obtain imports that would relieve bottlenecks. After the war, coal, cotton, petroleum, and other materials were in short supply. The Marshall Plan allowed them to be purchased at a higher rate than would have been possible otherwise. Marshall Plan dollars added to Europe's international liquidity and played a role in restoring intra-European trade. To the extent that the breakdown of the intra-European division of labor was reducing production, added liquidity may have relieved bottlenecks in foreign exchange.

In a well-functioning market economy, it is difficult to argue that such bottlenecks had more than a transient impact on the level of production. The European economy was not without possibilities for substitution. Market economies are very good at finding and utilizing such possibilities. However, assume for argument's sake that little active substitution of cheap goods for scarce imports was possible on the production side. It is still the case that Europe would not have seen lower production without Marshall Plan aid if governments had made sustaining production a priority when allocating foreign exchange. Absent the Marshall Plan, according to this scenario, imports of consumption goods would have been reduced as foreign exchange was diverted to purchase industrial raw materials, but output would not have been noticeably affected.

Had substitution possibilities been lacking in both production and use of foreign exchange, materials shortages might then have reduced production. But consider the following back-of-the-envelope calculation for the most severe bottleneck: coal. In 1938 Western Europe consumed 460 million tons of hard coal. It produced only 400 million tons in 1948. Over the life span of the Marshall Plan, Western Europe imported about 7 percent of its coal consumption from the United States. Assuming that coal was the most important bottleneck, that half of national product was produced in coal-burning sectors, and that these coal-burning sectors used fixed coefficients in production, then elimination of coal imports would have reduced Western European total product over the duration of the Marshall Plan by no more than 3 percent.

This back-of-the-envelope calculation neglects indirect effects and general equilibrium repercussions. One can imagine that, for example, a small decline in coal consumption might have produced a large decline in steel output, which in turn provoked an even larger fall in output in sectors for which steel was an essential input.

Input-output analysis is the classic way of analyzing such a situation. Consider Italy, for which Marshall Plan administrators prepared a 1950 input-output table.[22] Italy imported $72 million—L 13 billion—worth of coal during the Marshall Plan. Assume that all uses of coal would have been proportionately reduced in the absence of Marshall Plan imports, that all industry production functions were Leontief, and that slack resources would have remained idle.[23] Then input-output analysis reveals that industrial production would have fallen by 6.8 percent and transportation by 7.3 percent of a year's production.[24] The coal bottleneck would have produced secondary bottlenecks in steel production, refining, and transport. But agriculture and services would have been unaffected. Since industry and transport account for less than half of national product, the latter would have fallen by 3.2 percent of a year's production.[25]

This, of course, is an overestimate of the likely effects in 1950 of a coal bottleneck. The economy did possess substitution possibilities in production and foreign-exchange allocation. If the market was functioning and so uncovering substitution possibilities, it is plausible that losses due to all bottlenecks together would have been less than this calculation for coal. And even 3 percent is small relative to the speed of the remarkable European recovery. In individual periods—such as the winter of 1947—bottlenecks, primarily in coal, were present. Earlier in recovery, bottlenecks and resource scarcities may well have been very important. But the elimination of bottlenecks more than three years after the end of the war as a result of Marshall aid is unlikely to have been a significant factor driving the rapid Western European recovery, at least if the counterfactual is one in which the market is doing its job of adjustment and reallocation.

6 The Political Economy of European Reconstruction

But would the market economy have been allowed to do its job? The thirties had seen not chronic bottlenecks but chronic deficiencies of aggregate demand. Production had fallen far below normal for the entire decade; market forces had failed to restore demand to normal levels. Circumstances during the Great Depression had been exceptional, but circumstances in the aftermath of World War II were exceptional as well. Many feared the return of the Depression.[26]

Thus a live possibility in the absence of the Marshall Plan was that governments would not stand aside and allow the market system to do its job. In the wake of the Great Depression, many still recalled the disastrous outcome of the laissez-faire policies then in effect. Politicians were predisposed toward intervention and regulation: no matter how damaging "government failure" might be to the economy, it had to be better than the "market failure" of the Depression.

Had European political economy taken a different turn, post–World War II European recovery might have been stagnant. Governments might have been slow to dismantle wartime allocation controls and thereby severely constrain the market mechanism. In fact the Marshall Plan era saw a rapid dismantling of controls over product and factor markets in Western Europe and the restoration of price and exchange rate stability. An alternative scenario would have been the maintenance and expansion of wartime controls in order to guard against substantial shifts in income distribution. The late forties and early fifties might have seen the creation in Western Europe of allocative bureaucracies to ration scarce foreign exchange and the imposition of price controls on exportables in order to protect the living standards of urban working classes.

Europe in the Argentine Mirror

The consequences of such policies can be seen in the Argentine mirror. In response to the social and economic upheavals of the Depression, Argentina adopted demand stimulation and income redistribution. These policies were coupled with a distrust of foreign trade and capital and an attraction to the use of controls instead of prices as allocative mechanisms. Argentina's growth performance in the post–World War II period was very poor. Figure 8.9 displays the post–World War II growth of Argentine GDP per capita along with that of the four largest European economies. Even in the fifties, and even relative to Britain, Argentine growth was slow.

Díaz-Alejandro (1970) provides a standard analysis of Argentina's post–World War II economic stagnation. According to his interpretation, the collapse of world trade in the Great Depression was a disaster of the first magnitude for an Argentina tightly integrated into the world division of labor. While Argentina continued to service its foreign debt, its trade partners took unilateral steps to shut it out of markets. The experience of the Depression justifiably undermined the nation's commitment to free trade.[27]

In this environment Juan Perón gained mass political support. Taxes were increased, agricultural marketing boards created, unions supported, urban real wages boosted, international trade regulated. Perón sought to generate rapid growth and to twist terms of trade against rural agriculture and redistribute wealth to urban workers who did not receive their fair share. The redistribution to urban workers and to firms that had to pay their newly increased wages required a redistribution away from exporters, agricultural oligarchs, foreigners, and entrepreneurs.

J. Bradford De Long and Barry Eichengreen   212

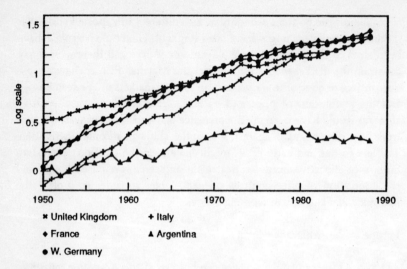

Figure 8.9
Post–World War II GDP per capita growth in Argentina, Britain, France, West Germany, and Italy
Source: Robert Summers and Alan Heston, *Penn World Table V.*

The Perónist program was not prima facie unreasonable given the memory of the Great Depression, and it produced almost half a decade of very rapid growth. The exports fell sharply as a result of the international business cycle as the consequences of the enforced reduction in real prices of rural exportables made themselves felt. Agricultural production fell because of low prices offered by government marketing agencies. Domestic consumption rose. The rural sector found itself short of fertilizer and tractors. Squeezed between declining production and rising domestic consumption, Argentinian exports fell. By the first half of the fifties the real value of Argentine exports was only 60 percent of the depressed levels of the late thirties, and only 40 percent of twenties levels. Due to the twisting of terms of trade against agriculture and exportables, when the network of world trade was put back together, Argentina was by and large excluded.

The consequent foreign exchange shortage presented Perón with unattractive options. First, he could attempt to balance foreign payments by devaluing to bring imports and exports back into balance in the long run and in the short run by borrowing from abroad.[28] But effective devaluation would have entailed raising the real price of imported goods and therefore cutting living standards of the urban workers who made up his political base. Foreign borrowing would have meant a betrayal of his strong nationalist position. Second, he could contract the economy, raising unemployment and reducing consumption, and expand incentives to produce for export by decontrolling agricultural prices.[29] But once again this would have required a reversal of the distributional shifts that had been the central aim of his administration.

The remaining option was one of controlling and rationing imports. Not surprisingly, Perón and his advisors chose the second alternative, believing that a dash for growth and a reduction in dependence on the world economy was good for Argentina. Díaz-Alejandro writes: "First priority was given to raw materials and intermediate goods imports needed to maintain existing capacity in operation. Machinery and equipment for new capacity could neither be imported nor produced domestically. A sharp decrease in the rate of real capital formation in new machinery and equipment followed. Hostility toward foreign capital, which could have provided a way out of this difficulty, aggravated the crisis..." Subsequent governments did not fully reverse these policies, for the political forces that Perón had mobilized still had to be appeased. Thus post–World War II Argentina saw foreign exchange allocated by the central government in order to, first, keep existing factories running and, second, keep home consumption high. The third and last priority under the controlled exchange regime went to imports of capital goods for investment and capacity expansion.

As a result, the early fifties saw a huge rise in the price of capital goods. Each percentage point of total product saved led to less than half a percentage point's worth of investment. Díaz-Alejandro found "[r]emarkably, the capital ... in electricity and communications increased by a larger percentage during the depression years 1929–39 than ... 1945–55," although the 1945–55 government boasted of encouraging industrialization. Given low and fixed agriculture prices, hence low exports, it was very expensive to sacrifice materials imports needed to keep industry running in order to import capital goods. Unable to invest, the Argentine economy stagnated.

In 1929 Argentina had appeared as rich as any large country in continental Europe. It was still as rich in 1950, when Western Europe had for the most part reattained pre–World War II levels of national product. But by 1960 Argentina was poorer than Italy and had less than two-thirds of the GDP per capita of France or West Germany. One way to think about post–World War II Argentina is that its mixed economy was poorly oriented: the government allocated goods, especially imports, among alternative uses; the controlled market redistributed income. Thus neither the private nor the public sector was used to its comparative advantage: in Western

Europe market forces allocated resources—even, to a large extent, for nationalized industries—the government redistributed income, and the outcome was much more favorable.

The European Analogy

In the absence of the Marshall Plan, might have Western Europe followed a similar trajectory? In Díaz-Alejandro's estimation, four factors set the stage for Argentina's relative decline: a politically-active and militant urban industrial working class, economic nationalism, sharp divisions between traditional elites and poorer strata, and a government used to exercising control over goods allocation that viewed the price system as a tool for redistributing wealth rather than for determining the pattern of economic activity.

From the perspective of 1947, the political economy of Western Europe would lead one to think that it was at least as vulnerable as Argentina to economic stagnation induced by populist overregulation. The war had given Europe more experience than Argentina with economic planning and rationing. Militant urban working classes calling for wealth redistribution voted in such numbers as to make Communists plausibly part of a permanent ruling political coalition in France and Italy.[30] Economic nationalism had been nurtured by a decade and a half of Depression, autarky, and war. European political parties had been divided substantially along economic class lines for a generation.

Yet Europe avoided this trap. After World War II Western Europe's mixed economies built substantial redistributional systems, but they were built on top of and not as replacements for market allocations of goods and factors. Just as post–World War II Western Europe saw the avoidance of the political-economic "wars of attrition" that had put a brake on post–World War I European recovery, so post–World War II Western Europe avoided the tight web of controls that kept post–World War II Argentina from being able to adjust and grow.

7   The Role of the Marshall Plan

Did the Marshall Plan play a role in Western Europe's successful avoidance of these traps? In answering this question, it is important to distinguish three effects of the American Marshall Plan program: its immediate contribution to the restoration of financial stability, its role in restoring the free play of market forces, and its part in the negotiation of the social contract upon which the subsequent generation of supergrowth was based.

The Restoration of Financial Stability

Financial instability was pervasive in post–World War II Europe. Relief expenditure sent budgets deep into deficit. Governments responded to inflation by retaining controls, prompting the growth of black markets and discouraging transactions at official prices. Farmers refused to market produce as long as prices were restricted to low levels. With receipts vulnerable to inflation or taxation, they were better off hoarding inventories. The post–World War II food shortage reflected not merely bad weather in 1947 but also the reluctance of farmers to deliver food to cities. Moreover, manufactured goods farmers might have purchased remained in short supply. Manufacturing enterprises had the same incentive to hoard inventories. As long as food shortages persisted, workers had little ability—or incentive—to devote their full effort to market work. Few were willing to sell goods for money when inflation threatened to accelerate at any time.[31]

The liberal, market-oriented solution to the crisis was straightforward. Prices had to be decontrolled to coax producers to bring their goods to market. Inflation had to be halted for the price mechanism to operate smoothly and to encourage saving and initiative. Budgets had to be balanced to remove inflationary pressure. With financial stability restored and market forces given free reign, individuals could direct their attention to market work. Without financial stability, the allocative mechanisms of the market could not be relied on—and government controls over the process of goods allocation would appear the more attractive option.

For budgets to be balanced and inflation to be halted, however, political compromise was required. Consumers had to accept higher posted prices for foodstuffs and necessities. Workers had to moderate their demands for higher wages. Owners had to moderate demands for profits. Taxpayers had to shoulder additional liabilities. Recipients of social services had to accept limits on safety nets. Rentiers had to accept that the war had destroyed their wealth. There had to be broad agreement on a "fair" distribution of income, or at least on a distribution of the burdens that was not so unfair as to be intolerable. Only then could pressure on central banks to continually monetize budget deficits and cause either explicit or repressed inflation be removed.

Here the Marshall Plan may have played a critical role. It did not obviate the need for sacrifice. But it increased the size of the pie available for division among interest groups. Marshall Plan aid as a share of recipient GDP was 2.5 percent—not an overwhelmingly large change in the size of the pie. But if the sum of national demands exceeded aggregate supply by

5 or 7.5 percent, Marshall Plan transfers could reduce the sacrifices required of competing distributional interests by a third or as much as a half. The presence of Marshall Plan aid could thus have significantly reduced the costs of compromise relative to the benefits.[32]

Dangerous instability arises if the failure to compromise leads to a "war of attrition." Suppose that the difference between the total sum of claims to output and output itself shows up as a deficit in the government's budget. Then even small conflicts over "fair shares" can easily lead to aggregate demand that exceeds supply by some 7 or 8 percent. To meet such a shortfall of revenues relative to demands for services and transfers through money creation, the government has to increase the high-powered money supply by 8 percent of GDP each year. The consequences of such a rate of increase in high-powered money are likely to be disastrous.

Marshall Plan aid of 2.5 percent of national product goes a substantial way toward closing this excess demand gap. Moreover, its potential availability if the government's stabilization plan meets the criteria required by Plan administrators provides a powerful incentive for governments to impose financial discipline. With Marshall Plan aid available, the benefits for quick resolution of "wars of attrition" were greater, and so the Plan in all likelihood advanced the date of financial stabilization. While internal price stabilization after World War II took four years, the German hyperinflation took place in the sixth year after the end of World War I, and France's post–World War I inflation lasted for eight years. Some large part of the credit for this early stabilization goes to the Marshall Plan and to earlier aid programs.[33]

Along with the carrot of Marshall Plan grants, the United States also wielded a stick. For every dollar of Marshall Plan aid received, the recipient country was required to place a matching amount of domestic currency in a counterpart fund to be used only for purposes approved by the United States government. Each dollar of Marshall Plan aid thus gave the United States government control over two dollars' worth of real resources. Marshall Plan aid could be spent on external goods only with the approval of the U.S. government. And the counterpart funds could be spent internally only with the approval of the Marshall Plan administration as well.

In some instances the United States insisted that the funds be used to buttress financial stability. Britain used the bulk of its counterpart funds to retire public debt. Vincent Auriol claims that the United States refused to release French counterpart funds in 1948 until the new government affirmed its willingness to continue policies leading to a balanced budget.[34]

French officials were outraged: nevertheless, they took steps to obtain release and raised taxes. This was policy: nations undergoing inflation could not draw on counterpart funds until the Marshall Plan administration was satisfied that they had achieved a workable stabilization program (Price 1955).

Marshall Plan administrators believed that their veto power over the use of counterpart funds considerably increased U.S. leverage over Western European economic policies. Moreover, counterpart funds were only one of several available levers. Plan administrators believed that if governments could afford to divert funds from reconstruction to social services, Marshall aid could be eliminated proportionately. Britain lost its Marshall Plan timber line item as a result of the government's entry into the construction of public housing. West Germany found the release of counterpart funds delayed until the nationalized railway had reduced expenditures to match revenues (Arkes 1972). Marshall Plan administrators and Lucius Clay, military governor of the American zone of Germany, viewed with alarm British schemes for unifying and nationalizing the coal industries of the Ruhr, then part of the British zone of occupation, and successfully lobbied against them. The United States was not interested in having Marshall Plan aid support policies of nationalization. The United States even put pressure on Britain's Labour government to delay and shrink its own nationalization programs.

The Free Play of Market Forces

Renewed growth required, in addition to financial stability, the free play of market forces. Though there was support for the restoration of a market economy in Western Europe, it was far from universal. Wartime controls were viewed as exceptional policies for exceptional times, but it was not clear what was to replace them. Communist and some Socialist ministers opposed a return to the market. It was not clear when, or even if, the transition would take place.

On this issue the Marshall Plan—specifically, the conditions attached to U.S. aid—left Western Europeans with no choice. Each recipient had to sign a bilateral pact with the United States. Countries had to agree to balance government budgets, restore internal financial stability, and stabilize exchange rates at realistic levels. Europe was still committed to the mixed economy. But the United States insisted that market forces be represented more liberally in the mix. This was the price that the United States charged for its aid.

The demand that European governments trust the market came from the highest levels of the Marshall Plan administration. Dean Acheson describes the head administrator, Economic Cooperation Administration Chief Paul Hoffman, as an "economic Savonarola." Acheson describes watching Hoffman "preach ... his doctrine of salvation by exports" to British Foreign Secretary Ernest Bevin. "I have heard it said," wrote Acheson, "that Paul Hoffman ... missed his calling: that he should have been an evangelist. Both parts of the statement miss the mark. He did not miss his calling, and he was and is an evangelist."[35]

European economic integration was pursued intensely by the Plan administration. Even where domestic markets were highly concentrated, they believed competition could be injected via intra-European and international trade. Government intervention and other efforts to interfere with the operation of market forces would be disciplined by foreign competition. As a condition for receiving Marshall Plan aid, each country was required to develop a program for removing quotas and other trade controls. In 1950, discussions culminated in the European Payments Union, a system of credits to promote multilateral trade among European countries.[36]

It was not inevitable that Western Europe would have accepted the bargain. Marshall aid was ostensibly offered to Eastern Europe and even to the U.S.S.R. Moscow's rejection can be seen in part as unwillingness to allow the United States to sidetrack its satellites' progress toward central planning. It is critical to acknowledge that the price charged for the aid was a price Western Europe might have paid for its own sake in any event. Support for the market was widespread, although just how widespread was uncertain. The Marshall Plan at most tipped the balance.

Post–World War II Europe was far from laissez-faire. Government ownership of utilities and heavy industry was substantial. Government redistributions of income were large. The magnitude of the "safety nets" and social insurance programs provided by the post–World War II welfare states were far beyond anything that had been thought possible before World War I. But these large welfare states were accompanied by financial stability and by substantial reliance on market processes for allocation and exchange.

The Social Contract and Long-Term Growth

The restoration of financial stability and the free play of market forces launched the European economy onto a two-decade-long path of unprecedented rapid growth. European economic growth between 1953 and 1973 was twice as fast as for any comparable period before or since. The growth rate of GDP was 2 percent per annum between 1870 and 1913 and 2.5 percent per annum between 1922 and 1937. In contrast, growth accelerated to an astonishing 4.8 percent per year between 1953 and 1973 before slowing to half that rate from 1973 to 1979.[37]

Because the roots of postwar Europe's supergrowth are not adequately understood, it is difficult to isolate the contribution of the Marshall Plan. We will nonetheless hazard some speculations about the role that U.S. aid might have played.[38]

Europe's rapid growth in the fifties and sixties was associated with exceptionally high investment rates.[39] The investment share of GNP was nearly twice as high as it had been in the last decade before World War II or it was again to be after 1972. Accompanying high rates of investment was rapid growth of productivity. Even in Britain, the laggard, productivity growth rose sharply between 1924 to 1937 and 1951 to 1973, from 1 to 2.4 percent per annum.[40] This high investment share did not, however, reflect unusual investment behavior during expansion phases of the business cycle. Rather, it reflected the tendency of investment to collapse during cyclical contractions and the absence of significant cyclical downturns between 1950 and 1971.

It would be tempting to ascribe Europe's cyclical stability to the advent of Keynesian stabilization policy but for the fact that Keynesian policy was not forgotten when increasingly volatile cyclical fluctuations recurred after 1972. A possible reconciliation is that Keynesian policy was effective only so long as labor markets were accomodating. So long as increased pressure of demand applied by governments in response to slowdowns produced additional output and employment rather than higher wages and hence higher prices, the macroeconomy was stable. Investment was maintained at high levels, and rapid growth persisted.

The key to Europe's rapid growth, from this perspective, was its relatively inflation-resistant labor markets.[41] So long as they accommodated demand pressure by supplying more labor input rather than demanding higher wages, the other pieces of the puzzle fell into place. What then accounted for the accommodating nature of postwar labor markets?

The conventional explanation, following Kindleberger (1967), is elastic supplies of underemployed labor from rural sectors within the advanced countries and from Europe's southern and eastern fringe. Elastic supplies of labor disciplined potentially militant labor unions. A problem with this argument is that the competition of underemployed Italians or Greeks or Eastern European refugees was hardly felt in the United Kingdom, yet labor market behavior was transformed in the United Kingdom as in other countries after World War II.[42]

Another explanation is history. Memory of high unemployment and strife between the wars served to moderate labor-market conflict. Conservatives could recall that attempts to roll back interwar welfare states had led to polarization, destabilizing representative institutions and setting the stage for fascism. Left-wingers could recall the other side of the same story. Both could reflect on the stagnation of the interwar period and blame it on political deadlock.

Yet another potential explanation is the Bretton Woods system. Bretton Woods linked the dollar to gold at $35 an ounce and other currencies to the dollar. So long as American policymakers' commitment to the Bretton Woods parity remained firm, limits were placed on the extent of inflationary policies. So long as European policymakers were loath to devalue against the dollar, limits were placed on their policies as well. Price expectations were stabilized. Inflation, where it surfaced, was more likely to be regarded as transitory. Consequently, increased pressure of demand was less likely to translate into higher prices instead of higher output, higher employment, and greater macroeconomic stability.

A final potential explanation is the Marshall Plan. Putting the point in this way serves to underscore that the Marshall Plan was but one of several factors contributing to observed outcomes. In principle, the Marshall Plan could have mattered directly. Marshall Planners sought a labor movement interested in raising productivity rather than in redistributing income from rich to poor. With labor peace a potential precondition for substantial Marshall Plan aid, labor organizations agreed to push for productivity improvements first and defer redistributions to later. Moreover, money was channeled to non-Communist labor organizations. European labor movements split over the question of whether Marshall aid should be welcomed —which left the Communists on the wrong side, opposed to economic recovery (Maier 1987).

In practice, we believe, the Marshall Plan's indirect effects were important. One way to think about the post–World War II settlement, and the contrast with the interwar period, is as a coordination problem. Labor, management, and government in Europe could, in effect, choose to try to maximize their current share of national income—as after World War I. Inflation, strikes, financial disarray, cyclical instability, and productivity problems can all be seen as corollaries of this equilibrium. Alternatively, the parties could trade current compensation for faster long-term growth and higher living standards, even in present-value terms. Workers would moderate their wage demands, management its demands for profits. Government agreed to use demand management to maintain employment in return for wage restraint on the part of unions. Higher investment and faster productivity growth could ensue, eventually rendering everyone better off.

Such a social contract is advantageous only if it is generally accepted. If workers continued to aggressively press for higher wages, management had little incentive to plow back profits in return for the promise of higher future profits. If management failed to plow back profits, workers had little incentive to moderate current wage demands in return for higher future productivity and compensation. If labor relations were conflictual rather than harmonious, productivity would be the casualty. The Marshall Plan could have shifted Europe onto this social contract equilibrium path, for once workers and management began coordinating on the superior equilibrium they had no obvious reason to stop.[43]

The Marshall Plan provided immediate incentives for wage moderation in the late forties. U.S. policy encouraged European governments to pursue investment-friendly policies. Productivity soared in the wake of financial stabilization and the advent of the Marshall Plan. The advantages of the cooperative equilibrium were suddenly clear.

It is intriguing that, within the group of reconstructing nations, those where the United States had most leverage had the fastest-growing economies. U.S. influence was strongest in Germany, weaker in France and Italy, and weakest in Britain. In the post–World War II period the German economy was the most successful, the British economy least. Japan, where MacArthur was proconsul, might be seen as an even more extreme case of this process at work.

8 Implications for Eastern Europe

Do conditions like those that made the Marshall Plan a success after World War II exist in Eastern Europe and the Soviet Union today? There are important parallels. Just as in Western Europe in 1947–48, enterprises hold back inventories in anticipation of higher prices once controls are relaxed. Excess liquidity and government budget deficits create the specter of rampant inflation. Belief that reform must occur soon, but uncertainty about its nature, provides a powerful incentive to delay investment and rationalization until the situation is clarified.

A paradox of reform in Eastern Europe is that the workers in heavy industry who initiated the rebellion against Communist domination were, from an economic standpoint, relatively unproductive at world prices and thus "privileged" under the ancien régime. Their wages were relatively high. The industries in which they worked were massively subsidized. Their real wages will be among the first to fall, and must fall the farthest. Their jobs are most likely to disappear during transition. Ironically, those in the vanguard of rebellion against the ancien régime may be the first to withdraw their support for reform. Even with substantial aid to cushion the fall in consumption during adjustment, it is not clear that adjustment can be successfully completed.

As in Europe after World War I, political struggles over economic structure could lead to damaging "wars of attrition." Conflict over distribution could produce inflation, price controls, and foreign-exchange rationing. Alternatively, market prices could be controlled in the interest of stabilizing income distributions. The government's fiscal and investment stance would be used to allocate resources. This would result in stagnation, for the market should handle the allocation of resources and the government's welfare state structure should moderate the distribution of income, not the other way around. If post–World War II Argentina is any guide, such a controlled, semiplanned economy could persist for a generation before being discredited.

To avoid both the post–World War I "distributional conflict" trap and the Argentinian "populist overregulation" trap, Eastern Europe will have to be lucky. A substantial aid program might help them to make their own luck. Supporting Eastern European living standards could limit public opposition to economic reform when output initially falls during the transition to a market economy. Hard currency would allow higher imports of much-needed commodities from the West. Reserves would make monetary stabilization and currency convertibility possible.

Important differences weaken the case for a Marshall Plan, especially for the regions of the Soviet Union. In post–World War II Western Europe there already existed widespread support for and experience with the market. The Marshall Plan only tipped the balance. It is not clear that comparable support exists in the Soviet Union today, or in much of Eastern Europe. Powerful elements still oppose economic liberalization. And many advocates have no clear idea of what liberalization entails.

In post–World War II Western Europe, Marshall Plan aid was effective at least in part because Europe had experience with markets. It possessed the institutions needed for their operation. Property rights, bankruptcy codes, court systems to enforce market contracts—not to mention entrepreneurial skills—all were in place. None of this holds in Eastern Europe today. For fifty years potential entrepreneurs have been labeled as "speculators" and attacked as public enemies. One principle of a market economy is that entrepreneurial profits tell not how much the entrepreneur is an exploiter but how wasteful of resources the situation would have been in his absence. This principle is not yet established, and so political leaders will be tempted to try to earn populist applause by renewed crackdowns on speculators.

In post–World War II Western Europe, U.S. aid and U.S. conditionality encouraged the reductions in government spending needed for financial stability. It encouraged the elimination of controls and the liberalization of trade. It is far from certain that aid today will have the same effect. Transfers to the central government may delay rather than accelerate the process of privatizing industry and creating a market economy. It is critical that whatever programs are adopted, aid should be provided on the basis of actions taken rather than need.

These observations all point toward caution on the part of those contemplating the extension of Western aid to the East. They are reminders that aid for Eastern European reform is a gamble. But the stakes are high, the downside risk limited, and the potential gain enormous.

The original Marshall Plan was a gamble as well. The Marshall Plan's Senate floor leader, Arthur Vandenberg, did not promise success. In his final speech before the Senate vote he warned that "... there are no blueprints to guarantee results. We are entirely surrounded by calculated risks. I profoundly believe that the pending program is the best of these risks..."

Notes

Prepared for the Centre for Economic Performance and Landeszentralbank Hamburg conference on Post–World War II European Reconstruction, Hamburg, September 5–7, 1991. We thank Marco Becht for research assistance, and Marc Uzan, Lawrence Summers, Steven Schran, Richard Layard, Charles Kindleberger, Rüdiger Dornbusch, Alessandra Casella, and Geoffrey Carliner for helpful comments. Barry Eichengreen's research was supported by the Center for German and European Studies of the University of California at Berkeley. Bradford De Long's was supported by the NBER and by the National Science and Olin Foundations.

1. Wartime relief, post–World War II UNRRA aid, and pre–Marshall Plan interim aid may well have significantly speeded up the reconstruction process. Although we do not address the question of the role of pre–Marshall Plan aid in this chapter, we hope to examine its effects in future work.

2. Without the Marshall Plan, the pattern of the post–World War II European political economy might well have resembled the overregulation and relative eco-

J. Bradford De Long and Barry Eichengreen   224

nomic stagnation of post–World War II Argentina, a nation that has dropped from First to Third World status in two generations. Or post–World War II Europe might have replicated the financial instability—alternate episodes of inflation and deflation—experienced by much of Europe in the twenties as interest groups and social classes bitterly struggled over the distribution of wealth and in the process stalled economic growth. This is not to say that post–World War II Western Europe was a laissez-faire economy.

3. Among others, Italy, Turkey, Portugal, Spain, Bulgaria, Greece, Rumania, Yugo-slavia, Hungary, Albania, Poland, Estonia, Latvia, Lithuania, Austria, Germany—not to speak of Japan, China, and many Central and South American countries—tried and then abandoned representative governments in the interwar period. See John Lukacs (1991).

4. See for example Hogan (1987), van der Wee (1986), Mee (1984), Price (1955), and Tinbergen (1954).

5. See Block (1977) for a discussion of reasons U.S. private investors were unwilling to loan money to Europe after World War II. Eichengreen and Portes (1989) describe the very different post–World War I experience when U.S. private invest-ment bankers were relatively eager to channel capital for European reconstruction.

6. For example, see Wexler (1983), Mee (1984), Mayne (1973), Gimbel (1976), and Arkes (1972). At variance with the folk image conveyed by these accounts is Milward (1984), one of the few who pays close attention to the quantitative dimensions of the American aid program. Milward's revisionist downplaying of the importance of the Marshall Plan and his conclusion that the pace of European recovery would not been very different in its absence have recently colored discus-sions of policy toward Eastern Europe. See for example *The Economist* (15 June 1991), or Collins and Rodrik (1991). As shall become apparent, we believe that Milward's revisionism is overstated.

7. See Sweezy (1943) for an extreme but surprisingly widely held contemporary view. See Maier (1987) for a historian's account of attitudes toward the market. In the immediate aftermath of World War II, the remaining pillar of market economics was the United States, but its performance during the Great Depression had been far from inspiring. Maier (1987) quotes British historian A. J. P. Taylor as speaking in late 1945 to how "nobody in Europe believes in the American way of life—that is, in private enterprise; or rather those who believe in it are a defeated party—a party which seems to have no more future."

8. One of us has suggested previously that Harris's estimate of realized returns is overly pessimistic. See Eichengreen and Portes (1989). But Harris could not antici-pate the settlement negotiations between U.S. creditors and debtor governments that would occupy the first postwar decade and return to American investors at least a portion of their principal. If Harris could not anticipate this outcome, neither were contemporary investors likely to do so. Thus, from the perspective of 1947, the returns on post–World War I loans to Europe appeared disappointing.

9. TRB, *The New Republic*, May 5, 1947.

10. Costs of the German occupation, however, were largely borne by Germany.

11. The remaining 7 percent was spent employing the U.S. merchant marine rather than lower cost competitors.

12. On the consequences of World War II and the situation at its end, see Milward (1984), Calvocoressi and Wint (1972), and Halle (1967).

13. We do not pass judgment here on the economic implications of strategic bombing. See U.S. Strategic Bombing Survey (1976) for a contemporary assessment. Also see Milward (1965, 1984), and Ellis (1990).

14. Although 1938 was a recession year in the United States, its use as a baseline for post–World War II comparisons should not be misleading for Europe. The European slowdown in economic activity in 1938 was relatively minor.

15. Italian industrial production had fallen to one-third of its pre–World War II level. In the three Western-occupied zones of Germany (including the Saar), industrial production had fallen to one-fifth of that of 1938.

16. The existence of war debt liabilities to the United States complicates the picture. But typically service of these obligations did not begin until the second half of the twenties, facilitating immediate post–World War I adjustment.

17. Holtfrerich (1986) analyzes the massive flow of short-term capital from the United States to Germany in 1919–21.

18. A strict loan embargo was imposed against the Soviet Union, the absence of a war-debt funding agreement led to the disapproval of a Romanian loan in 1922, and refunding issues for France were delayed. But Eichengreen (1989a) concludes that U.S. government restrictions were more bark than bite, and that "in almost all cases where the government entered an objection, [they] could be gotten round." Eichengreen (1989a), quoting Feis (1950).

19. William Clayton, Undersecretary of State for Economic Affairs, was the strongest voice. See Mayne (1973). The influential Harriman Report (1947), *European Recovery and American Aid*, a key piece of the administration's lobbying effort, took the same perspective. On U.S. State Department thinking before the Marshall Plan, see Acheson (1966), Bohlen (1973), and Pogue (1990).

20. Olson (1982) argues that World War II destroyed distributional coalitions and delayed the development of new ones, thus limiting the extent to which post–World War II European political economy could follow the post–World War I pattern of intensive redistributional strife. Below we suggest, however, that there was no absence of distributional coalitions after World War II; the difference lay rather in their behavior—and in the selective incentives to which they responded.

21. Similarly, the rapid repair of other forms of publicly provided infrastructure prevented them from constraining recovery. Water systems were quickly restored. The electrical grid was put back into operation (although there was not always coal to fuel the power plants). In fact, public spending did not rise in countries receiving large amounts of Marshall Plan aid. Countries that were major aid recipients saw

the government spending share of national income fall relative to other nations (see Eichengreen and Uzan 1991). The Marshall Plan did not accelerate growth by releasing resource constraints that prevented governments from rebuilding infrastructure. Earlier pre–Marshall Plan post–World War II aid may, however, have helped in the speedy reconstruction of Europe's infrastructure.

22. 1950 is almost precisely the midpoint of the Marshall Plan. The MSA mission, led by Hollis Chenery, in fact provided several such tables. We use the 16-sector input-output table provided by U.S. Mutual Security Agency (1953), pp. 132–133.

23. Of course, these assumptions are patently false, a point whose implications we explore below.

24. We derive these estimates by reducing each element of the vector of final demands by the same proportion until the coal constraint is just binding.

25. Compare the back-of-the-envelope calculation in the preceding paragraph, which came to 3 percent.

26. In fact, aside from the possibility that fear of a renewed Great Depression would act as a self-fulfilling prophecy, the return of the Great Depression was not likely in the forties. The memory of the Depression, and the greater strength and incorporation of social democratic political movements in government, kept right-wing governments from adopting policies of out-and-out national deflation. The availability of the large U.S. market to European exports—especially with the coming of the Korean War Boom and NATO in the early fifties—prevented any large world-aggregate demand shortfall as in the Great Depression. With the American locomotive under full steam, Western European economies were unlikely to suffer from prolonged Keynesian demand-shortfall depressions.

27. Moreover, conservative dictatorships in the thirties had sharpened lines of political cleavage. Landowner and exporter elites had always appropriated the lion's share of the benefits of free trade. They had in the thirties shown a willingness to sacrifice political democracy in order to stunt the growth of the welfare state.

28. Foreign borrowing would have appeared even less attractive to Argentines who recalled the extraordinarily high, real-effective interest rates that their foreign debt had carried during the deflation of the thirties. See Díaz-Alejandro (1970).

29. The experience of the previous generation, however, suggested ex ante that Argentina did not need to further specialize in the international division of labor. Demand for its export products had been depressed for twenty years.

30. For details, see Casella and Eichengreen (1991).

31. Wallich (1955) describes how German industries that made consumer goods would pay their workers in the factory's output so that its workers would have something with which to barter, while industries that made producer goods paid their workers some of their wages in coal, which managers had diverted from power generation.

32. This is the argument developed for Italy and France in Casella and Eichengreen (1991).

33. Banca Italiana Governor Menichella attributed Italian stabilization to the pre–Marshall Plan interim aid program. In his belief, "stabilization was made possible by interim aid.... Interim aid and the prospect of the Marshall Plan made it possible to maintain stability in prices." See Price (1955).

34. Auriol (1970), p. 162. Other sources do not contradict Auriol's memoirs. See, for example, Price (1955).

35. The Marshall Plan was not left to professional politicians, potentially interested in getting along with recipient countries and building bureaucratic empires. Because Republican senators like Arthur Vandenberg had feared either the Marshall aid would be wasted or—like New Deal programs—used to solidify Democratic political bases in the United States, the Economic Cooperation Administration had "sunset" provisions built into its enabling legislation and a peculiar status as an administrative agency formally subordinate to but not reporting to or responsible to the president. Republican worries moreover set in motion a chain of events that led the Economics Cooperation Administration to be headed by a businessman: Paul Hoffman had previously been president of Studebaker.

Truman originally sought Dean Acheson as Marshall Plan administrator, but Acheson demurred. Senator Arthur Vandenberg had been the key to getting the program shell fueled with appropriations. Vandenberg had worked hard to separate Marshall Plan administration from the ongoing governmental bureaucracy. Acheson believed—correctly—that the appointment of a State Department insider like himself would be taken as a rejection of what Vandenberg had worked for. Acheson suggested that Truman, instead, ask Vandenberg for his choice—and he speculated that Vandenberg would recommend Paul Hoffman. Truman did ask, and Vandenberg did so recommend.

36. Between 1948 and 1952, trade among European countries increased more than five times as fast as European trade with other continents. The economies of Europe were once again permitted to specialize in the production of goods in which they had a comparative advantage. Productivity received another boost.

37. Statistics in this section are from Boltho (1982).

38. The hypotheses advanced in this and the succeeding paragraph are developed at more length in Eichengreen (1989b).

39. This point, made forcefully for Britain by Matthews (1967), applies to other European countries as well. See Glyn et al. (1990).

40. Broadberry (1991), table 6, computed from Matthews, Feinstein, and Odling-Smee (1982).

41. This, of course, is the famous conclusion of Kindleberger (1967), although the mechanism there linking labor markets to economic performance is somewhat different.

42. See Broadberry (1991).

43. We leave for another paper the question of what caused the postwar settlement to break down in the seventies. Two intriguing treatments of this question are

J. Bradford De Long and Barry Eichengreen   228

those of Marglin (1990) and Broadberry (1991), both of whom argue that the postwar settlement contained the seeds of its own destruction.

References

Acheson, Dean (1960). *Sketches from Life*. New York: Harper & Bros.

Acheson, Dean (1966). *Present at the Creation*. New York: New American Library.

Alesina, Alberto and Allen Drazen (1992). "Why are Stabilizations Delayed?" *American Economic Review* (forthcoming).

Auriol, Vincent (1970). *Mon Septennat, 1947–1954*. Paris: Armand Colin.

Arkes, Hadley (1972). *Bureaucracy, the Marshall Plan, and the National Interest*. Princeton: Princeton University Press.

Bohlen, Charles (1973). *Witness to History 1929–69*. New York: W.W. Norton.

Block, Fred (1977). *The Origins of International Economic Disorder*. Berkeley: University of California Press.

Boltho, Andrea (1982). "Growth." In Andrea Boltho, ed., *The European Economy*. Oxford: Clarendon Press.

Broadberry, S. N. (1991). "Why Was Unemployment in Postwar Britain So Low?" Unpublished manuscript, Warwick University.

Calvocoressi, Peter and Guy Wint (1972). *Total War: Causes and Courses of World War II*. New York: Pantheon Books.

Casella, Alessandra and Barry Eichengreen (1991). "Halting Inflation in Italy and France After World War II." In Michael Bordo and Forrest Capie, eds., *Monetary Regimes in Transition*, Cambridge: Cambridge University Press (forthcoming).

Collins, Susan and Dani Rodrik (1991). *Eastern Europe and the Soviet Union in the World Economy*. Washington, DC: Institute for International Economics.

Cowan, Tyler (1985). "The Marshall Plan: Myths and Realities." In Doug Bandow, ed., *U.S. Aid to the Developing World*. Washington, D.C.: Heritage Foundation.

De Cecco, Marcello (1986). "On Milward's Reconstruction of Western Europe." In *Political Economy: Studies in the Surplus Approach* 2:1, 105–14.

Díaz-Alejandro, Carlos (1970). *Essays on the Economic History of the Argentine Republic*. New Haven: Yale University Press.

Dumke, Rolf (1990). "Reassessing the *Wirtschaftswunder*: Reconstruction and Postwar Growth in West Germany in an International Context." *Oxford Bulletin of Economics and Statistics* 52:2, 451–491.

Eichengreen, Barry (1989a). "The U.S. Capital Market and Foreign Lending, 1920–1955." In Jeffrey Sachs, ed., *Developing Country Debt and Economic Performance. The International Financial System*. Chicago: University of Chicago Press, 107–158.

Eichengreen, Barry (1989b). "European Economic Growth After World War II: The Grand Schema." presented to the Conference Marking the Retirement of William N. Parker, New Haven.

Eichengreen, Barry and Richard Portes (1989). "After the Deluge: Default, Negotiation, and Readjustment during the Interwar Years." In Barry Eichengreen and Peter Lindert, *The International Debt Crisis in Historical Perspective*, Cambridge, MA: MIT Press, 12–47.

Eichengreen, Barry and Marc Uzan (1991). "The Marshall Plan: Economic Effects and Implications for Eastern Europe." *Economic Policy* (forthcoming).

Ellis, John (1990). *Brute Force*. New York: Viking.

Feis, Herbert (1950). *The Diplomacy of the Dollar, 1919–1932: First Era*. Baltimore, MD: Johns Hopkins University Press.

Gimbel, John (1968). *The American Occupation of Germany: Politics and the Military, 1945–1949*. Palo Alto: Stanford University Press.

Gimbel, John (1976). *The Origins of the Marshall Plan*. Palo Alto: Stanford University Press.

Glyn, Andrew, Alan Hughes, Alain Lipietz, and Ajit Singh (1990). "The Rise and Fall of the Golden Age." In Stephen Marglin and Juliet Schor, eds., *The Golden Age of Capitalism*. Oxford: Clarendon, 39–125.

Halle, Louis (1967). *The Cold War as History*. New York: Harper and Row.

Harris, Seymour (1948). *The European Recovery Program*. Cambridge, MA: Harvard University Press.

Hazlitt, Henry (1947). *Will Dollars Save the World?* New York: Appleton-Century.

Hogan, Michael (1987). *The Marshall Plan: America, Britain, and the Reconstruction of Western Europe, 1947–1952*. Cambridge: Cambridge University Press.

Holtfrerich, Carl-Ludwig (1986). "U.S. Capital Exports to Germany. 1919–23 Compared to 1924–29." *Explorations in Economic History* 23:1–32.

Kindleberger, Charles (1967). *Europe's Postwar Growth*. London: Oxford University Press.

Kindleberger, Charles (1987). *Marshall Plan Days*.

Kostrzewa, Wojciech, Pater Nunnenkamp, and Holger Schmeiding (1990). "A Marshall Plan for Middle and Eastern Europe?" *World Economy* 13:1 (March), 27–50.

Lukacs, John (1991). *The Duel*. New York: Ticknor & Fields.

Maier, Charles S. (1977). "The Politics of Productivity: Foundations of American International Economic Policy after World War II." *International Organization* 31:607–633.

Maier, Charles S. (1981). "The Two Postwar Eras and the Conditions for Stability in Twentieth-Century Western Europe." *American Historical Review* 86:327–352.

Maier, Charles S. (1987). *In Search of Stability*. Cambridge: Cambridge University Press.

Marglin, Stephen (1990). "Lessons of the Golden Age: An Overview." In Stephen Marglin and Juliet Schor, eds., *The Golden Age of Capitalism*. Oxford: Clarendon, 1–38.

Matthews, R. C. O. (1968). "Why has Britain had Full Employment Since the War?" *Economic Journal* 82:195–204.

Matthews, R. C. O., C. Feinstein, and J. Odling-Smee (1982). *British Economic Growth, 1856–1973*, Stanford: Stanford University Press.

Mayne, Richard (1973). *The Recovery of Europe, 1945–1973*. Garden City, NY: Anchor Books.

Mee, Charles (1984). *The Marshall Plan: The Launching of the Pax Americana*. New York: Simon and Schuster.

Milward, Alan S. (1965). *The German Economy at War*. London: Methuen.

Milward, Alan S. (1984). *The Reconstruction of Western Europe 1945–51*. London: Methuen.

Pogue, Forrest C. (1990). *George C. Marshall: Statesman 1945–49*. New York: Viking Press.

Sweezy, Paul (1942). *The Theory of Capitalist Development*. New York: Oxford University Press.

Tinbergen, Jan (1954). "The Significance of the Marshall Plan for the Netherlands Economy." In Kingdom of the Netherlands Ministry of Finance, *The Road to Recovery: The Marshall Plan, Its Importance for the Netherlands, and European Cooperation*. The Hague: Kingdom of the Netherlands Ministry of Finance.

United Nations (1948). *International Capital Movements During the Interwar Period*. Lake Success, NY: United Nations.

United Nations (various years), *Economic Survey of Europe*. Geneva: United Nations.

United States Mutual Security Agency (1953). *The Structure and Growth of the Italian Economy*. Rome: MSA.

Wallich, Henry (1955). *Mainsprings of the German Recovery*. New Haven: Yale University Press.

van der Beugel, Ernst Hans (1966). *From Marshall Aid to Atlantic Partnership: European Integration as a Concern of American Foreign Policy*. New York: Elsevier.

van der Wee, Hermann (1986). *Prosperity and Upheaval*. Berkeley: University of California Press.

Wexler, Imanuel (1983). *The Marshall Plan Revisited: The European Recovery Program in Economic Perspective*. Westport, CN: Greenwood Press.

[2]
Regional Plans for European Trade, 1945–1957

Wendy Asbeek Brusse

1. Bilateral Trade Agreements

At the end of the Second World War, few leading politicians were immune to the 'lessons of the past' so widely discussed by experts on the inter-war period. Economic and political instability, the lack of an internationally coordinated reconstruction plan after the First World War and the prevalence of bilateral commercial relations were widely held to be responsible for the disastrous effects which the Great Depression had had on social and economic welfare. Multilateralism, promoted by a worldwide International Trade Organization (ITO), was therefore considered a key element for post-war stability and prosperity. For instance, the League of Nations warned in 1945:

> It is essential ... that multilateral trading, which was severely restricted in the 'thirties, should be restored. (...) any widespread recourse to 'bilateralism' or other forms of trading relationships involving discrimination against other third parties would involve not only the immediate danger of engendering trade warfare but also the ultimate risk of sapping the bases of political co-operation between peoples and consequently of world peace.

Yet severe distortions in the European economies caused by shortages of raw materials, goods essential for reconstruction and foreign exchange, by the elimination of Germany from the European trade scene and also by the changed balance of payments position of the United Kingdom from deficit to surplus *vis-à-vis* Europe, forced countries to impose restrictions on most of their trade after the war. Governments suspended tariffs and relied on quotas and exchange controls to allocate their scarce resources for reconstruction purposes. At the same time they exhausted their foreign currency reserves in order to meet constant demand for hard currency imports. The exchange of goods was usually conducted along strictly bilateral lines, based on the exchange of specific, mostly 'essential', goods and on reciprocal credits allowing for some flexibility in the volume of imports and exports. Despite a general awareness among politicians of the dangers of bilateralism, commercial relations between the European countries were dominated by bilateral trade and payments agreements, and in fact it was only as a result of bilateralism that intra-European trade managed to recover quite as rapidly as it did in the first year after the war.

By 1947 most governments realized that the controls imposed as temporary measures to overcome the transition to a stable multilateral trade system had become indispensible instruments to maintain high levels of dollar investments and economic activity. Rather than reducing restrictions, all nations imposed more drastic measures of control which protected the domestic economy from deflation; despite an even more rigid system of bilateral balancing in intra-European trade and a continuously growing European deficit with the dollar area. And as the prospects for a general balance of payments recovery and of currency convertibility appeared more remote than before, the willingness of countries to extend further credits for financing bilateral surpluses clearly diminished. As a consequence, there developed a permanent imbalance between creditor and debtor countries which forced trade into inefficient channels and in the long run might have curbed European trade expansion altogether.

The answer to Europe's two-fold problem of internal disequilibria and dollar shortages seemed to be provided by Marshall's announcement of financial aid for Europe and the new initiatives to deal with the prevalence of trade restrictions within Europe. The first and probably most ambitious of these initiatives, the European Recovery Plan, aimed to develop a united and politically and economically strong Europe by creating a multilateral European payments mechanism, removing the barriers to intra-trade and giving it a truly international forum for decision-making. Not only had Europe to recover from the disintegrative impact of the thirties and the war, but it had to be rebuilt into an economically and politically integrated area.

Their immediate aim was to close the widening gap between Europe's imports for domestic consumption and capital investments and its domestically produced exports, reduce the danger of inflation, increase production and social stability and hence lessen the danger of a 'communist take-over' in France and Italy. This would pave the way for realising the ultimate political objectives of the American state department's European policy: the transformation of Europe into an economic and military stronghold of the democratic and free world against Soviet communism. A strong and united economic ally would be a strong military ally and could eventually share in the common defence burden. Moreover, a powerful Western European economy would be an essential condition for the reconstruction of a worldwide international system of trade and payments. Economic growth through rising productivity, the American philosophy dictated, formed the key to Europe's transformation.

One way of transforming the old continent which was strongly in vogue with American policy-makers (and public opinion on both sides of the Atlantic), was the creation of a customs union. Customs Union theory provided an intellectual framework that appeared remarkably easily adaptable to their economic and political plans for Europe. It assumed that market size was one vital determinant of economic growth and productivity. Small, national markets, the argument ran, are no longer adequate to exploit the advantages of modern technology such as mass production and specialization to their full extent because their domestic demand is too limited. In addition, such markets eventually lag behind in competitiveness since they are dominated by a small group of producers who tend to limit production by concluding restrictive agreements. By removing the trade barriers between these previously separated markets and uniting them into one large customs union, producers and consumers can reap the full benefits of large-scale production and specialization on productivity. With the rise in the number of producers it becomes more difficult to enforce restrictive agreements so that competitiveness and efficiency will increase. Furthermore, the higher degree of specialization and maximization of comparative costs resulting from the elimination of trade barriers would also induce a gradual convergence of levels of productivity and income between the previously separate areas. As a consequence, social tensions would eventually fade, thereby eroding the soil for communism.

However, not all incentives for a European customs union were American-inspired. Well before the announcement of the European Recovery Plan, French politicians had explored the opportunities for a customs union with one or more Western European countries. And despite their difficulties at the time in overcoming Benelux resistance to a regional agreement dominated by France, they had not completely abandoned the idea of a customs union in Europe. The fact that Benelux refused to participate in any agreement from which the German economy would be excluded actually stimulated France to consider proposals for a customs union of a different composition. In this context, Marshall Aid, and the European economic cooperation it conditioned, provided a very suitable opportunity for presenting these alternative customs union options.

2.   The European Customs Union Study Group

When the sixteen European countries of the Committee on European Economic Cooperation (CEEC) met in Paris in July 1947, the Italian minister of foreign affairs, Count Sforza, made an appeal for a customs union between Italy and France as the first step towards a wider European union. However, since the Benelux countries held to their demand for German participation on an equal basis and since the United Kingdom was hesitant, the CEEC's final report did not contain any decisive plans for a customs union. It promised instead a careful and detailed study of a customs union of as many countries as possible and warned against any hasty undertakings: 'the formation of a customs union, particularly between several large and highly industrial countries, necessarily involves complex technical negotiations and adjustments which can only be achieved by progressive steps over a period of years'.

In September 1947 an independent European Customs Union Study Group (ECUSG) met with most European members of the CEEC taking part (Norway and Sweden sent only observers). Even at this stage, some American observers noted, there was a general tendency among the members to view the problems involved as being far greater than the possibilities offered. The conclusion reached in the first tentative report of November 1947 was deliberately vague. The long-term welfare effects of a large European customs union, it read, 'would depend on the proper solution of a great many problems and the nature of the compromise reached'.

The Study Group had meanwhile created a Tariff Committee to deal with technical problems and an Economic Committee to examine the effects of the customs union on the economies of the member states. They based the latter examination on the following major assumptions: all internal tariffs, quantitative restrictions and exchange controls between members and non-members would be removed; preferential tariff agreements against outside countries would be maintained, and the common external tariff of the union should not be higher than the average of the existing tariffs of the members. This last assumption appeared the most controversial of all.

The Charter for the ITO gave no clear indication of a method of calculating an average tariff for all products. Depending on which calculation method one preferred, the common tariff could be either protectionist, relatively low or somewhere in between. On the whole, there was a tendency for low tariff countries such as Benelux, Sweden and Denmark to demand a moderate tariff level in order to prevent their export interests with outsiders from being damaged. 'High tariff' countries like Portugal, Greece, Italy and France, on the other hand, wanted a more protectionist tariff to safeguard domestic producers against competition from third countries. Every country, however, including the so-called 'low tariff' ones, had some vulnerable industries for which it hoped to receive special protection measures and therefore did not want to commit itself to any calculation method before the outcome of that method for the average tariff in these sectors was known. As a consequence, the Tariff Committee had to draw up a complete specimen tariff for all products of the nomenclature without knowing whether the end result would be accepted by the delegations.

Using this specimen tariff and the conclusions of the technical sub-committees, the Economic Committee reported on the expected consequences of a customs union at the end of October 1948. The report rather optimistically stated that the sectoral studies had revealed 'fewer difficulties in the way of the formation of a Customs Union than might have been expected'. A study which divided industries according to the social and economic opportunities and difficulties they could reasonably expect from the creation of the customs union showed an impressive list of branches listed as 'unproblematic'. On closer examination, though, it revealed no cause for optimism. Firstly, a number of them had received the label of unproblematic only under protest from predominantly exporting countries and only after highly protectionist measures had been recommended for their adaptation to the customs union. For cereals, for example, the Committee had advised maintaining import quotas in importing member countries, but there had been no unanimity on this. The same situation occurred for coal and cokes. Moreover, the optimism over the removal of trade barriers for organic dyestuffs, machine-made lace, electrical equipment, and coal, tar and pitch was based on the assumption that producers within the union would make private producer arrangements to avoid competitive struggles, thereby confirming the suspicion of some American observers that the Study Group's technical experts, if left to decide on their own, had every intention of cartelizing Europe.

Turning to the sectors classified as 'problematic' in the creation of a customs union, their suspicion is merely strengthened. Here, too, fears of 'keen or abnormal competition' resulted in the advice to 'mitigate the most damaging effects of competition' in the pharmaceutical industry, to 'regulate the trade' in the paper industry and to maintain import restrictions in the machine tool industry. On iron and steel products opinion was strongly divided; France and Benelux favoured placing them in the category of 'unproblematic' products but received no support from the other countries. The report of the sub-committee on iron and steel actually hinted 'that the European iron and steel market was very stable before the war, due to the existence of the International Steel Agreement, of which nearly all the Study Group countries were members'. Not surprisingly, many foodstuffs were also classified as problematic, because most countries had maintained extensive systems of domestic protection, preferential agreements with their overseas partners and very often had conflicting interests in their European export markets. Agricultural products and foodstuffs, the delegates anticipated, formed a group on its own for which the removal of trade barriers, even after temporarily maintaining protectionist measures in a transitional period, seemed unfeasible. Any European customs union would have to leave room for quantitative restrictions, minimum export prices, subsidies and (seasonal) tariffs. To sum up, as the Benelux delegation rightly complained, there was 'a tendency towards establishing a system whereby there would no longer be a Customs Union in the true sense, but rather a free circulation of only a very limited number of the products studied, while no decision would be made about the others'.

This was in part due to the many uncertainties with which the delegates were forced to cope. First and foremost, uncertainty about the future of the German economy paralysed the negotiations. By June 1947, the French government had been forced to abandon plans to use German resources to boost exports to the German market and, instead, seemed determined to contain the German economy through a European customs union from which the Germans would either be excluded or incorporated on French terms. That the Benelux countries, who were indispensable to any kind of customs union, would accept the French conditions was in any case unlikely, whereas the Americans and the British might also reject them. The British role represented a second factor of uncertainty. Many governments doubted from the beginning that the British would be willing to surrender part of their preferential access to Commonwealth markets in exchange for the customs union. The British government decided against joining the Europeans only in May 1948, and few countries had been willing to reveal their policy before they knew the British verdict. A third important problem was caused by the fact that Europe's trade was still heavily restricted by quota and payments restrictions so that tariffs were largely ineffective and suspended. To discuss external tariff levels and assess the effects of a free internal market seemed bound to be a very speculative undertaking.

Given these highly unpredictable factors, it did not come as a surprise that new plans to remove European trade barriers were to concentrate on quantitative restrictions rather than tariffs. Thus, while the Study Group's work on customs unions was brought to a halt attention shifted to other, less ambitious projects. One of these was the OEEC's Plan of Action for European trade liberalization.

3. The OEEC's Trade Liberalization Programme

'No matter what door we go in – whether it be marked "Employment" or "Development" or "Commercial Policy" or "Commodity Policy" – the door where we come out is always marked "Q.R." [Quantitative Restrictions – WAB]. What we are talking about is protectionism, protectionism in its most extreme form. Of all forms of restrictionism ever devised by the mind of man, Q.R. is the worst.' These words, pronounced by an American delegate to the International Conference on Trade and Development in 1947, are characteristic of the American government's devotion to the battle against quantitative restrictions. Although initially imposed to control currency flows, the importance of quotas as protective and bargaining instruments had gradually increased and the American government feared that the longer a radical and systematic attack on quotas was postponed, the harder it would be to ban them from the European market. Thus, the Americans in the OEEC promoted the cause of a programme for their gradual removal, backed by a European payments union.

The OEEC's programme was ready in June 1949 and in November it was decided that by December members had to remove quotas on at least 50 per cent of their total imports on private account from the rest of the group in 1948 in each of three sectors of goods: food and feeding stuffs, raw materials and manufactured goods. Meanwhile, negotiations for a European payments organisation and for the next steps in the scheme continued in Paris.

To meet the requirement of the first liberalization effort, most countries began by removing quotas in those sectors where restrictions were either no longer necessary or no longer effective. This was mostly the case for raw materials and other essential goods for which there was a shortage on the home market. Thus, all countries reached the required limit by the end of 1949 without too many difficulties. They anticipated that the next step could cause more problems for their payments position and might actually reduce protection for domestic industries. The time limit for this next step towards a liberalization percentage of 60 per cent, retarded by the tiresome negotiations for the European Payments Union, was formulated in the OEEC 'Code of Liberalization of Trade' which eventually came into force on 19 September 1950. The delay meant that the 60 per cent stage did not become effective until October.

The adoption of the Code urged OEEC members to remove quotas 'as fully as their economic and financial position would permit' and with a view to balanced and similar efforts by their partners. It further committed them not to discriminate in their import policy with regard to both the liberalized and non-liberalized sectors. Moreover, the specific liberalization percentages were fixed at 60 per cent of all imports to be reached before October and 75 per cent as from the end of January 1951, with a minimum limit of 60 per cent in each of the three categories of goods. The latter obligation especially was expected to contribute to a major step forward in removing trade barriers and distortions in European trade resulting from bilateral trade agreements.

The degree of import liberalization achieved differed from country to country. By March 1950, the target date for the liberalization of 50 per cent of intra-European trade, six countries had failed to reach this minimum level. The overall percentages of the countries were, in most cases, not much above or below the required 50 per cent; the great exceptions being Turkey with no liberalization whatsoever and Switzerland with a percentage of 84. The real problem arose in meeting the minima for the sector of food and feeding stuffs and that of finished products. Germany, for example, only reached 44 per cent in the former and 24 per cent in the latter sector. Denmark, Italy and Norway were also well below the minimum level required for finished products. When at the end of 1950 the required overall and sectoral percentage of 60 had to be met, two of these countries were able to meet it. Germany had now removed 65 per cent of its restrictions on food and feed imports, but this was done partly by the expedient of shifting imports to state trade organizations and thereby removing them from the calculations. With 25 and 29 per cent of their respective manufactures liberalized, Denmark reached an overall liberalization percentage of 50 whereas Norway managed only 45 per cent.

Although the liberalization minima and non-discrimination rule adopted in the OEEC scheme were meant to trigger off a more radical removal of quotas, their actual impact was very modest. When the deadline of February 1951 arrived progress stagnated and was soon followed by widespread de-liberalization in Germany under the influence of the Korea boom. This immediately had an adverse effect on the liberalization efforts of the Netherlands and Denmark, who saw their major export market for agricultural products being closed. Both countries had been cautious about removing quotas from the start because, unlike other European partners, they had hardly any protective tariffs left to use as bargaining instruments. The introduction of the non-discrimination principle made them even less willing to remove quotas. As they rightly suspected, the principle not only gave a free ride to countries with a low liberalization percentage but also enabled them to damage the export opportunities of their less protected partners. Thus, the de-liberalization of Germany gave Denmark and Holland the signal to refuse further steps until other countries really opened up their markets.

This resistance to the OEEC scheme provided the incentive for a Dutch plan for the removal of trade barriers in Europe. Launched by minister of foreign affairs, Stikker, in the second half of May 1950, it claimed to offer a much more balanced approach to freeing European trade by attacking *all* barriers to trade instead of quotas only. Through a sector-by-sector method, quotas, tariffs and other barriers would be removed at the same time, thus leading to the gradual creation of a truly 'integrated' European market. A European Integration Fund would support participating industries with the financial aid needed for modernizing and re-allocating labour in the transitional phase. To prevent ministers in the Council of the OEEC from blocking the plan with their veto-right, the decision to implement the plan in each sector would depend on a 3/4 majority of the Council. Those countries that had voted against the integration of a particular sector were allowed to abstain from the operation whilst the other twelve or more countries went ahead with the removal of trade barriers. However, the latter construction proved to be the weakest element in the whole plan. Followed through in its entire logic, it would mean that for every sector to be integrated a constantly changing group of countries would have to form one market. Instead of integrating European markets this was likely to cause more imbalances and fragmentation of economies and trade patterns than the original situation.

Stikker's presentation of the plan as a genuine attempt at integrating Europe at a time when the ECA was waiting impatiently for European integration efforts, explains why the many critics of the plan could not simply reject it. If it were to be rejected, which hardly any government doubted, this could only be done after careful study of its merits and those of the alternatives. The Italian government understood this and managed to push the plan into a study group along with its own 'Pella plan' for European economic cooperation. The latter plan aimed at a preferential zone in which intra-European tariff reduction in the framework of the OEEC would have to be achieved through multilateral negotiations, the outcome of which would be subjected to an automatic reduction of all intra-European tariffs by 15 per cent within a period of three years. Apart from the method of automatic reductions which would influence other tariff plans at a later stage (see below), both the Pella and the Stikker plans disappeared in one of the drawers of the OEEC's 'Working Party No. 6', which spent about a year studying the proposals. Meanwhile, the Council of the OEEC continued to concentrate on the more serious problem of de-liberalization in Germany and, by November 1951, also the United Kingdom.

Faced with the danger of trade stagnation or even contraction, the OEEC adopted a French initiative to remove quotas on the basis of a common list of goods. Whereas previously hardly any good could move freely across the European borders because there was always some country that had put it under a quota regime, the liberalization of goods on a common list might actually create a quota-free market on a product-by-product basis. As the negotiations on the common list showed, however, it took almost a year before the OEEC eventually agreed on a list of products which, on balance, gave most countries a large enough interest in the liberalization effort to secure its implementation. And despite these cumbersome efforts the common list approach was not a success. Many products on the list had already been liberalized to a considerable extent in the previous period and, more importantly, not all countries in the end followed the rules of the game by removing quotas on all of them.

The experience of the percentage approach and the common list clearly showed how difficult it was to subject sixteen different economies to the discipline of one uniform liberalization method. One factor causing diversity was the difference in trade regimes within the OEEC countries. Countries like France, Germany and the United Kingdom, which had a considerable proportion of trade placed under state monopoly, had to liberalize a smaller proportion of total trade than countries with hardly any state trade. The impact of the liberalization scheme also varied according to the intensity of a country's intra-European trade and according to the commodity composition of its imports. For example, for a country importing only 10 per cent of total imports from the OEEC area, the burden of liberalization on total imports would be smaller than for one importing 30 per cent from the OEEC. For major agricultural exporters, too, the burden of liberalization would be relatively large because the level of liberalization in the agricultural sector was much lower than that in the other two sectors. The scheme had a different impact on every country and once these differences became wider over time, liberalization in Europe slowed down. Finally, as mentioned earlier, differences in tariff levels influenced the effects of liberalization. For countries with a high protectionist tariff the removal of quota restrictions could have less problematic effects than for those whose only barrier against foreign competition was the quotas to be removed under the liberalization obligations.

Given the unbalanced effects of liberalization it is hardly surprising that by the end of 1953, when the unchequered course of liberalization seemed to have ended, some countries demanded a radical departure from the method of gradual removal of restrictions. However, to suggest, as some countries did, that the OEEC should push all members over the last barriers of protectionism into the world of 100 per cent liberalisation is not only to ignore the strength of agricultural protectionism but also to ignore the events of the previous years. For already in 1949 it had become obvious that the OEEC would not evolve into the permanent supranational and political organization responsible for the creation of the European customs union which the Americans had originally planned. Like all schemes designed by the OEEC, the liberalization plan could only be implemented at a speed and with escape clauses which all participating governments were willing to accept. Lacking the economic powers of a supranational body, it would therefore take until 1955 before only a small 'hard core' of quotas was left to be removed.

4. The European Coal and Steel Community

With the formation of a customs union for coal and steel in 1952, the six governments of 'Little Europe' succeeded where the both the OEEC and the ECUSG had failed. The

European Coal and Steel Community (ECSC) united the coal and steel sectors of France, West Germany, Italy and the Benelux countries under a supranational High Authority, abolishing frontier barriers to trade, outlawing national discrimination and establishing trade rules in cases of glut or shortages. To most people European economic integration, so desperately pushed by the ECA and so energetically developed by the European Movement, seemed to take concrete shape for the first time since the war.

It is all too well known that the political dimension of a pool which united French and German coal and steel resources explains much of the origins of the ECSC and of its reputation in the history of European trade cooperation. Apart from political objectives, however, the project had economic objectives which had their origin in French policy making. It was aimed at safeguarding French access to the rich coal resources of the Ruhr after the dissolution of the International Ruhr Authority. At the same time it would allow Germany's production potential to recover beyond the artificial limits fixed by the Western Allies without posing the danger of German economic domination, because the supranational authority in charge would consist of independent experts rather than governmental delegates. Moreover, by aiming at pooling one sector of the economy only, the French steel industry would be able to profit while the other, weaker, sectors of the economy could remain protected.

To propose a customs union rather than the type of international planning institution for the steel industry suggested by the European Movement and French and British socialists, was to anticipate the negative reactions to any form of *dirigisme*. The idea of a planning authority, French insiders realized, would meet fierce resistance from German and French industrialists and possibly outright rejection on the part of the American administration. A customs union, on the other hand, tied in with American ideas and might appease those steel barons who had actually feared a socialist take-over in their industries. Ultimately, of course, the reactions to the pool for coal and steel would largely depend on the powers and tasks attributed to the supranational body during the international negotiations on the plan. These would determine if the High Authority was really to be the motor of efficient production and freer trade or just a modern version of the International Steel Cartel of the twenties, recalled with such nostalgic feelings by the ECUSG in 1948.

The negotiations between the governments of France, West Germany, the Benelux countries and Italy were concluded in April 1951 with the signing of the Treaty for the ECSC. With the support of the American delegation to the GATT the community received a waiver which permitted its exemption from the Most-Favoured-Nation rule. Less than two years later and without a transitional period (except for the Belgian coal industry and the Italian steel industry) the common market for coal, steel and iron ore was opened. The High Authority, although equipped with fewer powers than originally envisaged, not only abolished tariffs, quotas, subsidies and discriminatory freight rates but could also play a positive role in the field of social policy by improving working conditions and readapting redundant labour for other employment.

The rapid creation of the common market and the limited but real powers of the High Authority in fields other than trade probably explains why, even after having fulfilled its primary task of anchoring Germany into Europe, the ECSC remained such a powerful model for European cooperation throughout the 1950s. In fact, one sector where this model seemed to be especially applicable was agriculture. Here, too, market fluctuations had been so devastating in the past and protectionism was so persistent in the fifties that only a special, sectoral approach and a supranational body might change this situation.

5.   The Green Pool Negotiations

All efforts to remove trade barriers in Europe, whether in the framework of a European customs union, a trade liberalization scheme or a tariff reduction plan, almost automatically excluded dealing with agricultural protectionism. Agriculture, the ECUSG already observed in 1948, was too much of a special case for 'ordinary' plans and required measures different from any other economic sector. What explains this very special position of European agriculture? Part of the explanation can be found in the thirties, when agriculture was severely hit by the effects of the world economic crisis. By the end of the thirties most farmers in Western Europe could count on subsidies, high tariffs and levies, quota restrictions and high prices to guarantee their income.

After the war it seemed only natural to continue this policy for agriculture. The food shortages during and immediately after the war again confirmed the essential role of agriculture for the military, economic and political strength of a nation. As a matter of course, therefore, every national reconstruction plan accepted maximization of agricultural output as one of the main targets for the next five years. As long as the shortages persisted, food had to be bought overseas and paid for in dollars. Thus, the dollar gap gave an extra incentive to stimulate the expansion of agricultural production. Moreover, the prospect of a further increase in the population of Western Europe made maximizing agricultural output rational also as a long term target for reconstruction.

From the production figures one can conclude that the Western European performance in agriculture was still below the requirements of the post-war situation. Only in 1950 did agricultural output in Western Europe reach its pre-war level, and this was still not enough to meet the demand of a population that had in the meantime grown by about 12 per cent. The most characteristic feature of agricultural development in the post-war period was that the European countries had shifted their imports of cereals towards the dollar zone. Europe as a whole was now more dependent on cereal imports from this area than ever before; they made up 40 per cent of the OEEC foodstuffs deficit in 1951, more than 60 per cent of which came from the United States and Canada. As part of the total dollar deficit of that year for the OEEC countries this was about 40 per cent.

In 1951 the OEEC called for an increase in European agricultural production of 25 per cent. European self-sufficiency, already an accepted policy on the national level, would have to contribute to the solution of Europe's dollar problem. A number of barriers, however, prevented such a solution. Firstly, European countries did not change their pattern of production enough to free themselves from dollar imports. For wheat, for example, France increased her production and had actually planned a surplus in 1952–1953, while Turkey and Sweden both became net-exporters of cereals. But for Europe as a whole this development was too slow to guarantee self-sufficiency at some point in the future. Moreover, not all European countries were willing to import cereals from France and Turkey if the price was well above the world market level. Major dairy and meat producers like Denmark and Holland had an interest in keeping feed grain prices down and refused to finance the high-cost producers of Europe. This brings us to the second barrier to a European solution, namely that of the dominance of national programmes. European agriculture was merely the sum of national plans for agriculture resulting from national schemes, national pressures and national needs. In fact, all countries had some export trade, most had a large deficit and without actually closing the dollar deficit for food, most countries either had surpluses of some crops or developed them in the near future. France, though remaining a net-importer, had become a large exporter of agricultural products. Denmark, and to a somewhat lesser extent the Netherlands, were important exporters of dairy products, while Italy dominated in the export market for fruit and vegetables. It is against this background of growing surpluses in Europe that the first initiatives for a European agricultural market were developed.

Predictably, the initiatives came from the Netherlands and France, countries which both looked with increasing weariness to the trade barriers that continued to hamper access of agricultural surpluses to the European markets. The Dutch plan was originally prepared as a natural concomitant of the Stikker Plan for the removal of European tariffs and quotas on a sectoral base, which had mentioned agriculture as a sector requiring special treatment. Its author, the Dutch minister of agriculture Mansholt, however, proposed a gradual removal of barriers to agricultural trade along the lines of a predetermined scheme designed by a supranational body. During a long transition period allowing farmers to improve productivity by technological means, this body would allow countries to maintain their national price levels while quotas and tariffs were removed. The special fund mentioned in the Stikker plan would provide additional support to mitigate the adverse effects of the liberalization operation on inefficiently operating farmers. Once the market was completely free of barriers the body would fix maximum and minimum prices prevailing for all agricultural trade among the European countries and in doing so would further stimulate countries in rationalizing farming.

Although the OEEC might be the right forum to present the Mansholt plan, the organization never formally discussed it. Objections within the Dutch government against its allegedly *dirigiste* and supranational characteristics formed the main barriers to endorsement. Contrary to the majority in cabinet, Mansholt saw in a supranational authority the only possibility of breaking away from the national orientation of agricultural plans and creating permanently stable conditions for European farmers. That the exclusion of the British would be an automatic consequence he knew and accepted from the start, whereas others felt the British market would be an indispensable outlet for the exports of the future agricultural community.

How crucial the issues of supranationality remained in the following years can be seen from the negotiations on a French agricultural plan. Named after the then French minister of agriculture, Pflimlin, but also known as the 'Green Pool' proposal, it mentioned supranationality only as one of several possible organizational forms for the green pool since not only the British but also the German, Belgian, Italian and Danish governments would have great difficulty in defending any loss of sovereignty over domestic food and agricultural policy. Thus, the plan for a green pool was non-committal on its organizational form and directed to all countries of the OEEC. It suggested a product-by-product organization of the market in Europe (explicitly mentioning wheat, sugar, wine and dairy products – the French surplus goods) by guaranteeing markets and prices for European farmers. This would allow governments to remove trade barriers within the pool and to rely on common external barriers alone as a means of protection against exports from outside.

The Pflimlin plan received a very cool reception and escaped oblivion only through informal contacts between the Dutch and French agricultural ministries and preparatory meetings of a special European Agricultural Committee. However, in the course of the talks between the agricultural representatives of the OEEC countries during 1953/4 it became quite clear that disagreement on the institutional issue made compromises impossible. All the delegations of the Six, except the Dutch, were against any form of agricultural framework that took agricultural policy out of the hands of the national agricultural ministers, even if this kept them openly exposed to agricultural pressure groups. Diametrically opposed to this view were the governments of the Netherlands, the United Kingdom and the Scandinavian countries, who insisted on arrangements whereby this agricultural autonomy would be reined in. The best scenario, they felt, would be to have agricultural policy rules decided by unanimity in the Council of Ministers of the OEEC. This would give ministers of finance or economic affairs the final word on agriculture and allow them to anchor the agricultural sector firmly into the general framework of national policy.

In 1955 the negotiations on the green pool were finally brought to an end. Disillusioned by their complete failure the governments returned to the framework of the OEEC, without offering any permanent solution to the surplus problem of France and the Netherlands. The only result of the agricultural talks in the previous two years had been the setting up of schemes for 'freeing' agricultural trade in cereals, dairy products, meat, and fruit and vegetables, which left protectionist schemes entirely in the hands of the importing countries. This implied that whatever rise in trade might occur would be dependent upon crop conditions in individual countries and would always be reversible. Thus, with production increasing and surpluses still growing, the exporting countries were left to rely on the very same bilateral negotiating mechanism which they had sought to abandon because it had left them vulnerable and impotent in the 1940s and early 1950s.

6.   Plans for European Tariff Reductions

The slow but steady progress towards the removal of quotas in Europe brought tariff protection back into the limelight in the OEEC. Naturally, countries like the Netherlands, Denmark and Sweden, with low levels of tariff protection, were the first to draw attention to the tariff issue because they faced relatively high tariff walls against their exports while soon being deprived of quotas as their only possible instrument in trade bargaining. In 1949, the Danes had been the first to make the further removal of quotas conditional upon an OEEC investigation into the restrictive effects of high tariffs in Europe, whereas the Dutch had also tried to link tariff protection with quotas in proposing the Stikker Plan of Action. Although both attempts at attacking tariff barriers had failed, this low tariff club managed to trigger off new tariff plans in the course of the 1950s.

The first of these was a plan for multilateral tariff reductions presented by the Benelux countries at the GATT conference in Torquay in January 1951. Rather than following the usual GATT procedure of initial bilateral tariff discussions with the principal supplier countries, the plan suggested immediate tariff negotiations on a multilateral basis between the OEEC countries, the United States and Canada. The idea underlying this approach was to give real meaning to the GATT rules that a reduction was an equivalent concession to a binding of a tariff. Failing to meet the condition of principal supplier for most products, they had never really benefited from the rule because their bargaining position was simply not strong enough to enforce the rule on other GATT partners. In direct multilateral negotiations, however, the weight of low tariff countries would be larger and they might actually be able to embark on a greater equilibrium in tariff levels by receiving tariff reductions in exchange for bindings.

The decision to direct the proposal to Europe, Canada and the United States was based on two assumptions. The first was that the developing countries would not be interested in any scheme for tariff reduction since their young industries heavily depended on protection against lower cost competitors from the industrialized world. The second was that tariff reductions had a greater appeal when equally applied by Canada and the United States, the main competitors of European countries for manufactured goods. Both assumptions proved to be sound, but the question arises why the initiative was taken in the GATT if it was known from the start that it could never have worldwide implications. As its creators explained to their government, the plan was submitted to GATT merely for tactical reasons. It was not meant as a permanent relief for the low tariff countries but only as a demonstration of their commitment to GATT and as a way to convince the Americans of the need for a preferential European solution to the tariff problem to be worked out in the OEEC.

As a result of the Benelux memorandum eleven countries of the GATT reported in March 1951 on the problem of tariff disparity in Europe. These countries were France, the Federal Republic of Germany, Belgium, Luxembourg, the Netherlands, Sweden, Denmark, Norway, Italy, Austria and the United States. Their observation that the GATT negotiations were not likely to substantially 'contribute towards the creation of a *single market in Europe*' clearly showed the skill of those negotiators appealing to the 'Euromania' of the Americans to the detriment of their commitment to the GATT. But despite their skills, the low tariff club failed to shift discussions on European tariff disparity from the GATT to the OEEC, where progress in the field of tariff reductions could be bargained in exchange for the removal of quotas. For, although the American administration sympathized with a European approach to tariffs and allowed for the creation of a special GATT working group on the problem of tariff disparity, they did not prevent the British from blocking all real progress any time that an agreement between low and high tariff countries in Europe was in the air.

This was also the case with the Pflimlin plan, launched in the working party in September 1951, which is often referred to as the 'Group of Ten' or – in British documents – the 'Crazy Gang'. The plan proposed a 30 per cent tariff reduction across the board within a period of three years by annual cuts of 10 per cent. The reductions should not be applied to every individual tariff item (as suggested in the ECUSG) but instead to the weighted average tariff level in the major sectors of the economy, including agriculture. Contrary to the aim of the low tariff countries, the plan invited all contracting parties and envisaged waivers for developing countries in need of special protection. More essentially, however, it did not exempt low tariffs altogether from the reduction operation, as had been suggested by Benelux. Only sectors with a very low average tariff level might escape the tariff cuts.

Initially, the simplicity of the plan seemed to promise a speedy implementation by all GATT partners. But after a first survey of standpoints the underdeveloped countries backed out and negotiations continued within the group of eleven, supplemented by the United Kingdom and Canada. Moreover, even this smaller group of industrialized countries now proved heavily divided on the merits of the plan. The Benelux negotiators feared it only served the French in their efforts to escape a more sweeping attack on high tariffs. This fear seemed justified in so far as the plan offered high tariff countries the flexibility to spread the 'pain' of the 30 per cent tariff cuts within five very broad sectors of the economy. Delegates from the United Kingdom and Italy on the other hand denied the need for any form of tariff reduction, whereas their American counterpart seriously doubted the US government's ability to defend a 30 per cent tariff reduction in Congress. As a result of this divide the group's report of September 1952 marked the deadlock in discussions on the Pflimlin plan. On key issues such as the division of the sectors, the treatment of exceptionally low tariffs and the method of measuring tariff levels no compromises had been found. Officially, negotiators continued searching for an agreement. Unofficially, they agreed to stall the matter.

The low tariff countries had in the meantime tried to raise the tariff problem in a European forum. By the end of 1951, the Swedish economist and representative to the Assembly of the Council of Europe, Berthold Ohlin, presented an automatic scheme for tariff reductions among the European countries. He called for 'decapping' all tariffs above 35 per cent *ad valorem* within a fixed time span and maximum tariff levels of 5, 15 and 25 per cent in the sectors of raw materials, semi-manufactures and manufactures respectively. During the first year of the reduction operation the imposition of these maximum tariff ceilings was to be applied to 70 per cent of the total imports of each country for the three sectors. After a second and third year the maxima were to be extended to, respectively, 80 and 90 per cent of all imports. Although the plan was accepted by the Assembly, its vague formulation again allowed countries opposing tariff cuts to stifle it in the technical examinations of the GATT working group. The only trace it left there was through the decapping procedure for tariffs higher than 35 per cent; the group adopted this principle in one of its later drafts of the Pflimlin plan.

Another and more influential attempt at tariff reductions on a strictly European basis was made by the Dutch government. During the deliberations on the European Political Community (EPC) in September 1952, the Dutch extracted a commitment from the foreign ministers of the Six to entrust the political organization with economic tasks. Subsequently, their foreign minister, Willem Beyen, used this commitment as a stepping stone to push his version of European integration, a customs union between the Six. Building on the experience of previous plans in the OEEC, Beyen's plan introduced a rigidity in the timetable of the customs union which was meant to guarantee that no country could back out once it had agreed to join the scheme. The intermediate, automatic phases in the reduction of trade barriers and the formation of the common external tariff after a period of ten years, as well as the final date of completion of the customs union, should all be written into the treaty. The common external tariff on individual items should be based on the unweighted average tariff applied in the participating countries. In addition, the participants would be committed to schemes for the removal of restrictions in the transport sector and barriers to invisibles.

Although Beyen had left some flexibility in the scheme by allowing the authority of the future community to use safety clauses and financial aid from a European Fund in cases of fundamental difficulty, the plan simply appeared too rigid to be acceptable. Moreover, most governments rightly criticized it as being based on a very limited concept of a customs union which made no reference to the free movement of labour and capital or the harmonization of monetary and social policies. The economic committee studying the Beyen proposals between December 1953 and July 1954 therefore mainly discussed a number of ways to introduce more flexibility in the gradual formation of the customs union. Again, suggestions were made to decap the highest tariffs and exempt the lowest, to allow for differential time schemes for the different economic sectors and to introduce some form of weighting in calculating the average tariffs. But despite some signs of Dutch willingness to compromise, the level of the common external tariff and the time scheme for the customs union proved as always the ultimate stumbling blocks in the negotiations. Thus, the French parliament's death sentence on the EPC/EDC in August 1954 merely brought a formal end to the already failed economic negotiations.

7. Towards the European Economic Community

Although the failure of the EDC had brought down the Beyen plan for a European customs union, it did not prevent the Six from launching new attempts at economic cooperation as soon as two very urgent problems in European relations, the rearmament of West Germany and the status of the Saar area, were satisfactorily solved. Two different approaches dominated the talks on economic integration between the Six. The first, favoured by a circle of close collaborators of Jean Monnet, was to extend economic cooperation in the ECSC to the sector of classical energy and transport and to create a new European structure for the integration of the nuclear energy sector. The second approach, again put forward by the Dutch government, mentioned overall economic integration along the lines of a customs union. It was eventually on both approaches that the Benelux countries agreed to table the famous memorandum of 18 May for the meeting of the six foreign ministers of the ECSC at Messina.

The memorandum called for an economic community under a common authority as well as sectoral integration in the field of classical energy, transport and atomic energy. Despite numerous reservations from the governments, especially those of Germany and France, the memorandum was accepted during a meeting of the foreign ministers of the Six in Messina in 1955 as a departure point for further discussions. Here, the Six referred to a Common Market to indicate that they would not only aim at the removal of barriers to trade in goods but also at freeing the movement of services, capital and labour within the internal market. Moreover, they would explore possibilities for the harmonization of social, economic and financial policies, the application of safeguard clauses and the creation of a readaptation fund. Naturally, willingness to study these matters, even if representing a break with previous standpoints, was in itself no guarantee of tangible results. Crucial as a first measure of progress were in fact the negotiations between the governments of the Six after the appearance of the so-called Spaak report of April 1956 which gave an outline of the problems and solutions studied by a group of experts on the basis of the Messina resolution.

The Spaak report suggested the formation of the Common Market through the progressive elimination of tariffs and quotas within a period of twelve years, the gradual elimination of a common external tariff and the formulation of a common commercial policy. Internal tariffs were to be removed in three phases each of four years. In the first phase, all tariffs which were close to or below the future level of the common external tariff would be reduced by 10 per cent and all other tariffs by 30 per cent. In the second phase, tariffs would be reduced by another 30 per cent and in the last phase, the remaining tariffs would be completely removed. In order to meet the French demands for more flexibility in this automatic system of tariff reductions, the authors of the Spaak report had turned to a method resembling that of the Pflimlin plan; tariffs were arranged in broad groups according to their actual levels and each government was free to decide on the individual tariffs to be reduced as long as the overall reduction per group was achieved. To increase the flexibility of the system even further, the Commission of the community, supported by a majority in the Parliament and a qualified majority in the Council of Ministers, could decide on changes to the procedure of tariff reductions after the first phases and the extension of the transition period for another three years. Moreover, in agreement with the Commission, governments with special diffi-culties could be granted temporary exemption from the tariff reduction scheme for certain goods provided that these goods did not exceed a total of 5 per cent of all imports.

On the level of the common external tariff the Spaak report was far less detailed since it proved difficult to find a compromise between the extreme positions of the French and the Dutch. Initially, the former demanded a tariff that would be 'as high as possible' while the latter asked for a tariff around the same level as the low Benelux tariff. In the end the drafters of the Spaak report suggested a decapping procedure for the very high tariffs along the lines of the Pflimlin (and Ohlin) plan, after which the final average level would be calculated on the basis of the arithmetic tariff average of the French, Benelux, German and Italian tariff schedules.

The method of removing quantitative restrictions, too, remained an issue of bitter debate during the negotiations. The French saw no reason why the Six should depart from the OEEC's liberalization scheme but the other five favoured a separate scheme which would speed up their removal and would strengthen the rules on escape clauses. As a result of these divergent positions the Spaak report merely stated that in the last phase of the transition towards the Common Market quotas could only be applied by concerted action, after common agreement and for a maximum period of one year after the complete removal of internal tariffs. Moreover, the removal of quotas would be irreversible, with the exception of those applied according to the safety clauses laid down in the treaty.

If we compare the principles on tariffs and quotas of the Spaak report with the provisions in the EEC Treaty, there can be no doubt that it was the negotiations of the Six rather than the Spaak report that shaped the trade provisions of the Community. At the core of the Community remained the customs union, which was to be formed after 12 or 15 years, but the methods of achieving this goal and also the territory of the union had changed quite radically. Starting with this last point, in the final phase of the negotiations the French government had put forward the association of the French overseas territories with the Community as a *conditio sine qua non* for French participation. Although only Belgium supported this principle in the end, the French demands were met. The EEC Treaty stipu-lates that overseas territories with special links with the member states shall enjoy all the advantages of the tariff reductions within the Community. The member states in their turn will also, at least in principle, benefit from a gradual reduction of tariffs imposed by the associated countries, although the latter are entitled to tariff protection corresponding to 'the needs of their development and industrialization or produce revenue for their budgets'.

The provisions on the removal of internal tariffs and quotas that were incorporated in the Treaty had a more flexible character than those originally mentioned in the Spaak report. The first phase of four years would comprise three reduction stages. At the end of the first phase, every member would have reduced its tariffs by at least 25 per cent and at the end of the second phase by at least 50 per cent. In the last phase of the transitional period, every country should have removed all its tariffs towards the countries of the Community. The removal of quantitative restrictions between the members would take place through a method of gradually increasing the total value of imports under the quota regime by at least 20 per cent a year, with a minimum increase of 10 per cent for the quota on each individual item. Before this procedure took place, however, all bilateral quotas open to any of the members should be converted into global, non-discriminatory quotas.

At the same time that the internal barriers were removed, that is after 12 or 15 years, all countries would have reached the level of the common tariff. Tariff headings within a range of 15 per cent or less of the common tariff would have to be levelled towards the latter tariff before the end of the first phase. For all other tariffs the margin of difference with the common tariff would be gradually reduced in two steps of 30 per cent after the first and second phase and a final step in the third and last phase.

For once principles proved easy: it was determining the exact level of the external tariff which proved difficult. The final compromise laid down in the Treaty between the extreme positions of France and Benelux was as follows. The common tariff was to be calculated on the basis of the arithmetic average of the actually applied tariff schedules in the four customs areas (Benelux counting as one) as of 1 January 1957. Even so, seven different lists of exceptions had first to be agreed. The first of these lists, list A, contained no less than 73 tariff positions for which France was allowed to charge higher tariffs than those of the common external tariff. Lists B, C, D and E consisted of tariffs which were anchored at a level which would be above that obtained from the application of the general formula. List F only contained goods for which some member states had demanded less than the average tariff protection because these goods were inputs that they sought to import at low costs. List G, finally, was the result of product negotiations that had reached a deadlock and of technical difficulties in formulating the common tariff. Every member state was allowed to place products on this list which together did not exceed a value of 2 per cent of its total imports from third countries in 1956. The level of the common tariff for these goods would be determined in negotiations between the members before the end of the second year of the Treaty's implementation.

The negotiations on the seven special lists give just one of several illustrations of the hard bargaining and extensive compromising that eventually lead to the signing of the Treaty of Rome on 25 March, 1957. Another striking example is the debate on the special treatment of France, which was eventually allowed to maintain a system of export subsidies and import taxes until the French monetary problems were solved. Both issues led many observers to believe that the formation of the customs union might take much longer than the planned 12 or 15 years. It was thus all the more surprising that the Six went ahead far more rapidly with the removal of trade barriers than the original timetable of the Treaty planned.

Conclusion

This paper has tried to deal with the divergent nature and character of the various initiatives for the reduction or removal of barriers to intra-European trade. It demonstrates a continuous concern throughout the post-war period with this problem and it suggests a causal chain, alongside the more familiar links deriving from the force of federalist ideas, leading to the customs union incorporated in the Treaty of Rome. The EEC, it is true, went far beyond the removal of barriers to trade but the fact that, more than thirty years later, these concerns still loom large in the 1992 package suggests that even in this field it has not been completely successful. Vested sector and national interests have still remained entrenched and new forms of protectionism have been used to circumvent the spirit, if not the letter, of the Treaty.

The question still has to be answered why it was that a small group of six European countries in 1957 went as far as they did. This, however, falls outside the scope of the present paper. Obviously, political and military factors constituted important explanatory variables and to some extent the clauses on the common market were the fruits of linkages in what must be interpreted as a package deal. Nonetheless, the puzzle remains why the Benelux countries appeared so fixated with trade disarmament and why France in particular should have abandoned its almost traditional position of resistance. This can only be answered by a more detailed analysis of their perception of the changing international order, their position within it and the opportunities and constraints offered within new multilateral frameworks.

Bibliography

Asbeek Brusse, W. (1994), 'The Failure of European Tariff Plans in GATT, 1950–54', in G. Trausch (ed.), *La contruction de l'Europe du Plan Schuman aux Traites de Rome*, Milan/Brussels/Paris/Baden-Baden.

Boyer, F. and J. P. Salle (1955), 'The Liberalisation of Intra-European Trade in the Framework of OEEC', *International Monetary Fund Staff Papers*, **4**, (2).

Curzon, G. (1965), *Multilateral Commercial Diplomacy*, London.

Diebold, W. (1952), *Trade and Payments in Western Europe: A Study in Economic Cooperation, 1947/1951*, New York.

Gardner, Richard N. (1980), *Sterling–Dollar Diplomacy: The Origins and the Prospects of Our International Economic Order*, New York, [New, expanded edition].

Griffiths, R. T. (1988), 'The Abortive Dutch Assault on European Tariffs, 1950–52', in M. Wintle (ed.), *Modern Dutch Studies: Essays in Honour of Peter King, Professor of Modern Studies at the University of Hull, on the Occasion of his Retirement*, London.

Hieronymi, O. (1973), *Economic Discrimination Against the United States in Western Europe (1945–1958)*, Geneva/Paris.

Hogan, M. J. (1952), *The Marshall Plan: America, Britain and the Reconstruction of Europe, 1947–1952*.

Kock, K. (1969), *International Trade Policy and the GATT, 1947–1967*, Stockholm.

Kuesters, H.-J. (1982), *Die Gruendung der Europaeischen Wirtschaftsgemeinschaft*, Baden-Baden.

Milward, A. S. (1987), *The Reconstruction of Western Europe, 1945–1951*, London.

Milward, A. S. (1992), *The European Rescue of the Nation State*, London.

Poidevin, R. (ed.) (1986), *Histoire des debuts de la construction europeenne, mars 1948 / mai 1950*. Brussels/Milan/Paris/Baden-Baden.

Schwabe, K. (ed.) (1988), *Die Anfaenge des Schuman-Plans 1950/51. Beitraege des Kolloquiums in Aachen, 28–30. Mai 1986*, Brussels/Milan/Paris/Baden-Baden.

Serra, E. (ed.) (1989), *The Relaunching of Europe and the Treaties of Rome*, Brussels/Milan/Paris/Baden-Baden.

[3]

XII

THE SCHUMAN PLAN

PLANS AND REALITIES IN WESTERN EUROPE'S STEEL INDUSTRY

In 1983, when miles of major steel works are being closed down all over Europe, it may seem superfluous to remark that the manufacture of steel is one of the most volatile of all industries. Steel is the basic constructional material of the modern economy, its level of output immediately affected by any fluctuations in sales and investment. The peculiar problems of the steel industry derive from the instability and uncertainty arising from this extreme sensitiveness to economic trends conjoined with the massive scale of most of the manufacturing plant necessary. Since the invention of the Bessemer process in the mid-nineteenth century, a small number of huge investments, for the most part privately owned, have struggled to modify and equilibrate the effect on the steel industry of the fluctuations of the economy. In so doing in every western European country they have called into question the relationship of private ownership of the industry both to the state and to the common good, as well as the relative merits of free and controlled markets. The European steel industry has since its birth been at the heart of the controversy over the nature of the capitalist economy and the dramatic ebb and flow of its economic fortunes has been accompanied by insistent and far-reaching national and international political controversy.

In singling out the steel industry as a basic industry, an indispensable foundation of the economy, the French Modernization Plan did no more than incorporate into the formally planned pattern of investment a surge of investment in the steel industry which took place everywhere in western Europe after 1945 except in Germany. Public investment in the reconstruction of railways, mines, factories and housing meant a rapid rise in the demand for steel. When the Western European countries had to present national recovery programmes to CEEC they all incorporated into those plans proposals for a substantial increase in steel output. If the output of all the countries shown in table 49 (which comprises all the large and most of the small Western European steel producers) in their peak inter-war year is added together, it can be seen that they were still intending to exceed that quantity by a substantial margin even in 1948 and to have left it far behind by the time Marshall Aid should have come to a close.

Table 49 European steel plans, 1948–51, as presented to the CEEC in 1947 (crude and semi-finished steel, thousand tonnes, crude steel or ingot equivalent)

	Peak year in inter-war period	Actual output 1947	Planned output			
			1948	1949	1950	1951
Belgium	4,275	2,815	4,250	4,250	4,850	4,850
France	9,711	5,812	10,400	10,890	11,700	12,690
Italy	2,328	1,600	2,500	2,670	2,830	3,000
Luxembourg	2,696	1,800	3,000	3,000	3,000	3,000
Netherlands	57	207	303	393	473	503
Norway	65	57	67	72	92	92
Sweden	995	1,195	1,300	1,500	1,760	2,060
United Kingdom	13,192	12,700	13,970	14,200	14,480	14,990
Total	33,319	26,186	35,790	36,975	39,185	41,185
Western Germany and Saarland	20,782	3,562	5,725	8,188	10,188	12,688
Total	54,101	29,748	41,515	45,163	49,373	53,873

Source : CEEC, Vol. 2, *Technical Reports*, Appendices C(i), C(ii), C(iii).

For such ambitious programmes to be justified it would be necessary for the high domestic level of demand for steel to be sustained once the immediate reconstruction boom was over and for that boom not to turn into a period of contraction. The American administration was sternly critical of the programmes, seeing them as mercantilistic and nationalistic, inasmuch as each Western European country was interested in maximizing its own output of steel irrespective of the optimum distribution of the industry in Western Europe as a whole. This was the period in which the first major Dutch and Norwegian steel works, at Ijmuiden and Mo-i-Rana, were planned. Congress expressed the view, at the prompting of the ECA, that at a time when demand for steel in the USA was so high that in spite of record output levels steel rationing had nevertheless to be maintained, it would prove impossible for European countries to obtain the inputs to make so much steel.

The second underlying assumption of these European plans, however, was that the resources would be obtained at the expense of the reduced and restricted German steel industry. Table 49 shows that even when West German output would have reached the revised maximum limit imposed by the western Allies in 1947, total Western European output would still be lower than at the peak level of inter-war production. The targets set for the growth of the other Western European steel industries were in fact predicated on the restrictions to be maintained on the German steel industry.

364   *The Reconstruction of Western Europe 1945–51*

This had a double advantage; if domestic demand proved insufficient the large pre-war German export markets would be left for Germany's European competitors. This process, for example, was originally intended to account for about 3 million tonnes of the planned increase in steel output under the French Modernization Plan. In this light the objectives of the Western European governments in this sector were not so expansionist as they seemed in Washington, but they none the less assumed a regularity of demand for steel such as had been far from obtaining in the inter-war period. There might, the CEEC report suggested, be a slackening-off in demand in the early 1950s due to a weakening in the demand arising from the immediate needs of post-war reconstruction, but this would prove only a temporary phenomenon and continued prosperity would produce new sources of demand for steel. It was as though the Western European countries had taken a model of their economies in the inter-war period, injected into it full employment as a permanent factor and then simply read off the quantity of steel consumption which altering that variable would imply. *Per capita* steel consumption in France in 1951 was thus estimated at 234 kg ingot equivalent of finished steel compared to 162 kg in 1929, and in Italy at 87 kg compared to 59 kg in 1938.[1]

Most of the investment to meet this presumed demand was concerned with the modernization and rationalization of existing plant. The major, dramatic, single new projects which were launched in these years – the two continuous strip mills in France, the hot-rolled strip mill in South Wales, and so on – were only a part of a much more widespread programme of mixed private and public investment in the modification of existing plant sustained by boom conditions. Taken as a whole investment in the steel industry was not fitted into a rational programme of action but responded to the immediate situation where order books were full and steel sold at high prices. French steel investments were, of course, channelled through the Modernization Plan and this certainly contained a greater element of rationalization than was seen elsewhere, such as the linking of clusters of steel works to new, single, common electricity-generating stations. In a less rationalized framework the British steel manufacturers were also obliged to prepare a common development plan, but, as might have been expected from such a procedure, the plan seems to have contained something for almost every manufacturer.[2] The export capacity of the Belgian steel industry was so great that there was less anxiety that it might fail to meet the increased demand from the home market. In relation to the total output of the industry investment was lower in Belgium than in France and Britain, but in comparison to the previous thirty years it was at a high level.

[1] The actual levels attained in 1951 were France, 185 kg, and Italy, 75 kg, crude steel equivalents, UN, *Quarterly Bulletin of Steel Statistics*. Crude steel equivalencies based on suggested method in OEEC, *Industrial Statistics*.

[2] D. Burn, *The Steel Industry 1939–1959. A Study in Competition and Planning* (Cambridge, 1961).

The fact that government did no more than encourage and try to facilitate the modernization of the steel industry in Belgium was, however, exceptional in Western Europe. Elsewhere, no matter how unsystematic its actions, it was much more intimately involved in the process. In fact after 1914 there had been few years anywhere in western Europe where the steel industry's fortunes had been left to the untrammelled influence of the market. The scale and importance of the capital investments meant that even when governments did not regard the industry as being of such peculiar strategic and economic importance as to involve themselves closely in its fortunes the firms themselves protected the position of their investments through an intricate network of national and international agreements. Even after the great depression, the seizure of power by the Nazi government, and the rapid increases of steel output in Germany caused by reflation and rearmament there, the second

Table 50   Estimated values of investment in the iron and steel industry, 1947–51

	France	United Kingdom	Belgium	West Germany
	(million 1952 dollars)		(million current dollars)	
1947/8	190.4	305.2	24.6*	n.a.
1949	184.8	201.6	42.2	78.5
1950	246.4	212.8	41.0	90.4
1951	221.2	198.8	28.9	142.7

Sources: E. Baumgart, R. Krengel and W. Moritz, *Die Finanzierung der industriellen Expansion in der Bundesrepublik während der Jahre des Wiederaufbaus* (Berlin, 1960), pp. 51 ff.; D. Burn, *The Steel Industry 1939–1959. A Study in Competition and Planning* (Cambridge, 1961), p. 395; C. Reuss, E. Koutny and L. Tychon, *Le Progrès économique en sidérurgie. Belgique, Luxembourg, Pays-Bas 1830–1955* (Louvain, 1960), p. 290.

* 1948 only.

International Steel Cartel still regulated the export markets of European producers. These were allocated not so much on the basis of rationality as of previously established positions, traditions and business connections. Over the period 1925–9 steel exports in Europe had been about 38 per cent of total output of which exports to non-European countries had formed about 16 per cent. In the 1930s exports were of less importance, about 22 per cent of output over the period 1935–9.[3] Steel exports had been an important foreign currency earner for western Europe from the mid-nineteenth century onwards. They were closely tied to European investments in railways, harbours and other infrastructural developments in the underdeveloped world. In spite of the political fragmentation of Europe in the 1930s, co-operation within the International Steel Cartel was not found wanting in the face of attempts by

[3] UN, *European Steel Trends in the Setting of the World Market* (Geneva, 1949), pp. 7 ff. For American producers exports were relatively insignificant, about 5 per cent of output, and about four-fifths of world steel exports originated in western Europe.

366   *The Reconstruction of Western Europe 1945–51*

less-developed economies to develop their own steel industries. It was the Cartel's policy to keep export prices low, often at the expense of domestic prices, in order to maintain a hold on these markets.[4] The national domestic markets were, except for the well-established trades in semi-finished metals and in certain special steels, amply shielded from competition by outside producers.

The view of future policy which emerged from the national steel production programmes submitted to the CEEC was not significantly different in this respect from what had gone before. At higher levels of output exports would be more important, but they would be possible because of the absence of German exports and, except for Belgium and Luxembourg, they would continue to be seen essentially as useful regulators of the level of activity, a way of minimizing the fierce impact of cyclical fluctuations on the industry. The elimination of German exports would make the re-establishment of the Cartel easier. The outside world had, however, changed considerably. The war and its aftermath had stimulated the development of protected iron and steel industries in numerous markets which had been important in the inter-war period. It had also enormously increased the level of United States steel output, from an annual average of 44.1 million tonnes over the period 1936–9 to 80.3 million tonnes in 1948. In spite of the tightness of the home market, which meant that most United States steel exports only took place in the immediate post-war years through special licensing and controls, it was nevertheless implicit in all America's post-war international economic policy that this level of steel output would eventually imply a substantially greater volume of American steel exports than before. The steel output of the rest of the world, omitting Europe and North America, had run at an annual average of 9.2 million tonnes over the period 1936–9. The United Nations estimated its likely volume by the end of the Marshall Plan at 15 million tonnes. The submissions to the CEEC took little or no account of these changes in the extra-European world. In this light the objectives of the Western European countries looked much more ambitious, whatever happened in Germany.

In 1948 no significant producer in fact reached the forecast output. The reason for this, however, was certainly not a weakness in domestic demand. If Germany is excluded from the calculation, 1948 was a record year for steel consumption on the domestic markets of Western Europe. Exports had now fallen to a share of only about 18 per cent of total output and most countries maintained export quotas to ensure the availability of steel at home. Belgium suffered from export difficulties, but these were mainly attributable to high prices and to payments problems. The main reason for the failure of output to match the targets was the acute shortage of inputs, of which the most telling was the coke and coking coal shortage in France. Joined to this was the shortage of scrap. Before the war the United States had been a major exporter

---

[4] E. Hexner, *The International Steel Cartel* (Chapel Hill, 1943).

of steel scrap for use in European blast furnaces, but the growth of output in America had stopped this trade and the increased use of scrap in European furnaces in order to economize on coke meant that every European country, again with the exception of Germany, had by 1948 run into a bottleneck with supplies of steel scrap. Connected with both these causes, because due essentially to the same reasons, was the shortage of semi-finished steel imports from the United States.

If, however, the failure to reach the forecast level of output was caused until the end of 1948 by a bottleneck in the flow of inputs, in 1949 and 1950 it was due to a new and worrying cause, a noticeable slackening in the demand for steel everywhere except in Germany. The trend of rising output which had remained unbroken from the end of the war until summer 1949 then began to fall. The sudden downturn in production put the steel production targets in a quite different perspective. The end of the post-war restocking boom, which had not materialized in 1947, seemed now to be arriving. What made this even more alarming was West Germany's immunity to it. The backlog of demand for steel was so great there and there was so much spare capacity which could be taken up cheaply that the situation was entirely different.

German steel-making capacity had remained a long way above the limits set for it after Potsdam. When the report of the Humphrey Committee was accepted existing capacity was estimated at 19 million tonnes a year. The subsequent dismantling activities still left capacity far beyond the agreed output limit of 11.1 million tonnes. A comparison of plans with output achieved in Western Europe can be made by comparing tables 49 and 51,

Table 51   Crude steel output in Western Europe, 1946–52 (million tonnes)

	Belgium	Luxem-bourg	France	Saarland	Italy	Nether-lands	United Kingdom	West Germany
1946	2.26	1.27	4.34	0.29	1.13	0.13	12.70	2.72*
1947	2.84	1.69	5.64	0.70	1.66	0.19	12.72	3.12*
1948	3.86	2.41	7.12	1.21	2.09	0.33	14.88	5.47
1949	3.79	2.24	9.01	1.73	2.02	0.42	15.55	9.01
1950	3.72	2.41	8.52	1.87	2.33	0.48	16.29	11.93
1951	4.97	3.03	9.68	2.56	3.01	0.55	15.64	13.29
1952	4.99	2.95	10.70	2.78	3.48	0.67	16.42	15.56

Source: OEEC, *Industrial Statistics*.
* All Germany.

although the basis of calculation of the two tables is slightly different. Before 1950 all Western European countries were not keeping pace with their objectives as stated to the CEEC. By 1951 they had all reached those objectives except France. The shortfall in French output was, however, by that date made up by

368   *The Reconstruction of Western Europe 1945–51*

the great increase in West German output. In 1950 West German steel output passed the limits foreseen by the CEEC, passed the limits imposed on it by the Allies, and passed that of France. From the start of 1948 to the end of 1950 steel output doubled in the Federal Republic and its rate of increase did not slacken as output began to dip in the last quarter of 1949 in the other Western European countries. In 1951 it was only West Germany's contribution to the Western European total which finally justified the CEEC estimates of 1947!

In 1949 German steel exports made their re-entry into European markets and in that year they were about one quarter the value of British exports. In 1951 they were to exceed them. How this remarkable recovery in the German steel industry came about can be explained both by the general nature of the economic recovery in West Germany and by the specific situation of the steel industry relative to other industrial sectors.

Until the end of 1948 the recovery of output in the iron and steel industry in western Germany was further behind the level of recovery of the industrial economy as a whole, compared to pre-war levels, than that of any other significant industrial sector. From spring 1948 output in steel-consuming sectors rose vigorously, although unevenly, and sustained the demand for iron and steel when it was beginning to flatten out or even decline in other countries. At the end of 1948 when the index of total industrial production in the Bizone as compared to 1936 stood at 79 per cent, that of the iron and steel industry was still only at 55 per cent (table 52). Only one other industrial sector, the closely related 'other metallurgical industries', stood at a lower

Table 52   Index of industrial production in the British and American occupation zones of West Germany (1936 = 100)

	Industrial production	Iron and steel production	Iron and steel construction	Engineering and optical industries	Motor vehicles	Electrical industries
1946	34	20	42	35	15	33
June 1947	41	21	42	40	17	64
Dec. 1947	44	26	50	40	18	68
Apr. 1948	53	31	59	46	27	93
Sep. 1948	70	47	84	60	52	130
Dec. 1948	79	55	99	73	69	165

Source: W. Abelshauser, *Wirtschaft in Westdeutschland 1945–1948*, p. 43.

comparative level. Germany entered 1949 in potential boom conditions for the steel industry with a rapidly accumulating demand which remained unsatisfied only because of the need to repair plant and because of the bottlenecks in the supply of inputs. These two problems dealt with, as they largely were in 1949, the only restriction was that imposed by international agreement. This was already itself being relaxed in the course of 1949. In November, for example, the Petersberg protocols relaxed the limits on German shipbuilding and so opened up another domestic market likely to grow rapidly.

The combination of rapidly growing output and ample reserves of spare capacity and spare labour was an especially favourable one on the export market. Whereas other European steel manufacturers had full order books German manufacturers could accept immediate export contracts at less than profitable prices because of the gains they brought in economies of scale and in bringing idle plant into utilization. After the quota restrictions were eased on French steel exports in October 1948 actual exports over the ensuing twelve months fell about a third short of the newly permitted level.[5] For the first three quarters of 1950 they showed a slightly declining trend. If there was a sufferer from the increase in West German exports, however, Belgium/Luxembourg was the more probable candidate. In terms of national currency, exports of iron and steel products from Belgium and Luxembourg fell by more than 50 per cent between the third quarter of 1949 and the third quarter of 1950. No doubt some of this was due to the exchange rate readjustments in September 1949 when Belgium devalued by less than most of the other Western European countries and thus left her overpriced steel exports especially vulnerable. Although the dollar value of British steel exports, for example, fell by $27.5 million in the last quarter of 1949 their sterling value increased by £3.6 million. The fall in Belgium/Luxembourg's steel exports to the Netherlands in 1949 was roughly the equivalent of the increase in West Germany's exports to that destination (table 53). The Monnet Plan, however, had given an important place to steel exports; when output of crude steel reached 12.5 million tonnes a year, exports were to account for about three million tonnes. A double shadow of the failure of the domestic and foreign markets to absorb the Plan's output was thus thrown over the French economy.

From 1945 onwards the problem of Western European reconstruction had increasingly crystallized into the problem of future Franco-German relationships, and that of Franco-German relationships into the relationships of the coal and steel industries. The disindustrialization of Germany, the removal of most of its industrial capacity, had never been accepted as wise or feasible. The ceilings imposed on industrial output by the Levels of Industry Agreement had been calculated in order to make reparations out of current production possible. But the Soviet Union had wanted its reparations at once before output reached those limits (not an unreasonable interpretation of the Potsdam agreements), reparations had become meaningless as a guide to action, and the real interest of the western powers, even France, soon no longer lay in enforcing general limits on industrial output. That policy had in any case originally been devised without French participation. French interests had been more specific and focused on the control and regulation of the Ruhr

---

[5] M. Fontaine, *L'industrie sidérurgique dans le monde et son évolution depuis la Seconde Guerre Mondiale* (Paris, 1950), p. 160.

Economic Development of the EEC

Table 53 Total steel exports 1946–52, Belgium/Luxembourg, France, United Kingdom and West Germany (thousand tonnes)

	1938	1946	1947	1948	1949	1950	1951	1952
Belgium/Luxembourg	2314.3	1572.3	2268.9	3446.0	3745.5	3580.7	5160.9	5020.3
of which to Netherlands	287.0	319.6	357.3	586.2	521.1	727.2	856.5	646.1
of which to United Kingdom	300.3	12.8	71.4	238.3	511.0	142.2	262.8	489.0
*France**	1336.3	165.4	319.1	897.9	2117.1	3630.3	4537.8	3007.1
of which to Germany†	1.8	n.a.	0.7	157.7	92.9	203.6	105.6	297.1
of which to Italy	42.4	n.a.	1.3	8.8	44.4	261.4	298.7	157.5
of which to United Kingdom	206.9	n.a.	1.9	22.4	121.6	176.0	85.0	107.2
West Germany	‡2300.9	0	n.a.	**124.0	**608.5	1952.7	2345.6	2061.4
of which to Netherlands	315.8	0	3.0	101.8	91.9	196.3	217.1	198.8
United Kingdom	1549.8	2254.0	1919.6	2117.0	2493.9	2596.6	2142.2	2089.4

Source: British Iron and Steel Federation, *Statistical Yearbooks.* Includes all steel products.

* After April 1948 includes Saarland.
† After 1947 West Germany.
‡ Including Austria.
** Bizone.

industrial area. If at first this was acting under the strong influence of history and trying to force to a successful conclusion policies which had not been successfully enforced after 1918 it soon came to have a more modern rationale as well, since the success of the Modernization Plan seemed also to depend on the disposition of the Ruhr's resources. In this context the Ruhr meant coal, coke and steel. The Modernization Plan's targets depended on the allocation of the Ruhr's coal and coke resources and on what was to happen to the German steel industry.

When, after the second stage of the London conference, the Quai d'Orsay began to manoeuvre policy towards a Franco-West German economic association, the relationship between the French and German coal, iron and steel industries became even more central to the most crucial areas of foreign policy. It was precisely in these sectors that attempts at such an economic association had been made after the manifest failure of the Versailles treaty. In one sense, although at a very low level, the firm adherence of both France and Nazi Germany to the International Steel Cartel had been just such an association, but it fell far short of anything that the French had hoped might be produced by the occupation of the Ruhr in 1923. The problems requiring to be resolved could hardly be so by any agreement which avoided the whole question of regulation of domestic markets. The formation of the West German state, the long and detailed struggle over the powers of intervention of the International Authority for the Ruhr in those markets, and the enormous ambiguities which were left about the exact status and duration of the Ruhr Authority, had brought that question into a position from which it could hardly be removed by another unsatisfactory compromise like that of the Cartel. When the West German government took office the international bonds which restrained the Promethean strength of Germany's steel industry were already being tested and broken. Some new policy was needed if a Franco-German settlement was to become a reality and reconstruction to be achieved.

COMPARATIVE PROSPECTS OF THE FRENCH AND GERMAN STEEL INDUSTRIES

German steel output in 1938 had been more than 40 per cent of Western Europe's total output, most of it produced in the area which had now become the Federal Republic. In 1949 the Federal Republic's output was only 18.2 per cent of Western Europe's. Would the organized defence of Western Europe and the integration of the Federal Republic into the strategic bloc be accepted by the United States while so much steel-making capacity still lay idle or underutilized there? Had the occupying powers in fact succeeded in removing most of that capacity from Germany or replacing German output by their

372   *The Reconstruction of Western Europe 1945–51*

own the situation would have been different.[6] But they had not. An increase of defence expenditure in Western Europe would certainly increase once more the demand for dollar imports, and to expect the United States to provide increased aid which would logically be construed as payments to keep West German manufacturing capacity idle was hardly feasible. By autumn 1949 the American army seems to have espoused the cause of limited rearmament in West Germany; the rumours which tremulously ran on that subject in France were not without foundation. At the end of April 1950 the United States Joint Chiefs of Staff pronounced in favour of German rearmament.[7] The only barrier to its becoming official American policy was the knowledge of the consternation it would cause throughout Western Europe if it were adopted. In September formal proposals for German rearmament were in fact made by the United States. At the start of March 1950 Konrad Adenauer asked for a raising of the limits to German steel output and in that month the quantity of steel produced passed one million tonnes, suggesting the international limits might in any case be broken. Supposing all international regulation of the German coal and steel industries, including the International Authority for the Ruhr, to be ineffective, what would be the respective situations of the French and German steel industries now and in the likely future?

No entirely satisfactory answer could be given to that question at the time. Nor is it any easier to answer in retrospect. All that can be done is to strike a balance of probabilities, but in striking it a much more accurate appreciation of the two steel industries emerges. One of the reasons why the balance of probabilities is so hard to strike is because the patterns of comparative advantage in steel-making between Western European countries had been increasingly distorted for more than thirty years by government action. Any calculation of the relative production costs of the two industries shows that a more important part in production cost differences was played by government intervention than by differences in the overall balance of factor input costs. The relative difference in the prices of coke and ore to the two industries did of course contain an important element representing the natural comparative advantages of the two countries; German reserves of coking coal and French reserves of iron ore were each among the world's largest and most easily accessible. Even here, however, government intervention through freight rates and tariffs formed a substantial part of the final cost difference. And in this respect the immutable fact was that whereas France depended on German coal Germany consumed insignificant amounts of French ore.

---

[6] In Rhineland-Westphalia six blast-furnaces, forty-seven Siemens-Martin furnaces and two Thomas converters were dismantled entirely. Almost all the electro-steel capacity was removed, as were the rolling mills of the Hörder Verein and the one continuous wide strip mill at Dinslaken. K.H. Herchenröder, J. Schäfer and M. Zapp, *Die Nachfolger der Ruhrkonzerne* (Düsseldorf, 1954), p. 8.

[7] P. Melandri, *Les Etats-unis face à l'unification de l'Europe 1945–1954* (Paris, 1980), p. 291.

In comparing the relative costs of coke and ore the differences in the steel-manufacturing processes and the possibility of adjusting the mix of inputs within the blast furnace have to be considered. The French industry was less diversified than the German, a much greater proportion of its output coming from the relatively undifferentiated basic steel industry which had grown up in Lorraine on the low-grade minette ore field from the 1890s. The open-hearth process, which accounted for the greater part of West German output (table 54), was more capable of flexibility both in the mix of inputs and in the final product. On the other hand its costs were, except in very favourable

Table 54   French and German crude steel output by process, 1950 (thousand tonnes)

	France	Germany
Gilchrist–Thomas basic	5449.3	5129.0
Open–hearth, acid and basic	2587.9	6661.0
Electric arc, induction and crucible	539.6	331.0

Source: British Iron and Steel Federation, *Statistical Yearbooks*. The French figures are not comprehensive since they omit a small part of output not under the scope of the Chambre Syndicale de la sidérurgie française.

circumstances, higher than those of the Gilchrist-Thomas basic process. Because the Gilchrist-Thomas process is the best approximation to a standardized mass-production process in the industry the comparison of costs is easier there. It is, however, not possible to draw worthwhile comparisons between the cost structure of the Gilchrist-Thomas process and the open-hearth or other process. Indeed, even in respect of the Gilchrist-Thomas process it is only on the basis of an exact comparison between individual enterprises that the real situation could be accurately determined, since a global comparison has a manifest inapplicability to important individual cases. And this is to consider only the difficulties of comparing factor input costs at any moment in time. The way in which those costs could be adjusted in the final sale price, which was the crux of the matter, is a question of comparative productivity and the growth trend of comparative productivity. Although several ingenious methods have been devised for attempting such international productivity comparisons it must be said that there is still no econometric method satisfactory enough to justify its employment to take the issue further at this stage.[8] Not the least important reason for this is the purely political one that almost every element of the price structure of factor inputs into the two industries could be subject to radical alteration through

[8] The most satisfactory, especially as it was devised precisely for the steel industry, is that suggested by R.C. Allen, 'The peculiar productivity history of American blast furnaces, 1840–1913', *Journal of Economic History*, 37 (3), 1977, but in respect of the problem considered here the remark still applies.

374   *The Reconstruction of Western Europe 1945–51*

unpredictable political interventions at any moment, and that the aim of French diplomacy could be no more than to modify and control that political intervention in its own interests. A dubious comparison of relative levels of productivity in 1949/50 would be more or less worthless for establishing the relative final cost pattern of the two industries in 1952.

That having been said, it must also be said that the level of knowledge of and enquiry into the two industries by governments on the eve of embarking on extremely serious negotiations on the subject appears to have been quite astonishingly amateurish. That remark cannot exclude the Commissariat au Plan. As yet no written evidence has been discovered that they were really in a position to forecast with any reasonable accuracy the likely impact of their policies on the steel industry. There seems no reason why a historian should refrain from what may be blundering judgements when governments received advice which could be no more accurate.

In December 1951, six months before the European Coal and Steel Community entered into force, the material input costs of one tonne of Gilchrist-Thomas steel plate were estimated to be lower in West Germany than in France by almost 16 per cent.[9] The largest elements in the difference were the input price of coke in France, which exceeded the advantage France obtained from cheaper ore inputs by more than a thousand francs a tonne, and the greater cost of energy inputs into the manufacturing process, which reflected the higher cost of coal in France as compared to Germany. To this calculation, to establish final production costs, would have to be added wages and social security payments, any other incidences of national taxation which fell on the firm, internal transport costs, and an allowance for interest and depreciation on the capital. However, the costs of raw material inputs in Gilchrist-Thomas steel manufacture are by far the greater part of production costs, as much as 70 per cent of the total in some cases.

Differences in wage and social security costs ought theoretically in the conditions of 1950 to have been in West Germany's favour also, but in fact there is no evidence that wage rates in the West German steel industry were lower than in France, although the burden of social security payments on French producers made the total payment which the employer had to make considerably higher in France. The spread of wages in German steel works in 1950 seems to have been much wider than in French ones but this is the only indication that in West Germany there were 1.8 million unemployed in March 1950 whereas in France full employment still prevailed. The retrospective wage figures given in the Community's bulletin indicate that German steel workers' wages in August 1950 varied from 21.88 cents an hour to 30.91 cents; in France a skilled worker's wage was 29.99 cents.[10] It may emerge that

[9] J. Chardonnet, *La sidérurgie française. Progrès ou décadence?* (Paris, 1954), p. 102.
[10] Communauté Européenne de l'Acier et du Charbon, *Evolution des salaires et politique salariale dans les industries de la Communauté 1945–1956* (Luxembourg, 1960), p. 74.

the reason for this similarity was the maldistribution of the unemployed labour force in West Germany. The population of North Rhine-Westphalia had not increased, but had fallen in the immediate aftermath of the German surrender, and the influx of refugees into the Bizone had been mainly into the more rural Länder of Schleswig-Holstein and Bavaria. The metal-workers union, endowed with a remarkable gain in factory negotiating powers by the Allies, had been able to establish wage rates relatively free from the influence of the flood of unemployed *Ostvertriebene*, and the German steel industry did not gain the advantage of low wages common to almost all other West German industries, except of course coal, at the time.

Whatever the reasons for the similarity in wage levels it is clear that the social security element of the wage payment falling on the entrepreneur was much higher in France, especially because of the more generous family allowances paid there. The total burden of non-wage payments in the first quarter of 1950 in France was 53 francs, or another 50 per cent on the wage bill, and only 32 francs, or less than a third of the wage bill, in Germany.[11]

The nominal incidence of fiscal policy was quite different between the two industries, mainly because of the higher levels of direct taxation in the Federal Republic. The total fiscal burden on domestic steel prices in France was estimated in spring 1950 at about 23 per cent, in West Germany at 33 per cent.[12] Both countries, however, had a system of export rebates on turnover tax, but at different rates so that the incidence on export prices was entirely different. This was to be one of the most fiercely-fought issues of the Schuman Plan negotiations, especially when taken with the difference in protective tariffs. Finished steel sold in Germany paid a tax of 6 per cent; sold abroad it attracted a 6.5 per cent rebate. Imported steel had to pay a compensatory levy of 6 per cent. French steel sold on the domestic market paid taxes equivalent to 19 per cent of the price, while the corresponding export rebates and import levies were about 16.5 per cent. Thus the price relationships of German and French steel in their respective markets after tax were substantially different from those before tax. Although Gilchrist-Thomas plate f.o.b. the steel mill in Germany, discounting the difference in labour costs, was about 16 per cent cheaper than the equivalent product in France, this price advantage would be lost if it were exported to France. The same French Gilchrist-Thomas plate would then sell in West Germany at about 6 per cent less than the sale price of the equivalent German product in France.[13]

By the side of this scale of difference, differences in internal transport costs, capital costs and depreciation allowances could not have been especially

---

[11] FJM, AMG 22/5/4, Commissariat Général, 'Note relative aux effets du Plan Schuman sur les industries du charbon et de l'acier en France', 8 February 1951.

[12] C.H. Hahn, *Der Schuman Plan. Eine Untersuchung im besonderen Hinblick auf die deutsch-französische Stahlindustrie* (Munich, 1953), p. 80.

[13] See the prices given by H. Mendershausen, 'First tests of the Schuman Plan', *Review of Economics and Statistics*, 35 (4), 1953.

376   *The Reconstruction of Western Europe 1945–51*

significant. Everything we know about the period implies that capital must have been more expensive in Germany. Depreciation allowances, on the other hand, were set at a generous level by the Federal government. The extent to which capital costs and replacement were to be taken into account in deciding the future relationships of the two industries was by no means a negligible one; none the less it can be set on one side for the moment, because so much the main determinant of production costs were raw material inputs and fiscal policy.

Simply taking the most easily comparable sections of the French and German steel industries into account in this way suggests very strongly that in terms of basic input costs Germany was at a marked advantage. But this does not seem to have been the view of the Planning Commissariat, which seems rather to have believed that in any regulation of the European markets the Lorraine basic steel industry would be favoured.[14] Of course everything in such a comparison depended on the future growth of productivity and on what would be done about the element of government intervention in determining costs, for the variation in the government element was greater than that in factor input costs. Once fiscal and tariff policies, for example, were taken into account, Germany's cost advantages did not appear as an international comparative advantage, indeed some French Gilchrist-Thomas steel could be sold marginally more cheaply in West Germany than the equivalent German steel in France. But setting aside these matters the Planning Commissariat still took the view that the 16 per cent difference in material input costs between French and German Gilchrist-Thomas plate was due to lack of rationalization in the French industry and thus made this industry not only susceptible to being closed by planning but on the way already to being so.[15]

Once we widen the comparison to try to include the open-hearth producers and other producers of specialized steels the economics become even more problematic. The German industry, because so much more of it used the open-hearth process, required greater quantities of scrap and other iron inputs, and scrap prices were high after 1945. In this respect only the steel industry of Belgium and Luxembourg, 90 per cent of whose output was made by converters, was more favourably situated than the French. At the opposite extreme was Italy's small steel industry which was concentrated very heavily on special steel production. France used on average in 1949 312 kg of scrap combined with other inputs to produce one tonne of crude steel compared to West Germany's 429 kg, Britain's 629 kg, and Italy's 875 kg.[16] The input cost of scrap was about 20 per cent higher in France than in West Germany, because of the large amounts of scrap still lying around in the Federal Republic, but this still left the French industry's total scrap costs per tonne of steel produced considerably below the West German level.[17]

[14] FRUS, 1950, III, Acheson to Washington, 12 May 1950, p. 697.
[15] FJM, AMG 22/5/4.   [16] Hahn, *Der Schuman Plan*, p. 73.
[17] Although surely not 40 per cent lower as calculated by K.W.F. Zawadzki, 'The economics of the Schuman Plan', in *Oxford Economic Papers*, N.S., v, 1953.

An approximation of the average costs of material and labour for all steel-making was made by the United Nations Department of Economic Affairs in 1951. This shows that even when the open-hearth industry is included the principal differences in factor input costs betwen the French and German industries were still, on the French side, dearer coke and higher labour costs, and on the German side the higher costs of imported ore, and that the difference in labour costs balanced the difference in imported ore costs leaving the much greater relative cost of coke inputs the principal French disadvantage (table 55).

Table 55   Approximate costs of labour and main raw materials for steel making, 1951 (dollars)

	France		West Germany	
	Per hour or per tonne of raw material	Per tonne of steel	Per hour or per tonne of raw material	Per tonne of steel
Labour (inc. maintenance services)	0.63	21	0.63	16
Imported ore	0	0	20	5
Domestic ore	11	7	19	4
Scrap purchases	24	4	20	5
Coke	16	12	10	6
Costs per tonne of steel		44		36

Source: UN, *Economic Survey of Europe Since the War* (Geneva, 1953), p. 228.

A national assessment of the economic situation would therefore point to the following conclusions. The West German industry had significant cost advantages over that of France, of which the most significant was the input price of coke. The French government could hope to remedy this, as indeed it had been struggling to do since 1944, because West Germany was by far the most important foreign supplier of coke to the basic steel industry in France and France was West Germany's biggest market for coke exports. Given the relatively low level of investment (which, if the figures could be calculated net of the disinvestment which must also have taken place, would be even lower) in the West German steel industry since 1944 compared to its French counterpart, and given the high cost of capital in the Federal Republic, the view of the Planning Commissariat that differences in final sales prices to France's disadvantage would be eliminated or very much reduced by higher rates of productivity growth in the French industry was not necessarily wrong. Lastly, governmental pressures in any direct inter-governmental negotiations were likely to bring final sales prices closer together because government

378   *The Reconstruction of Western Europe 1945–51*

intervention, especially through fiscal policy, was so important a component of the final price in each country.

It was better for France to negotiate now while the West German state was in tutelage, before the extent of the Ruhr Authority's powers were finally discovered, and before the Federal German Republic was admitted more fully into the system of military alliances. But what form should the negotiations take? Certain issues relating to the regulation of the German steel industry and its domestic markets had already been hotly debated in the London conference and its aftermath. One was the difference made to final costs by the size of the firm. All the Allied powers, even though they had started from different philosophies, had made a facile identification of 'big business' with the Nazi regime. Powerful vested business interests and cartels were publicly branded at Potsdam as enemies of democracy and the trials of prominent German firms and industrialists at Nuremberg for war crimes were intended as a part of the process of 'democratization'.[18] Large, integrated firms were held to have exercised a malign influence on German history since the late nineteenth century and irrespective of the economic considerations involved there were powerful political pressures to break up the Ruhr firms into their component parts. Similar pressures had been exercised by French negotiators throughout the long discussions on the International Ruhr Authority and on dismantling. At least a third of Ruhr coal output was controlled by integrated steel firms. Such firms consumed coal and coke, not at market prices, but rather at more favourable transfer prices. Production costs may have been lower because in the larger integrated concerns economies of scale were greater and coal and coke input prices lower.

Another issue which had been important in the negotiations for the International Authority for the Ruhr was discrimination between domestic and export coal and coke prices. That is not to say that France and others did not also discriminate in the same way in respect of iron ore. But once the Saarland had been attached to France, Germany scarcely used French ores at all. The relatively high cost of imported ore in West Germany arose from the high transport charges on Swedish ores.[19] The price of German metallurgical coke delivered in Lorraine in spring 1950 was about 46 per cent higher than its price in the Ruhr, before compensatory fiscal adjustment in France.[20] The United Nations estimated that about 15 per cent of the delivered price was due to transport costs.[21] If this estimate is correct, using the rates of dependence of the French industry on German coke calculated in chapter 4, the difference made to final production costs in the French steel

[18] Two major steel manufacturers, Krupp and Flick, were prosecuted.
[19] Swedish Kiruna ore at 60 per cent fe. content retailed at $4 per tonne at the mine-head but at $7 per tonne fob Narvik in spring 1949. UN, *European Steel Trends*, p. 65.
[20] Zawadzki, 'Economics'.
[21] UN, *European Steel Trends*, p. 55.

industry by dual pricing of German coke could be estimated at about 2 per cent.[22]

During the Schuman Plan negotiations much evidence emerged that the freight rates charged by the railways through the Palatinate were highly discriminatory. Removing this further element of discrimination might therefore reduce the production costs of Lorraine steel by as much as 2.5 per cent. On the basis of 1950 steel prices this would have brought the price of Gilchrist-Thomas merchant bars in France down to equality with the equivalent German product although it would by no means have closed the gap between actual French and German prices for Gilchrist-Thomas plate, nor for open-hearth steel. The possible gain was, however, by no means negligible, for it might also preclude price discrimination in the future against the French steel industry, while the West German industry stood to gain little or nothing from the possible removal of French ore price discrimination against it.

If to this possible gain could be added a breaking-up of the integrated Ruhr firms the gains might be still greater. The average size of the producing unit was much larger in West Germany than in France. The assumption underlying the Modernization Plan's major investment projects in the French steel industry was that the optimum output level for unspecialized steel-producing plant which would be internationally competitive was one million tonnes of crude steel a year. No French plant was producing at that level in 1950; in September of that year three German works were operating at a higher level. In 1949–50 about half of German ingot output came from plant whose output was greater than 900,000 tonnes a year.[23] Most such firms were integrated upwards as far as the rolling mill and many owned their own coal supply, thus increasing the cost advantages which their greater steel-making capacity provided. The original Bizone proposals for 'deconcentration' made in February 1947, whose implementation had been postponed because of the dispute with the French government over ultimate ownership, had indicated that the major German steel companies would be broken up into twenty-five single firms. The French government could hope to develop the basic idea of these proposals while accepting in return the Allied *fait accompli* on the question of ownership. In this matter at least small might seem more beautiful to all except the Germans.

What, however, is by no means established is that the French coal and steel industries were any less integrated than the German. What seems more likely to have been the case is that integration brought greater savings in production costs in Germany because of the assembly on one continuous site by the larger firms of so many aspects of iron and steel-making and processing, with the

[22] The estimate of 4.8 per cent made by the UN, *European Steel Trends*, p. 65, is based on a set of coke prices which are not confirmed elsewhere and on inexact assumptions about the other elements in the calculation. [23] Burn, *The Steel Industry*, p. 402.

380   *The Reconstruction of Western Europe 1945–51*

consequent saving in transport costs. These savings would not be lost through breaking up the ownership of the capital in the enterprise. This would probably only reduce the advantage the German firms had, if any, in the external economies arising from the greater scale of management or the possibility of more flexible financing. There were numerous examples of similar forms of integration in France, which, even if the gains in productivity were less and the form of integration less direct and binding, no doubt brought similar internal price advantages to those in Germany. Of the thirty-seven companies which Lauersen lists in the French iron and steel industry, eight had the same degree of integration as the major German firms except that they had now lost control of their coal resources to the French state. A further five firms combined steel production with rolling mills and other finishing processes but had no blast-furnaces.[24] Before nationalization of the coal-mines at least ten of the French steel firms had owned their own coal supply and the Lorraine mines in particular had been intimately linked to particular steel works. This is to say nothing of the links between steel-makers and iron ore mines in France which were every bit as extensive as those between coal-mines and steel works in the Ruhr; sixteen of the French firms owned their own supply of ore.[25]

The issues discussed in this section may seem rather fine, even trivial, by the side of the grandiose language in which politicians wrapped the initial proposals for the Schuman Plan and beside the undoubtedly high ideals of some of its proponents. Variations in the price of coke and differences in productivity in steel works are not, it must be admitted, themes so apt to raise the enthusiasm as the waning of the nation state or the reconciliation of bitterly divided enemies. The intention of dwelling at such length on such uninspiring subjects is not to insist on the primacy of the economic objectives of the Schuman Plan. Far from it, the objectives of the Schuman proposals were overwhelmingly political. It is to explain precisely what the real possibilities for political initiative were, what their implications, and, above all, to show how the Schuman proposals, far from being a change of economic and political direction, evolved logically from the consistent pursuit of France's original domestic and foreign reconstruction aims.

THE POLITICAL ORIGINS OF THE SCHUMAN PLAN

The European Coal and Steel Community is sometimes criticized for having created so tangled a web of economic and political relationships between the member states as to have destroyed from the outset all possibility of economic

[24] W. Lauersen, *Ausmass und Formen vertikaler Verflechtung in der Eisen- und Stahlindustrie der Vereinigten Staaten, Grossbritanniens, Frankreichs, Belgiens und Luxemburgs* (Kiel, 1951).
[25] ibid., pp. 85–6.

rationality. But such a criticism disregards the previous history. To arrive at anything simpler the Community would have had to unravel a skein of politico-economic relationships which had already become almost untraceable in their complexity. There are certainly many justifiable economic criticisms of the Coal and Steel Community, but it was not more complex than what went before. It was in certain respects a simplification. In April 1950, on the eve of the Schuman proposals, the ECA confessed itself unable to understand what the effect of the French proposals to the coming foreign ministers' meeting to modify the relationship between the Allied High Commissioners and the International Ruhr Authority would be.[26] When Dean Acheson took over as Secretary of State he found American policy on the different issues negotiated so interminably at the London conference to be so piecemeal that 'he did not understand either how we ever arrived at the decision to see established a West German government or State. He wondered whether this had not rather been the brainchild of General Clay and not a governmental decision.'[27] A special sub-committee of the National Security Council was set up to review the whole range of American policy on Germany. It was through this procedure that the American army in Germany was eventually brought to heel and a final settlement with France on the uncompleted details of the London conference reached. Even this did not clarify the extent of French and Allied powers over the West German economy.

The deadline towards which events moved was set by the projected arrival of the Foreign Ministers in Washington to negotiate the North Atlantic Treaty Organization on 31 March 1949. Ten days before this Schuman met Clay and gave him the clearest indication that France was no longer especially interested in elaborate controls and control boards over the German economy, of the kind that the British government had favoured, and which the London conference had laboured so long to include in the preliminary versions of the Occupation Statute. French interest was now, Schuman indicated, more in the general principles by which French and German economic recovery might be harmonized.[28] The State Department had of course only accepted unwillingly the future operation of these complicated control boards and was glad to see them go. The agreed policy statement left with Truman on the eve of the NATO conference therefore sketched out an Occupation Statute much simpler and less restrictive than the London conference had discussed. It would contain the necessary security safeguards, the stronger because the North Atlantic Pact would mean that United States forces would remain in Germany 'until the present tense and insecure situation in Europe has been replaced by a satisfactory measure of international confidence and balanced

---

[26] ECA, 61, 'Problems of the International Authority for the Ruhr', 12 April 1950.
[27] FRUS, 1949, III, p. 102, Memorandum of conversation by Murphy, 9 March 1949.
[28] FRUS, 1949, III, p. 115, Caffery to Washington, 22 March 1949.

normal relationship'.[29] The Occupation Statute would now be only a short document reserving certain vital matters, such as foreign affairs and external security, to the Allied powers. The reign of the army would come to an end and with the birth of the Federal Republic the Allies would appoint civilian High Commissioners to deal with a government which would be entirely independent except for those matters reserved in the simpler Occupation Statute.[30] The occupying powers would surrender all their administrative controls over the German economy to the West German government except where the Occupation Statute or the International Authority for the Ruhr took precedence.

This still left much to settle about the relationship between the Moscow sliding-scales, the OEEC, and the Ruhr Authority, as well as about the continuation of dismantling and 'decartelization' in Germany. The Moscow scales stopped at a level of 330,000 tonnes output of coal daily and France wanted them extended upwards so that at higher levels of output the same percentage of Ruhr coal would have to be made available without the possibility of any discretion being exercised by the Ruhr Authority. It also wanted the sliding-scales to cover coking fines and coke at this higher level. The European Coal Organization had been wound up, but coal availabilities still had to be listed to the UN Coal Committee of the Economic and Social Commission for Europe, a vestigial trace of the earlier attempt at a world-wide peace settlement, so that there were other possible complications on the question too. Furthermore, it was unforeseeable what France's allies would be prepared to support when the Ruhr Authority first met in Düsseldorf, although the decision had been quite firm that the Authority's decisions could not contradict the annual economic programmes approved by the OEEC.

At the first meeting of the International Ruhr Authority the French representatives had their worst fears more than confirmed. The total budget of the Authority was to be only about $280,000 annually. It was not to have its own statistical services. It would have no direct contact of its own with the German firms, but only through the offices of the Allied High Commission. It would rarely be able to make inspections. It would have no say in the formulation of the West German programmes tabled at the OEEC.[31] There was very little France could do there except ensure that the relevant powers vested with the High Commissioners were not given away before they might be inherited by the Authority, a somewhat long-term course of action which was now only marginally relevant to French policy.

Until the Federal government entered into office its votes on the Authority were exercised by the occupying powers. There was no certainty that the new

[29] FRUS, 1948, II, p. 122, US Policy respecting Germany, 22 March 1949.

[30] Clay's verdict was, 'We have lost Germany politically and therefore it really does not matter except that history will prove why there was World War III.' Clay Papers, II, p. 1063.

[31] Y.62.3, Account of first meeting of the Ruhr Authority. Telegram, Dejean to Paris, 1 June 1949.

government would agree to serve on it or accept its rulings. The first Bundestag of the German Federal Republic was elected on 14 August 1949. On 20 September Konrad Adenauer came into office as Federal Chancellor, by the narrowest possible margin, and at the same time the Economic Council (Wirtschaftsrat) and the Administrative Council (Verwaltungsrat) for the Bizone were dissolved and the three civilian High Commissioners entered office as the Allied High Commission, replacing the separate Military Governments.[32] In opposition in Bonn the Social Democratic Party clamoured against the Ruhr Authority and pressed the government not to join it. On 16 September the High Commissioners agreed that Germany should be represented on the Authority by full voting members. The real problem for the High Commissioners was not whether to ratify this decision but how to disguise the fact that, in sharp contrast to the view of it taken by the Social Democratic opposition in Bonn, the Authority had few real powers anyway! As the British High Commissioner put it,

> Germans now think of IAR as a very powerful body and if they join they will soon discover that real powers lodged in other agencies. Therefore Germans likely go other extreme with impression that Authority has no important job to do and not to bother to work with it except in perfunctory way.[33]

It was not until 28 October that the Federal Republic took its seat in the OEEC and three days later a German representative attended the Council meeting. The problem was that although a seat on the Executive Committee had been kept warm for Germany when that Committee was first set up, any German representative now occupying it would mean an immediate breach in the Occupation Statute's prescription that the Federal Republic could not control its own foreign policy! Robertson suggested he might speak for Germany when the Executive Committee met at ministerial level, but that might have presented the Americans with the perfect excuse for insisting that their High Commissioner should also be involved in the OEEC.[34] In September the French High Commissioner, André François-Poncet, cut the tangled knot by suggesting that this one exception to the rule that the West German government be excluded from the sublime heights of foreign affairs be allowed, and the Federal Republic attended in October its first international conference as an equal.[35]

[32] The British High Commissioner was the same person, Sir (rather than General) Brian Robertson. General Koenig was replaced by André François-Poncet, a former ambassador to Berlin. The American High Commissioner was John J. McCloy.

John J. McCloy, 1895– . A lawyer. Educated at Harvard. Assistant Secretary of State 1941–5. President of World Bank 1947–9. United States High Commissioner for Germany 1949–52. Chairman of Board of Chase National, then Chase Manhattan Bank, and of the Ford Foundation, 1953–61. Disarmament adviser to Secretary of State Dulles. Co-ordinator of US Disarmament Activities 1961–3. An energetic and strong-willed person who exercised much influence.

[33] FRUS, 1949, III, p. 486, Riddleberger to Acheson, 16 September 1949.

[34] FO 371/76937, Robertson to Kirkpatrick, 23 February 1949.

[35] ibid., UK High Commission in Bonn to London, 13 September 1949.

384   *The Reconstruction of Western Europe 1945–51*

The new government chose well its first ground to fight. Although at first it declined to send full members to the Ruhr Authority, this was not in protest against the Authority but against the continuation of dismantling activities. It was on those grounds that the occupying powers were weakest; there was as much dismantling of German firms in 1949 as in the earlier years and the Americans had scarcely disguised their wish that it should end. With a change of heart in this direction by the occupiers Adenauer made it clear that the Federal Republic would accept its place in the Ruhr Authority.

The status of the specific controls on the level of output in West Germany had been decided in a set of separate negotiations in London which culminated on 31 March 1949. The United States had agreed to the continuation of the Potsdam limits as revised in 1948 on the annual output of steel in West Germany until the end of the ERP. The Bizone's limit was raised from 10.7 million tonnes to 11.1 million to allow for the incorporation of the French zone. The list of 'prohibited and restricted industries' had also been maintained in principle with only a few significant differences from the list first drawn up after the Potsdam conference. But as far as individual works went there were great changes. Of the 167 plants originally scheduled for dismantling whose removal from the list the Humphrey Report had recommended, 159 were removed from it. Yet among the six which were conceded to the British and French opposition and remained on the dismantling list was the Thyssen steel works at Hamborn, and the six between them represented as much as 30 per cent of the total employment provided by the full 'Humphrey list'. The insistence by Britain and France on putting up a harder fight in respect of the list of prohibited industries reflected the fact that domestic political opposition to relaxing the restrictions on the German economy would obviously focus on questions of future strategic security.[36] All shipyards with a capacity of more than 277,000 tonnes a year were also prohibited. The limits on the size and speed of new German ships remained. All these limitations were to apply until summer 1952 at the earliest. France had wanted them to be of indefinite duration.

In September both Adenauer and Kurt Schumacher, the leader of the Social Democratic Party, jointly urged John McCloy to try to end the dismantling activities, before Germany joined the two international organizations. Adenauer offered as a bait a willing acceptance by his government of 'some form of internationalization if such works as Thyssen could be preserved.'[37] The Americans agreed that they would try to persuade their allies at talks scheduled for that month in Washington, although Acheson thought there was little chance of success. Bevin knew well enough, as did the British

---

[36] In the United States the argument ran the other way; should works which contributed to Germany's strategic strength be dismantled? The American negotiators insisted against strong British and French pressure on removing the electro-steel works, Deutsche Edelstahlwerke, from the dismantling list.   [37] FRUS, 1949, III, p. 595, McCloy to Acheson, 13 September 1949.

cabinet after the Humphrey Report, that dismantling was coming to an end because it was impractical politically, but that seemed to him all the more reason for going ahead at an accelerated pace while it was still possible. Bevin wanted until April 1950 to knock down, for it now did not really come to much more than that, the remaining plant he was entitled to claim as the outcome of the March agreements on the Humphrey Report.[38]

This was not a very sensible policy, in so far as it made an intensification of the dismantling programme coincide with the Soviet moves to establish a government in their own zone of Germany. The effect of the Soviet actions on the western powers was a very powerful one, for it institutionalized a direct rivalry for the future allegiance of Germany. The wait to see whether the Federal German government would subscribe with some reasonable degree of conformity to the Western European institutional framework which had been devised, in the face of the very strong domestic opposition to that policy which it was encountering, was an anxious one and seems to have given many in Washington the feeling that they had lost control of the situation in spite of the ERP. Demonstrations against the dismantling squads in the British zone,[39] where most of the dismantling had to be undertaken, pressure from the United States, and agitation within the Labour Party against the policy worked to change Bevin's mind and on 28 October he proposed a compromise solution to be worked out through the High Commissioners, which would establish a definitive final programme with only a small remaining number of plants for dismantling. It was to be the last Allied attempt to grapple with the problem from a position of relative strength.

Accordingly the High Commissioners met in closed session in Paris with their three foreign ministers on 10 November. The main problem was the French anxiety about the level of German steel production. Providing the West German government gave an understanding to work with the Ruhr Authority and the Military Security Board France was prepared to remove from the list of prohibited industries, and thus from the list of works to be dismantled, synthetic oil plant, synthetic rubber plant, all factories in Berlin, and all major steel works including the Thyssen factories in Hamborn, but excepting the Hermann Goering works in Salzgitter and the Krupp works in Essen. As far as steel was concerned Schuman insisted, however, that all steel plant should be placed under a special statutory authority so that it could not exceed the permitted limits of production.[40] All Schuman could obtain was that the High Commissioners would be empowered to put any or all of the steel works now to be retained out of action once more if in fact German steel output did exceed the permitted limits.[41] Any further extension of German

[38] ibid., p. 599, Memorandum of conversation by Acheson, 15 September 1949.

[39] In March 1950 a serious riot stopped the dismantling of the Watenstedt plant of the former Reichswerke Hermann Goering at Salzgitter.

[40] CP (49) 237, Memorandum by Bevin, 'Germany: meeting of British, United States and French foreign ministers', 16 November 1949.

[41] When this happened, in 1950, they did not do so.

386   *The Reconstruction of Western Europe 1945–51*

steel-making capacity would require a licence from the Military Security Board. These terms were then embodied in the Petersberg agreements signed on 22 November, and thenceforward the German representative on the Ruhr Authority served as a full representative. To the embarrassment of all other member countries, who had appointed technical personnel, the German government nominated Franz Blücher, the Vice-Chancellor.

The possibility of a Franco-German association had not therefore been ruled out by the first actions of the West German government and the French government had pursued a careful, conciliatory path towards its objectives. French anxieties were more about the tendency of American policies to eliminate the bargaining advantages France still had over Germany. The Americans had given no support to France in the Ruhr Authority and in almost the first independent economic action of the West German government, the devaluation of the Deutschmark, France found only lukewarm support from the United States. The outcome was a further slight weakening of the French position.

The devaluation of the pound took place three days before Adenauer presented his government and its policy to the Bundestag. The first decision of any consequence which the Federal Government was called on to make, to establish a new exchange rate for the Deutschmark against the dollar, thus bore immediately on all issues which concerned the French government. Too large a devaluation would increase the competitiveness of German exports in Europe. The pound had been devalued by 30.5 per cent, the official export exchange rate of the franc by 22.5 per cent. The French proposed the mark be devalued by only 15 per cent. The German government proposed 22.5 per cent.

When the French ministers were in Washington in September Schuman had made a particular plea for direct American pressure to be brought to bear on the German government on the question of coal export prices.[42] The French government now insisted that the question of a new value for the mark should be tied by the High Commissioners to the end of dual coal and coke pricing by Germany. If the domestic and export prices of German coal and coke were equalized the French government would reluctantly accept a 20 per cent devaluation of the mark against the dollar.[43] Ironically, this was the level at which Erhard had originally wished to establish the mark, but he had been overruled by bankers, financial advisers and the Chancellor on the grounds that such a rate would cripple Germany's export capacity.[44] The French protest was followed by one in similar terms from Belgium and Luxembourg claiming that the new exchange rate proposed in Germany would 'wreck the

[42] ECA, 5, 'US-French conversations on economic problems', 15 September 1949.
[43] FRUS, 1949, III, Bruce to Washington, 22 September 1949, p. 451.
[44] ibid., McCloy to Washington, 22 September 1949, p. 452.

economies of France and the Benelux countries'.[45] America was not, however, prepared to tie the question of coal export prices to the new exchange rate.

There were good grounds for the American resistance. America's policy was to end dual pricing throughout Europe, not to enforce on the Federal Republic the abolition of a practice which was still standard in Britain. Nevertheless McCloy was now ordered to urge on Bonn a devaluation of only 20 per cent. At the High Commissioners' meeting on 24 September François-Poncet, the French High Commissioner, refused to agree to ratify any rate without an agreement to terminate dual coal pricing.[46] Once McCloy had persuaded the Bonn government to change its mind to conform to Erhard's original suggestion Acheson and Schuman met again for the second time in three days and Schuman agreed to the new rate on the understanding that American policy would actively pursue the ending of dual pricing by both West Germany and Britain.[47] The High Commissioners did not formally agree to the new German exchange rate until 28 September, by which date a further procedure had been established. A study group was to be set up to enquire into disparities in German coal prices with a view to eliminating them by the first day of 1950, 'if possible'.[48] Adenauer objected vigorously; he 'could not see what relation the internal price of coal had to the purposes of the occupation'.[49]

Needless to say the British cabinet had no intention of ending the dual price for British coal. They flatly declined to do so in December leaving the United States once more face to face with the Franco-German problem.[50] On 1 January 1950 the West German government did not abolish the dual pricing system but reduced the official differential between export and import prices from DM8.00 a tonne to DM5.82, later readjusted to DM5.46. As part of the readjustment domestic coal prices were increased, but by an amount which still left them well short of French domestic coal prices. This could be seen as a concession in view of Adenauer's categorical statement to the Bundestag in September that he would not increase the domestic coal price.[51] The German government, while insisting that the question of the price of coal exports was not, in its view, one to be settled either through the High Commission or the International Ruhr Authority, implied that it would be amenable to settlement through a more general European agreement which would change the status of the Federal Republic.

The worst tensions likely to emanate from the International Authority for

[45] ibid., Memorandum of conversation between Schuman and Acheson, 23 September 1949, p. 454. [46] ibid., McCloy to Washington, 24 September 1949, p. 458.
[47] Acheson Papers, 27, Visit of M. Schuman, 26 September 1949.
[48] FRUS, 1949, III, McCloy to Washington, 28 September 1949, p. 471.
[49] ibid., McCloy to Washington, 1 October 1949, p. 472.
[50] FRUS, 1949, IV, Kenney to Harriman, 13 December 1949, p. 460.
[51] F.R. Willis, *France, Germany and the New Europe, 1945–1967* (Stanford, 1965), p. 64.

388   *The Reconstruction of Western Europe 1945–51*

the Ruhr were in fact avoided at the start of its existence by the sluggish performance of the French economy in 1949 and the fact that steel output in West Germany, although rising rapidly, was still so low. In the conditions briefly prevailing on the Western European coal market in winter 1949–50 German coal producers were by no means reluctant to see their output allocated a secure niche in a large export market by an international organization! The opportunity was taken to end the interest which the UN Economic Commission for Europe still had in the allocation of German coal. By summer 1950 the situation would again have changed completely and in the coal shortage which the 1950 steel boom once more produced France would invoke every power it could inside the Authority to obtain supplies of coal in a time of coal penury in Germany. Before that, however, the possibility of an economic understanding was brought nearer by the sudden, temporary relaxation of the fierce scramble for coal and coke and the postponement of the struggle expected inside the Ruhr Authority.

Three days before the Petersberg agreements France had embarked on a last attempt to get the full powers of the Allied Coal and Steel Control Boards transferred intact to the International Ruhr Authority. America, however, was determined that they should remain in the hands of the High Commission, thus giving the American High Commissioner the decisive voice.[52] When this attempt failed the French government followed it with an attempt to vest some of the powers of the High Commissioners themselves in the Ruhr Authority. These proposals, which were to go to the foreign ministers' conference in May 1950, were that the final decision about allocation be transferred to the Authority and that the commission should give a firm guarantee at once that when its powers on decartelization were transferred these too would go to the Authority and not to any other agency. The French proposals were both vague and complex, vague because numerous hints seem to have been dropped that if these powers were transferred France might in turn agree to the Ruhr Authority being extended in some way to cover the Saarland, Benelux and France. Although the State Department and the ECA readily agreed that this would make the Authority more palatable to Germany, it was not a suggestion which the ECA looked on with favour. An extended Authority of this kind 'could hardly fail to become engaged in the maintenance of prices and the restriction of production in the interests of producers'.[53] And

[52] FRUS, 1949, III, p. 295, United States interests, positions and tactics at Paris, 5 November 1949.
[53] ECA, 61, Problems of the International Authority for the Ruhr, 12 April 1950. 'Can one' asked the State Department briefing for the May meeting, 'confidently hope that a new organization consisting of the present members of the Ruhr Authority could undertake investment planning with respect to their steel industries (or their coal industries) in a manner which would be less open to objection than the only organized inter-governmental attempt in this field that has actually taken place? This would appear to be extremely doubtful since the OEEC at least has the advantage of including in its membership countries whose interests are primarily those of consumers of steel rather than producers.'

since it meant weakening the powers of the American High Commissioner the State Department could not ultimately agree to it either. All roads to a Franco-German settlement through the Ruhr Authority seemed to be closed politically, in spite of the temporary peace which prevailed there.

Yet the international scope for a direct French initiative towards Germany outside the sphere of the Authority had increased. Adenauer's foreign policy left no doubt of his desire for a close co-operation with France. After September 1949 the United States had been obliged to accept that its policy of integrating western Europe through British political and economic leadership was neither possible nor, indeed, necessarily in American interests if it were to provoke British actions which would prevent the achievement of a wider multilateralism. In spite of the prevailing view in the ECA that to extend the Ruhr Authority's powers to Benelux and the Saarland would be against American interests, in so far as it would open the door to the return of the coal and steel cartels, the fact of the matter was that the integration of Western Europe was now only likely to be obtained through supporting a French initiative, and that this was the area where the scope for a French initiative was not diminishing.

Although the Occupation Statute contained a promise that within eighteen months it would be revised to extend West German jurisdiction, the areas in which it imposed limits on the freedom of action by the Federal government made up a forbidding list; defence, foreign affairs, occupation costs, matters relating to the federal and land constitutions, reparations, foreign trade and exchange controls, and international borrowing, as well as the powers over decartelization, the power to restrict ownership of Ruhr industries and the power to allocate Ruhr coal between domestic and foreign markets which was retained by the International Ruhr Authority. From the moment Adenauer was elected Chancellor he made it the prime objective of his foreign policy to have these restrictions on the full sovereignty of the Federal Republic removed. The path he chose was one of the closest possible collaboration with the western powers, probably in the hope that German economic strength would fairly soon establish the country as an indispensable and perhaps even the strongest member of the Western European bloc. Whatever the variety of public arguments put forward to defend this policy, Adenauer's basic assumption seems to have been that no short-term solution to the problem of German reunification was now possible. Once the time came when such a solution might be envisaged it would only be a satisfactory one if the Federal Republic could act from a position of strength, and this it could only obtain within the western bloc. If the time did not come, it would be even more dangerous to abandon the closest possible co-operation with the western powers.[54] It was

[54] For an analysis of Adenauer's motives see W. Besson, 'Die Anfänge der bundesrepublikanischen Aussenpolitik' in G. Lehmbruch (ed.) *Demokratisches System und politische Praxis in der Bundesrepublik* (Munich, 1971).

390   *The Reconstruction of Western Europe 1945–51*

this policy which offered the political opportunity to the French government which the Schuman Plan proposals were to seize, and without Adenauer's autocratic imposition of his own foreign policy on the Federal government these proposals would surely not have been made.

While tenaciously disputing the questions of dismantling and the mark exchange rate, Adenauer hinted at a solution on the largest possible scale. This was, even more strikingly, his attitude towards French actions in the Saarland. The Saar Landtag had approved in November 1947 a constitution instituting a monetary and customs union with France and effectively making the Saarland independent from Germany. Over the course of 1949, as the Federal Republic emerged, these earlier decisions proved increasingly displeasing to a broad spectrum of political opinion in the Saarland and it no longer looked as though France could rely on them as a way of retaining control of the Saar's resources. In February 1950 the French began to negotiate a convention by which the Saarland would receive autonomy but remain separated from Germany. The outcome of the convention, signed in March, was that France retained financial and customs authority in the Saarland and was given a long-term lease on the Saar coal-mines which would thus continue to operate in a French administrative framework and contribute to French supply, even though the rest of the area became independent of France in matters of day-to-day administration. The mines would remain under French control until a peace treaty was signed and in return the French government would pay a rent of 400 million francs ($1.14 million) annually. The convention also agreed on an attempt to equalize production costs in the coal and steel industries between the Saarland and France. The origins of this attempt were that the earlier proposals for a complete merger had not been at all welcome to the Lorraine steel industry, subjected to full competition on its own market from a steel industry operating at production costs nearer to the German than the French level.[55] The day after the convention was signed Adenauer described it as 'a decision against Europe'.[56] The West German government then announced its decision to delay its entry into the recently formed Council of Europe. At the same time Adenauer repeatedly offered through various unofficial channels to negotiate an association of French and German industries on equal terms or even a Franco-German economic union. He left no doubt that any initiative in this direction would be welcomed. This had been the attitude of several German politicians in the Ruhr itself to the Ruhr Authority. During the last debates on the 'socialization' bill in the Landtag of North Rhine-Westphalia the Minister-President, Karl Arnold, had publicly held out the hope that the bill would not be killed but serve as the basis of an equal agreement between

[55] J. Freymond, *The Saar Conflict 1945–1955* (London, 1960), pp. 61 ff; P. Fischer, *Die Saar zwischen Deutschland und Frankreich: Politische Entwicklung von 1945–1959* (Frankfurt, 1959), pp. 81–90.
[56] Willis, *France*, p. 76.

France, the Benelux and West Germany on the coal industry, and in a new year broadcast after the publication of the Ruhr Statute he repeated the wish.[57]

In the United States the opinions of the new Secretary of State, Acheson, had moved strongly in one direction. He had come to believe that negotiations over Germany's role in Europe had been so long and tortuous, and even by November 1949 had still not clearly produced the result that America wanted, because it was not really in the power of the United States alone to produce such an outcome. It was in the end only France which had the power to fulfil America's ambitions. German economic recovery was indispensable, but 'the goal of ERP is fundamentally political and France is the keystone of continental Western Europe'.[58] This conviction was finally established by Britain's actions in the 1949 sterling crisis.

On 21 October the more important American ambassadors in Western Europe, together with Harriman, McCloy and Admiral Alan G. Kirk, from Moscow, were brought for two days to Paris to discuss the whole range of American policies in Europe. Acheson provided them with an analysis of his own thinking. He asked them to recognize the limits on British actions and on American power and to accept that 'the key to progress towards integration is in French hands'.[59] But what could France specifically be expected to do? The answer came in the conclusion of his letter.

> By progress towards integration, as mentioned above, I have in mind the earliest possible decision by the Europeans as to objectives and commitments among them on a timetable for the creation of supra-national institutions, operating on a less than unanimity basis for dealing with specific, economic, social and perhaps other problems.[60]

The ambassadors thought this unrealistic.[61] Three days after they had told Acheson so he received Bevin's statement of the limits of Britain's commitment to Europe, that Britain could not 'accept obligations to western Europe which would prevent or restrict the implementation of our responsibilities elsewhere'.[62] Five days later Acheson decided, in spite of the ambassadors' pessimism, to reject their advice and make a personal appeal to Schuman to take an initiative along the lines he had suggested to the ambassadors' meeting and thus reconcile West Germany to Western Europe.

> I believe we would be wise to give an 'advance' of good will to the Germans in view of the strength of the safeguards which we have erected and our ability to call upon the powers we have reserved. Although we have these powers we cannot reasonably hope to recreate a German will to co-operate if we once permit it to die for lack of nourishment.

[57] D. Hüwel, *Karl Arnold. Eine politische Biographie* (Wuppertal, 1980), pp. 179–80.
[58] ECA, RG286, 53A 405, 1, State Department briefing papers, 'France', 31 December 1948.
[59] FRUS, 1949, IV, p. 470, Acheson to Paris, 19 October 1949.   [60] ibid., p. 472.
[61] ibid., p. 342, Bruce to Acheson, 22 October 1949.
[62] ibid., p. 347, Personal message to the Secretary of State from Bevin, 25 October 1949.

392   *The Reconstruction of Western Europe 1945–51*

I believe that our policy in Germany, and the development of a German Government which can take its place in Western Europe, depends on the assumption by your country of leadership in Europe on these problems.[63]

If France were now to come forward with a specific plan coupling a solution of the Franco-German problem to the idea of European integration, that plan could fly in the face of all the former, grander, more liberal American ideas of economic integration. In the interests of American foreign policy the State Department would now support it. When Acheson next left for Paris in May 1950 Congress still refused to delete from the appropriations bill the statement that the object of Marshall Aid was the economic unification and federation of Europe. For France, it was now or never. Before the Federal Republic burst its economic shackles asunder it might be brought, in return for entry into the western European community on more equal terms, into the sort of regulated market sharing agreement on which the United States government had so far looked with abhorrence as a basis for the economic reconstruction of Europe. In Washington, too, the way was suddenly open for the Schuman Plan.

But once we pass to the question, why did the Schuman proposals take the precise form they did, it becomes obvious that this analysis confined to the international level is insufficient. The nature of the proposals was also determined in Paris by purely domestic considerations, both political and economic.

Very little is said anywhere in this book about the various European political movements advocating some form of European political integration, because they exercised so little influence on policy decisions and on events. But as a political constituency they were there, particularly in France, Italy and West Germany, and to their ideals could be attached powerful, if transient, political emotions. The strength of these emotions brought these disparate groups from many countries together in 1947 in the European Union of Federalists, and from the conjoint pressures of this and associated groups there met in 1948 The Hague Congress of the European Movement where so many resounding speeches proclaiming the ideal of European unity were made by politicians of no little prominence.

When Count Richard Coudenhove-Kalergi polled European parliamentarians, albeit in an unsystematic way, to discover whether they approved in principle of European federation, 57 per cent of the Italian deputies and 44 per cent of the French replied in the affirmative before Marshall's speech.[64] It was evident in 1949 that a settlement between France and Germany might be more pragmatic if it could obtain the support of all those diverse groups who pinned

[63] FRUS, 1949, III, pp. 624–5, Personal message from Acheson to Schuman, 30 October 1949. Melandri, in his otherwise thorough account of American attitudes and policy towards European integration, seems not to have noticed that Acheson rejected the advice of the ambassadors' meeting. He emphasizes rather the ambassadors' own conclusions.
[64] W. Lipgens, *A History of European Integration 1945–1947*: vol. 1, *The Formation of the European Unity Movement* (Oxford, 1982), pp. 437 ff.

their hopes on some form of supra-national European organization. It would probably be a great mistake to underestimate the changeability and fluidity of political opinion in occupied Germany, but public opinion surveys there showed a high and consistent level of support for the idea of a western European union.[65] It was seen chiefly as a barrier to any further war and to the spread of communism, and a smaller proportion of respondents saw it as a barrier to undue American influence over western Europe. But the rapidity with which the idea developed in 1949 and 1950 probably drew on deeper wells of emotion. Sacrifice of national interest in a united Europe offered redemption from the awful sins of the past. A month after the Schuman Plan was proposed, before any of the details were negotiated, it met with a greater degree of approval in Germany than at any time in the subsequent six years.[66]

This strand of political opinion in both countries was brought into greater prominence by the formation of the Council of Europe. The Hague Congress had made the creation of a European council, a prototype European parliament, its main demand and had instituted a working party to devise a scheme under the former French Prime Minister, Paul Ramadier. The French government had then taken up the idea at the Consultative Council of the Brussels Pact countries, seeing it as yet another possible route to supporting a reconstruction which provided security against Germany. The British government had reluctantly accepted, determined that the Council of Europe should remain entirely powerless. The negotiations over its constitution between July 1948 and January 1949 had thus been disputatious. The French government wanted the Council of Europe to exercise certain parliamentary functions in order to make it a credible political framework into which West Germany could be inserted – and held. France wanted more members in the Council, wanted them to be elected or chosen in some way other than by government nomination, and wanted them to vote freely.[67] The British government, on the contrary, was determined to avoid any suggestion of a popular European assembly.[68] Had it not been for a threat by France to take the initiative and create such an organization unilaterally the Council of Europe might never have come into being. The long wrangle did however serve to keep the idea of a 'European' solution before parliamentary and public opinion and the outcome was yet another loose association between Western European countries, one more buffer poised for the shock of the encounter with the politics of the Federal Republic.

When the Assembly of the Council of Europe met it was, not surprisingly,

[65] A.J. Merritt and R.L. Merritt, *Public Opinion in Occupied Germany. The OMGUS Surveys, 1945–1949* (Urbana, 1970), pp. 217, 296–7.

[66] K.W. Deutsch and L.J. Edinger, *Germany Rejoins the Powers. Mass Opinion, Interest Groups, and Elites in Contemporary German Foreign Policy* (Stanford, 1959), p. 157.

[67] FO 371/79214, Paris embassy to London, 21 January 1949.

[68] 'We must avoid creating a kind of chamber of echoes where cranks could make their voices heard,' Ernest Bevin in ibid. Events have shown this to have been an impossible ambition.

inundated with a variety of motions calling for European integration. One proposal was that it should set up a powerful economic department, formed out of sections transferred from the OEEC and the UN Economic Commission for Europe, which would draw up proposals for the progressive integration of the economies of the member states. This was supported by both Guy Mollet and André Philip for the Section Française de l'Internationale Ouvrière (SFIO) and by Schuman and Bidault for the Mouvement Populaire Républicain (MRP) as well as by a bizarre collection of other people including the first post-war Prime Minister of Italy, Ferruccio Parri, a future Prime Minister of Britain, Harold Macmillan, and a future President of Sénégal, Léopold Senghor. The British government's view was that they 'would be opposed even to the study in Strasbourg of the many subjects covered by the Resolution'.[69] None the less, the debates on the succession of motions with similar implications, even if no commitment was involved, demonstrated the growing variety of groups to whom an economic solution of the problem of a Franco-German settlement which embodied a supra-national approach to European integration would appeal.

The interest in such a policy was emphasized by the re-emergence in 1949 of a school of opinion among both French and German steel-makers which repeated one idea of the Seydoux proposals for a Franco-German settlement in 1920, that there should be French investment in the reconstruction of the German steel industry.[70] The chairman of the board of trustees appointed under Law No. 75 to supervise the decartelization of the German industry and its transfer back to private ownership, Heinrich Dinkelbach, publicly espoused such a solution. So did Robert Lehr who was widely regarded as the spokesman in the CDU for the Iron and Steel Association and who, before the conclusion of the European Coal and Steel Community treaty, became a minister in the German government.

In February and in April 1949 the two congresses of the European Movement in Brussels and Westminster singled out the coal and steel industries as one area in which a common European organization could be created. But about what type of organization it would be they were not so clear. The impression given by the debates is that it would have been mainly controlled and managed by the firms themselves although there would have been an 'intergovernmental board' and, to retain the support of French socialists like André Philip who backed it enthusiastically at both conferences, trade union representation on the management committee.[71] Philip became chairman of the Basic Industries Sub-Committee of the Economic Committee of the Council of Europe and from this position he persuaded the Economic Committee of the Council to

---

[69] FO 371/78101, London to UK delegation in Strasbourg, 29 August 1949.

[70] The Seydoux proposals are analysed in M. Trachtenberg, *Reparation in World Politics. France and European Economic Diplomacy, 1916–1923* (New York, 1980), pp. 174 ff.

[71] FO 371/76694, Memorandum of conversation between Sir Harold Butler and Roger Stevens, 18 February 1949.

pass a resolution in December 1949 calling for a public authority for the European steel industry, to advise on investment, prices and production as the first step towards similar sectoral planning in coal, oil, electricity and transport.

Lastly, the argument in France over the status of the Modernization Plan and the Planning Commissariat has to be considered to understand both why the proposals took the form they did and why they were formulated in the way they were. Throughout 1949 the position of the Planning Commissariat had looked increasingly frail. The successful recovery of output in 1947 and 1948 followed by the faltering in 1949 had first soothed the anxieties about French recovery which had given the Planning Commissariat its initial opportunity and then raised doubts about whether the Modernization Plan could either achieve its economic targets or was necessary any longer as a basis for national reconstruction. In November 1949 the cabinet refused to give responsibility for the investment of public funds to the Planning Commissariat and prominent associations of employers launched a public campaign to abandon the principles and methods of the Modernization Plan on the grounds that a 'normal' situation had now been reached and persistence with the planning targets could only encourage over-investment.[72]

In the event the planners won the day and one reason for their victory was that the French cabinet could not face a future in which it was tied within Finebel to a much more liberal trade and payments relationship with West Germany. The opportunity had to be taken to reinstate the Monnet Plan as a guideline for foreign policy if it was to be safe as a guideline for domestic policy. The Schuman Plan was invented to safeguard the Monnet Plan.

The implication of the descriptions of the way the Schuman proposals were formulated is that the new policy was created in a daring and highly original way inside the Planning Commissariat and outside the normal channels of foreign policy formulation in the Ministry of Foreign Affairs. This is the view which Monnet and his colleagues and disciples have assiduously propagated.[73] A small cabal led by Monnet himself, it is suggested, acting in speed and secrecy, prepared the proposals, which were ignored by Bidault but then eagerly taken up by Schuman who was looking for a new policy. For fear that so revolutionary a departure in policy and in policy-making be stopped at the outset by vested interests Schuman, it has been implied, deliberately kept it secret from all but his most important cabinet colleagues, rushed it through cabinet with the Prime Minister's help, and announced it the same day. The new policy thus appears as the work of an enlightened cabal who by acting boldly and secretly changed the continent's history. This view, which owes much to Gerbet, has been accepted lock, stock and barrel by subsequent writers.[74]

[72] R.F. Kuisel, *Capitalism and the State in Modern France* (Cambridge, 1940), pp. 241 ff.
[73] Monnet, *Memoirs*, pp. 288 ff.
[74] P. Gerbet, 'La Genèse du Plan Schuman des origines à la déclaration du 9 mai 1950', *Revue française de science politique*, vi, 1956; Willis, *France*, pp. 83 ff.; R. Mayne, *The Community of Europe. Past, Present and Future* (New York, 1962), pp. 90 ff; W. Loth, *Die Teilung der Welt 1941–1955* (Munich, 1980), p. 249.

A certain saintliness has been conferred on all those who touched the Schuman proposals from Monnet and Schuman down to the professor of law who drafted a version of them, Schuman's *directeur de cabinet*, and Adenauer's chief of staff. Even now they do not lack their hagiographers, often from the ranks of those on whom the light shone. But from where else but the Planning Commissariat was policy likely to emerge? That the text was prepared in consultation with Monnet and other high officials of the Planning Commissariat was not at all exceptional. From Monnet's first proposals for an economic plan the Ministry of Foreign Affairs had sought to use the Plan as a justification of French policy in Europe to their allies. The common interest of the Ministry of Foreign Affairs and the Planning Commissariat had not weakened and, if there was no possibility of further advance to a settlement through the Ruhr Authority, it was up to the planners to think of something else.

How far the text of Monnet's first proposals was amended in the Ministry of Foreign Affairs is difficult to establish until all the relevant archives are made available. The versions of parts of the statement and the account of its preparation given by Monnet suggest there was considerable alteration. There were also alternative proposals which had to be rebuffed, such as the idea that at first only the Ruhr and Saar should be placed under a common regime.[75] That the substance of the proposals came from Monnet and the Planning Commissariat need not be doubted and the timing of their submission reflects Monnet's shrewd sense of the stage at which French policy had arrived. Alphand and indeed the Foreign Ministry as a whole had been in search of some such policy since June 1948. Civil servants have not been able to organize the same level of publicity for their actions since, and they were not so free to claim public credit at the time, but it would not be unfair on the evidence to say that some of them, who are never numbered in the gallery of European saints, had as much claim to the new policy as Monnet and his circle. The first origins of the Schuman Plan were really in the Ministry of Foreign Affairs during the London conference.

But the ultimate credit for the Schuman plan must go to Schuman himself. He had the courage to act quickly. Britain had not even been consulted and the proposals were made in the full knowledge that they might mean the end of the Franco-British co-operation in western Europe on which French policy towards Germany had been based since the end of the war. Such an outcome was not certain and was definitely not desired, but the risk was large. In taking it Schuman had the courage to seize the moment and translate into reality a complexity of vague interrelationships, suggestions and ideas which the fearfulness of others had left trembling on the brink of actuality.

[75] FJM, AMG 1/2 bis/1, Contre proposition pour une autre procédure, 6 May 1950.

THE SCHUMAN PLAN AND ITS RECEPTION

On 8 May Acheson arrived in Paris on his way to the foreign ministers' meeting in London. Schuman mentioned to him 'quite casually' and in general terms that he might, if he could, persuade the cabinet at its meeting the following morning to make a foreign policy initiative of some importance towards Germany.[76] That evening Monnet explained the full importance of what was happening to McCloy who had also come to Paris and McCloy told Acheson who, however, was obliged to keep the matter secret. The following day the proposals were approved by the cabinet and at six o'clock Schuman gave a press conference at which he read out his proposal, 'that the entire French-German production of coal and steel be placed under a joint High Authority, within an organization open to the participation of other European nations.' This would provide some real immediate function for a supra-national political body.

> By pooling basic production and by creating a new High Authority whose decisions will be binding on France, Germany and the other countries who may subsequently join, this proposal will create the first concrete foundation for a European federation which is so indispensable for the preservation of peace.[77]

The functions of that High Authority were then specified; to modernize production, to supply coal and steel on equal terms within a common market, to develop joint exports, and to equalize working and living conditions. This meant an investment plan, price equalization, a reconversion fund to permit closures in the cause of rationalization, and the standardization of freight rates. The setting up of the High Authority would not prejudge the question of ownership, but the Authority would take into account all the powers conferred on the International Authority for the Ruhr.

Although Schuman's statement was received at the time without many signs that it was an event of special importance, within a very short space it came to be thought of as a watershed in the post-war world, a moment when things going badly were reversed, a new vision of hope for post-war Europe, and it has been generally so considered since. Much of the emotion which was so quickly attached to it was attracted because it seemed to offer some prospect of European unity and peace at the very moment when those ideals seemed no longer to have any political force. After the disillusionment of the return of familiar national governmental figures and systems, after the worse disillusionments of 1947 with the division of Europe and the Cold War, after the failure once more to produce any real promise of a settlement acceptable to Germany, after the failure of pressure groups for European unity, Schuman

---

[76] FRUS, 1950, III, Acheson to Washington, 10 May 1950.
[77] There is a full text of the proposal in *Le Monde*, 11 May 1950.

398   *The Reconstruction of Western Europe 1945–51*

specifically linked the settlement with Germany to the hope of a united
Europe. In so doing he tapped a vein of hope and idealism which had been
buried even more deeply under the common earth of post-war history and
associated a diplomatic initiative with a cause. Thus 9 May 1950 and the
Schuman proposals soon came to be seen as the starting-point of a united
Europe. Especially was this so in the 1950s and 1960s, when large numbers
still believed the process of European integration to be progressive and
irreversible and the Schuman proposals to have been the first date of a new
historical epoch.

The immediate danger, however, was that the proposals would appear in
America as the first step in an attempt to revive protectionist cartels as a
framework for European industry. Thus into the proposal was inserted the
statement:

> Unlike an international cartel whose purpose is to divide up and exploit
> national markets through restrictive practices, and the maintenance of high
> profits, the projected organization will insure the fusion of markets and the
> expansion of production.[78]

This, nevertheless, was the aspect of the proposals which Acheson was least
convinced about when he was told about them and it remained the one major
worry which they presented to Washington. Well aware that this would be
the case, Monnet's group had presented a memorandum to McCloy on the eve
of the announcement setting out the reasons why the proposals would result
in an arrangement entirely different from the pre-war cartel.[79] McCloy, as
American High Commissioner in Germany, was a key figure because without
the permission of the members of the Allied High Commission West Germany
would not even be able to embark on the negotiations. The memorandum
stressed that what was at stake for France was a policy which would permit the
continuing increase of output and productivity by enlargement of markets
and rationalization of production. This was certainly the point at which
French and American conceptions of the economic future coincided. As the
Cold War became more frightening, as the rate of increase of output in the
French economy slowed down, and as more conservative voices were heard in
France, it became a matter of great concern to the Planning Commissariat that
the momentum gained in the first three and a half years not be lost through a
relapse into the defensive attitudes of the 1930s especially in the face of the
rapid German revival. If the means by which it sought to achieve this aim were
not so unremittingly liberal as the ideology which served America's ends, the
coincidence was sufficient to make it plausible that the Schuman Plan might

[78] FRUS, 1950, III, p. 694.
[79] CAB 134/295, Plowden to Makins, 10 May 1950. Almost certainly the same document
passed on to Acheson and translated in FRUS, 1950, III, Acheson to Washington, 12 May 1950,
p. 697.

eventually be firmly directed against restrictions on output. The existence of the High Authority would mean that all decisions taken would be open and public and those decisions would not be taken purely by representatives of the industries concerned. Later, France and America were to make joint representations to Adenauer not to appoint representatives of the steel industry to take an official part in the negotiations. In so far as price fixing and market sharing agreements would continue they would be only transitional.

Neither Acheson nor the State Department were ever entirely convinced by this view of the matter in spite of Dulles's enthusiastic recommendations. Dulles, it seems, had discussed similar ideas with Marshall at the Moscow Council of Foreign Ministers.[80] The State Department had three 'major difficulties' with the proposals – that they would result in a protectionist cartel, that Germany's association with it would slow down the pace of technological advance there, and that ultimately political considerations would override economic rationality.[81] From the documentary evidence at the moment available it seems these hesitations, which did not prevent the State Department from welcoming the proposals, were overcome by a change of heart and an almost wholly favourable verdict on the part of Harriman and the ECA. The proposals were now judged by the ECA to be an 'important step' towards trade liberalization and the concept of a single competitive market.[82] They implied the removal of tariffs, which of course was one of the ECA's main concerns, and the same ultimate goal of higher productivity which the ECA wished to achieve. The danger of a protectionist cartel was not absent, the ECA considered, but without the proposals it was surely greater.[83]

The American attitude was thus resolved, although a careful eye was kept on the course of the negotiations themselves. As they proceeded American anxieties began to develop again. The weakening of the powers of the High Authority in favour of those of the Council of Ministers which was added to it, the complicated price fixing for coal, the retention of coal distribution organizations, and above all the artificial coal prices fixed to allow subsidies to be paid to the Belgian mining industry, all confirmed some of the earlier fears.[84] But by this time the situation had radically changed. The Korean war and the rumour of West German rearmament had raised the possibility that the Federal Republic might not now have to accept the Schuman proposals as a way of getting rid of the limitations on its sovereignty. Whether the United States should back the French proposals for a European defence community became the determining question and when Washington decided to give full support to the concept of a European army it not only could no longer

[80] FRUS, 1950, III, Webb to Acheson, 10 May 1950, p. 695.
[81] ibid., Webb to Acheson, 11 May 1950, p. 696.
[82] ibid., Harriman to Acheson, 20 May 1950, p. 702.
[83] ECA, 33, Simons to Jeffers, 26 July 1950.
[84] FRUS, 1950, III, Byroade to Perkins, 9 September 1950, p. 747; Webb to Paris, 3 October 1950, p. 754.

400   *The Reconstruction of Western Europe 1945–51*

withdraw support from the Schuman Plan on economic grounds, but it had to back it and even cajole Germany to join it if the chance of West German rearmament was not to be irretrievably lost. All the United States could do after the outbreak of the Korean war was to try to salvage from the Schuman proposals whatever it could of the original American conception of a free-trade union in Europe. There was not much that could be saved and acceptance of the Schuman Plan meant a reversal of thirty years of American foreign policy.

In the 1920s the United States, like Britain, had had a vague vision of European unity as emerging, if it ever did, as the outcome of a network of most-favoured-nation clauses – just as the optimistic liberals of the 1860s had hoped – because this seemed the only way that European unity could be a stage towards world unity. This was the basis of American objections to proposals such as the Briand Plan or the Tardieu Plan, which in their attempts to create a European economic framework to contain Germany had foreshadowed the Schuman Plan. All this was now thrown over. In the face of such momentous issues the querulous voice of the American steel industry complaining that it would now be faced with a government-backed European steel cartel from which it would be excluded went unheeded. Thirty years later, at the moment of writing, its complaints are much louder, largely justified, and very much heeded.

When, in answering the few questions at the press conference where he made his proposals, Schuman agreed that they were 'a leap in the dark', the deepest obscurity was that which lay on the other side of the Channel. If the American government could be convinced that the proposals could be presented as in accordance with America's own interest in integration, if the German government could be convinced that the proposals were an offer to treat on almost equal terms, the voices in both countries which had been clamouring for some similar solution would be raised in enthusiastic support. But nothing could disguise the fact that France had this time taken a bold step towards creating her own Western Europe without regard to Britain and in the full knowledge that official British policy was opposed to such ideas. Acheson tells us that when Bevin was informed he flew into 'a towering rage'.[85]

Independently though the French had acted, however, they spared no effort of diplomacy and persuasion to bring the United Kingdom into the proposed European framework. Schuman travelled to London immediately after the announcement and on 14 May Monnet with other members of the Planning Commissariat arrived to explain and persuade. The task of finding out exactly what the implications were for Britain was delegated to Plowden, so that the meeting appeared in a rather ironical light as a continuation of the Monnet-Plowden talks of the previous year. Plowden was told to discover whether Britain would be able to go into the proposed talks 'without

[85] D. Acheson, *Sketches from Life of Men I Have Known* (New York, 1961), p. 39.

commitment'.[86] Monnet's own version of his approach to these talks, a version which seems to be borne out by the record, is that the one point on which he would make no concession was that all parties to the talks must accept beforehand the principle of the existence of a High Authority whose decisions would be binding. The political principles involved in the proposals were sacrosanct; the technical details were all negotiable, for the simple reason that none of them had yet been decided. As Monnet explained at the beginning of the talks France intended to reach an agreement with Germany anyway whatever the British reaction, so that great flexibility in the economic details was essential.

The talks with Plowden showed that the enthusiastic ideas of the Planning Commissariat were considerably removed from future political realities as they were to emerge from the negotiations. Monnet thought the appointment of a United Nations observer would be essential.[87] Hirsch, who was to be his successor as head of the Planning Commissariat, said that it would be a matter of indifference whether steel production were located in Germany or France since national frontiers would be wiped out. Members of the High Authority, he said, would be appointed for their technical expertise and nationality would be irrelevant. They could be British, or Swiss, or even American.[88] That last possibility, no doubt, was some way from the mind of Schuman and Adenauer.

Plowden's advice, based on these rather vague conversations, was that participation was likely to be economically advantageous to Britain and that Britain should therefore try to take part in the discussions. The Foreign Office did not, however, want Britain to do so 'unreservedly'.[89] Meanwhile the views were sought of the National Coal Board and of the British Iron and Steel Federation, the owners' association of the steel industry. At his final press conference before he left Britain Schuman seemed to leave open the possibility that Britain might indeed be able to be associated with the proposals without an entire acceptance of their political implications. This was the policy endorsed by the Economic Policy Committee of the cabinet on 23 May[90] and expressed in the official British notes of 25 and 27 May.[91] The French ambassador, René Massigli, in a conversation with Kenneth Younger, the Minister of State at the Foreign Office, on 28 May, did not rule out this possibility, but when the official French reply came back on 30 May it left no room for manoeuvre; the political negotiations must be begun by all on the basis that there would be a High Authority and a transfer of sovereignty.

[86] CAB 134/293, Meeting of Committee on Proposed Franco-German Coal and Steel Authority, 15 May 1950.   [87] CAB 134/295, Minutes of a meeting at the Hyde Park Hotel, 16 May 1950.
[88] CAB 134/295, Minute by Berthoud of conversation with Hirsch, 19 May 1950.
[89] CAB 134/293, Report by Plowden to Committee on Franco-German Coal and Steel Authority, 17 May 1950.   [90] CAB 134/293, Economic Policy Committee, 23 May 1950.
[91] Cmd. 7970, *Anglo-French Discussions Regarding French Proposals for the Western European Coal, Iron and Steel Industries*, May–June 1950.

402   *The Reconstruction of Western Europe 1945–51*

The outcome of the consultations with the relevant industrial bodies, with other industries, and with the leaders of the trade unions concerned justified the French stance, which seems to have stiffened after Schuman's return to Paris. The British Iron and Steel Federation was all in favour of an agreement to limit competition and feared exclusion from any such agreement, especially in so far as it might endanger ore supplies from Sweden and North Africa. On the other hand it would have wished any such agreement to preserve the home market and allow imports on equal terms only when there was 'excess' demand in the domestic market, like the pre-war International Steel Cartel. This seems to have been very much the view taken by its European associates also. All would have preferred to see a return of the Cartel, secure home markets, and no increase in governmental supervision. The steel manufacturer Hermann Reusch later resigned his post as economic adviser to the German government during the negotiations, publicly demanding a return to the pre-war Cartel as official policy. The dangers of competition on the domestic market and of ultimate government or international control over the industry were the chief subjects of attack in the national campaign launched against the proposals by the French owners' association.[92]

Although the British Iron and Steel Federation did not foresee a future without any agreement with its European rivals, exclusion from the proposed arrangements was scarcely a dangerous threat to sales. Western Europe accounted for less than 5 per cent of British steel exports (table 56). If the

Table 56   Proportion of total steel exports to future members of the ECSC (%)

	1938	1946	1947	1948	1949	1950	1951	1952
Belgium/ Luxembourg	27.0	22.2	19.3	19.4	18.9	26.3	20.7	27.9
France	15.2	–	–	23.4	11.3	17.3	12.1	18.3
West Germany	17.5	–	–	91.0*	22.2†	15.7	13.9	15.0
United Kingdom	3.8	n.a.	4.8	0.6	6.1	4.4	4.9	6.8

Source: British Iron and Steel Federation, *Statistical Yearbooks*.

* Includes Austria.   † Bizone.

political implications of the proposals did have to be accepted in full the Federation would on balance have preferred to stay out, in spite of the strong British competitive position, because it regarded the defence of a large acquired position outside Europe as more important than the possible opportunity of expanding a small position inside Europe.

Prices were lower and it was believed that productivity was higher in the British steel industry than in any of its continental competitors in 1950

[92] The campaign is analysed in H.W. Ehrmann, 'The French trade associations and the ratification of the Schuman Plan', *World Politics*, 6 (4), 1954.

(table 57) and it was at least as well equipped to withstand the revival of the German steel industry as was the French.[93] If wage levels were to be equalized

Table 57 An index of comparative domestic prices of steel (January 1950)

	Britain	France	West Germany	Belgium	Luxem- bourg	Italy	Nether- lands
Angles	100	127	109	121	129	200	145
Joists	100	107	100	–	123	–	–
Plates	100	134	104	119	125	222	145
Hot rolled strip	100	112	103	–	117	–	130
Rails	100	126	112	133	140	–	–
Sheets	100	124	115	–	–	–	–
Merchant bars	100	111	91	101	109	176	127

Source: CAB 134/295, Report of Working Party, 'Schuman proposals for an international coal and steel authority in western Europe', 16 June 1950. The prices are those supplied by the British Iron and Steel Federation.

it would be even better equipped, because this would mean a relative increase in production costs outside Britain. Britain had as much to gain, economically, in participating in any agreement as the other countries. When Schuman made his proposals steel markets were slack, which was some justification for the British manufacturers' response, although in the end the question resolved itself into one of Britain's willingness to compete in the future on relatively equal terms in its own as well as in export markets with the German steel industry.

Here we are touching on the unwritten and seldom spoken fears in Britain. The experience of the Labour government had been to start in a situation where only a seemingly impossible increase in exports could permit them to carry through their chosen domestic policy. That increase had been all but achieved, but only in a world market from which two of the most important competitors had been temporarily removed. The same anxieties for the future as governed the policy on international payments governed the attitude to the return of Germany to international markets. The natural reaction of the industry was to hold on to what it had and in a wider context the government's reaction was the same.

The National Coal Board's attitude was less ambiguous. For the coal industry anything resembling the Schuman proposals was a quite unwanted departure. Orders to reallocate output or to close pits emanating from a High Authority, as well as the apparent intention to give that Authority power over investment policy, were unacceptable because 'the NCB is sure of getting a fair hearing from His Majesty's Government.'[94] The shortsightedness of this

[93] CAB 134/294, Views of the British Iron and Steel Federation, June 1950.
[94] CAB 134/294, Views of the National Coal Board, 2 June 1950.

404   *The Reconstruction of Western Europe 1945–51*

view may be compared with that of the General Secretary of the Iron and Steel Trades Confederation, who argued that British steel workers would not wish in future to lose the wage benefits accruing from the generally higher level of productivity in the British steel industry than in the French and German industries.[95]

These unfavourable opinions were put forward as the close wrangle over whether Britain could alter the terms of participation came to a head. The French government obtained the initial acceptance of the terms of the negotiation from Germany, Italy, Belgium, Luxembourg and the Netherlands, although the Netherlands reserved the right to leave the negotiations at any time. This agreement was in the form of a draft communiqué and on 31 May the British government offered to put its name to the same communiqué providing there was still no firm commitment to the High Authority but instead a commitment to negotiate 'in a constructive spirit'.[96] It seems that at that stage Schuman still sought a compromise to allow Britain to join the talks. The Planning Commissariat made sure that in trying to amend the communiqué the French government did not alter the text in such a way as to abandon its original position, otherwise there would have been 'only some kind of OEEC'.[97] Thus, when it arrived in Britain the amended text made none of the hoped-for concessions and was accompanied by an ultimatum requiring a definite answer by 8 p.m. on 2 June. The British government made one last effort by proposing a meeting of the ministers of all the countries concerned to devise a different way of going about the negotiations, but this was certain to be declined.

The cabinet met on 2 June and there seems to have been a general, resentful agreement to give a negative answer. 'No British government could be expected to accept such a commitment without having had any opportunity to assess the consequences which it might involve for our key industries, our export trade and our level of employment.'[98] There was some foolish discussion about whether the Allied High Commission might not be used to stop the West German government taking part in the negotiations, followed by the conclusion that 'it should be made clear to the French government that we were surprised to receive such summary treatment in a matter of this importance.'[99] Britain had in fact already used its voice in the Council of the Allied High Commission to suggest that West Germany, since it was in economic and political tutelage, ought not to be freely allowed to negotiate and that an observer from the High Commission should be appointed.[100] But that suggestion had been firmly put down by McCloy and François-Poncet.

[95] ibid., Views of Lincoln Evans, 3 June 1950.   [96] Cmd. 7970.
[97] FJM, AMG 24/1/24, 'Note confidentiel pour le Gouvernement' by Pierre Uri, 1 June 1950.
[98] CAB 128/17, Cabinet conclusions, 2 June 1950.   [99] ibid.
[100] FRUS, 1950, III, McCloy to Acheson, 23 May 1950, p. 705. In Monnet's version the objections were made by Robertson, but in fact they were voiced by Sir G.N. Macready, his economic adviser, who stood in for him at the meeting.

There was no possibility of blocking the route in that way, although the High Commission did assert its right to be fully informed of the progress of the talks. As a last, ill-considered gesture the Foreign Office published its final secret compromise proposal for a ministerial meeting, even though that proposal had already been firmly declined in Paris. The idea, presumably, was to wean the other participants towards the British way of doing things.

There can be no doubt at all, reviewing the historical record, that the final French ultimatum was fully justified. There is ample evidence that the British government had no intention of accepting the High Authority or any surrender of sovereignty and that had Britain been allowed to join the negotiations they would have been of such a fundamentally different kind as to nullify completely the French initiative. There was a general acknowledgement in the British government that an international agreement on the organization of the Western European coal and steel industries was desirable. But it was felt that this should be essentially devised by the firms themselves, subject only to a loose supervision by consultative bodies of responsible ministers. This was the system that had applied in Britain since 1931 and the British government seems to have thought it more effective as a method of control than what was happening in France.[101] It is some indication of the lukewarm attitude of the government towards its own policy of nationalizing the steel industry that it was so concerned to preserve the powers of the entrepreneurs to make decisions. Industry and government together conspired to avoid a situation in which mandatory powers conferred on a special Authority and the surrender of national sovereignty which that involved might mean the disappearance of discriminatory practices and non-tariff barriers whose function was to preserve the home market and full employment.[102]

There is no need to do anything but briefly summarize the subsequent actions of the British government. The die was cast and London played a faintly absurd part in the following events. Either an assumption or a vain hope prevailed that the negotiations would fail. Such at least was the gist of the spiteful message put out by the British embassy in Paris. The cabinet set up a working party to devise an alternative scheme with less drastic implications, which would be submitted on the failure of the Schuman Plan negotiations. Whereas the essence of the negotiations was to start by taking away all barriers to equal competition and then gradually to replace some of them or devise

[101] 'It is very difficult to mix countries which for national reasons must exercise a large degree of state control over their economy with countries which for various reasons cannot do so even if they want to. ... France after the war, even under a socialist government, found she was incapable of doing so because the country did not have the necessary level of civic responsibility' (Mr Denis Healey in H.F. Havilland Jnr (ed.) *The United States and the Western Community* (Haverford Pa., 1957), pp. 41–2, exactly reflecting the views of the Foreign Office.) Five years later there would begin a spate of enquiries about why France was able to control its economy so much more effectively than the United Kingdom.

[102] See the discussion in CAB 134/293, First Report of Working Party on Schuman's Proposals, 19 June 1950.

new ones as the negotiations proceeded, the essence of the British alternative proposals was to take the barriers away by a series of gradual and carefully judged separate acts.[103] When the negotiations ended by producing a document which stressed exactly those aspects of the Schuman Plan which the British government could not accept, the working party's alternative proposals were shelved. The addition of the Common Assembly to the Plan did not meet the British wish that governments should control the High Authority, and the powers given to the Court of Justice were extra cause for objection. The single market would still be created too rapidly.[104] That the other parties to the negotiations had had the strongest objections to particular aspects of the proposals, many of which were noted with pleasure throughout July and August as the various leaks of information found their way to Whitehall, had not triumphed over their common interest and their need to belong to any joint regulation of the market by France and Germany.

   History cannot entirely avoid the bias of the moment at which it is written and it is impossible to avoid asking the question whether this was not a critical turning-point in Britain's post-war history. The answer, however, must be that the question is itself too simplified and too dramatic. Whether it was a turning-point economically would only be determined by the future economic relationships with the new economic bloc which was to be created. The events of 1950 and the signing of the Treaty of the European Coal and Steel Community on 18 April 1951 made no difference whatsoever at the time to the British economy and even the opening of the common market for certain of the products on 10 February 1953 made very little. No proper economic answer to the question can be given except by considering almost the whole span of time during which the framework created by the treaty has survived, and in that span of time so many other variables would come into account that the question would lose all precision and force. The decision not to join summed up past economic events and showed their influence, conscious and un-conscious, on diplomacy. The deep anxiety about Britain's international position in the 1930s, the protectionism which arose from that, the inability to find any certain way in which the high standard of living which trade and industrialization had created in Britain could be enhanced in the future, the conviction that no risks could be taken with exports, the war effort, the defeat of Germany and the influence which that had in preventing government from coming to terms with the longer view of history in which that enormous event was only a temporary aberration – all these things kept Britain out of the ECSC.

   Yet the prevailing mood while the decision was being made was more than natural anxiety. It was fear, and it is this which makes the contrast with French actions so striking and marks the event as more of a political than an

---

[103]   CAB 134/294, Report of Working Party, 30 June 1950.
[104]   ibid., 31 August 1950.

economic turning-point. In retrospect it is impossible to agree that the High Authority and the Court of Justice were at all as dangerous to the British economy, to full employment, to the principles of British political life, and to British foreign policy and defence as was suggested. They were in fact, for all the fine language about European unity in which they were wrapped, of limited scope and only narrowly specific application. They were certainly less dangerous to the economic and political future of the United Kingdom than the wild ideas of economic association or even union with the United States that were current in some circles in 1950. That the British reaction should have been both fearful and defensive may well have been of much more significance for the country's future than the decision not to join.

THE EUROPEAN COAL AND STEEL COMMUNITY

The political motivation for the ECSC remained paramount throughout the negotiations and because of that the economic implications had to be accepted in Germany. On the day the Bundestag ratified the treaty Monnet telegraphed to Adenauer, 'Europe is born, long live Europe.' 'Big Europe', the far-flung, liberal customs union with a low external tariff still waits to be born. In its stead came 'Little Europe' based on an incomplete, carefully regulated, sectoral integration, which, in the event, has not proved capable of extension to other countries without such serious modification as to call its meaning and its survival into question. Little Europe did involve a surrender to a supra-national body of certain formerly jealously guarded activities of the nation state and so was greeted with rapturous enthusiasm by many advocates of the greater union. Yet, seen from the admittedly short perspective of thirty years, its most lasting attribute, one which shows no substantial signs of weakening, has been its solution to a past problem and not its importance for the future. The Franco-German alliance has been the heart of all subsequent developments in the European Community and has taken on as permanent an air as the hostility which preceded it.

By contrast the tree of European integration, apparently planted by the conclusion of the treaty in April 1951, has shown almost every kind of mutation. Some of its branches grew rapidly at first in the same pattern until the sectoral integration of agriculture laid the basis for a common market covering a wider range of products. But their fruits were already different inasmuch as there was less talk about, and much less action to create, demo-cratically representative control of the executive machinery which itself was finally of a different kind. After that growth was stunted by the icy blasts of the 'Europe of the nations'. Recovering from that long winter the tree is proliferating in so diverse a way in the new climate, which is becoming more Mediterranean, as to become a quite different plant, a sort of dense, impe-netrable, rambling undergrowth clinging to the nations and holding them at

408   *The Reconstruction of Western Europe 1945–51*

times so firmly in place as to prevent all movement and at other times tempting them to hack it contemptuously to the ground.

The ECSC eventually emerged with large differences from Schuman's original proposals. Why it changed so much between conception and birth is a necessary appendage to the story. But it is impossible to tell it in any but provisional form at the moment because of the lack of documentary evidence. All that can be done is to round off the relevant aspects of the story and to hazard some suggestions as to why the changes came about.[105]

On the eve of the negotiations the proposals contemplated a wide range of drastic actions. They contemplated the removal of all customs duties within the market on the products covered, the removal of all discriminatory freight rates and export prices, the equalization of wages in the coal and steel industries, together with the appointment of the High Authority and of an 'arbiter' to ensure that its procedures in carrying out these changes were fair.

As they emerged in treaty form the proposals were for a five-year transitional period before the common market became complete. Some arrangement of this kind had always been thought of as necessary but the common market turned out to be much less perfect than foreseen. Italy was allowed to keep full tariffs for this period to protect its small, high-cost steel industry. The Belgian coal-mines received transitional subsidies from the German and Dutch mines and because the subsidies were paid out of sale prices the coal price policy took on straight away what the Belgian delegation called a 'very marked international dirigisme'.[106] The subsidies were to provide a breathing space for the modernization and rationalization of the Belgian mining industry, where productivity levels were lower than in the other countries. When they were due to end, the closure of a large number of mines in the Borinage was announced and the subsidies were hastily renewed to allow the mining of uncompetitive Belgian coal to continue. The production cost of a tonne of Belgian coal in 1950 was about a third higher than for French coal and the chances of closing such a gap over the transitional period could not have been good.[107]

Although coal prices were harmonized and dual coal pricing brought to an end, differential national and international rail freight rates remained in force. A fair transport rate for coal and coke on the German railways through the Palatinate would have made them cheaper in Lorraine than coal and coke from Nord and Pas de Calais! In May 1957 when genuinely equalized freight rates did come into force it was still only for distances of less than 400 miles. Thus the higher priced Italian producers still remained protected. As for the equalization of wages, that was a far too ambitious project once the market

[105] The best general account of the early history of the community is W. Diebold Jnr, *The Schuman Plan, A Study in Economic Cooperation 1950–1959* (New York, 1959).

[106] CAB 134/295, Note of conversations with the Belgian delegation to the Paris negotiations, 20 September 1950.

[107] FJM, AMG 22/5/4, Note relative aux effets du Plan Schuman, 8 February 1951.

included the two lower wage countries of the Netherlands and Italy. The difference made to steel prices by the incidence of turnover taxes, sales taxes and export rebates was not removed, in spite of Erhard's strenuous objections. The Tinbergen Committee appointed to report on the problem allowed France to maintain its equalizing levies on German steel imports, apparently letting its sense of what was politically feasible rule its economic heart. To insist that member countries harmonize their domestic taxation policies was to sail too close to one of the reefs on which American policy in the OEEC had stuck.

The Netherlands and Belgium objected to the great and undefined powers to be invested in the High Authority. The French conception was that the Authority should be set up first in order to create the common market and to define the economic functions and regulatory role which it would itself play. This would have left the other countries too much in the hands of a close Franco-German agreement on the powers of the Authority, so the Dutch and Belgian delegations insisted that the negotiations also define exactly what the economic purpose of the High Authority should be. This seems to have been the biggest blow to Monnet's hopes. The Benelux delegations insisted from the outset that the final treaty should lay down detailed and absolute provisions for the powers of the High Authority, and they were determined that there should be some governmental supervision over its decisions.[108] Both Dutch and Belgian delegations wanted a Council of Ministers to be able to issue directions to the High Authority. From this confrontation between France and West Germany on the one side and the smaller countries on the other the High Authority emerged in company with a Council of Ministers whose task was to review the Authority's decisions (although not to issue directives to it), with a court, with a powerless consultative committee of users, employees' representatives and so on, and with the annual Common Assembly which the French had tacked on to blunt the technocratic edge of the Authority and which was given the power to get rid of the High Authority itself by a two-thirds majority.

The specific economic issues with which French policy on the Ruhr had been concerned were also subject to compromise during the negotiations. Whether the differential export pricing of German coal had been worth the enormous effort France had devoted to the issue could perhaps be doubted. It was a function of the coal shortage and, given the importance of the French market to German producers, was not likely long to survive the moment when the supply of coal again came into equilibrium with demand, which it already showed signs of doing before the Korean war boosted demand again. It needed only a small increase of 4 marks a tonne in the price on the domestic market for the differential to be eliminated.

[108] CAB 134/295, Report of the Working Party on the Schuman Plan, 28 June 1950; ibid., Conversation between Labour attaché in Brussels and M. Vinck, 6 July 1950.

410   *The Reconstruction of Western Europe 1945–51*

One economic sacrifice which the Planning Commissariat seems to have regarded as inevitable and may, indeed, have actually welcomed, was the Plan's original ambitious target for coal output. The Plan had envisaged an annual output of 62 million tonnes of coal by 1955–6 and from the way Monnet and Hirsch presented the Schuman proposals in London they seem to have resigned themselves to reducing this target by about 10 million tonnes.[109] This would have been only a small increase, over the 1949 output. The proposals were conceived at a time when the European coal shortage seemed to be disappearing and when, as a consequence, the coal targets of the Modernization Plan, if they had ever been justifiable, no longer looked so. Output in fact fell in 1950 when it was still more than 11 million tonnes below the Plan's target, whereas the increase in output in West Germany continued unabated. Stocks of coal in France at the time of the proposals were higher than before or after.[110]

It was estimated that by 1953/4 Germany would have about 31.6 million tonnes of coal available for export. If transport rates were equalized France would nevertheless be able to export coal to areas south of Karlsruhe, which would compensate for the inevitable increase in non-coking coal imports from Germany. The agreement was eventually written in such a way that French output would never have to fall by more than one million tonnes a year in the transition period. The national distribution organization, Charbonnages de France, was allowed to maintain zonal prices. Furthermore the High Authority could, if it wished, levy a tax of up to 10 per cent of the value of net deliveries to France above the level of 1950 in order to reduce the price of French coal in the dearer zones. Since France had already decided to reduce coal output by one million tonnes the maximum possible theoretical decline in output under these arrangements, 5 million tonnes, was, even should it occur, not such a burden. It was only possible if coal was in very plentiful supply and it would be accompanied by a reduction in coal prices to producers. There would also be the readaptation fund which would help to cover the costs of any reduction in the labour force below the reduction of between four and five thousand already planned.

The extent of control of coal-mines by integrated steel works in Germany was, at least temporarily, much reduced, not in the Schuman Plan negotiations but by the contemporaneous exercise of the powers of the Allied High Commission implementing the 1947 Bizone plan for decartelization of the industry. It was made clear that this was a pre-requisite for the entry into power of the High Authority. Whatever the belief of the French planners in rationalization and modernization they did not for one moment take the view that the large size of the German steel companies was a laudable example of

[109] CAB 134/295, Meeting of Monnet, Makins etc. in Hyde Park Hotel, 16 May 1950.
[110] Coal stocks held at mines were 1.17 million tonnes in May 1948, 3.6 million tonnes in May 1950, and 1.8 million tonnes in May 1951. UN, *Monthly Bulletin of Statistics*.

either of these processes. Deconcentration of capital holdings in the German coal and steel industries thus went ahead, even though it meant reducing the annual crude steel output of some of the larger German firms below the one million tonnes level which the Planning Commissariat itself had regarded as the minimum level for optimum efficiency in a large integrated steel works. Ironically, this was achieved by insistence on the decartelization programme originally developed by the American and British Military Governments, the very programme which had originally been developed as a way of returning the German industries to private ownership and to which the French government had so strenuously objected.

Eleven days after the Schuman proposals were made public the High Commission approved Law No. 27 which re-enacted all the provisions of Law No. 75 of the Bizone Military Government, the law which had come close to breaking up the London conference in 1948.[111] It introduced a few modifications which would before have been even more offensive to the French. The absolute ban on works being returned to persons punished for political offences was replaced by the imposition of 'a reasonable and appropriate indemnity'. When the executive orders to the law were published in September 1950 the directors of the firms to be broken up were themselves appointed as overseers of the process. The six largest steel companies were broken up into twenty-four separate firms, with only a few variations from the original plans of the Military Government. Between September 1950 and March 1951 the United States brought pressure to bear on the German government to make it accept the separation of coal-mines from steel works. The twelve largest steel works, which had produced before the war about 90 per cent of the total output, were only allowed to own coal-mines up to 75 per cent of their required coal supply. In theory this should have left only 16.5 per cent of West German coking coal under the ownership of the German steel industry, instead of the pre-war proportion of at least a third. The coal companies were to have a separate management and were to sell to steel works only at established market prices. On this particular issue, therefore, the outcome was much more acceptable to France than what was likely to be achieved by the International Authority for the Ruhr.

Once the High Authority was functioning questions of concentration of capital, except where they concerned persons with a blatantly Nazi past or of especially unpleasant repute in France, did however come to be handled more as questions of economic convenience or rationality. The consequence was that the economic advantages of concentration reasserted themselves very quickly over the more political considerations which had prevailed in the decartelization programme. The amalgamations of the newly created Dortmund Hoerder Hütten Union with Howald shipyards, as well as of the

[111] The French High Commissioner placed a suspensive veto on the law which delayed it for one month, but during that month Schuman made his proposals.

412   *The Reconstruction of Western Europe 1945–51*

two very large Belgian coal, steel and engineering companies, Cockerill and
Ougrée, were both permitted by the High Authority in 1955 on the grounds
of rationalization. The smaller companies into which the central German coal
and sales agency, Deutsches Kohlen-Verkauf, was broken up by the executive
orders of February 1951 remained associated by numerous personal and
business links, the common device of interlocking directorates which normally
thwarts political interference of this kind.[112] The real powers of the High
Authority to supervise and regulate business practices within large and diverse
enterprises had obvious limitations. In 1954 a series of spot checks found
serious irregularities of business practice in thirty-five of the forty-eight firms
investigated.[113]

The fate of the Ruhr Authority depended on German willingness to reach a
settlement. It remained in place throughout the negotiations and in November,
against strong German protests, as the demand for coal again increased,
resumed the compulsory allocation of German coal to France, even though
there was a serious bottleneck in supply in Germany. This provoked a
demand from Germany that a definitive decision be made about the Ruhr
Authority in the light of the new negotiations. Monnet gave assurances to
Hallstein,[114] the chief German negotiator, that if the Federal Republic accepted
the gist of the Schuman proposals France would press for the International
Ruhr Authority to be wound up.[115] Towards the end of the negotiations the
Federal Republic obtained a formal written undertaking from the French
Ministry of Foreign Affairs that this would be their policy. Until then the
struggle within the Authority was every bit as discouraging as its opponents
had foreseen. Over the first six months of 1951 the German representatives
voted against every decision on allocation and the representatives of the other
countries voted for them until finally in August Franz Blücher, the Vice-
Chancellor, resigned from the Authority in protest. The background to the
negotiations for the ECSC could scarcely have been further from the international idealism which Monnet had preached.

There was an acute energy crisis in the Federal Republic in 1950 and 1951.
In the third quarter of 1950 West German industry only received about half

[112] The nationalized coal industry in France retained its own national coal importing and sales
organization. The national sales organization of the French steel industry, the Comptoir Français
des Produits Sidérurgiques, was proclaimed dissolved in 1952, but there is considerable evidence
that a very similar control mechanism was retained with tacit government encouragement
(W.G. Baum, *The French Economy and the State* (Princeton, 1958), pp. 265 ff).

[113] H.L. Mason, *The European Coal and Steel Community, Experiment in Supranationalism*
(The Hague, 1955), p. 76.

[114] Walter Hallstein, born 1901, university teacher of law at Berlin. Professor of law at
Rostock 1941, where he wrote a book not uncritical of legal tendencies under the Nazi regime.
Army officer 1942–5. Professor of Law and Rector of the University of Frankfurt, 1946.
State-Secretary in the Office of the Federal Chancellor, 1950. President of the Commission of the
EEC, 1958. President of the European Movement, 1968. Author of books on law and, later, on
European unity.

[115] FJM, AMG 22/4/23, Monnet to Schuman, 3 February 1951.

the average quantity of coal it had received for the first two quarters. About a quarter of Ruhr blast furnaces were not working because of coke shortages.[116] The operations of the International Authority for the Ruhr contributed only marginally to the situation. Nevertheless its actions and those of the Allied High Commissioners in breaking up the firms, together with the intervention by the OEEC to direct and control West German imports in order to save the EPU,[117] all showed the real nature of the choice before Germany. A spasmodic and haphazard economic regulation and intervention by the international diplomacy of the occupying powers was hardly to be preferred to whatever pressures might emanate from what was likely to be a more predictable and possibly more sympathetic source. Erhard's dislike of the ECSC as a needless restriction on German industry took little account of the other restrictions on the German economy which would persist unless the ECSC was accepted. Adenauer insisted throughout on the prime political priority for the Federal Republic of the removal of the Ruhr Authority and the weakening of the Occupation Statute.

Very little is yet known of what must have been a hard struggle inside the government of the Federal Republic. In August the representatives of the German Iron and Steel Manufacturers' Association were in Paris and Heinrich von Brentano, the CDU Party Chairman, was sent by Adenauer to impress on them that 'the political aim was in the foreground, and economic aims were more or less subordinate to it'.[118] The German steel industry had to agree to French steel-makers supplying the south German markets for two to three years and over that period sales to Germany made an important contribution to French exports.[119] The expansion of the German car industry provided, before Germany had reacquired the same technology, a market for products from the new wide strip mills whose construction the Modernization Plan had financed. At the same time the strength of domestic demand in Germany diverted German steel away from the export markets where France had most feared competition.

The reappearance of the coal shortage in 1950 benefited the French steel industry in a tangential way. Not only did Germany have to share the coking coal shortage but the special investment funds under the control of the High Authority were exclusively allocated to the coal industry until 1955, and by the end of 1958 High Authority loans had financed $205 million of investment in French coking plant. If West Germany had had any thought that the institution of the investment fund would ease the problems of capital investment in the reconstruction of the German steel industry those hopes had to be

[116] W. Abelshauser, 'Korea, die Ruhr und Erhards Marktwirtschaft: Die Energiekrise von 1950/51', *Rheinische Vierteljahrsblätter*, 45, 1981.
[117] See below, pp. 431–2.
[118] CAB 134/295, Views of the German Iron and Steel Association, 21 September 1950.
[119] French steel exports to West Germany
    1952 243,000 tonnes   1953 486,000 tonnes   1954 855,000 tonnes

414   *The Reconstruction of Western Europe 1945–51*

deferred. Investment had to come either from self-finance or from government short-term credits under the special programmes instituted in 1951, and that meant higher prices.[120] In 1952 German steel prices were raised twice so that when the common market came into operation the gap between French and German selling prices for a wide range of products had been almost eliminated.

It cannot be said that France came badly out of the negotiations. Negotiating from a position of political strength had proved as advantageous as Schuman had thought. Nevertheless, when the French negotiators presented the project of the draft treaty to ministers in Paris in December 1950 several important ministers demanded alterations which would have ended the negotiations on the spot. René Mayer wanted unilateral obligations to be imposed on Germany over the question of the ownership of the firms if the Ruhr Authority was to go. Petsche wanted the High Authority to have no greater powers than to receive reports about cartels and other forms of business association in French firms. He was opposed to allowing Italy to maintain its tariffs for a longer transition period and also to giving Italy access to North African ore on favourable terms. Ministers recommended to the Planning Commissariat that the existing rules covering business associations in France should not be affected by the treaty and that firms, presumably only French firms, should be protected against the powers of the High Authority to allocate all raw materials in times of scarcity.[121] In the circumstances Monnet's original insistence that the negotiators on the French and German side should not be ministers but men free from the weight of previous policy or of party politics had obviously been wise. The negotiators provided a buffer between the numerous members of both French and German cabinets who were increasingly opposed to what was going ahead.

Yet, assuming the original plans for French coal output to have been too ambitious, ministers were only being asked to make one major concession. That was over the Saarland. The protests from Germany over the conventions signed between France and the Saarland government in spring 1950 did not die down. The lukewarm enthusiasm of America and Britain for France's interest in the Saarland and the increasingly repressive nature of the unrepresentative Saarland government, as opposition to its policy of association with France mounted, so seriously weakened France's position there that the Bonn government felt strong enough in the negotiations to demand some change. This led the French government through various shifts of policy. Firstly it was proposed that the Saarland government should have its own representation in the ECSC or that both its autonomy and French control of its foreign relations be recognized by France signing every part of the ECSC treaty

[120] The methods of financing are discussed in H.R. Adamsen, *Investitionshilfe für die Ruhr. Wiederaufbau, Verbände und Soziale Marktwirtschaft 1948–1952* (Wuppertal, 1981).

[121] FJM, AMG 22/4/2, Documents relatifs aux observations des ministres. The concession that allocation within national boundaries should be a matter for national governments was made in February (ibid., AMG 22/5/3, Letter by Monnet, 9 February 1951).

twice, once for itself and once for the Saarland. There was a lot of discussion emanating from proposals made by Adenauer that the Saarland should become the first 'European' state, its territory governed by a special European legal status, and that Saarbrücken should become the headquarters of the ECSC. The Saarland elections of 1952, which were not fairly held, produced a substantial majority vote for the Saarland government and its policies of autonomous association with France and effectively ended the chances of this solution. The West German government, however, did not allow a position to arise where it would seem to be recognizing the post-war status of the Saarland, and in 1951 the French and West German governments exchanged letters in which it was expressly stated that the West German signature of the ECSC treaty would be in the full recognition by both governments that the current status of the Saar was not recognized by the German government, which would only accept a status determined by a treaty of peace.

When the treaty was presented to the French national assembly for ratification the government was obliged to accept further commitments which limited the force of its application. Among them was one to regulate the status of the Saarland. The others were that it should press for the canalization of the Moselle (which, it was thought, would reduce costs to French steel producers), that it should turn all loans made to the steel industry since 1947 into loans on the same terms as those to the nationalized coal industry, and that it should further pursue the harmonization of international transport costs, social service payments and indirect taxes so as to minimize the difficulties under which French producers would find themselves. In special steels the opening of the common market was delayed for three months at the last moment, a violation of the treaty by the High Authority's own rules.

In fact the sum total of concessions made to the Federal Republic during the negotiations not only scarcely modified the original French negotiating standpoint, but what the Federal Republic eventually accepted was considerably less than what Schuman had at first offered. Where France itself made concessions from the original proposals they were not to Germany but concessions which had to be made to secure the adherence of the other member countries to the bloc.

Once the complexity of the interests of the other countries, which were closely tied to conditions prevailing in the French and German steel industries, had to be taken into account, the more sweepingly simple ideas of the Planning Commissariat did not stand up to the test. Tariff policy, prices and freight rates had to take account of problems of regional adjustment and vested interest in areas long protected, and the difference between the ECSC and the concept of a single competitive market became wide.

Belgium and Luxembourg were more dependent on that market for their steel exports than the other members. Furthermore, steel was a fifth of their total exports (table 58). For them the issues, economically, were more crucial

416   *The Reconstruction of Western Europe 1945–51*

Table 58   Exports of iron and steel as a proportion (%) of the value of Belgium/
Luxembourg's total exports, 1937–51

	%	Total weight (000 tonnes)
1937	19	3909.0
1938	16	2314.3
1946	27	1572.3
1947	23	2268.9
1948	30	3446.0
1949	28	3745.5
1950	19	3580.7
1951	21	5160.9

Source: British Iron and Steel Federation, *Statistical Yearbooks*.

than for France or Germany. The Belgian industry was all in favour of sharing out exports but had no wish to sacrifice any part of its domestic market and aimed at a set of arrangements like the pre-war International Steel Cartel.[122] The reduction in the export price of Belgian merchant bars to a level about a third below that of British prices in February 1950 had been interpreted as an attempt to force the reconstitution of the Cartel.[123] For some time Belgium held out against giving the High Authority powers to co-ordinate investment, but received no support from the Dutch and, with so high a level of dependence on ECSC markets was not in the end in much of a position to argue.[124] The Netherlands was an importer on a large scale from the other countries, about 80 per cent of its steel imports coming from the ECSC. Its own small steel industry was highly competitive and it could hardly lose from the proposals unless the external common tariff of the ECSC was set too high. At this point the industry's interest coincided with that of the Dutch government which was afraid a high external tariff would preclude subsequent British membership.[125] Eventually the tariffs were set higher than those of the Benelux countries but lower than those of France. Only in the Netherlands were the economic advantages to the steel industry indisputable. It gained a safer access to imported raw materials and the new steel works at Ijmuiden which dominated the industry was protected from the price cutting and other discrimination which the International Steel Cartel had habitually employed against all

[122] FJM, AMG 3/3/1, Compte-rendu de la séance restreinte du jeudi 22 juin.
[123] *The Iron and Coal Trades Review*, vol. 160, p. 285. It could only have been effective for purchasers holding Belgian francs.
[124] MBZ, 602/50.6, Verslag van de Vergadering van de Commissie van Advies voer het Plan Schuman, 19 October 1950.
[125] MBZ, 602/50.9, Verslag van de Vergadering van de Commissie van Advies voer het Plan Schuman, 9 December 1950.

newcomers. But although the economic arguments were persuasive the reasons for accepting the ECSC were, as everywhere, political.[126] The ECSC was regarded as a decisive, long-term political choice and therefore not one to be lightly made. The Council of Ministers was added to the arrangements in order to meet Dutch objections that the high authority had handed power over to a group of officials who would be independent of elected government, and the addition to the original French proposals of a Common Assembly with the power to dismiss the High Authority was designed to meet objections of the same kind from the same source.

The Italian government did not object to the surrender of sovereignty and control 'in view of the relatively small scale of the Italian steel and coal industries'.[127] But it was nevertheless determined to bargain hard to mitigate the removal of protection from industries protected from birth. In the bargaining the Italian steel industry not only obtained a special protective regime during the transitional period but also obtained special treatment for ore and scrap. The Italian steel industry was different in nature from its partners because of the very high proportion of its output made up of special steels and steel made by the electric arc process. A quarter of the total output of steel in 1950 was made in electric furnaces compared to 6 per cent in France and less than 3 per cent in Germany. It was thus overwhelmingly dependent on scrap inputs. Its whole life had been spent behind very high protective tariffs and its cost structure bore no comparison to those of the other steel industries. The second post-war steel boom which arrived in Europe in the last quarter of 1950 threatened to recreate the acute shortage of steel scrap of the immediate post-war years. In those years western Europe had maintained a price for scrap lower than world scrap prices, mainly because of the rich stores of scrap left in Germany and the strict price and export controls covering the scrap trade. Italy insisted, to preserve this situation, that the common market should include scrap as well as coal, coke, ore and manufactured iron and steel. The ECSC emerged with a maximum price for scrap still artificially kept below the world price in order to keep the cost structure of the Italian steel industry within politically acceptable parameters. The excess demand for scrap within western Europe was met by an agreement to import from outside the ECSC at higher prices and to share between the other industries the cost of maintaining lower scrap prices to Italian manufacturers. Furthermore Italy was also guaranteed special access to ore from French territory in North Africa which France originally appeared to be hoping to exclude from the common market.

Although the ideas of the French architects of the Schuman Plan were very much influenced by their interpretation of France's own recent history, one

---

[126] MBZ, 602/50.6, Ministerie van Economische Zaken, Stand van de Besprekingen voer het Plan Schuman per 28 October 1950.

[127] FO 371/87167, Conversation between Makins and Grazzi, 13 July 1950.

of their weaknesses was their historical insensitivity, their assumption that the future could be cleansed of the influence of the past. In the formation of the ECSC history gave them a sharp reminder of its persistent influence. The High Authority emerged from the negotiations presiding over a highly imperfect single market in raw materials and manufactures, with powers to interfere in transport, with the capacity to make some decisions of its own about capital investment, and presiding over a common labour market which existed only in theory. Where the economic distortions of the nation state were replaced, it was less by the neutral, anonymous efficiency of the free market, or of an expert technocratic decision-making body, than by a set of complex regulations arising from the careful balancing and adjustment of the interests of the various nation states to allow them to achieve particular national objectives. The future political economy of the Treaty of Rome, the analysis of which by any neo-classical formulations is likely to reduce the analyst only to a state of bewildered despair, had already taken shape.

Yet in many respects this was a big improvement on what had gone before. It not only made a set of economic issues which had been closely intermingled with the causes of war and peace the subject of permanent government regulation but it provided a permanent international governmental organization, with some public appearance of neutrality, to regulate them. How well all this worked out in practice in the 1950s is another story, not yet known. But it survived, and the Franco-German alliance survived with it unweakened, thus providing the central tie in western European reconstruction which was so conspicuously missing in the 1920s. At no time after 1918 had any German government found itself able honestly to accept any French proposals for a settlement of the coal and steel problem or for a general western European reconstruction. In that sense the treaty of the ECSC ended eighty years of bitter and deadly dispute and made the reconstruction of western Europe possible. It did so by avoiding all major questions of war and peace and creating instead a formalized network of institutional economic interdependence. International regulation of the economy was institutionalized as the alternative to the formal diplomatic resolution of major areas of political conflict.

In this light it is hardly surprising that the national industrial associations failed in their opposition. They were asking to be allowed to regulate at an international level matters where their uncontrolled power to decide even on the domestic level had become unacceptable. The understanding by national governments of what was at stake was superior to that of the economic interests which opposed them, just as in most cases it already had been in the first two years of reconstruction when policies had been pursued in a purely national setting. The tensions between government and industrial interests over who was in control of economic policy, which had emerged at the end of the war in the various national battles over planning and nationalization, spilled over into the international setting in the battle over the Schuman Plan. The only industrial groups to support it everywhere were iron and steel users, who generally assumed that it would bring them lower prices. The iron and steel industries in Belgium, France, Germany and Italy all initially opposed it, in France with a vigorous national campaign and in Italy with the help of Confindustria which represented most of Italian industry. The objections raised in summer 1950 by the British Iron and Steel Federation were in fact very mild compared to those put forward to the draft treaty by their fellow organizations elsewhere. Opposition came as strongly from the coal owners' associations. It was fortunate that the French coal industry had been national-ized and could be made to accept government policy.

In retrospect these campaigns by industrial associations against arrangements which proved eventually to be more in their own economic interests than against them can be seen as the culmination of a struggle for political power in the reconstruction period. They were the last fierce resistance to the acceptance of real government power over the mixed economy in western Europe in peacetime. The alliance between government and industry could only be cemented if industry was prepared to concede that government had an over-riding political interest to which industry must subscribe. This had not been accepted, for example, by either the French or German coal and steel industries between 1918 and 1924. In the immediate aftermath of the Second World War the issue hung in the balance. The Monnet Plan had seemed to promise to French industrial interests a much more established and important position in policy-making than they had previously had, providing their weaker members accepted the implications of rationalization and the sanctions by which the Ministry of Finance and the Planning Commissariat could enforce them. But the intentions of the Plan were not ultimately protectionist, no matter how much the policy of the first years did provide a certain extra measure of protection. When the Plan had to be translated into the international setting which could alone guarantee French security the difference in objectives between industry and government could no longer be hidden. The ECSC represented the triumph of government in that struggle and the eventual reconciliation of the two industries to the domestic and international political realities of the post-war world. An external body backed by international hopes and itself an integral part of the peace settlement carried more force in bending industry to the will of government than any purely domestic body.

No durable framework of international interdependence could have been built without this domestic struggle for political power having been first decided. It was a major attribute of the importance of the Schuman proposals, as well as a decisive factor in their success, that they took a form which not only insisted on the primacy of an *international* regulation of the future of the French and German economies, but that they were able to use the international framework to force a solution in government's own interest to the purely

420   *The Reconstruction of Western Europe 1945–51*

internal national struggle for control over the economy. What the French and German steel industries could never be made to accept in the 1920s they were forced to accept in the 1950s.

In April 1951, the month when the treaty was signed, the other controls on the German steel industry, apart from the decartelization programme, were drastically modified. In October Britain agreed that all restrictions on West German output should be removed when the treaty came into force and that the International Authority for the Ruhr should be liquidated, policies to which, of course, American assent had been given most willingly. The High Authority was left, almost, face to face with the national governments. It was to be its great good fortune that for most of the first twenty years of its operation it would never be called upon to deal with one problem with which it was manifestly unequipped to cope, a severe and lasting contraction in the market for steel, for that would have torn apart its flimsy supra-national finery.

Keeping that finery in place meant that the ECSC was never so simple a basis for European reconstruction as its numerous enemies – left, right and centre – claimed, not the 'Europe Inc.' of Schumacher, not a charter for unbridled government intervention in the economy, and not the triumph of an undemocratic, uncontrolled, technocratic bureaucracy. It was a proto-plasmic organization able to take any shape it wished according to the pressures on it from the nation states. What other kind of organization could have resolved so complex and so long a historical problem? It was firmly based, as much as any previous European peace treaty, on the real interests of the nation states which signed it. Whether one of its protoplasmic attributes was that it could lead to a federation of Europe can only be judged by its subsequent history, and that remains to be written.

The Franco-German association which it created was in many respects a shotgun wedding. The German bride, although her other choices were not very enticing, had nevertheless to be dragged protesting by her aged father to the altar while numerous members of her family staged noisy protests on the way and an equally large number of the bridegroom's friends and relations prophesied disaster. Yet the knot once tied this surprising union soon settled into a safe bourgeois marriage in which the couple, rapidly becoming wealthy and comfortable as passions cooled, were held together, as such couples are, by the strong links of managing their complex joint economic affairs. To all those associated with the marriage and brought into the house the same bourgeois prosperity was vouchsafed. The United Kingdom was left in the position of a prim spinster who, having earlier rejected the bridegroom because of the lack of promise of his stormy adolescence, was later allowed into the household on not very flattering terms as a rather acidulous baby-sitter. If she leaves it will not make much difference, except to her. But if the marriage breaks up it will be the end of the peace settlement and perhaps of us all.

[4]

VIII

THE BEYEN PLAN

by
RICHARD T. GRIFFITHS

The failure of the Stikker Plan in the OEEC towards the end of 1950 had represented a set-back for Dutch commercial policy, but the sense of grievance felt at the inequity of the emerging post-war order and the determination to remedy matters remained undimmed. If one of the excuses made in the OEEC for not dealing with tariffs had been that tariffs were more properly the preserve of GATT, at least that particular excuse could not be raised in GATT negotiations. On the other hand, if the Netherlands felt that it faced a built-in protectionist majority in the OEEC, the situation was likely to be even worse in GATT whose membership also included developing countries heavily reliant on tariffs for their own industrialisation schemes.

Early in 1951 a Benelux plan calling for a multilateral round of tariff negotiations among the industrialised countries, whereby low tariff countries would agree to "bind" their tariffs in exchange for concessions from the rest, was tabled in GATT. These concessions were to be extended to other member countries in the normal way. Why multilateral talks of this kind should have led to any greater concession than the usual bilateral method is unclear and the plan should be interpreted more as the registration of a complaint than a serious proposal for a solution. To that extent it was a success insofar as a special group was constituted within GATT to consider the whole problem. Meanwhile Dutch officials began to consider some semi-automatic scheme for reducing tariff disparities. These ideas had yet to crystallise into definite proposals when, in September 1951 the French, in the person of Pierre Pflimlin, now minister of trade, presented their own scheme. Aimed at all GATT countries, it proposed a 30 per cent reduction in tariffs within three years, but the way in which this was to be done, left countries free to maintain protection in some sectors at the expense of others if they so chose.

The Dutch pinned some hopes on the fact French backing might at last raise the chances of something actually happening. They thus abandoned their own scheme and concentrated instead of introducing changes in Pflimlin's proposals which might make them more acceptable to themselves. These included ideas for 'decapping' the highest tariffs and introducing minimum tariff levels beneath which low tariffs would be exempted, both concepts from the last stages of the Stikker, Petsche, Pella plan negotiations. A special group of ten European countries, the USA and Canada had studied these various proposals sporadically before, in September 1952, producing a report which faithfully reflected a position of total impasse. There was little illusion in Dutch policy-making circles that any tariff scheme would fare better in the full GATT forum and the prospects of a Republican victory in the American elections, and a more protectionist shift in US trade policy, eclipsed the hopes of any support from that angle – support which it was recognised would be a precondition for success. The only reason for perpetuating discussions was seen as legitimising the search for a European solution and continuing in existence a ready-made forum for considering any scheme which might eventually emerge[1].

Whilst these developments were unfolding, in an entirely different and at first sight unexpected context events were moving in a direction which would afford the Dutch a new chance for an attack on the whole problem of quotas and tariffs. In February 1952, after a debate in the national Assembly, the French made clear that their acceptance of a European Army would be conditional upon it being subject to democratic control. These demands were backed by the Italians and as a result, although the European Defence Community treaty contained provisions for an assembly, section 2 of article 8 made clear that such arrangements would be temporary. Once the treaty came into force, the assembly itself would draft new arrangements.

There had also been indications previously that at least some of the "six" might not be averse to a situation whereby these new arrangements extended beyond the immediate confines of the EDC treaty. In September 1951, the French foreign minister, Robert Schuman had made a speech calling for the creation of a continental European community with a supranational, federalist political organ. In December he, together with chancellor Konrad Adenauer, and president Alcide De Gasperi, had addressed the Council of Europe to set out their vision for the future of Europe. This had immediately prompted a Council Resolution (recommendation 21b) for the creation of a political authority under parliamentary control and with competences over foreign policy and defence. It was not really surprising, therefore, that in May 1952, four days after the EDC treaty had been signed, the Council called for the *immediate* creation of an assembly to

BURIED ALIVE! The six ESCS ministers (at their first meeting in Luxembourg) gather to mourn the passing of "the old European vendetta". In the foreground, in a scene marked "the miracle of Strasbourg", the grave-digger Monnet discovers the foundling "United Europe".

consider the political organisation of the EDC rather than waiting for the completion of the ratification procedures in the individual countries (Resolution 14). A proposal to this effect was due to be submitted to the foreign ministers of the ECSC when it met in Luxembourg in September 1952.

These developments were coming to a head at a time when the Netherlands was without a government. General elections had been called on 25 June 1952 and a new cabinet was not installed until 1 September. In foreign policy, the major change had been the replacement of Dirk Stikker by the catholic Joseph Luns and by the non-party Jan-Willem Beyen. Beyen's nomination has been described as Willem Drees' "big mistake". Seeking to counter the integrationist tendencies among catholic politicians, Drees had called into the cabinet a banker whose career had been made in the Bank of International Settlements in Geneva and who, after the War, had spent much of his time in Washington: two qualifications which would supposedly have left him untainted by any European infection. To him fell the task of directing the country's European policy[2].

In a brief prepared for the new cabinet by the secretary-general for foreign affairs, Hendrik Boon, the point was made that the proposal for the immediate creation of a "political authority" seemed to assume that it would be the panacea for all Europe's troubles, but he wondered whether the reverse might not be true – that in working towards a political community, the drive towards solving fundamental economic issues might not be weakened even further. He doubted whether it made any sense to countenance a move towards European federalism without including the whole range of competences in the economic sphere[3]. This line of reasoning was adopted by Beyen at the Luxembourg meeting and was painlessly and unanimously endorsed. Reflecting the vagueness of any position which Beyen could adopt, the temporary assembly charged with drafting a treaty for a European Political Community was instructed to examine the question of economic integration as well. The ministers suggested that they would submit appropriate guidelines at a later stage[4]. The Luxembourg Resolution, therefore, was to provide the opportunity for the Dutch to reopen the question of the dismantling of trade barriers in a new but smaller forum. The reduced scope of the exercise, compared with the OEEC or GATT, was presumably compensated by the fact the Netherlands could expect to exercise greater political leverage by virtue of the linkages to the EPC initiative and the EDC treaty. However they first had to define the scope of their ambitions in this field.

In October the State Commission which had been established in August 1952 to advise the government on the question of European integration reported its preliminary findings. It warned against expecting quick results (especially in agriculture) and predicted that, left to itself, the drafting assembly would be unlikely to move beyond a statement that the EPC would concern itself with economic questions – and it might not even be able to agree which economic questions those should be ! It suggested that the only way to ensure progress would be to formulate definite and unambiguous proposals[5]. The next month Beyen was ready with his ideas. For a start he rejected political integration without economic integration as only bringing about "a very limited unity". Whilst he was personally willing to make some concessions in the direction of greater democratic political control, he did not consider the question relevant as long as it was confined to the existing communities (i.e. the ECSC and the EDC). Moreover, he was opposed to leaving all economic initiatives to the newly created EPC unless there were guarantees that something would emerge. He suggested that the six should aim at the creation of a customs union which would remove tariffs and quotas on intra-European trade and erect a common external tariff. The implementation could be left to the organs of the political community which could also prepare proposals for the coordination of monetary and social policy[6]. These views were transmitted to his fellow ministers of the "six" in December 1952, with two amendments – the end date for the achievement of the union was to be fixed in advance and a system of supranationally administered "safeguard clauses" was introduced for the first time[7]. A second memorandum, in February 1953, repeated most of these points but it was no added that the "automatic steps" for the achievement of the customs union should also be stipulated in the treaty and the concept of safeguard clauses was further defined and restricted. The possibility of some kind of adaption fund was also opened[8].

What was to become know as the Beyen Plan had come into existence. At a foreign ministers meeting of the six in Rome later in the month, Beyen suggested that it would be difficult to find a parliamentary majority in the Netherlands for an EPC treaty which did not include concrete steps for achieving European economic integration[9].

It would obviously have been much easier for the realisation of Dutch aims had the EPC treaty, which was being drafted by an assembly of parliamentarians constituted in a form identical with that envisaged in the EDC treaty under the chairmanship of Paul-Henri Spaak, actually included provisions along the lines proposed in the Beyen Plan. In December the Dutch catholic politician Pieter Blaisse had first tabled specific proposals along these lines[10], but got little further than an agreement in the restricted constitutional committee to give the EPC an advisory role in the economic sphere and possibly to include a separate protocol, which would require separate parliamentary ratification for concrete economic measures (which, incidentally, did not prescribe an end date for the creation of a customs union)[11]. The full assembly, led by the "homogeneous and impressively orchestrated voice of the Dutch", condemned these proposals as unsatisfactory[12], but the new proposals did little more than outline the procedural steps through which any common market proposals would have to pass. These served to include the common market within the community's competences but still failed to guarantee its realisation. If this concession failed to satisfy the Dutch, it equally began to attract more entrenched opposition from the French and Luxembourgeois delegations[13]. These articles were approved by the full session, with certain amendments. However the Dutch members, whilst also voting in favour, specifically stated that they reserved to themselves any action they might take in their own parliament because they could not agree with the creation of a political community without adequate guarantees in the economic sphere[14]. As if to lend credence to their concerns, a committee of the Council of Europe, reviewing the economic clauses, stated

> 'The European Community to be set up is endowed in the Draft Treaty with economic powers which would make possible a progressive development towards a common market. The Draft treaty does not, however, contain any obligatory provisions concerning economic integration, and the safeguards foreseen are such that if they are exploited they would make impossible any substantial progress towards achieving the objective proclaimed'[15].

The fate of the Beyen Plan now hung on the ability of the Dutch to convince the fellow governments of the six to amend the draft treaty in such a way as to reflect their own views of European integration. The portents were far from auspicious.

As with so many of these early European initiatives, the pivotal position was that of the French. Now, the introduction of the clauses for "democratising" the European Army could be interpreted as part of the general framework of supranationality which had characterised French policy towards Europe under Schuman's "reign" as foreign minister. In January 1953 that came to an end. A new cabinet was formed and invested with the support of the Gaullists. The price of their support was the replacement of Robert Schuman by Georges Bidault who, whatever the limitations of the new coalition, was anyway much cooler towards the idea of supranationality. A second factor was that these changes had occurred against a background of a rapid deterioration in the external position of the French economy which had already prompted the abandonment on the concessions made in the OEEC's liberalisation programme. If the EPC had originally been intended to ease the passage of the EDC through the French Assembly, it would certainly not do so if, in such circumstances, it carried the baggage of a customs union with it. At the February 1953 ministerial meeting in Rome, Bidault had questioned whether economic clauses should be included in the EPC Treaty[16] and even in the diluted form in which they were to appear, they were considered by the political division of the Quai d'Orsay to form an unacceptable infringement upon French sovereignty and to be incompatible with the Constitution[17]. The French delegation at the subsequent intergovernmental negotiations was instructed to press for a minimalist construction for the EPC whereby the object was to be confined to providing a political structure for the existing communities. Any advice it might have on economic questions would have to be the subject of a separate unanimous agreement of the states concerned[18].

In Germany the economics ministry showed a more positive attitude to the Dutch proposals from the start but tended to stress more especially the problem of currency convertibility[19]. In February 1953 this argument had been used by Ludwig Erhard, however, in a way as to suggest that the EPC was not the most appropriate place for an economic agreement – convertibility was essential to a customs union but since it could not be confined to the "six", neither should a customs union and thus a customs union should not be part of a treaty linked to the "six"[20]. Beyen, incidentally, in a conversation with the British ambassador in Rome, dismissed this type of logic as "all nonsense"[21]. Of more immediate concern to Adenauer and the foreign ministry, however, was the need to avoid anything which might complicate the ratification of the EDC treaty which was the cornerstone of his "European" policy. This was all the more urgent because of the impending elections where this policy would be tested against the "non-European", German reunification approach of the socialists. German policy was geared towards achieving a foreign policy "success" and if that meant an EPC treaty shorn of any content, so be it[22].

Once the elections, in September 1953, had passed, with a surprisingly large Christian Democrat victory, the way was opened for a more serious consideration of the Beyen Plan. These ideas went beyond what the Dutch seemed prepared to consider for whilst a start could be made in dismantling European trade barriers, it was felt that the process could not be completed until full convertibility had been achieved. In Erhard's own words, "The ordering of (some) areas with the continued disorder in others can never lead to an economically united Europe. A further partial union would mean the definite atomisation (lit. *Atomisierung*) of Europe." Accompanying this process, there should be the establishment of a permanent conference of central

172   **GRIFFITHS**

banks and the gradual transfer of the monetary and fiscal instruments of counter-cyclical policy to a supranational authority[23].

The initial Italian reaction was similar to that of Germany and for the same reasons. De Gasperi too was facing elections, this time in June 1953, and he too wanted a foreign policy coup. What he favoured was the acceleration of the procedure whereby the ministers of the six would endorse the draft EPC treaty intact[24]. In the event electoral fortunes were less kind to De Gasperi than they had been for Adenauer and in the new coalition he was replaced by the far less European-inclined Giuseppe Pella. Italian thinking, however, on the Beyen Plan itself was closer to that of France. The EPC treaty was interpreted more in the character of a constitution and although the Italians were willing to concede that the treaty's economic powers might require redefinition, they did not consider that there was a place for the kind of technical provisions which the Dutch seemed to be envisaging[25]. As far as the customs union itself was concerned, the feeling was that the political difficulties had been underestimated. They were totally opposed to any rigid timetable for its implementation and felt that progress should proceed within the limits dictated by the international cycle (viz. acceleration in times of cyclical upswing, freezing in times of recession). They also wanted the fund's scope enlarged to cover investment in backward (Italian) sectors, which would serve to promote the integration process[26].

The Belgian response was more positive from the start in the sense that they shared the Dutch conviction that the EPC's economic powers were hopelessly inadequate. However they felt that the concentration on a customs union would not, by itself, achieve market integration[27]. Like the Germans, their concern focussed on the absence of monetary considerations and other aspects of policy coordination, without which, it was felt, the whole edifice would be characterised by the same bickering as was marring Benelux[28]. In addition to the customs union, the community should be charged with "coordinating" by means of recommendations a wide range of monetary, fiscal, economic and exchange rate policy upon which, after a transitional period, the Council of Ministers would be able to take decisions binding on member states[29]. A "Benelux of the six", as the Beyen Plan was described, was seen as an essentially unstable construction, too vulnerable to being pulled apart by divergent national policies and then being fatally crippled by the reintroduction of protection as the safeguard mechanisms, envisaged in the Plan, came into operation[30].

The initial position for Luxembourg was to reject the Beyen Plan. Small countries, it was argued, had such little sovereignty anyway that they were naturally wary of signing it away to some supranational authority. As far as they were concerned it had nowhere been made clear why a customs union was an indispensable condition for creating a European political community[31]. Releasing, however, that a small country is ill-placed to deflect larger countries, if they are in agreement, from having their way, the strategy switched to pressing for the inclusion of concrete economic measures in a separate protocol, and to announcing the country's intention of claiming exemption for vital economic interests[32].

The elections in Italy and Germany and a cabinet crisis in France all served to postpone the moment at which the governments would be forced to pronounce upon the EPC treaty to September 1953. In the interval the Dutch, too, were able to reappraise their position. Within the cabinet, the new economics minister Jelle Zijlstra, was inclined towards the standpoint which was later to evolve in Germany and Belgium. He felt that the economic community should also embrace the liberalisation of payments and the free mobility of labour and he wanted policy harmonisation in the field of prices, wages and social security provisions, taxation policy and counter-cyclical policy[33]. Similar views were also expressed by an economic sub-committee which had been created. It warned,

'The opening of frontiers is almost impossible as long as a certain measure of coordination has not been achieved in the areas of general economic, financial monetary and social policy.'

It also argued against the stipulation of an end-date for the achievement of a customs union, partly because it was felt that its creation would be dependent upon progress towards policy harmonisation and partly because it anticipated that no one else would be likely to agree[34].

Even before the ink was dry, the cabinet had first to overcome the opposition of prime minister Drees to continuing with the EPC at all. He levelled a string of objections to the draft treaty and pointed out that it contained virtually nothing of Dutch demands. For good measure, he added that he thought that the six were incapable for forming a political community, because of the lack of political will and because some of the states themselves were too unstable, and if they were to agree a treaty, for these same reasons the institutional structure would probably fail anyway. This was strongly resisted by Beyen, supported by Sicco Mansholt, who contended that if this was the way the government felt, the Netherlands should not have embarked on the venture in the first place. Having started, however, it should continue its course. In the end Drees agreed to continuing with the Beyen Plan, making clear that he did not think other countries would accept it. However he would resign from the cabinet rather than sign a purely political treaty with no advantage to the Netherlands[35].

It was probably this uneasy compromise which kept the Beyen Plan

from deviating into other areas. Beyen ignored the sub-committee's
advice. In a reply on the Treaty, addressed to the six, which was not
discussed in advance by cabinet, he fell back upon the main lines of
the original plan[36]. When cabinet did get round to a more detailed
discussion, it was decided to push for the creation of a customs union
within ten years, despite the fact that both Drees and Zijlstra considered this too long. Beyen, however, argued that if the time-span
were further reduced, it would lead to an increase in the number and
complexity of escape clauses. The only other discordant note was pronounced by Mansholt who argued that a fall-back position should be
prepared for the eventuality that Dutch demands were not met in full.
He got no further than a concession (?) that the delegation would refer
back to cabinet any compromise suggestions but the feeling generally
was that the Netherlands should not join the EPC unless it had a real
economic content[37].

Given the line-up of the participating countries, it is not surprising
that the inter-governmental conference which spanned two weeks at
the end of September and the beginning of October 1953 turned into
a fiasco. There was barely enough time for the delegates to set out
their conflicting views before they had to turn their hands to producing an agreed report solemnly recording them all. The French position
alone, in rejecting any economic role for the EPC, itself made any
agreement impossible but even aside from that, the Dutch delegation,
tied to the narrow concept of the Beyen Plan, were unable to build any
bridges to the Belgian and German delegations, who were not unsym-
pathetic to Dutch goals but who simply did not think that they went
far enough[38]. At this juncture Mansholt had tried to get some relaxation of the Dutch instructions whereby concessions could be made on
matters of policy harmonisation. More critically, he argued in favour
of accepting a situation whereby the creation of the common market
be left to the EPC (as envisaged in the draft treaty) and dealt with in
a separate protocol. This was the position which had been adopted by
France, Italy and Luxembourg. The danger was, otherwise, that the
Dutch could be manoeuvered into a position where it might have to
accept a purely political treaty[39]. Given the fact that the discussion on
the institutional side of the draft treaty was equally deadlocked, the
danger of this happening seems somewhat exaggerated. Beyen,
however, refused point blank to shift the Dutch position before the
first study conference had ended[40].
  Among the concessions which Beyen was prepared to consider was
a lengthening of the time-scale for the achievement of a customs union
to fifteen years and a relaxation in the demands for automatism in the
reduction of barriers. He also considered that some move could be

made towards Belgian and German wishes for policy coordination.
However, he refused to make any gestures in the direction of leaving
matters entirely in the hands of the community institutions or of a
separate protocol[41]. Mansholt made a final attempt to prevent Dutch
intransigence from killing off the EPC treaty altogether but found
himself completely isolated. Drees' views, for once, reflected the
general position in cabinet,

> 'Even if the French only want a headdress for the ECSC and the
> EDC, the Netherlands should still say no, in view of the fact that
> we should not be prepared to surrender part of our sovereignty for
> the creation of an empty husk'[42].

Even this limited view of things probably exaggerated French ambitions. Still struggling with itself on the fate of the EDC treaty, the
political community project had become at best an irrelevance and at
worst an embarrassment. Although the ministers of the six had approved the continuation of discussions, a Quai d'Orsay report to
French embassies abroad made no bones about the fact that the decision had been taken to create the illusion that discussions were continuing without interruption or delay. It felt that further economic
negotiations would only reveal to the rest, the considerable difficulties
attached to the further surrender of sovereignty in the economic
field[43]. The delegation in the experts' conference tended either to
repeat the opinion that as far as they were concerned, the entire
discussion on economic clauses was inappropriate or to pile up difficulties and objections towards what the others were doing[44].

The should have made it easier to obtain a line-up of the remainder
"against" France possible but that was unlikely. In the first place,
Germany's "European" policy in its widest sense still depended on
French cooperation – there was still no European army, still no prospect of German rearmament, no solution to the Saar question and so
forth. Beside these concerns the question of whether or when to set up
a common market was of secondary importance. Italy, too, remained
far from the Dutch position. Although willing to discuss economic integration, their standpoint was still that it belonged to a separate
agreement. That left really little more than the possibility of a Benelux
front (minus Luxembourg !).

The continuing talks set up tensions in both camps. The delegate
from the Belgian finance ministry suggested dropping the insistence
on policy coordination and throwing support behind the customs
union, but the foreign ministry decided to quash such sentiments.
Firstly it was argued that the Dutch position was "not wrong but insufficient" but, more to the point "it would be absurd to renounce this
position and to cover ourselves with ridicule right in the middle of the
conference"[45]. In the Netherlands, too, disquiet was beginning to

build up at the restrictive nature of the instructions. In February
Johannes Linthorst Homan, who was chairing the economic study
group complained about the difficulty of holding fast the Dutch positions when the delegates themselves could privately acknowledge the
objections raised by the rest[46]. Also mentioned were the difficulties in
keeping the delegation together in the face of the inclination of
delegates from the economic ministry to cooperate in intensive discussions on policy coordination and rules for competition[47]. Still Beyen
refused to budge. To those who complained that on specific points the
delegates had veered from their instructions he replied cynically that
this would demonstrate that the Dutch, at least, had taken the
"study" character of the conference seriously – when the time came
for ministerial decisions, he could always reintroduce Dutch reserves.
Equally, he rejected a plea made on behalf of Mansholt to consider
concrete measures on policy coordination, especially since the country
was apparently willing to accept concrete measures on the movement
of goods. A relaxation of the delegates' instructions was considered
necessary if any agreement was to be reached. To this Beyen replied
that he considered coordination for its own sake to be dangerous. If
the others came with concrete proposals and if these could be shown
to be necessary for the achievement of a customs union, he would be
prepared to consider them on their merits[48]. The decision not to alter
the instructions was confirmed by cabinet in April 1954, notwithstanding Mansholt's plea to allow the EPC itself to implement the customs
union[49]. In fairness, however, it should be stated that that option had
already been passed long before. On the other hand, the opportunity
which was missed was that of cementing a more solid position with the
countries more sympathetic to Dutch aims.

   The situation in the summer of 1954 was that the fate of the EPC,
and the Beyen Plan, rested upon the position taken by France on the
EDC treaty. When, in August 1954, it was rejected by the French
Assembly the entire fragile edifice came tumbling down. But the one
thing that had emerged from the wreckage was that five countries were
willing, with greater or lesser degrees of commitment, to accept the
creation of a customs union as part of a more wide-ranging integration
of their economies. It was a "certainty" to which Beyen clung
throughout the confusion which surrounded the EDC failure and he
remained unmoved by various other schemes for "relaunching"
Europe which proliferated in its wake[50].

To Beyen these developments confirmed rather than denied the value
of automatic, time fixed and complete tariff removals provided for in
his Plan. If anything were to be achieved in the field of economic integration it would need a simple, supranationally implemented

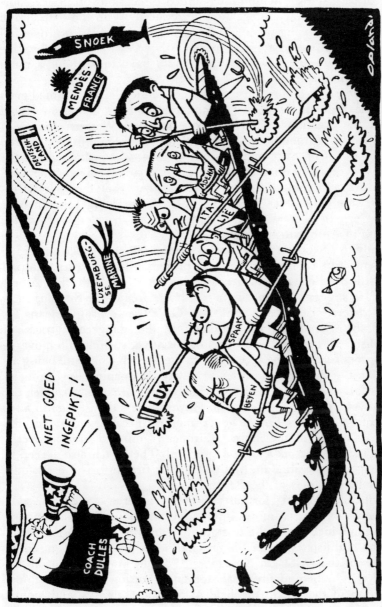

The Coxless Six   *DE GROENE AMSTERDAMMER 28.8.1954*

customs union as its basis. Only on these terms would all governments be forced to live up to the principles of free intra-trade and would the scope for "escaping" behind longwinded discussions on policy coordination and monetary integration be reduced. With the first step of a customs union being taken, Beyen insisted, the road towards a full economic union would actually more easily accessible[51]. For the time being, however, any new initiative would have to wait for a more favourable political climate in France[52].

On other fronts discussions on new economic plans continued even before the problem of West German rearmament had been solved through the creation of the intergovernmental Western European Union (WEU). Although Spaak, now Belgian foreign minister, shared Beyen's pessimism of premature initiatives, it was in fact within the Belgian government that economic plans again received attention. The nature and timing of these plans suggest that the Belgian initiatives were at least as much prompted by growing concern over Franco-German bilateral economic deals as by sheer enthusiasm for the cause of European integration.

Already in October 1954 French-German talks on long term trade agreements and a mutual investment project in French Africa caused alarm with the Belgian representative in the High Authority, Albert Coppé. He suggested proposing a free trade area of the Six plus their associated territories in the OEEC or GATT as a useful means for leading the French and Germans off the dangerous track of bilateralism[53]. Presented as a Benelux initiative, such an intergovernmental proposal might be acceptable to the French while still being attractive to the Benelux countries as a way for opening up European markets[54]. Eventually, this idea was abandoned because Spaak felt the time not yet right for such a move. However, less than a month after the fall of the Mendès-France government in February 1955 and the coming to power of the more "European"-minded Faure government, it received Spaak's formal approval. The Dutch also agreed to support it as a possible alternative to their first priority, a customs union along the lines of the Beyen Plan[55].

Notwithstanding this formal approval, the free trade area soon made way for other, more influential alternatives for economic cooperation which found their origin in Jean Monnet's close circle of European enthusiasts. After his resignation as president of the High Authority of the ECSC in November 1954, Monnet had put all his political weight behind proposals for an extension of supranational cooperation of the Six to the field of transport, energy and atomic energy. As he assured his close ally Spaak, the latter sector especially would offer "spectacular" possibilities for European cooperation because it was a relatively new, yet very promising source of economic growth[56]. Thus, when at a meeting of Benelux foreign ministers in March 1955, Beyen vigorously pushed forward his customs union plan he met in Spaak an ardent supporter of sectoral integration[57]. By way of compromise, the Benelux governments agreed to table a joint initiative which put forward both the sectoral and the general economic approach of a customs union as parallel and complementary ways for European integration. These ideas were considered and approved by the foreign ministers of the Six when they met at Messina in June 1955.

NOTES

ABBREVIATIONS

AD	Archives Diplomatiques (see MAE (Fr).
AN	Archives Nationals, Paris.
ARA	Algemeen Rijksarchief, The Hague.
BA	Bundesarchiv, Koblenz.
BBV	Buitenlands Betalingsverkeer (see MF).
BEB	Buitenlandse Economische Betrekkingen (see MEZ).
DGAP	Direzione Generale Affari Politici (see MDAE).
FO	Foreign Office (see PRO).
MAE(Bel)	Ministère des Affaires étrangères, Brussels.
MAE(Fr)	Ministère des Affaires étrangères, Paris.
MAE(L)	Ministère des Affaires étrangères, Luxembourg.
MAZ	Ministerie van Algemene Zaken, The Hague.
MBZ	Ministerie van Buitenlandse Zaken, The Hague.
MDAE	Ministero Degli Affari Esteri, Rome.
MEZ	Ministerie van Economische Zaken, The Hague.
MF	Ministerie van Financiën, The Hague.
MR	Ministerraad (see ARA).
PA/AA	Politisches Archiv des Auswärtiges Amtes, Bonn.
PRO	Public Records Office, Kew.

[1] These events are discussed more fully in R.T. Griffiths, "The Abortive Dutch Assault on European Tariffs, 1950-1952" in: M. Wintle (ed.) *Modern Dutch Studies. Essays in honour of Professor Peter King*, London, 1988, 199-207.

[2] See further Chapter seven, pp. 153, 155-156.

[3] ARA,MR (482) *Nota aan de ministerraad inzake ministers conferentie 9 en 10 September to Luxemburg* 29.8.1952 (MR 5.9.1952).

[4] ARA,MR (482) *Kort verslag van de eerste zitting van de bijzondere raad van ministers van de Europese Gemeenschap voor Kolen en Staal en van de daarop aansluitende conferentie der ministers van buitenlandse zaken van de staten-leden dezer Gemeenschap, gehouden op 8, 9 en 10 september 1952* (MR 15.9.1952).

180   GRIFFITHS

[5] ARA,MR (483) *Nota der Advies Commissie inz. de instelling ener Europese Politieke Gemeenschap, betreffende het van de zijde der nederlandse regeering in te nemen standpunt dienaangaande, en in het bijzonder omtrent de aan de Assemblé ad hoc voor te leggen vragen* (MR 16.10.1952).

[6] ARA,MR (484) *Grondslagen voor het nederlandse standpunt met betrekking tot het vraagstuk der europese integratie* (MR 24.11.1952).

[7] ARA,MR (486) Memorandum 11.12.1952 (MR 9.2.1953).

[8] ARA,MR (486) *Ontwerp van een memorandum bestemd voor de regeringen 28.1.1953. Europese politieke gemeenschap* 9.2.1953 (MR 9.2.1953).

[9] ARA,MR (487) *Verslag van de ministersconferentie van de zes Schuman landen te Rome op 24 en 25 februari 1953 (MR 2.3.1953).*

[10] MBZ, 913.100/14 *Commission constitutionelle, deuxième session, sous-commission des attributions. Remarques sur quelques options concernants la communauté politique presentées par M. Blaisse* AA/CC/SCA(2)7 11.11.1952, ML,GS 99 *De werkzaamheden der commission Constitutionelle en haar verschillende subcommissies* 3.12.1952.

[11] MBZ 913.100/18 *Inlichtingen en officiële documenten betreffende de constitutionele commissie,* December 1952. MBZ 913.100/15 *Commission constitutionelle, deuxième session, sous-commission des attributions, procès-verbal de la dixième séance,* AA/CC/SCA(2)PV10 3.12.1952. MBZ 913.100/17 *Constitutionele commissie, derde zitting. Overzicht van de amendementen op het rapport van de subcommissie Bevoegdheden ingediend,* AA/CC(3)21, 19.12.1952.

[12] ARA,MEZ,BEB 1033 *Samenvatting van de conclusies van de tweede zitting van de Assemblé ad hoc* 16.1.1953.

[13] MBZ 913.100/21 *Verslag van de werkzaamheden der constitutionele commissie en de subcommissies I, II en IV in de periode van 5 tot en met 12 februari 1953.*

[14] MBZ 913.100/24 *Verslag van de derde zitting van de Assemblé ad hoc* 16.3.1953.

[15] MBZ 913.100/26 Council of Europe. Consultative Assembly. 5th Ordinary Session, May 1953. *Recommendation 45. Appendix II.*

[16] See note 9.

[17] MAE (Fr) Generalité's 32 *Compatibilité du projet de statut avec la constitution française* 23.4.1953.

[18] AN,363 AP 23 *Instructions pour la délégation française à la conférence de Rome (22 Septembre 1953)* 18.9.1953.

[19] BA, B-102/11408 Erhard to the Foreign Office in Bonn 19.2.1953.

[20] MBZ 913.100/23 *Reacties van de verschillende ministers op de nederlandse voorstellen* 7.3.1953.

[21] PRO,FO 371/106076 Nevile Butler to J.E. Coulson 5.3.1953.

[22] PA-AA, II 224-20 *Gespräch zwischen dem Herrn Bundeskanzler, Ministerpräsident Mayer und Außenminister Bidault, 11.Mai 1953, abends* (Kurzprotokoll)

[23] BA, B-102/11409 *Protokoll der 24.Tagung des Wissenschaftlichen Beirats beim Bundeswirtschaftsministerium vom 24.April bis 1.Mai 1953 im Hotel Margarethenhof (Siebengebirge)* 10.6.1953.

[24] MDAE, DGAP, Pos.4215, No.255/6, 1953 Diplomatic telegram from Quaroni (Paris) the Ministry of Foreign Affairs in Rome 21.4.1953.

[25] MDAE, DGAP, Pos.4215, No.255, 1953 Telegramme (No.21/ 2202) of the Ministry of Foreign Affairs in Rome to the Italian Embassies in Bonn-Bruxelles-Paris-London-Washington ... 16.6.1953.

[26] MDAE, DGAP, Pos.4215, No.255/6, 1953, Italian delegation in Luxembourg (Cavaletti) to the Ministry of Foreign Affairs in Rome 30.5.1953: *Attribuzioni economiche della Communita' Europea (Documento di lavoro n.3).*

[27] MAE (Bel) 17.771/1 *Considération d'ordre économique sur le mémorandum néerlandais relatif à la création d'une communauté politique euoropéenne* 12.2.1953.

[28] Ibid., *Note pour monsieur le ministre des affaires étrangères. Etude du 3e Mémorandum*

Néerlandais concernant la Communauté Européenne n.d.

[29] Ibid., *Modifications proposées par le ministère des affaires economiques aux articles du projet de statut de la communauté européenne en matière d'attributions économiques* nd. probably August 1953.

[30] Ibid., *Notes sur les travaux de la commission économique de la conférence de Rome …* October 1953.

[31] MAE (L) 5960 *Déclaration de M. Bach à la conférence de Rome, février, 1953.*

[32] MAE(L)5944, *Procès-verbal de la réunion des six ministres des affaires etrangères Baden-Baden 7 et 8 août 1953.* This statement was endorsed as the official negotiating position MAE (L) 13170 *Conseil du Gouvernement. Séance du lundi 14 septembre 1953.*

[33] MBZ 913.100/14 *Het economisch substraat van een europese politieke integratie* nd but probably November 1952. Three times in this document he mentioned that these stipulations were to be considered as a minimum required.

[34] ARA, MR (488) *Rapport van der Economische Sub-Commissie* 22.4.1953 (MR 29.4.1953).

[35] ARA, MR (398) Minutes of cabinet 29.4.1953.

[36] ARA, MR (489) *Memorandum du Gouvernement des Pays-Bas concernant la Communauté Européenne* 5.5.1953 *Projet de dispositions économiques du Traité portant statut de la Communauté européenne* n.d. (MR 11.5.1953).

[37] ARA, MR (398) Minutes of cabinet 20.7.1953.

[38] For more detail see R.T. Griffiths and A.S. Milward, "The Beyen Plan and the European Political Community" in: W. Maihofer (ed.), *Noi si mura, Selected working papers of the European University Institute,* Florence, 1986 608-616.

[39] MAZ, Kabinet, 351.88(4)075 Mansholt to Beyen 28.9.1953.

[40] MAZ, Kabinet, 351.88(4)075 Beyen to Mansholt 3.10.1953. See also ARA,MR (398) Minutes of cabinet 5.10.1953.

[41] ARA,MR (495) *Resultaten van de conferentie van Rome, betreffende de Europese Gemeenschap* 22.10.1953 (MR 21./23.11.1953).

[42] ARA,MR (392) Minutes of cabinet 23.11.1953.

[43] MAE (Fr) Generalité 32, Parodi to Embassies 1.12.1953.

[44] See note 38.

[45] MAE (Bel) 17.771/3 Persoons to Upperts 26.1.1956, and annex *La position de la délégation belge en matière économique à la lumière des premiers travaux de la conférence.*

[46] MAZ, Kabinet, 351.88(4)075:32 *Notitie van de Heer Linthorst Homan* 25.2.1954; MF,BBV 1262/9 *Algemene beschouwing over de economische besprekingen ter Parijse studieconferentie EPG van 7 januari tot 8 maart 1954.*

[47] MF,BBV 1269/9 *Studieconferentie Europese Gemeenschap te Parijs* 10.3.1954.

[48] MF,BBV 1269/9 *Vergadering Commissie-Beyen inzake Europese Politieke Gemeenschap op 12 maart.*

[49] ARA,MR (399) Minutes of cabinet 13.4.1954.

[50] A.C. Harryvan and A.E. Kersten,"The Netherlands, Benelux and the Relance Européenne 1954-1955" in: E. Serra (ed) *Il Rilancio dell'Europa e i trattati di Roma,* Brussels/Milan/Paris/Baden-Baden 1989 132-136.

[51] MBZ 931.100/134 Beyen's note: appendix letter to Couvreur to Spaak 6-4-2955.

[52] Harryvan and Kersten, The Netherlands, Benelux and the "Relance Européenne", in Serra, *Il Rilancio dell'Europa* 133.

[53] MAE(Bel) 17.771/4 *(Notes du Département) Note pour Monsieur le Ministre* 29.10.1954.

[54] MAE(Bel) 17.771/4 *(Rapports des postes) Comment reprendre le problème de l'integration economique,* n.d.

[55] MAE(Bel) 17.771/4 *Note pour la Direction Générale de la politique* 1-4-1955; MBZ 913.100/134 Van der Beugel to Beyen 21-4-1955.

[56] P. Gerbet, "La 'Relance' Europeenne jusqu'a la conference de Messine" in:

182   **GRIFFITHS**

Serra, *Il Rilancio dell'Europa,* 66-70.
    [57] Harryvan and Kersten,"The Netherlands, Benelux and the Relance Euro-
peenne" 141-142.

Part II
The Creation of the EEC

3 Restoring France: the road to integration

Frances M. B. Lynch

The decision of the French government to sign the Treaty of Rome in March 1957 setting up the European Economic Community marked a sharp break with the policies of protection pursued since the end of the nineteenth century. So momentous was the decision to integrate the French economy with the five western European economies that the British were confident that the French government would not be able to take it. That the French government agreed to such an important surrender of sovereignty is generally portrayed in the literature as a sign of the weakness of the French state – a weakness which was confirmed when the entire regime of the Fourth Republic collapsed one year later.

Its political and military weakness is said to have been highlighted in the Suez fiasco – an episode which Pierre Guillen has argued was critical in tilting the internal debate in France in favour of signing the Treaties of Rome.[1] Its economic weakness is said to be demonstrated by the surge in growth which took place as a result of de Gaulle's decision after the collapse of the Fourth Republic to devalue the franc and to cut real wages, so enabling the French economy to respond successfully to the stimulus of the larger European market.[2] Yet although the French economy seemed to benefit from participation in the European Economic Community, with rates of growth of GNP rising from 4.4 per cent per annum in the period 1950–60 to 5.7 per cent per annum in the period 1960–70 making France the fastest-growing economy in the EEC in the 1960s, this has not been seen as the primary motivating factor. As William James Adams argues:

> despite its own predilection for self-sufficiency, France decided to surrender some of its economic sovereignty on political and military grounds. It did not choose economic integration to raise living standards through specialization in production. Nor did it choose economic integration to expose domestic producers to competition.

60   *The Frontier of National Sovereignty*

> Its primary goal was to achieve the greatest possible interdependence
> between Germany and its neighbours.[3]

In this argument precisely why interdependence should take the form of
economic integration is not explained, because by implication it was
inevitable. The Treaty of Rome was simply institutionalizing a set of
economic relations which already existed, or which would have existed
had the state not blocked them. It is at this point that classical economic
theory and political bias substitute for an explanation based on
historical research.

As this chapter demonstrates, the reason why the French state agreed
to sign the Treaties of Rome was due neither to the historical accident of
Suez, nor to the force of federalist political ideas, nor to the inevitable
process of economic development. It was rather the outcome of a
prolonged debate about how best to secure the French national interest
– a debate which was driven by the shock of defeat in 1940.

The experience of defeat and occupation had not only discredited the
Third Republic and the Vichy state but created a set of new expectations
which the Fourth Republic had to meet in order to establish its
legitimacy. As elsewhere in western Europe, the state was expected to
look after people's material well-being as well as their physical security.
These new demands necessitated both a new machinery of government
to articulate them and a new international framework to support and
sustain them.

The French played no part in negotiating the new international
monetary arrangements which culminated in the Bretton Woods
Charter, despite the attempt by two of de Gaulle's supporters in
London, Hervé Alphand and André Istel, to set out the French position
in a draft plan in 1943.[4] The emphasis was on domestic reconstruction. It
was to ensure control over domestic policy and policy-making that de
Gaulle set up the Commissariat au Plan under Jean Monnet in 1946. One
of the many weaknesses of the inter-war machinery of government had
been the vertical structure of policy-making. Each ministry represented
a particular sectional interest, but in the absence of a horizontal body
designed to co-ordinate or choose among conflicting interests, policy
tended to be dictated by financial criteria. The result had been disastrous
for the real economy; in 1938 the level of industrial output was 25 per
cent below that of 1929.

As in other countries, the French planners saw economic development
based on industrial expansion as the key to restoring the legitimacy of
the new state. Only by expanding the industrial base would the new
regime be able to solve the structural problem of the balance of
payments deficit and enable incomes, including agricultural incomes, to

France: the road to integration 61

rise. Industrial expansion would draw labour off the land, which would provide an extra incentive for mechanizing French agriculture and making it self-sufficient.

The planners inherited a number of ideas and instruments of control from both Vichy and the resistance which were to enable the plan to be implemented. These included controls over prices and external trade, the nationalization of key sectors, and the creation of a national credit council which would supervise the allocation of credit according to the priorities set by the plan. The ultimate objective as stated by the plan was to enable the French economy to be reintegrated into the international economic and monetary system – the first elements of which had been set out in the Bretton Woods Charter, signed by France in December 1945. However this did not inhibit the French government from adopting in the transitional period policies which were quite antithetical to the principles of Bretton Woods. The most notorious example was the decision to adopt a multiple system of foreign exchange rates for the French franc in January 1948 in an attempt to redirect imports away from the dollar area. Although the United States condemned this, it did not alter its support for the broad objectives of French economic policy as articulated in the Monnet Plan. This support took the form of a dollar loan in 1946 followed by dollar aid and its counterpart in French francs under the Marshall Plan.

The first real division over economic policy both within France and between France and the United States came in 1949–50 when the United States in the interests of promoting a multilateral trade and payments system in Europe diluted its support for national investment plans. The European Payments Union set up in 1950 was designed to increase the interdependence of European economies in order to reduce their dependence on the United States. Where the scheme divided the French was in its integral association with the earlier British and American scheme for liberalizing intra-European trade by the progressive removal of non-tariff barriers supervised by OEEC. When in February 1952 in the face of a payments crisis, the French had to reimpose trade controls, critics of this scheme seemed to be vindicated. The EPU provided the first real debate in France, as late as autumn 1949, over the nature and terms by which the French economy would be reintegrated into the international economy.

In 1949 the Ministry of Foreign Affairs had identified two ways of increasing trade. One was the market solution. This would entail exposing both competitive and uncompetitive sectors to foreign competition in the hope that the uncompetitive sectors would be stimulated into taking the steps necessary to survive. The alternative was to draw up

62   *The Frontier of National Sovereignty*

a list of those sectors which felt that they could withstand exposure to foreign competition but there was little doubt that such a list would be so short that it would not stimulate trade and competition.

For France the situation was complicated by the trading relations within the French Union. To adopt the second, progressive solution the government would have to consider first the effect on exports from the departments and territories overseas (DOM-TOMs) to metropolitan France, and second, metropolitan exports to these countries. These took place in a closed protectionist system. North African producers already felt menaced by metropolitan French imports of Mediterranean food-stuffs within the context of bilateral deals and were conscious of their own higher price levels. The reason that North African prices were uncompetitive was partly because these countries imported higher-priced French goods, particularly investment goods and textiles. Because French textile producers enjoyed a virtual monopoly in the North African market, it was certain that textiles would not feature on any list of goods to be exposed.

Unlike the textile industry, producers of investment goods and agricultural machinery were actually being encouraged under the Monnet Plan to expand output to satisfy the needs of North Africa and the overseas territories. If these countries were allowed by any change in international arrangements to turn to the sterling area, French industry would be saddled with overcapacity. The Ministry of Foreign Affairs felt that it would be possible in the short term to reconcile the two apparently conflicting objectives: namely an increase in intra-European trade with the maintenance of a closed trading system in the French Union, but not in the longer term.[5]

The debate over the EPU revealed the main cleavages of opinion within France which were to remain until 1957. On one level the dispute was simply over the timing of trade liberalization. It was argued that France should retain control over its external trade and payments until the Monnet Plan had been fully completed; in other words, that modernization had to precede liberalization.[6] On another level it was argued by the Ministry of Foreign Affairs that France would have a deficit with the sterling area and the German Federal Republic which it would be unable to cover with a surplus from the rest of OEEC. Therefore the EPU would not lead to the rebuilding of French reserves, the restoration of convertibility of the franc, and the reintegration of the French economy into the international economic system. This analysis was based on the inter-war experience when France had depended on the receipts from invisible transactions – and in the 1930s on its gold reserves – to balance its external payments. French gold reserves had been further

France: the road to integration   63

depleted between 1945 and 1947 to help finance the needs of reconstruction before Marshall Aid arrived, so that by 1949 they amounted to
a mere 464.6 tonnes compared with a maximum of 4900.4 tonnes in
1932.[7] It was assumed that receipts from invisible transactions had also
largely disappeared. This reasoning led to the recommendation that
France would be better off expanding trading links with complementary
economies in eastern Europe and the French Overseas Territories in the
short term at least.

A third argument centred on the nature of the trade liberalization
programme and on the inclusion of the German Federal Republic in it.
Within OEEC, the United Kingdom and France had very different views
about the best method of reducing quantitative restrictions on trade.[8]
Whereas the British advocated a simple percentage reduction in each
of the three main categories of 1948 private trade, the French Ministry of
Finance wanted it to be done on the basis of common lists of products
to be liberalized. Only in that way it was argued would liberalization lead
to an increase in intra-European trade and competition between
producers. However it was the British proposal which was adopted by
OEEC. In view of the arguments which the announcement of the French
proposals for a common list provoked within France, this was probably
the wisest course of action. Within the Ministry of Industry, which had
not been consulted, the Directorate of Mechanical and Electrical
Industries objected to the fact that steel was not on the list whereas
industries using steel were to be liberalized.[9] Given the lower price of
West German steel, all users of French steel would be at a comparative
disadvantage and yet they were to be exposed to European competition
before the steel industry itself.

This of course was not the only factor identified by the Ministry of
Industry as responsible for West German economic superiority. The
inadequacy of Allied military action during the war and their reparations policy after the war meant that the German Federal Republic had a
production potential in 1950 equal to that of 1938. The stock of machine
tools in France – 500,000 – was one-third that of the Federal Republic
and they were twice as old, averaging twenty years. Whereas French
industry was saddled with debts, the West German monetary reform had
amortized those of the Federal Republic. West German industry also
benefited from cheaper basic products – the price of coal was 15–20 per
cent less and electricity 25–30 per cent less than in France. West German
social charges were lower. Vertical concentrations in West German
industry led to savings in fiscal charges. Overcapacity and surplus labour
in West German industry would reduce marginal costs of production,
allow increases in productivity, and enable West German industry to

64   *The Frontier of National Sovereignty*

dump abroad in the future. The conclusion though was not that French industry should be protected permanently against West German exports, but that trade liberalization should be gradual and be accompanied by a harmonization of the two economies and an end to all West German discriminatory practices: in other words that something closer than interdependence as it had been earlier defined was to precede liberalization.

A fourth argument put forward by the Confédération Générale de Travail (CGT), the main communist-dominated trade union, was that exports from the French overseas territories would be exposed to competition on the French market with exports from the overseas territories of other OEEC countries, and that this would undermine the cohesion of the French Union. Rather than be forced to liberalize trade and payments with western Europe as a condition for further American aid, the CGT preferred to cut back on imports from the dollar area, accept a decline in living standards and forgo American aid.[10]

The main supporter of the EPU was the Ministry of Finance, on the grounds that it was only by restoring competition among European producers that the price and productivity gap with the United States would be closed and with it Europe's need for dollar aid. Without making it a precondition for accepting the EPU it continued to argue that competition would only be restored if countries agreed to liberalize trade in the same products.[11] It also considered that the attempts to re-create a trading structure based on the supposed complementarity of industrialized countries and developing ones were completely misguided. Few developing countries wanted it. France had no option but to trade and become competitive with other industrialized economies.

Two events of major importance were responsible for overcoming some of the criticisms of the EPU within the French administration. One was the announcement of the Schuman Plan which was directed towards removing the most significant advantages which the West German steel industry benefited from at the expense of its French counterparts. An initiative of Jean Monnet, head of the Planning Commission, it succeeded in removing some of the grounds for objection to the EPU of both the Ministry of Foreign Affairs and the Ministry of Industry. The second was that, quite contrary to expectations, as the West German economy got going again, its demand for imports from France increased and far outstripped French imports from the Federal Republic. Thus instead of running a deficit with the Federal Republic, France had a very healthy surplus.

As a result between July 1950 and April 1951 France registered a net surplus each month with the EPU. This enabled the government to

France: the road to integration 65

comply with the OEEC trade liberalization code so that by February 1951 it had removed quotas on 75 per cent of its 1948 private trade. After that the situation deteriorated and it was not until autumn 1954 that French payments with the EPU were back in surplus.

The obvious conclusion to be drawn is that the critics were correct and that France could not survive when exposed to a degree of competition within Europe. But in fact it could be argued that the deterioration in the payments position was due entirely to the effects of the Korean War. After the war broke out both the French government and French producers took the decision not to join in the international race to stockpile raw materials. Their argument was that it was an exaggerated response to the international situation and would be inflationary.[12] As a result French exports increased quite dramatically – particularly to the German Federal Republic, the United Kingdom and the United States, between the second and fourth quarters of 1950. But in 1951 the restrictions first on German imports and then later on British imports – both countries temporarily restoring the import restrictions earlier removed under the trade liberalization scheme – together with the inflated price of raw material imports from the sterling area caused the serious reversal of the French payments position in EPU.

The balance of payments deficit which reached a crisis in February 1952 was tackled in the same way as in the 1930s. Trade liberalization was suspended, planning was abandoned and an orthodox deflationary policy was implemented by the Pinay and Mayer governments in 1952 and 1953. Between 1952 and 1955 the French economy remained one of the most protected economies in OEEC.

This was tolerated initially by France's partners on the grounds that the state of the French balance of payments in EPU did not permit any relaxation of import controls. The evidence presented by the French was that in the period between October and December 1953 when imports had been liberalized slightly the volume of imports had increased by about 30 per cent in both industry and agriculture.[13] Nevertheless the government was under increasing pressure from the rest of OEEC to participate in the trade liberalization programme again. The Ministry of Foreign Affairs, under the guidance of Georges Bidault, wanted to resist this pressure on the grounds that the best way to overcome what was still seen to be a structural deficit in the balance of payments was to restrict imports and exploit the resources of the entire French Union to the full. The option of devaluation, which had been tried several times since the war to solve the balance of payments deficit, would not work since, it was argued, it did not solve the underlying causes of inflation in France. These were held to be lower levels of productivity and higher wages

66   *The Frontier of National Sovereignty*

relative to France's competitors in OEEC. However to cut wages, devalue and liberalize trade would lead to the sort of stop-go policies which were to become so familiar in the United Kindom and which would, in the Ministry of Foreign Affairs' view, soon undermine investment and growth and further damage French competitiveness.

But this was a policy which the rest of OEEC and the French Ministry of Finance were opposed to on the grounds that prolonged protection of the French economy destroyed European trade flows and would actually make it harder for French industry to compete. For this reason Edgar Faure, when he became Minister of Finance in June 1953, advocated devaluing the franc and resuming the OEEC trade liberalization programme. But because of the opposition of the Ministry of Foreign Affairs he agreed to set up a commission chaired by Roger Nathan to investigate the reasons for higher prices in France which caused the balance of payments deficit.

The conclusions of the Nathan Commission were that it was essentially the policy of protection which was responsible for the proliferation of small firms and for the higher prices in France. Lower productivity was not the real reason since levels of productivity varied from one firm to another and depended very much on the size and degree of concentration of the firms. Nor were higher wages the reason, since wages in France were higher than in the German Federal Republic, Italy or the Netherlands but lower than in the United Kingdom, Belgium or Switzerland. French interest rates were higher than in the United Kingdom, Belgium or Switzerland but lower than in the Federal Republic or Italy.[14] This more or less reinforced the view of the Ministry of Finance, so that Faure continued to advocate a devaluation of 15 per cent and a resumption of trade liberalization.

Bidault as Foreign Minister was not prepared to accept this. He insisted that France was unable to liberalize trade and should return to earlier ideas and implement the Second Plan, left in abeyance since 1952, to improve the levels of productivity and competitiveness of the economy. This would prepare for the day when the economy could eventually be liberalized.

A problem with putting the Second French Modernization Plan into practice was that it would be hard for France to insist that the EPU be retained if it was at the same time refusing to co-operate in its trade liberalization programme and there had been plans afoot since 1952 in the United Kingdom to get rid of it. With the improvement in British reserves in early 1954 the French government fully expected the United Kingdom to announce in the summer the convertibility of sterling, which not only would probably have meant the end of the EPU but as a consequence might have entailed also the convertibility of the Deutschmark, leaving France with the choice of retaining a non-convertible currency or being forced into a more competitive multi-lateral system at a time not of its own choosing.

Whereas the American government had previously been opposed to British plans to make sterling convertible on the grounds that it would break up the EPU and undermine the process of European integration, the situation was rather different in 1954. In view of its declining commitment to the European Defence Community treaty and its associated Political Community and in view of its reluctance to participate in the OEEC trade liberalization programme, France could no longer claim, as it had been able to in 1950–2, to be taking the lead in the integration of Europe. If the franc did not become convertible this would obstruct the workings of the ECSC through which the French steel industry was exporting increasing amounts of steel to the German Federal Republic. It would also undermine the modernization of French industry which was being stimulated with imports of German machines, machine tools and parts – the demand for which far exceeded the capacity of France itself to supply. But if the franc did become convertible then French industry would lose most of the protection which it enjoyed in the French overseas territories. Since many of these countries did not have tariffs it was largely through exchange control that France was able to ensure privileged access for French exports. Not only would convertibility open up these markets to foreign competitors but it would reveal the full extent of French privilege at a particularly sensitive time politically.[15]

The compromise worked out was that France would agree to participate in the OEEC trade liberalization programme but on condition that it could apply import taxes on a selected range of products. This would enable France to maintain its credibility as a European leader particularly in view of the threatened convertibility of sterling and the break-up of the EPU, while exposing French industry to a greater degree of European competition, without endangering the balance of payments. The imposition of import taxes had the advantage over a devaluation of the franc in that it was not applied to raw material imports or imports into the overseas territories. A further condition was that France would implement the Second Plan which had been drawn up in 1952 but not adopted for financial reasons and in view of the likely move to make sterling convertible it was agreed to set up a commission to explore the consequences of forming a customs union with the overseas territories.

68   *The Frontier of National Sovereignty*

FRENCH POLICY TOWARDS THE FRANC AREA[16]

An integral part of the strategy for restoring France after 1945 had been to strengthen the French empire, renamed the French Union for political reasons. As in France itself, it was recognized that this could best be achieved by improving living standards largely through a programme to stimulate economic development. Originally the plan for the social and economic development of the overseas territories was to be spread over ten years but in 1948 this was reduced to four years to bring it into line with the European Recovery Programme (ERP). Each of the three North African countries drew up its own plan and in 1948 these plans were also dovetailed with the time-scale of the ERP. One of the main issues at the end of the war had been whether these development plans should be carried out by giving the colonies full tariff autonomy, and thus not oblige them to import from metropolitan France if they could buy the imports more cheaply elsewhere, or whether France should control trade with these countries even more tightly in order to make them run a balance of payments surplus with the rest of the world and thereby help solve France's external deficit.

In 1934 the French government had considered the conclusion of a French-style Ottawa agreement with its colonies. It was rejected however because in certain important products the French colonies were considered to be competitors either amongst themselves or with respect to France. The government chose instead to restrict the trade in, and in some cases the production and transport facilities for, colonial products.[17]

In 1941 and 1942 the Vichy government, largely for practical reasons, had given the colonies full tariff autonomy for the duration of the war, so that after the war a decision on their future had to be taken. The reason that tariffs were the central issue was largely because in its white paper on trade and employment published in December 1945 the United States had talked of eliminating imperial preferences and of rejecting any preference or customs agreements which were not a full customs union. The French government itself was divided over the issue. The Ministry of Overseas France was in favour of giving complete customs autonomy to the colonies to enable them to buy at cheap world prices and to protect their own economies from competition from metropolitan France. Other ministries called for a return to a system of preferences to provide metropolitan France with both supplies and markets. The steel industry wanted colonial markets, especially if the colonies were going to be industrialized, whereas agriculture wanted greater complementarity between metropolitan and colonial agricultural production.

What the French government realized was that whereas the United States treated the countries of the French Union as a set of quite distinct customs territories, the entire franc zone, despite having different currencies, was treated as one unit in the IMF. Alphand, head of the economic section of the Ministry of Foreign Affairs, who was himself in favour of granting a large degree of autonomy to the colonies, felt that it was a matter for the French government and not the American government to decide. But sometime in the course of 1946 American policy softened somewhat and the US administration began to accept the continuation of a preferential regime if it was needed to safeguard the vital interests of a country. The Ministry of Overseas France in turn modified its opposition to preferential tariffs and in October 1946 argued that a preferential regime would be acceptable provided that it did not result in higher prices for the French Overseas Territories.[18]

However the whole debate was to prove largely irrelevant, since in the years after the war France controlled the trade of the DOM-TOMs through the use of exchange controls and quotas rather than tariffs. Largely on account of the shortage of foreign exchange and their development needs the countries of the French Union ran a trade deficit with both metropolitan France and the rest of the world between 1948 and 1952. The size of the trade deficit with metropolitan France was 537,600 million francs in this period. Over the same period French investment in the DOM-TOMs totalled 1,340,000 million francs of which 662,700 million francs were loans from the French Treasury and 533,800 million came from the counterpart of Marshall Aid.[19]

While metropolitan assistance to the Overseas Territories under the first plan was 55 per cent subsidy and 45 per cent loans from the Fonds de modernisation et d'équipement (FME) through the intermediary of the Caisse Centrale de la France d'Outre-mer, 100 per cent of the metropolitan contribution to the development plans of North Africa took the form of loans from the FME. Largely for political reasons the first plan put more emphasis on social rather than economic investment in North Africa which meant that those economies were not growing fast enough to finance the increased demands on the general budget arising from the better provision of social amenities. Given that most of the resources of the FME came from the counterpart of Marshall Aid, as this ended the metropolitan budget had to assume all the costs. For these two reasons the financing of the second plan for North Africa threatened to be contentious. Either investment had to be cut or the contribution from metropolitan France had to be increased.

Furthermore because the metropolitan contribution took the form of loans rather than grants, albeit at interest rates lower than those

70   *The Frontier of National Sovereignty*

prevailing in the market, France did not gain the benefit of any political capital.[20] When the FME was replaced by the Fonds d'expansion economique (FEE) the French government lost all control over the uses of it made by the North African governments. The loans simply became part of the local budget.[21]

As we have seen, the Ministry of Foreign Affairs saw the trade and payments arrangements within the French Union as offering a more stable and secure basis for restoring French independence than the closer association with western Europe advocated by the United States and supported by the Ministry of Finance. However in 1954 this concept of stability was called into question. Quite apart from domestic political unrest in North Africa, it was events in western Europe which threatened the French system of economic control. Currency convertibility would remove the main form of protection which France enjoyed in many of the markets of the French Union. Second, the agreement reached by OEEC in April 1954 to extend trade liberalization to members' overseas territories threatened France's trade monopoly even more directly and immediately.

Trade liberalization in OEEC between 1949 and 1952 had not been applied automatically to all the countries of the French Union. The French government decided to extend it to Algeria, New Caledonia and the overseas departments as well as Saint-Pierre and Miquelon but not to Morocco, French Equatorial Africa, Togo and Cameroon. Each of the latter group had an international statute which prevented it from discriminating in favour of OEEC member states.[22]

Even if the franc were not made convertible immediately after a declaration of sterling convertibility, France would still have to begin to revise tariffs if it were to get preferential access to these markets or even renegotiate their international statutes in view of the cost to the French exchequer of financing development in them. Since any upward tariff revision was contrary to GATT, one alternative was to turn the entire French Union into a customs union. It was to assess the implications of such a policy as well as to draw up a balance sheet of the existing arrangements that a major study was initiated on 10 May 1954 under the direction of General Corniglion-Molinier, a minister of state. He set out to identify a coherent long-term direction to the economic relations between metropolitan France and the departments and territories overseas. Quite apart from the external pressure to change the system it was coming under internal attack both in the colonies and in France itself. The DOM-TOMs blamed their relative underdevelopment on having to import investment goods and other manufactures from metropolitan France which, apart from steel, were at prices higher than world prices, whereas the French complained at having to cover both the external and the domestic budget deficits of the colonies while domestic agriculture faced increasing competition from colonial exports.

There was plenty of evidence to support each case. A study quoted by the Ministry of Overseas France calculated that in 1953 the overseas territories had paid 1,320 million francs above world prices for flour, 1,870 million francs for cars and lorries and 16,090 million francs for investment goods. In the case of Algeria, which was by far the largest single market in the franc area for goods from metropolitan France, the price difference was considerable. In 1954 Algeria imported 21 per cent of all French car exports. Belgium–Luxemburg, the second largest market, was far behind, taking 12 per cent. Furthermore the unit value to Belgium–Luxemburg was much lower, 42 million francs compared to 53 million francs to Algeria. Similarly Algeria was the single largest market for metallurgical goods taking 16 per cent of all exports. The average unit price was 19 million francs compared with an average unit price of 7 million for exports in the same category to Brazil. Whereas metropolitan goods sold in the DOM-TOMs at a level of prices on average 19.7 per cent above world prices of similar goods, goods from the DOM-TOMs sold in France itself at a price level only 9.5 per cent above that of world prices. Thus French industry benefited to the extent that it was able to export to the departments and territories overseas at much higher prices than to the rest of the world, and that when it exported to Europe at a loss it was able to make this up on exports to the DOM-TOMs.

Not surprisingly given such a level of protection and given the emphasis of the Monnet Plan on increasing production to supply the markets of the franc area France ran a large trade surplus with the rest of the franc area. Between 1949 and 1955 it amounted to 1,075,800 million francs. In this period however the French invested 1,340,000 million francs of public funds in those territories and less than 100,000 million francs in private funds. Any reduction in the level of protection enjoyed by metropolitan producers in these markets threatened to undermine confidence in the investment plan. Yet as the study directed by Corniglion-Molinier concluded, given the very high level of trade between the DOM-TOMs and metropolitan France – 72.5 per cent of all their imports and 76 per cent of their exports – it would be difficult if not dangerous to increase the links by forming a customs union. The Ministry of Foreign Affairs still believed that in the short term a policy of liberalization in the context of OEEC could be combined with a protection of the French Union as long as the time was used to modernize production in both France and the DOM-TOMs.[23]

72   *The Frontier of National Sovereignty*

In February 1955 the Commissariat au Plan carried out its own investigation into the implications of integrating the French Union into Europe of the Six. The broad conclusions were that it would benefit Europe because the French overseas territories would provide markets, sources of supply and investment opportunities. It was expected that it would also probably benefit the overseas territories because they would pay less for imports, which would lead to an improvement in their living standards, to an increase in their exports, and possibly to an increase in productive investment provided that such investment was not solely for the purpose of extracting raw materials. But the planners concluded that it would probably not benefit France. In economic terms France would lose valuable export markets or would no longer be able to charge higher prices to pay for subsidizing exports in world markets. And if France had to carry the costs of financing unproductive investment while sharing productive investment with others then it would bear a disproportionate burden.

On the other hand it was clear that the French government could no longer cope with the burden of financing investment in the overseas territories on its own and it was failing to mobilize private investment. At the same time it was under increasing pressure to develop these economies if only because of the example from elsewhere in Africa. It was for that reason that the planners saw an advantage in some form of closer association between the French Union and western Europe if in return for opening up the markets of the French Union they could secure a contribution to investment in their economies.[24] Thus even before the Benelux relaunched proposals for a common market in spring 1955 the French planners were already coming to the conclusion that the future of the French Union lay in some form of integration with Europe of the Six.

THE ROLE OF AGRICULTURE IN FRENCH ECONOMIC DEVELOPMENT

After the war official policy, enshrined in the Monnet Plan, had been based on expanding the basic sectors of the economy. Agricultural machinery was selected as one of the six priority sectors on the grounds that the mechanization of agriculture would release labour for the expanding industrial sectors while improving the productivity of those remaining on the land. It was accompanied by a pricing policy designed to restructure cultivation to match more closely changes in domestic consumption. This meant that output of wheat was to decline relative to that of meat, dairy products, fruit and vegetables, with the ultimate objective of making France as nearly self-sufficient as possible in foodstuffs. This was to correct the pre-war situation in which France, despite having a third of the labour force employed in agriculture, was a net food importer. However, one bad harvest in 1947 revealed how precarious this policy was. As a result of the relatively low price for wheat, the area sown was cut back and France had to import extra wheat from the United States, causing the severe balance of payments crisis of 1947.

This led to a shift in policy in 1948. Under the revised version of the Monnet Plan the whole of agriculture was made a priority sector in terms of access to investment and supplies. The understanding was that if surpluses were generated as a result, the government would not allow prices to fall but would negotiate export contracts instead. And to confirm its commitment the French government registered as a net exporter in the International Wheat Agreement. However since voting strength there was based on trade rather than production France had only seven votes out of 2,000 and thus had no effective influence over prices. Partly for that reason and partly because in the conditions of global food shortages which prevailed until 1952 better deals were available, the French preferred to dispose of their surpluses by negotiating bilateral contracts in which agricultural products were exchanged for industrial raw materials.[25]

However by 1953 the situation had changed. The global food deficit had turned into a surplus. The price of wheat exported under the International Wheat Agreement fell from 87 dollars per tonne to 73 dollars compared with French producer prices of 102 dollars.[26] It was in this context that the French planners announced their second plan to increase agricultural output by 20 per cent above the 1952 level. While it was clear that considerable gains in productivity could be achieved from investing in French agriculture there was no incentive to do so if as a result output increased and prices fell. And indeed the budget submitted by the Ministry of Agriculture for 1954 reflected this fear on the part of French farmers. The President of the Committee for Agricultural Production and Rural Equipment wrote to the Planning Commissariat in October 1953 expressing its concern that the planned increase in output would lead to overproduction and a crisis similar to that of 1930–6. The commission also complained about subsidized production in the overseas territories competing with French agriculture. Yet the expansion was justified by the planners on the grounds that of the three possible policy options for agriculture, expansion was the only one which would stimulate the development of the whole economy.

One option was to increase productivity without increasing production simply by ending protection and by running down the

74   *The Frontier of National Sovereignty*

agricultural labour force. This was ruled out on the grounds that the industrial sector was not large enough to absorb the labour transfers. The other option was for the state to continue protecting agriculture but not take any part in restructuring or modernizing it. This would result in a widening gap between living standards in industry and agriculture and an acceleration of the rural exodus with the youngest and most able leaving first. Since the planners felt that both of these options would provoke considerable political discontent and instability and exacerbate the balance of payments deficit neither was entertained for serious consideration.[27]

Of course to try to increase agricultural production and exports required the co-operation of farmers and this was seen to depend on state guarantees that an increase in production would not lead to a collapse in prices. This meant guaranteed export markets. But as the French governments' experience between 1947 and 1952 had demonstrated, it was exceedingly difficult to negotiate export contracts with foreign governments until export surpluses actually existed. Yet without such contracts French farmers would not increase production. To break the vicious circle the planners argued that if need be France would have to be prepared to import food in the first instance in order to provide exports. It would also have to subsidize these exports if it was necessary to find purchasers.

So whereas under the revised version of the first plan the objective behind increased agricultural production was dollar saving with exports being a welcome but uncertain bonus, by 1953 the experience of an expansion in agricultural production together with falling prices and peasant riots led to a change in policy. While the underlying objective of the second plan was still to modernize the sector it was now argued that the most painless, indeed perhaps the only, way to do this was by negotiating export contracts. This new awareness necessitated a much clearer understanding of the food import needs of other European countries and of how French agriculture could be restructured to meet those needs best.

What was essentially a policy choice based on domestic factors was then given a wider but quite spurious justification by the planners. French agricultural surpluses which were intended as a result of diverting increasing amounts of public funds into agriculture would, the planners argued, meet Europe's need for increasing amounts of basic foodstuffs. They seemed to think that rising incomes together with a greater equality of income distribution in Europe would result in a higher per capita consumption of foodstuffs whereas most of the historical evidence pointed to the contrary. The second assumption,

France: the road to integration   75

Table 5 Relative shares in Europe's food trade, 1952 (per cent)

	Imports	*Exports*
United Kingdom	38	
German Federal Republic	20	
Switzerland	7	
France	7	8
Belgium–Luxemburg	7	8
Netherlands		19
Denmark		18
Italy		8
Sweden		8

Source: French national archives Commissariat au Plan CGP, 'Projet de rapport général des Commissions de la production agricole et de l'équipement rural', 22 September 1953.

equally mistaken, was that rising prices in developing economies, from which Europe had traditionally imported cheap food, would lead to a closure of the price gap and a reduction in trade between Europe and the developing economies and particularly of exports of manufactured goods in exchange for imported food.

If France was going to benefit from these assumed trends and increase its food exports its main competitors in meat and dairy products would be Denmark and the Netherlands, and in wheat the United States and Canada. In sugar the main exporters were the United States and Central America which together accounted for 50 per cent of Europe's imports, with the rest supplied by Denmark, France and Benelux. Since French agriculture was relatively undermechanized and productivity per worker was lower than that of its major competitors the planners were quite confident that France had considerably more potential for growth and price reductions than had its main competitors. But France would only be able to exploit this potential market in Europe if it undertook the modernization which had been called for since the war. However it was not until 1954 as table 6 shows that public investment in agriculture mirrored the public rhetoric. Although there were substantial wheat surpluses for export in 1950 and 1951, in general it was not until after 1953 that the problem of finding a market for food surpluses became a serious one.

When the French National Assembly failed to ratify the European Defence Community (EDC) treaty in August 1954, Prime Minister Mendès-France tried to recapture the initiative by proposing the creation of a Franco-German economic committee to bind the two economies more closely together. However in view of the West German

76 The Frontier of National Sovereignty

Table 6 Public expenditure in agriculture and industry (as percentage of OEEC total)

Year	Agriculture	Trade and industry
1947	1.6	10.0
1948	1.1	23.0
1949	1.8	21.5
1950	1.3	16.6
1951	1.8	8.2
1953	1.5	6.6
1954	4.6	9.6
1955	5.5	10.6
1956	5.3	9.8
1957	3.7	8.9
1958	4.2	7.8

Source: C. André and R. Delorme, *L'état et l'économie. Un essai d'explication de l'évolution des dépenses publiques en France 1870–1980* (Paris, 1983).

government's hostility to any structure which brought together industrialists and civil servants along the lines envisaged by the French, all that actually emerged from the initiative was a commercial agreement governing non-liberalized trade. Since the German Federal Republic had liberalized most of its imports of raw materials and manufactured goods the main French interest in the agreement was to get guaranteed markets for some key agricultural products, particularly wheat and sugar. On the other hand since France was still edging tentatively towards liberalizing 20 per cent of its 1948 private trade by December 1954, the German Federal Republic was anxious to get greater access to French markets. For that reason the Germans wanted to negotiate a three-year agreement allowing for some exceptions to be negotiated on an annual basis, whereas the French wanted the reverse. In the end the Germans agreed to the French proposal and offered long-term contracts for French agricultural products to a value of 9,000 million francs above the level of the current year. This was to include 500,000 tonnes of wheat in the first year and 400,000 tonnes in the two subsequent years, as well as 250,000 tonnes of other cereals each year, but the Federal Republic refused to give any commitment for sugar, meat or milk products.

At the same time the German side insisted on being able to export to France goods of the same value which were still under quota restrictions. This meant that as the French reduced their import restrictions they would have to find additional items which the Federal Republic could export freely. The total value of imports into France from the Federal Republic which were subject to quantitative restrictions was 18,000

France: the road to integration   77

Table 7 French wheat exports to the United Kingdom and the German Federal
Republic, 1951–4

Year	United Kingdom		German Fed. Rep.	
	Quantity (1,000 tonnes)	*Price (per 1,000 tonnes in million francs)*	*Quantity (1,000 tonnes)*	*Price (per 1,000 tonnes in million francs)*
1951	32.3	34.9	227.5	30.0
1952	21.9	36.6	55.8	24.8
1953	17.1	22.7	175.5	30.5
1954	332.5	20.8	371.0	23.3

Source: *Statistique mensuelle du commerce extérieur de la France.*

million francs. Since the Germans were proposing to import an extra
9,000 million francs of goods and demanding full equality of treatment,
this would effectively mean widening French quotas by 50 per cent in
respect of imports from the Federal Republic.

In the final negotiations at the end of April 1955 France tried to avoid
complete reciprocity, bargaining for exports of 500,000 tonnes of wheat
to the Federal Republic each year for three years as well as 85,000 tonnes
of sugar, without having to widen quotas on the same value of imports.
The real worry was that if the French accepted reciprocity with the
Federal Republic they would find it difficult not to extend it to the United
Kingdom and Switzerland which until then had not made any such
demands in return for French agricultural exports.[28] And as table 7
indicates, in 1954 the United Kingdom had imported nearly as much
wheat as the German Federal Republic although at a lower price. What
is clear is that when Benelux proposed to reopen negotiations to set up a
common market among the six member countries of the European Coal
and Steel Community the implications for French industry, in terms of
exposure to competition, were not very different from what the West
Germans were demanding in return for accepting French agricultural
exports.

NEGOTIATING THE TREATY OF ROME

It was the French Ministry of Foreign Affairs which still remained
opposed to joining a European common market when Benelux relaunched the idea. Given that the option they had favoured earlier of a
closer association within the French Union was being dismissed at the
official level, the Quai d'Orsay was in the embarrassing position of not

78   *The Frontier of National Sovereignty*

having an external economic policy at all both before and for some time
after the Messina conference. The internal debate revolved once again
around the ability of French industry to compete in a common market.

The situation at the beginning of 1955 was that, given the way it was
calculated within OEEC, trade liberalization in France had reached 79
per cent – albeit with special taxes on imports. The breakdown for the
three main categories of imports was 96 per cent for raw materials, 65 per
cent for manufactured goods and 64 per cent for agricultural products.
Import taxes were applied only to 3 per cent of raw materials – mainly
lead, some fertilizers, cement, tar and some skins. The increase in
imports of raw materials which had taken place was not considered to be
due to liberalization but to the increase in demand from industry itself. It
was thus not felt that the formation of a common market for raw
materials would make any difference – except that national tariffs, which
were 5–10 per cent, would be removed to be replaced by an external
tariff. French production should not decline. The problems lay elsewhere.

As far as manufacturing industry was concerned a special committee
was set up in 1955 to calculate the effects of trade liberalization on
machine tools, agricultural machinery and automobiles. The main
European producers of machine tools were the German Federal
Republic and the United Kingdom where production was over three
times higher than in France. Other suppliers were Switzerland and Italy
where production was less than in France. They had all removed their
quantitative restrictions on imports. Tariff protection on machine tools
ranged between 7 and 25 per cent in Italy, but only between 6 and 8 per
cent in the Federal Republic, and was fixed at 20 per cent in the United
Kingdom, which was similar to France. It was concluded that the main
reason why the French machine tool industry was not competitive was
that social and fiscal charges were higher in France and that France did
not have the same need as the Federal Republic to export given that the
German machine tool industry was so over-equipped. But the committee did not fear the effects of a common market on the French
machine tool industry, judging the market to be much less open to new
suppliers than the trade in consumer goods. It recommended a gradual
liberalization accompanied by an import tax. Since preserving the
special taxes on imports would not have been possible either in OEEC or
the separate negotiations with the Federal Republic, the committee's
recommendations were not acceptable either to the industrialists
themselves or at ministerial level.

Price disparities were also a problem for agricultural machinery. But
in this case the reasons were not considered to be the higher wages and

Table 8 Structure of costs in the European car industry

	Price of steel products	Weight of steel price in car retail price before tax	Per cent difference in car price due to steel price	Level of wages including social charges	Weighting of labour costs in car retail price before tax	Per cent differences in car price due to labour costs	Total per cent difference
France	100	20	–	100	40	–	–
German Fed. Rep.	100	20	0	75	40	10	10
United Kingdom	80	20	4	93	40	2.8	6.8
Italy	100	20	0	74	46*	6	6

* Including the obligatory cost of retaining surplus labour

Source: Quai Branly, Interministerial Committee for Questions of European Integration, SGGI 121.9.

social charges in France but rather the lack of concentration and specialization in this sector in France and the high cost of investment. If the French were to specialize in the production of petrol-driven engines for tractors leaving diesel ones for the German Federal Republic then trade liberalization could, it was argued, be very beneficial.

The car industry was heavily protected by tariffs in all the main producing countries. Tariffs were highest in Italy at 35–45 per cent, 30–35 per cent in the Federal Republic, 33.3 per cent in the United Kingdom and 30 per cent in France. The Federal Republic had, though, removed its quotas. French car imports represented 1 per cent of production and were fifteen times less than car exports. But the committee identified a number of obstacles to trade liberalization. French prices were higher than those of France's main competitors mainly due to higher wages and social charges as table 8 indicates. Other explanations for differences in car prices were that French prices incorporated a margin for financing exports which amounted to about 1.5 per cent of the construction price. Prices in both the German Federal Republic and the United Kingdom were said to benefit from greater economies of scale. If French car production could reach the same level, it was argued, savings of 2–4 per cent could be achieved through replicating the same scale economies. At the same time it was suggested, somewhat oddly, that the West German car industry was under much greater pressure to export since car ownership was very much lower in the Federal Republic than in France –

80 *The Frontier of National Sovereignty*

Table 9 Output and exports of motor vehicles, 1955

	Passenger cars	Commercial vehicles, etc	Total	Exports	Exports as percentage of production
United Kingdom	897,500	339,500	1,237,000	536,300	43
German Fed. Rep.	692,000	216,400	908,800	409,000	45
France	553,300	171,700	725,000	164,000	22.5
Italy	230,800	38,000	268,300	74,650	28

Source: Quai Branly, Interministerial Committee for Questions of European Integration, SGGI 121.9.

one car for every thirty-four inhabitants there compared with one car for every fourteen inhabitants in France. This justified rather than explained the situation since the lower level of car ownership in the Federal Republic could have resulted in fewer exports and a greater concentration on exploiting the potential of the domestic market.

The only condition under which the French car industry could be liberalized was in the committee's opinion if a compensation tax of 15 per cent were added to tariffs of 30 per cent and if the car industry was liberalized at the same time in both the United Kingdom and Italy. Even then the risks to the French car industry were, it was estimated, serious.

The committee also investigated the effect of trade liberalization on intermediate products and consumer goods. Nearly half of total French imports of these goods came from the German Federal Republic, Italy, Belgium and the Netherlands. Even with an import tax imports tended to be very sensitive to trade liberalization. This was with tariff protection of 25 per cent and import taxes of more than 10 per cent. The committee selected three sectors for detailed study: the cotton industry, artificial textiles, and paper and card.

Its conclusions for the cotton industry were extremely pessimistic. Most OEEC countries had removed quotas and their tariffs were lower than those in France, while the French industry was further protected by an import tax of 15–20 per cent. This was necessary because apart from the usual explanations for higher French prices – namely, higher wages and social charges – the cotton industry faced declining demand and was saddled with overcapacity. Thus even though the industry was relatively concentrated, the institution of a common market would still, it appeared, threaten a large number of French firms.

The situation for artificial fibres was little better. France was the only country in OEEC not to have removed quotas on rayon and one of the few not to have liberalized staple fibres. French tariffs were also higher – 20 per cent and 18 per cent compared with 13 per cent in the Federal Republic and 10 per cent and 6 per cent in Benelux. The committee considered that liberalization, if accompanied by an import tax of 15 per cent, would compensate for differences in price due to differences in labour costs. But if tariffs also were eliminated, as in a common market, then the fact that French prices were 15 and 30 per cent higher than those of the other member states would have serious consequences.

Only the paper industry presented few problems. Quotas had been removed, tariffs on paper and card were 18 and 25 per cent and they also had special import taxes of 7 and 15 per cent. Most imports came from Scandinavia although the German Federal Republic supplied some. Provided that the industry was given time to reorganize itself into larger production units the committee saw few obstacles in a common market of six.

The committee's overall conclusions were that the problems raised by liberalizing trade within 'Little Europe' were really no less than within OEEC. Since imports from the Federal Republic, Benelux and Italy represented 70 per cent of imports from OEEC, unless the formation of a customs union were accompanied by a devaluation of the franc, safeguard clauses would be crucial for most branches of industry. But the alternative of retaining quotas temporarily would not ensure that industries made the necessary conversions to ease their entry into a common market. This was true even for modernized industries for which demand was growing such as the car industry, the machine tool industry or the electrical construction industry.

It is somewhat surprising, given the pessimistic nature of this committee's conclusions, that the French government did sign the Treaty of Rome and that French exports did so well as a result. Since subsequent studies showed that the devaluation of 1958 was not the only factor responsible for this successful performance it indicates that French industry was stronger than it liked the French government to believe.

The Ministry of Foreign Affairs was equally dissatisfied and sceptical about the findings of the committee and consulted Milton Gilbert, the director of Statistics and National Accounts at OEEC.[29] It found him sceptical about the worth of studies which tried to compare prices and competitiveness. Gilbert dismissed the view which had been held consistently by the Ministry of Finance that the French external deficit

82 *The Frontier of National Sovereignty*

was an indication of the lack of competitiveness of the French economy
and could be solved by devaluing the franc. It was, said Gilbert, not a
global problem which could be tackled with global remedies. On the
other hand it was practically impossible for a government to carry out
detailed studies comparing production costs to find out which industries
were not competitive and why, since industries would never reveal the
real situation. The only purpose of such studies was the political one of
justifying or recommending particular levels or forms of protection.[30]

What Gilbert recommended was that specific factors should be
identified which distorted costs and prices so that these could then be
harmonized. These included disparities between male and female wages,
the length of the working week and the age of retirement.

This was not a new argument of course. It had already given rise to
studies carried out by the High Authority of the European Coal and
Steel Community as well as the Institut National de Statistique et des
Etudes Economiques (INSEE) and the French Ministry of Industry, and
with very conflicting results. The High Authority argued that rather than
a comparison of wages and social charges only, all costs to the employer
needed to be taken into account. These included family allowances,
perks, costs of recruitment and professional training. While social
security costs in France were higher than in the other member states, all
costs were not. In the car industry social charges were 45 per cent of
hourly wages in France, 35 per cent in the German Federal Republic
and 25 per cent in Belgium, but the overall costs of labour were
0.55 dollars per hour in France, 0.53 dollars in the Federal Republic and
0.76 dollars in Belgium. The average hourly wage in the steel industry
was 284 francs for the Federal Republic and 262 francs for France.
Indeed the differences in the overall wage cost between regions in the
same country was often greater than between countries. Once again in
the case of coal, the differences in the overall wage cost between France
and the German Federal Republic was 36 francs per hour, while that
between Lorraine and the mines in the centre of France was 59 francs
and between Lorraine and the Nord/Pas-de-Calais mines 47 francs.[31]
The French contention that taxes were higher in France was also
rejected. While it was true that indirect taxes were high in France, these
were completely reimbursed when production was exported, whereas
imports were subjected to the same tax as national production.

However the French government refused to accept these findings also.
One major omission of such a study based on the coal and steel
industries was, it argued, that since virtually no women were employed
in these industries the great disparity between male and female wages
which affected such industries as the textile industry, was ignored. Since,

Table 10 Production costs in the woollen industry

	France	UK	Belg.	Neth.	Italy
Wages: male	100	122	107	84	65
female	100	104	88	56	55
Obligatory charges on wages (as % of wage)	52		30.9	30.7	68.2
Cost per man-hour	100	male 88	92	72	72
		female 75	76	48	61
Energy: electricity	100	72	110	115	75
coal	100	64	104	93	117
petrol	100	73	68	56	108
Maintenance	100	70	96	74	70
Amortization:					
spinning equipment	100	89	87	86	80
weaving equipment	100	85	90	90	91
Wool credits	100	99.53	99.43	99.2	100

Source: Quai Branly, Interministerial Committee for Questions of European Integration, SGGI 121.9, Direction Générale des Prix et des Enquêtes Economiques, 23 May 1956.

it argued, France was the only country to apply the Geneva Convention relating to equal pay for women, this was critical to explaining differences in production costs.

A comparison of costs in the woollen industry goes some way to bearing out this contention (table 10), although it does not show the relative proportion of male and female labour in the different countries. INSEE had carried out its own study published in May 1955 which concluded that of all the factors entering into the calculation of wage costs, the length of the working week and therefore of overtime and differences between male and female wages, were the most important. This made the calculation of average costs fairly irrelevant. In France overtime pay started at 40 hours, in the United Kingdom at 45 and in the German Federal Republic, Benelux, Italy and Switzerland it was at 48 hours.

The debate remained inconclusive leaving France still with no clear line of policy on how to fit its great effort at national reconstruction into the evolving multilateral international economic system. What forced the issue was the United Kingdom's first proposal in July 1956 to OEEC for a free trade area covering OEEC members including the Six, but excluding agriculture. Although the Spaak Committee, to which the proposals for a customs union of the six ECSC states had been referred without any positive commitment on the French side, had made no

84   *The Frontier of National Sovereignty*

recommendations regarding agriculture which pointed the way to
solving France's problems, it accepted that it would be included in the
common market but would require special treatment. As we have seen,
French plans for developing the economy were seen to depend on the
success of the policy of agricultural modernization which in turn
depended on securing access to the West German market for food
exports. The fear was that the British proposal of a free trade area might
be more attractive to the West Germans and undermine at a stroke
French economic policy as well of course as French foreign policy in
Europe which aimed at closer links with the Federal Republic. When the
government met to decide its policy towards the common market in
September 1956 it was ironically the Minister of Finance, the Socialist
Paul Ramadier, who now opposed it. His position was based on the
deteriorating situation in Algeria which, he argued, would require
France to operate a closed economy if not a war economy for some time.
But his was a minority voice.

Both Prime Minister Guy Mollet and Foreign Minister Christian
Pineau argued that a policy of European integration was the only way to
solve France's economic and colonial problems. What was agreed was
that provided a number of conditions were met including the harmonization of social legislation and arrangements for the French
overseas territories then France should sign the treaty.[32] Despite the
opposition of the German negotiators to any harmonization of social
legislation on the grounds that the French problem was a monetary one
which should be solved by altering the exchange rate, Adenauer for
political reasons overruled them during his highly secret talks with
Mollet in November 1956.[33]

Similarly, although everyone apart from Belgium rejected the connection made by France between trade liberalization and investment in
the member states' overseas territories, a compromise was reached. Von
Brentano, the German Minister of Foreign Affairs, proposed that in
return for an annual investment allocation of 100 million dollars shared
among the Six over a period of twelve to fifteen years, the same
programme of trade liberalization would apply on trade with these
countries as on trade within the Six. The Italian government, which was
already committed to a ten-year investment programme in the South of
Italy, objected to such a long-term commitment in the overseas
territories of France, Belgium and the Netherlands. As a compromise
Spaak suggested that the German proposal apply in the first instance for
five years. In that case, the Germans argued, it should take the form of a
Marshall Plan – in other words investment with no commercial strings
or obligations. But Pineau found this politically unacceptable on the

grounds that it would mean that French territories were being subsidized by the German Federal Republic.

The compromise arrangement which was eventually settled upon was that the six states would contribute 581 million dollars in investment over five years with France and the German Federal Republic contributing 200 million dollars each. But there were to be different arrangements for agriculture for France and its overseas territories. France was offered long-term purchasing contracts for agricultural exports until such time as the special arrangements for a common agricultural policy, announced in the treaty, were completed. The overseas territories were excluded from this, but they were to have preferential tariffs. In return the tariff concessions which they granted to exports from the five other common market countries at the end of the five-year period were not to be the same as for France but rather to be equal to the difference between French tariffs and those previously applied to the other five.[34]

CONCLUSIONS

Despite frequent changes of government under the Fourth Republic there was a basic continuity in the debate over the best framework in which to promote French economic development. The Ministry of Finance, which until the Socialist Paul Ramadier took over in 1956 was held by centre-right politicians, advocated a policy of increased interdependence in OEEC as a prelude to participation in the one-world system announced by Bretton Woods. The assumption was that greater exposure to competition would lead to an improvement in productivity and help correct the external deficit. But the Ministry of Finance no longer had the monopoly which it had enjoyed in the inter-war period over economic policy-making in France, and particularly where foreign economic policy was concerned it had to take account of the views of the Ministry of Foreign Affairs. Although the political leadership of this ministry changed quite frequently between 1954 and 1956 there was considerable continuity in its recommendations throughout the entire period from 1945. Basically it opposed trade liberalization on the grounds that it would weaken the French economy, escalate the disintegration of the French Union and exacerbate the external deficit. But its preferred policy, which was based on economic expansion within the protected confines of the French Union, was not viable in the long term. France could not continue to resist the pressure from OEEC to participate in the trade liberalization programme, because it wanted to retain the EPU with its easy credit arrangements and wanted also to

86   *The Frontier of National Sovereignty*

resist moves by the United Kingdom to take over the leadership of
Europe by dismantling European institutions and re-establishing the
one-world system of Bretton Woods according to its own timetable.
Furthermore the trade and payments arrangements within the French
Union were coming under pressure from both France and the countries
of the Union.

Where the planners played a key role was in offering a long-term
perspective for economic policy. In many respects the first plan had
avoided the critical problems raised by French economic interdependence by arguing that as a result of an investment programme
implemented within the protected confines of the French Union the
French economy would be able to participate freely in a one-world
multilateral trade and payments system. By 1952 this had been proved to
be wrong. A basic problem was that although the investment programme increased the external deficit, without it French industry could
not meet domestic demand. As the level of protection was reduced this
demand was met from imports which in the absence of external aid could
not be financed. Moreover although the internal financing of investment
in metropolitan France was increasingly met from private sources, as
American aid declined, this was not true for investment in the French
Union. The longer-term solution advocated by the planners was based
on an expansion of agricultural exports and the participation of other
countries in the investment programmes of the French Union. Mendès-
France hoped to achieve these economic objectives through bilateral
inter-governmental arrangements particularly with the German Federal
Republic. However given the conditions demanded by the Federal
German government in return for accepting French agricultural
exports, the result was not particularly advantageous for France and
risked setting a precedent for other governments to follow. While the
integration of the French economy with the other five European
economies was not a French initiative in 1955, the form which it took
owed much to French conditions drawn up to ensure what was perceived
to be the French national interest.

As the debate outlined in this chapter has shown, integration was a
policy choice which was not forced on the French government through
the pressure of technological developments, or trading patterns, or
external political events such as the Suez fiasco. While the need to
contain the German Federal Republic played a part in the decision this
does not in itself explain the form which the European Community was
to take. Where the decision was to a certain extent inevitable was that by
1956 it was clear that the French government could no longer achieve its
objectives within the existing framework of interdependence in OEEC or

in the alternative one offered by the one-world system of Bretton Woods and GATT.

Notes

1 P. Guillen, 'La France et la négociation des Traités de Rome: l'Euratom', in Enrico Serra (ed.), *The Relaunching of Europe and the Treaties of Rome* (Brussels, 1989).
2 François Caron, *An Economic History of Modern France* (London, 1979), p. 327.
3 William James Adams, *Restructuring the French Economy. Government and the Rise of Market Competition since World War II* (Washington DC, 1989), p. 122.
4 One of the main concerns of this 'plan' was to safeguard the value of official reserves in the event of a devaluation of sterling against the dollar, but this was not taken into consideration by either the Americans or the British.
5 French Ministry of Foreign Affairs (hereafter MAE) DE-CE, 1945–60. Service de Coopération Economique, 'Effet de la libéralisation des échanges sur les territoires d'outre-mer', 16 July 1949.
6 MAE, DE-CE, 1945–60, 351 Conseil Economique, 26 January 1950.
7 French Ministry of Finance, the Budget and Economic Affairs, *Inventaire de la situation financière* (Paris, 1951).
8 A. S. Milward, *The Reconstruction of Western Europe, 1945–1951* (London, 1984).
9 French Ministry of Industry (hereafter Min. IND) 830587 Ind 11, report by Bellier, January 1950.
10 MAE, DE-CE, 1945–60, 351 Conseil Economique, 26 January 1950.
11 French national archives (hereafter AN), Interministerial Committee for Questions of European Integration (hereafter F[60ter]) 474, 12 May 1950, Schweitzer to Filippi.
12 AN, French Ministry of Agriculture (hereafter F[10]) 5628. French Ministry of Finance and Economic Affairs, Comité des Importations, 'Compte rendu de la séance', 24 August 1950.
13 MAE, 1945–60, 353, Comité de direction des échanges, 3 April 1954.
14 French Ministry of Finance and Economic Affairs, *Commission créée par arrêté du 6 janvier 1954 pour l'étude des disparités entre les prix français et étrangers* (Paris, 1954).
15 AN, Commissariat au Plan (hereafter 80AJ) 71, Deuxième Plan de Modernisation.
16 The franc area included metropolitan France, Algeria, Tunisia and Morocco, as well as the territories and departments overseas. The French Union excluded Tunisia and Morocco.

17 S. Moos, 'The Foreign Trade of West-European Countries', *Bulletin of the Oxford Institute of Statistics*, 7, 1 and 3, 1945.

18 MAE, Gatt A-10–13, dossier 1, Direction des Affaires Economiques, 22 October 1946.

19 Commissariat Général au Plan, *Rapport sur la réalisation du plan de modernisation et d'équipement de l'Union française* (Paris, 1953), p. 84.

20 French Ministry of Finance (hereafter Min. Fin.) B24947, Relations de trésorerie, 'Note au sujet du financement des dépenses d'équipement en Afrique du Nord', 22 October 1952.

21 Min. Fin. B24929, Fangent to Bissonnet, 17 November 1954.

22 AN, 80AJ 71, Commissariat Général au Plan, document from Ministry of Foreign Affairs.

23 MAE, DE-CE, 1945–60, 197, note from Service de Coopération Economique, 12 June 1954.

24 AN, 80AJ 72, 'L'integration de l'Union française dans l'Europe des Six', 9 February 1955.

25 AN, F^{10} 5620, 'Rapport au sujet de la quatrième session du Conseil International du BIE', 24–7 October 1950.

26 Food and Agriculture Organisation, *Commodity Policy Studies*, no. 2, April 1953.

27 AN, 80AJ 54, CGP, 'Projet de rapport général des Commissions de la production agricole et de l'équipement rural', 22 September 1953.

28 MAE, Accords Bilatéraux, France: Allemagne, note, 28 April 1955.

29 Gilbert was the joint author of an official study which compared national products and the purchasing power of currencies in OEEC countries and the United States. M. Gilbert and B. Kravis, *An International Comparison of National Products and the Purchasing Power of Currencies* (OEEC, Paris, 1954).

30 MAE, DE-CE, 1945–60, 613, note, Service de Coopération Economique, 30 August 1956.

31 Quai Branly, Interministerial Committee for Questions of European Integration (thereafter SGG1), 122.22A, note from the High Authority of ECSC, 27 June 1956.

32 SGG1, 122.21, 'Réunion du Comité interministériel', September 1956.

33 SGG1, 122.13(b), 'Réunion Mollet, Adenauer', 6 November 1956.

34 MAE, DE-CE, 1945–60, A-30–6 Marché Commun, Bousquet to Pineau, 21 Febraury 1957.

[6]

WERNER BÜHRER

German Industry and European Integration in the 1950s

According to Fritz Berg, President of the Federation of German Industry (Bundesverband der Deutschen Industrie or BDI), achieving a united Europe counted among the most important goals of German industrialists. Since politicians still seemed to be captivated by ideas of prestige and national sovereignty, he even claimed some sort of European pioneering role in this respect for German industry.[1] Four years later, in September 1954, Wilhelm Beutler, general manager of the Federation, while rejecting any hegemonic ambitions, confirmed this declaration by stressing the seriousness and honesty of German endeavours towards European unity. He conceded, however, that in the meanwhile European 'enthusiasm' had been replaced by 'realism'.[2] Although one may doubt whether there had been such enthusiasm at the beginning of the integration process, attitudes had obviously changed as West Germany gained more independence.

In 1949, when the Federal Republic of Germany was founded, some major decisions on post-war Germany's international relations and its role in Europe had already been taken by the occupying powers. Among these, the decision to incorporate the western part of Germany into the framework of a comprehensive European recovery programme was particularly important. This meant that, despite some *discussion* in West German political and economic circles on the perspectives and implications of European integration, the *decision* to take part in these efforts had been made in Paris, London, and especially in Washington. This should be kept in mind although the Federal Government, for example by the accession to the Organisation for European Economic Co-operation (OEEC) at the end of October 1949 or by the approval of the Schuman Plan, subsequently 'ratified' these decisions. Moreover, since participation in common reconstruction efforts seemed to be the only chance for West Germany to recover in due time, German officials and industrialists most likely would have made the same decisions even without Allied interference.

Compared with the other participants, however, the Germans took particular interest in European cooperation and integration. It is true that they were looking for goods in short supply, markets and funds as were the French or the Italians. But they were just as much interested in achieving *Gleichberechtigung* – treatment on equal terms. This, for instance, would have meant that all Allied restrictions such as the limits on steel production, the foreign trade controls and decartelisation would have to be abolished. This also implied that the government should be able to decide foreign policy matters on its own. In short, seen from the German point of view, European integration seemed to be by far the best and most effective means to regain sovereignty.

To achieve this goal the Federal Republic was ready to fulfil Allied – especially American and French – expectations and requirements to an extent it certainly would have rejected under 'normal' conditions. This was one of the reasons why German attitudes towards European integration became more rigid and criticism increased during the 1950s; step by step, its political and economic elites became more self-confident and less inclined to adapt to schemes that seemed to hamper their amibitions. This was especially true for German industry. Its outlook on European integration changed between the end of the 1940s and the end of the 1950s from almost full support, first to cautious reluctance and then to pragmatic participation.

This process – the formulation and modification of integration conceptions and policies by German industry, its motives and expectations, and the attempts to influence, with the help of powerful businessmen and trade associations, the integration policy of the government – is the subject of the following article. In the first section the article outlines the relative strength of the various branches of industry in the post-war period and the interest group structures. Subsequently it focuses on the more general aspects of industry's attitudes towards cooperation and integration, and on the ways and means of active participation in the building up of

European connections and in the work of European institutions. The fourth section concentrates on the main steps of European integration and the efforts of important industrial associations to put through their ideas and goals, and tries to evaluate the role of German industry in the integration of Western Europe.

Structural changes and the organisation of German business

How important were the various sectors of industry in post-war Germany, and did differences in economic strength have any impact on the influence of the different sectors over their industry-wide associations? During the Second World War the influence of the various sectors depended on the extent to which they contributed to the war economy. Although the production of consumer goods remained at a relatively high level, those industries involved in armaments production ranked at the head of the intra-industrial hierarchy. After the war, these sectors understandably became the main targets of Allied dismantling and control measures. Moreover, despite some evidence that 'wartime investment had increased the industrial capital stock by more than the extent of wartime damage', individual industries such as coal-mining, steel, electricity generation and transportation 'had been seriously affected by wartime destruction and post-war disintegration'.[3] And until late summer 1947 it was by no means clear whether the German economy would be restored in its capacity as one of the biggest industrial 'workshops' in Europe or would become instead a supplier of raw materials such as coal.

The mere fact that coal and steel were vital to economic reconstruction was therefore not enough to give those industries a privileged position. In the case of coal mining, the reconstruction period seemed to be nothing more than a short respite in the decline of this formerly so powerful industry.[4] In contrast to the coal sector the iron and steel industry was able to establish during the 1950s, for at least two decades, a position not so far from its pre-war rank. Nevertheless, the so-called Investment Aid Act (Investitionshilfegesetz) of 1952, which obliged the other sectors to support investments in the energy sector, the railways and the coal and steel industries,[5] was one of the last great victories of Ruhr heavy industry over finishing and consumer goods industries.

Leading sectors of the 1950s and the following decades became the chemical industry, mechanical engineering, motor manufacturing and electrical engineering.[6] The following tables may give an impression of the rapid growth of production in these branches and the growing shares of employment and sales.

Table 1 Index of industrial production, 1950–65

Year	Industry (Total)	Mining	Basic raw materials	Capital goods	Consumer goods	Food products	Energy	Construction
1950	100	100	100	100	100	100	100	100
1955	176	128	176	216	167	158	172	188
1960	248	132	254	323	235	219	245	260
1865	327	135	348	423	304	286	351	365

Table 2 Employees and sales in individual sectors, 1950–65

Year	Totals		Mining %		Basic raw materials %		Capital goods %		Consumer goods %		Food products %	
	Empl. 1000	Sales Mio. DM	Empl.	Sales	Empl.	Sales	Empl.	Sales	Empl.	Sales	Empl.	Sales
1950	4.935	82.061	11.6	5.5	22.4	27.4	29.0	22.3	27.3	24.8	6.8	18.1
1955	6.815	171.568	9.5	4.8	21.1	29.9	33.4	28.9	26.3	19.3	6.1	14.3
1960	8.081	266.373	7.6	4.3	21.0	30.3	37.6	31.8	24.1	17.6	6.0	13.0
1965	8.460	374.612	4.9	3.6	22.3	31.8	42.9	38.8	23.8	19.4	6.4	14.9

Source: Winkel, *Wirtschaft*, p. 98 and 100.

German Industry and European Integration   91

Did these structural changes find expression in the system of industrial federations and in the power hierarchy of the various industrial associations? On the face of it, the former organisational pattern – regional, social policy and economic policy organisations – and even the traditional hierarchy were soon reestablished. 'Thus, of the national organisations in the business sphere, the Federation of German Industry may very well rank first in prestige, financial strength, and influence.' The BDI is composed of federally structured associations of the various branches of industry – thirty-four in 1949 and thirty-nine in 1964. The coal and steel associations formally joined the BDI in 1953. In 1961, according to a BDI official, '98 per cent of all West German industrialists are represented through the BDI'.[7] Fritz Berg, the owner of a medium-sized metal manufacturing firm, was elected president, and the BDI's political influence resulted not least from his close personal contacts with Chancellor Konrad Adenauer.[8] On the other hand, these relationships occasionally gave Adenauer the possibility to manipulate the Federation for his own purposes. W. Alexander Menne (chemical industry) and Otto A. H. Vogel (textile industry and president of the Augsburg Chamber of Industry and Commerce) were elected vice-presidents. The presidential board of the BDI consisted of Alexander von Engelberg (gravel industry), Otto A. Friedrich (rubber), Franz Linsenhoff (construction), Gustav Möllenberg (machine tools) and Hermann Reusch (steel).[9]

Some historians, for example Volker Berghahn, argue 'that the informal balance of power was clearly tilted towards heavy industry, and it was to be some time before a change occured in this respect'.[10] In particular, Reusch's role as some sort of 'grey eminence' of the BDI seems to furnish some evidence in favour of this interpretation. I do not share this view, however, and the Federation's position concerning European integration speaks particularly against there being a predominant position for heavy industry. Besides this, the number of votes possessed by the individual associations in the Membership Assembly did not allow heavy industry to control the BDI's affairs. In 1954, for example, the coal industry had fifteen and the steel industry eight votes. In contrast, the chemical industry disposed of eight votes, mechanical engineering thirteen, electrical engineering nine and textiles eleven votes out of a total of 113 votes.[11] In any case, the associations of all these industries, with the exception of coal, played an important role in BDI politics.

The second 'pillar' was formed by the employers' associations headed by the Federation of German Employers' Associations (Bundesvereinigung der Deutschen Arbeitgeberverbände, or BDA). They were engaged mainly in labour and social policies. As stated by Braunthal, the BDA ranked between the BDI and the Diet of German Industry and Commerce (Deutscher Industrie- und Handelstag, or DIHT), the umbrella organisation of about eighty regional chambers of commerce. In the field of European integration, however, the DIHT far surpassed the employers associations in importance. According to Berghahn, the DIHT, 'its heterogeneity notwithstanding, was by and large outward-looking and liberal-capitalist', whereas the BDI 'represented the conservative traditions of large-scale industry, but also mirrored the old tensions between its various branches...'[12] However, as far as European integration was concerned, the BDI, too, opened up new paths.

Types and characteristics of European attitudes

During the First World War prominent industrialists, for example Emil Kirdorf, Hugo Stinnes and August Thyssen, and various associations counted among the most nationalistic and expansionistic circles of the German *Reich*.[13] After the defeat, other businessmen like Max M. Warburg, Carl Melchior, Emil Georg von Stauß, Wilhelm Cuno, Richard Merton, Carl Bosch and Felix Deutsch, representing banking, shipping, metal, chemical and electrical industries, rejected old-fashioned *Machtpolitik* in favour of a new, cooperative economic foreign policy.[14] Later, after the Treaty of Versailles had been signed, even such hard-boiled heavy industry representatives as Stinnes changed course and searched for cooperative solutions – for instance to the Franco-German coal problem.[15] The various international cartels, too, although their 'de-nationalising' effects should not be overestimated,[16] might have contributed to the emergence of some sort of internationalistic mentality.

This did not of course mean that nationalism had lost its attraction, as the experience of the Third Reich showed. Did German businessmen learn something from this experience? The American political scientist Gabriel A. Almond, on the basis of some fifty interviews during the summer 1954, came to the conclusion 'that the learning has been incomplete, the lessons are undigested, and present responses to the political situation are based upon simple power calculations and situational adjustments'. Since there were 'no realistic grounds for hopes of vindication or revenge', the revival of an 'adventurous nationalism' seemed highly improbable. What was apparent, however, among all groups of the population was a demand, varied in degree, 'for more independence in the conduct of foreign policy'.[17] According to Almond and other researchers, heavy industry elites were particularly predisposed to such nationalist trends. It is not without its ironic aspects, therefore, that coal and steel after the war had to play the pioneering role in the integration of Europe.

Almond distinguished three different streams of pro-European attitudes among German businessmen:

> In the first place, there is a genuine European current based upon one or a combination of religious, cultural, economic, and political considerations. Secondly, there is a phenomenon which may be appropriately characterized as an 'escape into Europe'. And, finally, there is a kind of 'crypto-nationalist' Europeanism, a belief that German economic and political dominance may be attained through European integration. These attitudes occur most typically in combination, but it is possible to distinguish among individuals according to the type of attitudes that predominates in the thinking of each.[18]

In his study on the BDI, Braunthal came to similar conclusions:

> Many businessmen evidently support integration because they favor the economic and political strengthening of the European continent and the doing away with the narrow focus on nationalism. Others apparently see integration as giving Germany a dominant role in a supranational union. Whatever the motivation, industrialists have unquestionably broadened their horizons.[19]

In reality, however, it is quite difficult to decide which of these motives might have been predominant as far as certain industrialists were concerned. Günter Henle of Klöckner steel works, for example, was an ardent supporter of Franco-German reconciliation and avowed opponent of traditional power politics. Yet during the Schuman Plan negotiations, when the Ruhr *Verbundwirtschaft,* i.e. the efficient and cost saving exchange of fuels and supplies

within *one* company, was attacked by the French and the
Americans, he, too, was afraid to loose this structural advantage –
one of the steel industry's, and therefore Germany's, trump
cards.[20] Hermann Reusch by contrast, who in 1950 counted
among the critics of the Schuman Plan, later worked to obtain a
fair judgement on the ECSC.[21] And, of course, it was and is not
unusual, for German industry in particular, for European attitudes
to be based on national or even sector and company interests.
Perhaps it is more useful to distinguish not between different types
of Europeanism, but between different characteristics or components of pro-European thinking.

One strong characteristic of German Europeanism was its
strong anti-communist motivation. As BDI president Berg once
put it, German industry was closely attached to the western world;
western civilisation was the source of its resistance against the
'Asiatic flood'. Only European unity therefore would guarantee
the power to withstand the 'Eastern storm'.[22] Typical, too, was the
fact the Germans, businessmen and politicians alike, were compelled to a larger extent than other Western Europeans to subscribe to European integration and to use European 'packaging'
in order to achieve their specific national goals.

Another essential of the industry's conception of European
unity was the reconciliation with France. In particular Günter
Henle of Klöckner steel works, who was one of the more prominent 'political' industrialists, and not only because of his Christian
Democratic Party membership and his seat in the Bundestag,
became a committed advocate of Franco-German rapprochement.
In an analysis of November 1949 he stated that the situations of
both countries, as a consequence of the 'massive landslide...in
Germany since 1945', had come to resemble each other. The
Federal Republic wished to cling to the West because it saw itself
'today threatened, exposed and defenceless', and was therefore
'itself gripped by the demand for *sécurité*' that had been dominant
in France 'as strongly ever since 1918'. Pointing to the fact of the
Iron Curtain, he set German relationships in a wider context,
stressing that 'yesterday's world had vanished, with all its ambitious
goals and aspirations'. Old rivalries had become 'suicidal and
senseless'. The Federal Republic, he asserted, had no new objectives of 'future power politics in the West' and was aware that 'in
the age of the atom bomb old-style power politics can no longer
exist'. By contrast with the 1920s, it was clear from the circum-

stances of the Cold War that 'the idea of sovereignty had to give place to higher requirements', when the common welfare and the existence of Europe was at stake.

And, alluding to widespread fears in France, he explicitly stressed that there was no wish to 'swallow up' Germany's neighbour since this was well beyond German strength, even if such a belief in German capabilities might be flattering. Ideas such as 'predominance', so Henle concluded, had now become outdated; whoever really wanted to be in Europe ought to get rid of 'sentiments of this kind'.[23] This analysis, in particular the appraisal of some sort of 'special Franco-German relationship', was representative of the decisive circles in West German industry, and it corresponded precisely with the convictions of Chancellor Konrad Adenauer. Since German industry, and heavy industry in particular, had a long tradition of cooperation with the French, this accord should not be taken as proof that Adenauer succesfully manipulated German businessmen and their associations.

Finally, the absence of any thinking of Europe as a 'Third Force', at least as far as the prominent industrialists were concerned, should be mentioned. Close contacts to the United States as the dominating Western power were considered to be very important. This attitude resulted from security needs as well as economic considerations.[24] Surprisingly, the possibility of conflicts between these two political options seems to have been ignored.

Institutionalised participation in European politics

Already during the inaugural meeting of the BDI's predecessor organisation in October 1949 several spokesmen declared their belief in European cooperation. To them, this cooperation was the only chance to save western civilisation. Hermann Reusch, managing director of one of the six leading West German steel works, the Gutehoffnungshütte, who, as mentioned before, became one of the most influential persons in the BDI, emphasised moreover the important role of the Federal Republic in general and of a powerful German industry in particular. According to him, any European community would be impossible without German participation.[25]

To demonstrate its European conviction to the public, the Federation founded a special committee on European questions

96   *Werner Bührer*

in December 1950. Berg was elected as chairman.[26] After this impressive overture, however, the committee disappeared from the public scene almost completely. In 1953 its name was changed into 'Committee on International Relations' – to signal its 'expanded field of activity', as the semi-official history of the BDI put it.[27]

Of course, the presidential and the executive boards talked frequently about integration questions, and within the BDI executive staff the international relations branch was responsible for integration issues. But not until 1957 did the DIHT install a department of European economic integration; in 1958 two committees on European problems were established in order to cope with the increasing number of tasks after the foundation of the European Economic Community (EEC).[28] Before that time European problems had been discussed by the *Hauptausschuß*, the Foreign Economic Policy or the Tarifs Committee of the DIHT. The various branch associations proceeded similarly. To deal with the problems arising out of the Schuman Plan negotiations, the steel association, for instance, installed several working groups and a coordinating committee for the technical subcommittees.[29] As far as the BDA was concerned, integration matters fell under the competence of the International Social Policy Department and the Committee on EEC Social Policy.[30]

Besides this, the European activities of the individual associations were made public in detail. Each annual report, for example, included a special chapter summing up the work of the past year. During the annual sessions of the membership assemblies, too, the problems and prospects of integration, played an important role. In October 1952 the BDI held a 'Europe Day' at Trier with Paul-Henri Spaak, Ludwig Erhard and Georges Villiers, president of the *Conseil National du Patronat Français*, addressing the audience. The Federation wanted this congress to be understood as an appeal to the political leaders to overcome still existing reservations and to intensify integration efforts – and as a demonstration of the high level of cooperation that already had been reached by European industry.[31]

Another field of European activity was the engagement of national associations and individual businessmen in various transnational and international organisations. The first of these 'clubs' joined by the Federation of German Industry was the Council of European Industrial Federations (CIFE), established in

September 1949 with headquarters in Paris as a consultative body to the OEEC. Berg became member of the steering committee even before the BDI's foundation, and soon a liaison office was set up to deal with the routine work of the Council. The Federation used this organisation as a platform to re-establish contacts with the industrial associations of the Western European countries.[32] In 1957 Berg was elected President of the CIFE.[33]

Within its framework, again at French prompting, a new 'club' was formed in September 1952, the Union of Industries of the Schuman Plan countries. This organisation grouped 'the national associations of the six countries into a tight body, meeting far more frequently than the parent organisation, largely independent of it, and determined to gain recognition as the sole ECSC employer organisation'.[34] The Union allowed the member associations to coordinate their economic policies and to influence the activities of the High Authority of ECSC. Therefore the BDI was quite satisfied with the Union. 'During the short time of its existence', the 1952–53 BDI annual report said, 'a close cooperation has developed enabling the Union to resolve even difficult problems in a spirit of friendly understanding'.[35]

The various branch associations also succeeded in setting up transnational organisations. While the steel associations of the six countries formed in 1952 a rather informal *Club des Sidérurgistes*, the coal associations in the same year established a much more formal organisation, the West European Coal Producers' Study Committee.[36] It might have been the steel associations' fear of being suspected of cartel ambitions that explains their refusal to found a well organised 'club'. The German branch associations participated in the activities of these transnational groups as they did in the case of, for example, the Liaison Committee of European Metallurgical Industries, the Common Office of Scrap Consumers, or, later on, in the *Organisme de Liaison des Industries Métalliques Européennes* or the *Sécréariat International des Groupements Professionnels des Industries Chimiques des Pays de la Communauté Economique Européenne*.[37] The DIHT concentrated its efforts during the first half of the 1950s on the International Chamber of Commerce.[38] In the field of social policy, too, cooperation was institutionalised, and the Federation of German Employers contributed to the work of the respective organisations.[39]

In 1958, after the European Economic Community had been established, the Union of Industries of the Schuman Plan

Countries gave way to a new Union of Industries of the European Community. Although this organisation was regarded as a proper instrument to press for the achievement of economic principles and structures similar to those in the Federal Republic, BDI spokesmen left no doubt that they looked upon the EEC as a starting point for an all-European integration.[40] Thus, from the BDI's point of view, it would have been wrong to concentrate organisational efforts almost exclusively on the Community. Correspondingly the Federation opposed the establishment of a strong Union machinery in order to protect the autonomy of the national associations.[41] The BDI, however, did not play a dominant role within these various European industrial associations, nor did the BDA or DIHT; it was the French *Patronat* that held the leadership.[42] This might have been one reason why, in addition to these multilateral cooperation efforts, bilateral contacts with the industrial organisations of France, Italy, the Netherlands, the United Kingdom or the United States remained important for the BDI as well as for the BDA and the DIHT. Furthermore, several national associations maintained liaison offices in Brussels in order to maintain close and permanent contacts with European institutions.[43]

But the representatives of the associations and individual industrialists also demonstrated their pro-European attitudes and commitments in another way. They supported, personally and financially, 'private' pressure-groups such as the *Europa-Union* or more academic 'clubs' such as the European League for Economic Co-operation (ELEC) or the *Comité Européen pour le Progrès Économique et Social* (CEPES).[44] While the industrialists were in a minority position in the pressure-groups – but nevertheless tried to exploit them for different purposes – [45] they played a dominant role in ELEC and CEPES. In 1953, for example, Berg, BDI general manager Beutler, Otto A. Friedrich and W. Alexander Menne of the presidential board were members of the German group of CEPES. The BDI planned to give DM 35,000 to support the activities of the group in 1953–54. To avoid duplicating work and, more important, duplicating funding, the Federation demanded the cooperation or even fusion of ELEC and CEPES.[46] Although it is difficult to evaluate the importance of all these activities from the BDI's point of view, surely the *Europa-Union* or CEPES were less important than the European 'clubs' of industrial associations. But as a platform to establish or intensify transnational contacts they undoubtedly were quite useful.

German Industry and European Integration   99

All these ways of influencing the integration process described
hitherto represent more or less indirect forms of participation.
There was, of course, direct participation as well. Members of several branch associations – steel, coal, non-ferrous metals, chemicals and textiles – engaged themselves in the work of the technical
committees of the OEEC. Not all of the German businessmen or
association officials appreciated the efforts of these committees.
The general manager of the textiles association, for example, felt
embarrassed to pass on the official OEEC documents because he
regarded them as being of poor quality.[47] Whereas participation in
the OEEC was restricted to the period after its foundation, the
BDI, the Iron and Steel Association and the semi-governmental
Deutsche Kohlenbergbauleitung (DKBL) had a voice in the drafting of
the ECSC treaty. Berg and Reusch represented the Federation on
one of the advisory commissions that had been set up to support
the German delegation during the negotiations in Paris, but did
not often attend meetings. Reusch resigned in September 1950 in
order to protest against the Allied decartelisation policy, but what
might have been meant as an appeal to his colleagues to reject the
ECSC project failed.[48] In short, as far as the Schuman Plan was
concerned, the influence of the steel association and the DKBL
clearly exceeded that of the BDI.

In January 1956, when the negotiations on the common market
and Euratom started, the associations tried to intervene. The BDI
established an ad hoc presidential board to establish contact with
members of the German delegation 'sympathetic to the BDI's
objectives'. But once again the Federation was discontented with
the degree of its influence. According to Braunthal, Berg 'was
reported to have protested personally to Adenauer that industrial
associations in other EEC countries were being consulted more
frequently than the BDI had been in Germany'.[49] Paradoxically,
similar associations in other West European countries made the
same complaints to their respective governments about the supposedly greater influence of German industry.

After the various treaties had come into force, the associations
were busy trying to 'infiltrate' the individual boards and committees of the European organisations. Franz Etzel and Fritz Hellwig,
who successively held one of the German seats in the High
Authority of the ECSC, were closely allied to industrial circles.
Rudolf Regul and Hermann Dehnen of the DKBL and Wilhelm
Salewski, former general manager of the steel association, became

leading officials of the ECSC bureaucracy. Berg and, from 1957 to
1967 Hans-Günther Sohl, president of the BDI between 1973 and
1976, represented German industry in the Consultative
Committee.[50] Finally, two of the eight business seats in the German
group of the Economic and Social Committee of the EEC went to
the BDI and one to the BDA.[51] In the 1960s Beutler played a very
active role in this committee.

To sum up, by using both direct and indirect methods, the
German industrial associations contributed to the process of
European integration. So which conceptions of cooperation and
integration did they prefer, and to what extent did they succeed in
realising their ideas and goals?

Integration conceptions and policies

The OEEC was the first international organisation after
the Second World War to give the Germans the chance to learn
what it meant to participate in a joint, cooperative European programme. It soon became apparent that this meant something different than the type of 'cooperation' practised during the war.[52] In
the beginning, West German interests were represented by the
Military Governors of the three Western zones. German advisers
were admitted and were allowed to attend the negotiations, but
they had to take their seats in the second or third row and were not
permitted to speak for themselves. When the Federal Republic
officially joined the OEEC in the autumn of 1949, it was the first
time since the war that Germany was able to become a member of
an international organisation on equal terms – at least formally.
The Western powers considered this step to be some kind of test of
West Germany's ability and willingness to adapt to modern standards of behaviour in international relations.[53]

Industry in general in West Germany welcomed the Marshall
Plan and the OEEC. The reasons, leaving *Gleichberechtigung* out of
consideration, are easy to understand: since the OEEC dealt with
problems concerning economic integration it seemed to be the
proper platform for West Germany, which lacked political power
but had the economic potential that would be required in order to
reconstruct Europe in due time. Moreover, the ERP was seen as a
chance to revive traditional forms of cooperation between national industries including international cartels, as Salewski of the steel

association explained in an immediate reaction to Secretary of State George C. Marshall's famous speech at Harvard University.[54] And, finally, the OEEC type of cooperation did not greatly restrict the members' freedom of movement.

Though some historians explicitly or implicitly deny any decisive contribution on the part of the OEEC to the process of European integration,[55] the organisation – in particular by its efforts to liberalise trade and, with the help of the European Payments Union (EPU), to multilateralise payments – actually did play an important role. German industry in principle supported these efforts because the Federal Republic depended more than ever on liberal foreign trade structures. This did not mean that each association agreed with the liberalisation programme – steel, textiles and even the chemical industry raised some objections – but this criticism was directed mainly against the pace of liberalisation and supposed discrimination against the Germans.[56] Most industrialists and association officials were well aware of the urgency – and the advantages – of trade liberalisation. Despite some objections in detail a large majority within the DIHT, for example, took a positive position on liberalisation since it seemed to be the first step towards an 'integrated European *Wirtschaftsraum*'.[57] After the Federal Government stopped liberalisation in February 1951, the BDI was counted among the first to come out in favour of re-liberalisation.[58]

In contrast to this, as far as the division of Marshall aid and the coordination of industrial investments were concerned, there was a general and growing discontent in Germany. BDI staff members accused the OEEC of misdirection and other OEEC countries of parochialism and misuse of Marshall aid, insinuating that this aid might be used more effectively in West Germany.[59] The 'investment policy' of the organisation, particularly in the steel sector, was repeatedly attacked by representatives of the German steel industry.[60] Sometimes it seemed that in West Germany only measures and policies to the country's own advantage were regarded as *European*.

But, in spite of some harsh criticism, the BDI in particular valued the OEEC very highly. The BDI's annual report of 1954–55 praised the Paris organisation as the 'most successful instrument of European economic integration...working without supranational powers'.[61] The DIHT was less enthusiastic: while stressing the remarkable progress in economic cooperation, the 1957–58 annual report at the same time emphasised the limits of the liberalisation policy of the OEEC.[62] Nevertheless, the DIHT also held the Paris organisation in esteem. In addition to the reasons mentioned above, the impressive development of the Federal Republic within the OEEC since 1952 might be another explanation. From not initially being allowed to make independent decisions and subject to embarrassing examinations during the balance of payments crisis in 1950–51, Germany became the largest and most consistent creditor of the European Payments Union.[63] Thus, and because interference with national politics was kept at a tolerable level, the OEEC type of European integration had many supporters among German industrialists.

The fact that the High Authority would have supranational powers explains why the European Coal and Steel Community was less popular than the OEEC. Thus, after a number of mostly positive immediate reactions,[64] more and more critical comments were to be heard. The Iron and Steel Association raised a number of objections against the 'dirigistic' elements of the French plan, and against 'harmonisation' of production factors and prices and of labour costs: '"pro-European" sentiment was widely mingled with anti-supranational demands, indicating that for many businessmen integration meant little more than the removal of Allied controls'. It should not be left unmentioned, however, that several steel industrialists, in spite of some criticism, spoke in favour of the Schuman Plan.[65] The Federation of German Industry did not oppose the French initiative in public, but Berg and his colleagues took a rather critical view of the negotiations. The prospect of replacing the highly unpopular Allied Ruhr Authority by the Coal and Steel Community was welcomed, but at the same time, 'German weaknesses due to war losses, damage and reparations were mentioned incessantly in order to buttress the argument of sacrifice'.[66] Therefore the BDI stressed in particular that the treaty should take into account the 'economic realities' and, of course, should ensure that the activities of businessmen and their associations should not be restricted.[67] The BDA was interested principally in the social provisions of the treaty. As it soon became obvious that the ECSC's powers in this field would be quite small, the BDA's anxiety eased.[68]

It was the Korean War and the following boom that decisively influenced the attitudes of most German industrialists towards the Schuman Plan. Suddenly it seemed possible to get rid of all the

Allied restrictions without accepting new schemes of control, even if such control might no longer be unilateral, as in the past five years. As mentioned above, Hermann Reusch of *Gutehoffnungshütte*, a member of the BDI's presidential board, took the lead in attacking the Schuman Plan. He became annoyed at the thought of Germany accepting economic disadvantages for political reasons, even though the country was economically stronger than its competitors.[69] But he and others who agreed with him did not succeed in building up a powerful front against the coal and steel pool. Ludwig Erhard, Minister for Economics, and Franz Blücher, Minister for the Marshall Plan, though showing some sympathy with the critics, did not dare to support them openly.

It seems remarkable that neither the steel association nor the coal interests backed the opponents of the ECSC. Obviously they knew very well that there was hardly any realistic alternative to the Schuman Plan, in spite of their considerable dissatisfaction with the decartelisation and deconcentration clauses of the ECSC.[70] Was this, to use Almond's terms, some sort of 'escape into Europe' – or was it a sign of growing, honest 'Europeanism' within German heavy industry? Or should this be taken as evidence that 'those branches of industry, such as coal, which equate supranational action with their own survival', differ from the general pattern?[71] As far as industrialists like Günter Henle of Klöckner steel works were concerned, European cooperation and integration was felt to be inevitable for political and economic reasons. Others, like the senior officials of the iron and steel association, adapted pragmatically to the new political conditions in Western Europe. In any case, 'declining' industries seem to be more open to integration efforts than 'strong' ones.

The BDI, however, adhered to its criticism, while the coal and steel leaders remained reluctantly supporters. After the ECSC treaty had been signed, but before its ratification, the Federation switched over to the offensive and, in the spring of 1952, publicly declared that economic integration in the future should not be accomplished by sectoral approach but by trade liberalisation and broader 'horizontal' arrangements which would aim at the harmonisation of the economic policies of the participating countries.[72] Harmonisation measures, in other words, had to be restricted to those fields, in which the Germans expected advantages. And 'harmonisation', without doubt, meant that the other participants had to adjust themselves to the German practice. Objections that were raised during the common market negotiations, that sectoral integration might distort the individual national economies, did not play a decisive role. Despite spectacular activities like the *Europa-Tag* in October 1952, scepticism and criticism within the BDI increased. In May 1953, after the European Defence Community treaty and the so-called Contractual Agreements with the Western Powers had been signed, Berg stated that the time of occupation had come to an end: 'We start a new period of our political and economic life as a self-responsible state.'[73] Although it took another two years until the Federal Republic achieved formal sovereignty, Berg's statement was typical of a new German self-confidence which was demonstrated not only in economic but in political circles as well.

After 1945, most initiatives and plans to integrate Europe had been characterised by the intention to control Germany. Now, from the German point of view, any further restriction or supervision had to be avoided. Taking into account Germany's dependence on foreign trade, the BDI and DIHT tried to adjust future methods of cooperation to the needs of the West German economy. They urgently demanded, for example, the harmonisation of the trade and economic policies of the NATO member states[74] – again understood as harmonisation on German terms. Supranational sectoral integration was no longer seen as a proper means to protect German interests. Therefore the failure of the European Defence Community was regarded as a striking proof of the unsuitability of the sectoral approach. In contrast to Chancellor Konrad Adenauer, the BDI demonstrated coolness at this setback: it was not integration as a whole, but only one possible method that had failed.[75] During the preparatory discussions for the Messina conference the BDI consequently declared that the process of integration should not be continued by abandoning sovereign rights. Now, after the Paris treaties had been ratified, the OEEC type of integration was praised by the BDI as the only possible way in the future.[76]

In any case, the readiness to participate in European projects declined after May 1955. This became particularly clear when nuclear energy cooperation was discussed. Some members of the German government, especially the Minister for Atomic Energy, Franz-Josef Strauß, strongly supported by the BDI and several associations and firms, opposed the foundation of an European atomic community. They favoured bilateral arrangements with the United States or the United Kingdom in order to obtain what seemed necessary to build up national nuclear energy capabilities. It was American disapproval, assisted by individual Western European governments, that convinced Adenauer at least of the necessity to join the European scheme.[77] French insistence on Euratom, however, made pressure in favour of a common market easier for the German government.

Although the Federal Republic was still not in a position to take the political lead in integration efforts, the Germans succeeded in gaining acceptance for their market economy principles. The BDI therefore commented favourably on the common market negotiations.[78] In particular the reduction of supranational powers of the new community, as compared to the ECSC, and the overall approach met with general consent. The projected common trade policy was also approved, not least because of the strengthening of the community's 'bargaining power'. Trade policy was therefore no problem to the BDI. Criticism concentrated on the insufficient harmonisation of economic policies, the possibility of turning away from the German-type *Ordnungspolitik* and eventual problems resulting from the coexistence of EEC and ECSC, but none of the BDI representatives and officials would have run the risk of failure due to opposition from German industry.[79] The BDA raised objections against a possible harmonisation of social costs and labour law to the disadvantage of the German side and demanded that each member state should be responsible for its social policy.[80]

While stressing general consent to the common market programme of the Adenauer government, the DIHT criticized the traffic policy and tariff provisions of the projected treaty and the special rules in favour of agriculture. Since all participants had to make certain sacrifices in the interest of international cooperation, however, the DIHT supported the common market and Euratom.[81] Did the industrial associations have any influence on the negotiations at all? According to Hanns Jürgen Küsters, the role of the industrial associations – and trade unions – was not very important.[82] One should not, however, jump to conclusions from the fact that there seemed to be little direct participation on behalf of the associations. Their positions were by no means unknown to the officials of the ministries involved, and the close contacts between Berg and Adenauer have already been mentioned.

What were the attitudes of the steel and of the coal associations? The steel association, until then not among the principal critics, attacked sector integration severely in a statement of February 1956. Only full-scale economic integration was seen as a proper means to avoid undesirable trends and to effect a real economic fusion of the individual economies of the participating countries.[83] The mining association shared this view, although its opinion about the ECSC was less negative. In particular, according to a memorandum of February 1956, the association expected that market economy principles should be implemented much more strongly.[84] Thus, under changed circumstances, both associations took a more critical view of the ESCS than they had done before.

To sum up, German industry supported the common market and, very reluctantly, Euratom, not least because of the flexibility of the EEC treaty which seemed to make possible necessary 'improvements' of the EEC. The projected common trade policy and common tariffs were welcomed, assuming a non-protectionist policy and relatively low tariffs. This pragmatic outlook on EEC and Euratom was of course far from Adenauer's enthusiastic prognosis that the economic power of 'little Europe' would have an impact on world affairs.[85] Whereas the Chancellor also believed in the political effects of the EEC, the BDI, for example, was less optimistic. But the Federation's main interest was elsewhere: by analysing the production costs and competitive situation of German industry, the BDI came to the conclusion that 'a certain confidence and optimism in joining the Common Market was quite justified'.[86] Nevertheless, there can be no doubt that the process of protracted bargaining over interests was not liked by the German industrialists. And it was also obvious that from their point of view the EEC was not the end, because the Europe of the Six might endanger the economic community created by the OEEC and lead to a division of Western Europe into two trade blocs. To understand these fears, one has to remember the percentage shares in the Federal Republic's overall foreign trade: in 1957, 26 per cent of German exports and imports were with the Six and 23 per cent with the Seven.[87] Thus German industry was interested in any proposal or measure directed against the threatened economic division of Western Europe.

As is known, during the negotiations about the common market and Euratom the British government had proposed the foundation of a free trade area composed of the Six and the rest of the

German Industry and European Integration   107

OEEC members. Agriculture was to be excluded from the free trade provisions. As Miriam Camps put it, 'the adoption of free trade in industrial products with important competitors like the Six would mean a major change in British trade policy, which for nearly twenty-five years had been highly protectionist',[88] so this initiative should not be seen merely as an attempt to torpedo the common market project. Ludwig Erhard, German Minister for Economics, welcomed the British proposal enthusiastically, as did German industry. Erhard's consent seemed to have been mistaken by the British as the consent of the whole German government. But Chancellor Adenauer, despite some promises to Macmillan, did not support the British initiative wholeheartedly.[89]

The OEEC then began to discuss the plan. A special working group came to the conclusion that a free trade area of the kind proposed was technically possible. During a meeting of the OEEC Council in February 1957, Erhard praised the free trade project as an 'important, not to say the most important political and economic initiative to integrate Europe for years'.[90] Whereas Paul-Henri Spaak in the name of the Six stressed the priority of the common market project, the German minister spoke of the two plans as belonging together.

After the Treaties of Rome had been signed, the climate of the negotiations on the free trade area proposal gradually worsened. The BDI nevertheless continued to support the project because, as a BDI official emphasised, 'the Germans wanted the free trade area, they had to support it and should do all they can to solve the problems'.[91] Moreover, the Federation saw it as its great task to act as a mediator between French and British interests.[92] There were, however, warnings not to get involved too deeply in the Franco-British conflict because this might endanger the existence of the OEEC and EPU which had proved to be 'the most successful European institutions so far'.[93] The DIHT shared the BDI's position. A free trade area seemed to be the best means to support the efforts of the EEC: 'The area of European integration has to be extended as far as possible'.[94] Both associations maintained their point of view even after the breakdown of the free trade negotiations in November 1958.[95] In a letter to Adenauer BDI president Berg worried about the possibility of trade conflicts in Western Europe and encouraged the Chancellor to continue the negotiations. Adenauer, however, as Berg stated with a tone of resignation, obviously wanted to avoid putting any pressure on the French.[96]

108   *Werner Bührer*

Nevertheless, from German industry's point of view towards the end of the 1950s, there was a need to break out of 'European narrowness' and join the Atlantic Community.[97] The attempts to expand trade into the so-called developing countries and the achievement of convertibility of the most important European currencies were directed to this same goal.[98] In short, Western Europe was getting too small for the 'economic giant' West Germany. The integration into European schemes without being able to dominate them economically and politically caused dissatisfaction. But since money cannot buy everything, the Germans had to accept their new role in international relations – and they did.

This interpretation may be illustrated by a statement of an economic association official in 1960. According to him, there were no longer any ambitions of power politics in Germany as well as in Western Europe. In spite of the extraordinary boom during the 1950s, he considered Europe's traditional powerful position to be lost. What was his point of view regarding the new European hierarchy? The glory of spiritual leadership he conceded to Rome. Political leadership he ascribed to Paris, because after the recent past any German ambitions in this field would be impossible for a long time, if not forever. Economic leadership, however, he claimed for the Federal Republic.[99] European integration, despite some discontent within German industry, started to become 'irreversible'.

Recapitulating the first half of the EEC's transition period, a BDI publication underlined that the Federation had supported the establishment of the EEC from the beginning. Obviously the BDI had come to realise that 'bigger markets encourage technical progress and economic development in general'. Although the authors of the report denied the possibility of verifying the effects of integration precisely, they left no doubt that 'the economic boom of the last few years can be put down to the EEC to a considerable extent'.[100] German industry therefore remained interested in the continuation of the integration process according to the principles of the EEC treaty, i.e. without supranational elements. The German industrialists, one could say, had become 'pragmatic Europeans'.

Notes

1. Speech by Berg during the foundation of the 'Europa-Ausschuß' of the BDI, 18 December 1950, BDI-Altregistratur (BDIA), Aufsätze Präs. Berg ab 1950.

German Industry and European Integration 109

2. Beutler, 'Die politische Bedeutung wirtschaftlicher Zusammenarbeit' in *Vortragsreihe des Deutschen Industrieinstituts* No. 38, 20 September 1954.

3. Klaus Hinrich Hennings, 'West Germany', in Andrea Boltho (ed.), *The European Economy: Growth and Crisis*, Oxford, 1982, pp. 472–501 (p. 477). See also Werner Abelshauser, *Wirtschaft in Westdeutschland 1945–1948. Rekonstruktion und Wachstumsbedingungen in der amerikanischen und britischen Zone*, Stuttgart, 1975; Alan Kramer, *The West German Economy, 1945–1955*, New York/Oxford 1991.

4. See Werner Abelshauser, *Der Ruhrkohlenbergbau seit 1945. Wiederaufbau, Krise, Anpassung*, Munich 1984; Mark Roseman, *Recasting the Ruhr, 1945–1948: Manpower, Economic Recovery and Labour Relations*, New York/Oxford, 1992.

5. See Heiner R. Adamsen, *Investitionshilfe für die Ruhr. Wiederaufbau, Verbände und soziale Marktwirtschaft 1948–1952*, Wuppertal, 1981; Kramer, *The West German Economy*, p. 171.

6. See Harald Winkel, *Die Wirtschaft im geteilten Deutschland 1945–1970*, Wiesbaden, 1974, pp. 96–104; Gerold Ambrosius, 'Wirtschaftlicher Strukturwandel und Technikentwicklung' in Axel Schildt and Arnold Sywottek (eds), *Modernisierung im Wiederaufbau. Die westdeutsche Gesellschaft der 50er Jahre*, Bonn, 1993, pp. 107–28.

7. Quoted in Gerard Braunthal, *The Federation of German Industry in Politics*, Ithaca, N.Y., 1965, p. 31. On industrial associations see also Hans-Peter Ullmann, *Interessenverbände in Deutschland*, Frankfurt am Main, 1988; Werner Bührer, 'Unternehmerverbände', in Wolfgang Benz (ed.), *Geschichte der Bundesrepublik Deutschland*, bd. 2, Wirtschaft, Frankfurt am Main, 1989, pp. 140–68.

8. See Arnulf Baring, *Außenpolitik in Adenauers Kanzlerdemokratie. Westdeutsche Innenpolitik im Zeichen der Europäischen Verteidigungsgemeinschaft*, vol. 2, Munich, 1971 (paperback edition), pp. 53–7.

9. See BDI (ed.), *Fünf Jahre BDI. Aufbau und Arbeitsziele des industriellen Spitzenverbandes*, Bergisch Gladbach, 1954, p. 44.

10. Volker R. Berghahn, *The Americanisation of West German Industry 1945–1973*, Leamington Spa/ New York, 1986, p. 66; also Ullmann, *Interessenverbände*, pp. 243–4.

11. 'List of number of votes of the member associations', 28 April 1954, Archives of the IHK Augsburg (AIHKA), NL Vogel, BDI Allgemein, 1 December 1953–31 December 1954. Braunthal, *The Federation of German Industry*, p. 36, nevertheless thinks that the 'weighting of the vote could lead to oligarchic control by the heavy industry of the Rhine-Ruhr-complex'.

12. See Braunthal, *The Federation of German Industry*, pp. 26–9; Berghahn, *Americanisation*, pp. 66–8.

13. See Fritz Ficher, *Griff nach der Weltmacht. Die Kriegszielpolitik des kaiserlichen Deutschland 1914/18*, Kronberg/Ts., 1977 (paperback reprint).

110   *Werner Bührer*

14. See Leo Haupts, *Deutsche Friedenspolitik 1918–19. Eine Alternative zur Machtpolitik des Ersten Weltkrieges*, Düsseldorf, 1976; critical of this view is Peter Grupp, *Deutsche Außenpolitik im Schatten von Versailles 1918–1920. Zur Politik des Auswärtigen Amts vom Ende des Ersten Weltkriegs und der Novemberrevolution bis zum Inkrafttreten des Versailler Vertrags*, Paderborn, 1988, esp. pp. 43–9.

15. See Peter Wulf, *Hugo Stinnes. Wirtschaft und Politik 1918–1924*, Stuttgart, 1979.

16. See Clemens A. Wurm, 'Politik und Wirtschaft in den internationalen Beziehungen. Internationale Kartelle, Außenpolitik und weltwirtschaftliche Beziehungen 1919–1939: Einführung' and Ulrich Nocken, 'International Cartels and Foreign Policy: The Formation of the International Steel Cartel 1924–1926' in Clemens A. Wurm (ed.), *International Cartels and Foreign Policy: Studies on the Interwar Period*, Wiesbaden, 1989, pp. 1–31 and 33–82.

17. Gabriel A. Almond, 'The Politics of German Business' in Hans Speier and W. Phillips Davison (eds), *West German Leadership and Foreign Policy*, Evanston/White Plains, 1957, pp. 195–241 (223–4).

18. Almond, 'The politics of German Business', p. 232–3.

19. Braunthal, *Federation*, p. 288.

20. See Werner Bührer, *Ruhrstahl und Europa. Die Wirtschaftsvereinigung Eisen- und Stahlindustrie und die Anfänge der europäischen Integration 1945–1952*, Munich, 1986, esp. pp. 132–5 and 198–9.

21. See Werner Bührer, 'Die Montanunion – ein Fehlschlag? Deutsche Lehren aus der EGKS und die Gründung der EWG' in Gilbert Trausch (ed.), *The European Integration from the Schuman-Plan to the Treaties of Rome*, Baden-Baden, 1993, pp. 75–90.

22. 'Report on the Membership Assembly of the BDI', 28 March 1950, in *Drucksache* Nr. 4, p. 18.

23. 'Gedanken zu einer deutsch-französischen Aussprache', 22 November 1949, Klöckner Archives, NL Henle, Europäische Bewegung/ Der Deutsche Rat/ Exekutiv-Komitee/ 1.6.–1.12.1949.

24. See Werner Bührer, 'Der BDI und die Außenpolitik der Bundesrepublik in den fünfziger Jahren' in *Vierteljahrshefte für Zeitgeschichte*, vol. 40, 1992, pp. 241–61, esp. pp. 251–3.

25. 'Report on the Foundation of the Commission for Economic Questions of the Industrial Associations', p. 6. See also 'Gemeinsame Willensbildung', in *Handelsblatt*, 21 October 1949.

26. Speech by Berg on the occassion of the foundation of the *Europa-Ausschuß*, 18 December 1950, BDI Archives (BDIA), Aufsätze Präs. Berg ab 1950.

27. *Der Weg zum industriellen Spitzenverband*, Darmstadt, 1958, p. 350.

28. DIHT, *Tätigkeitsbericht für das Geschäftsjahr 1957/58*, p. 53 and *Tätigkeitsbericht 1958/59*, p. 325.

German Industry and European Integration 111

29. Wirtschaftsvereinigung Eisen- und Stahlindustrie, *Tätigkeitsbericht Juni 1950*, p. 5.
30. See Hans-Wolfgang Platzer, *Unternehmensverbände in der EG – ihre nationale und transnationale Organisation und Politik*, Kehl am Rhein/Straßburg, 1984, p. 258.
31. See BDI, 'Europa-Tag in Trier 30–31 October 1952' in *Drucksache* Nr 18.
32. See *Fünf Jahre BDI*, p. 172–3; Platzer, *Unternehmensverbände*, p. 37–40; Ernst B. Haas, *The Uniting of Europe: Political, Social and Economic Forces 1950–1957*, London, 1958, p. 324.
33. *Jahresbericht des BDI 1957/58*, p. 23.
34. Haas, *The Uniting of Europe*, p. 324.
35. *Jahresbericht des BDI 1952/53*, p. 25
36. See Hans Dichgans, *Montanunion. Menschen und Institutionen*, Düsseldorf/Vienna, 1980, pp. 136–9; Haas, *The Uniting of Europe*, pp. 325–7.
37. Haas, *The Uniting of Europe*, pp. 327–30; Platzer, *Unternehmensverbände*, pp. 199–220.
38. See, for example, DIHT, *Tätigkeitsbericht 1954/55*, pp. 230–2; Walther Herrmann, 'Internationale Bestrebungen der Unternehmerverbände' in *Europa-Archiv*, vol. 7, 1952, pp. 5247–8.
39. See Platzer, *Unternehmensverbände*, pp. 257–62.
40. See Braunthal, *Federation*, p. 326.
41. See Platzer, *Unternehmensverbände*, pp. 57–8.
42. See Sönke Reimers, 'The "Union des Industries de la Communaute Européenne" (UNICE) between the Common Market and a European Free Trade Area' in *Historians of Contemporary Europe Newsletter*, Vol. 7, No. 3–4, December 1992, pp. 147–55.
43. As far as the BDI is concerned see Platzer, *Unternehmensverbände*, p. 58.
44. As regards ELEC see Michel Dumoulin and Anne-Myriam Dutrieue, *La Ligue européenne de coopération économique (1946–1981). Une groupe d'étude et de pression dans la construction européenne*, Bern/Paris, 1993; on CEPES see Anne-Myriam Dutrieue, 'La CEPES, un mouvement patronal européen (1952–1967)' in Michel Doumulin, René Girault and Gilbert Trausch (eds), *L'Europe du Patronat. De la guerre froid aux années soixante*, Bern et al., 1993, pp. 213–30.
45. See Wilfried Loth, 'Die Europa-Bewegung in den Anfangsjahren der Bundesrepublik' in Ludolf Herbst, Werner Bührer and Hanno Sowade (eds), *Vom Marshallplan zur EWG. Die Eingliederung der Bundesrepublik Deutschland in die westliche Welt*, Munich, 1990, pp. 63–77, esp. p. 74.
46. BDI to members of the presidential board, 11 July 1953, AIHKA, NL Vogel, BDI-Außenhandelsausschuß, Juli 1951–September 1953.

112   *Werner Bührer*

47. Textiles association to Vogel, 26 July 1950, AIHKA, NL Vogel, Marshallplan/Pariser Verhandlungen, April 1949–October 1950. See in general Werner Bührer, 'Die deutsche Industrie und der Marshallplan 1947–1952' in Comité pour l'Histoire Économique et Financière de la France (ed.), *Le Plan Marshall et le relèvement économique de l'Europe*, Paris, 1993, pp. 449–65, esp. 457–60.
48. See Bührer, *Ruhrstahl*, pp. 179–85.
49. Braunthal, *Federation*, pp. 321–2.
50. See Dichgans, *Montanunion*, pp. 188–90.
51. See Braunthal, *The Federation of German Industry*, pp. 322–3.
52. See, for example, John R. Gillingham, *Industry and Politics in the Third Reich: Ruhr Coal, Hitler and Europe*, Wiesbaden, 1985.
53. The problems of the incorporation of West Germany into the ERP and OEEC are described by Werner Bührer, Auftakt in Paris. Der Marshallplan und die deutsche Rückkehr auf die internationale Bühne 1948/49' in *Vierteljahrshefte für Zeitgeschichte*, vol. 36, 1988, pp. 529–56.
54. See Bührer, *Ruhrstahl*, pp. 85–8.
55. See Alan S. Milward, *The Reconstruction of Western Europe 1945–51*, London, 1984, esp. pp. 168–211; Wilfried Loth, *Der Weg nach Europa. Geschichte der europäischen Integration 1939–1957*, Göttingen, 1990, esp. pp. 66–8.
56. See Werner Bührer, 'Erzwungene oder freiwillige Liberalisierung? Die USA, die OEEC und die westdeutsche Außenhandelspolitik 1949–1952' in Herbst, Bührer and Sowade (eds), *Vom Marshallplan zur EWG*, pp. 139–62, esp. p. 154.
57. Statement by Carl-Gisbert Schultze-Schlutius, general manager of the Hamburg Chamber of Commerce at a DIHT *Hauptausschuß* conference, 26 January 1951, verbatim report, p. 58, in DIHT Archives, Bonn, Hauptausschuß, Sitzungen 1951; furthermore see 'Report on the 5th session of the foreign economy experts' working group', 27 October 1950, ibid., 300–12 Außenwirtschaftsreferenten, Sitzungen bis 1953.
58. See 'Memorandum regarding re-liberalization', 25 July 1951, Bundesarchiv-Koblenz (BA), B 146, 858.
59. See 'Report on the BDI conference at Bad Dürkheim', 28 March 1950, p. 9.
60. See, for example, 'Report on the session of the OEEC steel committee', 2–3 March 1949 and 9–10 March 1950, Archiv der Wirtschaftsvereinigung Stahl, Düsseldorf, 0308, Eisen- und Stahlkomitee der OEEC, 9.3.1949–30.9.1950. In general, see Jan van den Heuvel, 'Co-ordination of industrial investments' in *At Work for Europe: An Account of the Activities of the Organisation for European Economic Co-operation*, Paris, 1956, pp. 79–83.
61. *Jahresbericht des BDI 1954/55*, p. 18.

62. DIHT, *Tätigkeitsbericht 1957/58*, p. 42.
63. See Jacob J. Kaplan and Günther Schleiminger, *The European Payments Union: Financial Diplomacy in the 1950s*, Oxford, 1989, pp. 245–65.
64. See Bührer, *Ruhrstahl*, pp. 170–2.
65. Haas, *The Uniting of Europe*, p. 165; positive comments are mentioned by Bührer, *Ruhrstahl*, pp. 178–9. See furthermore John Gillingham, 'Solving the Ruhr Problem: German Heavy Industry and the Schuman Plan' in Klaus Schwabe (ed.), *The Beginnings of the Schuman-Plan*, Baden-Baden, 1988, pp. 399–436, esp. 413–22.
66. Haas, *The Uniting of Europe*, p. 163.
67. *Geschäftsbericht des BDI 1950/51*, p. 12.
68. See Werner Bührer, 'Die "Europäisierung" des Arbeitsrechts aus unternehmerischer Sicht 1950–1990' in *Archiv für Sozialgeschichte*, vol. 31, 1991, pp. 297–311, esp. pp. 301–3.
69. Wellhausen to Reusch, 25 August 1950, Haniel Archiv, NL H. Reusch, 40010146/44.
70. See Bührer, *Ruhrstahl*, pp. 185–206; Gillingham, 'Solving the Ruhr Problem', pp. 422–32.
71. Haas, *The uniting of Europe*, p. 176.
72. 'Declaration of the BDI regarding sectoral integration', 26 March 1952, BA, NL Blücher, 103.
73. 'Meeting of the BDI', 17–19 May 1953, p. 15.
74. See, for example, *Jahresbericht des BDI 1952/53*, p. 16.
75. See *Jahresbericht des BDI 1954/55*, p. 23.
76. 'Meeting of the presidential board', 8 June 1955, BDIA, Sitzungsprotokolle 1955/56.
77. See Foreign Relations of the United States, 1955–57, vol. IV, pp. 335ff.; Christian Deubner, *Die Atompolitik der westdeutschen Industrie und die Gründung von Euratom*, Frankfurt am Main/New York, 1977; Michael Eckert, 'Die Anfänge der Atompolitik in der Bundesrepublik Deutschland' in *Vierteljahrshefte für Zeitgeschichte*, vol. 37, 1989, pp. 115–43.
78. See 'Meeting of the presidential board', 23 May 1956, BDIA, Sitzungsprotokolle 1955/56.
79. See *Jahresbericht des BDI 1956/57*, pp. 33–42; Platzer, *Unternehmensverbände*, pp. 49–55.
80. See Bührer, '"Europäisierung" des Arbeitsrechts', pp. 303–4.
81. See DIHT, *Tätigkeitsbericht 1956/57*, p. 25.
82. Hanns Jürgen Küsters, *Die Gründung der Europäischen Wirtschaftsgemeinschaft*, Baden-Baden, 1982, pp. 275–6.
83. See 'Provisional statement regarding European economic integration', February 1956, Archiv der Wirtchaftsvereinigung Stahl, Düsseldorf, NL Salewski.
84. See 'Memorandum concerning full-scale European integration', 14 February 1956, BA, B 116, 7296.

114   *Werner Bührer*

85. 'Kanzler-Tee', 22 February 1957, in *Adenauer. Teegespräche 1955–1958*, Berlin, 1986, p. 181.

86. *Jahresbericht des BDI 1957/58*, p. 27.

87. See Braunthal, *The Federation of German Industry*, p. 303.

88. Miriam Camps, *Britain and the European Community 1955–1963*, Princeton, 1964, p. 100; see also Küsters, *Gründung*, p. 280–94.

89. See Daniel Koerfer, *Kampf ums Kanzleramt. Erhard und Adenauer*, Stuttgart, 1987, pp. 201–5.

90. OEEC, Council, Minutes of the 355th Meeting, 12–13 February 1957, BA, B 146, 867.

91. 'Meeting of the presidential board', 26 February 1958, BDIA, Sitzungsprotokolle 1958/59.

92. 'Meeting of the presidential board', 29 March 1958.

93. 'Meeting of the presidential board', 29 April 1958.

94. 'Statement concerning questions of the free trade area', 4 December 1957, in DIHT, *Tätigkeitsbericht 1957/58*, pp. 437–9.

95. See Camps, *Britain*, pp. 153–72.

96. See 'Meeting of the presidential board', 9 December 1958, BDIA, Sitzungsprotokolle 1958/59.

97. 'General Assembly of the BDI', 23 June 1959, BDIA, Sitzungsprotokolle 1959.

98. See, for example, *Jahresbericht des BDI 1957/58*, pp. 37–41, and *Jahresbericht des BDI 1958/59*, pp. 74–80; DIHT, *Tätigkeitsbericht 1958/59*, p. 36–7.

99. 'Meeting of staff members of industrial associations', 8 April 1960, BDIA, Sitzungsprotokolle 1960.

100. BDI (ed.), *Die deutsche Industrie im Gemeinsamen Markt. Bericht über die bisherigen Auswirkungen der Europäischen Wirtschaftsgemeinschaft 1958–1963*, Bergisch-Gladbach, 1965, pp. 3–6.

[7]

IX

THE COMMON MARKET

by

RICHARD T. GRIFFITHS

One of the constant themes running through this volume has been the relentless Dutch search for a multilateral trade agreement which would reduce or eliminate protectionist barriers to their exports. If one remembers, however, that these years also represented an unprecedented period of economic expansion which, for the Netherlands too, is identified with the phenomenon of "export-led growth"[1] then we are left with something of a paradox. This can also be illustrated by an examination of Table 9.1 which measures the evolution of the penetration of Dutch exports in the markets of the major trading partners[2].

Table 9.1 *Weighted share of Dutch imports in the major Dutch export markets*

Year		Year		Year		Year	
1923	66	1931	81	1947	44	1955	88
1924	70	1932	75	1948	55	1956	87
1925	77	1933	69	1949	66	1957	86
1926	78	1934	69	1950	87	1958	95
1927	75	1935	65	1951	74	1959	100
1928	76	1936	63	1952	83	1960	97
1929	74	1937	62	1953	86		
1930	78	1938	65	1954	89		

Source: Calculated from League of Nations, *International Trade Statistics,* various years (1923-1938) and United Nations, *Yearbook of International Trade Statistics,* various years (1947-1960).

The table demonstrates quite clearly the terrible problems the Dutch experienced in regaining a foothold in their traditional markets in the immediate post-war years since the index is much lower than even the abysmal levels achieved in the 1930's. However the picture then changes dramatically. In 1950, reflecting the trade agreement achieved with Germany the previous year, and again consistently after 1952 the Netherlands achieved market shares which surpass not only those of the 1930's but even those of the boom years of the 1920's. The question thus arises, why, if export performance was so favourable, did Dutch policy-makers keep producing one trade initiative after the other. There are probably two explanations. The first is that policy-makers became trapped in a set of assumptions, based upon the immediate post-war experience, which continued to shape thinking even after the objective circumstances had changed. Whilst I believe that this did play a role, more important still was the second explanation, namely that they did not believe that such changed circumstances would last. In the case of Germany, France and the United Kingdom the Dutch had already experienced the partial suspension of OEEC liberalisation measures which had demonstrated the fragility of the programme. They had witnessed the persistence of protectionist measures even during the prosperous years of the early 1950's and they expected such barriers to increase once the trade-cycle turned downwards. We now know that such cyclical disturbances had relatively little impact on European growth in the 1950's and 60's but in the early 1950's there were few who would have anticipated such a situation occurring. After a number of years of strong economic growth, they expected a period of recession with all the painful consequences which that would entail for small, trade-dependent economies like the Netherlands. What the Dutch wanted, and what the Beyen plan had been designed to provide, was a mechanism which would limit the freedom of their trading partners over their own commercial policies. For them, a customs union would represent a definite economic peace treaty to end forever the trade war which had begun in the 1930's.

It is often said that the Dutch interest in realising a customs union in western Europe was a logical consequence of the relative openness of the economy. But whilst the relatively high ratio of imports and exports to national income (higher still if services are included) can explain the attractiveness of removing trade barriers in general, it cannot explain why the Dutch should be willing to enter into a framework for economic interdependence which combined internal free trade with external protective tariffs. To answer this question and therefore to explain the Dutch conduct during the negotiations it is necessary to examine the structure of Dutch trade more closely.

Table 9.2 *Intra-exports of the EEC countries in 1955. (as percentages of total exports)*

Country	Total EEC	Nether-lands	Bleu	West-Germany	France	Italy
Netherlands	38,3	—	13,8	17,1	5,0	2,4
BLEU	44,7	20,7	—	11,8	10,0	2,2
W.Germany	28,8	9,4	6,7	—	7,0	5,7
France	24,0	3,0	7,0	10,5	—	3,5
Italy	23,5	2,4	2,7	12,6	5,8	—

Source: UN, *Economic Survey of Europe, 1956,* Geneva 1957

The data in Table 9.2 would seem at first sight to confirm the Dutch interest in reaching a commercial agreement with the "six". Its dependence on the rest as an export market is exceeded only by the Belgian-Luxembourg Economic Union (BLEU). But before reaching the inevitable conclusion it is necessary to note that within Benelux, the Dutch already enjoyed a position of no tariff barriers and quantitative restrictions on its industrial exports and a position as preferential agricultural supplier to the Belgian market. It had little extra to gain in this direction with the negotiations. Remove this island of (quasi-) free trade and the proportion of exports going to remaining partners falls back to the level of the rest. There was one area, however, in which the Dutch could be said to have had a particular interest not shared by the rest and that was in foodstuffs. This category accounted in 1955 for 28 per cent of Dutch exports to the Six (still over 20 per cent if BLEU is excluded) whereas for the others it accounted for only 5 per cent of intra-exports. If there were to be a common market, it was a major Dutch priority to ensure that agriculture was part of it[3].

The import composition of the Netherlands also differed from that of the others. It is typical of a small country's trade with a relatively larger share of end products in the total than was the case for Germany and France which had more diversified industrial structures. However, a glance at Table 9.3 reveals another specific feature of Dutch trade which played a vital role during the negotiations. The Dutch economy relied heavily upon imports of semi-manufactures and end-products from countries *outside* the area of the proposed community. The Dutch derived almost 60 per cent of their imports in these categories from outside the proposed bloc compared to the six-country average of 28 per cent.

Table 9.3 *Import composition of Dutch and comunity trade with third countries (as percentages)*

	Netherlands	EEC Countries
Primary Products	41	72
Semi-Manufactures	26	13
End Products	33	15

Note:　　　　　Dutch statistics refer to 1955 and the EEC Statistics to 1958
Source:　　　　ARA, Ministerie van Economische Zaken, Buitenlandse
　　　　　　　　Economische Betrekkingen, 1700, *Europese Integratie. Buitentarief der
　　　　　　　　douane-unie in de industriële sector*, 22.1.1957
EEC Statistics:　P. Maillet e.a., *L'économie de la Communauté Européenne*, Paris, 1968,
　　　　　　　　246.

This short summary has focussed on four essentials: the weight of earnings from trade and services in national income, the importance of the common market as a (potential) export market for Dutch foodstuffs, the importance of BLEU as an importer of Dutch products and the large share of semi-manufactures and end products from outside the group in total imports and total industrial inputs[4].

It is obvious from this list that Dutch governments would have a difficult task in weighing up the pros and cons of joining a common market. Although, in theory, the community offered an attractive prospect for Dutch exports of foodstuffs, the government was aware that any real liberalisation of agricultural trade, still at the time of the most protected areas in Europe, would be difficult to achieve and would take a long time to realise. Furthermore, the comparative advantage which Dutch exporters enjoyed in Benelux would almost certainly disappear with only negative consequences for Dutch trade and Dutch national income[5]. And, finally, the government knew that the structure of Dutch imports made it absolutely necessary for the future community to be as "open" as possible if a deflection of imports from third countries to relatively high price producers within the community were to be avoided. Since the Benelux tariffs were the lowest among the Six (see Table 9.4) the danger was ever present that the Dutch could end up having to accept a relatively high common external tariff. This would carry the danger of increasing the price of industrial inputs and worsening the competitive position of Dutch industry in general[6].

Table 9.4 *Weighted indices of tariffs (excluding fiscal duties): tariff revenue as a percentage of import values*

Category of Goods	BLEU	W. Germany	France	Italy
I	1	11	11	27
II	5	21	9	23
III	14	15	9	19
IV	0	2	2	2
V	4	15	17	20
VI	10	14	15	21
VII	13	18	18	22
VIII	4	10	6	22
IX	10	12	16	23
X	9	8	14	20

I-Primary products for food (excl. fish); II-Manufactured products for food (excl. fish); III-Fish and fish products; IV-Raw materials incl. petroleum; V-Chemicals; VI-Leather, leather products, furs, rubber, wood, cork, paper and printer matter; VII-Textiles and clothing; VIII-Base metals and manufactures thereof; IX-Machinery, electric and transport equipment; X-Misc. manufactures.

Source: GATT, *Basic Instruments and Selected Documents, Second Supplement*, Geneva 1954.

The question which needs to be posed is why, if the prospects were so gloomy, would the Dutch want to run the risk of being isolated in a protective community of six if their real interests lay in a wider framework? One part of the answer lies in the experience they had already had in trying to negotiate the removal of trade barriers in the forums of the OEEC and GATT. Not only had these organisations represented members' economic interests that were too diverse for much to be achieved, but the experience had also shown that the Dutch were in a weak negotiating position because their level of protection was too low to offer much bargaining power[7]. In the talks with the Six, however, they could at least join forces with Belgium and Luxembourg against the protectionist tendencies in other countries. The other motive for joining was the Dutch fear of renewed protectionism in a future recession. Within a customs union they hoped that trade barriers once down would stay down, excluding certain carefully controlled, limited and temporary exemption situations. But if the Dutch were to agree to the new community it had shown a liberal face towards the outside world and could not be allowed to damage sectors considered vital for Dutch economic survival. These goals were deemed so important that neither the realisation of the customs union itself nor the level of the external tariff were to be left in any uncertainty whatever.

The foreign ministers of the six at their meeting in Messina had agreed to setting up a conference of experts to study the various proposals before it, including that of forming a common market. The Belgian foreign minister Paul-Henri Spaak was chosen to chair the conference. To lead the Dutch delegation, the cabinet chose a "balanced ticket" – Professor Verrijn Stuart, whose views on integration were strictly functional and whose inclination was to reject any institutional arrangements not immediately necessary for a common market, was to lead the delegation but his immediate subordinate was Johannes Linthorst Homan, whose aspirations were openly more federalist but whose conduct of the EPC negotiations on the Beyen Plan had shown that he could be relied upon to toe the line where necessary[8]. Although the conference initially included committees on transport and classical energy alongside those on the common market and atomic energy, it did not take long before the focus concentrated on the latter. As early as the second week of the conference itself, the delegation reported back on this happy development[9] and Spaak himself confirmed his own conversion to this standpoint when reporting to the foreign ministers in Noordwijk in September 1955. All the various other questions, as far as he was concerned, had to be seen in the light of need to create a common market, as had been agreed at Messina[10].

During the negotiations leading to the Spaak Report, the cabinet spent very little time discussing developments. This is not to say that the delegation did not liaise with different ministries on particular problems but rather it reflected the fact that the Netherlands at least treated the conference for what it was – a study group whose task was to draw up a report; once the report was ready would come the time for political decisions. Only towards the end of the proceedings, when the delegation began to encounter real difficulties in getting put Dutch demands written into the final report, did this position begin to waver. This pattern of different delegations reflecting their national positions but without operating under strict instructions, characterised the conduct of virtually the entire negotiations[11], but there was one interesting exception which is worth following because it did lead to a lengthy debate in cabinet which demonstrated the fragility of cabinet unity in these early stages.

Since the first launching of the Beyen Plan, official Dutch policy had been that the customs union should be worked out in the treaty down to virtually the last detail. This alone sheds much light on the early conversion to "supranationality" which also characterised the Dutch negotiating position. Not only was the neo-federalist conviction that this should be the way forward not shared throughout the cabinet but even among a number of apparent adherents, supranationality was a means to an end rather than an article of faith. It was to be used when the Dutch thought they could get a better deal later compared with what might flow from the negotiations themselves or when they thought such arrangements could better prevent independent action on the part of others. It was not an easy or even elegant position to have to try to maintain.

These questions came to the surface when the cabinet turned to discuss a note setting out the French position on the customs union in October 1955. France, it will be recalled, had adopted a minimalist position towards a custom union throughout the EPC negotiations and there had been deep concern whether it would accept anything along the lines of the Benelux memorandum at Messina. This hesitancy had been demonstrated time and again by its delegation throughout the early weeks of the work of the study conference but, even so, there was some surprise that the government should have chosen to stake out a (semi-)official position at this stage of proceedings. The French note contained three points of contention – a proposal to equalise working conditions (on which more will be said below), a demand that countries in balance-of-payments problems be allowed unilaterally to reintroduce trade restrictions and a suggestion that tariffs on intra-trade be reduced by 30 per cent over the first four years and that the rest of the operation be left to a *magistrature commun*[12].

The French demand for the possibility of temporary exemption status came close to the idea of *clauses de sauvegarde* which the Dutch had backed since the EPC negotiations. If a country experience a "fundamental disequilibrium" in its balance of payments within the market, there should be a supranational mechanism allowing the temporary reimposition of quantitative trade restrictions. However, there should be no going back on tariff reductions already granted. This placed the delegation in the curious position of arguing at one and the same time for the quickest implementation of a common market and the possibility of suspending it at any time in the future. Yet the Dutch clung to this position because of a dislike of any of the alternatives. These included a commitment to fund any country in balance-of-payments problems, a far-reaching degree of policy coordination which would reduce or eliminate the chances of such disequilibrium appearing in the first place or a levelling (upwards!) of working conditions, wages and social security payments[13]. None of the other delegations had shown much inclination in supporting this position until the French note which, in demanding that the *autonomous* reimposition of quotas *and* tariffs, took the Dutch ideas one step further. This struck a positive chord with the finance minister Johan Van der Kieft who argued that he preferred import restrictions to open-ended credit commitments. He pointed out that since national governments and parliaments would still exist after the market had been created, it should be left to them to decide upon the timing and nature of the measures to be taken. This opened the door for other skeptics on the value of supranationalism to have their say. The defence minister, Cornelis Staf, chipped in with the observation that the six were only a small group and that the supranational solutions proved impossible to agree. Willem Drees also replied in the same vein, pointing out for good measure that all the French were offering was a small drop in tariffs but were demanding in return the expensive measures of social harmonisation. Beyen held out for this original position and was strongly supported in his stance by Jelle Zijlstra, who, whilst echoing the feeling in cabinet that it was necessary to avoid being "sucked into dangerous harmonisation ideas", nevertheless rejected the right of states unilaterally to reimpose import restrictions. He then went on to proclaim that there was no point in progressing towards a customs union if there was "no complement in the political sphere". Unusually for cabinet, the question was put to the vote and a majority emerged for continuing to push for supranationality, on this issue at least[14].

The reaction to the French suggestion to leave the implementation of the later phases of the customs union to a supranational body was roundly rejected. Beyen now argued that the fact that the other five delegations refused to concede supranationality on the *clauses de sauvegarde* issue, and were unwilling to go as far as the Dutch on the supranationality question in general, made it easier for the Dutch, in turn, to reject any supranational solution as far as the customs union was concerned. He made absolutely clear that the government should stick to its original policy "that the group of six countries is only acceptable if it arrives at a closer bonding. If this does not occur, there is no reason to remain within the group of six"[15]. It was this basic principle which united the skeptics, opportunists and idealists within the cabinet. It was also, incidentally, the hope that the Dutch could realise this goal which prompted a brusque rejection of the United Kingdom's ideas for a free trade area. The only response, as Zijlstra put it, was to "carry on resolutely" and to ignore attempts to form, what he called "a crippled customs union"[16].

The Dutch delegation had done their best to have the principles of an automatic customs union with a low external tariff written into the Spaak report. However, with none of the other five delegations agreed and with Spaak's determination to present a unanimous document to the six governments, this was easier said than done. It was Drees who was most irritated by this. He rejected the "intimidation" employed to get the Dutch delegation to soften its position[17] and scorned the efforts to present a unanimous report when "it is not true". Only Sicco

Mansholt supported the Spaak method. He argued that if every country acted as apparently the cabinet wanted the Dutch to do, the months of negotiation would have accomplished nothing. The majority of cabinet, however, sided with Drees that, "one cannot force experts to be agreed about a report on which they are not, in fact, agreed". The very least they wanted was a statement included that the report was not unanimous[18]. When this demand was met, Dutch qualms were stilled. As far as the report itself was concerned, it received nothing but praise. Zijlstra saw it as "a satisfactory basis for a governmental conference". Mansholt felt it offered "a new beginning for European integration". Even Drees was forced to concede that it was "a clever report"[19].

Within the negotiations leading to the Spaak report the "ideal" Dutch solution of an automatic reduction of internal tariffs and a common external tariff (CET) based upon the Benelux schedules had quickly proved unrealisable. However, the Dutch had come closer to success on the former demand than on the latter. The Spaak report had recommended the abolition of all internal duties in three stages of four years each. In the first stage, all tariffs which were close to or under the target for the external tariff were to be reduced by 10 per cent and all other tariffs by 30 per cent. In the second stage a further 30 per cent reduction would be achieved and during the last stage, they would be eliminated entirely. Since, from the start, the French objections to a completely automatic system were accepted, three further elements had been introduced to allow individual governments some room for manoeuvre. Firstly, the tariffs were arranged in groups according to the actual tariff levels[20] and governments were left free to decide which exact tariff posts to reduce in order to achieve the overall reduction. Secondly, on the basis of a proposal by the commission, endorsed by a majority vote in the Parliament and a qualified majority in the Council of Ministers, a decision could be taken to alter the procedure in the second and third stages and to extend the transition period for a further three years. Finally, if the Commission agreed, governments with special difficulties could apply for temporary exemption status for certain posts with the understanding that these could never cover more than 5 per cent of total imports[21]. Thus, the Spaak report seemingly guaranteed the creation of a common market whilst at the same time introducing an element of flexibility aimed at overcoming the resistance of high-tariff countries.

Far less satisfactory for the Dutch were the results on the level of the common external tariff. Against the initial Dutch bid for using the Benelux tariff as a basis for the CET with, possibly, some small percentage increases[22] lay a French demand that the level be "as high as possible''[23]. A further danger to the Dutch position lay in a Belgian proposal to adopt the GATT maximum tariffs as "fighting tariffs" and to work towards a new CET via multilateral negotiations[24]. In this way the new community would avoid the need for making unilateral reductions vis-à-vis third countries without getting anything in return. The discussions were muddied even further in October when the French suggested that the CET be based upon the weighted average of all the existing tariffs above the GATT recommended maximum. Spaak had then tried to build a compromise round the earlier Belgian proposal for fighting tariffs. He also suggested that the "floor" for the new tariff structure be the arithmetic average for those products where existing tariffs[25] lay close together and the weighted average for the remainder. Products for which "particular difficulties" existed would be resolved by further negotiation. The fear of the Dutch was still that the subsequent GATT negotiations would fail to yield the expected results and that the new community would be left saddled with a high tariff. Besides, if there was to be a "floor", it should be the existing Benelux tariff. Since the Dutch delegation was isolated on this point, Spaak suggested that it come with its own counter-proposal[26]. This brought some movement in the Dutch position. Zijlstra informed Spaak that the Dutch wanted a zero tariff on raw materials and the existing Benelux tariff on manufactures. However, for end products he was willing to make the following concession: all the extremely high tariffs should be "de-capped" to the GATT maximum and then the final level should be determined by the arithmetic average of the four tariff schedules[27]. By using an arithmetic average, the Benelux level would account for a quarter of the weighting: using a weighted average it would more often than not count for less. This method was the one enshrined in the Spaak report, but it was to apply to *all* product groups[28]. Examining this position, Zijlstra concluded that it seemed likely that a low tariff on raw materials was within reach since, within the group, low tariffs were the norm. On finished consumption goods he considered that "the economy would not collapse if the import duty on such goods were raised, for example, from 20 to 30 per cent". The real fight, as he saw it, would come on semi-manufactures upon which the economy was so import dependent. Moreover, the "really dangerous point" remained the French demands for social harmonisation[29].

Zijlstra's concern was really to understate the difficulties since it was far from certain that the French would accept the Spaak report at all. However, when the foreign ministers met in Venice at the end of May 1956, the French foreign minister Christian Pineau announced his governments approval for new negotiations to commence, on the basis of the Spaak report, towards separate treaties for Euratom and a common market. At the same time, however, he reiterated the French position outlined in the note of October 1955 and mentioned, for the first time, the need to consider arrangements for French overseas territories[30].

At the beginning of September 1956 Maurice Faure outlined the specific French demands – equalisation of wages for women within two years and the harmonisation of the length of the working week and the number of paid holidays two years after that. Moreover, at the end of the transition period, there should be an equalisation of wage levels (on the basis of commission proposals effectuated by unanimous, later majority, decision of the Council of Ministers)[31]. Within the cabinet, the general reaction was that the French demands, no matter how desirable in themselves, did not allow for a sufficient time-scale for implementation. Drees added what was rapidly becoming his common refrain that he was only in favour of integration as long as did not harm the country's interests. Thus it was felt that if a more reasonable time-table could be agreed, there should be room for compromise on the questions of equal pay and holidays. It was decided, for the moment, to say nothing on the 40-hour week[32].

Before anything could be decided on the social harmonisation issue, Faure tabled a second set of French demands. He claimed that whilst France was willing to ratify the treaty, its provision should be suspended for France until the Algerian question had been solved. Since devaluation was politically unachievable, France should be able to maintain its current measure of import restriction and export subsidies for as long as necessary and, in the case of urgent balance-of-payments problems, it should be allowed autonomously to impose import restriction (subject, afterwards, to Council of Minister approval). Furthermore, he wanted the decision to move on to the second phase for creating the common market to be dependent on a unanimous decision of the Council of Ministers. The only concession was that if these demands were agreed to, France might soften its standpoint on harmonisation[33].

Within cabinet, Beyen attempted to put a positive gloss on the latest turn of events by suggesting that they demonstrated that France was serious about creating a common market. Cabinet was willing to countenance some concessions but was not inclined to accept the Belgian proposal of an "empty chair". On the other hand, Drees was worried about creating as situation whereby France could join in making future decisions which would be binding on others whilst not itself being bound by the results. Both he and Zijlstra were of the opinion that a common market in which the French could maintain protection would not be a *common* market. If a definite time limit could not be agreed in advance, the least he wanted was for a procedure to be fixed

in which France would not have a *de facto* veto right in determining
when the period in which it would be exempt from common rules
would come to an end[34].

This was the last time the old cabinet, Drees III, met to discuss
European questions. In the new cabinet the most important change
for foreign policy was the absence of Beyen. Joseph Luns, who was
noticeably less Europe-inclined than Beyen, assumed control over the
direction of foreign policy as a whole[35]. On the other hand, the pro-
European element in cabinet was strengthened by the inclusion of two
new ministers, Marga Klompé and Ivo Samkalden[36].

Whilst this had been going on, the French demands had been
meeting stiff opposition from the other delegations in the negotiations,
where matters had been muddied even further by a new set of German
proposals on Euratom. Moreover, over the whole spectrum of issues,
the negotiations appeared to be coming bogged down in endless commission discussions not least because a final standpoint on economic
questions was dependent upon the institutional construction chosen
and vice-versa. If not exactly drifting towards an impasse, the negotiations were nonetheless in need of some political breakthrough. That
came not, as expected, at the ministers' conference in Paris but at a
summit, at the height of the Suez crisis, between Guy Mollet and
Konrad Adenauer in November 1956. It was a deal so fragile that
tinkering with any one element might unravel the entire package.
Luns accepted that the exemption status accorded to France was not
especially favourable but he recommended that cabinet should accept
he compromise because it would allow matters in Brussels to get going
again[37].

Luns' advice was not accepted so easily. The course which events had
taken served to reawaken the reserves of the skeptics for whom they
proved a vivid illustration of what might await the Netherlands in the
future[38]. Equally important they dismayed those on the pro-European
wing who had seen so many of their early ideals ever more watered
down the further the negotiations had proceeded. In particular, the
supranational dimension on which they had pinned their hopes was
fading fast as, time and again, the decisive role in the decision-making
process was given to the Council of Ministers. It was these ministers,
Samkalden and Klompé, together with Mansholt, who took the initiative in raising neo-federalist arguments in particular and the entire
institutional structure in general at cabinet level. This new element in
the discussion cannot be explained simply by reference to the stage
which the negotiations had reached. Repeatedly Dutch demands in
this area had been rejected by the rest without the matter becoming
a cabinet matter possibly because Beyen had felt that Drees would ac-

cept almost anything so long as the common market was realised. This new approach carried the inherent risk of waking sleeping dogs best left to lie and evoking the response from the skeptics: if you're not happy with things, we're not either, so let's forget about the whole thing.

The first point which united cabinet across the spectrum from Drees to Mansholt was the fact that the Mollet/Adenauer agreement, however important politically, must be open for discussion. In particular it was felt that the fault of affording France an almost open-ended exemption status was merely compounded by opening the possibility for other states to impose countervailing duties on French exports. The common market should be irreversible. In the end Zijlstra suggested that the Dutch could concede a special regime for seven years, but that this concession be kept in reserve for horse-trading in the course of the forthcoming negotiations[39].

There then followed a long discussion on the interlinked questions of the institutional arrangements and the provisions in the treaty for agriculture and transport. Throughout the Brussels negotiations the Dutch had insisted that a common market should be arrived at for both of these sectors at the same time as the common market for trade. It was recognised that there should be some common policy within which this should occur but it had been the goal to make that policy as liberal as possible for in this the Dutch saw their greatest national advantage. The problem was that these (and previous!) negotiations had demonstrated that the other five governments had visions on these questions considerably more dirigist and more protectionist than those cherished by the Dutch and possibly for this reason there had been no great pressure to obtain a detailed set of arrangements written into the treaty. They would probably not have liked the result. The alternative, therefore, was to try to obtain a procedure for arriving at a common market in these sectors which was not dependent on a decision by national governments, represented in this case by the Council of Ministers[40]. Unfortunately there was no agreement in cabinet on how best to achieve this. Mansholt, Samkalden and Klompé felt that proposals made by the Commission should go to the Assembly before being discussed by the Council. The independence of the Commission and the pro-Europeanism of the chamber representing the *peoples* of Europe, would together guarantee the kind of results the Dutch wanted and there would then exist the necessary pressure to force the council, otherwise trapped by national sectoral pressure groups, to heel. On the other hand Zijlstra, Drees and the minister for transport, Jacob Algera, preferred to seek the solution in strengthening the rights of initiative of the Commission and ensuring majority decision-making in the Council. They did not see the Assembly contributing very much to any discussion and were reluctant to allow the Assembly to do more than control the *overall* policy of the Commission. Besides, they felt that the ministers had first and foremost to answer to their own parliaments. It was in this direction that cabinet agreed to seek a solution[41]. The furthest the Dutch were to get was an agreement to introduce majority decision-making on the question of the form of the common agricultural policy from the end of the second phase (i.e. after eight years). Since, in the meanwhile, countries could autonomously maintain their own price support systems, the Dutch had to console themselves with the addition of a passage pronouncing the intention that such measures should not (further) reduce trade. On the somewhat more positive side, they did manage to avoid the full French demands for preferential purchasing contracts and they did get an acknowledgement in principle that import duties on foodstuffs destined for the processing industry and then for reexport could be refunded. As far as transport was concerned, the Dutch had to realise that they had not the slightest chance of shifting the rest in the desired direction and had thus to make do with broad procedural clauses "in the spirit" of the treaty as a whole.

The Dutch had initially had problems in getting agriculture onto the agenda at all. It was seven weeks into the Spaak negotiations before the question was seriously raised and even then France, Germany and Luxembourg had argued against synchronous treatment with the rest of the common market on the grounds of the wide gulfs in existing levels of development[42] and even then the French held out for a separate review of the situation after four years[43]. Spaak's secretariat, however, came out early and firmly in favour of including agriculture in the common market after a suitable transitional period[44] in a document which now only attracted German opposition. This was probably because Luxembourg had retired from the fray by announcing the intention of claiming exemption status and because France was without a government, which made it difficult to push a firm position[45]. Whilst the Spaak report, itself, therefore was relatively favourable to Dutch interests, whether any policy would eventually be agreed and, equally importantly, what kind of policy would emerge, were still in doubt.

The agricultural discussions did not resume in the intergovernmental negotiations until October 1956. It is instructive to pause at the discussions which took place on something as straightforward as the "aims" of a common agricultural policy to get an idea of the protectionist spirit which still haunted the discussions. The draft articles had suggested that one of the aims be a level of income sufficient to support a "normally productive" enterprise[46] which presumably, after a period of adaptation, meant sacrificing the incorrigibly inefficient.

This was resisted by the Germans, who wanted a goal of augmenting the incomes of *all* those engaged in agriculture, and the Italians, who wanted a statement added that an aim should be the maximum employment in agriculture[47]. To counter this the Dutch had secured French support for an amendment to the effect that agriculture should aim at creating the best possible technical conditions and securing "reasonable" prices[48], adding a stipulation the output structure be adjusted so that it was more in line with global specialisation[49]. This fell foul of virtually everyone. Italy and Luxembourg argued that "reasonable prices" would be carried on the backs of the farmers whilst France and Germany resisted any mention of global specialisation. Eventually the Dutch had to settle for a construction whereby rising living standards were made conditional on raising productivity[50]. This might all seem rather cosmetic, but it was indicative of the general atmosphere.

No one, however, was under any illusions that what was of crucial importance was what was to go into the policy and who was to control it. The Germans wanted national organisation to stay in place throughout the transitional period (which was to be between 12 and 15 years) and even beyond, envisaging the "common policy" as little more than a set of rules governing their operation[51]. This was supported by France insofar as they did not consider that an organisational vacuum should be left until a common policy was in place, but to ensure, for example, that the German state grain purchasing monopoly bought French grain, they wanted the conclusion of preferential purchasing agreements[52]. These suggestions met Dutch and Italian resistance since they saw themselves trapped between restricted German markets and expensive purchasing deals involving overpriced French surpluses[53], but in view of the fact that those surpluses were likely to be small, the Dutch were prepared to accept them in return for French support[54]. Instead what they received was another nasty shock, for the French claimed that in order to give their producers certainty, any decision to move towards the second phase of the policy (when common pricing rules were to be introduced) should be dependent upon satisfactory progress in the first four years[55]. Gradually the French position softened and the issue of preferential purchasing was successfully resolved – the issue of timing was not.

Both the French and Germans now supported a position whereby national price regimes and national organisations should remain autonomous for the first two phases (8-11 years!) and should only be phased out if there was sufficient agreement. This brought a pained Dutch reaction that such provisions would rob the achievement of a common agricultural market of any incentive, as far as they were concerned[56]. This brought the discussion back to square one whereby common price rules would be prepared in the first phase and implemented in the second[57], but still left open the question, in whose hands would the decision to move from phase one to two, to three lie?

The original draft articles had been clear – all rights of initiative lay with the Commission, whose proposals would have to be accepted by the Council of Ministers, voting unanimously in the first phase and by majority thereafter, and by the European Assembly. Very early on, the Dutch had protested that the unanimity provision could effectively "freeze" the policy in its first phase[58]. Worse was to follow because the French had promptly proposed extending unanimous voting procedures into phase two and removing any decision-making function from the Assembly[59]. Later they were to attempt to stretch unanimity into the third phase as well[60]. Of course, if implemented, this could have had the effect of continuing national price fixing etc. in perpetuity, since their disappearance was contingent upon reaching agreement on a common policy. The argument was that since there would be no opportunity for governments to consider specific proposals in the treaty itself (because there were none), the least one could do was to allow their dissent to be respected afterwards[61]. The Dutch now dug in their heels, stating that they would not accept the treaty unless the original draft procedures were reinstated. This served to restore the Assembly and to remove the threat of unanimous voting and veto rights in the third phase[62], but they were totally isolated in the demand for majority voting in the second phase. At the ministerial conference in February 1957 they were forced to concede this position in return for a (platonic) statement that in the second phase, national price regimes should not act in a way as to restrict trade[63]. At least the Dutch had won the position that decisions on common price levels under the common policy would not be subject to national veto rights. When that point was reached, however, in 1965 the French boycotted the Commission and got unanimity rules reinstated – with all the consequent results! Moreover, there was one consolation: unless a decision was taken to the contrary the timing of the stages for achieving a common agricultural policy were tied to the stages by which the internal trade barriers for industrial goods. A breakdown in progress in agriculture could be used as a legitimate reason to veto progress in other directions. The final shape of the agricultural policy was left in the hands of the Commission and a Council of Ministers who may or may not be exposed to the same pressures which had made such a farce of the green pool negotiations. "Progress" thus seemed reasonably guaranteed, in which direction it would be remained a matter of faith.

At this point the vital negotiations on the level of the external tariff were coming to a head. The crucial point for the Netherlands remained that of "decapitating" the highest tariffs before the arithmetic average was arrived at. The question which had remained vague in the Spaak report was the exact level of these permitted maximums. The Dutch demand was for a maximum of 5 per cent for raw materials, 10 per cent of semi-manufactures and 20 per cent for end-products. This was countered by the Italians who demanded 10, 15 and 20-30 per cent respectively but even more threatening was the position adopted by the French who wanted no decapitation at all. Moreover, they wanted all tariffs of 3 per cent or lower excluded in calculating the average[64]. This went altogether too far for Linthorst Homan who complained that the Benelux countries were already disadvantaged by counting their tariff schedules as one rather than three and that now it was proposed to exclude them from the calculations altogether! A German compromise proposal eventually formed the basis for a solution to the decapitation problem: 3 per cent for raw materials, 10 per cent for semi-manufactures but no decapitation for end products[65]. This solution was accepted by the ministers in Paris in February 1957. However, at the insistence of the French, the Dutch had to concede that for organic chemicals there would be a ceiling of 25 per cent and that for purposes of calculating the average, Benelux tariffs of 3 per cent or less would be entered as 12 per cent[66].

The new cabinet's disgruntlement with the course of the negotiations, which had been apparent since the Mollet-Adenauer agreement, increased even further when it was confronted with the results of yet another bilateral deal, namely the Franco-Belgian note of 16 November on the inclusion of overseas territories. Luns was more than a little annoyed that the Belgians should have committed themselves so far without even informing the Dutch beforehand. He did not fell it "self-evident" that Eurafrica should be created and certainly not at a time when it was still not clear what the implications of creating a common market would be for the six European nations. He considered that the Dutch should not accept a special regime for agricultural imports from the overseas territories and that they should not accept "co-responsibility" for other countries' colonies, let alone pay towards their upkeep[67]. Within cabinet, Zijlstra defended the inclusion of the overseas territories but he felt that the French and Belgians had erected barriers which were unacceptable. He questioned, however, whether "the soup should be eaten quite as hot as it has been served". Drees, in particular, focussed his objections upon the demands for a joint investment fund both economically and in terms of the political implications whilst Mansholt was concerned primarily about the implications of the preferential purchasing agreements for Dutch agriculture and food industries[68]. Before the ministerial con-

ference in Brussels, Linthorst Homan and Van der Beugel suggested
that the Dutch try to force the French and Belgians to acknowledge the
distinction between a trade regime for association and ''the launching
of a Marshall Plan for Africa''. The Dutch, they felt, could agree to
examining the former whilst rejecting the latter or leaving it to the
Commission to work out[69].

The position in which the Dutch found themselves shifted with the
appearance of an alternative German proposal which diluted the
political rhetoric of the original, which rejected preferential purchasing agreements and which, whilst accepting the principle of economic
and social help, seemed to hold the promise of reducing the sums involved. Moreover, it mentioned the inclusion of all overseas
territories[70]. Luns suggesting supporting the German position if only
because the limited financial contribution envisaged made a refusal to
participate politically untenable. Moreover it opened the prospect of
isolating the French who would have then to chose between a common
market with association and modest aid or no common market and no
aid[71]. Luns advised the cabinet to accept the German compromise and
to concentrate upon trying to limit the financial consequences. Drees,
however, was not yet ready to take such a step. He felt that the Dutch
delegation had already strayed considerably from the original cabinet
standpoint and he was particularly wary of agreeing to anything
before the cost was known[72]. That answer came very quickly from the
German side: a contribution of 7 per cent of the $500 million which,
at the time, was envisaged to be the size of the fund. Drees responded
by dropping his last reserves, as long as 7 per cent were indeed the
maximum. It was also decided to get Dutch New Guinea introduced
into the scheme in order to recoup some of the costs[73]. At a marathon
session in Paris on 20 February Drees succeeded in realising a net contribution for the Netherlands equivalent to 6 per cent of the investment fund. As far as the rest of the arrangements were concerned he
was content largely to support the German position[74]. Luns was able
to inform cabinet that Belgium had got less out of the fund than the
Netherlands despite the fact that the Congo, with 15 million inhabitants, was larger than New Guinea with 700,000. He doubtlessly
derived some satisfaction, too, from the news that Spaak was experiencing some measure of discomfort from his own cabinet[75].
However, when, at almost the last hurdle, to save face Belgium
demanded equal treatment to the Netherlands, the concession was
painlessly made[76].

The cabinet never got round to a review of the treaties as a whole
before they were signed in March 1957. The remorseless tempo which
Spaak forced upon the negotiations in order to get the treaties signed

and ratified before the West German elections could unfavourably change the composition of the Bundestag or before a renewed crisis could topple the existing French administration meant that the cabinet was forced to meet twice a week in order to keep pace with the changing situation. Locked into a process of incremental decision-making, there was simply no time to step back and take stock. The nearest we can get, therefore, to an overall assessment are the cabinet discussion documents themselves.

One of the clearest statements of the dilemma in which the Dutch found themselves was prepared by Linthorst Homan and Van der Beugel in January 1957. In looking at the situation they suggested that one could either start from the Spaak report and look to see what had survived or one could look at the treaties and see whether they offered a reasonable chance of accomplishing the goal of European integration. They preferred the latter. As far as the common market was concerned, they acknowledged that the direction of events since the Spaak report had served to weaken the treaty both economically and politically. The Dutch had failed to realise their aims on agriculture[77]. They had failed to raise the issue of including transport *services* beyond the level of a commitment in principle. The external tariff level was higher than they had wanted. Competences which they felt belonged with the Commission had been transferred to the Council of Ministers in which the weighted voting procedure further damaged the representation of Dutch interests. Prices would rise because of the social harmonisation measures and finally, they were saddled with an association of overseas territories which they had never wanted in the first place. Their conclusion was that nonetheless the Dutch should sign, preferably after extracting more concessions[78]. Drees, in cabinet, had in his possession a note from the cabinet secretary Drs. J. Middelburg. In the later stages of the negotiations he had acted almost as a mirror on the dark side of Drees' nature and was the author of a number of similarly blood-curdling notes. What he argued in this one was that whilst Linthorst Homan and van der Beugel "tended ... towards eventual acceptance, accompanied by a number of "buts", my view ... is rather the opposite, namely tending towards rejection of the treaty, accompanied by a number of "unlesses" "[79]. Drees, however, refrained from making any such statement and merely joined in the discussion on how best to extract the concessions which the Dutch deemed necessary.

If the cabinet's attitude towards the common market treaty was one of deep reservation, feelings towards the Euratom treaty were downright hostile. Klompé, at one point, wondered aloud if the treaty should be accepted since it would make the population who, according to her, were expecting a supranational treaty look like fools. At that

meeting only Zijlstra had a positive word to say, and that was only that
Euratom might actually develop into something important[80].
However, the Dutch were trapped into the logic of the equal treatment
of both treaties and, whatever their feelings, could not reject the one
without torpedoing the other. In a note to cabinet, Luns summed up
the situation on the Euratom treaty as follows: "it is difficult to show,
in concreto, what the advantages for the Netherlands are compared with
the existing possibilities for bilateral and multilateral cooperation. Important principles which played a fundamental role in the Spaak
report have disappeared.... It boils down to a choice between this treaty or no treaty"[81].

The choice between "this treaty or no treaty" applied to the common market as well. The Dutch had, after all, obtained the binding
commercial agreement they had wanted and much else besides. If the
end result was far from perfect, there was at least the consolation that
rejecting it would prove much worse. Such considerations, however,
did not stop Drees in April 1957 commenting, "In signing this treaty
the Netherlands has joined a relatively small, protectionist combination"[82]. On the other hand, for those with greater ambitions, the
treaties represented a stride, albeit faltering, in a new direction –
towards a democratic and federated Europe. For them disillusion
would come later.

The Dutch experience within the common market negotiations differed considerably from their previous experience in concluding a successful treaty with the six, namely the Coal and Steel negotiations.
Within the ECSC its interests had been relatively small and could be
accommodated without destroying the balance of the community as a
whole whilst in the Treaty of Rome negotiations its aims touched vital
sectors of commercial policy and protectionism in all the participating
nations. Moreover, the nature of the treaties themselves differed. The
Treaty of Paris creating the ECSC consisted of a set of rules binding
the exercise of supranational powers. In such circumstances it had
been easier to represent specific national interests. By contrast, the
Treaty of Rome must be seen more as a set of procedures by which
rules would be established at some point in the future. Although the
Dutch would have preferred to see many more issues settled in the
treaty itself, they were forced to accept this procedure because they too
ultimately realised that any delay would jeopardise the parliamentary
majorities required for ratification. Finally, in the ECSC negotiations,
the Dutch had benefitted from the fact that for the "major players",
France and Germany, the negotiations were almost foredoomed to
succeed. The uncertainty which would result in the event of failure
was simply too great. However, for at least a full year of the Treaty

The European Family... Bon Appetit. Belgium dines on
a plate of coal and steel, Italy on the Investment Bank,
France on Euratom and Germany on the common market.
The Netherlands forms the book-mark in the volume entitled
European Law.

VOLKSKRANT 11.1.1958

of Rome negotiations this same imperative did not exist. It is even possible to argue, in view of the "last minute" dictates of the French, that this was true virtually to the end. By this stage, however, the Dutch had so much at stake that they were simply forced to swallow many of their reserves. Yet the fact remained that *if the treaty were implemented* the Dutch would have secured their major aim of dismantling frontier barriers to trade, and stabilising the situation thereafter, in an area including three of their major trading partners including, most importantly of all, West Germany. Moreover, and this is equally clear from this book as a whole, without the constant pressure from the side of the Netherlands, there might never have been a common market at all. That would have left European integration continuing along the path of sector integration envisaged in 1955 by Jean Monnet. A fair indication of where that path might have ended is provided by the parallel set of negotiations, those leading to the creation of Euratom, which are considered in the next chapter.

NOTES

ABBREVIATIONS

ARA   Algemeen Rijksarchief, The Hague.
BEB   Buitenlandse Economische Betrekkingen (see MEZ).
MAZ   Ministerie van Algemene Zaken, The Hague.
MBZ   Ministerie van Buitenlandse Zaken, The Hague.
AMEZ   Ministerie van Economische Zaken, The Hague.
MR   Ministerraad (see ARA).

[1] See for the application of various growth models to the Dutch case R.T. Griffiths, "Het Nederlandse economische wonder" in H.W. von der Dunk e.a., *Wederopbouw, welvaart en onrust*, Houten, 1986, 147-167.
[2] The table is based on all countries which accounted for one per cent or more of Dutch exports in 1929 (for the period 1923-1938) and in 1959 (for the period 1947-1960). In addition, in 1959, Indonesia is also included, despite the fact that its share was less than one per cent, because of its importance in the earlier period. The composition of the two lists show a large degree of overlap. Belgium/Luxembourg, Denmark, France, Germany, Italy, Indonesia, Spain, Sweden, Switzerland, the USA and the UK are represented in both periods, joined by Argentina, Canada and India in the interwar years and by Australia, Austria, Brazil and South Africa in the post-war period. In 1929 these countries accounted for almost 88 per cent of Dutch exports and in 1959 for almost 80 per cent. The data was then found for the share of the Netherlands in the imports of each of these countries and the results weighed by their individual importance in Dutch exports in either 1929 or 1959. For statistical pur-

poses the two series were linked by a back projection to 1938 using 1959 weights and reduced to a single index whereby 1959 = 100).

[3] A more detailed breakdown of trade by commodity classes is given in UN, *Economic Survey of Europe, 1956*, Geneva, 1957.

[4] It is impossible to illustrate this last point briefly within the scope of this chapter. See for data, UN Statistical Commission and Economic Commission for Europe, *Standardized Input-Output Tables for ECE countries for years around 1959*, New York, 1972.

[5] This negative "Benelux effect" is known as trade erosion. In a contemporary estimate of the welfare effect of a customs union of the six. P.J. Verdoorn, "Welke zijn de achtergronden en vooruitzichten van de economische integratie in Europa en welke gevolgen zou deze integratie hebben, met name voor de welvaart in Nederland?" *CPB Overdrukken No. 22* (1952).

[6] ARA,MEZ,BEB 1700 *Europese Integratie, Buitentarief der douane-unie in de industriële sector*, 22.1.1957.

[7] R.T. Griffiths, "De eerste fase van de Westeuropese eenwording" in: T.P.W.M. van der Krogt e.a. (eds.) *Big is Beautiful? Schaalveranderingen in overheid en samenleving*, 's-Gravenhage, 1987, 435-453, and "The Abortive Dutch Assault on European Tariffs, 1950-1952" in: M. Wintle (ed.) *Modern Dutch Studies, Essays in Honour of Prof. P. King*, London, 1988, 186-208.

[8] ARA,MR (401) Minutes of cabinet 13.6.1955.

[9] MAZ, Kabinet, 351.88(4)075:32 Nederlandse delegatie bij de intergouvernementele commissie ingesteld door de conferentie van Messina *Weekbericht No. 2, Periode 26 t/m 29 juli 1955*.

[10] ARA,MR (515) *Verslag van de Conferentie der Ministers van Buitenlandse Zaken der zes landen, leden der EGKS, gehouden te Noordwijk op 6 September 1955* 9.7.1955 (MR 12.9.1955).

[11] See for example, MAZ, Kabinet, 351.88(4)075:32 *Weekbericht No. 3, Periode 2 t/m 5 augustus 1955*.

[12] MAZ, Kabinet, 351.88(4)075:32 *Memorandum de la délégation française sur l'établissement d'un marché commun général* 14.10.1955 MAE/CIG No. 337.

[13] For the discussions on these points in the Brussels discussions see MAZ, Kabinet, 351.88(4)075:32 *Weekbericht No. 4, Periode 29 augustus t/m 1 september 1955, Weekbericht No. 5, Periode 5 t/m 16 september 1955, Weekbericht No. 6, Periode 20 t/m 23 september 1955*.

[14] ARA,MR (402) Minutes of cabinet 7.11.1955.

[15] ARA,MR (402) Minutes of cabinet 14.11.1955.

[16] ARA,MR (402) Minutes of cabinet 19.12.1955.

[17] ARA,MR (403) Minutes of cabinet 20.2.1956.

[18] ARA,MR (403) Minutes of cabinet 16.4.1956.

[19] ARA,MR (403) Minutes of cabinet 22/23.5.1956.

[20] The first two categories grouped tariffs 0-5% and 5-10% respectively. Tariffs between 10% and 50% were divided into categories each with a band of 2-5% whilst those above 50% were divided into 5% bands.

[21] ARA,MEZ,BEB 1400 *Rapport des Chefs de Délégation aux Ministres des Affaires Etrangères* 21.4.1956, henceforth *Spaak Report*.

[22] This formula had provided the basis for agreement in the European Coal and Steel Community negotiations.

[23] MAZ, Kabinet, 351.88(4)075:32 *Weekbericht No. 3, Periode 2 t/m 5 augustus 1955* Appendix: *Algemeen Overzicht der z.g. "eerste lezing"*.

[24] MAZ, Kabinet, 351.88(4)075:32 *Weekbericht No. 4, Periode 29 augustus t/m 1 september 1955*.

[25] See note 14.

[26] MAZ, Kabinet, 351.88(4)075:32 *Weekbericht No. 11, Periode 28 november tot 4*

206

december 1955.
[27] ARA,MR (403) Minutes of cabinet 5.3.1956.
[28] *Spaak report,* 32.
[29] ARA,MR (403) Minutes of cabinet 22/23.5.1956.
[30] ARA,MR (524) *Verslag van de conferentie der zes ministers van buitenlandse zaken van de leden staten der EGKS op 29 en 30 mei 1956 to Venetië* (MR 4.6.1956).
[31] MAZ, Kabinet, 351.88(4)075:32 Nederlandse delegatie bij de intergouvernementele conferentie voor de oprichting van een gemeenschappelijke markt en van Euratom *Weekbericht No. 6, Periode 3 t/m 7 september 1956.*
[32] ARA,MR (404) Minutes of cabinet 10.9.1956. There was some confusion as to whether the French were suggesting that for a week of 40 hours, the Dutch worker should be offered the same wage as he had received for 48 hours and that the rest be paid as overtime or whether he should receive the hourly rate he had received for 48 hours for the first 40 hours and then be paid overtime. Later clarification showed that the latter was indeed intended.
[33] MAZ, Kabinet, 351.88(4)075:32 *Weekbericht No. 7, Periode 10 t/m 13 september 1956.*
[34] ARA,MR (404) Minutes of cabinet 1.10.1956; ARA,MR (528) *Nota inzake de conferentie over de gemeenschappelijke markt en Euratom* 25.9.1956 (MR 1.10.1956).
[35] Luns' brief had previously excluded the European negotiations. His "support" for Beyen's policy within the cabinet discussions from 1952 to 1956 had been characterised by almost total silence.
[36] Klompé was minister for social work and Samkalden became the justice minister.
[37] ARA,MR (529) *Nota inzake de voortzetting der onderhandelingen over de Gemeenschappelijke Markt en Euratom* 13.11.1956 (MR 19.11.1956).
[38] At this stage Spaak was still thinking of weighting the votes in the Council of Ministers for the taking of majority decisions with four each for France, Germany and Italy, 2 each for the Netherlands and Belgium and one for Luxembourg. A majority of 12 would be necessary for a decision which would mean that the three large countries could force through a decision against Benelux opposition or that two large countries could effectively block a Benelux interest.
[39] ARA,MR (404) Minutes of cabinet 19.11.1956.
[40] For a description of the state of play in the negotiations see ARA,MR (529) *Nota inzake de voortzetting der onderhandelingen over de Gemeenschappelijke Markt en Euratom* 13.11.1956 (MR 19.11.1956).
[41] ARA,MR (404) Minutes of cabinet 19.11.1956.
[42] MAZ, Kabinet, 351.88(4)075:32 Nederlandse delegatie bij de intergouvernementele commissie ingesteld door de conferentie van Messina *Weekbericht No. 7, Periode 27 t/m 30 september 1955.*
[43] MAZ, Kabinet, 351.88(4)075:32 *Memorandum de la délégation française sur l'établissement d'un marché commun général* 14.10.1955 MAE/CIG 337.
[44] MAZ, Kabinet, 351.88(4)075:32 *Document de Travail No. 5 L'agriculture* 7.11.1955, 11.1.1956.
[45] MAZ, Kabinet, 351.88(4)075:32 *Verslag van de besprekingen over de agrarische zijde de Douane Unie, Brussel, 11 januari 1956.*
[46] ARA,MEZ,BEB 1398 *Projet d'articles relatifs à l'agriculture présenté par le Groupe de Rédaction* 12.9.1956 MAE 270.
[47] MAZ, Kabinet, 351.88(4)075:32 Nederlandse delegatie bij een intergouvernementele conferentie voor de oprichting van een gemeenschappelijke markt en van Euratom *Weekbericht No. 10, Periode 1 t/m 4 oktober 1956.*
[48] MAZ, Kabinet, 351.88(4)075:32 *Weekbericht No. 11, Periode 8 t/m 10 oktober 1956.*
[49] MAZ, Kabinet, 351.88(4)075:32 *Proposition de rédaction des articles bis 36 à 39*

présentée par la délégation néerlandaise 24.10.1956 Mar Com 90.

⁵⁰ MAZ, Kabinet, 351.88(4)075:32 *Weekbericht No. 13, Periode 24-25 oktober 1956, Weekbericht No. 18, Periode 3-6 december 1956.*

⁵¹ ARA,MEZ,BEB 1399 *Proposition de la délégation allemande en vue de la rédaction de l'article 38,* 4.10.1956 Mar Com 64 MAE 376.

⁵² ARA,MEZ,BEB 1399 *Note sur l'agriculture dans le marché commun (Proposition de la délégation française)* 3.10.1956 Mar Com 60 MAE 367.

⁵³ MAZ, Kabinet, 351.88(4)075:32 *Weekbericht No. 10, Periode 1 t/m 4 oktober 1956, Weekbericht No. 11, Periode 8 t/m 10 oktober 1956.*

⁵⁴ MAZ, Kabinet, 351.88(4)075:32 *Weekbericht No. 18, Periode 3-6 december 1956.*

⁵⁵ MAZ, Kabinet, 351.88(4)075:32 *Weekbericht No. 19, Periode 10-14 december 1956.*

⁵⁶ MAZ, Kabinet, 351.88(4)075:32 *Weekbericht No. 19, Periode 10 t/m 14 december 1956.*

⁵⁷ MAZ, Kabinet, 351.88(4)075:32 *Weekbericht No. 20, Periode 17-20 december 1956.*

⁵⁸ MAZ, Kabinet, 351.88(4)075:32 *Weekbericht No. 10, Periode 1 t/m 4 oktober 1956.*

⁵⁹ ARA,MEZ,BEB 1399 *Proposition de la délégation française concernant les articles 38 et 39,* 9.10.1956 MAE 391.

⁶⁰ MAZ, Kabinet, 351.88(4)075:32 *Weekbericht No. 19, Periode 10-14 december 1956.*

⁶¹ MAZ, Kabinet, 351.88(4)075:32 Intergouvernementele conferentie voor de oprichting van een gemeenschappelijke markt en van Euratom *Weekoverzicht No. 15, Periode 2-5 januari 1957.*

⁶² MAZ, Kabinet, 351.88(4)075:32 *Weekoverzicht No. 17, Periode 14-20 januari 1957.*

⁶³ MAZ, Kabinet, 351.88(4)075:32 *Kort verslag Ministersconferentie Gemeenschappelijke Markt, Brussel 4 februari 1957.*

⁶⁴ MAZ, Kabinet, 351.88(4)075:32 *Weekbericht No. 18, Periode 3-6 december 1956.*

⁶⁵ MAZ, Kabinet, 351.88(4)075:32 *Weekbericht No. 19, Periode 10-14 december 1956, Weekbericht No. 20, Periode 17-20 december 1956.*

⁶⁶ ARA,MR (522) *Nota: De Ministersconferentie in Parijs over de verdragen voor de Gemeenschappelijke Markt en Euratom 28.2.1957* (MR 22.2.1957).

⁶⁷ ARA,MR (530) *Nota: De Europese Gemeenschappelijke Markt en de overzeese gebieden der leden-landen 29.11.1956* (MR 3.12.1956).

⁶⁸ ARA,MR (404) Minutes of cabinet 3.12.1956.

⁶⁹ ARA,MR (531) *Nota betr. de integratie* 14.1.1957 (MR 21.1.1957).

⁷⁰ Ibidem.

⁷¹ ARA,MR (533) *De overzeese gebieden en de gemeenschappelijke markt* 11.2.1957 (MR 15.2.1957).

⁷² ARA,MR (405) Minutes of cabinet 15.2.1957.

⁷³ ARA,MR (495) Minutes of cabinet 4.1.1957, 18.1.1957.

⁷⁴ ARA,MR (532) *De Ministersconferentie in Parijs over de verdragen voor de Gemeenschappelijke Markt en Euratom 22.2.1957 (MR 22.2.1957).*

⁷⁵ ARA,MR (405) Minutes of cabinet 4.3.1957.

⁷⁶ ARA,MR (411) Minutes of the "Ministerraad van het Koninkrijk" 18.3.1957. This was a cabinet committee designed to discuss colonial affairs. Because of the tempo of the last phase of the negotiations and the overloaded cabinet agenda, in the course of 1957 it was used for discussions on the common market and Euratom as well. MBZ 100.93 Texeira de Mattos (Dutch embassy Brussels) to Luns 18.3.1957 and reply Luns.

⁷⁷ This statement, it must be remembered, was made before the Dutch had extracted the *minimum* concessions they wanted.

⁷⁸ ARA,MR (531) *Nota betr. de integratie* 14.1.1957 (MR 21.1.1957).

⁷⁹ ARA,MR (531) Middelburg to Drees 16.1.1957 (MR 21.1.1957).

⁷⁹ ARA,MR (531) Middelburg to Drees 16.1.1957 (MR 21.1.1957).

⁸⁰ ARA,MR (411) Minutes of the "Ministerraad van het Koninkrijk" 1.2.1957.

208

81 ARA,MR (532) *Brussels conferentie* 30.1.1957 (MR 1.2.1957).
82 ARA,MR (405) Minutes of cabinet 29.4.1957.

[8]

Italy and the EEC Negotiations: An Economic Perspective*

Francesca Fauri*

1. Historical background

At the start of the European Recovery Programme in 1947, the European member countries were urged by the US government to make the 'integration' of Western European economies into a single market one of their major aims. Within Western Europe the idea found considerable support in some countries. In 1947 a customs union study group (CUSG) was set up in Brussels to carry on studies on the feasibility and economic implications of a European customs union. Yet, within two years the CUSG found itself constrained, by lack of support from member governments, to concentrate on technical questions, such as the development of a standard tariff nomenclature. Within the Organization for European Economic Cooperation (OEEC), proposals for economic integration, such as the Stikker, Petsche and Pella Plans, received little support in 1950. Other OEEC attempts to coordinate recovery programmes and to promote integration by sector, were soon eclipsed in importance by the programme of liberalization of intra-European trade and payments and the establishment of the European Payments Union (EPU).

Thus, attempts at a closer integration of the economies of Western European countries were pursued mainly outside the OEEC. Most of them had a political as well as an economic inspiration. Yet, except for the Benelux Economic Union, they were all doomed to fail (like the project for a Franco-Italian customs union or the much more ambitious goal of instituting a European Defence Community, EDC).[1] Much more successful was the first experiment in a sector approach to economic integration, which led to the establishment of the European Coal and Steel Community (ECSC), and the opening of a common market for these products among the six member countries in 1953.[2]

Other suggestions for moving to a single market in Western Europe had met with little success. Discussions on the 'green pool' proposals for joint marketing schemes for agricultural products continued from 1951 to 1954 with little result.[3] Other plans were also put forward in the Council of Europe and elsewhere. One of these proposed the formation of a new preferential system comprising the Western European countries and their associated monetary areas, with the provision of mutual assistance in financing economic development and for the support of primary production by means of long-term contracts (Strasbourg Plan, 1952).[4] Another proposed tariff reductions within the GATT framework (GATT Plan, 1953) on items of particular importance in Western European trade.

Of course, it is not possible here to give a full account of the plans for free trade in Western Europe that followed one another from the end of the 1940s. This brief survey just wants to underline that, first, such intense negotiating activity was in most cases leading nowhere, but provided a set of international forums where the European countries had the opportunity at least to confront one another on issues relating to freer trade. Second, the emergence of all these different plans reflected very specific disappointments at the results of the OEEC trade liberalization campaign and of successive tariff negotiations under the GATT. In particular, the low tariff countries saw their bargaining power being constantly reduced. As the OEEC Working Party on the Common Market pointed out: 'it became clear that liberalization in its present form had practically reached the limit of its possibilities. In particular, countries with moderate tariffs consider that they cannot proceed further with the abolition of quotas until a start has been made on the problem of tariff disparities'.[5] The driving force behind the EEC Treaty was indeed the low tariff countries, which constantly sought the permanent removal of intra-European tariffs by creating a supranational European customs union.

In 1955, the fact that the OEEC activities in this field had come to a full stop pushed the Dutch to relaunch the customs union plan (Beyen Plan) which they had already tried to add to the 'shaky EDC/EPC (European Political Cooperation) structure'.[6] With the German question finally resolved through the creation of the intergovernmental Western European Union, Beyen stubbornly pursued his plan for a supranationally implemented customs union. He believed that the countries' delegations had not just been wasting their time in trying to build the fragile EDC structure; even though the French Assembly had rejected the Treaty, the negotiations had shown that 'five countries were willing, with greater or lesser degrees of commitment, to accept the creation of a customs union as part of a more wide-ranging integration of their economies'.[7] In February 1955 a more 'European-minded' government had come to power in France, sensitive to Monnet's proposals for an extension of supranational cooperation of the Six in the field of transport, energy and atomic energy. The Benelux countries were swift in incorporating this last aspect into the memorandum which they addressed to the ECSC members in the spring of 1955. As has been observed, when the Six met in Messina and opened the way for the 'relaunch', their contrasting views on the ways to shape such a relaunch could have just led to another failure.[8] Yet, this time the events took an unusual, quick and favourable upturn, which in two years of negotiations led to the signing of the Treaties of Rome.

2.   Italy's Trade Performance in the 1950s

If the second half of the 1950s represented a period of intense export growth and commercial success for Italy, in 1952 the country was burdened with a large trade deficit with the EPU countries which compromised the survival of a set of the more traditional export industries. The causes were: a downward trend in international demand at the end of 1951 (caused by the end of the 'Korean boom'); a parallel upsurge of import restrictions and quotas, particularly harmful in the case of France and Great Britain – their suspension of trade liberalization caused a slump in Italy's exports; and finally the import policy pursued by the Italian authorities which, with the last liberalization provisions of October 1951, had made foreign exporters' access to the Italian market considerably easier.[9] This decision in favour of liberalization and tariff reductions exerted a major impact not only on Italy's production conditions, but also on its international financial position. The deterioration in the trade balance was in large part due to the increase of imports of raw materials and semifinished goods and to the doubling of finished products imports. At the same time, the unexciting behaviour of exports was blamed, besides international factors, on the inadequate provisions for export promotion in Italy when abroad subsidies and guarantees to export trade were common practice.

On the foreign trade side, in fact, the 1952 balance-of-trade crisis owed much to decreased exports primarily of textiles (from 385 billion lire in 1951 to 207 billion lire) and agricultural produce (from 205 billion lire in 1951 to 197 billion lire) and to lower prices of these two commodity groups.[10] As mentioned before, British and French suspension of trade liberalization also severely hit Italy's exports, because trade with those two countries had previously accounted for as much as 84 per cent of EPU trade.[11] When Great Britain cut imports in 1952, it was Italian exports that were hardest hit, in particular textile exports already suffering from overproduction at home. Between January and September 1952 British imports of fruit and textiles from Italy dropped by 45 per cent and from France by 35 per cent. On the other hand, Italian imports (of coal and machinery) from the United Kingdom and France remained stable and particularly significant in the case of Britain, thanks to the credits granted by the Italian government for purchase of industrial equipment in this country (see Table 1).

Table 1   Trade with France and Great Britain (millions of dollars)

	Imports		Exports	
	1951	1952	1951	1952
Great Britain	592	593	620	372
France	132	134	166	124
Other EPU countries	461	586	418	455

Source: *Italian Economic Survey*, May–June 1953, p. 31

This situation caused Prime Minister Pella, in October 1953, to present a petition to the OEEC Council in favour of issuing restrictive measures that would render it more difficult to appeal to the escape clause of balance-of-payments problems and suspend trade liberalization. According to Pella, 'the Italian government, even though deeply convinced that the achievement of complete liberalization is a useful necessity for all countries, feels that the lack of effective reciprocity could question its engagement'.[12]

But the situation of Italy's export trade had already improved by the end of 1953 and in 1954 the value of exports registered an increase of 8.6 per cent (81 billion lire) as compared to the preceding year. Simultaneously, the value of imports decreased by 0.8 per cent, helping to reduce the negative trade balance by 93 billion lire. The improvement in the balance-of-trade deficit was thus determined not by a decrease in imports, but by a decrease in prices of raw materials and semifinished products (which represented, in 1954, 61 per cent of Italy's import trade) together with an increase of finished industrial goods prices (the main item in Italy's export trade, 471 billion lire – 46 per cent of 1954 export trade) and a decisive expansion of exports. Italy was going through a period of intense economic development sustained by a strong industrial apparatus, modernized thanks to Marshall Plan funds and the adoption of American machinery. Such an important modernizing step was, in part, the result of a change in the industrialists' mentality in favour of production increases based on the belief of an expansion of the market. Their betting on the future was met by the astonishing performance of their exports, easing the way to the forthcoming EEC negotiations among the Six.

2.1   Interdependence and Trade Interests

Italy's political and alleged economic interests in bringing about a customs union in Western Europe have been extensively dealt with in the literature.[13] Yet, a closer look at the trade interests that might have pushed Italy to enter into a framework of economic interdependence might be useful. In order to better access Italy's trade interests in a possible customs union, it would be useful to examine closely the structure of Italian trade and its relative importance in the national income. As far as the latter is concerned, 'a relatively high ratio of imports and exports to national income can explain the attractiveness of removing trade barriers in general'.[14] Italy at the time was the least endowed with such a feature among the Community countries. In 1955, its exports ratio to national income was 8 per cent, against 11.2 per cent for France, 13 per cent for Germany, 25 per cent for the Belgo-Luxembourg Economic Union (BLEU) and 34 per cent for the Netherlands.[15] Thus, in order to see what was the Italian interest in reaching a commercial agreement with the other five nations it is necessary to focus on the structure of Italy's trade.

The data in Table 2 show that, first of all, Italy's dependence on the outside as an export market was the least significant among the community countries. Second, if we analyse the composition of Italy's export trade directed to the future partners as a percentage of total export trade, it is clear that in 1955 the EEC was already an attractive export market for agricultural goods (37 per cent of total exports) and, to a lesser extent, for manufactured products (20 per cent). More specifically, it is worth noting that agricultural and manufactured exports account, respectively, for 35 and 48 per cent of total exports to the EEC.

2.2   Agriculture

In 1955, the area of foodstuffs was the one in which the Italians could be said to have had a particular interest, shared only with the Dutch, who were exporting 45 per cent of their total agricultural exports to the Six. This category for the others accounted for from 15 per cent of intra-exports in total for France, to 4.1 per cent for Belgium–Luxembourg and 2.4 per cent for Germany (see Table 2). As has been shown by a recent work on the subject, if there were to be a common market, it was a major Italian priority to ensure that agriculture was part of it.[16]

Table 2 Exports of the six Common Market countries in 1955 by commodity classes to countries within the group and to the world (millions of dollars)

Areas of destination	BLEU	Nether.	France	Germany	Italy	Total EEC(a)	World (b)	(a)/(b)%
Exporting country and commodity group								
BLEU								
1. Food, beverages, tobacco		19	13	16	3	51	104	
2. Fuels, crude materials		91	73	74	14	252	418	
3. Chemicals		26	12	14	4	56	187	
4. Machinery and transport		90	22	22	5	139	310	
5. Manufactured goods		347	156	199	34	736	1 725	
Total		575	278	327	61	1 241	2 779	44.6
Netherlands								
1. Food, beverages, tobacco	97		42	205	37	381	838	
2. Fuels, crude materials	79		36	90	7	212	527	
3. Chemicals	22		7	18	5	52	193	
4. Machinery and transport	48		21	30	8	107	416	
5. Manufactured goods	124		27	113	7	271	691	
Total	371		133	459	66	1 029	2 688	38.3
France								
1. Food, beverages, tobacco	30	26		89	32	177	747	
2. Fuels, crude materials	133	31		139	62	365	821	
3. Chemicals	15	12		15	14	56	360	
4. Machinery and transport	55	29		19	21	124	786	
5. Manufactured goods	101	43		239	54	437	1 930	
Total	337	144		504	185	1 170	4 798	24.4
Western Germany								
1. Food, beverages, tobacco	9	10	14		9	42	147	
2. Fuels, crude materials	103	78	154		81	416	735	
3. Chemicals	34	48	39		38	159	680	
4. Machinery and transport	159	227	131		117	634	2 457	
5. Manufactured goods	107	216	95		96	514	2 113	
Total	413	578	434		342	1 767	6 135	28.8
Italy								
1. Food, beverages, tobacco	10	9	21	113		153	412	
2. Fuels, crude materials	3	4	12	29		48	296	
3. Chemicals	2	2	10	9		23	127	
4. Machinery and transport	11	9	36	21		77	371	
5. Manufactured goods	23	20	30	60		133	650	
Total	50	45	108	233		436	1 857	23.5
Total Common Market								
1. Food, beverages, tobacco	146	64	90	423	81	804	2 248	
2. Fuels, crude materials	318	204	275	332	164	1 293	2 797	
3. Chemicals	73	88	68	56	61	346	1 547	
4. Machinery and transport	273	355	210	92	151	1 081	4 340	
5. Manufactured goods	355	626	308	611	191	2 091	7 109	
Total	1 171	1 342	953	1 523	654	5 643	18 257	31

Notes:
1. Food, beverages, tobacco (SITC, Sections 0 and 1).
2. Fuels, lubricants, crude materials including animal and vegetable oils and fats (SITC, Sections 2 to 4).
3. Chemicals (SITC, Section 5).
4. Machinery and transport equipment (SITC, Section 7).
5. All other manufactured goods (SITC Sections 6 and 8).

Source: UN, *Europe Economic Survey*, 1956.

If the data imply an association between the Netherlands and Italy as far as the quantity of their agricultural exports to the other five is concerned, their aims were on opposite stands. Dutch agriculture was labour-intensive, efficient and one of the most productive in Europe: 'it transformed the import of cereals and fodder into exportable and more valorised horticultural and animal products'.[17] Thus, the Dutch aimed at liberalization in order to conquer new markets for their highly competitive foodstuffs production. Italy's agricultural production suffered from a chronic imbalance between the more advanced production of the North and the neither efficient nor very productive land cultivation in the South. Yet, if we analyse the composition of Italy's agricultural exports, it is interesting to note that in 1955 its trade balance was positive only for unprocessed horticultural products – legumes, fruit and vegetable exports – coming to a large extent from the South[18] (see Table 3).

Table 3   Location of Italy's horticultural production in 1955 (percentage)

	North	Centre	South	As a % of hort. exp.
Legumes	17.4	12.6	70.0	
Vegetables	37.5	18.9	43.6	21.5
Fresh and dry fruits	38.2	6.2	55.6	57.5
Citrus fruits	0.7	2.9	96.4	21.0

Sources: ISTAT, *Annuario and Annuario del commercio con l'estero*, 1956, and Relazione Bonomi al XII Congresso Nazionale de i Coltivatori Diretti Roma, April 1958.

To some economists EEC membership was seen as a chance to expand Italy's exports of horticultural products,[19] which would act as an important stimulus to the expansion of production and income rate in the undeveloped southern zones. In particular, as Table 3 shows, the South by itself was contributing 20 per cent of Italy's horticultural exports through its production of citrus fruits, which could count on traditional well-established export flows.[20] In 1955 the Six were buying from Italy 44.7 per cent of the oranges, 60.2 per cent of the tangerines and 53.8 per cent of the lemons they imported.[21] What was asked from the government was increasing supplies of fertilizers, selected seeds, machinery, electric power, fuels and credit facilities so as to obtain higher per unit yields and, consequently, lower production costs. Lower costs, increases in production and exports thanks to EEC membership could improve – according to contemporary agronomics – the living conditions in those wide southern areas where agriculture represented the most important source of income. In these zones the lack of a process of accumulation and diversification of capital in line with population growth had had the consequence of spurring peasants towards the land as towards the sole means that could in some way guarantee them subsistence and the sole factor with which they could combine their capacity for work.[22] By looking at the share of population employed in agriculture in 1955, 51.6 per cent of the labour force was still working in the fields in the South (against 30.1 per cent in the North) often as day workers in areas almost lacking mechanization[23] and industries engaged in the processing of farm products.[24] As a result, the South suffered from widespread underemployment in agriculture, the traditional solution for which lay in emigration.[25] Unsurprisingly, during the EEC negotiations on a common agricultural policy in 1956, Italy proposed to add to the draft articles that were being discussed, a statement that an aim should be 'maximum employment in agriculture'.[26]

Government intervention in favour of the poor agricultural South went through different phases. If the Netherlands believed that 'the agricultural sector had to contribute in the largest possible measure to the creation of national wealth',[27] in Italy in the aftermath of the Second World War the agricultural sector was not among the priorities of government intervention (whose investment policy was mainly directed towards the industrial sector).[28] At the same time, the government long-term programme limited itself to acknowledging the existence of 'a vast region that may be defined as a "depressed area" in which industrial progress demands, at the outset, the development of basic services'. But it was only with the beginning of the 1950s that the problem of southern development was tackled. Things started to change with the approval of a series of laws that solved the problem of '*latifondo*'[29] and set up the '*Cassa per il Mezzogiorno*'[30] to assist the land tenure reform in the South, but in economic terms results were negligible, especially in the short run.[31]

Besides, although the Community offered an attractive prospect for Italian agricultural exports, any real liberalization of agricultural trade would have been very difficult to achieve in the short term. Italy itself was not in favour of liberalizing its very protected agricultural market (the average legal tariff was about 19.4 per cent, while the tariff in use was 14.4 per cent),[32] fearing an invasion of foodstuffs from the Netherlands and France, which could further worsen its negative trade balance in this sector with these two countries (respectively, –6.5 billion lire and –5.8 billion lire in 1955). Furthermore, the average *ad valorem* tariff on agricultural products ranged around 15 per cent in Germany (in France it was about 20–25 per cent and in the Benelux countries the average level was 10 per cent), which in 1955 was buying 74 per cent of Italy's agricultural exports going to the EEC. Last but not least, the weight of agriculture on total exports had decreased from 25.2 per cent in 1950 to 22.6 per cent in 1955,[33] and over the same years there had not been any major change in the negative trend of Italy's trade balance for agricultural products. The only groups of items with a positive balance were fruits and legumes and vegetable exports, while Italy remained strictly dependent on cereal imports. More specifically, as Tables 4 and 5 show, the trend of Italy's agricultural trade with the EEC countries underwent limited increases (or even a decrease in the case of France) on the export side, with the sole exception of Germany, which remained the main importer of Italian fresh and dry fruits. On the import side, Italy between 1950 and 1955 had seen its dependence on agricultural goods increase by 51 per cent in the case of France and 86 per cent in the case of the Netherlands.

All Italy's governments had traditionally been in favour of expanding the country's agricultural exports, especially when in the nineteenth century they represented, along with raw silk, the two leading export sectors. Yet, the agricultural sector never became a priority of government capital investments. The end result was that the southern regions, where private investments went towards expanding property rather than modernizing means of production, remained dependent on traditional labour-intensive production unable to set in motion any virtuous circle of growth.[34] There being no alternative in the short term, the government, as in preceding trade negotiations, considered Italy's agricultural exports of vital importance in order to defend its weakest southern regions.[35] However, according to

Table 4   Trend of Italy's import trade with future EEC partners, 1950–1955 (more than 1,000 million lire)

	BLEU		France		Germany		Netherlands		EEC
	1950	1955	1950	1955	1950	1955	1950	1955	1955
TOTAL	2,157	37,679	41,764	108,366	75,887	214,732	8,921	41,234	402,011
1–45 AGRICULTURE	3,366	8,926	17,652	2,196	3,553	2,918	21,498	32,029	46,069
23 Cattle	1,624	7,171			1,161				
46–57 Mining	11,522	3,607	8,169	23,824	38,702	48,635	213	587	76,653
49 Iron and steel scraps			3,256	19,485	1,292	13,400			
53 Coke	10,702	2,726	4,021	2,841	34,404	33,918			
59–94 FOOD MANUFACT.	987	1,513	2,101	11,836	203	4,148	1,524	4,709	22,206
95–140 TEXTILE	2,658	3,945	4,258	11,957	1,366	7,518	216	1,018	24,438
101 Wool		1,859	1,369	4,279					
141–152 WOOD and CORK	195	219	757	2,255	996	3,738	22	358	6,570
153–168 IRON and STEEL	9,885	13,317	6,936	19,765	7,118	15,106	417	1,857	50,045
154–155 Iron and steel works	7,405	7,070	5,232	7,362	4,257	6,143			
160 Copper	1,305	4,012							
169–196 ENGINEERING	909	3,904	2,882	10,460	11,720	67,198	469	3,048	84,610
172 Agricultural machinery						2,717			
174 Textile machinery						3,957			
182 Telecommunications		1,757				4,605			
187–194 TRANSPORT MEANS	251	143	690	1,741	877	7,108	2	88	9,080
189 Cars						1,115			
190 Tractors						2,221			
191 Spare parts						3,163			
195–205 NON-MET. ORES	1,306	3,813	1,534	5,726	5,989	22,166	362	637	32,342
196 Tools					1,014	3,725			
203 Pottery					1,477	4,759			
204 Glass works	1,102	2,413				2,853			
206–229 CHEMICALS	1,742	3,096	4,483	10,297	5,839	28,349	2,298	4,752	46,494
206 Fertilizers				1,275	1,197	1,283			
213 Ink, enamels									
229–236 MISCELLANEOUS	564	756	1,028	2,853	881	7,233	480	2,686	

Source: Own calculations from ISTAT, Annuario del commercio con l'estero, 1950–1956.

Table 5   Trend of Italy's export trade with future EEC partners, 1950–1955 (more than 1,000 million lire)

	BLEU		France		Germany		Netherlands		EEC
	1950	1955	1950	1955	1950	1955	1950	1955	1955
TOTAL	19,515	31,192	65,313	67,539	11,760	27,946	73,799	145,664	272,341
1–45 AGRICULTURE	5,772	4,825	11,986	11,773	2,362	3,665	32,032	69,893	90,156
6 Legumes and fresh		1,372					3,587	15,562	
8 Citrus fruit			4,021	1,863			8,246	9,714	
10–11 Fresh and dry fruit				6,291		1,415	13,169	36,077	
46–57 MINING	836	575	2,422	1,247	174	242	830	1,895	3,959
58–94 FOOD IND.	2,203	2,170	7,091	3,932	892	2,786	12,276	11,207	20,095
58 Rice			4,755				4,890	1,721	
84 Skins								3,049	
88 Wines						1,223	1,098	1,735	
95–140 TEXTILE IND.	4,965	5,854	31,752	7,917	3,807	4,441	17,532	29,776	47,988
106 Silk			6,465				1,109	3,161	
111 Synthetic fibres							4,605		
114 Cotton cloth			19,239						
115 Wool cloth							2,561	12,754	
141–152 WOOD and CORK	402	613	877	1,512	138	490	686	1,456	4,071
153–168 IRON and STEEL	242	418	214	5,785	702	837	573	6,925	13,965
154 Iron and steel works				4,318					
169–196 ENGINEERING	1,685	3,499	5,802	15,198	1,509	3,475	1,526	7,150	29,322
187–194 TRANSPORT MEANS	1,155	3,785	813	7,294	715	2,460	3,334	6,357	19,896
189 Motorcycles		1,325							
189 Cars		1,848			229	1,221	1,959	5,107	
195–205 NON-MET. ORES	879	1,111	788	1,584	501	740	434	1,125	4,560
206–229 CHEMICALS	453	1,757	1,941	7,521		2,040	4,149	7,402	18,720
216 Plastic mat.								1,044	
220 Petrol				1,594				1,035	
229–236 MISCELLANEOUS	923	6,585	1,627	3,776	731	6,770	427	2,478	

Source: Own calculations from ISTAT, *Annuario del commercio con l'estero*, 1950–1956.

the data, agriculture could not be the sector on which the government was betting for its future economic expansion inside the Common Market. Furthermore, in the following decade 'the government started thinking it useless to go on with a development project and started addressing towards the South a constant flow of public welfare expenditure waiting for the definitive abandonment of rural areas'.

2.3 Manufacturing

As far as manufactured trade was concerned, in 1955 80 per cent of manufactured goods exported were still directed outside the Community. Yet, as shown in Table 2, if we analyse the relative importance of the different groups of items traded within the Community, it is worth noting that the largest share – 48 per cent – of Italy's exports going to the EEC countries consisted of manufactured goods, including machinery and transport equipment, while foodstuffs took up 35 per cent of Italy's exports to the other five. What Table 2 also highlights is that the trade of the six countries of the Common Market with the outside-world largely took the form of exports of manufactures and imports of food and raw materials, while intra-trade consisted overwhelmingly of manufactures.

In the case of Italy, if we analyse the composition of imports in 1955, the Italian economy relied heavily upon EEC imports of engineering chemical and iron and steel products, accounting, respectively, for 48, 47 and 38 per cent of total imports.[36] Liberalization would thus reinforce Italy's dependence on a set of manufactured goods and chemical imports coming from the Community, and in particular from Germany (providing 62 per cent of the chemical and manufactured goods coming from the EEC countries in 1955). A significant example, as Table 4 shows, is that of German machinery imports, which increased from 11 to 67 billion lire between 1950 and 1955, representing 31 per cent of total German exports to Italy and 79 per cent of Italy's machinery imports from the Common Market members in 1955.

A special case is that of crude materials, which were undoubtedly important items playing in favour of Italy's participation to the EEC, representing 25 per cent of Italy's imports from the Community members in 1955. In quantitative terms Table 4 clearly shows that it was the mining sector on which Italy relied the most and which provided vital items (such as coke and iron and steel scraps) for its industrial expansion. Germany and France were the main suppliers, increasing their mining exports to Italy from 8 to 23 billion lire in the case of France and from 39 to 49 billion lire in the case of Germany, which remained Italy's main supplier of coke (representing 16 per cent if its exports to Italy). More specifically, for both countries mining exports accounted for 22 per cent of their total exports to Italy.

As far as the trend of manufactured exports to the EEC partners is concerned, between 1950 and 1955, if textile and food, beverage and tobacco manufactures exports continued holding important quantitative positions (apart from a consistent drop from 31 to 7 billion lire in textile exports directed to France), the most significant increases are to be found in the engineering, machinery and transportation sectors, as shown by Table 5. Over the period analysed, Italy's exports of engineering products increased by 96 per cent in the case of France and by 92 per cent in the case of Germany.

3. Italy's Economic Objectives at Messina

As we have seen, between 1950 and 1955, the expansion of Italy's trade relations with the future EEC countries provided a not unfavourable background to Italy's decision to participate. Yet, after the failure of the EDC, into which Italy had put so much effort, there was no real autonomous initiative on the part of the Italian government to bring back discussion on integration in the European forum. It was only in April 1955 that numerous reports were sent from Grazzi and Scamacca (Ambassadors in Brussels) to Martino announcing that Spaak and Beyen were on the verge of resuming talks on the Beyen Plan of 1952. By the end of month it was clear that 'new plans on European integration would be presented at the Luxembourg meeting of the ECSC'.[37] Things were to proceed even more swiftly. Before the upcoming official ECSC meeting, the ECSC countries' foreign ministers met in Paris on 10 May 1955 for a conference of the Atlantic Council. During the Paris meeting Martino managed to change the site of the next ECSC meeting from Luxembourg to Messina (where he had to campaign for important elections).[38] And, more importantly, Spaak gave the ECSC countries' foreign ministers a 'Memorandum Project' of the Benelux countries formulated on the basis of the Beyen Plan. On the same occasion, Martino gave to his ECSC colleagues a (very vague) Italian document on 'European Economic Integration'.[39]

Although not particularly innovative in its contents, to a certain section of the Italian Foreign Office the Benelux memorandum came as a welcome surprise. The reaction of the Italian Foreign Office was to circulate a document (which had been ready since 5 May) prepared by Cattani, head of the Economic Department in the Foreign Office, which analysed the different proposals on European economic integration, and recognized in Messina the necessity to 'go forth on the path of European integration'.[40]

Italy's memorandum presented at Messina highlighted the leading principles that accompanied the Italian delegation during the negotiations and will be analysed below: 'the realization of horizontal integration ... in order to take care of all economic and social life sectors, including the labour sector (which will be translated into Italy's struggle for the free movement of labour); the creation of an investment found and of a readaptation fund'.[41]

3.1 The Free Movement of Labour

The free movement of labour, for which Italy had often sought a solution in the international arena, contained in its formula the solution to two strictly correlated problems: unemployment and emigration. In the long-term programme the solution to 'the problem of a surplus population' consisted in 'developing an emigration policy adequate to the demographic needs of the country' which in quantitative terms was to correspond to an emigration flow of 832,000 people in four years (364,000 to Europe and 468,000 to other continents), a forecast which was overly optimistic of future trends.[42]

In 1946 the government calculated that the excess manpower was about 2 million official unemployed to which had to be added an estimated unofficial number of between 1 million and 4 million. Comparative unemployment figures after the war only confirmed Italy's 'special problem', which also remained one of the country's major problems during the 1950s.[44] Again in 1949, a report of the 'Direzione generale dell'emigrazione' recommended as a solution the planning of 'adequate migration'.[45]

Historically, all Italy's democratic governments had favoured high emigration flows. From an economic point of view, the incentive given to emigration was finalized by creating 'an extremely important source' for helping Italy's balance of payments: the emigrants' remittances. The long-term programme had foreseen that emigrants' remittances could cover 10 per cent of imports by the early 1950s. It has been calculated that between 1950 and 1955, on average, official remittances were able to pay for 4.7 per cent of imports, but if unofficial remittances are taken into account, the percentage goes up to 8–10 per cent as foreseen by the programme.[46] Another aspect of emigration that was considered very important from a political point of view, was the role of 'safety-valve' which it had always played in reducing social tensions.[47]

From the end of the nineteenth century, and with the exclusion of the fascist period, Italy's emigration levels had been on average 2,500 million per decade, with peaks of 6,027 million between 1900 and 1910.[48] During the 1950s, out of a total of 2,937 million emigrants, the majority 1,767 million went to Europe, a considerable number left for South America (514 million) while only 193 million left for the US, confirming a downward trend started from the early 1920s when new restrictive laws on immigration were introduced and in Italy the new fascist government started opposing it. After the war the United States, although acknowledging its interest in 'plans for the migration of surplus population from western Europe'[49] allowed only very limited flows of people to enter and were in part responsible, together with an increase in demand from the European countries, for the re-direction of Italy's emigration flows (which from the South were traditionally orientated overseas), towards European destinations.[50] The main difference between these two types of geographical location was that in the case of the European countries, emigration resulted in a highly temporary and fluctuating shift of single workers rather than a permanent movement of entire families. The high percentage ratio of returns on emigration outflows for all European countries between 1946 and 1957 (%R/O = 52), greatly reduced the extent of the phenomenon in net terms.[51]

The goal of relieving Italy's manpower surplus problem through emigration meant an untiring effort, on the part of postwar governments, to involve the international community; in the words of the interministerial reconstruction committee 'the problem of unemployment has been tackled at the international level, in the conviction that it affected not only Italy, but the entire Western Community'.[52] Yet, if from the end of the war the problem of free movement of labour had been discussed in various international forums, the solutions proposed were mere statements of intent. The OEEC in 1948 had established a Manpower Committee – in which the Italian delegation took an active part – whose work terminated in 1950 with a recommendation addressed to member countries which stressed the necessity for bilateral or multilateral agreements for the liberalization of manpower movements. Successively, an OEEC 'liberalization code' for standardization of the rules concerning the employment of foreign workers within the member countries was finally approved in 1953, but in practice, in the words of the OEEC itself 'it was still impossible to talk of a European labour market'.[53] In 1950, Italy's unemployment problem was also submitted in terms of 'manpower surplus' to the European Council in the form of a memorandum.[54] The 1951 final report of the Expert Committees within the Council limited itself to acknowledging the necessity of free mobility of labour forces in the world. More practical results were obtained through ECA (European Cooperation Administration), OEEC and Italian government financing for the 'Migration Field Mission' (1950), which made some funds available for the financing of travel expenses of Italian overseas emigrants.[55] A similar result on a European level was obtained through the setting up of the Intergovernmental Committee on European Migrations, which thanks to US funds was able to pay for the travel expenses of half the European emigrants leaving for overseas destinations by 1957.[56] A limited step forward in the direction of a more open-minded attitude on the free circulation of workers was also made with the setting up of the ECSC. Since Article 69 of the Treaty was very vague on the free movement of workers inside the Community and left room to different interpretations, in the end an agreement was reached on a 'working pass' (*carta di lavoro*), which would allow demand-induced migrations of specialized workers after a transition period of 15 years.[57]

None the less, the Italian government's most important practical result in postwar years as far as exporting its labour surplus is concerned was the *programmazione* of emigration through successive bilateral agreements. In the case of Belgium, for instance, the agreement was considered a success since it also set up a compensation scheme between emigrants' savings and Belgian coal supplies to Italy.[58] Among the EEC countries, Italy's labour force provided the main source of manpower for France and Belgium between 1950 and 1955.[59] However, according to the Italian government forecasts, German demand for foreign workers was going to increase the most after unification.[60] The institution of supranational organizations among the European countries was seen by many economists as a good and radical solution to the migration problem that would thus become 'an internal movement of workforce' aimed at balancing the internal labour market.[61] At the same time, further reduction or abolition of tariffs was closely linked with and subject to the establishment of 'perfect labour mobility'.[62] It was also thought that thanks to the institution of the European Community there would be a reduction of production costs both in the agricultural sector and in the industrial sector. 'Nevertheless, such reduction would be undoubtedly helped through the implementation of the Treaty clause regarding the free movement of labour that would eliminate capital and labour underoccupation.'[63] Thus, Italian productivity increases depended upon the free circulation of capital and labour resources.

Also, at government level the Italian interpretation of European economic cooperation was marked from the beginning by a belief in the 'indissolubility' between free movement of goods and workers. During the EEC negotiations, in the subcommittee on social problems, the Italian delegation made clear from the beginning that the movement of labour had to be as free and extensive as possible. Still, if the idea could be accepted in principle, the reports from Brussels spoke of the difficulties that arose in trying to reach an agreement on the 'time and means to allow the free movement of labour'.[64]

Fears of excessive mobility were still too strong among the other participants, and 'in spite of Italy's pressure, no right for the unemployed to seek for jobs abroad was contemplated. The guiding principle remained the primacy of demand-induced migration.'[65] Such limited liberalization of manpower movements also meant that under the Treaty, the Italian government had no legal instruments to force other members states to hire Italian rather than extra-EEC workers, as had been foreseen by those parliamentary forces opposing ratification[66] and as became clear in the 1960s.[67] This powerful political and institutional resistance to Italian emigration showed that, according to national economic priorities, free movement of labour was much more difficult to accept than free movement of goods, especially since Italy was the only EEC country that had a direct interest in the matter.

In the course of the EEC negotiations, because of the alternative solutions for the unemployment problem proposed in Italy's new programmatic document (the Vanoni Plan), and also the realization that the free movement of labour could find no solutions in the short term, the Italian delegation progressively relaxed its position on free manpower circulation. The negotiators concentrated their efforts on obtaining tangible results as far as the European investment and readaptation funds were concerned[68] and on drawing international attention to the ten-year programme.[69] The ten-year programme, never officially approved by the government, had already been presented by the Minister of the Budget, Ezio Vanoni, at the OEEC Council in January 1955, in order to highlight two among Italy's major economic problems – unemployment and the economic development of the South – and propose concrete solutions. In the face of the existing difficulties in increasing emigration, the Vanoni Plan proposed to concentrate more on stimulating internal demand in order to alleviate unemployment.

> It should be possible by rational and persevering efforts to eliminate in a few years this undesirable phenomenon (unemployment) especially if these efforts are backed by international understanding and assistance. ... Unemployment has placed my country in a position of marked inferiority. In the past the situation was alleviated by large-scale emigration, but today owing to reduction in that flow, it can be corrected only through large-scale capital investment.[70]

Following the same strategy, 'a concentration of investment in the South has been considered so as to promote a greater expansion of income in these regions as compared with the North'.

3.2   The European Investment Bank, the Social Fund and the Protocol Concerning Italy

Both the Italian memorandum presented at Messina and a section of the Spaak Report asked for the creation of Community sources of capital that could be invested in the development of Italy's southern areas.[71] The Italians were responsible for the long section of the Spaak Report entitled 'The development and full utilization of European resources' in which it was held that 'as shown by the experience of Italian unification after 1860 ... the divergence (between regions) can grow in aggregate if the fundamental conditions for the development of production are not immediately created by public bodies'.[72] Thus, according to this approach, it was in the interest of all member states to provide funds in order to develop the depressed areas of the Community, which for the most part were located in southern Italy.

During the Paris meeting of October 1956, Italy's Foreign Minister, after illustrating the 'economic situation of certain underdeveloped areas and the risks which the Italian economy was running in setting up a common market' asked for EEC support in the implementation of the Vanoni Plan.[73] Martino asked that a common statement be annexed to the Treaty recognizing that the ten-year development plan was of common interest and that 'the Community institutions were to help the Italian government in such effort through a proper use of the investment and readaptation funds'. What Italy obtained in the end was the setting up of the two different funds and a statement of moral support included as an appendix to the Treaty ('Protocol Concerning Italy').[74] In the Protocol, the Six recognized that the ten-year plan for the economic development of the South and the elimination of unemployment was in 'their common interest' and they agreed that the Community should 'facilitate the accomplishment of this task ... through the adequate utilisation of the resources of the European Investment Bank and of the European Social Fund'. The first task of the European Investment Bank was indeed the financing of 'projects for developing less developed regions'. At the same time, through the European Social Fund, the EEC was going to pay 50 per cent of expenses incurred by member states in ensuring productive re-employment of workers by means of occupational retraining, resettlement allowances and granting aids.

As far as the institution of the funds was concerned, the Italian delegation considered it its own success, pursued from the beginning against much understandable resistance.[75] In the subcommittee on investments, headed by Di Nardi, the 'cautious attitude of the German and to some extent of the Benelux delegation on the readaptation fund' was to be understood since 'they will have the role of suppliers rather than beneficiaries of the resources'.[76] Along the same lines, a Foreign Office memorandum, prepared for a visit by Martino to Germany in February 1956, underlined the fact that 'the German government must be reassured that its future contribution to the development of the Italian economy, in the course of the European integration process, won't be excessive'.[77]

In the end, the Italian government considered an important diplomatic victory the insertion in the Treaty of what the Cabinet called 'three safeguard elements for Italy inside the Common Market ... the Bank, the Social Fund and the Protocol, which turn the ten-year Italian program into a Community problem'.[78]

4. Tariff Provisions

Two important factors that had to be considered on joining a common market were the timetable for reducing tariff protection internally and the level of the common external tariff. The abolition of all internal duties in three stages of four years each as recommended by the Spaak Report and accepted with some modifications by all governments,[79] reproposed a similar automatic system for tariff reductions contained in the Pella Plan presented at the OEEC in 1950.[80] The Italian delegation accepted the principle of automaticity and irreversibility of the integration process and supported the position of Germany and the Benelux countries on the issue of automatic tariff reductions and – more importantly for its export possibilities within the EEC countries – progressive abolition of import quotas.[81] The basic rates subject to reductions were defined as the duties in force on 1 January 1957 ('legal duties'). Thus, although, according to the report of the EEC Parliamentary Commission on the occasion of ratification, Italy believed in the positive effects tariff reductions could have on its firms' 'competition strength',[82] the impact of such reductions was mitigated by the fact that Italy's legal tariff was much higher than its tariff in use. Therefore, when the Common Market came into effect, on 1 January 1959, in practice Italy's customs duties did not undergo any modification. With a legal tariff on average more than 10 per cent higher than the tariff in use (by 1953 the average incidence of the legal tariff – 24.4 per cent – had been reduced to the much lower average incidence of 14.5 per cent of the working tariff) the first 10 per cent cut had no effect on the Italian economy.[83] None the less, the inclusion of Article 109 in the Treaty on the resumption of tariff controls or 'measures of safeguard ... where a sudden crisis in the balance of payments occurs' was a concession made to Italian industrialists.[84] Italy's industrial world still considered itself comparatively weak and still had a great fear of a recession, which would undoubtedly undermine many industrial success stories.[85] As Guido Carli recalls

> I remember the angry phone calls from Vittorio Valletta [Fiat's general manager] to the Italian delegation in Paris trying to convince them to soften as much as they could the Treaty obligations … The emphasis on Article 109 must be attributed to the strong pressures of Prof. Valletta, scared by the progressive reduction of tariffs.[86]

Moreover, at the time, Valletta's fears were reinforced also by the threat of progressive abolition of quantitative restrictions, which could mean the possibility of seeing foreign car imports increase from an allowed quota of 2,803 vehicles coming from the EEC countries in 1957 to a much bigger quota of 10,500 vehicles in 1959.[87]

Much more difficult to agree upon was the level at which to set the common external tariff (CET) and in particular the exact level of the permitted maxima which would be the crucial factor in determining the final arithmetical average. Apart from the initial French position, which wanted no decapitation at all, the Italians' requests were the most protective, demanding a maximum of 10 per cent for raw materials, 15 per cent for semimanufactures and 20–30 per cent for end products.[88] The Treaty had to conciliate, among the six countries, national policies that originally were wide apart. France and Italy were protectionist minded with high tariff barriers; the Benelux countries were traditionally attached to liberal trade practices, with low or even non-existent customs duties. As Roberto Ducci, a member of the Italian delegation in Brussels, observed in 1957: 'France and Italy think that – for reasons of political presentation more than economic ones – with the falling of all internal impediments to trade, the external barriers should be set as high as possible'.[89] In the end, a compromise was reached on the basis of a German proposal. It was finally agreed that, as a rule, the CET should be based on the arithmetical average of the effectively applied tariffs on 1 January 1957. Here Italy could not hide behind the protection of its legal tariff, and the delegation in Paris fought to obtain a special solution. In the end, the Italians were allowed to define their applied tariff as that levied before 1951, without the temporary 10 per cent reductions and successive autonomous tariff cuts. In cases where their legal tariff exceeded the applied level by more than 10 per cent they could add 10 per cent to the applied duty.[90]

Still, there remained many exceptions to the general rule setting the CET. For some commodities, enumerated in four lists appended to the Treaty, the common tariffs were not to exceed certain maximum limits (lists B, C, D and E).[91] For items on list F (mainly agricultural products) the tariff was fixed directly by the Treaty. Finally, tariffs on list G had to be left for further negotiations between the governments. This list was of course the most critical one, since the Six had not been able to agree on the level of external protection to grant to this group of sensitive products. The general rule was that items were placed on the list because a country wanted special protection for an industry that was important to it, but unable to face foreign competition.

5.   Conclusion

At the end of the Second World War, American help for reconstruction was made dependent upon collaboration among European countries and upon acceptance of a new wave of liberal trade policies. The unexpected pace of recovery, thanks to the firm basis of Italy's industrial apparatus built up over many decades, made foreign competition an acceptable threat. After the war, Italy's industrial structure was able to set the country in motion again and, thanks to Marshall Plan funds, the machinery and production methods of many firms were modernized. Productivity levels increased and Italian competitiveness on the international market soon ushered in the trade boom of the 1950s.

The good trade relations and economic interdependence with the future EEC partners, and especially with Germany, provided an important favourable setting for a positive outcome of the negotiations. Furthermore, the 1950s trade boom undoubtedly helped industrialists relax their negative stance towards liberalization and economic integration. The acceptance of a progressive loss of protection due to the abolition of internal tariffs as provided by the EEC Treaty, was mediated through the insertion of safeguard clauses. What can be derived from the analysis of the Italian case from an economic perspective is that in times of cyclical upswing, and corresponding industrial and trade boom, negotiations on economic integration have better chances of success.

Finally, if Italy's struggle for the free movement of labour found no sympathetic acceptance by Community partners, the Investment Bank and the Social Fund can be considered two Italian victories going in the projected direction of long-term investments in favour of southern development.

Notes

*   I gratefully acknowledge the comments of Prof. R.T. Griffiths and Vera Zamagni on earlier drafts of this work.
** The author is in the Department of Economic Science, University of Bologna.
1.   On the Franco-Italian customs union project, see F. Fauri, 'Italy in International Economic Cooperation: The Franco-Italian Customs Union and the Fritalux–Finibel Negotiations', *Journal of European Integration History*, No. 2, Brussels, October 1995. On EDC, see E. Furdson, *The European Defence Community, A History*, London: Macmillan, 1980; D. Preda, *Storia di una speranza. La battaglia per la CED e la Federazione europea*, Milan, 1990 and J. van der Harst, 'The Pleven Plan', in R.T. Griffiths (ed.) *The Netherlands and the Integration of Europe 1945–1957*, Amsterdam: NEAH, 1990.
2.   On the ECSC negotiations, see R. Ranieri, 'L'espansione alla prova del negoziata L'industria italiana e la comunità del carbone e dell'acciaio, 1945–1955', EUI (European University Institute) PhD thesis Fiesole, June 1988.
3.   On the green pool negotiations, see R.T. Griffiths and A.S. Milward, *The European Agricultural Community 1948–1954*, EUI Working Paper No. 86/254, 1986; R.T. Griffiths (ed.), *The Netherlands and the Integration of Europe*, Amsterdam, 1990; G. Noel, *Du Pool Vert à la politique agricole commune. Les tentatives de Communauté agricole européene entre 1947 et 1955*, Paris: Economica, 1988. On Italy and the green pool negotiations, see G. Laschi, 'L'Italia e il processo di integrazione europea: il caso dell'agricoltura, 1947–1957', EUI PhD thesis, Florence, 1992, pp. 151 ff.
4.   On the plans for freer trade in Europe, see W. Asbeek Brusse, 'West European Tariff Plans 1947–1957 From Study Group to Common Market', EUI PhD thesis, Florence, 1991.
5.   OEEC, *Report on the Possibility of Creating a Free Trade Area in Europe*, Paris: OEEC, January 1957, p. 7.
6.   R.T. Griffiths, 'The Stranglehold of Bilateralism', in R.T. Griffiths (ed.), *The Netherlands and the Integration of Europe, op. cit.*, p. 23.

244 *Economic Development of the EEC*

7. R.T. Griffiths, 'The Beyen Plan', in R.T. Griffiths (ed.), *The Netherlands and the Integration of Europe*, op. cit., p. 176. On the long-term process leading to the 'European relaunch' and its aftermath, see also Pierre Gerbet, *La construction de l'Europe*, Paris: Impr. National, 1983.
8. 'Ainsi à la veille de la Conférence de Messine, les oppositions apparaissaient nettement sur les modalités de la relance', Pierre Gerbet, 'La relance européenne jusqu'à la conférence de Messine', in E. Serra (ed.), *Il rilancio dell'Europa e i trattati di Roma*, Milan: GIUFFRE, 1989, p. 91.
9. In this respect, criticism was often levelled at government commercial policies, by stating that 'Italy could not remain prisoner of ideal (free) trade principles when others disregarded them'; see 'La politica commerciale ad una svolta', in *Esteri*, Vol. IV, No. 21, 15 November, 1953, p. 19.
10. Banca d'Italia, *Relazione Annuale*, 1953, p. 165.
11. See *Italian Economic Survey*, February–March 1953, p. 3; A. Cassuto, 'Anno di mutamenti radicali il 1952 per gli scambi italo-britannici', *24 Ore* (Panorama Economico), January 1952, p. 5; and M. Badi, 'Scambi italo-inglesi e sistema OECE–UEP', in *Rivista italiana di scienze commerciali*, Vol. XVIII, Nos 11–12, November–December 1952, pp. 701–5.
12. 'Déclaration de M. Giuseppe Pella président du Conseil des Ministres d'Italie au Conseil de l'OECE, le 29 Octobre', in Archivio Storico Politico del Ministero degli Affari Esteri, (ASMAE), Buste OECE, n.1001.
13. On this issue, see E. Di Nolfo, 'La "politica di potenza" e le formule della politica di potenza. Il caso italiano (1952–1956)', in A. Varsori, *La politica estera italiana nel secondo dopoguerra (1943–1957)*, Milan: LED, 1993, pp. 413–34; and E. Serra, 'L'Italia e la conferenza di Messina', in E. Serra (ed.), *Il rilancio dell'Europa e i trattati di Roma*, op. cit., pp. 93–124.
14. R.T. Griffiths and W. Asbeek Brusse, 'The Dutch Cabinet and the Rome Treaties', in E. Serra (ed.), *Il rilancio dell'Europa e i trattati di Roma*, op. cit., p. 465.
15. Banca d'Italia, *Assemblea Generale Ordinaria dei Partecipanti*, Rome, 1961, p. 197.
16. 'Italy, Belgium and the Netherlands were the countries in favour of including agriculture in the Common Market ... refusing the idea of a special status for agriculture', see G. Laschi, 'L'Italia e il processo di integrazione europea: il caso dell'agricoltura, 1947–1958', op. cit., p. 305.
17. T.E. Mommens, 'Agricultural Integration in the Benelux', in R.T. Griffiths (ed.), *The Netherlands and the Integration of Europe*, op. cit., p. 50.
18. The southern region in economic terms was among the less-developed in the Italian context, 'all its characteristics gave the picture of an area fallen in the classic backwardness cycle', see M. D'Antonio, *Aspetti dell'economia italiana*, Rome: SVIMEZ, 1968.
19. 'When the Treaty comes into force it will certainly offer advantages for Italy's vegetable and fruit production, since it is impelled by the consideration that the present level of demand for farm products must be increased in order to level up current disequilibriums between the levels of consumption of the Community countries with those of more advanced nations (UK, USA, Canada ...)', see G. Fazio, 'La produzione ortofrutticola italiana e la CEE', *Rivista di Economia Agraria*, No. 4, December 1957, pp. 445–71.
20. See V. Zamagni, 'Le radici agricole del dualismo italiano', *Nuova Rivista Storica*, 1975.
21. Fazio was of the opinion that Italy could expand its trade in citrus fruits, juices and derivates and consequently their cultivation centres in Sicily, Calabria, Puglia, Campania and Latium. He also believed that an increase in citrus fruit exports would give the people of the South the possibility for better living conditions and therefore increase imports of other products from the EEC countries; see G. Fazio, 'Produzione, consumi e prospettive di sviluppo dell'agrumicoltura italiana nel quadro dell Communità Economica Europea', *Rivista di Economia Agraria*, No. 4, December 1958, pp. 440–72.
22. 'At the same time the bourgeois categories, within the modest range of choices offered them for investments, have been induced to seek in the land the place that was safest for their capital and even now do not find ... enough stimuli or reliable opportunities as to induce them to withdraw their savings from their first refuge, the land', see G.G. Dell'Angelo, 'Aspetti economici e demografici del diverso grado di sviluppo degli ambienti agricoli italiani', *Rivista di Economia Agraria*, No. 4, December 1958, p. 437.

23. *Percentage employment distribution by region in agriculture and industry in 1955*

	Agriculture	Industry
North	30.1	40.8
Centre	39.3	28.4
South	51.6	23.6
Islands	44.4	26.1

Source: ISE, *Annuario della congiuntura 1954–55*, Milan, p. 49.

Tractors in 1955   (percentage distribution)

North	68.7
Centre	15.1
South	5.3

For more details on the development of mechanization in agriculture in Italy, see G. Stefanelli, 'Trattrici e meccanizzazione agricola in Italia all'inizio del 1959 e sviluppi nel decennio 1948–1958', in *Rivista di Economia Agraria*, No. 1, 1960, pp. 3–28; Conferenza nazionale dell'agricoltura, *Rapporto finale*, Rome, 1961 and G. Barbero, 'Produttivita' e progresso tecnico nell'agricoltura italiana', *Rivista di Economia Agraria*, No. 1, 1974. On the North–South divide in agriculture, see M. Rossi-Doria, *Analisi zonale dell'agricoltura italiana*, Rome, 1968.

24. A study examining all aspects of production and exports of processed vegetable crops and the potential consumption of the EEC, underlined the importance of setting in motion in southern Italy a balanced development of industries forming a complement to farming, in the light of the favourable repercussions that the Rome Treaty could have on Italian exports of processed vegetable crops. See G. Fazio, 'Produzione ed esportazione dei prodotti vegetali conservati e prospettive di consumo nella Comunità Economica Europea', in *Rivista di Economia Agraria*, No. 4, October–December 1959, pp. 558–99. Along the same lines, see A. Buffa, (Unione delle Camere di Commercio Industria e Agricoltura della Regione Sicilia), *Integrazione europea dell'agricoltura siciliana*, Palermo, 1965.

25. At the moment of EEC entrance 'agricultural wages are still at very low levels and in wide rural areas emigration causes everything go to rack and ruin', see G. Fabiani, *L'agricultura in Italia tra sviluppo e crisi (1945–1977)*, Bologna: Il Mulino, 1979, pp. 152 ff. According to Ugo Ascoli, 'We are speaking of a massive exodus, of biblical proportions, that comes from the fields in the South and invades the industrial centres in the North-West of Italy and Central Europe', in *Movimenti migratori in Italia*, Bologna: Il Mulino, 1978, p. 52.

26. R.T. Griffiths, 'The Common Market', in R.T. Griffiths (ed.), *The Netherlands and the Integration of Europe 1945–1957, op. cit.*, p. 197.

27. T.E. Mommens, 'Agricultural Integration in the Benelux', in R.T. Griffiths (ed.), *The Netherlands and the Integration of Europe, op. cit.*, p. 50.

28. The relative weight in government discussions given to the problem of the development of the South are extensively documented by Barucci, who concludes by saying that it should not surprise that the southern problem was overlooked in the aftermath of the war ('non abbia trovato praticamente eco concreta nel dibattito sulla ricostruzione') given the climate of economic emergency and delicate political equilibrium; see P.Barucci, *Ricostruzione e Pianificazione, Mezzogiorno. La politica economica in Italia dal 1943 al 1955*, Bologna, 1978, pp. 277–309. Moreover, one of the most important economic ministers of the postwar period, Giuseppe Pella, deliberatedly overlooked the problems of the South, 'Il punto debole della impostazione di Pella era la su evidente connotazione "nordista". Nel suo approccio i problemi del sottosviuppo meridionale erano infatti assenti o solo marginalmente considerati', see B. Bottiglieri, 'Tra Pella e Vanoni: la politica economica degli ultimi governi De Gasperi', in *Keynes in Italia*, IPSOA,

1984, p. 143. See also F. Barbagallo, *Mezzogiorno e questione meridionale 1860–1980*, Naples, 1982.

29. The principal laws were: Provvedimenti staordinari per la colonizzazione dell'altipiano della Sila e dei territori jonica contermini, 12 maggio 1950; norme per la espropriazione, bonifica, trasformazione ed assegnazione dei terreni ai contadini, 21 ottobre 1950; which was successively extended to other areas (Maremma, Fucino, Delta del Po, Comprensorio del Volturno e del Sele, Puglia, Lucania, Molise, Sicilia e Sardegna). The land tenure reform was intended to redistribute land and farm income for social and political reasons, as well as to increase productivity in connection with land improvement and irrigation projects. In the words of the OEEC, this was to be 'a far reaching reform ... which could increase farm production so as to ease the strain on the balance of payments for food imports', see OEEC, *Europe the Way Ahead Towards Economic Expansion and Dollar Balance*, Fourth Annual Report of the OEEC, Paris, 1952, p. 293. On the reform, see also P. Villani and N. Marrone, *Riforma Agraria e Questione Meridionale, Antologia Critica, 1943–1980*, Bari: Laterza, 1981 and M. Bandini, *La riforma agraria* Rome, 1956, p. 43, who underlines that the land reform concerned unpopulated areas with no infrastructure. With the elimination of *latifondo*, the law aimed at setting up small family-owned properties partly also as a response to the social tension arising in the South, poor and unable to offer prospects to the ex-servicemen. Yet, many authors have criticized its practical results: 'From an economic point of view, the land tenure reform gave priority to the formation of micro-economic business units with a family orientation, which were not able to stand competition coming from the modern EEC agro-industrial firms', T. Fanfani, *Scelte politiche e fatti economici in Italia nel quaratennio repubblicano*, Turin, 1988, p. 76.

30. The *Cassa per il Mazzogiorno* draft law was drawn up by Donato Menichella (*governatore* of the Bank of Italy) on the basis of an innovating project for the development of the South elaborated by a new research centre (SVIMEZ). The draft law was presented to Parliament by De Gasperi on 17 March 1950, see Camera dei Deputati, *Atti Parlamentari*, Seduta del 17 Marzo 1950, pp. 16296–313. On the role of Donato Mecichella, see M. Finoia, 'Il ruolo di Donato Menichella nella creazione della SVIMEZ e della Cassa per il Mezzogiorno', in AAVV (Autorivari), *Donato Menichella. Testimonianze e studi raccolti dalla Banca d'Italia*, Bari, 1986. On SVIMEZ, see V. Zamagni and M. Sanfilippo, *Nuovo Meridionalismo e intervento straordinario. La Svimez dal 1946 al 1950*, Bologna: Il Mulino, 1988.

31. In the longer run, at least, it may be said that thanks to the Mezzogiorno development policy the North–South divide did not worsen. 'From 1954 to 1966, the gross product of the South grew slightly less than that of Italy as a whole – taking 1954 = 100, the South's index rose to 280 while the index for Italy as a whole reached 289 ... Given the high growth rate of Italy, this result may be deemed a success', see Commission of the European Community, *A Regional Policy for the Community*, Brussels, 1969, p. 107. See also D. Yuill, K. Allen and C. Hull, *Regional Policy in the European Community. The Role of Regional Incentives*, London, 1980.

32. The calculation of the average legal tariff for the agricultural sector is taken from E. Corbino, 'Le nuove tariffe doganali', *op. cit.*, the estimates of the tariff in use in 1953 have been calculated from Ministero delle Finanze, *Tariffa dei dazi doganali di importazione della Repubblica italiana*, Rome, 1953. The other countries' tariff levels are taken from Commissione della Comunità Economica Europea, *Relazione sull situazione economica dei paesi della Comunita'*, Brussels, September 1958, p. 99.

33. As has been observed, from a social point of view these investments – especially in infrastructure – were important in bettering the living conditions of the population in the South; see P. Bevilacqua, *Breve Storia dell'Italia Meridionale dall'Ottocento a oggi*, Rome: Donzelli, 1993, p. 102; see also T. Fanfani, *Scelte politiche e fatti economici in Italia nel quarantennio repubblicano*, Turin: Giappichelli, 1988, 'Ma tutto cio' (le carenze negli esiti costruttivi) non puo' annullare il significato dei risultati raggiunti che nel lungo periodo porteranno ad un incontrovertibile livello di miglioramento delle condizioni sociali e civili delle popolazioni del Mezzogiorno' (p. 84).

34. On this point, see V. Zamagni, 'Le radici agricole del dualismo italiano', *Nuova Rivista Storica*, *op. cit.*, 1975. And also L. Cafagna, *Dualismo e sviluppo nella storia d'Italia*, Venice: Marsilio, 1989.

35. From the beginning of the twentieth century 'a large part of Italian industrialists accepted the government trade policy aimed at favouring agricultural exports, even though the price of these concessions was to be paid by industry', F. Coppa, 'Commercio estero e politica doganale nell'Italia liberale', in G. Mori (ed.), *L'industrializzazione in Italia (1861–1900)*, Bologna: Il Mulino, 1977, pp. 229–30. Quotation from: F. De Filippis and L. Salvatici, 'L'Italia e la politica agricola del mercato comune europeo', in P. Bevilacqua (ed.), *Storia dell'agricoltura italiana in eta' contemporanea III Mercanti e istituzioni*, Venice: Marsilio, 1991, pp. 560–61.

36. Banca d'Italia, *Relazione Annuale*, 1955; on this point, see also P. Saraceno, *La situazione economica italiana all'atto dell'entrata in vigore del trattato di Roma*, Rome: Istituto Poligrafico dello stato (ISP), 1959, p. 22.

37. ASMAE, Ambasciata Italia Parigi (1951–55), b.58, Letter from Brussels to Ministero Affari Esteri on 18 April 1955, and TE 1831/992 from Scamacca to Esteri, 21 April 1955.

38. On this point, see E. Serra, 'L'Italia e la Conferenza di Messina', *op. cit.*, pp. 114 ff.

39. Ibid., pp. 109–10.

40. ASMAE, b. 58, 'Direttore general degli affari economici: considerazioni di natura orientativa sul problema dell'integrazione economica europea', 5 May 1955.

41. The text of the memorandum has been reprinted in R. Ducci and B. Olivi, *L'Europa incompiuta*, Padua: Cedam, 1970, pp. 279 ff.

42. In the four years between 1949 and 1952, a total of 1,025,367 emigrants left Italy; if returns are considered, the net number of people who emigrated was 645,903. The data are from ISTAT, *Annuario del statistiche del lavoro e dell'emigrazione*, 1954.

43. G. De Meo, 'Aspetti quantitativi dell'economia italiana in rapporto alla disoccupazione ed alla politica degli scambi con l'estero', *Commissione Parlamentare*, Vol. IV, No. 4, 1946, pp. 41–2.

44. In a situation of large and rising unemployment, liberalization on the part of Italy as we have analysed in the preceding section, was in sharp contrast with the statements contained in a Report which a group of experts appointed by the UN Secretary-General had prepared at the end of 1949. It was stressed there that 'The system of bilateral trading and exchange control is undoubtedly a most powerful weapon for maintaining full employment' and that 'in the successful attainment of the twin goals of full employment and a relatively free multi-lateral trading system, the former must certainly take precedence over the latter'. Unilateral tariff cuts and elimination of quantitative restrictions went in the opposite direction. Interestingly enough, during the 1950s Italy experienced both high levels of unemployment and significant net emigration. The experts were: J.M. Clark, N. Kaldor, A. Smithies, P. Uri and R.E. Walker, United Nations, *Report 1949*, p. 32.

45. Ministero degli affari esteri, Direzione generale dell'emigrazione, *Emigrazione italiana (Situazione-Prospettive-Problemi)*, 31 March 1949, Rome 1949. On the government emigration policy in postwar years, see, A. Fontani, *Gli emigranti*, Rome, 1962.

46. On this point, see Banca d'Italia, Gruppo di studio sulla politica monetaria e fiscale, *Bilancia dei pagamenti dell'Italia (1947–1957)*, fasc.II, tavola 'rimesse degli emigranti'; F. Balletta, 'Le rimesse degli emigranti iltaliani 1961–1975', in F. Assante, *Il movimento migratorio italiano dall'unità ai nostri giorni*, *op. cit.* pp. 207–86; S. Mantovani and U. Ascoli, 'Riflessi dell'emigrazione sullo sviluppo economico italiano (1945–1970)', in F. Angeli, *L'emigrazione dal bacino del Mediterraneo verso l'Europa industrializzata*, AAVV, Milan, 1976, p. 498. For an international comparison on the level and trends of the emigrants' remittances during the 1960s, see M. Livi Bacci (ed.), *The Demographic and Social Pattern of Emigration from the Southern European Countries*, Florence: Arti Grafiche, 1972, pp. 19–22.

47. 'Emigration will always be seen in all moments of national development as the most efficient "valvola di sicurezza" for the maintenance of social peace', in U. Ascoli, *Movimenti migratori in Italia*, Bologna: Il Mulino, 1979, p. 28. On this point, see also R. Villari, 'L'emigrazione e le classi dirigenti', in R. Villari (ed.), *Il Sud nella storia d'Italia*, Bari: Laterza, 1974.

48. The data are taken from ISTAT, *Annuario di statistiche demografiche*, Vol. XXII, 1973, Rome, 1975. For the US laws on immigration between 1921 and 1924, see M. Livi Bacci, 'L'emigrazione italiana verso l'Europa', in G. Vaciago (ed.), *Lezioni sull'economia italiana nell'integrazione internazionale*, Milan: Ed. Comunità, 1974, pp. 413–14.

49. *FRUS* (Foreign Relations of the United States), 'Interest of the United States in Plans for the
     Migration of Surplus Population from Western Europe', 1951, Vol. VI, pp. 171–82, where it was
     suggested that 'the US should provide for a continued intake of immigrants in excess of the
     numbers permitted by our basic immigration laws ... in order to solve the overpopulation
     problem and improve the security aspect, since this idle people are extraordinarily susceptible to
     propaganda designed to undermine our indulgence upon and help to these countries' (p. 179).
     Italy's repeated diplomatic attempts to convince the Americans to soften the immigration rules
     for the Italians were worthless. At a conference with the US Deputy Representative on the North
     Atlantic Council, De Gasperi held that 'the Americans should not lose sight of the fact that
     Italy's biggest surplus are babies', *FRUS*, Vol. IV, 1951, p. 608. Other more formal requests on
     the need to reopen US borders to Italian emigrants were made by De Gasperi during his visit to
     Washington in September 1951, see *FRUS*, Vol. IV, 1951, p. 699–719.
50. As underlined by E. Sori, this long-term trend in the origin and destination of Italy's migration
     flows was also due to the fact that if someone had to leave from Sicily, 'it was more expensive to
     reach Germany by land than take a ship to New York', E. Sori, *L'emigrazione italiana dall'Unità
     alla seconda guerra mondiale*, Bologna: Il Mulino, 1979, p. 29. On southern Italy's postwar
     migration overseas, see also S. Cafiero, *Le migrazioni meridionali*, Rome: Svimez, 1963, and
     the following table:

*Percentage distribution of unemployment and emigration per area of origin between 1950 and
1960*

	Official unemployment 1955	Continental emigration	Overseas emigration	Total
North	42	42	17	33
Centre	16	12	11	11
South	42	16	72	56

Sources: Calculated from ISTAT, *Annuario di statistiche demografiche*, Vol. XXII, 1973,
Rome, 1975; ISE, *Annuario della congiuntura economica italiana*, 1955, p. 57.

51. Ministero degli Affari Esteri, *Problemi del lavoro italiano all'estero, relazione per il 1971*, Vol.
     III, Appendici Statistiche.
52. CIR (Comitato interminsteriale per la ricostruzione), *The Development of Italy's Economic
     System in the Framework of European Recovery and Cooperation*, Rome, 1952, p. 337.
53. OEEC, *From Recovery to Economic Strength*, Sixth Report, Paris, 1955, I, p. 19; and F. Romero,
     Emigrazione e integrazione europea 1945–1973, Rome: Edizioni Lavero, 1991, pp. 51–7.
54. ASMAE, DGAP (Direzione generale affari politici), 'Documentazione sul problema della
     sovrapopolazione presentata al Consiglio d'Europa', 1950, Annex 1, b. 333.
55. Successive international conferences on emigration (in chronological order from April 1950:
     Geneva, London, Paris, Naples and Brussels), only served to let everybody know that Italy's
     population surplus constituted an element of serious imbalance and that it was willing to 'make
     available to the western community its excess of manpower', CIR, *The Development of Italy's
     Economic System*, *op. cit.*, p. 339. At the Conference of Naples the ILO (International Labour
     Organization) was denied US financing for a migration agency on the basis that the ILO was
     also including Eastern countries, see *FRUS*, Vol. IV, 1951, pp. 191–4.
56. F. Romero, *Emigrazione e integrazione europea 1945–1973*, *op. cit.*, pp. 45–7.
57. If Italy's fight on the issue of the free movement of labour had been accepted in principle, 'there
     had been a clear choice on the part of foreign governments, for reasons of economic policy and
     social consensus, to keep the labour market under full control'. See R. Ranieri, 'L'espansione
     alla prova del negoziato', *op. cit.*, p. 287.

58. A. Oblath, *Problemi dell'emigrazione italiana*, Rome: ISP, 1946, pp. 367–8. Underneath the rhetoric of European integration, Italy's policy aimed at soving national problems, see Adstands (Paolo Canali), *Alcide De Gasperi nella politica estera italiana, 1944–1953*, Verona: Mondadori, 1953; G. Pella, 'European Economic Integration', Banco di Roma, *Review of the Economic Conditions in Italy*, 1951, pp. 163–73; M. Ferrari Aggradi, *Europa. Tappe e prospettive di unificazione*, Rome: Studium, 1958.

59. Net emigration flows to Belgium and France in 1950–1955 amounted respectively, to 70,503 in the case of Belgium and 99,641 in the case of France. Calculated from ISTAT, *Annuario di statistiche del lavoro e dell'emigrazione*, 1957. Pasquale Saraceno calculated that between 1950 and 1957, in the face of the natural increase of Italy's population amounting to 0.81% per year, 44% of such increase had been absorbed through migrations of which 25–30% was directed to the EEC countries. See P. Saraceno, *La situazione economica italiana all'atto dell'entrata in vigore del trattato di Roma*, Rome: ISP, 1958, pp. 17–18.

60. See Cabinet report to Parliament on the occasion of ratification of the EEC Treaties in Presidenza del Consiglio dei Minstri, Servizio Informazioni, *Communità Economica Europea*, Rome: ISP, 1958, pp. 234–5.

61. 'While internal migrations always represent a balancing factor, international migration might carry dangerous unbalancing consequences', C. Gini, 'Delle migrazioni internazionali', *Rivista di politica economica*, March 1955, pp. 173–86. Among these unbalancing consequences, can be underlined 'the impoverishment of the best human energies ... which would negatively affect the abandoned areas in the long term', in R. Volpi, *Storia della popolazione italiana dell'unita' a oggi*, Florence: NIS, 1989, p. 62. At the end of the 1960s also the EEC Commission was convinced that: 'a particularly serious problem, which still has to be resolved, is the uninterrupted (Italian) emigration from the South ... This exodus deprives the South of valuable and enterprising manpower whose absence might be a major handicap in subsequent growth phases', in Commission of the European Communities, *A Regional Policy for the Community*, op. cit., p. 110. On emigration seen as a loss of the most qualified-enterprising workers, see also F. Masera, 'L'equilibrio della bilancia dei pagamenti nel quadro del Mercato Comune e della zona di libero scambio con particolare riferimento all'Italia', *Bancaria*, No. 12, 1957, p. 1380 and C. Urcioli, 'Il Mercato comune europeo', *Stato sociale*, February 1957, p. 204 and B. Barbieri, 'La circolazione delle persone nell'economia europea' conference speech published in *Operare*, No. 4, 1958.

62. G. Gamberini, 'I dazi doganali e la libera concorrenza nel mercato internazionale', *Rivista di politica economica*, 1955, p. 944.

63. Istituto Nazionale di Economica Agraria, *Annuario dell'agricoltura italiana*, Vol. X, 1956, pp. 39–40.

64. ASMAE, DGAP, 'Appunto sullo stato di avanzamento dei lavori della commissioni', from Benvenuti, Brussels, 5 September 1955 to MAE, b.480. For an overview of Italy's negotiating policy on the question of the free movement of labour, see F. Romero, *Emigrazione e integrazione europea 1945–1973*, op. cit., and also M. Doumulin (ed.), *Mouvements et politiques migratoires en Europe depuis 1945: le cas Italien*, Brussels: CIAGP, 1989.

65. F. Romero, 'Migration as an issue in European interdependence and integration: the case of Italy', in A.S. Milward (ed.), *The Frontier of National Sovereignty History and Theory 1945–1992*, op. cit., p. 52. The articles in the EEC Treaty on the free movement of labour are: Art. 3, Part I, on the 'principles' and Arts 48 and 49, Part II, on the 'Community fundamentals'; also some contemporary observers considered these provisions 'extremely vague and evasive', see F. Compagna, 'Domanda europea e offerta italiana sul mercato internazionale del lavoro', *Mondo Economico*, 6 July 1957 and L. Solari, 'La Comunità Economica Europea', *Civiltà delle Macchine*, March–April 1957, in particular p. 21. On the successive directives and regulations relating to the free movement of workers, see G. Del Gaudio, 'Libera circolazione e priorità comunitaria dei lavoratori nei paesi della CEE', in F. Assante (ed.), *Il movimento migratorio italiano dall'unità nazionale ai giorni nostri*, op. cit., pp. 147–53.

66. 'The country that could more likely absorb Italian emigration is France. Yet, a conspicuous number of workers from French Africa has been moving to France in search for a job since the

end of the war, offering conditions at which Italian labour could hardly compete'. See the report to Parliament of Berti 'Relazione di minoranza', in Presidenza del Consiglio dei Ministri, *Comunità economica europea, op. cit.,* p. 322.

67. In a Memorandum on the EEC employment policy presented at the EEC Council of Ministers for Social Affairs by the Italian Minister of Labour, the preference many EEC countries showed for extra-EEC workers was related to the lower cost of manpower and to the lack of specific EEC agreements to balance internal offer and demand: 'De facto existing discriminations in wages, housing, and social security treatment between Community and extra-Community workers hits Italian emigration in particular, which (in the 1960s) has been the principal component of Community emigration ... in 1970 the quota of labour force requested by the EEC countries was covered by Italian workers only up to 16–17% of the total', see Ministero del Lavoro e della previdenza sociale, *La politica dell'impiego nella CEE,* Memorandum presentato al Consiglio dei Ministri degli affari sociali della CEE dal Ministro Donat Cattin il 24-6-1971 and published in *Mondo Economico,* Supplement No. 39, 'La politica di impiego nella CEE', October 1971, pp. xiv–xv. Successive EEC comments on the Italian memorandum underlined the Community's 'impermeability' to Italy's complaints; on this point, see G. Mottura and E. Pugliese, *Agricoltura, Mezzogiorno e mercato del lavoro,* Bologna: Il Mulino, 1975, pp. 227 ff.

68. The Italians argued that southern Italy would be the first to feel the increased competition and that the Fund should therefore; (1) relieve unemployment 'independent of its cause and form' since it would be impossible to differentiate between unemployment caused directly by the EEC and that due to other causes; (2) share in the cost of retraining and relocating the unemployed. See U. Munzi, 'The European Social Fund in the Development of Mediterranean Regions of the EEC', *Journal of International Affairs,* Vol. 2, 1965 and F.R. Willis, *Italy Chooses Europe,* New York, 1971, pp. 62–4.

69. On the connection between the Vanoni Plan and the Common Market, see G. Vedovato, 'Mercato Comune ed Euratom', *Rivista di studi politici internazionali,* 1957, pp. 369 ff; P. Saraceno, 'Schema Vanoni e MEC', and 'Schema Vanoni e integrazione europea nella politica meridionalistica degli anni '50', in P. Saraceno, *Gli anni dello schema Vanoni (1953–1959),* Milan, 1982.

70. European University Institute Archives (EUIA): OEEC, Council, Minutes of the 270th Meeting, 13–14 January 1955, b.22/4. Also in E. Vanoni, *Discorsi sul programma di sviluppo economico,* Rome, 1956, pp. 59–70. For Vanoni's opinion on the importance of asking for international cooperation for the implementation of the plan, see E. Vanoni, 'Lo sviluppo economico italiano e la cooperazione internazionale', in P. Barucci, *La politica economica degli anni Degasperiani,* Florence, 1977, pp. 377–88. For the text of the Plan, see also ACS (Archivio generale dello stato), Ministero Industria e Commercio, Gabinetto, b.4.

71. *Distribution of agricultural underemployment in Italy (as a percentage of the available labour force)*

	1949	1960
North west	35.6	17.1
North east–Centre	44.3	32.1
South	50.7	46.8

Source: Calculated in an unpublished work by SVIMEZ and reproposed by G. Fabiani, *L'agricoltura in Italia tra sviluppo e crisi (1945–1977),* Bologna: Il Mulino, 1979, p. 150.

Indeed, in the following years, the solutions aimed at reducing unemployment to tolerable proportions went in different directions. International observers such as Vera Lutz, gave rise to many voices when she proposed among the possible means of reducing unemployment 'a substantial transfer of population from South to North' since 'underemployment was a problem prevailing in the South, where poor natural resources and an unfavourable geographical location associated themselves with high population density'. The alternative solution to internal migration proposed by Vera Lutz was 'subsidization of Southern industry on a much larger scale, and for a longer period than legislation and official policy-makers have so far explicitly comtemplated', V. Lutz, *Italy A Study In Economic Development*, Oxford: Oxford University Press, 1962, pp. 152–239. For a critical opinion on Vera Lutz's assessments, see G. Chapman, *Development and Underdevelopment in Southern Italy*, London, 1976, where the author claims that 'She is unable to perceive the structural nature of the political consideration behind the evolution of the South ... Her proposals for the revival of the South are rendered irrelevant' (p. 17ff.).

72. 'Through the construction of roads, ports, means of communications, public works for drainage, irrigation, and land reclamation, and with the creation of schools and hospitals'; for the text of the Spaak Report, see Presidenza del Consiglio dei Ministri, *Comunità Economica Europea, op. cit.*, pp. 49–65. On the negotiations preceding the Spaak Report, see M. Doumulin, 'Les travaux du Comité Spaak (juillet 1955–avril 1956)', in R. Serra (ed.), *Il rilancio dell'Europa e i trattati di Roma, op. cit*, pp. 195–210.

73. ASMAE, DGAP, b.480, 'Relazione sulla riunione del consiglio dei Ministri degli affari esteri dei sei paesi della conferenza di Bruxelles sul mercato comune e Euratom', 27 October 1956.

74. Treaty establishing the EEC and connected documents, Annexes, 'Protocol Concerning Italy'. The quotations were taken from Art. 125 and Art. 130 of the EEC Treaty.

75. The Italian memorandum, which called for a common market that 'should cover the whole economic and social life of the countries concerned, without neglecting the social or labour field' was also of the opinion that 'general economic integration should be moderated through a readaptation fund for retraining workers and modernizing or converting factories', reprinted in Ducci and Olivi, *L'Europa incompiuta, op. cit.*

76. R.T. Griffiths, 'The Common Market', in *The Netherlands and the Integration of Europe, op. cit*, p. 200.

77. ASMAE, DGAP, b.420, 'Visita ufficiale a Bonn (6–9 febbraio 1956)'.

78. Cabinet report to Parliament on the occasion of the ratification of the EEC Treaties in Presidenza del Consiglio dei Ministri, *Comunità Economica Europea op. cit.*, p. 170.

79. This point is extensively dealt with in R.T. Griffiths, 'The Common Market', in *The Netherlands and the Integration of Europe, op. cit.*, p. 191.

80. Pella, as we have seen in Section 2, had proposed automatic tariff reductions on the third and sixth year of the union. The proposed tariff cuts of 15% could eventually be increased through parallel negotiations.

81. On 1 January 1957, the situation of trade liberalization as far as import quotas were concerned was the following:

	Total	Food	Manuf. products	Raw materials
Italy	99.1	97.5	100.0	99.2
Benelux	95.6	89.3	99.2	94.4
Germany	91.5	81.3	98.0	96.2
France	82.3	79.2	96.3	71.6

Source: Presidenza del Consiglio dei Ministri, *Communità Economica Europea, op. cit.*, p. 218.

'The abolition of tariffs and quotas among the member countries will push demand towards the best and more convenient products and will expand the consumer market to those potential buyers who have been excluded so far by tariffs and quantitative restrictions', see the Cabinet Report to Parliament for the ratification of the EEC Treaty, in Presidenza del Consiglio dei Ministri, *Comunità Economica Europea, op. cit.*, p. 115.

82. 'La politica commerciale e tariffaria comune, basandosi sulla soppressione dei dazi, fra gli stati membri stimolera' l'aumento della forza concorrenziale delle imprese di questi stati', see the

Commission report to Parliament for the ratification of the EEC Treaty, in *Presidenza del Consiglio dei Ministri, Comunità Economica Europea op. cit.*, p. 211.

83. On the administrative provisions leading to a significant divergence between Italy's legal and current tariffs, see F. Fauri, 'La fine dell'autarchia: le prime tappe del processo di liberalizzazione del commercio estero italiano nel secondo dopoguerra', *Rivista di Storia Economica*, No. 3, October 1995.

84. With the benefit of hindsight, Bino Olivi, member of the Italian delegation in Brussels, observes that such safeguard clauses inserted in the Treaty as a result of Italian pressures were successively used more by those states that had opposed them during the negotiations than by Italy itself. See B. Olivi, *L'Europa difficile*, Bologna, 1993, p. 47.

85. On the position of Confindustria during the negotiations, see F. Fauri, 'L'atteggiamento Confindustriale di fronte alla prospettiva del mercato comune europeo', *Rivista di Politica Economica*, primavera/estate 1996.

86. G. Carli, *Cinquant'anni di vita italiana*, Bari: Laterza, 1993, pp. 164–5.

87. See F. Masera, 'L'equilibrio della bilancia dei pagamenti', *Bancaria*, 1957, *op. cit.*, 'the major exception to liberalization is the car industry that will enter into tough competition through the progressive abolition of quantitative restrictions' (p. 139). Vittorio Cito had calculated that Italy's car quota was to be enlarged by 275% in 1959, corresponding to an increase in imports of 10,500 automobiles. See V. Cito, 'Le restrizioni quantitative al commercio nel Trattato per la Comunità Economica Europea', *Bancaria*, No. 6, 1958, p. 664. Some authors also believed that the abolition of quantitative restrictions was to be balanced internally by special government provisions in order to avoid 'ruinous falls' among the industries concerned, see A. Lazzati, 'In margine alla questione dei contingenti nella Comunità Economica Europea', *Bancaria*, No. 4, 1959, pp. 448–51.

88. 'The Dutch demand was for a maximum of 5% for raw materials, 10% for semi-manufactures and 20% for end-products'; the solution in the end consisted in a German compromise proposal: 3% on raw materials, 10% for semi-manufactures and no-decapitation for end products', see R.T. Griffiths, 'The Common Market', *op. cit.*, p. 197.

89. R. Ducci, 'Un mercato comune per l'Europa', *Civitas*, 1957, p. 23

90. W. Asbeek Brusse, 'West European Tariff Plans', *op. cit.*, p. 275.

91. These maximum limits were: 3% for products on list B (raw materials); 10% for products on list C (semifinished items); 15% for products on list D (inorganic chemicals); 25% for products on list E (organic chemical products).

[9]

U.S. Attitudes towards Integration and Interdependence: The 1950s

Federico Romero

United States policy toward European integration in the 1950s grew out of the ideas of the Marshall plan.[1] Western Europe was to be stabilized, revived, and united and, along with American military power, serve as a pillar of an anti-Soviet containment strategy. Europe's economic recovery and its integration gradually but surely altered the terms of Atlantic interdependence. By the end of the decade, changed American domestic interests required a redefinition of national priorities, and therefore of the United States's international economic aims. In addition, the European and Atlantic settlements of 1947–1950 had produced new conditions. The turning point came in 1958. A new policy would slowly emerge thereafter. This paper examines change and continuity in U.S. integration policy in an increasingly interdependent Atlantic world.

The Postwar Rationale for European Integration

Both contemporary U.S. government officials and recent historians of the Marshall Plan assume that the United States had two chief reasons for pursuing West European integration. The first was a conviction that containment could succeed only if Western Europe made peace with itself and grew cohesive, stable, and united in the face of the Soviet threat. The second was

104   Federico Romero

the belief that a stable and prosperous Western Europe could only be founded upon a large unified market where competitive pressures, economies of scale, and a rational allocation of resources would improve productivity, incomes and consumption. One rationale was, in other words, essentially geopolitical and aimed at building up Europe's strength by enhancing its cohesiveness and by reconciling Germany's recovery with the security of the other nations, especially France. The other derived from customs union theory. It elevated America's own historical experience to a paradigm of modernization: A vast single market would create a context within which rapid productivity growth and a high level of consumption would supersede class conflict and assure the viability of democratic governments. European unification, it was thought, provided the means to defeat economic nationalism and introduce market discipline and multilateralism. Further American aid would then be unnecessary, since economic growth would close the dollar gap. It could thus be sold to Congress as a policy in the American interest not only in the field of security but on economic grounds as well.

The two approaches that coexisted in U.S. policy-making still provide useful interpretative frameworks for historical analysis. Even though the former featured prominently in State Department thinking and the latter developed within the European Cooperation Administration (ECA), they were complementary and mutually reinforcing rather than contradictory. The economic and social ideas of postwar America provided the cultural foundations for its international security strategy. With Marshall Plan aid, European integration in fact became the "interlocking concept in the American Plan for Western Europe." Integration was to be the source of Western economic and political strength, and at the same time would offset Soviet power on the Continent.[2]

Marshall Plan aid policy nevertheless failed to fulfill all these promises. As the plan progressed it became clear that the United Kingdom would neither move towards unification nor disband the sterling area. The Organization for European Economic Cooperation (OEEC), though a worthwhile intergovernmental forum for trade liberalization, was not an avenue toward integration. Most importantly, the liberalization of trade and payments proved to be feasible only at the regional level and on a discriminatory basis. The European Payments Union (EPU), an offshoot of the Marshall Plan, successfully encouraged economic recovery. It took place, however, within a framework of limited, rather than worldwide, multilateralism. It discriminated against dollar imports. The European Coal and Steel Community (ECSC) achieved the crucial goal of Franco-German reconciliation but in so doing reduced the scope of European integration, both geographically and sectorally.[3] Although by the early 1950s American containment was gradually becoming successful, Western Europe had not moved toward either political unification or economic integration. The latter followed an irregular course that bore only a faint resemblance to the American route to a united Europe.

While the Marshall Plan created an effective framework for cooperation, economic trends promoted political stability. The specter of further fragmentation no longer haunted the Western European scene. NATO had successfully built strength through unity. It linked Western Europe to the United States and cemented an Atlantic bloc around the idea of containment. Europe's economic solutions nevertheless deviated markedly from the federalism and functionalism preached at the ECA. The supranational institutions of the ECSC embraced only a limited number of core countries; its sectoral policies reinforced, rather than transcended, national industrial plans; and the community could very well have developed into an updated version of a cartel. The discussion surrounding the so-called green pool indicated that almost any regional agricultural agreement would be so clearly protectionist and discriminatory that it would alienate even the most ardent pro-Europeans in the American administration. The liberalization of trade and payments within the OEEC involved a Germany-centered pattern of industrial trade and entailed deep and durable discrimination against dollar imports. The mechanics of Europe's economic growth produced, in other words, an indefinite postponement of the return to multilateralism and currency convertibility that remained the central ingredient in America's recipe for the world economy.[4]

American policymakers realistically accepted modification of their plans. Discriminatory though it was, a viable system of trade and payments had been made to work and, with the help of dollar aid, to engender sustained economic growth and stabilization. The foreign policy establishment recognized that these strategic gains were well worth both the sacrifice of American exports and the temporary shelving of plans for multilateralism and currency convertibility. The U.S. Treasury, though wary that EPU might evolve into a soft-currency bloc that would put the dollar at a disadvantage in future world trade, had to accept European regionalism in the short run. In the early 1950s protectionist claims did not greatly affect the bipartisan consensus around internationalism. Obviously there was little public concern about the international competitiveness of the American economy. Temporary discrimination against the dollar area could be tolerated because it did not infringe upon any conspicuous interest in an economy that appeared to be almost invulnerable.

Transatlantic economic interdependence was a concept that rarely entered into American policy discussions, which continued to rest on the premise that Western Europe depended on dollar aid. Thus there was no nationalistic response to European regionalism or even any major change in the American position. Certain ECA officials, skeptical of Europe's ability either to catch up on productivity growth or narrow the dollar gap, nevertheless advocated the creation of an Atlantic reserve system that would pool dollar, sterling, and Continental monetary reserves. To stop the drain on American resources, the United States was to accept an "interdependent and organic relationship" with Western Europe, which would become one of two parts in an institutionalized Atlantic community. Neither the Treasury Department nor Congress would ever consider such a possibility.[5]

The State Department more realistically focused on improving existing institutions. However much its scope was to have been narrowed, European integration remained of utmost importance, indeed it was deemed "vital to the security of the United States." The ECSC, based as it was on the principle of supranationality and crucial as it had been in binding the Federal Republic to the West, was viewed in the State Department as the core of a set of "mutually reinforcing concentric circles."[6] The others were the OEEC for economic cooperation and NATO for security. After the outbreak of the Korean War and the resumption of Western armament, hopes for progress toward European integration turned to the negotiations for the European Defense Community (EDC); together with the development of the ECSC, it rapidly grew into America's main integrative hope.

Political support for integration could be generated more easily by emphasizing strategic rather than economic considerations. American interest in the EDC treaty became almost obsessive. The State Department could best secure backing for the ECSC by playing up the importance of the security issues involved. This was clearly the case in discussions surrounding a U.S. loan to the ECSC High Authority. Concerns expressed by the Treasury and the U.S. steel industry that the ECSC could evolve into a powerful new international cartel were overridden by the State Department's insistence on the need to show support for an organization that represented the only instance of supranational integration in Europe. The strategic argument for European unity gained the full backing of the White House, and the State Department thus won its battle. The advancement of the Six toward economic federation and increasing political unity had become Washington's preferred road to European integration.[7]

The Debate on Currency Convertibility

In the Eisenhower years American support for European integration, though increased as a result of cold war tensions, gradually lost its economic justification. Indeed the rapid growth of the European economy, its productivity improvements, and its comeback as a challenger in international markets would call into question the postwar tenets of U.S. aid policies. How long could American foreign economic policy be geared to the single, overarching goal of filling the dollar gap? An era of interdependence was dawning across the Atlantic, vulnerabilities in the American economy were coming to light, and established postwar views were being opened to attack. European economic regionalism, once accepted as a transitory stage toward multilateralism, threatened to become an obstacle to U.S. foreign economic policy. By the mid-1950s European integration no longer appeared to be neatly consistent with America's commercial and financial interest. As a consequence, the Eisenhower administration faced recurring clashes of diverse impulses and priorities, often embodied in conflicts between the foreign policy establishment and the economic departments.

In 1953, with the appointment of the Commission on Foreign Economic Policy chaired by Clarence B. Randall, President Eisenhower embarked on the difficult task of squaring an Atlanticist belief in a strong and united Western Europe with commitments to fiscal restraint, free trade, and private enterprise. The Randall Commission conducted the first general review of U.S. foreign economic policy since the Marshall Plan. In its report, the commission did not challenge the desirability of multilateral free trade, which continued to be regarded as the main avenue to international stability as well as the best possible trading environment for the then highly efficient American producers. Currency convertibility remained the overriding long-term goal and everybody in official Washington agreed on the need to overcome the separation of currency areas. Prompting this consensus was a British request for American credit and support for the introduction of sterling convertibility. Difficulties arising from the persistent world payments imbalance highlighted the Administration's deep divisions on essential strategic considerations. The Treasury and the Federal Reserve Bank considered convertibility essential: The economic strength of the West had to be based upon full multilateralism and international market discipline. In their view, the American national interest required a prompt end to discrimination against the dollar; interdependence had to be created in an open system of trade and payments in which competition from more efficient American producers would cause Europeans to increase their productivity.

108   Federico Romero

The British proposal seemed therefore to present a welcome opportunity to begin the dismantlement of regionalism. The Treasury prepared to support openly Britain and any other European country inclined to introduce convertibility. It regarded the resulting breakdown of the EPU as well as the deflation that would consequently occur in the deficit nations as symptoms of a healthy return to financial discipline.[8]

But such a step appeared dangerous, both to the State Department and to the Foreign Operations Administration (FOA). They maintained that European unity and integration could be defended even at the cost of dollar discrimination and were convinced that the termination of EPU would jeopardize the centerpiece of their postwar policy. Some State Department officials openly argued for global trade and payment arrangements and opposed regionalism, but they believed that Europe's low level of reserves and huge needs for dollar imports made convertibility unsustainable. Without a trade increase, the dollar gap would continue to be large and convertibility remain futile. Only a gradual "orderly transition" to convertibility was conceivable to them, since any move toward freer trade in the Atlantic area had to be reconciled with further progress in European integration.[9]

FOA officials also wanted to move toward convertibility but argued that it ought to result from a new American commitment to an institutionalized Atlantic community, either in the form of a tripartite Atlantic reserve system, consisting of the United States, the United Kingdom, and the Six, or by means of full U.S. membership in a trans-Atlantic OEEC. Convertibility would then be established between the dollar and the currencies of the EPU, treated as a unit. Such an outcome would both assure that deeper continental integration remained possible and encourage "an expanding trade and payments relationship" between the EPU and dollar areas.[10]

Between the Treasury's view of a hegemonic interdependence resulting from free multilateral trade and payments and FOA's dreams of currency blocs linked by transatlantic institutions and upheld by dollar reserves, there could evidently be no convergence. The first approach seemed financially and politically unsustainable since the size of the trade imbalance would push most European countries to adopt tighter national restrictions. It was therefore worthless from the standpoint of American interests. At the same time, FOA's plan involved a financial commitment and—something all but inconceivable to Washington—a renunciation of American autonomy.

A more cautious approach eventually emerged along lines suggested by the State Department. Regional integration, OEEC liberalization, and dollar discrimination remained pillars of the postwar stability of Europe. EPU continued to serve as the main institution upon which European growth rested; it, too, had to be preserved and regional discrimination tolerated until a better alternative could be found. The issue could only be approached gradually. The Randall Commission report, though silent on matters of regionalism and European integration, restated U.S. support for EPU as a way station to convertibility.[11] The successes of regionalism were thus not sacrificed to a dogmatic, nationalistic assertion of U.S. monetary and commercial hegemony; nor were they overblown into fancy designs for a tighter, unnecessary Atlantic interdependence. The Randall report left U.S. international monetary policy largely unchanged.

Reassessing U.S. Trade Policies

As the U.S. quest for multilateralism moved from monetary to trade policy, it became linked to the administration's commitment to reduce expenditures. Since the Treasury insisted that foreign aid had to be cut, the dollar gap could only be reduced by increasing Europe's foreign dollar earnings. The State Department wanted to lower American tariffs to give European producers access to larger markets, and assumed that the American economy enjoyed "a relative invulnerability to changes from abroad." That was not the opinion of the Department of Commerce, which opposed deep tariff reductions: Free trade had to be accompanied by protective measures for sectors that would suffer from low-wage competition.[12]

The Randall Commission eventually recommended increasing mutual trade and encouraging increased outflows of dollars for private investments to replace government aid. Eisenhower endorsed the new approach in a message to Congress in March 1954 that requested authority to negotiate new tariff cuts. In calling for increased trade and import competition on the American market, the administration had closed the gap between foreign and domestic economic policy and at the same time opened the door to many powerful domestic pressure groups. The durable goods exporting sectors with high productivity lobbied for more liberal tariff policies. Such "Detroit free traders" had to deal with pressure exerted by low-technology, low-wage, small-scale producers who feared European competition.[13]

Congress remained reluctant to remove commercial protection for the sake of foreign allies. With the renewal of the Reciprocal Trade Agreement Act, the White House received authority for modest tariff cuts but the two main statutory instruments for the protection of American trade, the "escape clause" and the "peril point clause," were retained. They entitled American producers to request suspension of tariff reductions when foreign competition became threatening. If the Tariff Commission upheld the petitioner's case, as it usually did, the president had to restore import duties. These clauses allowed the unilateral repeal of trade concessions; they made U.S. trade policy unpredictable and discouraged foreign competition from entering the American market. The same applied to the agriculture sector, where the United States maintained the right to impose restrictions, in violation of GATT, whenever imports threatened domestic price support policies.[14]

Congress has traditionally upheld the view that no international obligation could override the national interest or limit American sovereignty. Such an attitude could only frustrate the State Department's "trade rather than aid" campaign. The administration frequently yielded to the refusal to accept even a moderate degree of economic interdependence. While the State Department continued to preach about the urgency of mutual trade liberalization, the Tariff Commission accepted several requests for new import duties on items that were beginning to hurt marginal or backward sectors of the American economy. Between 1953 and 1955, tariffs were unilaterally raised on bicycles, pipes, fur hats, watches, lead, and zinc.[15]

A bold new trade policy never took shape. As with convertibility, American relations with Europe continued to be based largely on doctrines and frameworks devised in 1947–48. But the cracks were widening in the institutions created after the war. As European recovery progressed, it became increasingly more difficult to fit Europe's integrative arrangements into the mold of America's economic aims. From the American point of view the value of European integration was now entirely strategic and political; it strengthened Western Europe vis-à-vis the Soviet bloc. Support for integration never disappeared during the cold war but it faced powerful challenges from domestic economic interests that clamored for thorough review of America's relations with a Europe that was no longer weak and marginal. In the mid-1950s, U.S. attitudes towards integration turned increasingly on America's changing economic situation as well as on the negotiations begun by the Six for a Common Market.

The Common Market

Though the failure of the EDC had brought disillusionment and skepticism, steady progress towards integration remained a key U.S. strategic objective, one made even more critical by the need to reconcile France with the inclusion of Germany in NATO. Both the State Department and the White House took a keen interest in the so-called Euratom project for a European

U.S. Attitudes 111

atomic energy authority. Euratom might also have prevented national European nuclear development programs from becoming military ventures. According to the terms of the scheme, American industry was to have been the main supplier of atomic technologies. This added an economic dimension to the project's appeal. The United States was fully supportive of Euratom. The Common Market idea did not receive a similarly warm welcome: the State Department thought it "a pretty nebulous project" with little chance of success.[16]

Other agencies were equally dismissive. FOA viewed regional arrangements primarily as means to promote trade liberalization and to narrow the dollar gap: its "baby" was the OEEC. Sectoral integration risked restoring cartels. More ambitious arrangements like the Common Market were deemed to be unrealistic. The Treasury and the Federal Reserve System hesitated to take an official stand but their leading officials did not conceal a distaste for Europe's regionalism and anticipated a harsh American reaction if the Common Market led to increased commercial discrimination. In their opinion, "US interest in an economically united Europe" was "ill considered" and no longer appropriate.[17]

This deprecation of the Common Market left the strategic and political aspects of American interest in a unified Europe unchallenged. Eisenhower personally emphasized "the desirability of developing in WE a third great power bloc" by means of further progress towards "the unity of Western Europe," and Secretary of State Dulles never failed to stress the importance of integrating Germany irrevocably into the West. He continued to perceive "the greatest hope" in "the six-nation grouping approach." The process set in motion at Messina was worthy of America's strongest support, he thought. Euratom may have been the State Department's new pet project but in its trail the Common Market also came to be seen as a positive development. As early as December 1955 the department reached the conclusion that the political importance of integration rendered commercial issues "necessarily subordinate." The State Department was prepared to accept a certain degree of discrimination for the sake of its broader political goals.[18]

With the progress of the Brussels negotiations and the concurrent discussions arising from the British proposal for a Free Trade Area, the future of Europe's economic institutions brightened. In July 1956 the State Department outlined the future pattern of U.S. policy. Regional trade arrangements could be accepted if they contributed to the attainment of U.S. political objectives in the area and to an overall expansion of international trade. The Common Market met the first criterion since it enhanced the integration of Western Europe, and received a more cautious but largely favorable

112   Federico Romero

judgment on the second one. The department was "gratified" by the all-encompassing character of the customs union, the apparent lack of protectionist leanings, and the "attention given to the international obligations" of the participating countries. The Free Trade Area, which disavowed political aims, was less welcome since its discriminatory effects could not be offset by progress toward European unity.[19]

The White House directed the Interdepartmental Council on Foreign Economic Policy to prepare a special assessment of the impact of the new projects on the U.S. economy and foreign trade. A surprisingly upbeat mood pervaded the CFEP review, reminiscent of the optimism of integration theories of the Marshall Plan. As though nothing had happened in the intervening years, integration was again treated as an abstraction and viewed through the lenses of customs union theory. CFEP thought further European integration desirable for political as well as economic reasons. By accelerating its internal growth, the Common Market would become "a better market for US exports." Supranational institutions were also thought to promote liberal trade policies; a healthy rollback of national protectionism was predicted as the sequel to integration. Tariff discrimination by the Common Market was expected to be moderate, and could be negotiated away in GATT without "net adverse effects upon US trade." CFEP chairman Clarence Randall concluded that the Common Market could be "the most significant economic events in [his] generation."[20]

Evidence of current economic conditions and trade flows seemed to warrant such optimism. They pointed to the existence of a buoyant, highly competitive U.S. economy that could benefit from European growth. In 1955–57 the trade balance with Western Europe was not only positive but rapidly improving, with a surge in export growth. Highly competitive industries, like automobiles, machinery, and chemicals, welcomed creation of the Common Market as a "juicy opportunity" for massive direct investment. Their spokesmen predicted that any short-term displacement of exports would be more than offset by profits from future direct investments in the huge new market.[21] Some export interests, such as aircraft and farming, pressed the administration hard to intervene against both steep external tariffs and discriminatory "organized" markets. This did not, however, amount to a generalized effort by a powerful export lobby. Nothing like that materialized in 1956–57. The Department of Agriculture managed to send representations to Brussels during the final stages of the treaty negotiations, but they had little overall influence. Nor did the protectionist, inward-looking sectors make their influence felt: the Common Market did not appear to pose an immediate threat of increased competition, and no explicit linkage with a further round of mutual tariff reductions was publicly suggested by the administration prior to 1958. Even the Department of Commerce sided with State during the policy review process.[22]

The emerging concern about the balance of payments did not change this view, although the Treasury worried about the yearly accumulation of payments deficits. The trade balance remained healthy. The Treasury's focus was on the reduction of public expenditures abroad. Together with the Federal Reserve Bank, the Treasury expressed reservations about European regionalism but did not call for a new offensive in trade policy. Moreover, it doubted that the Six could overcome their internal differences enough to integrate their economies effectively. The Treasury probably also recognized that an open struggle to prevent U.S. endorsement of the Common Market was pointless. A Common Market, if ever actually created, could have two faces. A true internal liberalization would force Europeans, particularly France, to "put their own house in order" and replace inflationary policies with financial discipline and fiscal orthodoxy. This would certainly be a positive step toward the Treasury's goal of convertibility. At the same time, it could develop into a protectionist and restrictive arrangement, presumably to accommodate France.[23] How could the United States influence these choices? The State Department chose to support the most liberal elements among the Six.

Eisenhower therefore once again praised European unity, and the CFEP concluded that integration appeared "desirable on political and economic grounds"—provided that it did not lead to "an inward-looking regional bloc." The United States promised to support both the Common Market and the EFTA insofar as the new arrangement neither hampered progress towards multilateralism and convertibility nor increased discrimination against dollar goods. The CFEP emphasized the U.S. interest in a stronger British linkage with the Six through a free trade area but expressed a clear preference for the political approach of the Common Market as opposed to the purely economic objectives of the EFTA.

The CFEP review inaugurated a policy of official support for the Common Market. The State Department's view of a Europe integrated around the Six, and still beneath the umbrella of dollar discrimination, remained at the core of U.S. policy. European unity was, as previously, the supreme goal, and multilateral trade and convertibility were still subordinated to it. The alternative concept of interdependence was not taken into consideration. When the idea of an integrated Atlantic economic community was mooted in NATO, the State Department replied that there was no need for a more tightly knit interdependence; integration in Europe and cooperation across the Atlantic were quite enough![24]

114   Federico Romero

During the final stage of the negotiations for the Treaty of Rome, the Treasury and the Department of Agriculture advocated the use of pressure to assure that U.S. commercial interests received due consideration. The State Department publicly expressed strong support for the Common Market, offered milder backing for the EFTA project, and submitted an aide-memoire to the Six requesting no increase in the current level of discrimination, particularly against agricultural products. It also advocated further liberalization of dollar imports. Even though the replies were largely noncommittal, the department saw no reason for pessimism. It maintained that economic expansion would be strong enough to accommodate increasing imports from third countries into the Common Market. The political priority of seeing the treaty safely completed furthermore induced American diplomats to shelve queries concerning commercial issues. The GATT debate on the new customs union was deliberately postponed till after the treaty ratification.[25]

Secretary Dulles had by now elevated the integrative effort of the Six to a central role in America's world view. It was now described as a step in the building of a powerful bloc, a "cornerstone in [the] Atlantic construction." In April 1957 the department triumphantly reported to the CFEP that the Treaty of Rome was "in accord with the US policy objectives" and therefore deserved U.S. support. The treaty paid heed to "the interests of third countries." Any remaining problems (such as the level of the external tariff, agricultural policy, and preferential treatment for overseas territories) were left to future GATT negotiations. Since from a commercial point of view these issues were crucial, the Treasury complained that the State Department had underestimated the economic consequences of the Common Market. Yet no attempt was made to override State's essentially political approach. The report was approved by the CFEP as the official U.S. position. Later on, in GATT, the State Department rejected the widespread criticism of the Common Market's protectionist features and helped assure its international acceptance. Thus the shelter of America's friendly diplomacy enabled Europe to strengthen, indeed crucially advance, the regional integration of Europe.[26]

1958: A Turning Point

America's support for the EEC originated primarily in strategic considerations. The debate within the administration, and in the country at large, remained anchored to the axioms that had guided U.S. policy since 1948, and they gave priority to the political and economic strengthening of Western

Europe in the interests of containment. Such persistent concern could well justify a further sacrifice of America's short-term commercial interest. Strategic motives nevertheless do not entirely explain why so little attention was devoted to the changing terms of interdependence. Momentous decisions in transatlantic economic relations were indeed underway. Within a year they would force the United States to review its policy towards West European regionalism.

With the sudden jump of the U.S. payments deficit to $3.5 billion in 1958, up from a previous yearly average of $1 billion, the situation came to be seen in a different light. The rise was almost entirely due to a large drop in trade surplus from $6.1 billion to $3.3 billion. More than half of this decline came from decreases in trade with Western Europe. In spite of the American recession, imports from Western Europe had increased by 10.6 percent while U.S. exports to Western Europe had decreased by 23.6 percent. It was no longer just a matter of tightening restraints on public spending: the trade performance of the American economy had now become a matter of explicit concern. For the first time since World War II American policymakers were confronted with a "weakening of [our] ability to compete with other countries in world markets."[27]

By the end of the year Western Europe was ready to disband the EPU, as most currencies had become convertible into dollars. Convertibility brought to an end a decade of postwar recovery and was obviously very welcome in Washington. The State Department considered the move, along with French financial stabilization, as a vindication of its support for a liberal-minded EEC. But convertibility also raised the stakes in the mounting trade conflict. The Treasury, for once in agreement with the State Department, demanded rapid action to prevent the Europeans from preserving a "deeply embedded" discrimination against dollar goods. Import restrictions had to go. Regional discrimination could no longer be tolerated to the same extent. The era of U.S. commercial sacrifices for the sake of European growth and stability was finally over.[28]

By mid-1959 the trade surplus dropped to $1 billion, the lowest level in the decade, and the balance of payments became the paramount concern in U.S. policy toward Europe. American attitudes underwent a swift and deep change. In trade as in other issues a new assertiveness in defense of the national interest was evident. After the shift to convertibility, the United States declared at GATT in May 1959 that trade discrimination no longer responded to any "financial logic" and had to be superseded by nondiscrimination and multilateralism. "The period of postwar adjustment" was now recognized as being over. The old arguments about "dollar shortage" had

116   Federico Romero

"lost their relevance."[29] At the OEEC the United States demanded action
from the European allies; aid and increased imports from the United States
were to help redress the American deficit.[30] Interdependence had now
reached the United States as well, and it carried a price. An entirely new
game had begun.

Facing Interdependence

The new attitude brought noticeable changes. Any attempt to reduce the
contrasts between the Six, the United Kingdom, and other OEEC states on
a regional basis would meet with explicit U.S. hostility. From now on,
liberalization had to proceed on a worldwide and multilateral basis, as well
as within GATT's framework. The OEEC itself was to be transformed from
a regional organization into a larger forum with U.S. direct participation (and
rebaptized as the OECD: Organization for Economic Cooperation and Development), in the hope that it could serve as an instrument for overcoming
the U.S. payments deficit. The EEC also came to be seen in a new light. The
United States still had a strong strategic interest in "maintaining the political
cohesion of the Six," as Undersecretary Douglas Dillon declared during a
trip to Europe in December 1959, but American commercial interests were
now paramount; discriminatory policies would no longer be accepted. For
the first time since the war, an American statesman toured Europe not to
organize recovery, strengthen NATO, or preach integration but with the task,
according to Dillon, of "promoting US exports and removing discrimination."[31] The subsequent "Dillon round" in GATT gave the United States a
chance to begin bargaining down commercial tariffs with the EEC and
EFTA. In the 1960s, under President Kennedy, this approach would become
the centerpiece of U.S. international economic policy.

The timing was crucial; had it come about just one or two years later
the EEC certainly would have received a very different treatment in Washington. But in 1956 the dollar shortage and Europe's productivity gap were
still accepted as unalterable realities. In the frame of mind shaped by the
strategy of containment, they still governed America's responses to European economic issues. The strengthening of Europe through integration was
held to be an imperious necessity in light of the Soviet threat, not something
that should be influenced by U.S. commercial interests that, after all, were
only mildly damaged by European regionalism.

Even as late as 1956–57 the strategic importance that the United States
attached to integration by the Six prevented a thorough reassessment of U.S.

U.S. Attitudes 117

long-term economic goals. The Free Trade Area proposed by the United Kingdom should, in theory, have advanced Washington's objectives of healing the split between Britain and the Six, accelerated Europe-wide liberalization, expedited convertibility, and reinforced liberal tendencies within the Six. Of course, a larger preferential area might have entailed a bigger commercial disadvantage to the United States, and chances were that a compromise between the Six and the United Kingdom could be reached only on highly discriminatory terms. This was not, however, the main reason for Washington's persistent support of the Six at the expense of the EFTA. From the State Department's perspective the EFTA proposal was mainly a threat to the political unity of the Six and the success of the Common Market. First priority went to the conclusion of the Treaty of Rome and the establishment of the EEC. Thereafter, the Six could negotiate with the Britain as a cohesive and strong unit. For Washington the EFTA proposal was not a viable alternative; it merely reinforced the decision to support the EEC.[32]

As long as the current interpretations of U.S. payments difficulties did not focus on trade, the persistent American deficit could be rationalized, and even welcomed, as signaling the success of the U.S. postwar policy of fostering European growth and international recovery. To most concerned parties the Treasury's multilateralist criticism of regionalism appeared dogmatic and impractical; without regionalism there would have been even less liberalization. Concern for the U.S. balance of payments did not yet shake established axioms and would have done so only if intense domestic pressures raised transatlantic economic relations to the status of a major national policy issue.

Public reaction in the United States to the changing terms of interdependence was long delayed for various reasons. The weak, uncompetitive sectors remained sheltered behind the special provisions of American trade legislation and had no incentive to coalesce into a national force lobbying against U.S. international economic policy. They in fact managed for quite some time to take advantage of U.S. hegemonic privileges by wringing out ad hoc protection. Many advanced, competitive manufacturers, furthermore, chose the path of multinationalization. They preferred to invest abroad and transfer production to Europe rather export to it. Even labor unions were solidly within the large postwar multilateral free trade consensus. They endorsed aid to Europe and did not question America's support of regionalism in Europe. With no awareness of any serious threat to America's productivity, investment and employment did not yet seem worth defending aggressively in the national arena.[33] In the crucial months when the EEC was brought to life, this attitude was essential.

118   Federico Romero

Within a few years it became evident that the Common Market was not harmful to the American economy. Rapid European growth drew in increasing quantities of U.S. exports. Even more striking was the boom in U.S. direct investment in fast-growing sectors of the EEC. This did not, however, help solve America's payments problem. European integration certainly did not help provide the expanding trade surplus that the U.S. would have needed to contain its payments deficit. The American ability to shape the framework of international economic relations was significantly reduced by the payments problem. Even with convertibility, multilateral interdependence did not equate multilateral free trade but implied the emergence of stronger regional blocs. The so-called Kennedy round of GATT negotiations would make clear that the EEC was a main trading power and a new actor that could force the United States to concessions.

A decade of support for integration had mixed results for the United States. Dollar discrimination and integration had enabled Western Europe to overcome the dollar gap, thereby accomplishing America's primary postwar international economic and strategic goal. At the same time, the establishment of a regionally segmented pattern of interdependence strengthened the competitiveness of America's allies, facilitated the outflow of investment (which would gradually dilute the U.S. domestic manufacturing base), and accelerated the erosion of the international role of the dollar. In these contrasting achievements were rooted the rivalries and tensions that characterized Atlantic interdependence in the 1960s.

Notes

This research was supported by the Lverhulme Trust and by the Economic and Social Research Council (Grant E 0023 2270).

1. Michael Hogan, *The Marshall Plan, America, Britain, and the Reconstruction of Western Europe, 1947–1952* (New York, 1987), 294.
2. See Alan S. Milward, *The Reconstruction of Western Europe, 1945–1951* (London, 1984), and Charles S. Maier, ed., *The Marshall Plan and Germany* (New York, 1991).
3. See John Gillingham, *Coal, Steel, and the Rebirth of Europe, 1954–1955* (Cambridge, 1991).
4. The proposal is National Archives (hereafter NA), Files of the State Department Lot (hereafter SD), RG 59, File 55 D 105, b. 2 f. "1954 Green Book": Memo from H. Cleveland to L. Gordon and E. Martin, 17 July 1952. For the ECA/MSA internal debate and the Treasury's opposition, see NA, Records of the U.S. Foreign Assistance Agencies 1946–1961, RG 469, Regional Organizations Staff, Subject Files

U.S. Attitudes 119

1948–1957 (hereafter RG 439 ROS), b. 15 f. "Integration: Atlantic Reserve System," and b. 20 f. "Integration: memoranda."

5. NA, SD, RG 59, Lot File 55 D 105, b. 1 f. "Briefing papers": Memo, "European Integration," 11 July 1951.

6. See NA, SD, RG 59, Lot File 55 D 105, b. 1 "EPC 1952": T. Tannenwald to D. Bruce, 17 October 1952, and Boneright to D. Bruce (draft for circular telegram) 15 November 1952. On U.S. policy on the EDC, see Pierre Melandri, *Les États-Unis face a l'unification de l'Europe, 1954–1955* (Paris, 1980). For attitudes toward the ECSC and the debate on the loan, see *FRUS,* 1952–1954, vol. 6, 311–80, and John Gillingham, *Coal, Steel.*

7. NA, FRC accession no. 68A2809, Records of the Office of International Finance (Treasury Dept.), Europe (EUR) 1941–1959 (hereafter *OIF–EUR,* b. 28 EUR/3/11; Memo "A New Payments System for Europe," 23 March 1953, and Memo "Next Steps in Free-World Monetary and Trade Arrangements," 21 May 1953. NA, OIF-EUR, b. 28 EUR/3/12; A. Marget to Chairman Martin, "FOA Memorandum on Relations between EPU and the Dollar Area," 15 January 1954, and W. R. Burgess, Memorandum to the Director, FOA, 25 January 1954.

8. NA, RG 59, 840.00/3-2053, tel. from Dulles-Stassen-Humphrey to Draper, 20 March 1953; NA, RG 59, 840.00/1-653, Memo from Ben T. Moore to R. Perkins, "The Dollar Problem," 6 January 1953. See also *FRUS,* 1952–1954, vol. 6, 921–62 and 1028–29.

9. NA, Records of the U.S. Foreign Assistance Agencies 1946–1961, RG 469, Office of the Director, Subjects File 1948–1955 (hereafter *RG 469 OD,* b. 21, f. "EPU 1953": Memo by H. Stassen, "The Next Session of OEEC in March 1954," 3 November 1953 (also memos from D. A. Fitzgerald to H. Stassen, 22 October 1953, and from R. Bissell to H. Stassen, 30 April 1953).

10. See Commission on Foreign Economic Policy, *Report to the President and the Congress* (Washington, 1954), and *FRUS,* 1952–1954, vol. 1, 340–48, Memo by John H. Williams (of the Randall Commission), 15 December 1953.

11. *FRUS,* 1952–1954, vol. 1, 74, Memo by the State Department Bureau of Economic Affairs, "Foreign Economic Relations of the US," 17 May 1954; NA, Records of the Office of the Secretary of Commerce, RG 40, Central Files 1950–1955 (hereafter *RG 40*), f. "Finance, public duties and tariffs": Sinclair Weeks to Ward LaFrance, 1 June 1953. See also NA RG 469 OD, b. 33, f. "Trade": William M. Rand to Harold E. Stassen, Memo: "Discussion of the RTAA at the White House," 16 March 1953.

12. CFEP, *Report to the President*; Eisenhower's message in DSB, 19 April 1954, 602–7. On diverse sectoral interests, see NA, RG 40, f. "Finance, Public Duties and Tariffs," Craig R. Sheaffer to Secretary Sinclair Weeks, 5 February 1953, and Craig R. Sheaffer to Samuel W. Anderson, 3 March 1953. Also NA, RG 469 OD, b. 13 f. "Randall Commission: the Randall Commission Minority Final Report," by Daniel Reed and Richard Simpson, 30 January 1954.

13. See the reconstruction of the Congressional debate in B. Kaufman, *Trade and Aid: Eisenhower's Foreign Economic Policy, 1953–1961* (Baltimore, 1982), 18–29.

14. See *FRUS,* 1955–1957, vol. 9, pp. 110–51, and Kaufman, *Trade and Aid,* 30–45.

15. NA, RG 273; National Security Council Directive No. 5433, 16 September 1954; *FRUS* 1955–1957, vol. 4, 301–3, B. Eisenberg to J. Palmer. See also J. Helmreich, "The United States and the Formation of Euratom," *Diplomatic History* 15 (1991): 387–410.

16. NA, RG 469 ROS, b. 93 f. "OEEC 1955": memo by E. E. Lachman, "Discussion with Dr. Emminger, German Executive IMF Director," 1 December 1955. On FOA's views, see NA, RG 469 ROS, b. 106 f. "SPEC": "Summary Record of the Conference of Senior Economic Officers," Paris, 19–21 September 1955.

17. Eisenhower's remarks in *FRUS,* 1955–1957, vol. 4, 348–49; Minutes of NSC meeting, 21 November 1955. For Dulles's remarks, see ibid., 363, The Secretary of State to Foreign Secretary Harold Macmillan, 10 December 1955. NA, RG 469, b. 59, f. "CSC 15—general": undated [but December 1955] State Department position paper "Considerations regarding the proposed European Common Market."

18. *FRUS,* 1955–1957, vol. 4, 450–53, Circular airgram from the Secretary of State to certain diplomatic missions, 13 July 1956.

19. *FRUS,* 1955–1957, vo. 9, 24–25, Report by the Chairman of the CFEP, Clarence B. Randall, September 1956. *FRUS,* 1955–1957, vol. 4, 469, C. B. Randall to the Secretary of State, 4 October 19(64).

20. *FRUS,* 1955–1957, vol. 4, 556, memo, I. Frank to D. Dillon, 24 May 1957. See also American Management Association, *The European Common Market: New Frontier for American Business* (New York, 1958).

21. NA, RG 59, 440.002/7-2357, O. R. Cook to D. Dillon, 23 July 1957; NA, RG 59, 440.003/8-2157, memo "European Agriculture, the C. M., and the F. T. A.," 21 August 1957. See also Pierre Melandri, *Estate–Unis.*

22. NA, Office of the Secretary of the Treasury, RG 56, (hereafter *RG 56*), Sec. G. Humphrey Subject Files, b. 10, f. "President," and b. 12, f. "White House" respectively: Humphrey to Eisenhower, 21 December 1956, and Humphrey to Hauge, 24 September 1956. NA, OIF-EUR, b. 27, EUR/0/42, memo, "Inflation as an Obstacle to European Integration," 6 November 1956. Also NA, RG 56 NAC, minutes of National Advisory Council meeting no. 256, 19 February 1957.

23. *FRUS,* 1955–1957, vol. 4, 482–86, J. S. Davis, "Report to the CFEP," 15 November 1956. NA, SD, RG 59, Lot file 66 D 487, PPS records, b. 75, "Summary of US Reply to the NATO Questionnaire," 30 November 1956, and J. C. Holmes to the Secretary, "Atlantic Working Group Report," 3 August 1956.

24. NA, OIF-EUR, b. 27 EUR/0/42, Memo from Fields to Willis, 4 January 1957, and tel. 3786, Embassy Paris to Department, 2 February 1957. NA, RG 59, 840.05/2-157, "Aide-memoire," 31 January 1957; NA, RG 59, 440.002/2-2857, Memorandum of conversation with Eric Wyndham White.

25. *FRUS,* 1955–1957, vol. 4, 534ff., Circular telegram 735, 6 March 1957; "The Euratom and Common Market Treaties," in *Current Economic Developments* (April 1957): 11–15.

26. NA, OIF-EUR, b. 27 EUR/0/42, memo from Fields to Willis, 21 February 1957. NA, RG 59, 840.00/3-3158, Circular instruction 913. Also Curzon and Curzon, "The Management of Trade Relations in the GATT," in *International Economic Relations of the Western World 1959 -1971,* ed. Shonfelt (London, 1976), vol. 1, 228–41.

27. NA, RG 56, Subject files of Secretary Robert B. Anderson, b. 24, f. "Foreign Aid": Memo "US International Position re Development Financing Programs," 15 November 1958; see also B. Kaufman, *Trade and Aid,* 152–53 and 175–79; data are from OEEC, *Foreign Trade Statistics.*

28. NA, RG 56, 840.00/1-359, Sec. Anderson sub f., b. 25, f. "IMF": F. Southard to Secretary Anderson and Acting Secretary Dillon, 18 May 1959, and Memorandum

for the President, 30 December 1958; NA, RG 59, 440.002/1-659: Circular telegram 942, 3 January 1959, and Circular telegram 826, 6 January 1959.

29. NA, RG 59, 840.00/6-1359 and 840.00/9-1459, D. Dillon to various embassies, 13 June 1959, and Herter to Paris embassy, 14 September 1959.
30. NA, RG 59, 440.002/10-1359, Circular telegram 476; 440.002/11-2459, "Proposal for US Membership in a Reorganized OEEC," 24 November 1959; 440.002/12-859, Dillon's statement in Memorandum of conversation at the Foreign Office, 8 December 1959; and 440.002/12-1059, tel. 3021 from London, 10 December 1959.
31. See *FRUS,* 1955–1957, vol. 4, pp. 564–65, Herter to Paris embassy, 10 October 1957. NA, RG 59, 440.002/2-1358, Circular instruction 7021, 13 February 1958, and 440.002/3-2058, and Circular instruction 8151, 10 March 1958. For a critique of U.S. policy, see Melandri, *Etats-Unis,* 200.
32. The major labor unions turned towards protectionism only in the late 1960s. See AFL-CIO, *Needed: A Constructive Foreign Trade Policy* (New York, 1964).
33. See Lawrence B. Krause, *European Economic Integration and the United States* (Washington, 1968), and Randall Hinshaw, *The European Community and American Trade* (New York, 1964).

Part III
The Economic Development of the EEC
1957–92

[10]

The Economic Impact
of the EEC

MICHAEL DAVENPORT*

Introduction

This chapter deals with the economic impact of the EEC. But it should be recognized that the establishment of the EEC is a step in the search for an ideal in which economics has never been the dominant motive. The ideal of a United States of Europe can perhaps be traced back through Napoleon and Charlemagne to Julius Caesar. The modern concept, however, is to be found *inter alia* among the non-Communist resistance movements in occupied Europe in the early 1940s.[1] The Council of Europe was established by ten Western European countries in the summer of 1949, but this was an inadequate instrument to satisfy the ambitions of federalists such as Jean Monnet and his Action Committee for the United States of Europe. Monnet proposed the establishment of a European Coal and Steel Community (ECSC) in 1950, an idea taken up enthusiastically by Robert Schuman, French Foreign Minister at the time, Konrad Adenauer, the German Chancellor, and Alcide De Gasperi, the Italian Prime Minister. But Monnet stressed from the outset that the ECSC or any other economic institutions on the European scale were primarily instruments to further political integration. Political integration *per se* found expression in the proposals for a European Defence Force in 1950, but these proposals were effectively buried by the French assembly in 1954.

In 1955, the Benelux countries sought to maintain the momentum towards European integration with the Messina Conference. This directly led to the signing of the Treaty of Rome in 1957, which established the institutions of the European Economic Community. The Treaty also laid down the competences of the different institutions, the Council of Ministers, the Commission, the Assembly, the Court.

The major achievements of the Community were, in the early days, the establishment of a customs union or common market and the development of the Common Agricultural Policy (CAP). Customs duties between member states were eliminated over a ten-year transitional period. The first part of this chapter examines the economic gains to the original six members which were expected to derive from the customs union, and, to some extent, the gains of the United Kingdom, Denmark, and Ireland, who joined the customs union definitively, that is after a five-year transitional period, in 1978.

While the establishment of the common market paid some respect to liberal

---

*Wharton Econometric Forecasting Associates, Philadelphia.
[1] W. Lipgens, 'European Federalism in the Political Thought of Resistance Movements during World War II', *Central European History*, March 1968.

trading principles, the CAP was founded on a belief that protectionism was essential in the agricultural sector. The CAP has often been described as the French quid pro quo for the free market in manufactured goods which was foreseen as benefiting most of all the German economy. That is perhaps an over-simplification, and the Germans have never been notable for their reforming zeal as regards the CAP. The economic impact of the CAP is examined in the second part of this chapter.

The third major goal was from the beginning that of Economic and Monetary Union. The EMU, like its avian homonym, never took off. The history of plans – from Barre, through Werner and Marjolin to MacDougall – is witness to the failure to develop the necessary unified institutions such as a European central bank or effective European policy instruments. On the other hand, some progress was achieved in the later 1970s in the areas of the co-ordination of demand management policies, the development of centralized loan instruments, particularly for member states in balance of payments difficulties, and most notably in the establishment of a zone of relatively fixed exchange rates, the European Monetary System (EMS). The economic impact of these developments is discussed in the third section of the chapter. That section also incorporates some brief discussion of the major so-called structural policies of the Community, industrial, regional, commercial (i.e. tariff) policy, and so on. Important though these policies may have been to certain firms or even industries, they have been of little macroeconomic significance, with the possible exceptions of steel and textiles. This is not to disparage the importance of the micro-project approach, which characterizes the regional, social, and agricultural guidance funds, and only slightly less so the industrial and transport policies, or the case-method approach of competition policy. But this chapter sets out to get some feel for the macroeconomic impact of the first twenty-two years of the Community, and this, together with space constraints, justifies the short shrift given to these activities and those in the fields of energy, education, and so forth which are getting under way at the beginning of the 1980s.

I. The Community as a Customs Union

The theoretical literature on the economic gains associated with the formation of a customs union makes an important distinction between 'static' gains (or gains deriving from 'trade creation' net of losses due to 'trade diversion') and 'dynamic' gains linked to the favourable impact of larger markets and greater competition. It also distinguishes between the static effects of customs unions on consumption and on production and is, on the whole, rather agnostic as to whether customs unions will or will not increase overall economic welfare. The empirical literature is more limited in scope and almost entirely confined to estimates of trade creation and trade diversion. There seems to have been no quantitative work following the analytical division between production and consumption effects and very little on dynamic effects – admittedly, these are inherently difficult to quantify. This section presents a brief overview of the main results that have been reached in trying to determine whether the creation of the Common Market has had beneficial effects on member countries.

Trade creation and trade diversion

The literature on static trade creation and trade diversion effects is extensive, and a survey of some of the major studies is attempted in the Appendix to this chapter. A summary impression of the main results can be obtained from Table 8.1, which presents various estimates of trade creation and trade diversion due to the Common Market for the six original EEC member countries combined at the turn of the 1960s. Though the studies cited in the table usually obtained a

TABLE 8.1. *Estimates of trade creation and trade diversion in the EEC*[a]

	Date	Coverage	Trade creation ($ billion)	Trade diversion ($ billion)
Truman	1968	manufactures	9.2	1.0
Balassa	1970	manufactures	11.4	0.1
Balassa	1970	all goods	11.3	0.3
Verdoorn and Schwartz	1969	manufactures	11.1	1.1
Aitken	1967	all goods	9.2	0.6[b]
Kreinin	1969–70	manufactures	7.3	2.4
Resnick and Truman	1968	manufactures and raw materials	1.8	3.0

[a] Original six member countries only
[b] Diversion from EFTA countries only
Sources: see Appendix.

number of alternative results, the ones shown tend to be the authors' preferred estimates or those which appear to be based on the most defensible assumptions. The methodologies used to obtain the figures differ quite substantially, yet a cursory look at the table suggests that the divergence in estimates is relatively limited, with the majority clustered in a range going from $7½ to $11½ billion for trade creation and from $½ to $1 billion for trade diversion. Indeed, standardization to a common year would have brought the various estimates marginally closer. A major exception is provided by the Resnick and Truman study – apparently the only one in the whole literature on the subject which obtains an excess of trade diversion over trade creation – but the approach used by these two authors probably underestimates the positive effects of the elimination of tariffs on trade flows, for reasons which are discussed in the Appendix.

If the amount of trade creation is taken as, say, $10 billion in 1970 and trade diversion as $1 billion, the net gain would represent some 10 per cent of the combined imports of goods of the EEC at the time, or nearly 2 per cent of Community GDP – a non-negligible gain from the creation of a free trade area. What this could have meant in terms of static welfare gains, that is the greater satisfaction of consumer wants through access to lower cost and more diverse sources of supply, has received scant qualitative attention. On the basis of the so-called 'welfare triangles', Balassa tentatively suggests that an $11.4 billion increase in trade in manufactures is associated with a welfare gain of only $0.7 billion or 0.15 per cent of GNP.[2] These conjectures are however fraught with conceptual

[2] B. Balassa, 'Trade Creation and Trade Diversion in the European Common Market: An Appraisal of the Evidence', in B. Balassa (ed.), *European Economic Integration*, Amsterdam 1975.

as well as statistical problems. The net stimulation to trade following the form-ation of the Common Market was expected to have, and almost certainly had, a greater overall impact on real incomes through increased opportunities for economies of scale, increased competition, and the expansion of investment activity, the 'dynamic' effects, than it had through the static gains and losses of trade creation and diversion.

Dynamic effects

By 'dynamic effects' are usually meant all the direct and indirect influences of the formation of a customs union on the rate of economic growth in the member countries. Because of the many and complex channels through which such in-fluences may operate, the concept has remained vague and ill-defined, and to a large extent a cover-all phrase for all the effects excluded from the static gains and losses associated with trade creation and diversion. In general, though, three principal 'dynamic effects' have been identified and emphasized in the literature:

(i) The opportunities presented by the elimination of tariffs for the exploitation of a larger market and thus economies of scale;

(ii) The gains in productivity and cost reductions associated with the in-centives of greater competition – the often-cited 'cold shower of competition' argument;

(iii) The spur to investment presumably to a large extent associated with economies of scale or greater competition, and thus the acceleration of economic growth.

Certainly the dynamic effects played a considerable part in the early economic justifications offered for the formation of the Common Market. They also played a prominent role in the debate in the United Kingdom both before the enlargement and subsequently in the referendum campaign.[3] Nevertheless, the arguments are difficult to subject to rigorous theoretical analysis and certainly do not easily lend themselves to quantitative appraisal.

There are a number of weaknesses, for instance, behind the economies of scale effect. If the ability to exploit economies of scale is limited by the sizes of tariff-free markets, one would expect production costs to be higher and living standards lower in small countries. This was certainly not the general pattern in Europe before the EEC and EFTA were established.[4] Nevertheless, whether the welfare gains are 'dynamic' or 'static', the formation in Europe of two customs unions with free trade in manufactured goods between them and the opportu-nities for scale-economies must have furthered rationalization and concentration in, for example, the motor-car industry. To what extent the market would have been unified and the scale economies exploited without the elimination of customs duties is speculative. Certainly Japan and Spain were able to remain competitive in this market despite the tariff barriers. The economies of scale

[3] For Example, J. Williamson ('Trade and Economic Growth', in J. Pinder (ed.), *The Economics of Europe*, London 1971) estimated that, by 1978, the static welfare gains for the United Kingdom would amount to some £19 million, while benefits from economies of scale would add another £210 million, or 4 per cent of GDP.

[4] M.B. Krauss, 'Introduction', in M.B. Krauss (ed.), *The Economics of Integration*, London 1973, p. 14.

gains can only be assessed industry by industry in the context of the interplay of trade creation and diversion, changing industrial structures due to new technologies, relative factor costs, and so on. But they cannot be dismissed out of hand.

The 'cold shower of competition' argument is equally difficult to pin down. It presupposes that producers do not follow the cost-minimizing rules postulated in neo-classical theory, but that their effort to minimize costs, or reduce 'X-inefficiency', will be greater the more they are exposed to competition, in this case from foreign suppliers following the abolition of tariffs. The argument is plausible – as are the various 'satisficing' theories of firm behaviour to which it is obviously related – but it is clearly not easily subject to verification.

The third major dynamic effect is that of the spur given to investment by the formation of a customs union. This is closely related to the foregoing arguments, since the exploitation of economies of scale of the galvanizing impact of foreign competition are often realized through investment in new plant and equipment. New investment merely designed to take advantage of the increased market size is presumably offset by reduced investment in sectors where foreign producers can now dominate the home market. Here, again, verification is bound to be difficult, but an attempt to estimate the increased growth due to higher investment following the formation of the EEC and EFTA was made by Krause.[5] He took the increase in the average ratio of business investment to GDP between the periods 1955-7 and 1960-4, and using Denison's methodology imputed to the increased investment an average annual increment to the GDP growth rate. The methodology, however, is suspect – the incremental capital–output ratio was for several countries higher in the latter period for cyclical reasons, while the translation from investment ratios, through capital–output ratios, into GDP growth rates raises numerous methodological problems. For what the results are worth, they show that the growth effect of the formation of the EEC ranged from 0.18 per cent per annum in Germany to 0.22 per cent in Italy.

Much more impressionistic evidence as to whether the 'investment effect' was at all important is presented in Table 8.2, which shows GDP and machinery and equipment investment growth rates in the original EEC countries over selected periods. The years 1954-8 predate the establishment of the customs union, while the periods 1958-63 and 1963-8 are years of transition, since the last tariffs on intra-Community trade in industrial products were not eliminated until 1968. Obviously, the comparisons of growth rates over these three quinquennia are fraught with problems. They are not, for example, adjusted to eliminate business cycle effects (which are particularly important in the case of Italy). Also, the growth rates in the earlier period may to some extent have been pushed up by investment in anticipation of the formation of the Community. Still, it is probably reasonable to conclude that the increase in the growth rates of investment and GDP in the period 1958-63 in Italy and Belgium were to some extent due to the stimulatory impact of tariff reductions. No clear impact is, however, apparent in France, Germany, and the Netherlands.

The Italian example is particularly interesting since Italy joined the EEC at a lower stage of development than the other five countries – its per caput income

[5] L.B. Krause, *European Integration and the United States*, Brookings Institution, Washington 1968.

TABLE 8.2. *Growth of GDP and investment in machinery and equipment*
(average annual percentage changes)

	GDP			Investment		
	1953–58	1958–63	1963–68	1953–58	1958–63	1963–68
France	4.7	5.6	5.1	10.0	(8.2)	7.5
Germany	7.2	5.7	4.2	10.0	(6.1)	2.8
Italy	5.0	6.6	5.1	5.3	14.0	–0.8
Belgium	2.7	4.6	4.3	..	8.7	4.8
Netherlands	4.0	4.9	5.6	9.1	9.3	7.5

Source: OECD, *National Accounts of OECD Countries* (various issues).

in 1958 was only 60 per cent of the Community average at the time and agriculture still represented some 18 per cent of output and 35 per cent of total employment, against figures elsewhere in the range 7 to 11 and 8 to 24 per cent respectively. Yet, according to Johnson, a country will only wish to enter a customs union, or an existing union will only want to accept a new member, if the new and the old members are at a similar stage of development. The new member must believe its industrial production will gain from being within the union, and the existing members must believe their own industrial competitiveness able to withstand competition from the new member.[6] This raises the possibility that not all countries need necessarily benefit from dynamic effects and that, for instance, the industrially more competitive partners may, in the longer run, gain at the expense of weaker members, particularly if exchange rate changes are either not possible or ineffective. The apparent success which Italy had in the early days of the EEC in weathering the competition of its more advanced neighbours suggests, however, that the country benefited from dynamic effects on scale economies, competition, and investment. Over the period, the capital goods industries, in particular chemicals and iron and steel, and the durable consumer goods industries developed very rapidly, and in Italian exports there was a marked decline in the share of agricultural products.

Among the newer member countries, Ireland was also relatively less developed when it joined the Community in 1973, but it was in a particularly advantageous position to gain from the CAP. In 1974, the guarantees section of the CAP subsidized Irish agriculture to twice the extent of the pre-accession 1972/3 Irish budget. Apart from large transfers aiding both the balance of payments and public revenues, farm incomes benefited greatly, and this no doubt to some extent encouraged investment in agriculture and related industries.

But the possibility that the dynamic effects of a customs union may not be positive has been raised in connection with United Kingdom membership. In 1970, the government described the advantages of membership as:

The creation of an enlarged and integrated European market would provide in effect a much larger and a much faster growing "home market" for British industry. It would provide the stimuli of much greater opportunities — and

[6] H.G. Johnson, 'An Economic Theory of Protectionism, Tariff Bargaining, and the Formation of Customs Unions', *Journal of Political Economy*, June 1965.

THE ECONOMIC IMPACT OF THE EEC   231

competition – than exist at present or would otherwise exist in future. There would be substantial advantages for British industry from membership of this new enlarged Common Market, stemming primarily from the opportunities for greater economies of scale, increased specialisation, a sharper competitive climate and faster growth. These may be described as the "dynamic" effects of membership on British industry and trade.[7]

And in the concluding section:

This would open up to our industrial producers substantial opportunities for increasing export sales, while at the same time exposing them more fully to the competition of European industries . . . The acceleration in the rate of growth of industrial exports could then outpace any increase in the rate of growth of imports, with corresponding benefits to the balance of payments. Moreover, with such a response, the growth of industrial productivity would be accelerated as a result of increased competition and the advantages derived from specialisation and larger scale production.[8]

These quotations have prompted a study which set out to measure *ex post* some of the benefits and costs of United Kingdom membership.[9] The main argument advanced was that the welfare benefits of trade creation would not be realized if the trade accounts of a member country in a weak competitive position deteriorated and forced the authorities to contractionary policies reducing real national income. Using alternative values for demand and relative cost elasticities of imports and exports to adjust the deviations over the years 1973 to 1977 from the extrapolated 1958–72 trend, the authors of the study estimated the amount by which British manufactured trade had been affected by membership. Depending on the elasticities used, the average export effect varied from + £0.4 billion to − £0.6 billion and the average import effect from + £0.1 billion to − £2.4 billion (all at 1970 prices) – a very wide range. The authors' preferred estimate – of a net import effect of £1.1 billion ($1.9 billion) – led them to conclude, following simulations made on the Cambridge Economic Policy Group econometric model, that, in view of a balance of payments constraint, the authorities had to constrain the level of real national income by an average 6 per cent per annum below what it would otherwise have been, and nearly double this figure in 1977. If the transfer costs of the Community budget, which they estimated to be of the order of £1 billion ($1¾ billion) in 1977, were added, the total cumulated cost to real national income by 1977–8 was of the order of 15 per cent.

Though the exact calculations may be disputed, the conclusion that the United Kingdom suffered a 'dynamic loss' is a serious charge. It implies that Britain was unable to withstand the 'cold shower' of European competition, and it presumably means that the promised dynamic gains of economies of scale, greater efficiency, and induced investment were not realized on a substantial scale. The conclusion hinges, however, on the idea that over the period examined

---

[7] *White Paper on Britain and the European Communities* (Cmnd. 4289), HMSO, London 1970, p. 26.
[8] Ibid., p. 37.
[9] M. Fetherston, B. Moore, and J. Rhodes, 'EEC Membership and UK Trade in Manufactures', *Cambridge Journal of Economics*, December 1979.

it was the balance of payments deficit which called for demand-restraining policies, and inflation played no role.

The argument that the balance of payments impact was negative has, in any case, not gone unchallenged. A subsequent study argued that British exports of manufactures benefited significantly from EEC membership, so that despite the increase in imports, there was a net gain to the balance of payments.[10] By comparing actual United Kingdom exports of manufactures to the EEC to what these exports would have been had the United Kingdom's share in EEC imports moved with the United Kingdom's share in the rest of the world, the author estimated that, by 1977, the total cumulative export 'gain' was of the order of £1 billion. The tariff cuts associated with joining the EEC were estimated to have increased British imports by some £0.7 billion, leaving a small net improvement of about £0.3 billion ($½ billion) in 1977, compared with the Cambridge estimated loss for that year of over £3 billion or $5 billion (both at current prices).[11]

The methodologies used in the two studies are, of course, different, but even if one were to adopt the more optimistic analysis of the balance of payments effects, it would be difficult to argue that the small gains in the trade account could offset the substantial and increasing budgetary costs of membership. Nor do there seem to have been any studies which have claimed that the United Kingdom reaped significant dynamic gains. This is not, of course, to say that Britain's relative industrial decline might not have been faster without the net gains in exports of manufactures which are consistent with the calculations in both papers.

Foreign direct investment

Creation of the Common Market might also have stimulated an inflow of non-EEC direct investment into the area. The so-called 'tariff discrimination hypothesis' states that the erection of a common external tariff higher than the average earlier rates of duty will reduce the levels of trade in goods with the rest of the world but increase the inflow of foreign investment aimed at avoiding the higher tariff barriers. Mundell demonstrated the thesis theoretically by relaxing the usual assumption of trade models that factors of production are internationally immobile.[12] The conditions for the hypothesis to work seem to have been satisfied, as shown by Table 8.3, which provides information on the 1962 EEC external tariffs and on the previous national tariff of the dominant supplier of each product.

The empirical studies testing the hypothesis as it pertains to United States investment in the EEC have produced conflicting evidence. The major difficulty lies in developing a robust econometric model to explain direct foreign investment, since merely looking at gross or trend-adjusted flows before and after

[10] A.D. Morgan, 'The Balance of Payments and British Membership of the European Community', in W. Wallace (ed.), *Britain in Europe*, RIIA, London, 1980.

[11] For the sake of completeness, a third set of unpublished estimates prepared by the British Treasury should also be mentioned. According to *The Economist* (5 January 1980), the study's conclusion is that 'the best central estimate may be to regard the net balance unchanged'.

[12] R.A. Mundell, 'International Trade and Factor Mobility', *American Economic Review*, June 1957.

union leaves too many alternative explanations available. A review of the literature over a decade, from the late 1960s to the late 1970s, shows that some authors found no evidence of increased United States investment due to the formation of the Common Market,[13] whereas others claim to have found such evidence.[14]

TABLE 8.3. *Comparison between 1962 EEC*[a] *external tariff and previous national tariff of dominant supplier country* (number of commodities)

	Higher	Equal	Lower
Chemicals	10	–	2
Textiles	3	1	3
Other manufactures			
Classified by material	14	3	2
Machinery and transport	11	–	–
Other	8	1	3
Total	46	5	10

[a] Original six member countries only
Source: L. B. Krause, 'European Economic Integration and the United States', *American Economic Review*, May 1963.

Such direct foreign investment from outside the EEC as was stimulated by the external tariff has probably been distributed unevenly among the member states. Belgium seems to have been particularly attractive to foreign investors in the 1960s, with the United States the predominant source. Between 1959 and 1969 the United States accounted for 64 per cent of foreign direct investment projects in Belgium, and the latter, in turn, represented half of all net manufacturing investment in the Community.[15] Belgium seems to have gained from its skilled labour force, favourable geographic situation, good infrastructure, attractive tax and credit incentives, and the *laissez-faire* attitude of the public authorities. Less foreign investment went to Belgium in the later 1970s, but multinational enterprises still accounted for 20 to 25 per cent of industrial employment. In the 1970s it was Ireland which attracted a good deal of foreign investment. A wide range of fiscal and credit inducements clearly played a role, but 'jumping' the external tariff may also have been an important factor.

In summary, there would seem to be some evidence of substantial dynamic

---

[13] A. Scaperlanda, 'The E.E.C. and U.S. Foreign Investment: Some Empirical Evidence', *Economic Journal*, March 1967; R. d'Arge, 'Note on Customs Unions and Direct Foreign Investment', *Economic Journal*, June 1969; and A. Scaperlanda and L. J. Mauer, 'The Determinants of U.S. Direct Investment in the E.E.C.', *American Economic Review*, September 1969.

[14] K. F. Wallis, 'The E.E.C. and United States Foreign Investment: Some Empirical Evidence Re-examined', *Economic Journal*, September 1968; A. Schmitz, 'The Impact of Trade Blocs on Foreign Direct Investment', *Economic Journal*, September 1970; and A. Schmitz and J. Bieri, 'EEC Tariffs and U.S. Direct Investment', *European Economic Review*, No. 3, 1972.

[15] See Ch. 20 below.

gains from the customs union, but these have probably been short-lived adjustments to the extension of free trade to a larger market. They may also have been concentrated in countries which for a number of reasons, including an important policy emphasis, were attractive to direct foreign investments, such as Belgium and Ireland, or offered major opportunities for a technological catch-up, such as Italy. The static gains are easier to identify, but in absolute terms seem to have been fairly insignificant relative, say, to year-to-year fluctuations in growth rates.

II. The Community as an Agricultural Regime

Before attempting to assess the economic impact of the Common Agricultural Policy, it is useful to recall its objectives and briefly review the basic mechanisms that it has used to pursue them. Article 39 of the Treaty of Rome set out the five objectives of the CAP as:

(i) To increase agricultural productivity (the productivity of labour being especially mentioned);
(ii) To ensure a fair standard of living for the agricultural community;
(iii) To stabilize markets;
(iv) To assure the availability of supplies;
(v) To ensure that supplies reach consumers at reasonable prices.

Furthermore, these objectives were meant to be pursued within the more general aim of the Community to develop an integrated market. This section will not make a balance sheet for each of these objectives, which in very general terms would show that there have been dramatic rises in agricultural labour productivity, that farmers are on average no longer relatively poor, that products reach the market, and that although prices are high relative to world prices, food takes up a small and shrinking share of income. It will instead briefly outline the mechanisms of the CAP and then consider the impact of agricultural policies within member states, between member states, and on the rest of the world.

The structure of the Common Agricultural Policy

At the start it is worth recalling that setting up the CAP was the result of hard bargaining between the original member states. While they agreed that some agricultural policy was necessary, they each had different domestic policies.[16] It was thus a much more delicate political affair than merely reducing tariffs to create the common market for industrial goods. The basic agreement was to follow three principles: (a) free internal trade; (b) preference for member countries, and (c) common financial responsibilities. Given that preference for the agricultural sector was accepted, the policy was not illiberal — in fact rather the opposite, as it frequently replaced quantitative controls by market-dependent mechanisms. The main policy instrument was to be the setting of common prices, not necessarily because that was considered to be the most efficient way, but because it was the method which minimized the direct budgetary cost of

---

[16] For a detailed account of the development of the CAP between 1958 and 1970, see J. Marsh and C. Ritson, *Agricultural Policy and the Common Market*, RIIA, London 1971.

the system. This was of importance both because unseen transfers were (and still are) politically more acceptable than seen ones (the more so when the transfers are between states rather than between sectors within a given nation), and because of the limited size of the EEC budget. Price has therefore always been the crucial variable, and even at the start of the system the compromise on the common price level was at the top of the existing range of national prices. It will be seen that, as the CAP developed, this tendency persisted.

The CAP has two basic parts: a market policy which guarantees prices, and a structural policy which is meant to make funds available for improving agricultural efficiency. Despite the continuing lip-service being paid to enlarging the share of structural policy from the 'Mansholt Plan' of 1968[17] onwards, this aspect has been mostly covered by the member states acting individually. In 1979, out of a total budgetary expenditure of over $14 billion on agriculture, only $450 million was spent on structural policy. The main mechanism of the market policy is a price-support system, or in the jargon of the Community, the guarantee section of the European Agricultural Guidance and Guarantee Fund (EAGGF). The support arrangements are not the same for all agricultural commodities,[18] but they include at least some of the following basic features:

(i) Prescribed prices for products. The exact system differs from product to product, but, as an illustration, the system for cereals links three prices: a *target* price in the wholesale market set to enable farmers to plan production and give an economic indication to all market users; a *threshold* price for imports, calculated such that threshold price plus transport costs equals the target price; and an *intervention* price at which national intervention agencies are obliged to purchase produce meeting quality requirements;

(ii) Variable import levies to bridge the gap between the lowest price at the EEC community frontier and the threshold price;

(iii) Export subsidies granted to enable Community-produced excess supplies to be sold on lower-priced world markets while maintaining the internal price;

(iv) Subsidies for domestic markets.

The direct financing for these general support arrangements is borne in common by all the member states through the EEC budget. This cost has grown very considerably in the 1970s, from around $1.8 billion in 1968 to $3.5 billion in 1974, and was over $14 billion in 1979, or about 3½ per cent of total expenditure on food. Table 8.4 shows this budgetary expenditure in 1979 for the largest part of the system, the guarantee section of the EAGGF. The table does not include expenditure by the guidance section, which only accounted for some $410 million in 1979, but does include spending on monetary compensation amounts (MCAs), which accounted for about $1 billion.

The reason for these payments stems from the existence of so-called 'green'

[17] 'Memorandum on the Reform of Agriculture in the EEC', submitted to the EEC Council of Ministers, 1968.

[18] For details of workings of each market organization, see EEC, *The Common Agricultural Policy*, Brussels 1978.

TABLE 8.4. *CAP expenditure by sector,* [a] *1979*

	$ million	Per cent of total
Cereal and rice	2,213	15.7
Milk products	6,055	42.9
Sugar	1,376	9.7
Fruit and vegetables	571	4.0
Beef, veal, pigmeat, poultry, and eggs	1,150	8.1
Oils and fats	812	5.7
Wine and tobacco	420	3.0
Other	478	3.4
Monetary compensation amounts	1,055	7.5
Total	14,131	100.0
of which: Refunds	6,438	45.6
Intervention	6,639	47.0

[a] Expenditure by Guarantee section of the European Agricultural Guidance and Guarantee Fund (EAGGF)
Source: EEC, *The Agricultural Situation in the Community*, Brussels 1980.

currencies, which introduce a further complication into the system.[19] Although there is a common market in that the whole of the EEC can be regarded by any producer or trader of agricultural products as an extension of his own domestic market, there is no common market for consumers. Casual empiricism shows that food prices differ between member states, and it is not only food prices that vary but also guaranteed prices of basic agricultural products. Common prices are set at the annual price-fixing in units of account, but these are converted into national currency using representative (or 'green') exchange rates. As these rates have been set by decision of the Council of Ministers the relationship between them has not necessarily been the same as the relationship between market exchange rates. In fact, as 'green' rates have only been changed infrequently and have been set primarily to determine national price levels, there have been persistent differences between the two sets of exchange relationships. Germany's 'green' currency has been undervalued between 1969 and 1979, and the United Kingdom's has been overvalued most of the time between accession and 1979. This resulted in the so-called common price for guaranteed products being higher in Germany than in Britain when valued using market exchange rates. Without a system of border taxes and subsidies, all United Kingdom produce would have been sold to German intervention stores to collect the guaranteed price in DM which could have been exchanged on the market for more pounds than could have been obtained by selling the produce in Britain. Furthermore, no German produce would ever have been exported to the United Kingdom, as the DM equivalent of the price there would have been less than the intervention price in Germany. These taxes and subsidies, the MCA system, do not balance out and have normally resulted in a substantial cost which is borne by the Community budget.

[19] For a full account of this system, see T. Josling and S. Harris, 'Europe's Green Money', *The Three Banks Review*, March 1976.

Transfers within member countries

Within each country the total size of the transfer from the non-agricultural to the agricultural sector depends (a) upon the size of the agricultural sector, and (b) upon how high prices are set above the level which they would otherwise have reached. While the first of these variables can be measured relatively easily, there is no clear measure of the second, which, it should be remembered, over time will have an effect on the first. For want of anything better, the measure often used is the world price level. Some idea of how EEC price levels have stood in relation to world market prices for certain key products is provided in Table 8.5. The figures show a high degree of variability, but on average Community prices have been well above world prices over the period surveyed. In the late 1970s, for a large number of products, they were nearly twice as high, and for some commodities (e.g. butter and skimmed milk powder) a staggering four or five times higher.

TABLE 8.5. *CAP – ratio of selected EEC prices to world market prices*[a]

	1968/69	1970/71	1972/73	1974/75	1976/77	1978/79
Soft wheat	195	189	153	107	204	193
Rice	138	210	115	81	166	157
Barley	197	146	137	107	147	225
Maize	178	141	143	106	163	201
White sugar	355	203	127	41	176	276
Beef	169	140	112	162	192	199
Pigmeat	134	134	147	109	125	155
Butter	504	481	249	316	401	403
Skimmed milk powder	365	218	145	139	571	458
Total[b]	(229)	(195)	(149)	(139)	(208)	(229)

[a] The world market prices used are not necessarily those at which the EEC could import more than marginal quantities of the products in question

[b] Roughly obtained by applying the average of production, total domestic use, and final private consumption weights to the price differentials

Source: EEC, *Yearbook of Agricultural Statistics* (various issues).

However, as mentioned above, world prices are not a wholly satisfactory benchmark, partly because they have been in themselves highly influenced by EEC prices. For a number of products the EEC is a major world supplier and consumer, and hence its own prices have had a marked effect on world prices. This raises, of course, major problems for calculating the transfer to the agricultural sector as a function of the difference between the two price levels. The world price could not be expected to remain unchanged if the EEC were to abandon its price support policy. Though admitting to the existence of this problem, a 1980 study has made some estimates of the total transfers between consumers and producers in each member state on the simplifying assumption that, in the absence of the CAP, world prices would not have been very different from what they were.[20] The estimates are subject to two further methodological difficulties which relate to the values of the demand and supply elasticities

[20] C.N. Morris, 'The Common Agricultural Policy', *Fiscal Studies*, March 1980.

(which in some cases are either not known or seem to be highly variable) and to the problem of aggregation over products which are substitutes. Given some fairly arbitrary assumptions to overcome these difficulties, the author arrived at the estimates shown in Table 8.6.

TABLE 8.6. *CAP – estimates of consumer losses and producer gains,*[a] *1978*
($ million)

	Consumer loss	Producer gain
France	6,081	6,993
Germany	8,828	7,747
Italy	6,553	4,333
United Kingdom	3,431	2,204
BLEU	1,392	1,306
Denmark	559	1,369
Ireland	336	783
Netherlands	1,713	2,694

[a] Due to within-country transfers resulting from the CAP
Source: C.N. Morris, 'The Common Agricultural Policy', *Fiscal Studies*, March 1980.

Even allowing for measurement problems, the magnitudes shown are substantial and raise distributional issues as well as the question of whether the transfers are having the desired effect – in particular whether the expressed aim of the CAP of ensuring a fair standard of living to the agricultural community has been achieved or whether relatively rich farmers became richer and whether this was at the expense of the relatively poor. The second question can be answered fairly easily. As the basic mechanism of the CAP support system is to hold food prices above the level at which they would otherwise have been, the cost is borne by consumers. Since Engel's law, which states that the proportion of income spent on food decreases as income rises, is well substantiated, the cost of the CAP must in the first instance fall more heavily on the relatively poor, though of course governments can correct this effect. An estimate for the United Kingdom shows, for instance, that in 1965 a two-adult family with no children in the lowest income bracket would have borne costs equivalent to 5.75 per cent of after-tax income (the estimate for pensioners was even higher), whereas the cost borne by the same type of household in the highest income group would have been of only 0.14 per cent.[21]

The other question, of whether the already rich farmers were made richer by the CAP, cannot be considered from the distributional point of view alone. Though there is evidence suggesting that richer farming regions obtained a disproportionate amount of the CAP's budget, it may be that the rich are more efficient, and a perfectly legitimate aim of the system is to encourage the efficient.[22] The evidence on the distributional question is scarce, not least because farmers on the whole have traditionally been rather inefficient at filling in

[21] T.E. Josling and D. Hamway, 'Income Transfer Effects of the Common Agricultural Policy', in B. Davey, T.E. Josling, and A. McFarquhar (eds.), *Agriculture and the State*, Trade Policy Research Centre, London 1976.
[22] Whether it has done so is, virtually impossible to document.

income tax forms. Overall, farm income, measured in terms of gross value added at factor cost, increased in real terms at an average annual rate of 3.3 per cent between 1970 and 1978, compared with the rate of 3.0 per cent for the rest of the economy.

Transfers between member countries

The CAP, however, cannot be considered only in the light of its effects within countries. Both because of the very large trade flows between them, and because the whole system is financed through the Community budget, in which the contribution key is very different from the expenditure key, the consumers in one member state may make transfers to the producers in others, and large flows of funds are generated between countries, not least because of the MCAs. Taking into account the different national price levels and the MCA system, the magnitude of the inter-country transfers then depends for each product upon:

   (i) The amount of trade between member states that is subject to preferential pricing arrangements. There is a transfer to exporters to enable them to export products to other EEC markets at the same conditions as they could obtain on their own markets, and the importing countries bear the cost;

  (ii) The flows through the EEC budget because of the common financing of the system.

In what follows the first amounts are called trade effects and the second budgetary effects.

As the pattern of agricultural expenditure is related to the output of the subsidized producers in each country and is therefore independent of the pattern of member state contributions,[23] some countries who make large contributions to the budget receive relatively little, and vice versa. The overall budget problem is relatively well documented, and there have been a large number of estimates of its magnitude, especially in conjunction with various British demands to pay a 'fair share'.[24] Estimating the net budgetary flows attributable to the CAP from these overall figures needs some assumptions, but the scope for error is relatively small, as agricultural expenditure has been the dominant item (nearly three-quarters) of total expenditure. The major problem is how to treat the MCAs, i.e. whether to attribute MCA payments on imports as expenditure in the exporting or importing country. The Commission's studies have presented both sets of figures. However, although the data on net budgetary transfers give the correct direction of the flows, the magnitudes involved are in themselves misleading until the trade effects are also considered. A number of estimates of these effects

[23] At the margin, the contribution key is determined by relative amounts in the total VAT potential; this gave the following percentages in the late 1970s: France 24.7, Germany 32.8, Italy 10.9, United Kingdom 17.4, Belgium 4.5, Denmark 2.6, Ireland 0.8, Luxembourg 0.2, Netherlands 6.1. For a complete description of the budgetary financing system, see D. Strasser, *Les finances de l'Europe*, Paris 1975.

[24] In conjunction with the 1975 'renegotiation', see M. Emerson and T.R. Scott, 'The Financial Mechanism in the Budget of the European Community', *Common Market Law Review*, May 1977, and for the late 1970s position, EEC, 'Net Cash Transfers in 1978 between Member States Resulting from the Community Budget', Press Release, 6 April 1979.

have been made.[25] The studies are not strictly comparable because of different periods covered, different concepts of costs and benefits, and different valuation methods.

The two studies which will be used to illustrate the magnitudes involved are by the Cambridge Economic Policy Group and by Rollo and Warwick.[26] The latter authors abstract from the problem of using a direct measure of world prices and use instead current rates of levies and 'restitutions' (i.e. export subsidies), as a measure of the difference between EEC and world price levels. This method avoids the problem of the price effects of CAP itself on world price and supply levels and hence facilitates the calculation of the trade costs and benefits consistent with the amounts shown in EEC budgets. It implies that the member states would have had the same price level in the absence of the CAP as they had with it, and that support would have been given in the same way. The study therefore measures the balance of payments effect of the common system rather than the effects of the price level itself. It is however quite doubtful whether some of the countries which receive large net benefits from the common system, especially Denmark and Ireland, would have been prepared to maintain prices at EEC levels if all the financing had had to come from within.

The Cambridge study, on the other hand, uses an estimate of world prices to assess the net trade receipts and payments on internal trade on the assumption that trade would have taken place at these world prices in the absence of the CAP. For some products, like beef and grains, for which there is a substantial volume of trade, it considers that importers would have had no difficulty in obtaining any desired supplies at current market prices; for other products, like sugar, butter, and cheese, it assumes that importers would have had to obtain supplies at a price considerably higher than the world one. It also makes an estimate of the prices that exporters might have got on the world market. For all products this was lower than what could have been obtained by selling within the EEC, and substantially lower for some products.

The results of the two studies are presented in Table 8.7. Though the figures are not strictly comparable because of differences in coverage, reference periods, and approach, the divergence in the estimates is not very pronounced. In absolute terms, the United Kingdom, Italy, and Germany (in that order) were the largest contributors to the CAP, while the Netherlands, Denmark, France, and Ireland reaped the greatest benefits. On a per caput basis the net gains of the latter three smaller countries were, of course, much more pronounced.

The CAP and world agricultural trade

The EEC is a very substantial trader in agricultural products. It is the world's

---

[25] Josling and Hamway, 'Income Transfer Effects'; E.A. Altwood, 'The Consequences of Participation in the Common Agricultural Policy to the Irish Economy', in M. Whitby (ed.), *The Net Cost and Benefit of EEC Membership*, Centre of European Agricultural Studies, Wye 1979; and P. Blancus, 'The Common Agricultural Policy and the Balance of Payments of the EEC Member Countries', *Banca Nazionale del Lavoro Quarterly Review*, December 1978.

[26] *Cambridge Economic Policy Review*, April 1979, and J.M.C. Rollo and K.S. Warwick, 'The CAP and Resource Flows among EEC Member States', *Government Economic Service Working Paper*, No. 27, 1979.

TABLE 8.7. *CAP – estimates of net gains/losses to member countries*[a]
($ million)

	Rollo and Warwick 'central' estimate 1978	Cambridge Economic Policy Group estimate 'composite' year[b]
France	1,100	1,350
Germany	−950	−950
Italy	−1,600	−1,150
United Kingdom	−1,500	−1,700
BLEU	−50	100
Denmark	1,200	1,000
Ireland	950	750
Netherlands	1,400	1,100

[a] Due to inter-country transfers resulting from the CAP
[b] Obtained by adding estimated 'trade costs' and 70 per cent of 'net budget costs' as given in the original source
Sources: J.M.C. Rollo and K.S. Warwick, 'The CAP and Resource Flows among EEC Member States', *Government Economic Service Working Paper*, No. 27, 1979; *Cambridge Economic Policy Review*, April 1979.

largest single importer on either a net or gross basis and is also well up in the ranking of exporters. In 1979, for example, its gross food exports amounted to some $22 billion compared with a figure of $35 billion for the United States. The CAP has, however, been generally inward-looking and it can justly be accused of being protectionist and of adding to instability on the world markets.[27]

The protectionist nature of the CAP has come under international examination on several occasions. In 1958, a GATT committee critically looked at the agricultural articles of the Treaty of Rome. In 1960–2, before the mechanisms of the system had been fully worked out, the 'Dillon Round' also attempted to weaken the CAP, and indeed some EEC agricultural duties (e.g. on cotton, soya beans, and protein meals) were eliminated. But the EEC achieved what it really wanted, i.e. an international acceptance of the whole concept of a common agricultural support system. This was a major concession, mainly on the part of the United States, which had most to lose. But America at the time wished to encourage European integration; moreover its bargaining position was weakened by its own illiberal attitudes to agricultural trade, which included claiming unlimited rights to restrict trade by quotas and duties.[28] Though the CAP came under much greater attacks during the 'Kennedy' and 'Tokyo' rounds of trade negotiations, its protectionist nature escaped largely unchanged.

As well as being protectionist and thereby limiting world agricultural trade, the mechanisms of the CAP have added to the instability of world markets[29]

[27] T.K. Warley, 'Western Trade in Agricultural Products', in A. Shonfield (ed.), *International Economic Relations of the Western World, 1959–1971*, RIIA, London 1976.
[28] V. Sorenson, 'Contradictions in US Trade Policy', in E.F. Ferguson (ed.), *United States Trade Policy and Agricultural Exports*, Iowa State University Centre for Agriculture and Rural Development 1973.
[29] T.E. Josling, 'Agricultural Protectionism and Stabilization Policies. An Analysis of Current Neo-Mercantilist Practice', paper presented to the Symposium on International Trade and Agriculture, Tucson, Arizona 1979.

since the EEC has purchased agricultural products abroad only when domestic supplies were short and has sold on world markets at a subsidized price. It is this latter policy instrument which has caused the major problems – on an increasing scale, as the level of EEC surpluses rose in line with prices. It could be argued that the effects of a variable import levy are the same as those of a variable export subsidy in that it does not matter to other suppliers how demand for their products is decreased. In practice, however, the export subsidy has tended to be more disruptive than the import levy for a number of reasons. Traditional suppliers to a given market were badly affected by the sudden influx of some subsidized produce, and even if they were not put out of business they found it hard to re-establish themselves in the market. There has also been (and still is) a much greater political acceptance, both internally and externally, that high cost countries protect their producers by restricting imports, than that they should continue this support to such a degree that their producers eventually become exporters. In this case the formerly largely hidden subsidy becomes clearly evident and is resented, both by the foreign producers and the domestic taxpayers who see that they are subsidizing foreign consumers.

While the overall judgement on the customs union which was ventured above was clearly favourable, a similar overall judgement on the CAP must be negative. The system has almost certainly kept European food prices somewhat above the levels they would otherwise have reached; it has required significant financial transfers between member countries which from an international equity point of view would seem largely inappropriate; it has, similarly, led to substantial internal redistribution from consumers to producers which may well have conflicted with the distributional aims which governments were pursuing; finally, it has generated vast surpluses of some commodities whose subsidized exports have at times de-stabilized world markets and (much more than the CAP's protectionism, shared after all by most major agricultural areas) created a good deal of international ill feeling. It is true that against this must be set the fact that the EEC is, broadly, agriculturally self-sufficient – no mean achievement in a world in which food, just like energy, can be used as a weapon. But self-sufficiency could probably have been reached in a less expensive and economically more rational way.

III. The Community as a Policy-Maker

A glance at the *General Report on the Activities of the European Communities for 1979* indicates that in that year the EEC undertook a project with the aim of drawing up a consolidated balance sheet of ground water resources with a view to better use thereof, completed an initial screening of 30,000 human blood samples for lead content, and decided that certain stockbrokers were 'natural persons' to whom, therefore, freedom of establishment did not appear to be of practical interest. The Community, at the initiative of the Commission, has endeavoured to implement policies in an enormous range of fields. To an important extent these policies are seen to be necessary to protect competition in the customs union. Anything from bathing-water to tractors' rear-view mirrors may be harmonized to prevent member states obtaining an advantage for their own suppliers by making 'safety' or other rules designed to prevent imports of certain goods. But over and above the monitoring of the customs union, and the agricultural, external, and economic policies which are discussed separately, the EEC also has or is attempting to define an employment and social policy, an industrial policy, an energy policy, a regional policy, an environmental and consumer protection policy, a fisheries policy, a transport policy, all of which have been developed with much time-consuming negotiation. Many of these areas can be subsumed under the vague heading of structural policy. This section begins with a discussion of structural policy, inevitably selective, goes on to survey EEC policy *vis-à-vis* the outside world, and ends by looking at the EEC as a centre for macroeconomic policy, and, in particular, as a monetary union. If, at the end, any broad theme has emerged, it is one of small, hesitant steps towards integration and eventually unity of policy.

'Structural policy'

The words 'structural policy' are used as a portmanteau for a large range of different activities at the EEC level. Some of these are of potential macro-economic importance, in particular industrial policy, energy policy, and regional policy. Only the first of these has already had a significant impact particularly as regards the steel sector, and will be discussed in this section. Energy policy up to the late 1970s was still very much at the debating stage, and the Commission's efforts to push the member states along this road had not got very far. Regional policy at the EEC level has suffered from the major drawback that 'additionality' has been difficult to ensure. In other words, the regional grants and loans provided by the EEC institutions on proposal by the member states did not always represent additional finance for regional development, but were offset by less finance from national administrations. But even if it were assumed that all the expenditure under the regional fund had represented additional resources, the total in 1979 still only amounted to 5 per cent of Community budgetary expenditure, or 0.04 per cent of the EEC's GDP. Clearly, no matter how wisely utilized, the macroeconomic impact of such expenditure was bound to be insignificant. Social fund expenditure has been even more limited, though its operation in industrial retraining, assistance to migrant workers and handicapped persons, and so forth has shown an imaginative approach often absent at the national level.

Regional policy stemmed largely from fears that regional disparities in productivity or living standards were a political obstacle to further integration. It has also been argued that economic integration, by encouraging industrial concentration in certain areas, with superior infrastructure, lower transport costs, and the availability of skilled labour would itself aggravate these disparities. There is little information on regional output per head with which to assess the argument that integration has increased the differentials between regions. Regional income data are more readily available, but are, of course, affected by interregional transfer payments. As they stand, they show perhaps some reduction in relative disparities between the early 1960s and the late 1970s.[30] But the regional fund can only have played a very unimportant part in these relative changes. In terms of EEC redistributive mechanisms, agricultural expenditure

[30] See Ch. 14 below.

has been many times more significant, but it has been based on criteria essentially unrelated to income levels.

The importance of a common industrial policy was in the early years stressed by the French and Belgians, whose economic policies were fundamentally *dirigiste* and in favour of medium-term planning, and opposed by the Germans who were economically more liberal (regardless of the party or coalition in power). The typically Community compromise was for a mixture of limited financial powers (outside the separate funds for the coal and steel industries), and substantial EEC legislation originally designed to remove legal obstacles and to encourage concentration within European industries, believed necessary to counter competition from United States firms. The steel industry (which falls under the somewhat different ECSC regime) provides an example of the sort of intervention which can arguably be best practiced at the EEC level. The European steel industry was the first important sector to experience the problems of overcapacity, fierce competition from Japan and newly industrialized countries, regional concentration, and a high-age-group labour force, problems which have since become manifest in other sectors, such as shipbuilding and textiles. By the late 1970s the industry had not yet recovered from the 1974–5 recession. Between December 1974 and June 1978 some 12 per cent of the EEC's steel workers were made redundant, while output fell by 20 per cent.

Since the ECSC was established, with particular interventionist powers, the EEC has spent a lot of money on plant modernization (close to $½ billion in 1978), loans to establish alternative industrial plants, and social aids for supplementary unemployment benefits, retraining, and relocation costs. More radically, the 1977 'Davignon Plan', which was accepted by the European steel industry, restricted imports from the most serious competitors outside the EEC, imposed ceilings on productive capacity and compulsory minimum prices for particularly sensitive products, tried to outlaw national aids to the steel industry which gave rise to unfair competition, and provided aid for modernization and rationalization of companies and for industrial reconversion and diversification in the major steel-making areas. The 'Davignon Plan' represented a radical intervention by the EEC into the affairs of one industry. It was agreed upon by both the member countries and the major private steel firms in the Community as an acceptable way of cushioning the social problems of a declining industry, while gradually modernizing it and rendering it competitive with the low-cost producers outside the EEC.

External policies

It is interesting to speculate on the impact which the development of the EEC has had on the balance between free trade and protectionism in the outside world. It is sometimes argued that because the Commission has been responsible for the Community's commercial policy *vis-à-vis* the rest of the world, it has served to limit concessions to the demands of special interest groups in individual countries for further protectionist devices. At the very least, the national governments may have been able to use the Commission as a scapegoat in this respect. On the other hand, in sensitive areas, it is likely that the EEC has, at times, come closest to the most restrictive position. But probably the most important contribution the EEC has made to greater freedom of trade is that its

existence as a customs union has made possible such wide-reaching and substantial negotiations as the 'Kennedy' and 'Tokyo' rounds. Without the EEC
there would have been no interlocutor of sufficient weight for the United
States to justify such time-consuming negotiations and the attendant domestic
problems of a distrustful and often openly protectionist Congress. To the
extent that the United States or any other country could have taken liberal
initiatives, these would have tended to be through sets of bilateral agreements
specific to particular products and hence very much more limited in scope.

While the 'Kennedy Round' was initiated by the United States, the 'Tokyo
Round' followed a Community initiative. Though the outcome of the negotiations was not dramatic (apart from the adoption of some 'codes of conduct'
in international trade, EEC tariffs on industrial goods were cut from 9.8 to 7.5
per cent), it was considered important to maintain the momentum of trade
liberalization, particularly in a period of world recession. The one area which
gained least from the 'Tokyo Round' was the developing world, which failed to
obtain the concessions it was seeking on such key products as steel, fertilizers,
or leather goods. Indeed, in the field of textiles, the 'Multi Fibre Agreement'
reimposed bilateral quotas for individual developing countries. But arguably
the EEC's greatest contribution to the Third World resides in the two Lomé
Conventions of 1975 and 1979 (themselves inheritors of the older Yaoundé
Convention of 1963).

The second Lomé Convention was signed by fifty-eight developing countries.
These countries, known collectively as the ACP (African, Caribbean, and
Pacific) states, include all of Africa south of the Sahara, except for Zimbabwe,
South Africa, Angola, and Mozambique, and most former English and French
colonies in the Caribbean and in the Pacific. The overall conception of the conventions and the many years of negotiation which preceded them were remarkably free of ideological arguments. The ACP countries, despite their political
differences, displayed a high degree of cohesion, and this certainly contributed
to improving the terms of the conventions from their point of view. There have
been three main aspects to the agreements: (a) non-reciprocal trade co-operation;
(b) a guaranteed export earnings scheme, and (c) provisions for aid.

The principal idea behind trade co-operation has been that of a common
market extending to all the EEC and ACP countries. An important aspect of
these provisions has been that of non-reciprocity. This has been often demanded
by developing countries in the past, but rarely achieved and certainly never on
the same scale. Whereas almost the total of ACP exports to the EEC have been
freed of import quotas or duties, the ACP states have not been required to offer
more than the existing preferences, or if none, then 'most favoured nation'
status, and to refrain from discrimination between EEC countries in return.
Over 90 per cent of ACP exports to the EEC were admitted duty-free in 1977.
The only major goods still subject to import duties were those which competed
with EEC agricultural products (in particular beef and sugar). Beef was given
further preferential treatment in the 1979 convention. For sugar, particularly
crucial to the West Indian economies, it was agreed that the ACP countries
would receive a guaranteed price for annual quotas (of some 1.4 million tonnes
a year) defined country by country. In practice, since 1976, the first operating
year, the negotiated price has followed the price guaranteed to sugar-beet farmers

in the EEC and considerably exceeded the world price. In 1978–9, for instance, the average world price was $16.15 per tonne, while the guaranteed price was $36.78 per tonne.

The 'Stabex' mechanism of guaranteed export earnings has been claimed as a model for future aid schemes for developing countries. It was the first scheme to assure a minimum revenue for raw material producers, whose export earnings were especially subject to vagaries in production or fluctuations in world market prices. Under 'Stabex', shortfalls in export earnings have, under certain conditions biased in favour of the poorest countries, been compensated for by interest-free loans by the European Development Fund (EDF). The commodities covered have included most ACP agricultural exports. By mid-1979, the fifth year of operation, $365 million had been transferred under the scheme, including $216 million in the form of grants. The $365 million only represented 2½ per cent of the value of EEC imports from the ACP countries in 1978, but for some of the poorer ACP countries the importance of 'Stabex' was considerable.

Financial aid (channelled through the EDF) during the five years of the first convention came to $4.3 billion, of which the bulk (some $2.7 billion) was earmarked for outright grants. The 1979 convention planned for an average annual aid flow of $1¼ billion over five years. These figures compare with a sum of more than $19 billion of net official development assistance from the Western developed countries (members of the Development Assistance Committee of the OECD) to the developing countries in 1978, and a total of more than $6 billion of official bilateral aid from individual EEC countries in the same year. Though the EDF flows may thus seem relatively unimportant, they are concentrated on fifty-eight, generally small, countries. Total net bilateral development aid to all the ACP countries was about $5 billion in 1978. Thus if there is no reduction in bilateral aid – and the EEC member countries have committed themselves to not partly offsetting their payments through the Lomé Convention by cutting their direct aid – the convention could increase the total flow of aid to the ACP area by as much as a quarter.

Two features of the conventions appear to have been of great value to the ACP countries. First, aid has been provided on a contractual basis with the contract including the maintenance and extension of free access to markets on a multilateral basis. This has been an important advance on the bilateral trading privileges which have tended to characterize bilateral aid. Second, the conventions have provided for a measure of security. The ACP countries have been enabled to plan ahead in agriculture and industrial development with some confidence that development aid would be available over a five-year period and with certain export earnings guarantees. This is not to deny that the conventions have been of economic and of course political value to the EEC as well. Some 40 per cent of EEC exports to the outside world were in the late 1970s going to the developing countries. Increased aid has thus had a quick return in the form of additional EEC exports given that the imports of the ACP countries have been heavily weighted towards the Community.

Macroeconomic policies

Until the mid-1970s, macroeconomic policy co-ordination did not really figure in the armoury of EEC policies. The Commission was not hesitant to proffer advice on short-term economic policy to the member states through its quarterly reports on the economic situation. This advice, however, was not particularly EEC-oriented. It tended to pick some point on the 'expand to reduce unemployment – contract to reduce inflation' locus depending on the relative severity of the problems in the countries concerned – without looking at the issues from a Community viewpoint, perhaps because there was no very apparent EEC business cycle till the early 1970s. The advice quite often took the form of a tough monetary stance to cut inflation with an expansionary fiscal policy to reduce unemployment. To the extent that there was policy co-ordination it was at the sharing-of-information level.

The greater synchronization of cyclical fluctuations since the first oil crisis prompted a search for greater co-ordination not only at the OECD, but also at the EEC level. This found its first expression in the 'concerted action' programme prepared by the Commission and national authorities and adopted at the Bremen 1978 European Council meeting. This programme, in some cases, defined precisely the contribution of each country to fiscal expansion. Germany, the Netherlands, and Luxembourg were, for instance, to take stimulatory measures so as to boost demand initially by about 1 per cent of GDP. The contribution of the other member states was expressed in various terms, for some more precisely than others, but in all cases referred to instruments of fiscal policy including the central government budget as a whole. What was striking about the programme was that no references were made to monetary policy. This was partly because the Commission had not up to that point ever made a quantitative recommendation about a member country's monetary policy, and on the eve of the establishment of the EMS this did not seem an appropriate innovation, and partly because detailed discussions about monetary policies tended to be conducted behind the very closed doors of the committee of governors of central banks at the BIS. Though a monetary dimension was subsequently introduced in EEC discussions, monetary policy co-ordination tended to be confined to technical matters of central bank co-operation, largely in exchange rate intervention.

Yet the ideal of a monetary union is as old as that of the EEC itself. Through most of the 1960s the Community had been relatively complacent about monetary integration, which seemed to be taking place of its own accord. During that period the idea gained ground that, with the increasing integration in trade and especially with the fixing of common agricultural support prices in units of account, exchange rate adjustments had become nearly impossible and the EEC had *de facto* become a monetary union. As the 1960s drew to a close (and international currency crises became more frequent) the flow of reports and proposals for closer economic and monetary co-operation started. Thus, the Hague summit of December 1969 set up a committee to prepare a plan to establish economic and monetary union by stages. That plan (the 'Werner Plan')[31] stated that: 'The group considers that economic and monetary union is an objective realizeable in the course of the current decade,' and monetary union was taken to imply the irreversible fixing of parity rates. Overall, the plan was a compromise

[31] EEC, 'Report of the Council and the Commission on the Realization of Stages of Economic and Monetary Union in the Community', *Bulletin of the EEC Commission*, Supplement No. 11, 1970.

between a 'monetary' school of thought which considered linking exchange rates and monetary policies as a necessary and sufficient condition for integration, and an 'economic' school of thought which considered (as Chancellor Erhard is quoted as having said) that 'the use of monetary schemes to promote economic integration is like putting the bridle on the tail of the horse'. In any case, the up-heavals of 1971 and the breakdown of the Bretton Woods system made it im-possible to implement the first steps of the plan, let alone its final goals. The idea that the Community was a viable currency area persisted, however, and a number of proposals were put forward in following years.[32]

The year 1972 also saw the establishment of an exchange rate mechanism – the 'snake'. This did not for any length of time encompass all member states and could not be compared in comprehensiveness to the Bretton Woods system, but, despite many gloomy predictions, it not only survived the turbulent years to 1979 but it can also be seen as one of the major ingredients in the setting-up of the EMS.

The EMS should be seen as as much of a political as an economic achievement. Extensive political and technical discussions accompanied its birth and led to the adoption of measures designed to strengthen the economies of the less pros-perous member states. The latter was the quid pro quo for Italy and Ireland to join the system. These countries' argument was mainly based on the 'economist' side of the 'economist' versus 'monetarist' controversy. It was maintained that monetary integration could not take place without economic integration, and that as well as strengthening co-operation and co-ordination, it would be neces-sary to give special aid to the less prosperous countries which would have extra adjustment costs in keeping up with the discipline of the richer and stronger currency member states. The argument was further supported by the proposition from the 'MacDougall Report' that in an integrated Europe there would have to be much larger interregional transfers.[33] The measures consisted of loans of up to $1.4 billion available each year over a five-year period and subsidized by up to $300 million per year.

The economic impact of these transfers is unlikely to be large, and that of the EMS itself is extremely difficult to assess. At the time of writing the system was in a transitional phase, and its eventual impact will depend upon as yet un-answered questions about the existing mechanisms, the reserve asset and settle-ment instrument of the system, the ECU, and the development and characteris-tics of the new institution (the European Monetary Fund, or EMF). The EMS will have a significant economic impact if the Fund is set up in such a way that it can grow over time into a European Central Bank with discretionary powers over liquidity creation through control over the supply of its liability, the ECU.

[32] For a comprehensive review of monetary integration in the EEC before 1972, see A.I. Bloomfield, 'The Historical Setting', in L.B. Krause and W.S. Salant (eds.), *European Monetary Unification and Its Meaning for the United States*, Brookings Institution, Washing-ton 1973. For post-1972 developments, a chronology of the 'snake' is given as an annex to N. Thygesen, 'The Emerging European Monetary System: Precursors, First Steps and Policy Options', in R. Triffin (ed.), 'The Emerging European Monetary System', *Bulletin de la Banque Nationale de Belgique*, April 1979.
[33] EEC, *Report of the Study Group on the Role of Public Finance in European Inte-gration* (MacDougall Report), Brussels 1977.

The exchange rate mechanism adopted in 1979 was neither a fully fixed nor a fully floating system.[34] Each participant declared a central rate and was obliged to intervene to hold its currency within 2¼ per cent margins (6 per cent for Italy) around this rate; but central rates could be, and have already been, changed. The important provision was that central rates had to be adjusted by 'mutual agreement and by a common procedure'.[35] Depending upon how these words will be interpreted, this could represent a significant shift away from the position that determining one's own exchange rate is an essential pillar of a national economic sovereignty. A further important question will be how the system as a whole will behave *vis-à-vis* the rest of the world. Originally, the 'snake' was in a 'tunnel', i.e., there was a declared rate against the dollar, but this arrangement only lasted until March 1973. Subsequently, the choice lay predominantly with the dominant economy, Germany. This solution would not seem to be open to the EMS, which contains more than one large economy. Again, the Brussels resolution admits the problem but does not provide a specific answer. The second set of questions concerns the role of the ECU as the EMS's reserve asset. Under the transitional arrangements, each central bank transferred 20 per cent of its gold and dollar reserves to a fund in return for a quantity of ECU. This mechanism, which through gold price changes resulted in just over one year in a spectacular growth in the quantity of ECU from 26 to 46 billion (or from some $36 to $64 billion), is hardly appropriate for a system whose declared intention is to create a zone of monetary stability. The quantity of ECU reserves available to the system will also depend on the credit facilities, which were expanded to a potential total of nearly $30 billion. The stated intention is that in the next phase these credit arrangements will be consolidated into the system, although it is neither clear what is meant by that term nor what role credit can or should play within a regional grouping which seems to have more than adequate liquidity and which is composed of participants able to get all the financing they may need from the international markets.

The answers to these questions about the nature of the exchange rate mechanism, the reserve asset, and the credit facilities will in part determine whether the system survives in its original form or not. Failure in any of the fields is more likely to lead to adapting the arrangements than to abandoning the whole attempt,[36] and so a more important question than survival is success. The latter must be judged in terms set by the system itself — monetary stability, implying both internal price stability and external exchange rate stability. This brings one back to the old 'monetarist' versus 'economist' debate. Can the EMS alone lead to stabilization and create economic and monetary union? The answer is almost

[34] For a comprehensive account of the mechanisms of the EMS, see Deutsche Bundesbank, 'The European Monetary System: Structure and Operation', *Monthly Report*, March 1979; and EEC, *European Economy*, July 1979.

[35] 'Resolution of the European Council of 5 December 1978 on the Establishment of the European Monetary System and Related Matters', in EEC Monetary Committee. *The Compendium of Monetary Texts*, Brussels 1979, Article 3.2.

[36] See C. McMahon, 'The Long-run Implications of the European Monetary System', in P.H. Trezise (ed.), *The European Monetary System: Its Promise and Prospects*, Brookings Institution, Washington 1979, in which he concludes that 'if the EMS did not exist, it — or something similar — would have to be invented' (p. 92).

certainly no. A well designed monetary system would greatly contribute to achieving these goals, just as the lack of order during the 1970s contributed to the growing divergences in the EEC in terms of growth, unemployment, and inflation rates. It is, however, also essential that other measures be taken and that political will be engaged. Supporters of the EMS would say that the system both provides the first elements of the necessary monetary dimension and clearly demonstrates the existence of political will.

Conclusions

The previous discussion has shown that in most areas it is difficult to say whether the economic effect of the EEC has been positive or negative, let alone to assess quantitatively its impacts. A major difficulty in trying to answer such a question is the benchmark against which to make any measurements. The economies of the member states have changed fundamentally since the formation of the EEC, but so have those of non-member states. And though the EEC is essentially an economic community, its political dimension must also be taken into account in any assessment. The initial intention was that gradual step-by-step integration in specified areas would have spill-over effects and lead to political integration. In the late 1970s, with direct elections to the European Parliament, increased co-operation in foreign policy, and the setting-up of the EMS, there have been renewed signs that this approach could work. Previously it had seemed as if the strategy had been dealt a death blow in 1965 by de Gaulle's blocking of the evolution of the Community to the phase prescribed in the treaty, when certain decisions might be taken by less than unanimous vote, and by his dashing of the hope that the Commission might be able to strengthen its independence *vis-à-vis* the national governments. Certainly there have been achievements, but they remain far short of the dreams of a unified Europe.

Returning to the specifically economic areas, the corner-stone of the EEC is the customs union. The EEC speeded up the process of reducing tariffs between its member states, a process which would probably have in time happened to much the same extent in any case. The direct impact of the customs union on trade flows does not appear to have been very large — probably less than 1 per cent of GDP. The beneficial effects of the customs union also arise, however, in unquantifiable ways such as increased consumer choice and indirect stimuli to growth, at least in some countries. *Vis-à-vis* the rest of the world the EEC may appear more protectionist. Yet it is not clear whether the overall degree of protectionism has been greater or less as a result of negotiating as a Community rather than as individual nations. On the positive side is the fact that a smaller number of parties may facilitate agreements, and that one negotiator representing a block with slightly different interests may be able to offer more permutations for compromises than if each different interest was seeking only its own goal. On the negative side is the powerful argument that the compromises adopted as the EEC solution before negotiations began with other parties may have been closer to the most restrictive position than to the mid-position. This is closely tied to the problem of veto and unanimous voting used in Community matters, which has often resulted in common policies representing the lowest common denominator.

Agriculture has always been treated as a special case, and the EEC's record in that sector is certainly protectionist. It is also, as was suggested in Section II, disruptive to world trade. The EEC's high price policy has made it more than self-sufficient in a number of agricultural products, leading to surpluses which have often been sold off on the world market with subsidies. This has been even more disruptive than the policy of taxing imports with a system of variable levies on the difference between the world and the EEC price. Internally, the CAP's impact is difficult to assess with any accuracy, again mainly because the individual national policies in the absence of the CAP cannot be known. Most studies looking at the effects of the CAP have assumed that world prices would prevail in the EEC if the CAP did not exist, but, especially for products for which the EEC represents a substantial share of the world market, the validity of this assumption is dubious. It is, however, almost certain that the common financing of the CAP has resulted in a higher degree of transfers to the agricultural sector of some countries, especially Denmark and Ireland, than would have been available from the national exchequers.

Agriculture was responsible for the two most pressing problems the EEC faced in the late 1970s. The high price policy leading to structural surpluses and disruption of the world market had pushed the EEC budget to its financing limit, and had caused unjustifiable financial flows between member states. Whereas it may have made sense in terms of the wider goals to have made substantial transfers to Ireland, the same cannot be said for Denmark, which had the highest per capita income in the EEC. This problem came to a head again in 1979, with United Kingdom demands for substantial reductions in its own contributions, and crisis was only averted by a temporary solution which involved adapting the so-called 'financial mechanism' which had been created in 1975 in answer to exactly the same problem. The major reason for the difficulties was that nearly three-quarters of total expenditure went to the agricultural sector. This situation had been allowed to persist because the EEC's 'own resources' (customs duties, agricultural levies, and up to 1 per cent of national VAT revenues) had grown sufficiently rapidly to allow the financing of these expenditure flows. But the prospect of the CAP taking an ever-increasing share of the budget, and of a budgetary ceiling being reached, may provide the necessary spur to reform that was lacking previously.

So far the so-called 'neo-functional' approach to integration has failed to live up to expectations. The underlying idea, associated particularly with the thinking of Monnet, was that of taking small steps in specified areas, selected by a politically motivated bureaucracy as symbolic, but sufficiently technical and uncontroversial that the decisions would be left to experts. Integration was to be achieved almost behind the backs of the governments who had been unwilling to take the underlying political decision. The process was meant to gather momentum and spread from the initially chosen areas. Events have worked out differently. Instead of spill-overs from the original areas and growing momentum, some institutions like Euratom never got off the ground, and other areas like agriculture gave rise to reticence about, rather than enthusiasm for, further efforts. The bureaucracy might have lacked ingenuity and motivation, but, above all, the governments were not taken in by the strategy.

In many ways, it seems as if the EEC in the late 1970s was running out of steam. International organizations, it is sometimes said, are always designed to prevent the last war, and to some extent the cold war made the EEC redundant from the start. Europe has been held together not by the Treaty of Rome but by geopolitical circumstances. If it had not found itself between two opposed superpowers, developments might have been very different. As it was, the underlying political aims as opposed to the explicit economic goals could largely be attained without surrendering sovereignty through integration. In foreign policy and defence, as well as in the economic sphere, co-ordination was perhaps achieved more through the tutelage of the United States than through the efforts of the EEC member states.

Appendix: A Survey of the Literature on Trade Creation and Trade Diversion

The theoretical literature on customs unions and economic integration more generally has been closely associated with the formation of the Common Market. The first important works were by Viner and Meade.[37] Viner first developed the concepts of trade creation and trade diversion, and made the fundamental point that there can be no general presumption as to whether the formation of a union increases overall economic welfare. Trade creation takes place when there is a shift from higher-cost domestic sources to sources in the partner country of the union which have become relatively cheaper since tariffs have been abolished. Trade diversion takes place to the extent that trade is switched from lower-cost foreign sources to domestic or partner country producers due to the erection of the common external tariff.

Later, Meade and Lipsey introduced the distinction between the effects of the formation of a customs union on consumption as distinct from production. Lipsey argued that when 'consumption effects are allowed for, the simple conclusions that trade creation is good and trade diversion bad are no longer valid'.[38] While trade diversion implies a switch to higher-cost but tariff-free sources of supply, it eliminates the divergence between domestic and international (customs union) prices caused by tariffs. Therefore consumers who were previously purchasing a more-than-optimal quantity of domestic goods can usefully reallocate their expenditures between commodities. Whether the loss in welfare due to the shift to a higher-cost source of supply is greater or less than the gain due to the removal of the tariff constraint on consumer equilibrium is, in principle, an empirical question, but not one to which a straightforward empirical test can be applied.

Quantitative research on the impact of the European Common Market *qua* customs union has been almost entirely confined to the estimation of the Vinerian trade creation and trade diversion effects. The following text surveys a selection of this research, concentrating on relatively recent works that appear methodologically sound.[39] The studies chosen can be grouped under four broad headings:

    (i) Single-country demand for imports approaches;
    (ii) Gravitational models;

[37] J. Viner, *The Customs Union Issue*, New York 1950; J.E. Meade, *Problems of Economic Union*, London 1953, and *The Theory of Customs Unions*, Amsterdam 1955.
[38] R.G. Lipsey, 'The Theory of Customs Union: Trade Diversion and Welfare', *Economica*, February 1957.
[39] A complete survey of the literature can be found in D.G. Mayes, 'The Effects of Economic Integration on Trade', *Journal of Common Market Studies*, September 1978.

   (iii) Control-country approaches;
   (iv) Multi-country models.

   Examples of studies that have adopted the *single-country demand for imports approach* are those by Truman and Balassa.[40] The approach is based on the assumption that had it not been for the formation of a customs union, the imports of the member countries would have increased over time according to some rule, for example that of constant shares of domestic and foreign supplies in total absorption (Truman), or constant income elasticities of import demand (Balassa), and that the difference between the actual level of imports and that implied by the rule can be attributed to the formation of the customs union.

   The approach has a number of drawbacks. First, the chosen rule is all-important. The validity of the results depends on how accurate is the representation of the hypothetical path of imports over time in the absence of the customs union (the counterfactual). Second, the choice of the base period over which the elasticities or shares are estimated is critical, and in particular there is the danger of cyclical distortions. Third, a number of variables are implicitly or explicitly assumed to be unchanged by the establishment of the customs union. In the foregoing case of an elasticity with respect to GDP rule it is assumed that GDP is independent. If, in fact, the formation of the customs union accelerates economic growth, the application of the rule will underestimate the extent of trade creation.[41] Finally, in the specific case of the EEC, both before and after the abolition of all tariffs among the original six countries, trade liberalization on a broader scale was taking place within the framework of the 'Kennedy Round' and later on between the EEC and EFTA.

   Truman's methodology is richer than that of most earlier studies in that it allows for double trade creation where both non-member countries and member countries gain shares at the expense of domestic production in the importing member country. This is most likely to happen when the new common external tariff is lower than the tariff previously protecting the importing country. Also, Truman distinguishes internal and external trade erosion, which occurs when the share of domestic suppliers rises after the customs union is formed and either the share of member or non-member countries or both fall. External trade erosion may occur when the common external tariff is higher than the previous national tariff. It is difficult, however, to understand how the formation of a customs union alone could lead to internal trade erosion.

   To counter the argument that the assumption of share constancy will lead to overestimates of trade creation and underestimates of erosion because during the 1960s trade shares were growing under the impact of multinational tariff reductions, Truman, in a second set of comparisons, took the shares for 1968 as predicted by regressions of shares against a cyclical variable and a time trend estimated over the period 1953–60. The results indicated less trade creation ($2.5 billion rather than $9.2 billion), less internal trade creation and external diversion ($0.5 billion rather than $1.0 billion), and more trade erosion. It seems likely that the inclusion of a linear time trend, which assumes that the multinational tariff reductions induced the same average annual rate of growth in trade between 1961 and 1968 as they did between 1953 and 1960, will seriously

---

   [40] E.M. Truman, 'The Effects of European Economic Integration', and Balassa, 'Trade Creation and Diversion', both in Balassa (ed.), *European Economic Integration*.
   [41] It is true that this is going somewhat beyond Viner's definition of trade creation. But the various methodologies on the whole cannot distinguish between trade creation in the pure Vinerian sense and that consequent upon an increased growth rate in the union.

overestimate the level of trade in the counterfactual, and thus underestimate the effects of the customs union. But the wide divergence in estimates indicates the problems in quantifying the pattern of trade as it would have been if duties had not been abolished.

A similar 'residual-imputation' methodology was adopted by Balassa, only rather than use a shares-in-consumption rule, he preferred an elasticity rule. Like Truman, Balassa ignores the effects of changes in relative prices (or assumes that they are all brought about by the integration process), and such dynamic changes as might affect income or consumption. Following a criticism of an earlier study,[42] he is careful in selecting the periods over which he takes percentage changes in imports and GNP to calculate the elasticities. The periods chosen are 1953-9 and 1959-70, with the following elasticities for all EEC imports taken together.

	1953-59	1959-70
total	1.8	2.0
intra	2.4	2.7
extra	1.6	1.6

Thus, at the global level there is indication of internal trade creation but not of trade diversion. Values of trade creation and diversion are calculated for each sector by taking differences between the actual and the hypothetical (constant elasticity) trade flows.

The difficulty of ignoring other factors affecting the elasticities is well exemplified by considering Balassa's analysis of the food category. The GNP import elasticities of food imports do not show evidence of trade creation. However, if GNP is replaced by total food consumption or industrial production there is evidence of trade creation, because 'the income elasticity of demand for food fell during the period under consideration and the rate of growth of industrial production declined while that of GNP increased slightly'.[43] All the results are interpreted in terms of particular *ad hoc* factors, which throws doubt on the usefulness of the basic methodology.

A second group of studies of trade creation and diversion in the European Common Market by Verdoorn and Schwartz, and by Aitken, is based on the so-called *gravitational models*, first developed in the regional science field and only later applied to international trade problems.[44] The basic idea is that the size of a trade flow between any pair of regions or countries is a positive function of demand in the importing country and supply in the exporting country, and a negative function of tariff and non-tariff barriers including transport costs. The most straightforward empirical application of the gravitational model for the assessment of the trade impact of the formation of a customs union is through cross-section estimation of bilateral trade functions with dummy variables or average tariff time series to measure the customs union effect.

Verdoorn and Schwartz estimate a number of such functions, among which the most satisfactory yields the estimates for trade creation and diversion shown in Table 8.1. But perhaps the most interesting conclusion of their work is that

[42] W. Sellekaerts, 'How Meaningful are Empirical Studies on Trade Creation and Trade Diversion', *Weltwirtschaftliches Archiv*, No. 4, 1973.

[43] Balassa, 'Trade Creation and Diversion', p. 83.

[44] P.J. Verdoorn and A.N.R. Schwarz, 'Two Alternative Estimates of the Effects of EEC and EFTA on the Pattern of Trade', *European Economic Review*, No. 3, 1972; N.D. Aitken, 'The Effect of the EEC and EFTA on European Trade: A Temporal Cross-Section Analysis', *American Economic Review*, December 1973.

the relative price variables, which compare alternative sources of supply after taxes and tariffs, only capture a minor part of the extra trade flows which follow the establishment of a customs union – the greater part seems due to the dummy or average tariff variables. This is explained by the fact that prior to the union some of the duties, even though possibly fairly low in percentage terms where there was considerable competition, effectively prohibited trade for the commodity in question. When those tariffs were eliminated, trade in that commodity could expand rapidly, but this rate of expansion would not be caught in the coefficients on the price relatives. In addition to the impact of the abolition of effectively prohibitive tariff barriers are what Verdoorn and Schwarz call the 'promotional effects' (e.g. increased flow of information to markets, development of repair and distribution networks, reduced risk of the re-establishment of tariff or non-tariff barriers), all of which are best captured by dummy variables.

In another application of the gravitational model, Aitken uses cross-section regression analysis to estimate the customs union impact, but he estimates successive equations for each year, with dummy variables to represent tariff cuts, deriving a measure of the customs union effects over time. The original seven EFTA members and the original five EEC trading countries (Belgium and Luxembourg being aggregated in the trade statistics) are included in the study. Two alternative estimates for trade creation in the EEC for 1967, of $11.1 billion and $9.2 billion, are obtained. In the case of EFTA they are of $2.4 billion and $1.3 billion. The lower projection estimates are marginally to be preferred in that their equations take more explicit account of trade diversion between the two communities. Trade diversion was estimated at the relatively small levels of $0.6 billion and $0.2 billion for the EEC and EFTA respectively. Thus, despite the apparent advantages in capturing the effects of increased integration, the gravitational models have not yielded much higher estimates of trade creation than the residual-imputation approach discussed earlier.

The first major study using a *control-country approach* was that of Williamson and Bottrill.[45] Their basic hypothesis is that the share performance of a given supplier in markets where there are no preferential tariff changes gives a good indication of that supplier's hypothetical performance in markets being affected by integration. In their case they use the rest of the world as the 'control country'. Thus the difference between the 'control-country' and the 'residual-imputation' approaches is that rather than invoke some rule of constant elasticities or shares or other measure to reconstruct the counterfactual, the control-country approach adopts the assumption that the performance of countries outside the union, when appropriately evaluated, permits the estimation of the hypothetical trade flows as they would have developed in the absence of the union.

Kreinin takes the control-country approach further and more heroically than Williamson and Bottrill both in terms of country and product-disaggregation.[46] His principal method is to compare percentage changes in the United States and EEC import–consumption ratios in different manufacturing industries. It is initially assumed that the EEC external import–consumption ratios would have moved by the same amount as the United States total import–consumption ratios without the customs union. This gives a measure of trade diversion. It is

---

[45] J. Williamson and A. Bottrill, 'The Impact of Customs Unions on Trade in Manufactures', *Oxford Economic Papers*, November 1971.

[46] M.E. Kreinin, 'Effects of the EEC on Imports of Manufactures', *Economic Journal*, September 1972.

further assumed that the ratios of external to total EEC imports would have remained unchanged at their 1959–60 values. The change in the EEC ratio of total imports to consumption minus the change in the American ratio, 'blown up' by the EEC base year total-to-external-imports ratio, gives an estimate of trade creation. In fact between 1959–60 and 1969–70 the United States import-consumption ratio for all manufactures rose by 2.1 per cent, while the EEC external import–consumption ratio rose by only 1.3 per cent, implying trade diversion of some $1.1 billion. The EEC total import ratio rose by 7.5 per cent, which implies trade creation of $8.5 billion.

The methodology might appear excessively simplistic, in particular in that it assumes away differential price and income movements. Kreinin tries crudely to adjust for the effects of these on import–consumption ratios. First, using an independent estimate of the income elasticity of import demand, he raises the United States import–consumption ratio to reflect the country's lower income growth over the period. Second, he adjusts for the loss of United States competitiveness in certain industries by reducing imports in those industries by a percentage equal to the decline in the United States share in third markets.[47] After these adjustments, the estimate for trade creation in 1969–70 falls to $7.3 billion and that for diversion rises to $2.4 billion.

Finally, among the studies discussed here, Resnick and Truman adopt a *multi-country model approach.*[48] They propose a model for the imports of ten EEC and EFTA countries (excluding Portugal and Finland, and combining Belgium and Luxembourg) which takes the form of a decision tree. Total non-food imports of each country are assumed to be a function of relative domestic and import prices, real income, and a pressure of demand variable. Total imports are then allocated to suppliers on the basis of relative prices in a hierarchical way. First, the shares in total imports from the other nine European countries and those from the rest of the world are separately related to relative import prices. The first group is then divided into the shares from the EEC and the shares from EFTA. Finally, in each customs union the shares coming from each country are related to all relative prices in that union. Thus there is one total import equation to be estimated for each of the ten countries, one Europe and one non-Europe share equation, one EEC and one EFTA share equation, four EEC member and five EFTA member share equations. In some cases difficulties in obtaining good ordinary least squares estimates led to the combining of some of the supplying countries' shares.

Once estimated, this set of import-allocation equations permits the simulation of any number of different customs union arrangements, provided the arrangement can be translated into a relative price change. For example, the impact of the 'Dillon Round' of multilateral tariff cuts can be isolated from that of the formation of the EEC customs union, provided that some view is taken as to what the 'Dillon Round' would have meant for the tariffs of the six if the first EEC tariff reductions had not intervened. In fact, it was assumed that the tariffs of the six would have been reduced by 10 per cent, the average cut for other participants in the 'Dillon Round'. The trade creation and diversion effects

---

[47] This is justified on the grounds that 'in quantitative terms U.S. manufacturing imports happen to be roughly equal to U.S. manufacturing exports to markets outside the EEC' (ibid., p.911). If this is merely a question of coincidence, the logic of adjusting in this way is difficult to see.

[48] S.A. Resnick and E.M. Truman, 'An Empirical Examination of Bilateral Trade in Western Europe', in Balassa (ed.), *European Economic Integration.*

following the formation of the two customs unions can be calculated from the price elasticities.

After abstracting the effects of the 'Dillon Round', the EEC is calculated to have generated only $1.9 billion of trade creation and $3.0 billion of trade diversion in 1968 at current prices. These are apparently the only results in the literature which show trade diversion in excess of trade creation. Resnick and Truman suggest some biases which may have arisen because of the use of particular time-series. In addition, the only regression coefficients which can pick up the effects of membership of the same trading bloc are those attached to relative prices, and Verdoorn and Schwarz showed that these will only pick up a minor part of the effects of tariff cuts. The effects of the elimination of prohibitive or nearly prohibitive duties will be all but missed.

Bibliography

There seems to be a lack of historical surveys of the EEC. An introduction to the economics side is D. Swann, *The Economics of the Common Market*, London 1978 (4th edn.). Some general books which provide historical background are: J. Pinder (ed.), *The Economics of Europe*, London 1971; A. Cairncross et al., *Economic Policy for the European Community*, London 1974; L. Tsoukalis, *The Politics and Economics of European Monetary Integration*, London 1977; B. Burrows, G. Denton, and G. Edwards, *Federal Solutions for European Issues*, London 1978; H. Wallace, W. Wallace, and C. Webb, *Policy-Making in the European Community*, New York 1977; P. Coffey (ed.), *Economic Policies of the Common Market*, London 1979; A.M. El-Agraa (ed.), *The Economics of the European Community*, Oxford 1980.

On the customs union issue, the two most complete surveys are B. Balassa (ed.), *European Economic Integration*, Amsterdam 1975, and D.G. Mayes, 'The Effects of Economic Integration on Trade', *Journal of Common Market Studies*, September 1978. An earlier account can be found in E. Dalbosco and F. Pierelli, 'Evoluzione della struttura del commercio estero dei paesi membri della CEE', in Banca d'Italia, *Contributi alla ricerca economica*, No. 3, 1973.

The Common Agricultural Policy is surveyed in: J. Marsh and C. Ritson, *Agricultural Policy and the Common Market*, RIIA, London 1971; Commission of the European Communities, *The Common Agricultural Policy*, Brussels 1978; C.N. Morris, 'The Common Agricultural Policy', *Fiscal Studies*, March 1980; R. Fennell, *The Common Agricultural Policy of the European Community*, London 1979. A continuing useful source is the *European Review of Agricultural Economics*.

General issues about economic and monetary union are raised in M. Fratianni and T. Peeters (eds.), *One Money for Europe*, London 1978. More specific references to EMS can be found in P.H. Trezise (ed.), *The European Monetary System: Its Promise and Prospects*, Brookings Institution, Washington 1979, while the original system is explained in EEC, *European Economy*, July 1979. The implications of economic union for financial transfers are investigated in EEC, *Report of the Study Group on the Role of Public Finance in European Integration* (MacDougall Report), Brussels 1977. Regional policy is analysed in T. Buck, 'Regional Policy and European Integration', *Journal of Common Market Studies*, December 1975. For discussion of the operation of the Lomé Convention and relations with the Third World in general, see the Commission's own journal, *The Courier* (various issues), as well as P. Coffey, *The External Relations of the EEC*, London 1976.

258   THE EUROPEAN ECONOMY

Other aspects of EEC economic policy not treated in the chapter are covered in, *inter alia*, M. Shanks, *European Social Policy, Today and Tomorrow*, Oxford 1977; N.J.D. Lucas, *Energy and the European Community*, London 1977; A.P. Jacquemin and H.W. de Jong, *European Industrial Organisation*, London 1977; L. Tsoukalis, *The European Community and its Mediterranean Enlargement*, London 1981. Finally, some more general essays on EEC problems can be found in W. Hallstein, *Die europäische Gemeinschaft*, Düsseldorf 1974, and in R. Triffin, R. Aron, R. Barre, and R. Enalentio, *L'Europe de la crise*, Brussels 1976.

[11]

Journal of Common Market Studies
Volume XVII, No. 1   September 1978

THE EFFECTS OF ECONOMIC
INTEGRATION ON TRADE

By David G. Mayes*

Department of Economics, University of Exeter

ABSTRACT

This article provides a critical analysis of the models and methods which have
been used to estimate the effects of economic integration on trade and suggests
the most fruitful lines of further development. Both the problem of the
examination of the effects of past events and problems in the prediction of
future changes are tackled. In particular the drawbacks of the method of
estimation of the effects of previous integration as a residual from models which
explain what would have happened had the integration not taken place are
shown. It is concluded that the most fruitful avenue of approach lies in the
estimation of models which provide an economic explanation of trade flows and
their changes, and can hence be used for both the explanation of the effects of
previous integration and the prediction of future events.

Over the past twenty years a vast literature has sprung up
attempting to explain what happens to trade when countries
reduce or abandon some or all of the barriers to free trade between
them. Although the subject is by no means so new the upsurge in
interest stems from the formation of trading areas in many parts of
the world. The irony of the situation is however that despite such
an accumulation of effort there is widespread disagreement
between investigators as to the most appropriate method of
analysis. To some extent this disagreement stems from the
pursuance of different aims; however, most of it revolves round
the lack of any yardstick against which to measure the accuracy of
any results. Furthermore, since most estimates belong to different
time periods and are recorded in different units of measurement it
is extremely difficult to make meaningful empirical comparisons
between the results. It is therefore the purpose of this article to
appraise the methods of analysis which can be used and to see
which differences have any bearing on the quantitative results so
that conclusions can be drawn on the most profitable line of
further advance.

* I am grateful for the helpful comments of John Black, John Kay, Frank Oliver, Paul
Richards and the SSRC International Economics Study Group on earlier versions of this
paper.

2   DAVID G. MAYES

I. THE TWO METHODS OF APPROACH

In most areas of economic analysis it is possible to use models which have been developed to estimate the effects of events in the past to predict the results of similar behaviour in the future. This is not true of the majority of estimated models of the effects of economic integration on trade because they estimate (ex-post) the effects of integration to be the residual between what actually occurred and the trade predicted on the basis of the continuation of previous economic relations. The remaining models (let us call them 'analytic') which can also be used for predictive purposes provide a direct economic explanation of the value of trade flows after economic integration.[1]

In general, despite their great variety, the determination of the level of trade between countries in the models considered here stems from some or all of four categories of variables:

(1) economic variables explaining behaviour in the importing country (economic activity, population, prices, pressure of demand, etc.)

(2) economic variables explaining behaviour in the exporting country (economic activity, population, prices, pressure on supply, etc.)

(3) variables explaining specific characteristics of trade between the two countries (geographical separation, trading preferences, etc.)

(4) variables explaining relevant behaviour in third countries (imports, exports, prices, economic activity, etc.).

We shall argue that unless the full range of these variables is included in the model, the estimation of the effects on trade cannot hope to be unbiased, but we shall also consider how valid simplifications of this structure are in producing results where the biases are unimportant. Of necessity ex-ante models consider fewer of the variables as prediction requires not only a model to predict the future values of endogenous variables but also the derivation of a set of future values of the exogenous variables in the model. The degree of heroism required in this latter derivation is such that most authors wisely keep it to a minimum. This also helps to explain why so much more effort has been expended on the ex-post models.

[1] Running right across these two categories are differences in aggregation by country and industries, in static or dynamic form and in whether more than just the effects of changes in tariffs is considered. The flavour of the model is also greatly affected by whether it seeks to explain trade flows for a single country or the world at large.

EFFECTS OF ECONOMIC INTEGRATION ON TRADE   3

2. THE EFFECTS OF ECONOMIC INTEGRATION

The theory underlying our expectations of the effects of economic integration is well known,[2] all we need to note here is that if barriers to trade, tariffs, quotas, national buying policies, etc., are removed then we would expect trade to expand (trade creation), and if barriers are removed from trade with one country but not from trade with another we would also expect imports from the first country to increase at the expense of imports from the second (trade diversion).[3] Further effects will also stem from 'positive' actions in integration—such as the adoption of common standards—in addition to the 'negative' actions of merely abandoning discrimination.

In view of the concentration in empirical work on short-run effects on trade flows it is easy to lose sight of the fact that these are only one type of effect. Furthermore the use of simple measures such as trade creation and trade diversion tends to obscure the existence of several causes of the one event. The formation of a trading area, Lipsey suggested (1957), results in changes in the international economy from five main sources:

(1) the specialisation of production according to comparative advantage which is the basis of the classical case for the gains from trade (2) economies of scale (3) changes in the terms of trade (4) forced changes in efficiency due to increased foreign competition (5) a change in the rate of growth.

The bulk of the empirical work which has been undertaken so far is concerned with sources (1) and (3), some of the other sources are included in passing but not often dealt with specifically. It is only right, however, that in a general appraisal such as this that all these factors should be borne in mind. In particular influences on the rate of growth will have important repercussions on trade.

It is a matter of major importance to distinguish between short-run static effects, whereby a change in the barriers to trade result in a single change in trade and its pattern, and longer-run dynamic effects, where the rate of change of economic variables over time is permanently altered by economic integration. We shall therefore examine both of them with respect to trade.[4]

By drawing the line at the consideration of the effects on trade we must also be aware that we are omitting consideration of other

[2] See for example, Balassa (1961), Krauss (1972; 1973) and Robson (1972).
[3] These two terms have many different detailed definitions, see Truman (1972) for example, we have merely opted for the most straightforward.
[4] Some of the controversy over estimation methods (see Sellekaerts (1973) for example) stems from whether the intention is to measure the static effects alone or the static and dynamic effects combined (a common result in residual methods).

4   DAVID G. MAYES

factors which may be of greater importance. Much of the theoretical interest in customs unions stems not from the fact that the balance of trade of participants may be affected either positively or negatively, but that the overall effect on world welfare is contingent upon the particular relationship. Also, there is what Kaldor (1971) terms a 'resource cost' for some of the participants in economic integration. In so far as the static trade effects are negative a country will have to indulge in offsetting economic policies if it wishes to rectify the situation. The cost of this rectification is the resource cost of integration, the value of the resources which have to be used in sustaining integration.

3. RESIDUAL MODELS

Let us turn our attention first to residual models as they form the bulk of estimated models and then extend it to consider models which can also be used for prediction. Residual models have the common characteristic that they seek to quantify the hypothetical situation (often referred to as the anti-monde) of what would have happened had the trading agreement not been implemented. As with any such hypothetical circumstance we have no means of testing its validity other than the plausibility of the results and the behaviour of the model in different observable situations. The problem of establishing such an anti-monde is expressed excellently by Duquesne de la Vinelle (1965) in a survey of some early attempts:

La philosophie profonde de cette aporie se trouvait déjà chez le philosophe Heraclite lorsqu'il écrivait 'on ne se baigne deux fois dans le même fleuve'.

Clearly we would expect that the more of the explanatory variables we set out on p. 21 are taken into account the better determined the anti-monde, so we have structured the rest of this section by considering the problem in increasing order of complexity of model.

3.1 *Import Models*

There is a strong tendency to concentrate on explanatory variables drawn from the importing country alone as this considerably reduces the complexity of data collection. Our concern here is to establish whether the gains from convenience are outweighed by the losses in accuracy.

EFFECTS OF ECONOMIC INTEGRATION ON TRADE   5

(a) *The demand for imports*

The form of argument which is used is that imports would have increased over time without the trading agreement at exactly the same rate as they did before the agreement came into effect. Clearly such trend extrapolation will have severe drawbacks for a cyclical activity like international trade, so authors such as Clavaux (1969), Walter (1967) and Wemelsfelder (1960) have assumed that imports will retain the same linear relation to total expenditure, GDP and GNP respectively in the anti-monde as they did in the pre-integration period. These studies, as pointed out by Williamson and Bottrill (1971), make the thoroughly unlikely assumption that the marginal propensity to import remains constant, whereas the evidence points to its rising with income. Further, any estimation of the actual marginal propensity to import over previous periods will always be clouded by the other changes in trading arrangements which took place then, and will not represent an anti-monde where no change takes place.

While it is possible to make a critical examination of these hypotheses purely on the basis of economic theory and experience without any consideration of the numerical values of their results, the relative importance of changes in the assumptions can only be shown by looking at their quantitative effects. We have therefore drawn up in Figure 1 a graph comparing the published results of the various models for the effects of the formation of the EEC. The choice of the EEC is dictated purely by the relatively larger number of results relating to that grouping than to any other. Obviously the best form of comparison would be to use each of these models with the same set of data, and where the amount of recomputation involved is small, this has been done and is included in specific tables in the text. However in many cases the data required are so different that we have chosen to use the original results, and these are included in Figure 1, with a time axis to denote the year for which they are estimates.

It is possible to improve the results by use of more observations; Sellekaerts (1973) for example uses ordinary least squares to estimate a linear relation between imports from extra-area suppliers and GNP in the EEC allowing for a shift in both parameters in the period after the formation of the EEC, but interestingly enough he estimates that in aggregate trade diversion is in favour of non-members to the tune of $24,037 mn–$26,404 mn by 1967, not at their expense.

6   DAVID G. MAYES

FIGURE 1

PREDICTIONS OF TRADE CREATION AND TRADE DIVERSION IN THE EEC

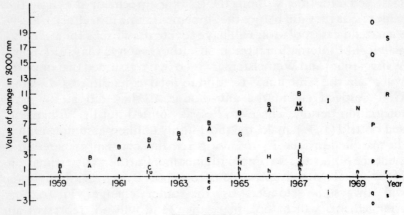

KEY TO FIGURE 1

Capital letters denote Trade Creation and small letters Trade Diversion

A Aitken (1973) (projection)
B Aitken (1973) (dummy variable)
C Waelbroeck (1964) (method 1)
D Truman (1969) disaggregated 1958 base
E as D 1960 base
F Balassa (1967c)
G Clavaux (1969)
H EFTA (1972)
I Major-Hays (1970) 1958 base
J Resnick-Truman (1974)
K Truman (1972)

L K (adjusted)
M Verdoorn-Schwartz (1972)
N Williamson-Bottrill (1971)
O Kreinin (1972) not normalised
P O US normalised & adjusted
Q O UK normalised
R Balassa (1964)
S Prewo (1974)
t Lamfalussy (1963)
u C method 2

Values denoted:

	(i) Trade Creation					(ii) Trade Diversion		
Year	Estimate	Value in $000 mn	Year	Estimate	Value in $000 mn	Year	Estimate	Value in $000 mn
1959	A	0·9	1965	H	1·7	1962	t	0·5
	B	1·1	1966	A	8·6		u	0·5
1960	A	1·6		B	9·8	1965	d	−1·6
	B	2·5		H	2·2		e	−0·3
1961	A	2·3	1967	A	9·2	1965	f	0·1
	B	3·3		B	11·1		h	0·6
1962	A	3·2		H	2·3	1966	h	0·7
	B	4·1		J	1·8	1967	h	0·9
	C	1·0		K	9·2		j	3·0
1963	A	4·7		L	2·5		k	−1·0
	B	5·2		M	10·1		l	0·5
1964	A	5·7	1968	I	10·8		n	1·1
	B	6·4	1969	N	9·6	1968	i	−2·9
	D	4·5	1969/70	O	20·8	1969	n	0·0
	E	2·6		P	7·2	1969/70	o	−4·0
1965	A	6·9		Q	16·0		p	2·4
	B	8·2	1970	R	11·4		q	−2·8
	F	1·9		S	18·0	1970	r	0·1
	G	5·0					s	−3·1

(b) *Shares in Apparent Consumption*

The problem can also be approached by considering the relative shares of the various suppliers in total consumption, rather than the absolute value of imports. Truman (1969) takes the simplest solution and assumes that the shares of each supplier will remain constant over time, but it is clearly preferable to allow for some change in the ratio over time on the basis of historical change. The EFTA Secretariat Studies (1969, 1972) incorporate this by assuming that the linear trend in shares between 1954 and 1959 would have been maintained by the member countries in the anti-monde. The particular trend they estimate is open to objection on the grounds, first, that the two years chosen may not lie on the actual trend, and second that the form of the trend is too simple. Further estimation by say regression is not really profitable given the simplicity of the original assumption.

The effect of assuming a linear trend in the shares in the anti-monde as opposed to no change from the pre-integration period on the aggregate trade flows is shown in Table 1 for EFTA. Both Truman (1969) and EFTA (1969) disaggregate their analysis by manufactured commodities, but while this prevents some of the bias from aggregation, it makes the rigidity of the hypotheses about import shares rather more unlikely. We must therefore emphasise that the basis of the comparison in Table 1 is in aggregate. All the same the dissimilarity of the results and the almost random distribution of positive and negative signs is striking.

These projections of trade flows relating solely to the performance of import demand in previous periods make too strong assumptions for their validity to be very great. They assume that past trends will continue into the future without considering either the exact nature of the relationship[5] or whether it is really likely that events such as multilateral tariff reductions can be expected to continue at the same rate in the anti-monde. Furthermore, they tend to assume that many of the determining variables, GNP, apparent consumption, etc., would be unchanged in the anti-monde from their actual observed values. Since we would expect these variables themselves to be affected by economic integration this assumption will not be valid. The use of shares rather than absolute values does not avoid the problem

---

[5] Sellekaerts (1973) is an exception to this as he does allow for cyclical factors.

8   DAVID G. MAYES

TABLE I
Alternative estimates of aggregate effects of EFTA, 1965 $mn

Country	Trade creation		Trade diversion	
	Hypothesis		Hypothesis	
	(1)	(2)	(1)	(2)
Austria	−121·5	163	178·3	79
Denmark	−180·6	−122	322·1	−166
Finland	−204·9	−59	149·0	−136
Norway	−32.7	63	261·6	−73
Portugal	63·8	62	−15·1	43
Sweden	364·4	276	96·5	−110
Switzerland	−357·8	218	288·3	117
United Kingdom	831·0	−343	−619·1	−594
Total	361·7	258	661·6	−840

SOURCE: EFTA (1969).
(1) Using the EFTA (1969) method.
(2) Assuming that shares in 1965 would have been the same as those in 1959 in the anti-monde.

unless we can assume that income (and to some extent sub-stitution) effects are zero. Yet EFTA (1969, 1972) explicitly include an income effect.

(c) *Changes in the Income Elasticity of Demand for Imports*
It is also possible to look at the problem of changes in shares from the opposite direction, and see what the actual changes imply for the elasticity of demand for various sorts of imports with respect to income. Balassa (1969b, 1974) estimates separately income elasticities of demand for imports from fellow members and for imports from non-members. He argues that a rise in the elasticity of demand for imports from all sources indicates trade creation, and that a fall in the elasticity of demand for imports from non-members, while the elasticity for imports from other members shows a rise, indicates trade diversion. It is presumably these results which are reported, Balassa p. 115, and are reproduced here in Figure 1. The anti-monde is thus that income elasticities of demand would not have changed. Since the estimated elasticities are not unitary and not equal for imports from member and non-member countries, this means that changes in the shares of total imports in apparent consumption and imports from non-member

EFFECTS OF ECONOMIC INTEGRATION ON TRADE   9

countries (and hence member countries) in total imports can and do take place in the anti-monde. Allowances are made for changes in prices and the effects he calculates are similar to the general trend in Figure 1 although both positive and negative effects occur.

Whether the problem of the anti-monde is approached by Balassa's (1967b) method or the EFTA (1969) method it is still clear that the period before the formation of EFTA and the EEC was one of considerable trade liberalisation, and hence the estimation of trade relationships during that period will be affected by it. The implicit assumption of the anti-monde may in fact be that nothing new occurred, but that liberalisation continued at previous rates. Clavaux (1969) estimates that if we take into account the existence of liberalisation in the estimation period and exclude it from the anti-monde then Balassa's estimates of trade creation by 1966 should be more than doubled. It is not clear that the bias that Clavaux claims is actually so important. In the light of the other drawbacks we have mentioned it is clear, however, that precise elasticities suggest a degree of sophistication which is not really present in these models. As Orcutt (1950) points out, if there are no supply equations there is an identification problem which biases estimates of price elasticities towards zero. The neglect of supply conditions implicitly rests on the strong assumption of infinite supply elasticities. Balassa's (1974, p. 93) estimation of ex-post income elasticities will take supply constraints into account implicitly, but so will it of course for the pre-integration period.

Balassa's approach is also questioned closely by Sellekaerts (1973) who suggests (p. 526) that the estimates will be biased unless 'the following ceteris paribus assumptions are realistic: no autonomous changes in relative prices, no changes in exchange rates, no changes in extra-area trade flows caused by the dynamic effects of a customs union'. Clearly any trends in relative prices either before or after the formation of the area will bias estimates based on income elasticities of demand alone. The third point about dynamic effects merely makes the point that since Balassa is using a 'residual imputation model' all effects, not just the static ones will be included in the residual. Far more important is Sellekaerts' clear demonstration, (pp. 529 and 544), that income elasticities vary widely over both the pre- and post-integration periods. Thus the choice of periods for comparison is crucial. Elasticities will vary with the pressure of demand and it is thus important either to compare time periods where activity was in the same sort of phase of the economic cycle, or to allow for changes in the economic cycle explicitly in the estimation.

3.2 *The Inclusion of Supply Variables*

All these models we have mentioned so far only consider the first area of economic variables affecting trade, namely the variables in the importing country. They are thus largely demand determined, although *ad hoc* supply constraints were introduced in some cases. Obviously the specification of the model will be improved if explicit allowance is made for supply conditions. Thus trade between any pair of countries is a function of variables within both of them.

The simplest approach has been to suggest that under 'normal' circumstances trade between any pair of countries is purely a function of the total trade of each of the two countries. In particular, in the anti-monde the trade between any pair of countries will vary proportionately with total exports of the exporting country and total imports of the importing country. The original model, dubbed RAS, was developed by Stone and Brown (Cambridge, 1963) in the context of input–output analysis, and was turned to the present context by Kouevi (1965) and Waelbroeck (1964).[6] Its major drawback is that total predicted imports and exports are constrained to their actual values so it is not possible to measure trade creation. Further, the whole point of the original RAS was to minimise the errors in the predictions rather than our current purpose. This can be overcome to some considerable extent as is shown in Baron (1968) and Mayes (1971; 1974) in a model which I christened RASAT by adding a commodity dimension and relaxing some of the constraints, but the estimated results for trade diversion are small. In a 32 commodity breakdown for EFTA, however, substantial trade diversion was observed for most of the major categories (Mayes, 1974, Table 5).

A much more satisfactory means of incorporating determining variables from both the importing and the exporting countries is the so-called 'gravitational' model pioneered by Tinbergen and developed by Pulliainen (1963), Poyhonen (1963) and Linnemann (1966) with a large number of applications to the present context.

---

[6] A somewhat similar model to RAS was proposed by Savage and Deutsch (1960) and used to measure changes in the trade of EFTA and the EEC after their formation by Carney (1970).

EFFECTS OF ECONOMIC INTEGRATION ON TRADE   11

A major advantage is that the model is no longer 'mechanical' and incorporates explicit economic variables in both countries which makes its interpretation much easier. The gravitational model suggests that the trade flow between any pair of countries is a multiplicative function of their respective national incomes, populations and the distance between them (thus also incorporating part of our third category of explanatory variables (see p. 21) relating to specific factors affecting trade between a pair of countries). The model is estimated using cross-section data and the effects of any trading arrangements are calculated by the unexplained residual in the regression, or, as suggested in Aitken (1973) and Aitken and Lowry (1973), by the inclusion of a dummy variable for trade between partner countries. These two methods can give strikingly different results as the parameters of the model seem to vary substantially over time. Aitken (1973) estimates that trade creation by EFTA in 1967 using the 1958 parameters is $1264 mn (this method is labelled 'projection' in Figure 1) while using the 1967 values themselves and the dummy variable the result is 92% greater (labelled 'dummy'). Since Aitken's results are the only ones which are estimated for a sequence of years they have a heavy influence on the overall pattern of Figure 1. While in general they are coherent with other estimates although they form the upper bound, in some cases, e.g. 1965, they are 3 to 4 times as large as the lower bound. Against this substantial relative difference must be held the fact that the absolute magnitude of all the results is small. The main reason for these differences, as is confirmed by Bluet and Systermanns' (1968) disaggregated study, is the variability in the estimated parameters from year to year, hence projection with fixed parameters should be treated with care. Much of the variability in the estimators occurs because a

TABLE II

Gross trade creation in the CACM and the LAFTA, $ mn

Year	CACM	LAFTA
1963	55·1	239·4
1964	97·0	297·4
1965	121·3	404·9
1966	160·5	503·2
1967	200·0	357·5

Source: Aitken and Lowry (1973, p. 334)

12   DAVID G. MAYES

cross-section cannot represent a relationship which responds to
cycles in economic activity and the very process of trade
liberalisation in general. Pooling data helps to some extent but the
model's main disadvantage is the omission of relative prices.

This deficiency is overcome by Verdoorn and Schwartz (1972)
in the second of their models. They combine the advantages of the
gravitational model with the effects of price, both on the overall
demand for imports and the substitution between imports from
various sources. This model really provides the link between the
residual models and the analytic models in the next section. While
results are still largely calculated on a residual basis, two dummy
variables are used to explain some of the 'residual', although they
are only explanatory in a statistical rather than an economic sense.
The results are shown in Table 3 and, as can be seen from Figure 1,
they correspond with the general run of results, which is
comforting in the sense that the different methods agree, but it
also implies that this more highly developed model does not tell us
much which is new. The unexplained variation is still large (22%)
so there is still room for considerable improvement particularly in
the rather harsh constraint that the parameters of the model shall
be the same for all countries.

TABLE III

*Resnick and Truman's (1974) estimates of trade creation and trade diversion in EEC and
EFTA compared with those of Verdoorn and Schwartz (1972) $ mn*

Country	Trade creation		Trade diversion	
	R & T 1968	V & S 1969	R & T 1968	V & S 1969
EEC				
BLEU	152	913	281	183
Netherlands	93	868	190	216
W. Germany	−659	3,874	1,732	267
Italy	1,022	1,336	62	154
France	582	3,073	737	248
Total	1,190	10,064	3,002	1,068
EFTA				
UK	81	204	394	249
Other EFTA	131	161	231	547
Total	212	365	625	796
EEC+EFTA	1,402	10,429	3,627	1,864

3.3 *The Incorporation of Information from Third Countries*

We argued on p. 21 that relevant behaviour in countries excluded from the trading area both before and after the agreement comes into force should be incorporated into the analysis. While the share approach to estimation does not include supply factors directly it can include third country behaviour as is shown with great clarity by Lamfalussy (1963). He showed that if we take the change in shares of trade of non-members and member countries of the EEC in other markets, where neither suffers nor benefits from discrimination, as the basis of our expectation about how shares in the member countries' markets would have changed without integration, we get a very different set of answers from those from trend extrapolation in the members' markets alone. This can be seen in Table 4. The differences have a fairly clear pattern: the share of EEC exports in both EEC and EFTA imports is substantially greater under the first hypothesis and the share of ROW in both markets falls under the first hypothesis but rises under the second. EFTA shares in both markets are greater under the second hypothesis but only very marginally so in the case of intra-EFTA trade. It is also clear, as Williamson and Bottrill (1971) demonstrate, that Lamfalussy's pessimistic con-

TABLE IV

A comparison of the effects of different anti-mondes on the imports of the EEC and EFTA in 1969 ($ mn)

Anti-monde	Exporter	Importer	
		EEC	EFTA
(1)		5,091	−1,042
(2)	EEC	1,018	−3,610
(1)/(2)		5·00	0·29
(1)		−2,258	2,542
(2)	EFTA	−1,594	2,644
(1)/(2)		1·42	0·96
(1)	Rest of world	−2,833	−1,500
(2)		576	966

(1) Share of exporter i in the market of importer j would change between 1959 and 1969 at the same linear rate as the share of i's exports in the imports of Rest of World (ROW) changed during the same period (shares constrained to sum to unity).

(2) Share of exporter i in the market of importer j would change between 1959 and 1969 at the same linear rate that it did between 1954 and 1959.

Source: Data drawn from Williamson and Bottrill (1971).

clusions are largely due to the fact that he was only able to consider the first three years of the Common Market's existence; over a longer period an obvious EEC effect would have been observed. They, therefore, develop his method further by using a long run of data and more sophisticated extrapolation methods of the anti-monde shares. However, this method does not enable us to determine the derivation of trade creation and diversion until further assumptions are made about their relative sizes. This is not, however, too dramatic a drawback for as is shown in Mayes (1976), the estimates are not unreasonably sensitive to the choice of the relative magnitudes.

The idea of the use of non-member countries as a control group or form of 'normalisation' in order to estimate what the anti-monde would have been, can be incorporated explicitly into the model, and is done so most thoroughly by Kreinin (1972) where he adapts the technique of projecting the anti-monde on the basis of predicted import/consumption ratios described at the beginning of Section 3.1. This enables us to see far more clearly how the normalisation procedure works, so that we can evaluate the plausibility of the assumptions on which it rests. It is too easy to assume that we can actually find a control group for arrangements such as the EEC, because the control variables themselves are affected by the very experiment we are seeking to isolate. In the case of say the CACM and LAFTA the particular arrangement does not have important feedback effects on the control variables, but there again the control variables are affected by other examples of economic integration which occurred simultaneously during the period of estimation. Kreinin in seeking to estimate the effects of the EEC on imports of manufactures uses the US, the UK and Japan as normalisers. The percentage increases in the total import/consumption ratio and the ratio of imports from non-members to consumption are reduced by the increase in the normalising country's import/consumption ratio. From these two normalised ratios he estimates trade creation and trade diversion respectively. Additionally, in the case of normalisation by the US alone he further adjusts the EEC import/consumption ratio firstly for the fact that the real GNP of the US had grown more slowly than that of the EEC during the period and that its income elasticity of import demand is 1·69, and secondly for the different rates of inflation and hence competitiveness. This second change is estimated by assuming that US imports should be reduced by the same percentage as the decline in the US share in third markets. These adjustments are rather ad hoc and it is helpful to see the full

EFFECTS OF ECONOMIC INTEGRATION ON TRADE   15

range of estimates set out in Table 5.[7] 'Normalisation' is highly dependent upon the choice of normaliser, as is suggested in Mayes (1974); it is unfortunately true that no one country appears to be 'normal'. Hypothetical normality is bound to be difficult to assess, and unless a model is used which explains differences from the norm such attempts at normalisation will be unsatisfactory.

TABLE V

Estimates of trade creation and diversion in the EEC in manufacturing industry in 1969/70 ($ mn)

	Trade creation	Trade diversion
Not normalised	20,777	− 4,024
Not normalised but +		
income adjustment	10,481	1,431
US normalised	8,543	1,721
US normalised		
+adjustments	7,256	2,426
UK normalised	16,044	− 2,848
Japan normalised	20,500	− 4,161

Source: Kreinin (1972): Tables VI, VII, VIII

3.4 *The Estimation of the Anti-Monde*

In Sections 3.1–3.3 we have shown that the number and range of estimates of the effects of economic integration by imputation of the unexplained residual are large, and it is evident that the more of our four categories of variables included in the estimation of the anti-monde the more satisfactory is the result. Further refinements such as disaggregation and the incorporation of a clear distinction between final and intermediate products should further improve the estimates, although the work by Prewo (1974) shows a strikingly different pattern of results from the other models (see Figure 1), probably due to the simplicity of some of his other assumptions. Yet the problem of estimating a hypothetical anti-monde is in itself not an attractive proposition. While it is possible to point out the existence of biases it is not possible to know whether an unbiased estimate has been achieved, one can merely judge on the grounds of plausibility. Plausibility depends upon the factors taken into account not just in the importing and exporting countries, but as they affect the trade cycle and movements in world prices. There is therefore a considerable incentive to find an analytic model which can explain actual trade flows and their

[7] These results are deliberately chosen to show how wide the range of estimates can be, they do not represent Kreinin's considered views in his article—the subtraction of processed foods has a considerable equalising effect on the results.

16   DAVID G. MAYES

changes, rather than to have to resort to the derivation of an anti-monde and the imputation of residual differences to the effects of integration.

4. ANALYTIC MODELS

We have already suggested that some of the models which employ the residual form of analysis are partly analytic, for example there is the demand analysis side of Verdoorn and Schwartz (1972) second model (p. 31). However, let us repeat the meaning of 'analytic' in this context, namely 'providing an economic explanation of the actual post-integration situation'. This is a necessary requirement for all ex-ante models as of course the actual values of trade flows in the future are unknown. Because of the difficulties inherent in prediction ex-ante models are usually simple, concentrating on economic behaviour in the importing country. In particular[8] it is suggested imports are a function of some measure of income or economic activity and the relative prices of imported and domestic products. Hence trade creation can be predicted from the change in tariff levels if the relation between tariff changes and price changes is assumed and trade diversion can be estimated if the elasticity of substitution with respect to price changes between partner and excluded countries is known.

This approach is clearly simplistic and although it can be improved by the use of more sophisticated import demand functions it will not give really satisfactory estimates until the relation between tariff changes and price changes can also be explained. The expectation which is normally used—that prices fall by the full amount of tariff changes—is shown in EFTA (1968) to be an overestimate; only part of the tariff change appears to be passed on. There is considerable evidence at a micro-economic level that the pricing of imports of many products depends largely on the prices of existing competing domestic products. Walter (1967) suggests that the problem is even worse as importers tend to anticipate tariff changes and hence trade growth will lead the 'determining' tariff changes. Thus not only is price used as a proxy for all the other non-price factors in economic integration, such as decisions to set up marketing networks, which affect trade flows but it is not the true measure of the actual change in 'price' either.

---

[8] See Houthakker and Magee (1969), Ball and Marwah (1962), Kreinin (1969), Mayes (1971) and Barker and Lecomber (1967).

EFFECTS OF ECONOMIC INTEGRATION ON TRADE 17

Attempts (Krause, 1962; Kreinin, 1961) to estimate tariff elasticities directly have not been very successful and as Mayes (1971, 1974) shows, the results from this approach do not correspond closely with those from residual models.

The greater the degree of disaggregation the more plausible the results as there is no reason to expect different commodities or countries to behave in an identical manner. The results from Mayes (1971) for a projected 'Atlantic' Free Trade Area composed of US, Canada, EFTA and Japan are shown in Table 6 for a 97 commodity breakdown of manufactured products. Not only do the results have the expected pattern of signs for overall trade creation and diversion but they are fairly robust to quite substantial changes in the parameters. While I tried to allow for a complete system of demand equations with the volume and price of imports from each country being distinguished to give a whole matrix of direct and substitution elasticities[9] other authors have tried to use more global values based either on assumption or crude extrapolation from estimates for the United States. The effects on the estimates of using three different sets of assumptions proposed by Balassa (1967), Kreinin (1967) and Krause (1968) are shown as columns (2), (3), and (4) respectively in Table 6.[10] To quite an extent the similarity between the various results is due to offsetting changes, greater trade creation is balanced by greater trade diversion. The main feature of the results is their smallness compared with residual models (Kreinin (1969), for example, gives estimates for the effects of the formation of the EEC during the period 1962–65 which are all less than $100 mn).

More substantial models which allow for the determination of import levels by a series of allocative decisions have been developed, Armington (1970) and Resnick and Truman (1973, 1974) and simple assumptions can be made for supply constraints as in Balassa and Kreinin (1967), but as can be seen from Table 3 and Figure 1 these results do not accord well with those from the residual models. Compared with Verdoorn and Schwartz (1972), for example, Resnick and Truman's estimates for trade creation in the EEC are only one-eighth the size (although the ratio is three-fifths for EFTA). Second because Germany had to revise its tariffs upward to the CET, trade creation is negative in the analytic case

[9] Along the lines of Barten (1970). It was also shown that the hypothesis that elasticities of substitution are the same for all countries should be rejected.

[10] It should be stressed that the results shown are the results of my calculations based on my interpretation of their assumptions and not the published results of the authors themselves.

DAVID G. MAYES

TABLE VI

A comparison of ex-ante predictions of the effects of economic integration on trade

An Atlantic free trade area[1] *(Effect on total exports) ($ mn) 1972 (estimated)*

Country	(1)	(2)	(3)	(4)
US	2,454	2,318	2,509	2,645
Canada	2,141	2,610	2,547	2,650
Belgium-Luxemburg	−88	−124	−93	−117
France	−127	−146	−159	−199
Germany	−444	−538	−538	−673
Italy	−131	−144	−163	−204
Netherlands	−48	−56	−64	−80
TOTAL EEC	−838	−1,008	−1,017	−1,273
Denmark	22	30	24	24
Norway	15	23	18	18
Sweden	128	156	144	148
UK	607	821	726	756
Rest of EFTA	241	263	225	269
TOTAL EFTA	1,013	1,293	1,167	1,215
Japan	1,879	2,380	2,301	2,448
Rest of the world	−646	−806	−719	−898
TOTAL	6,002	6,786	6,786	6,786

[1] Defined here as an area comprising US, Canada, EFTA and Japan—this corresponds closely to the definitions used by Balassa (1967a) and Maxwell-Stamp (1967).

[2] Commodity categories are different so these results do not represent an exact up-dating of the original results.

(1) Mayes (1971).

(2) Using elasticities used by Balassa (1967b).[2]

(3) Using same import elasticity as Balassa but assuming elasticity of substitution is −2·5 as does Kreinin (1967b).[2]

(4) As (3) but assuming elasticity of substitution is −2 as does Krause (1968).

but the largest positive effect for any country in the residual model. This tells us that other factors besides tariff changes had a strong positive effect on Germany's trade after the formation of the EEC. There is clearly much more to be explained which *is not* covered by the analytic models and *cannot* be covered by the residual ones.

The major advantage of the analytic models is that they can be tested after the event and can be used for forecasting as well as ex post estimation. Clearly they need substantial improvement and

EFFECTS OF ECONOMIC INTEGRATION ON TRADE 19

some hope lies in the detailed work on particular industries,[11] especially since Williamson (1971), for example, has found that the formation of the EEC has resulted in intra-industry specialisation rather than the *inter*-industry specialisation we might have expected. Further they must make allowance for supply factors, the behaviour of third countries and cycles in trade (Adams et al (1969) points the way forward) and most important they must try to reduce the disparity between their results and those of residual models caused by factors other than the impact effect of tariff changes.

5. DYNAMIC EFFECTS

It is clear that in concentrating on the impact effect of price changes alone, the largest part of the total effect may be omitted altogether. The feedback on to incomes and the rate of economic growth or the need for expenditure switching policies to accommodate movements in the balance of payments may be substantial and either positive or negative—Kaldor (1971), for example, in his gloomy assessment of the likely effects of UK entry into the EEC, thinks that adverse impact effects will be aggravated by adverse dynamic effects. Despite this there are very few attempts to estimate such dynamic effects. The most important exception is by Krause (1968) who seeks to explain changes in the rate of real economic growth in EFTA and the EEC by increasing business investment and increasing efficiency. The impact of these factors is straightforward, an increased ratio of investment to GDP leads to an increase in the capital stock, and if the marginal capital output ratios are constant, then output and hence the rate of growth must increase. This fixed relation between capital and output of course automatically excludes economies of scale, one of the factors we specifically wanted to include. The increase in efficiency comes from a decrease in input costs from imports, hence the increase in the ratio of imports to output is calculated and this, multiplied by the average tariff rate, gives the income effect of the reduction in costs which can be expressed as an annual rate.

This analysis is clearly crude in that it makes the assumptions we have considered before about the equality of tariff changes and

[11] Bond and Wonnacott (1968), Haviland et al. (1968) and Singer (1969) in the 'Canada in the Atlantic Economy' series, for example, and the detailed studies of comparative competitive position in Han and Liesner (1971) and Wonnacott and Wonnacott (1967).

20
DAVID G. MAYES

consequent price changes. As is shown in Mayes (1971) these two effects can also be applied to Japan where over the same period Japan shows a larger rate of growth effect from the establishment of the EEC and EFTA than do all of the actual members.[12] It is clear that the procedure of attributing all changes which occur during the period after formation of the two areas to their formation is not satisfactory; other economic factors are at work and a satisfactory model must explain them. In Mayes (1971) I attempted a simple calculation of such effects over a limited time horizon of 10–12 years using a truncated dynamic model, and showed what the resulting changes in trade flows would be if each participant country were to alter their exchange rate in such a way as to return to their original balance of trade before the formation of the trading area, but this does not provide a full explanation of the factors at work. This area of growth is probably the most important for future research as its effects can prove far more substantial than any once and for all static effects on trade flows which at maximum result in a gain of around 1% of GNP.

6. CONCLUDING

It is clear after such a wealth of research that bounds of magnitude have been established for the effects of economic integration on trade. If we take the many estimates shown in Figure 1 we can draw arbitrary bounds of the form suggested in Figure 2.[13] Several of the more extreme results lie outside these bounds, yet the range for 1970 is approximately $8–15,000 mn, so it is clear that we are a long way from achieving an agreed point estimate. However, the only really satisfactory bounds that we would wish to use would take the form of an interval estimate where a statement can be made in probability. To obtain this, whether by means of direct estimation with an 'analytic' model or imputation from a 'residual' model, requires a more carefully specified and estimated set of equations than have been presented here. These equations must, as we have established, explain both demand and supply factors and take account of cycles in world trade. The width of the interval estimate could then be brought down to a more reasonable figure.

[12] The respective figures for Japan are approximately 0·19% for the investment effect and 0·08% for the efficiency effect, 0·27% in total, the highest total effect for a member country is 0·25% for Denmark (Krause, 1968, p. 44).

[13] A number of the lower estimates for 1967 lie outside the bounds. To some extent their exclusion is deliberate but it is also somewhat arbitrary, the bounds have been drawn linear, but there is no reason to expect that they should have any such rigid functional form over time.

EFFECTS OF ECONOMIC INTEGRATION ON TRADE   21

FIGURE 2

APPROXIMATE BOUNDS TO PREDICTIONS OF TRADE CREATION
AND TRADE DIVERSION IN THE EEC

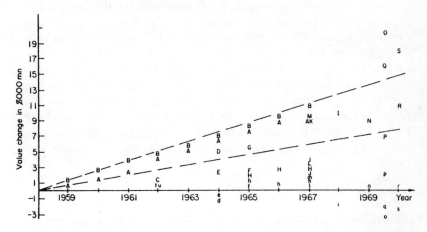

Furthermore it is also clear that the effects on trade flows are by
no means simple. Models seeking to isolate 'static' effects rarely do
so. Changes in trade flows will occur not only as a result of the
exploitation of comparative advantage when international discrimination is reduced or altered and from changes in the terms of
trade, but also from derived effects on variables such as business
efficiency, the exploitation of economies of scale, the abolition of
non-tariff barriers, international standardisation and changes in
the rate of economic growth. These derived or feedback effects
may far outweigh the simply static effects and for our estimates to
have any real meaning they must be included. Since integration
occurs over a period of time any ex post estimation is bound to
include an amalgam of the two types of effects, so any attempted
division between them is likely to be extremely difficult. It is clear
therefore that there is ample scope for further research.

We have expressed throughout a preference for an analytic
approach to the problem, not so much because of the substantial
problems in estimating a hypothetical anti-monde but because of
the unattractive nature of the estimation of an effect such as that
which cannot be explained by the model. There will always be an
unexplained residual in any stochastic model of economic
behaviour and it is therefore inevitable that the residual imputed
to the effect of integration will also include residuals due to other
unknown influences. It is intellectually far more satisfactory to be

22   DAVID G. MAYES

able to explain the effect of integration rather than to explain
everything else instead. We have shown that it appears to be
possible to estimate satisfactory price effects, but that the
estimation is complicated by problems such as the inequality of
price and tariff changes, the tendency of price to act as a proxy for
other effects and the poor determination of equations as the model
distinguishes between a larger number of different countries of
origin of imports. However, analysis has not progressed far
beyond price, because we become involved with the dynamic
effects beyond this point, but also because income is not taken
fully into account. What is clear from Figure 1 and elsewhere is
that the 'residual' models show that there is much more of the
effects of economic integration for the 'analytic' models yet to
explain.

TABLE VII

The effects of the enlargement of the EEC on the imports of manufactured goods (SITC 5–8)

Importing country	Trade creation			Trade diversion		
	(1)	(2)	(3)	(1)[1]	(2)	(3)[2]
Belgium-Luxemburg	52	68	—	—	58	—
France	39	126	—	152	104	—
Germany	273	314	—	236	249	—
Italy	124	97	—	34	77	—
Netherlands	58	134	—	15	111	—
TOTAL EEC	546	739	2,187	438	599	2,727
Austria	78	—		—	—	
Denmark	0	27	} 1,661[3]	48	51	} 698[3]
Norway	74	56		—	38	
Sweden	24	87		—	113	
United Kingdom	346	406	1,058	45	109	1,501
TOTAL EFTA	523	576	2,719	94	311	2,199
TOTAL	1,069	1,316[4]	4,906	531	910	4,926

[1] From rest of world only.
[2] These figures are derived and may underestimate trade diversion as calculated by
   Kreinin through aggregation.
[3] Continental EFTA + Eire.
[4] Does not sum through rounding error.

(1) Resnick and Truman (1974, p. 86), $ mn 1968.
(2) Mayes (1971, Ch. 6, p. 29), $ mn 1972 (estimated).
(3) Kreinin (1973, p. 95), $ mn 1970.

EFFECTS OF ECONOMIC INTEGRATION ON TRADE 23

In order to end on a speculative note and to keep as many issues as possible open we can look ahead to the assessment of the effects of the enlargement of the EEC to include Denmark, Eire and the United Kingdom together with the free trade arrangements between the EEC and the rest of EFTA. The integration began in 1973 and Table 7 gives three ex-ante predictions on the likely effects on the imports of the participating countries. All three models are analytic and measure the static effects alone, although a medium term estimate for the years 1981/2 is given by Mayes (1971, Ch. 7, p. 34) incorporating some dynamic effects. All these results should be testable in the light of experience over the next few years by ex-post methods. Resnick and Truman (1974) and Kreinin (1973) do not quote the years by which these effects can be expected to be observed, but provided the existing schedules of integration are followed I suggested (1971, Ch. 6, p. 29) that the results are for the years 1977/8. It will be interesting to see how wrong they are proved to be.

REFERENCES

Adams, F. G., Eguchi, H. and Meyer-Zu-Schlochtern, F. (1969) 'An Econometric Analysis of Trade: An interrelated explanation of imports and exports of OECD countries', Paris: *OECD* (Jan.).

Aitken, N. D. (1973) 'The Effect of the EEC and EFTA on European Trade: A Temporal Cross-Section Analysis', *American Economic Review*, (Dec.), Vol. LXIII No. 5.

Aitken, N. D. and Lowry, W. R. (1973) 'A Cross-Sectional Study of the Effects of LAFTA and CACM on Latin American Trade', *Journal of Common Market Studies*, (June) 11(4), pp. 326–36.

Armington, P. S. (1970) 'Adjustment of Trade Balances: Some Experiments with a Model of Trade among many Countries', *IMF Staff Papers* 17, pp. 488–523.

Balassa, B. (1961) *The Theory of Economic Integration*, London: Allen and Unwin.

Balassa, B. ed., (1967a) *Studies in Trade Liberalisation*, Baltimore: Johns Hopkins.

Balassa, B, (1967b) 'Trade Creation and Trade Diversion in the European Common Market', *Economic Journal* (March).

Balassa, B. (1967c) *Trade Liberalisation among Industrial Countries—Objectives and Alternatives*, New York: McGraw-Hill.

Balassa, B. (1974) 'Trade Creation and Trade Diversion in the European Common Market: An Appraisal of the Evidence', *Manchester Sch. Econ. Soc. Stud.*, (June), 42(2) pp. 99–135.

Balassa, B. and Kreinin, M. E. (1967) 'Trade Liberalisation under the Kennedy Round: the Static Effects', *Review of Economics and Statistics*, (May), Vol. XLIX No. 2.

Ball, R. J. and Marwah, K., (1962) 'The US Demand for Imports, 1948–58', *Review of Economics and Statistics* (Nov.).

Barker, T. S. and Lecomber, R., (1967) 'British Imports, 1972', University of Cambridge Department of Applied Economics, Report to National Ports Council, (Aug.).

Baron, C. G., (1968) 'A Multiproportional Growth Model for International Trade Flows', M.Sc. thesis, University of Bristol.

Barten, A. P., (1970) 'Maximum Likelihood Estimation of a Complete System of Demand Equations', *European Economic Review*, 1 (1).

24   DAVID G. MAYES

Bluet, J. C. and *Systermanns*, Y. *(1968)* 'Modèle gravitationnel d'échanges internationaux de produits manufacturés', *Bulletin du CEPREMAP*, (Jan.) Vol. 1 (new series).

Bond, D. E. and Wonnacott, R. J. (1968) *Trade Liberalisation and the Canadian Furniture Industry*, Toronto: University of Toronto Press for the Private Planning Association of Canada, No. 6 'Canada in the Atlantic Economy'.

Cambridge, Department of Applied Economics (Stone, J. R. N. and Brown, J. A. C.) (1963) 'Input-Output Relationships', London: Chapman and Hall, No. 3 in *A Programme for Growth*.

Carney, M. K. *(1970)*, 'Developments in Trading Patterns in the Common Market and EFTA', *Journal of the American Statistical Association*, (Dec.) 65 pp. 1455-59.

Clavaux, F. J. (1969) 'The Import Elasticity as a Yardstick for Measuring Trade Creation', *Economia Internazionale*, (Nov.).

Duquesne de la Vinelle, J. (1965) 'La Création du Commerce Attributable au Marché Commun et Son Incidence sur la Volume du Produit National de la Communauté', *Informations Statistiques*, EEC, Brussels, No. 4.

EFTA Secretariat (1968) *The Effects on Prices of Tariff Dismantling in EFTA*, Geneva.

EFTA Secretariat (1969) *The Effects of EFTA on the Economies of Member States*, Geneva. Jan.

EFTA Secretariat (1972) *The Trade Effects of EFTA and the EEC, 1959-1967*, Geneva. June.

Han, S. S. and Liesner, H. H. (1971) 'Britain and the Common Market', Cambridge: Cambridge University Press—Cambridge University Department of Applied Economics Occasional Papers, 27.

Haviland, W. E., Takacsy, N. S. and Cape, E. M. (1968) *Trade Liberalisation and the Canadian Pulp and Paper Industry*, Toronto: University of Toronto Press for the Private Planning Association of Canada, No. 5 in 'Canada in the Atlantic Economy'.

Houthakker, H. S. and Magee, S. P. (1969) 'Income and Price Elasticities in World Trade', *Review of Economics and Statistics*, Vol. LI, No. 2 (May).

Kaldor, N. (1971) 'The Dynamic Effects of the Common Market' in Evans, D. ed. *Destiny or Delusion: Britain and the Common Market*, London: Victor Gollanz.

Kouevi, A. F. (1965) 'Essai d'application prospective de la methode RAS au commerce international', *Bulletin du CEPREL*, No. 5 (Oct).

Krause, L. B. (1962) 'US Imports, 1947-58', *Econometrica*, (April).

Krause, L. B. (1968) *European Economic Integration and the United States*, Washington: Brookings Institution.

Krauss, M. B. (1972) 'Recent Developments in Customs Union Theory: An Interpretive Survey', *Journal of Economic Literature*, (June), Vol. X, No. 2.

Krauss, M. B., ed. (1973) *The Economics of Integration*, London: George Allen and Unwin.

Kreinin, M. E. (1961) 'The Effects of Tariff Changes on the Prices and Volumes of Imports', *American Economic Review*.

Kreinin, M. E. (1967) 'Trade Arrangements Among Industrial Countries: Effects on the US', in Balassa (1967).

Kreinin, M. E. (1969) 'Trade Creation and Diversion by the EEC and EFTA', *Economia Internazionale*, (May), Vol. XXII No. 2.

Kreinin, M. E. (1972) 'Effects of the EEC on Imports of Manufactures', *Economic Journal* (Sept).

Kreinin, M. E. (1973) 'The Static Effects of EEC Enlargement on Trade Flows', *Southern Economic Journal* (April), 39(4) pp. 559-68.

Lamfalussy, A. (1963) 'Intra-European Trade and the Competitive Position of the EEC', *Manchester Statistical Society*, 13th March, 1963.

Linnemann, H. (1966) *An Econometric Study of International Trade Flows*, Amsterdam: North Holland.

Lipsey, R. G. (1957) 'The Theory of Customs Unions: Trade Diversion and Welfare', *Economica*, Vol. 24.

EFFECTS OF ECONOMIC INTEGRATION ON TRADE 25

Major, R. L. and Hays, S. (1970) 'Another Look at the Common Market', *National Institute Economic Review* (Nov.).

Maxwell Stamp Associates (1967) *The Free Trade Area Option*, London: The Atlantic Trade Study.

Mayes, D. G. (1971) 'The Effects of Alternative Trade Groupings on the United Kingdom', PhD thesis, University of Bristol.

Mayes, D. G. (1974) 'RASAT, A Model for the Estimation of Commodity Trade Flows in EFTA', *European Economic Review*, Vol. 5, pp. 207–221.

Mayes, D. G. (1976) 'The Estimation of the Effects of Trading Areas on Trade', mimeo, University of Exeter.

Orcutt, G. H. (1950) 'Measurement of Price Elasticities in International Trade', *Review of Economics and Statistics*, (May).

Poyhonen, P. (1963) 'Towards a General Theory of International Trade', *Ek. Samf. Tidskrift*, No. 2.

Prewo, W. E. (1974) 'Integration Effects in the EEC: An Attempt at Quantification in a General Equilibrium Framework', *European Economic Review*, (3).

Pulliainen, K. (1963) 'A World Trade Study: An Econometric Model of the Pattern of the Commodity Flows in International Trade, 1948–60', *Ek. Samf. Tidskrift*, No. 2.

Resnick, S. A. and Truman, E. M. (1973) 'An Empirical Examination of Bilateral Trade in Western Europe', *Journal of International Economics*, Vol. 3, pp. 305–35.

Resnick, S. A. and Truman, E. M. (1974) 'The Distribution of West European Trade under Alternative Tariff Policies', *Review of Economics and Statistics*, No. 1. 56 pp. 83–91.

Robson, P., ed. (1972) *International Economic Integration*, Harmondsworth: Penguin.

Savage, I. R. and Deutsch, K. W. (1960) 'A Statistical Model of the Gross Analysis of Transaction Flows', *Econometrica* (July) 28, pp. 551–72.

Sellekaerts, W. (1973) 'How Meaningful are Empirical Studies on Trade Creation and Diversion?', *Weltwirtschaftliches Archiv*, (Dec.) 109 (4) pp. 519–53.

Singer, J. (1969) 'Trade Liberalisation and the Canadian Steel Industry', Toronto: University of Toronto Press for the Private Planning Association of Canada.

Tinbergen, J. (1962) *Shaping the World Economy*, New York: Twentieth Century Fund.

Truman, E. M. (1969) 'The European Economic Community: Trade Creation and Trade Diversion', *Yale Economic Essays*, Spring.

Truman, E. M. (1972) 'The Production and Trade of Manufactured Products in the EEC and EFTA: A Comparison', *European Economic Review*, Vol. 3, pp. 271–90.

Verdoorn, P. J. and Schwartz, A. N. R. (1972) 'Two Alternative Estimates of the Effects of EEC and EFTA on the Pattern of Trade', *European Economic Review*, 3, pp. 291–335.

Waelbroeck, J. (1964) 'Une nouvelle methode d'analyse des matrices d'échanges internationaux', *Cahiers Economiques de Bruxelles*, 21, I.

Walter, I. (1967) *The European Common Market: Growth and Patterns of Trade and Production*, New York: Praeger.

Wemelsfelder, J. (1960) 'The short term effect of lowering import duties in Germany', *Economic Journal* (March).

Williamson, J. (1971) 'On Estimating the Income Effects of British Entry to the EEC', Warwick: *Survey Papers in Economics*, No. 5 (June).

Williamson, J. and Bottrill, A. (1971) 'The Impact of Customs Unions on Trade in Manufactures', *Oxford Economic Papers* (Nov.), 23(3).

Wonnacott, R. J. and Wonnacott, P. (1967) *Free Trade between the U.S. and Canada: The Potential Economic Effects*, Cambridge (Mass.): Harvard University Press.

[12]

ASSOCIATION WITH THE EEC: ECONOMIC ASPECTS OF THE TRADE RELATIONSHIP

By Charles Young

I. INTRODUCTION

1. The accession of the UK to the European Communities means that the system of Commonwealth Preference will be brought to an end by 1975. As a replacement for the advantages and preferences which they previously derived from Commonwealth Preference, the independent Commonwealth countries[1] in Africa, the Caribbean, the Pacific and the Indian Ocean have been offered a choice of three formulae for regulating their relationship with the enlarged Community. The first formula is to take part in the re-negotiation of the Yaounde Convention which links the 18 Francophone African States[2]—the Associated African States and Madagascar, or AASM—with the EEC. The present, second Yaounde Convention expires early in 1975, and re-negotiation will commence in mid-1973. The second option is a more limited agreement offering reciprocal trade advantages, based on the existing Arusha Agreement which links the East African Community to the EEC. The third option is a straightforward, presumably non-preferential, trade agreement.

2. This paper attempts to clarify some of the issues relevant to the choice which the 20 Commonwealth countries concerned—the 'Commonwealth Associables'—will have to make. It is limited, however, to the trade relationship and does not discuss the other implications of association, namely aid from the European Development Fund,[3] institutional links with the EEC and the political implications[4] of

[1] The countries concerned are Barbados, Botswana, Fiji, the Gambia, Guyana, Jamaica, Kenya, Lesotho, Malawi, Mauritius, Nigeria, Sierra Leone, Swaziland, Tanzania, Tonga, Trinidad, Tobago, Uganda, Western Samoa and Zambia.

[2] Burundi, Cameroon, Central African Republic, Chad, Congo, Dahomey, Gabon, Ivory Coast, Madagascar, Mali, Mauritania, Niger, Rwanda, Senegal, Somalia, Togo, Upper Volta and Zaire.

[3] The current EDF provides an average of about £1 per head per annum, mainly as grants, to the AASM; the amounts received by the smaller states are proportionately much higher.

[4] The European Commission's document on a Community Development Policy specifically makes the point that 'association is in the first place a political option which aims at the maintenance and development of privileged relationships of every kind between Europe and Africa; the AASM say they have deliberately preferred the Community as the first foreign partner in their development', p. 11.

ASSOCIATION WITH THE EEC

association. The paper deals first and foremost with the results of the trade provisions of the Yaounde Convention: the Arusha Agreement has broadly similar trade provisions, but has not been in operation long enough to draw empirical conclusions. When the trade provisions of Yaounde and Arusha differ, this is clearly indicated in the paper. It must be borne in mind, though, that the trade and other provisions of the next Yaounde Convention may emerge as different from those of the present one. While an assessment of the effects of past Yaounde Conventions is very relevant, there is no intention of implying that the effects of the next Convention will necessarily be the same.

3. In section II of the paper the rather complicated 'free-trade' regulations in the Yaounde Convention and Arusha Agreement are set out and explained; their implications for various products of interest to Associables and Associates are drawn out; the general positions taken up in advance of the Yaounde III negotiations by the AASM and the Commission are roughly sketched; and finally the provisions relating to reverse preferences are set out. Next, in section III the theoretical background for attempting to analyse the economic effects of these preferential arrangements is rather crudely explained. Finally, in section IV an empirical analysis of the results of the Yaounde Convention is attempted. This is split into two sections, one dealing with the direct preferences accorded to Associates in the EEC market, and one dealing with the reverse preferences accorded by Associates to EEC exports. In both cases we are concerned primarily with the costs and benefits *to Associates* and not the costs and benefits to the EEC. A short concluding section summarises the main findings.

II. PREFERENCES EMBODIED IN THE YAOUNDE AND ARUSHA AGREEMENTS: PRINCIPLES AND PRACTICE

4. The provisions in the Yaounde Convention by virtue of which Associates receive preferential treatment in the EEC market are fairly straightforward. The Yaounde Convention assures Associates duty-free and quota-free entry to the EEC market for all goods other than petroleum products and those covered by the Common Agricultural Policy. The goods covered by the Common Agricultural Policy (CAP) are both those actually produced within the EEC, such as sugar and tobacco, and 'homologous' goods whose unrestricted entry would cause difficulty in marketing EEC produce. These latter include oilseeds, but do not as yet include bananas or tinned pineapples. The free trade provisions are qualified in general by Article 16, which states that 'if serious disturbances occur in a sector of the economy of the Community or of one or more of its member states, or jeopardise their

external financial stability, or if difficulties arise which result in a deterioration in the economic situation of a region in the Community, the latter may take the necessary protective measures'. This safeguard clause has not been invoked as yet, but might be if there were a large increase in exports of manufactured goods from Associates to the EEC, causing unwanted trade creation.

5. On goods covered by the CAP, the Community has been prepared to grant preferential access to the Associates under various agreements and regulations separate from the Yaounde Convention itself; these are essentially trade-diverting arrangements which are not allowed to constitute a threat to EEC production, but which give the Associates a head start in competing for whatever residual market there is in the Community once local production has been sold. The tool for ensuring protection for EEC production is the levy, in effect a variable tariff adjusted to whatever height is necessary to ensure that no imports have access to the market unless Community production is insufficient to meet demand. Associates are granted either a reduction on the levy payable, or waiver of the tariff, or percentage reductions in the tariff.

6. The EEC preferences to Associates thus come under two headings: those resulting from the free-trade provisions of the Yaounde Convention itself, and those embodied in the various separate agreements on products covered by the CAP which have as their basis Protocol No. 1 of the Yaounde Convention, stating that 'the treatment which the Community applies to these products shall be more favourable than the general treatment applied to like products originating in third countries.'

The rate of preference on the first category of products is of course equal to the Common External Tariff, which is shown below (see Table I) for some major products of interest to Associates and Associables.

7. In the second category, special arrangements exist for each of the various commodities which are of interest to Associates. For oilseeds and edible oils, regulation 518 of 1970 assures Associates of unrestricted duty-free and levy-free entry, subject to the proviso that if the volume of imports of these commodities originating in the Associates changes appreciably, the Community may introduce special measures to deal with the situation. Associates thus receive preference equal to the CET, which is 10 per cent on crude oil and 15 per cent on refined oil (but 9 per cent for palm oil). There is no duty for groundnuts themselves, though the Community may under certain conditions impose charges. On rice, they benefit from a reduction of the levy by about 45 per cent. They also receive duty-free entry for tobacco, for most of which the CET is 23 per cent. They have no preferential treatment on citrus, but this is probably because they have no interest in the crop and have not requested the preferential treatment accorded to countries of the Medi-

ASSOCIATION WITH THE EEC   123

TABLE I

Product	CET
Bananas (duty-free quota for Germany)	20%
Coffee, roasted or ground	15%
Coffee, other	7%
Cocoa	4%
Bauxite	Nil
Alumina	5%
Copper (wirebars)	Nil
Copper (wrought shapes, wire)	8%
Tea	Nil (9% suspended tariff)
Cotton	Nil
Cotton fabrics	13–15%
Clothing (outer and under garments)	17%
Canned pineapples	32%
Lead, zinc (unwrought)	$13.2 per tonne

terranean and the Maghreb. They do not at present export sugar to the EEC, as a result of increased EEC production and higher consumption within the Associates themselves.

8. Arusha Associates enjoy substantially the same access as Yaounde Associates, with the exception of commodities which the Yaounde Associates are sensitive about. On the three commodities exported by East Africa to the Community in competition with the AASM—coffee, cloves and canned pineapple—the East Africans were accorded duty-free quotas. Once the quota is filled, re-imposition of the duty is not automatic, but at the discretion of the EEC. In 1971 the quota for tinned pineapples was substantially exceeded, and the AASM were successful in persuading the EEC to reimpose the duty.

9. Apart from the preferences accorded to Associates and to some Mediterranean countries by the EEC, there are also some precedents for preferential treatment in the context of 'non-preferential' trade agreements. These precedents, which relate to beef from Yugoslavia and possibly Argentina, may be of some interest to non-Associables when they negotiate 'non-preferential' trade agreements with the EEC. They also embody a technique for having a preferential trade agreement without violating the most-favoured-nation principle in GATT. Thus the Yugoslavian agreement brought about a new, lower, rate of duty for a particular newly-defined product. This does not violate the most-

favoured-nation clause because the rate applies to any country able to export the product. The product itself however is 'beef having a Yugoslavian certificate of origin.'

10. These are the regulations existing at present for trade between the Associates and the EEC; but there are signs of incipient pressure from the AASM to reinforce their tariff protection by other methods. They welcome the entry of the UK into the EEC because they feel that the Commonwealth Sugar Agreement is an example and a precedent for the type of commodity agreement which they would welcome for a whole range of products—particularly groundnuts, cocoa and cotton.

11. The EEC's reaction to proposals of this nature has not yet been formulated in detail. On sugar they plan to 'accede to the International Sugar Agreement by pursuing an internal policy that will gradually reduce its (the EEC's) structural surpluses' (Commission memorandum on a policy for development co-operation, p. 32). This will in fact come about in any case as a result of enlargement. 'Under the International Coffee Agreement the Community should participate in a long-term action, for instance measures concerning production which are written into the agreement but on which a start has scarcely been made. For other products (cocoa, tea, oleaginous products, jute) the Community should renew its activity and take fresh steps where necessary. If it should prove impossible to conclude world agreements, or if the conclusions of such agreements were to suffer delays detrimental to the developing countries, or again if for a given product a world agreement were not justified, the Community could envisage—whether for all developing countries or a region—the possibility of applying temporarily, as either an independent or concerted action, the intended provisions of the world agreements. Alternatively it could in accordance with the priorities arising from its commitments, seek ad hoc solutions to which further developing countries could accede' (ibid).

12. This needs rather careful interpretation. The final sentence fairly clearly refers to agreements in the first instance with Associates or favoured Mediterranean countries (this must be the meaning of "in accordance with the priorities arising from its commitments'). Such an agreement would however be open-ended and provide access to other developing countries; the Community would not appear to favour discriminatory agreements which necessarily exclude non-Associates. The previous sentence does envisage the possibility of regional agreements from which non-Associates might be excluded—but only if these agreements applied 'the intended provisions of world agreements'. What seems to be ruled out here is an agreement which does not apply the intended provisions of a world agreement and from which non-Associates would be excluded; and this is broadly what the AASM

ASSOCIATION WITH THE EEC 125

want. The document cited however represents the view of the Commission, and has yet to be approved by the Council of Ministers.

13. It is certainly too early to be confident about the likelihood of discriminatory organised markets. But the evolution of the trade relationship between the EEC and the Associates has on the whole been away from special arrangements for Associates' exports and the quotation above does not seem to represent a reversal of this trend.

14. Turning now to the provisions relating to reverse preferences one encounters a considerably more complicated situation. In principle, the Yaounde Convention sets up a series of separate free trade areas between the EEC and each of the 18 AASM. Article 3.1 of the Convention states that 'products originating in the Community shall be imported into each Associated State free of customs duties and charges having equivalent effect'; and Article 7.1 states that 'subject to the provisions of this Article, the Associated States shall not apply any quantitative restrictions or measures having equivalent effect to the importation of products originating in Member States' (i.e. of the Community). However these clauses are hedged around with so many qualifications as to be without real force. Thus Article 3.2 states that 'each Associated State may, however, retain or introduce ... customs duties ... which are necessary to meet their development needs or which are intended to contribute to their budgets', and under Article 7.2 they may 'retain or introduce ... quantitative restrictions ... in order to meet their development needs or in the event of difficulties in their balance of payments.' One could hardly wish for more permissive escape clauses. The concept of 'development needs' and the conditions under which restrictions on imports from the EEC are permissible are set out in rather more detail in Protocol 2 of the Convention; basically it can be said that the only restriction on the Associates as regards their import regulations is a clause permitting the EEC to institute consultations in the Association Council on the way in which the Protocol is applied.

15. Associates are therefore permitted to impose import duties (and charges having equivalent effect such as 'fiscal entry' charges) on EEC goods. Furthermore there is no stipulation in the Convention that these import duties must be lower than those imposed on goods imported from third countries. Article II states that 'without prejudice to the special provisions for border trade or to Articles 12 and 13' (which allow Associates to set up and maintain regional integration schemes among themselves and with other African countries with similar economic structures) 'the treatment that Associated States apply by virtue of this Title to products originating in the Community shall not be less favourable than that applied to products originating in the most

favoured third country'; but this is of course quite compatible with a single-column non-preferential tariff.

16. There is thus nothing in the Convention calling specifically for the application of reverse preferences by the Associates; a refusal to grant preferential treatment to EEC exports is quite compatible with the letter of Convention. Protocol 2 of the Convention, which regulates the application of Article 3 stipulates that 'each Associated State shall, within a period of three months from the entry into force of this Convention, communicate to the Association Council its customs tariff or the complete list of customs duties and charges having equivalent effect which it imposes on products originating in the Community and in third countries. In this communication, each Associated State shall specify those duties . . . which remain applicable to products originating in the Community by virtue of . . . Article 3.2 . . . At the request of the Community there shall be consultations on the customs tariffs.' In principle the EEC might be able to object to a single-column tariff under this heading, but there have been indications from the Commission that states which wish, like Zaire and Togo do at present, to combine Association with non-discriminatory tariffs may not encounter difficulties in doing so.[5]

17. The Arusha Agreement between the East African Community and the EEC, which is the model for the second option open to Associables, has basically the same provisions relating to reverse preferences, but differs in the contents of the Protocol regulating the application of Article 3. This Protocol (No 3) has an Annex listing the 59 products on which East Africa accords preferential treatment to the EEC, and Article 6.1 of the Protocol states that 'the advantages accorded to Member States *vis-à-vis* third countries in respect of the products listed in the Schedule annexed to this Protocol shall not be reduced during the life of this agreement'. The Yaounde Convention imposes no such specific obligation on its signatories, and neither the Yaounde nor the Arusha Conventions imposes a similar obligation on the EEC (i.e. not to reduce the advantages accorded to Associates). Reverse preferences are thus 'written in' to this option more specifically than with the Yaounde Convention.

18. So much for the rather complex formal provisions relating to reverse preferences; it may now be useful to outline how they are at present applied in practice. Broadly speaking, one may distinguish

---

[5] The latest unofficial 'prise de position' by a Commission official was that Associates should initially provide some preferences to the EEC, but there would be no objection to them subsequently, *in the course of negotiations*, according the same 'preferences' to any—or presumably all—other countries. 'But there must be negotiations.' To the writer this seems a very curious position, explicable perhaps only in terms of the Commission's revealed preference for trade negotiations for their own sake.

ASSOCIATION WITH THE EEC 127

three groups of countries among the AASM in so far as reverse preferences are concerned. The 13 ex-French States (excluding Togo) accord fairly wide margins of preference to EEC products on quite a large range of goods—estimated at 12 per cent of the value of the product on nine-tenths of dutiable imports. Three other Associates—Burundi, Rwanda and Somalia—originally had non-discriminatory tariffs, but now grant limited preference margins on a wide range of goods. Finally, as mentioned above, Zaire and Togo have non-discriminatory tariff systems. Arusha Associates grant fairly limited preference on 59 products representing about 15 per cent of East African imports from the EEC.

III. ECONOMIC RESULTS OF THE EXCHANGE OF PREFERENCES

19. The same concepts can be used for analysing the static effects of a reciprocal exchange of preferences as for studying other, closer forms of regional integration. The fundamental concepts are of course those of trade creation and trade diversion.[6] The points to be borne in mind are that in static terms, trade creation will benefit everybody and trade diversion will harm everybody; in dynamic terms, trade creation will cause difficulties for the industries which are obliged to contract to make way for imports, while trade diversion will have a positive dynamic impact on the countries to which the trade is diverted (i.e. the countries which become the new sources of supply) and a negative dynamic impact on the countries away from which it is diverted. When one of the partners is a less developed country suffering from widespread unemployment, the dynamic disadvantages of trade creation can outweigh the static considerations, and there is consequently a case for permitting LDCs to be more protectionist than countries with full employment (the infant-industry argument).

20. It is for this reason that, as we have seen, the Yaounde Convention permits Associates to impose non-discriminatory charges on all imports, including those from the EEC and, when necessary, to reinforce these with import quotas. In other words, no trade creation takes place as a result of reverse preferences, lest the dynamic and distributional losses might outweigh the static gains. Their sole result, if any, is to divert trade away from third countries and in favour of EEC exporters. We shall consider later whether there is evidence that this has happened. To

[6] Trade creation is said to occur when country A runs down those industries which produce at a higher (comparative) cost than country B and expands those industries which produce at a lower (comparative) cost. Country A will import more of the former and export more of the latter. Trade diversion occurs when country A replaces a low cost source of supply from country C by a higher cost source in country B (which is a possible outcome of regional integration between country A and country B). Briefly trade creation is a change from a high-cost to a low-cost source of supply; trade diversion is a change in the opposite direction.

the extent that it does, reverse preferences impose a cost on LDCs, the amount of which can be computed as equal to the value of trade diverted multiplied by the percentage by which the new suppliers' prices exceed the cheapest suppliers' prices.

21. Turning from reverse preferences to direct preferences, the effect will be beneficial if direct preferences lead to trade creation. If they lead to trade diversion, there would I think be general agreement that the outcome is beneficial in so far as trade is directed from developed countries to LDCs. (Such an agreement forms the basis of the generalized preferences schemes that have been introduced by most OECD countries other than the USA and Canada over the last couple of years.) If trade is diverted from some LDCs to other LDCs the outcome is probably not desirable, though one might be able to make out some sort of a case for diverting trade to the countries that have been identified as 'least-developed'.

22. The value of direct preference for a homogeneous commodity marketed under competitive conditions is simply equal to the value of exports of the commodity times the preference margin. If we discard the assumption that marketing is competitive or that the preference recipients are a small proportion of total supply, the value of the preference will be much harder to calculate, but will in any case be smaller.

23. Basing our arguments on these considerations, let us now attempt to calculate very roughly the net value to the Associates of the trade provisions of the Yaounde Convention. We start with reverse preferences and our first task is to estimate whether they have led to trade diversion, and if so how much. The method will be an analysis of the evolution of trade shares.

24. The level of exports from any one country to any other can be held to depend on the following three factors:

(a) the overall level of effective demand for imports in the importing country
(b) the ability of the exporting country to produce at a competitive price the goods demanded by the importing country
(c) the existence of any special privileges favouring or disfavouring the exporting country. These fall into two categories:
  (i) Tariff preferences and discriminatory quota arrangements. These we may loosely call 'formal privileges'.
  (ii) Institutional ties, acquired tastes, better knowledge of particular countries' products, better trade channels and marketing arrangements favouring certain countries, linguistic and cultural factors. There may be heaped together under the heading of 'informal privileges'.

25. The task is to identify and quantify the specific effects of (c)(i). The method which suggests itself is to compare the trading performance of four groups of countries over the period since formal privileges were granted. On the exporting side, we have those countries receiving the

ASSOCIATION WITH THE EEC   129

formal privileges and those who did not; on the importing side we have
the countries extending the formal privileges and those who did not.
The rates of growth of trade may be set out in the following table,
where I_1 and I_2 represent respectively those importing countries which
did, and which did not, extend formal privileges, and X_1 and X_2
represent those exporters which did and which did not receive the
privileges; and r_{ij} represents the rate of growth of exports from
country i to country j.

	I_1	I_2
X_1	r_{11}	r_{12}
X_2	r_{21}	r_{22}

26. The problem is to identify the factors influencing r_{11}, the rate of
growth of trade within the preferential zone. A high rate of growth
may have been due to factor (a) above—a high rate of growth of
overall imports into I_1. To allow for this factor, we consider, not r_{11} in
isolation, but its relation to the growth of imports from other sources,
r_{21}. The ratio r_{11}/r_{12} indicates whether I_1 has increased its share of imports from within the preferential zone; this is the case if the ratio is
greater than one. This alone is sometimes erroneously cited as evidence
for the effectiveness of formal privileges. However it is clear that changes
in the ratio r_{11}/r_{21} may equally well be due to factor (b)—a change in
the relative ability of X_1 to supply the required goods competitively.
Now the ratio r_{12}/r_{22} provides an indication of the change in the overall
competitiveness of X_1 in relation to X_2. If this is the sole influence on
the ratio r_{11}/r_{21}, one would expect the equation

$$r_{11}/r_{21} = r_{12}/r_{12} \dots\dots\dots\dots(1)$$

to hold. This may also be written as

$$r_{11}r_{22}/r_{12}r_{21} = 1 \dots\dots\dots\dots(2)$$

27. If the left-hand-side of equation (1) is greater than the right-hand
side, this is evidence that r_{11} is greater than would be expected on the
basis of factors (a) and (b) alone; it would appear that there has been
a change in the way in which factor (c) influenced trade. It might be
that factor (c) had disadvantaged the X_1 countries in the markets of the
I_2 countries; but unless there is some evidence for this one may conclude that factor (c) has worked to their advantage in the I_1 countries.

28. This provides a heuristic way of identifying whether there has
been a change in the way in which factor (c) works to the benefit of
particular countries. But it will be recalled that it is specifically changes
due to factor (c)(i) which have to be identified. The best that can be
done is to exclude from the analysis any countries in the X_1 group for

D

which there is evidence of some change in the benefits due to factor (c)(ii). One would normally expect factor (c)(ii) to change very little in the short-run, but the sharp discontinuity and fundamental change in institutional links brought about by de-colonisation must reduce the 'informal privileges' accorded to both partners. It is for this reason that trade between ex-colonies and their ex-metropolitan countries will be excluded from the analysis.

29. Provided these points are taken into account, the fact that the left-hand-side of equation (1) is greater than the right-hand-side is fairly strong evidence for the effectiveness of 'formal privileges'. To estimate the amount of trade diverted by 'formal privileges' is a more speculative matter, particularly when much of the trade is with countries with past colonial links. One can calculate from either of the above equations what r_{11} and r_{21} would have been if the equality had held and given also that the overall rate of growth must be unchanged. This can give an indication of what the level of imports from the X_1 countries would have been without formal preferences.

EEC Exports to Associates

30. We now bring these considerations to bear on the evolution of exports from the EEC to the Associates; Tables II, III and IV show the levels in 1959 and 1969 and the rates of growth. The EEC (5) refers to the countries other than France; the other main metropolitan country, Belgium, is included since its three ex-colonies, Rwanda, Burundi and Zaire have been excluded from the Associates' figures in view of the fact that none of them applied reverse preferences during the period under consideration. (Separate figures for Togo and Somalia, the other two countries not then granting reverse preferences, are not available.)

31. Using the ratio described above, one arrives at the figure 1·45 (15·7/10·1 divided by 7·4/6·9). In other words there is a strong indication that special factors favoured the growth of exports from the EEC to the countries granting reverse preferences. Three special factors

TABLE II

1959 TRADE (UNIT $m.)

	Importers	
Exporters	AASM (15)	Other LDCs
EEC(6)	435	5,612
EEC(5)	61	3,694
Other OECD	76	13,534

TABLE III

1969 TRADE (UNIT: $m.)

	Importers	
Exporters	AASM(15)	Other LDCs
EEC(6)	888	10,095
EEC(5)	263	7,499
Other OECD	199	26,279

TABLE IV

AVERAGE ANNUAL TRADE GROWTH (%)

	Importers	
Exporters	AASM(15)	Other LDCs
EEC(6)	7.4	6·0
EEC(5)	15·7	7·4
Other OECD	10·1	6·9

can be identified; reverse preferences, procurement from the EDF, and the extension to the other members of the EEC of the quota privileges previously accorded only to France. Procurement from the EDF cannot by itself have accounted for all of the extra growth in exports from the EEC(5) to the AASM; even if all procurement had gone to the Five, and none to France or the AASM (which was far from being the case) the ratio would still have been greater than one. There does not seem to be any way of deciding which of the two forms of discrimination applied by the AASM—discrimination in quotas or in tariffs—was the more important. However there appears to be quite strong evidence that this discrimination did result in trade diversion.

32. How much trade was diverted in this way? One can calculate that for a given level of total imports by the Associates, a level of exports from the EEC(5) 21 per cent lower than that observed in 1969 would have caused our trade diversion ratio to be equal to unity. We assume that this measures the trade-diverting effect of the special privileges granted to the EEC as a whole, and that French exports would likewise have been lower by the same amount without reverse

preferences. This gives us an estimate of $190m. worth of trade so diverted.

33. For an estimate of the cost to Associates of this trade diversion, we would need to know by how much the price of goods so directed exceeded that of comparable goods from the cheapest source. This is of course virtually impossible, especially with heterogeneous manufactured goods. However the maximum extra cost is given by the average value of the preferences—12 per cent (if EEC prices were higher by more than an average of 12 per cent, the preferences would have been ineffectual). The maximum cost of reverse preferences to the Associates was thus equal to about $23m. or about 2 per cent of their total import bill.

34. It should be borne in mind that these calculations are based on the rather comprehensive discriminatory treatment accorded by the ex-French members of the AASM. The more limited discriminatory treatment offered by Rwanda, Burundi and Somalia, as well as the East African Community will have correspondingly smaller trade diverting effects and hence smaller costs. (Assessing the effects of the unimplemented agreement between Nigeria and the EEC, which quite closely resembled the Arusha Agreement, Bridget Bloom has estimated the value to the EEC of the small reciprocal concessions granted by Nigeria as 'probably somewhat in excess of the Community's expenditure on its negotiating team in Brussels', i.e. £175,000. The value of the EEC's concessions to Nigeria was estimated as 'hardly enough to cover the cost of sending the successive Nigerian delegations to Brussels —£50,000'. Quoted in I. W. Zartman, 'The Politics of Trade Negotiations between Africa and the EEC', p. 228. It must be borne in mind that the benefits to one partner are not necessarily equal to the costs to the other.)

35. In addition to the direct cost of reverse preferences, they may involve some additional indirect costs on account of possible retaliation by the non-EEC countries whose exports are discriminated against. For example, the U.S. has announced that countries which have not committed themselves to phase out reverse preferences by a definite date, probably 1975, will not be eligible to benefit from the U.S. generalised preference scheme. The importance of this cannot be assessed unless and until the U.S. GPS comes into operation.

Associates' Exports to the EEC

36. We now turn to an assessment of the effect of direct preferences. We can attack this in two ways; on the one hand we can apply a similar analysis to discover whether they were effective in diverting trade in favour of Associates, i.e. whether there were dynamic gains

for Associates, and on the other hand we can assess the static gains. We start with the trade flow statistics (Tables V, VI and VII) from the analysis of which the ex-metropolitan areas, France and the Belgian-Luxembourg Economic Union are excluded.

TABLE V

1959 TRADE (UNIT: $m.)

	Importers		
Exporters	*EEC(6)*	*EEC(3)*	*Other OECD*
AASM	853	191	228
Other LDCs	5,915	3,714	11,794

TABLE VI

1969 TRADE (UNIT: $m.)

	Importers		
Exporters	*EEC(6)*	*EEC(3)*	*Other OECD*
AASM	1,716	570	487
Other LDCs	13,069	8,972	20,962

TABLE VII

AVERAGE ANNUAL TRADE GROWTH(%)

	Importers		
Exporters	*EEC(6)*	*EEC(3)*	*Other OECD*
AASM	7·2	11·6	7·9
Other LDCs	8·2	9·2	5·9

37. Deriving the same ratio which was used to examine whether reverse preferences diverted trade, we reach a figure of 0·94. This is close to the expected value (unity), and suggests that there is no evidence that direct preferences were effective in diverting trade. (For the less relevant trade relation with the whole EEC the ratio is 0·7.) This difference in the effects of direct, and reverse preferences is, one supposes, largely a function of the different types of commodity involved—

homogeneous primary commodities seem to benefit less from preference than manufactured goods. In the latter case the lower duties are
likely to be passed on to the consumers as lower prices; in the former
case a competitive market will see to it that (when preference-receivers
are a small part of total supply) the reduction in duty means a higher
price for the producer.

38. Thus the absence of trade diversion does not mean that Associates did not gain from their preferential treatment; it will have enabled
them to get higher prices for their exports. The extent of this gain can
be computed as equal to the percentage of preference on each good
multiplied by the value of exports of that good. Table VIII indicates
the values by commodity. This covers the major dutiable exports of

TABLE VIII

Static gains from preference

Commodity	Exports (1969)$m.	CET(%)	Gain ($m.)
Cocoa	201·8	4	8·1
Coffee	163·4	7	11·4
Bananas	45·9	20	9·2
Tobacco	4·9	23	1·1
Palm oil	25·5	9	2·3
Other edible oils	51·3	10	5·1
Aluminium	23·3	9	2·1
Plywood, veneered sheets	114·7	13	1.9
Total	530·9		41·3

Associates to the EEC. (Other important non-dutiable exports such as
copper, wood in the rough, cotton, iron ore, oilseeds and oilcake,
petroleum and rubber make up the remainder; these plus the items
listed above account for over 90 per cent of AASM exports to the EEC.)
The gain from preferences works out at around 1·9 per cent of total
AASM exports. Preferential treatment on goods such as fish, preserved
fruit, rice and meat, which were exported to the EEC to a total value
of $27m, but on which it has not been possible to estimate the gain
from preference, may bring this figure up by half a per cent or so. On
the other hand the estimate might be somewhat reduced by abandoning the assumption that the countries receiving preference form a small
proportion of total supply, and the assumption that marketing is competitive. Clearly the decisive element in the calculation of gains from
preference as a proportion of total exports is the share of dutiable exports in total exports.

ASSOCIATION WITH THE EEC   135

CONCLUSIONS

39. The 'free-trade' provisions of the Yaounde Convention have caused no trade creation, but only a certain amount of trade diversion. That there has been no creation of trade from Africa to Europe is evidenced by the list of dutiable goods above, none of which can be produced within the EEC (with the exception of bananas produced in the French departments of Guadeloupe and Martinique, and of plywood). We may assume that there has been no trade creation from Europe to Africa in view of the wide scope Associates have for protecting their local industries. Direct preferences seem neither to have created nor diverted trade; reverse preferences seem to have diverted trade. Thus dynamic advantages have accrued only to the EEC, and not to the Associates (and, to be sure, the advantages accruing to the EEC from reverse preferences have been negligible in the context of the EEC's total trade).

40. The Associates have however derived some static advantages, probably equal to around 2 per cent of their exports, The costs of reverse preferences are virtually impossible to calculate, but at a maximum they may also have cost around 2 per cent of the import bill of those Associates granting reverse preferences. It is likely that in reality the costs were much lower than this. On balance, the net benefits to Associates in the field of trade have almost certainly been positive, but by no means large.

[13]

Agricultural Development and Agricultural Trade, 1945–1973*

Richard T. Griffiths**

Agricultural development and agricultural trade in Western Europe had, by 1945, long since ceased to be the outcome of free market forces. The agricultural sector had become almost the most regulated part of national economies, run virtually like giant national corporations. These determined the supply and demand parameters for domestic production and the conditions for any residual import requirements. Only for non-competitive (usually tropical) products were anything like unimpeded imports allowed, and then only when controls imposed for balance of payments reasons were relaxed. Most of intra-Western European trade was competitive in nature, at least at some time of the year, and could only take place if, and to the extent that, domestic import regimes permitted. None of this was a post-war invention, although both the levels and the pervasiveness of protection probably were. A further innovation was that six European countries decided in 1957 to subsume their individual efforts into a common agricultural policy. In this way agriculture, therefore, became intertwined with what in common parlance was known as 'the process of integration'.

. To understand these developments it is necessary to go back almost a hundred years to the Great Depression of the 1870s and 1880s.[1] The nature of the depression and its fundamental causes have been the subject of considerable debate among economic historians. For agriculture it was characterized by a sharp fall of the grain prices in Europe caused by the opening up of temperate farm lands in North America and Australasia and by a vast improvement of international ocean shipping which had slashed the prices of transporting bulk products to Europe. At the time of the outbreak of the crisis, the agricultural pressure groups in Europe were fragmented and lacking much political weight. Yet the slowness of government reactions to the crisis galvanized these loose peasant groups into powerful coalitions that articulated the demands of the agricultural sector for protection.

National governments responded to the fall in prices in two ways: either by granting that protection or by forcing the agricultural sector to adapt. Rather belatedly in France and in Germany tariffs were first imposed on imports of grain. Because grain is a key product in determining the price structure for the rest of agriculture, a network of protection spread outward from grain into other sectors of dairy and arable farming. For some other countries, however, the fall in grain prices produced a new opportunity. In the United Kingdom, for example, where agriculture employment was down to probably 13–14 per cent of the labour force at the time, the government responded by viewing lower grain prices as a contribution towards reducing the cost of living for the working classes. It would thus allow the majority of the working population to increase their purchasing power, leaving agriculture to adapt as best it could. In Denmark and the Netherlands, where agriculture was already highly developed and orientated towards the export of animal produce, the drop in the price of grain represented a fall in the cost of an important input into the dairy and poultry sector. For those countries, the Great Depression accentuated the trend already apparent from arable to animal farming.

By the mid-1890s the Great Depression had passed and prices were already recovering strongly. Despite more prosperous times, however, the framework of agricultural protectionism was not rolled back. And, after the First World War, it was augmented even further. Again the problem lay in the temperate agrarian countries. It was no longer a question of railways opening up vast new areas of agrarian land, it was the fact that newly discovered techniques of mechanization were better applied to the large farming units that were possible in Australasia and the Americas. This technology could not be replicated in the fragmented landholdings that typified most of Europe. In addition, because of the war, and the need for shipping across the Atlantic, there was a large surplus of peacetime capacity. This produced a corresponding depression in the freight rates, which further reduced the price of imports from overseas.

Once again, the grain area was uniquely depressed. There were probably no more than one or two favourable years for European grain producers during the entire decade of the 1920s. By 1928, a full eighteen months before the 'real' Great Depression hit the rest of the European economy, the crisis in grain had already started. Grain prices were falling fast, and again the response of governments in increasing the levels of protection was slow. Then, from late 1929 through into 1930, economic conditions throughout the rest of the European economy deteriorated.[2] As disposable incomes shrank, demand for what were now seen as luxury items (butter, cheese, eggs, milk, meat) especially declined. The prices for meat and dairy products fell dramatically and, from 1931, for the first time, animal production found itself in a serious crisis. By the time governments had reacted to these new demands for protection, the entire agricultural sector had been covered by a web of domestic regulations and frontier controls.

Ironically in countries such as the Netherlands and Denmark, which had previously seen themselves as free traders in agriculture because they were dependent on agricultural exports, the mechanisms of protection were more extensive and more profound than in the rest of Europe. The reason behind this is easy to understand. When the policy objective is simply to isolate the domestic market from cheap imports, the introduction of a tariff (which will increase the price of imports) or a quota (which, through arbitrarily limiting the volume of foreign produce will restrict supply and therefore raise the price) will be sufficient. For a country with an export surplus, these measures are also necessary, but they are not enough. Usually a central purchasing agency will also be required, to pay the farmers, to sell part of the product at a higher price on the domestic market and to use the 'profits' on these transactions to cover the losses on foreign sales. Only by acting as a monopoly could the farmers operate a system of differential pricing.

By the time the downward cycle of the Depression had passed in 1933–34, almost every sector of agriculture in Europe was subject to government interference. Yet nowhere were these measures particularly successful. There is not a case in Europe where agricultural incomes were restored to the level prevailing in more prosperous times. Nor were governments able to prevent an erosion in differentials with urban incomes. It is against this background that the farming communities, which saw themselves falling behind in terms of employment, incomes and social amenities, began to articulate demands for political change. The identity of farming discontent with anti-democratic, usually fascist, parties pledged to undermining or usurping the capitalist system also became a trademark of the 1930s.[3] Thus, by the end of the decade, ideological as well as practical considerations meshed together to justify a framework of agricultural protectionism that was already higher, and more pervasive, than ever before.

The Second World War, and its aftermath, served to drive agricultural protection to new peaks and to cement these pre-war systems even more firmly into place. The aims of all post-war agrarian policies can be summed up in one word – self-sufficiency, or as near self-sufficiency as possible. The reasons for this were broadly the same. First, the war had confirmed that the success of agriculture was vital to national survival – vital in the sense of 'necessary for life'. Had it not been for the dramatic reorganizations in European agriculture, the chances of survival for a large sector of the population would have deteriorated. These achievements lifted agriculture from the position it had occupied in the 1930s – a sectoral interest, albeit an import one – to the status where it became a scarcely veiled, and scarcely questioned, truly national interest. The need for reliable sources of sustenance, elevated agriculture to the status of a veritable 'cult of food'.

Second, the recovery of agriculture after the war took much longer than did that of industry. Around 1947–48, European industrial production had already regained its pre-war level and by 1950 it was about 20 per cent ahead of what it had been in 1938. Agriculture by contrast lagged behind and it was only in 1950–51 that European countries regained pre-war levels of output. Since, in the intervening period, the population had increased by about 12 per cent, there was still a long way to go before European agriculture regained its pre-war per-capita levels. In the interval, there was a gap between supply and demand. This, in itself, was nothing new. Western Europe had been an aggregate food importer since the 1870s. So, after the war, policy makers had to take account of the probability that they would have to import more food than before. The real problem was where to obtain it. The largest single source of disposable exports was in the dollar area. It was to the United States, in particular, that governments had to turn to make up the overall shortfall in domestic output. The situation was aggravated, however, by the fact that traditional Eastern European supplies had virtually disappeared and, to complicate matters further, food supplies from Asia had also diminished. The result was a total disruption of the normal pattern of international food trade. A few examples will illustrate this situation. In the 1930s Western Europe had obtained 35 per cent of its wheat imports from the dollar area; in 1948–50 the figure was 76 per cent. For sugar, the relevant figures were 37 per cent and 64 per cent respectively, and for coarse grains, 10 per cent and 24 per cent. Thus, a situation soon emerged in which food imports from the dollar area represented the single largest source of Europe's dollar deficit.[4]

In the longer term the cure for the dollar deficit lay in producing more food. When the Korean War broke out in 1950, the Americans urged the OEEC (the Organization for European Economic Cooperation, comprising 16 West European states that had come together to distribute Marshall Aid) to make it a priority to increase food production by 25 per cent. This would be a contribution to European security and a contribution to solving the dollar problem. Accepting these targets was, of course, no problem. This was, after all, the very policy that the agricultural lobbies had been urging upon their governments since the end of the war. If the government wanted more food, the agricultural sector was prepared to provide it, as long as governments implemented policies to facilitate that goal. Those policies centred on raising agricultural incomes and therefore raising the incentive to produce more food. If, in the process, agriculture improved its position relative to the rest of the economy, this would be an extra bonus for the agricultural pressure groups. These were not only advocating such policies but were also becoming increasingly integrated in their planning and execution.

It is a false dichotomy in this period to talk of a split between government and agricultural pressure groups. In many cases the agriculture pressure groups were the executive agent of government policy. In West Germany, for example, where there was no agricultural ministry, or national government, until the foundation of the Federal Republic in 1949, the *Bauernverband* had represented agricultural interests before the Allies. It never lost this comparative advantage in power and experience. In Denmark after the war, the government quickly dismantled the state-sponsored agricultural system and transferred many of the powers directly to the Danish agricultural cooperative societies. These are perhaps extreme examples but similar situations prevailed elsewhere in Europe. In many countries there was almost a revolving door between the agricultural lobby and agricultural ministries as they exchanged personnel and people in key areas. This was often complemented by strong cross-party representation in national parliaments that allowed direct and effective pressure on ministers. Thus post-war Europe was characterized by a situation where agriculture was seen as a national priority, where it performed essential economic functions, where the policies underpinning it benefited the farmers, and where the farmers' interest groups were strategically placed to articulate and exercise these policies.

There was just one problem: what did European self-sufficiency mean? The term had a different meaning for the different actors on the scene. For the Americans it obviously meant that Europe as a whole should become less dependent on the dollar area. But for each European country individually the term meant that each tried to liberate itself from imports. And so European self-sufficiency became nothing more than the sum of various, increasingly autarchic, policies that were not only reducing dollar imports but were cutting off imports from other European countries as well. This, in itself, was not a new situation. However, the levels of protection throughout Europe in the years 1945–50 made the 1930s look like a children's kindergarten playground by comparison.

Partly through European self-interest and partly through American pressure, the OEEC countries took the decision at the end of the 1940s to 'liberalize' European trade. This implied the removal of quotas for mutual trade, on the basis of a series of targets culminating, within a relatively short period of time, in their complete elimination. This should have been the perfect forum for freeing trade in agricultural products, since quotas were particularly prevalent in this sector. Yet the scheme failed for agriculture for a variety of reasons. First, no American government, and no European government for that matter, wished to interfere in the internal affairs of another country, and the OEEC's rules made sure that they did not. Whether a national government chose to have a free market for agriculture or to employ rationing through a central purchasing agency was not a question for decision at a European level. Thus, 'state trade', as it was called, was exempted from the scope of the entire operation. And state trade dominated agriculture. France and the United Kingdom both had large state purchasing monopolies from the start, and West Germany introduced the system in 1950–51. Second, it was argued that tariffs were the preserve of the GATT, and so the OEEC's scheme ignored the issue. In this way it ignored a situation whereby tariffs that had previously been suspended (since quotas had rendered their primary function redundant) were reimposed to compensate for quota removal. Third, and finally, countries could choose what to liberate within three broad categories: raw materials and semi-manufactures, industrial goods and agriculture. The usual strategy for agriculture was to eliminate quotas on non-competing tropical produce, to remove them on grain (where almost all countries had large deficits and anyway usually had them secreted under 'state trade'), to remove them on one or two areas of marginal importance, and to leave most of the remainder firmly intact.

By 1950–51 it was quite clear that the method by which Europe hoped to achieve freer trade in industry was not going to work for agriculture. Against this background another initiative was born, inspired partly by the failure of the OEEC and partly by the success of the Schuman Plan for a European community for coal and steel (ECSC). The idea for a European agricultural community, known as the 'green pool', originated almost simultaneously in France and in the Netherlands and in 1951 a conference was called of European agriculture ministers to discuss the project.[5] The discussions involved all the OEEC states and they lasted from 1951–52 until the 'green pool' was buried in January 1955. The negotiations revealed the extreme reluctance among virtually all the participants to accept the principle of a supranational authority over agriculture. The Dutch were the strongest protagonists but they were completely isolated in their demands for an effective supranational body. At times the French came close to the Dutch position but always retreated in the face of opposition from elsewhere, more concerned to reach some practical solution for their export surpluses than with the form of that solution. The other countries of the Six (Germany, Belgium, Luxembourg and Italy) which had embraced a supranational body for coal and steel certainly did not want one for agriculture. Nor did the United Kingdom. The opposition of the United Kingdom was particularly important. The six ECSC countries together faced the prospect that they would soon form an agricultural surplus area for many products; with the United Kingdom included they would be a deficit area. At the time, therefore, the presence of the United Kingdom was seen as essential for any scheme to work. But it also condemned any scheme to failure because the one thing the United Kingdom did not want to do was to sacrifice its Commonwealth preferences for the rather dubious advantages of an unformed European agricultural market.

Not surprisingly, during the green pool negotiations national delegations tended to favour agricultural schemes on a multilateral basis that would allow them to keep domestic protectionism intact and still allow them to share out any extra markets that might emerge. That, in turn, could only occur if extra-European suppliers were pushed aside to make room for high-priced European surpluses, which, of course, was exactly what worried the United Kingdom. A community of this nature would also serve to legitimize high levels of protection, especially where they were already being questioned. Indeed, so bizarre had become the negotiations that agricultural ministers were staking out positions way in advance of what would be backed by their national governments. It was schizophrenic, for example, that the German delegation were pushing for ever higher levels of protection, when national government policy was aimed in the opposite direction. Gradually, the national governments regained control over the conference, which was beginning to run away from them in rather dangerous directions. In 1955 they closed it down and transferred the forum to the OEEC.

Sicco Mansholt, who was to be pivotal in the development of the EEC's common agricultural policy, drew several lessons from the green pool experience.[6] Mansholt considered that if there were to be a common market, then agriculture had to be part of it. He had two main reasons for this opinion. First, agriculture itself did not provide sufficient scope for trade-offs that would lower protection – swapping concessions between highly shielded sectors would not succeed in lowering the overall level of protectionism. On the other hand, a trade-off of agricultural protection for gains in industry, or elsewhere, would increase the scope for bargaining. Second, the spectacle of the green pool had also persuaded Mansholt that agricultural ministers should never again be left alone to make international policy. He thought that, in a wider community, countries would largely be represented by ministers of foreign affairs and economic affairs, and that they would restrain their agricultural colleagues. Finally, more than ever, he was sure that agriculture had to be run with a supranational agency, that it could not be left to a set of *ad hoc* bilateral or multilateral deals.

There was never any guarantee that agriculture would have become part of the common market treaty. When the ECSC foreign ministers met in Messina, in early summer 1955, it was far from certain that the common market itself would ever have made it beyond the agenda. As they flew into Sicily, the French were not particularly enamoured by the idea of a common market, and the Germans were not inclined to cross the French on this issue. It was probably only the fact that an atomic energy community, which at the time was France's highest priority, was being discussed alongside the common market that kept it alive at all.[7] And once the subsequent intergovernmental conference on the Messina proposals, under the chairmanship of Paul-Henri Spaak, got under way, within the group working on the common market there was no will to tackle the question of agriculture. The topic was not even mentioned until seven weeks into the negotiations, and then only summarily. It was left for the drafters of the 'Spaak Report', who began work at the end of 1955, to sort out for themselves what to do with agriculture. At that time only the Netherlands was pushing for its inclusion. What changed the course of the negotiations was that a new, more European-inclined French government came into power in early 1956. In the delegation reports that have ben preserved in the archives, one can see a marked change in direction and tempo of the negotiations for a common market. A common market would come into being, but in a form that could accommodate specific French interests. It would therefore also have to include some arrangements for agriculture.

Many histories stop their interpretations at this point. It is a historical fact that requires no further explanation; there was a 'process of integration', the Treaty of Rome advanced that process and it embraced agriculture. Newly released archives, however, allow us to review the range of options discussed and to see the alternative clauses that were never signed, never even negotiated, because they were not acceptable. We can see now why the common agricultural policy was protectionist from the start.[8] It was because five agricultural ministers wanted it that way, and because the sixth had to accept an imperfect solution or risk everything. Within the context of this article, it is sufficient to demonstrate this simply by reference to the aims of the policy (enshrined in Article 39.1):

Article 39.1   The objectives of the common agricultural policy shall be:

a)   to increase agricultural productivity by promoting technical progress and by ensuring the rational development of agricultural production and the optimum utilisation of factors of production, in particular labour;
b)   thus to ensure a fair standard of living for the agricultural community, in particular by increasing the individual earnings of persons engaged in agriculture;
c)   to stabilise markets;
d)   to assure the availability of supplies;
e)   to ensure that supplies reach consumers at reasonable prices.

The critical statement is Article 39.1.b since upon this hangs the meaning one should attach to the rest. The Spaak Report had called for the maintenance of returns at a level sufficient for a 'normally productive' enterprise. At the time, the Germans had objected to this and had suggested instead that the goal be to augment the living standards of *all* engaged in agriculture. The Italians wanted this formulation further enlarged to include the aim of achieving maximum employment in agriculture. Of course neither the German nor the Italian amendment was compatible with the original version. Guaranteeing returns to the 'normally productive' implied, by definition, the sacrifice of the less than normally productive. Equally the aim of security of supply entailed a different degree of commitment in the German–Italian version than in the original draft. The latter was compatible with a degree of imports while the former implied an all-out drive for self-sufficiency. The Dutch insisted on the original version. At the same time, they secured French support for an amendment stating that the promotion of agriculture should aim at creating the best technical conditions. This would become Article 39.1.a.

The Dutch then tried to reinforce the direction of these proposals by suggesting that in raising productivity, governments should attempt to adjust the output structure so that it was more in line with global specialization. Simultaneously, and on this basis, they introduced the commitment that the provision of needs of the population was to be on the basis of 'reasonable prices'. These ideas received virtually no support at all. Both Luxembourg and Italy opposed any reference to reasonable prices which, they argued, would be carried on the backs of the agricultural population. The French rejected any mention of adjustment to global conditions, which, after all, would imply the sacrifice of much of its grain and sugar production. All these positions were supported by the Germans. The Dutch at this point were forced to retreat. By dropping any reference to global specialization, they could keep the endorsement of 'reasonable prices' (39.1.e). As a further concession, by inserting the word 'thus' at the start of Article 39.1.b, the goal of raising living standards became conditional on the increase in productivity levels.

The agricultural clauses in the Treaty of Rome established procedures for a policy rather than their contents. If any of the partners had qualms about this, or about the exact nature of the compromises, they suppressed them because there were significant compensatory achievements elsewhere. The lonely battle for a liberal set of clauses had been lost by the Dutch. Indeed, their hope was that the supranational elements in the Treaty would raise agriculture above the grasp of protectionist pressure groups and their captive ministers. The battle for realizing the common agricultural policy (CAP) had still to be joined. The German pressure, in particular, still hoped to use the procedures in the Treaty to perpetuate national protectionism. It is interesting that the real provisions guaranteeing that the CAP would be created were hardly debated at all in the buildup to the Treaty.

Although there were very few detailed commitments in the agricultural clauses, both phase one and phase two did stipulate stages to be reached in the preparation of the CAP. Moreover, the Treaty also contained Article 8, which specified that there would be no progression from the first stage unless all its objectives had been 'attained in substance'. Should there not be unanimity on the transition to the next stage, the first could be automatically twice prolonged by a year. Even then, if progress to stage two were decided by a majority, any state could demand that the question be referred to an arbitration tribunal whose (unanimous) advice would be binding on all parties. In this way, the Treaty made clear that if agriculture was to be treated on the same basis as other commodities, it could seriously impede progress on other fronts. Indeed, it might prevent advance beyond the first stage altogether since Article 8 was unclear what would happen if the procedures it contained were exhausted without a positive outcome. It was this linkage, forged outside the agricultural clauses themselves, that ultimately proved the driving force behind the CAP's creation. Unfortunately no similar linkages existed to steer its final direction.

Mansholt had no qualms about this. He recognized that if he went for a more concrete treaty at the time of the negotiations, it would become even more protectionist than the version actually agreed. Moreover, he was an institutional federalist who believed that if supranational agencies were given a task, they would do it differently from and better than individual governments since they could raise themselves above narrow national sectoral interests. He was wrong, because soon the agricultural ministers were alone together, fixing price and determining the future rules of the policy.

Western European agriculture in the post-war period experienced a transformation probably unmatched in its previous history. The growth of output of the six states that were to form the EEC surged from an already high average of 2.8 per cent a year in the 1950s (ranging from 1.9 per cent in France to 4.5 per cent in the Netherlands) to 2.8 to 3.1 per cent in the 1960s (ranging from 2.4 per cent in the Belgo-Luxembourg Economic Union (BLEU) to 3.5 per cent in France).[9] These growth rates are impressive historically, although they do lag behind the exceptionally high levels of expansion achieved by industry over the same period. More impressive still was the fact that, throughout most of Western Europe, improvements in labour productivity registered by agriculture outstripped those achieved elsewhere in the economy. Even where non-agricultural productivity grew faster, as in Italy, where in the years from 1953 to 1967 it increased by 4.9 per cent per annum, agricultural productivity grew by 5.8 per cent. In West Germany the respective figures were 3.7 and 6.0 per cent. Portugal was a clear exception to this trend since agricultural productivity increased by 2.9 per cent per annum compared to 4.7 per cent in the rest of the economy. This increase in productivity, in turn, was accompanied by a sharp decline in agricultural employment ranging, among the Six, from a decline of 1.8 per cent per annum in France to 3.9 per cent in Belgium. In the 1960s, this rate accelerated to range from 3.2 per cent per annum in the Netherlands to 4.7 per cent for Italy. Close on one million people a year, labourers and their families, left the land in an exodus that more than halved the agricultural employment. In the rest of Western Europe the figures for the decline in agricultural employment from 1953 to 1967 ranged from 1.8 per cent for Finland to 4.1 per cent for Sweden, with Portugal's 2.0 per cent at the bottom of the spectrum.[10] Part of this increase in productivity was a reflection that the attractions of the industrial boom of the 1950s and 1960s were pulling heavily underemployed manpower off the land. Indeed one eminent economic historian adapted the Lewis model of 'economic development with unlimited supplies of labour', originally designed for less-developed countries, to this process in Western Europe. Labour with virtually zero marginal productivity could be pulled off the land at virtually no cost and employed in higher productivity activities in industry to the benefit of both sectors.[11]

This approach contains an element of truth, but it implies an essentially passive role for agriculture. The reduction in agricultural employment was not only the result of the greater attraction of industry, it was also a symptom of momentous changes in the agrarian economy, as fundamental and as 'revolutionary' as any in its history. First, there was a sharp improvement in the land:labour ratio, an accelerated degree of consolidation of landholdings and a steady increase in farm size, caused partly by the migration of marginal farmers, but also actively encouraged by government policies. Yet it is important not to exaggerate the change in farm size. By the end of the 1960s, only in the United Kingdom did farm size average more than 60 hectares and in most of the rest of Western Europe the average was less than 20 hectares. This compared with an average farm size of more than 200 hectares in the United States and Canada.[12] Given the relatively small size of a farm unit, the fact of the sharp increase in mechanization is something of a surprise. It is true that it represented a substitution of labour for capital but it was attributable less to the upscaling in unit farm size than to technological changes towards more powerful small tractors and a wider range of appropriate implements. The introduction of tractors provides a useful indication of the extent of mechanization. By the end of the 1960s the ratio of 84 tractors per 1000 hectares engaged in the agriculture of the Six far outstripped the 24 per thousand in North America.[13] Third, although mechanization was important, it formed only part of the technical improvement in agriculture. The increasing use of fertilizers and pesticides also played a crucial role in improving yield. Restricting ourselves to fertilizers, the use of potash by the Six increased by 36 per cent, phosphates by 45 per cent and nitrogenous fertilizers by 110 per cent.[14] Fourth, and more difficult to quantify, agriculture adapted to new types of crop. Fruit farming was one area where this change is visually immediately apparent with regimented lines of dwarf trees replacing the traditional orchards. Less visible, but far more important, was the introduction of new disease- or drought-resistant crops. The impact of this change on the poorer countries of the Third World was sufficient to justify the term 'the green revolution', but few observers paused to consider the effect when applied by rich countries that could easily afford the changeover. Finally, since none of these innovations came cheap, there had to be means available to introduce these changes. These included government loans, grants, subsidies, guaranteed mortgage schemes and, of course, an attempt to provide a generous and stable margin of profit.

To an extent, these changes were encouraged by government policies. Security of supplies, foreign currency needs and, occasionally, the electoral concerns for vulnerable coalition governments pointed in the same direction – the promotion of farm output. None the less, the pattern of change that began to emerge in the 1950s was not universally appreciated within agrarian circles. The green pool episode may have suggested that the agricultural lobby was extremely powerful, but it saw its position as vulnerable and insecure. First, the flight from the land weakened their constituencies and, despite the improvement in rural living standards, in terms of relative employment and incomes, the sector was everywhere falling behind. Second, the dynamics of supply and demand were not moving in favour of the agricultural sector. As we observed earlier, for products where the national market was in deficit, national price levels could be maintained at the expense of imports. As the market approaches saturation, it becomes susceptible to sharp falls in prices (the consequence of a relatively elastic short-term supply curve and a relatively inelastic demand), at a time when existing forms of intervention will prove inadequate. In such circumstances, the lobby was likely to become more strident in its demands for security. By the end of the 1950s, when it became necessary to fill in the content of the EEC's common agricultural policy, these trends were already apparent.

The EEC's problem was that although its citizens were becoming richer, faster than ever before, they were spending proportionally less of their incomes on foodstuffs. Worse still, whatever increased expenditure there was, fell behind the rate of increase of output. In the 1960s, average consumption of agricultural products grew by 2.6 per cent per annum, compared with a growth in output of 3.1 per cent per annum. Only Italy provided an exception to this trend.[15] At the end of the 1950s the EEC was 85 per cent self-sufficient in grain. On the eve of the first enlargement in 1972–73, the figure was 97 per cent and for wheat and barley the figure was 112 per cent. Dairy produce, which hovered on the edge of self-sufficiency at the end of the 1950s, surpassed that achievement by a wide margin in 1972–73, with butter notching up a figure of 119 per cent.

In 1958, Sicco Mansholt became the commissioner in charge of implementing the common agricultural policy (CAP) for the new community. Given that agriculture was not usually associated with lengthy tenure or a high profile. Mansholt was uniquely experienced for the task of commissioner, having served as his country's agricultural minister uninterruptedly since the Second World War. His own experience had left him with little fear of the agricultural lobby. On the contrary, he considered that it was important to work with the farmers' organizations, if a CAP were to be successful. While weak ministers came and went, the barons of agriculture were both stronger and more permanent. It is significant that the policy was launched, and the outlines of the CAP agreed, at a conference with the various national agricultural associations in Stressa in 1959. Even so, it was far from evident that the policy would ever come into being, and it was helped along its way by several factors that could not have been anticipated when the original clauses had been constructed.[16]

The agricultural clauses had been framed in stages which, if read in a negative way, could be interpreted as saying that if the new arrangements had not been agreed, the status quo (and therefore national protection systems) would continue. Apparent reasons for pessimism could be further induced by the fact that agreement for passage to the second stage required a unanimous vote from the Council of Ministers. However, the Treaty also stipulated that the creation of the common market as a whole should be synchronized. Thus, a block on agriculture could hold up progress elsewhere. When the Six, therefore, with West Germany in the foreground, wanted to accelerate the dismantling of their industrial tariffs, the French maintained that the first stage for agriculture had to be agreed at the same time, thereby forcing German concessions. After intense negotiations, in 1962, market unity, Community preference and financial solidarity emerged as the principles of a future CAP. This still left important issues, such as the level of support prices and the financing of the system, to be settled before the CAP could become operative. Meanwhile, a regulation was passed establishing the FEOGA (*Fonds Européen d'orientation et de garantie agricole*) with provisions extended until mid-1965.[17]

The level of common prices as well as the financing of the CAP proved to be very controversial. The fierce negotiations brought the EEC to the brink of collapse. It took until the end of 1964 before German reluctance to accept a target price for grain below their prevailing national level could be overcome and before a common price level for cereals could be introduced. Proposals for common financing of the CAP were submitted in March 1965. Since these envisaged augmenting the EEC's institutional powers, via increasing the budgetary competencies of the European Parliament and through the introduction of majority voting. France flatly opposed the move. In summer 1965 it withdrew its representation at all EEC meetings and, with this 'empty chair' policy, precipitated a major crisis within the Community. It was resolved in January 1966 with the 'Luxembourg Compromise'. This stipulated that, notwithstanding the Commission's rights of initiative enshrined in the Treaty of Rome, it would consult with governments before adopting any important proposal. More significantly, even on issues normally decided by majority, it stipulated that if a country felt that its vital interests were at stake, the Commission was bound to continue discussion until unanimous agreement was reached. At the same time the financing of the CAP was resolved with a fixed scale of contributions agreed to run until January 1970.

The CAP was modelled on the system used in the Netherlands, which also mirrored those in operation in the other member states. Interestingly, when it was introduced after the war, it relied on high consumer prices rather than budget transfers in order to escape parliamentary scrutiny at times of fiscal stringency. If one accepts this premise, then the principles of the policy make a great deal of sense up to and including he moment when *occasional* surpluses appear. For much of the time, domestic supplies would satisfy much of the market without threatening the base price while imports would take care of the rest. Those imports would be taxed so that they did not undercut the domestic price and the revenues would feed into a central fund. When domestic supplies exceeded the market's capacity, the fund could buy up the surplus and cover the losses involved in selling them on the world market. There might even be sufficient cash remaining to finance schemes for agricultural improvement. If, however, the surpluses became structural, there would always be an obligation to buy up the excess and, without imports, the system would lack the automatic means to fund the operation. The system was the same when applied to one country or to several, with one exception. In a national system, the deficit country would only pay out the foreign exchange involved in buying at world market prices; in the CAP it had to secure those supplies at the same high price prevailing for domestic supplies. Originally, Mansholt had hoped that this mechanism would encourage finance ministers in the food-deficit countries (for instance, Germany) to act as a counterweight to the pressures anticipated from the agricultural lobby for higher intervention prices.

Matters did not turn out quite that simple. The CAP negotiations proved excruciatingly drawn-out and complex, and the agricultural ministers moved back into the more central role they had occupied during the 'green pool'. Moreover, there was little counterweight within the Commission. Agricultural policy conceived and executed by the Community's supranational arm and the CAP became the living proof of its achievements. Before long, agriculture was being described as the 'motor' for integration or the 'cornerstone' of the Community. Finally, since the German economy was generating one annual balance of payments surplus after another, its finance minister was really in no position to complain about the foreign exchange costs of the CAP. Meanwhile, the threshold for success or failure for the policy was determined by the price levels set. It is doubtful whether lower prices would have made for much higher consumption for many goods, but it would certainly have curbed production. For products already moving into 'overproduction' the prices were already way over those commanded on world markets, although one should remember that the world market is more of a dumping ground for surpluses than the 'invisible hand' beloved of free marketeers. Bearing this in mind, the prices of wheat and barley in 1967–68 were 70 and 65 per cent above world prices, that of butter 300 per cent higher. An American estimate suggested that already in 1968 the total transfer to agriculture (45 per cent from higher consumer prices and the rest from national and FEOGA budgets) was equivalent to 55 per cent of the value of gross output.[18]

Like the sorcerer's apprentice, Mansholt tried to undo the train of events he had set in motion. In 1968, the Commission published new proposals, dubbed the 'Mansholt Plan', designed to tackle the problem of surpluses (through production quotas and withdrawing land from production) and to accelerate structural change in agriculture (further reducing the labour force but hopefully closing the income gap with other sectors of the economy). The proposals created a storm of protest in agricultural circles and by the time they emerged from the decision-making process, nothing much of the original remained intact.[19]

The effect of creating a high price preference area among the six EEC countries had been to encourage their mutual trade at the expense of other producers. For produce covered by the CAP, the EEC obtained 25 per cent of its import requirements from other member states. On the eve of enlargement, the figure stood at nearly 50 per cent.[20] The losers in this process were American grain and poultry producers and, in Europe, the Danish meat and dairy farmers. The Danes had had a foretaste of this development. When, in 1949 in the context of Benelux, the Belgians had granted the Dutch a position as preferential supplier of agricultural products to the Belgian market, Danish trade had been virtually eclipsed.

At the end of 1956, the United Kingdom launched its proposals for a pan-European free trade area (FTA) to encapsulate the common market being formed by the Six. They deliberately excluded agriculture. This had been intended both to preserve the basis for Commonwealth preferences and to allow the government freedom to continue its policies of direct farm subsidies. If the Benelux example had provided a foretaste of the CAP, then the UK egg market provided a timely reminder of the dangers of unfettered British policy. A remorseless drive for domestic egg production, stimulated by subsidies, had in the 1950s driven out Danish (and other) suppliers. Moreover, countries which relied on agricultural export earnings resented the implication that they remove protection on industrial imports while gaining nothing in return. These reservations were expressed from the ranks of the Six (especially France, Italy and the Netherlands), from the Scandinavian countries and from the Mediterranean producers. The furthest the British came during the eighteen months of negotiations on the FTA within the OEEC was a meaningless concession that the others could negotiate agricultural arrangements among themselves, but that the UK would claim exemption status from its provisions. The FTA collapsed in November 1958 when the French government, led by Charles de Gaulle, refused to continue the negotiations. Although other, political and economic, factors probably explain the failure, the impasse on agriculture had acted as an irritant throughout.

When, several months after the FTA's failure, plans were discussed for a more limited European Free Trade Association (EFTA), it became clear from the start that, despite the UK's insistence that it would not be part of the EFTA Convention, some accommodation would need to be found for agriculture. Thus, before formal negotiations began, the UK and Sweden negotiated important bilateral preferential deals with Denmark. The most important arrangement was that with the UK, which removed tariffs on imports of Danish bacon, tinned meats and blue cheese (although not butter at this early stage). Other bilateral deals were concluded in the course of the negotiations. Portugal, for example, benefited from these since cork was already treated as an industrial raw material, sardines (and later purée tomatoes) were given 'industrial product' treatment and port wine imports into the UK were given a preferential revenue duty.

As a result, the treatment within the EFTA Convention was limited to a declaration of intent (Art. 22) to give 'reasonable reciprocity' to countries relying on agricultural exports, subject to safeguards for domestic producers, an encouragement of bilateral treaties (Art. 23) as a means to that end, and an obligation (Art. 24) to remove subsidies that might damage the exports of other members (which was never implemented). Under these agreements, the share of intra-EFTA trade in total EFTA agricultural trade increased from 8.7 per cent to 10.2 per cent, of which possibly half was attributable to EFTA's existence. It was not a very spectacular feat, but possibly not out of line with the goals and the chosen means of achievement. There were several reasons behind the failure. The slow growth of the British economy generally inhibited the expansion of intra-EFTA trade and the devaluation of 1967, in particular, disrupted markets. A second factor inhibiting an improved performance was the fact that other states continued to use domestic policy to promote their own outputs, clearly demonstrating the secondary importance attached to imports (even if Denmark was given some preferential treatment in their allocation). The UK, for example, increased its levels of self-sufficiency during the 1960s to virtually 99 per cent for eggs, 97 per cent for poultry and 100 per cent for pork. Other countries also augmented their levels of self-sufficiency and often reinforced their own export surpluses. A third factor that damaged intra-EFTA trade was the appearance of large EEC surpluses that were dumped on other European markets and, whatever the stipulations of the EFTA Convention, it was difficult to maintain a preference for higher priced, unsubsidized, EFTA exports.[21]

If Denmark was Western Europe's most efficient producer of meat and dairy produce, as most commentators seemed to agree, its position reflects most poignantly the growing irrationality of Europe's agricultural trade. As feared, its position in the EEC agricultural markets was marginalized by the diminished import requirements, by shifts in suppliers and by the operation of the preferences inherent in the CAP. In the course of the 1960s, Denmark's share of the EEC's agricultural import trade fell from 23 per cent in 1960 to 7 per cent in 1972.[22] Ironically the position was similar for the main EFTA importers. Denmark merely maintained its share of imports into the UK, which were anyway being held back by the increase in subsidized domestic production. It saw its share of Swedish imports fall from 74 to 65 per cent between 1960 and 1969, partly at the expense of imports from the EEC but also because of inroads from subsidized exports from Austria and Finland. Its share of Swiss imports also tumbled from 54 per cent to 31 per cent over the same period while, gallingly, the share for every other EFTA member state increased.[23] For Denmark, when the opportunity arose, it made increasingly more sense to secure EEC membership. Only then could it hope to recover lost market positions in continental Europe but could place the burden of finding and funding external markets on the shoulders of the other member states.

The institutionalization of the cult of food was too strong for governments to resist. As a result, far from a harmonious development of agriculture in balance with the needs of European societies and consistent with the dictates of the world economy, something very different emerged. Even its expansion to include the largest importer of foodstuffs in the world, in the form of the UK, did little to offset its inherent deficiencies. The CAP rapidly evolved into a policy that became so expensive that it throttled the movement and dynamism of the Community in any other direction. It was a policy that was so contentious that it absorbed between 70 and 80 per cent of the time of the Council of Ministers who tried to thrash it out and pitched the Community from one crisis to another. It was a policy that did meet its own goal of supplying food to its population at a reasonable price. It was a policy that did not even leave the rest of the world alone, but one where the dumping of subsidized European products on world markets undermined the efforts that were being promoted through other sectors of the Treaty of Rome for less-developed countries to sustain their development in a healthy direction. It was a policy that has never shaken itself loose from the dead hand of history, that has brought more than one set of international trade negotiations to the brink of collapse, and that still has the capacity for further harm before, and if, it is ever brought under control.

Notes

*   Translation of 'Desenvolvimento Agrícola e Comércio Agrícola, 1945–73', in *Portugal e a Europa, 50 anos de integraçao*, Lisbon, March 1996.

**   The author is at the University of Leiden, The Netherlands. He would like to thank Anne Christine Knudsen for her assistance in preparing this article.

1. J. Blum, *The End of the Old Order in Rural Europe*, Princeton, 1977, M. Tracy, *Government and Agriculture in Western Europe, 1880–1988*, London, 1989.

2. Some of the best works were written at or close to the time. See L.B. Bacon and F.C. Schroeder, *World Trade in Agricultural Products*, Rome, 1940; H.A. and A.D. Taylor, *World Trade in Agricultural Products*, New York, 1943; V.P. Timoshenko, *World Agriculture and the Depression*, Ann Arbor, 1953; P.L. Yates, *Food Production in Western Europe*, London, 1940.

3. P. Cioccia and G. Toniolo (eds), *L'economia italiana nel periodo fascista*, Bologna, 1976; J.E. Farqueson, *The Plough and the Swastika. The NSDAP and Agriculture in Germany, 1928–1945*, London, 1976.

4. A.S. Milward, *The Reconstruction of Western Europe, 1945–1950*, London, 1983.

5. B. Girvin and R.T. Griffiths (eds), *European Integration, the Green Pool and the Origins of the Common Agricultural Policy*, London, 1995; A.S. Milward, *The European Rescue of the Nation State*, London, 1992; G. Noel, *Du Pool Vert à la politique agricole commune. Les tentatives de Communauté agricol européenne entre 1945 et 1955*, Paris, 1988.

6. R.T. Griffiths, 'The Mansholt Plan', in R.T. Griffiths (ed.), *The Netherlands and the Integration of Europe, 1945–1958*, Amsterdam, 1990; W.H. Vermeulen, *Europees Landbouwbeleid in de Maak: Mansholts eerste plannen, 1945–1953*, Groningen, 1989.

7. H.J. Küsters, *Die Gründung der europäischen Wirtschaftsgemeinschaft*, Baden-Baden, 1982 (French edition 1990); E. Serra (ed.), *Il rilancio dell'Europa e i Trattati di Roma*, Brussels, Milan, Paris, Baden-Baden, 1989.

8. The following paragraphs have been taken from the delegation reports located in the Dutch central government archives in The Hague.

9. F. Duchène, E. Szczepanik and W. Legg, *New Limits on European Agriculture*, Ottawa, 1985, Appendix 1.

10. D.G. Johnson, *World Agriculture in Disarray*, place: 1973, 67–8, 70. United Nations (ECE), *The European Economy, 1950's to 1970's*, Geneva, 1970, 68.

11. C.P. Kindleberger, *Europe's Postwar + * 15* ole of the Labour Supply*, Cambridge, London, 1967.

12. UN, *The European Economy*, 70.

13. Johnson, *World Agriculture*, 73–4.

14. *Ibid.*, 78.

15. Duchène et al., *New Limits*, Appendix 1.

16. For accounts based on access to archives, see H. von der Groeben.... and A. Burger, *Voor Boerenvolk en Vaderland. De vorming van het EEG beleid, 1959–1966*, Amsterdam, 1993.

17. The first archive-based study is A. Burger, *Voor Boerenvolk en Vaderland. De vorming van het EEG-landbouwbeleid, 1959–1966*, Amsterdam, 1993. See further S. Harris et al., *The Food and Farm Policies of the European Community*, Chichester, 1983; J. Marsh and C. Ritson, *Agricultural Policy and the Common Market*, London, 1971 and the articles by A. Fearne and C. Saunders in C. Ritson, (ed.), *The Common Agricultural Policy and the World Economy*, Oxford, 1991.

18. Cited in Johnson, *World Agriculture*, 48–51.

19. G.G. Rosenthal, *The Men behind the Decisions. Cases in European Policy-making*, Lexington, 1975.

20. Quoted in Tracy, *Government and Agriculture in Western Europe*, 287.

21. V. Curzon, *The Essentials of Economic Integration. Lessons of EFTA Experience*, London, 1974, 183–93.

22. Duchène, *The Limits of Agriculture*, 123.

23. Curzon, *The Essentials of Economic Integration*, 180–83.

[14]

Journal of Common Market Studies
Volume XXVII, No. 2 December 1988
0021–9886 $3.00

The Effects of the Common Agricultural Policy of the European Community: A Survey of the Literature

DIMITRIOS G. DEMEKAS, KASPER BARTHOLDY, SANJEEV GUPTA, LESLIE
LIPSCHITZ AND THOMAS MAYER*

This survey deals with the costs and benefits of the common agricultural policy for EC Member States and the effects of the CAP on world markets and the well-being of the Community's trading partners. It presents and discusses recent empirical literature that attempts to estimate quantitatively the domestic and international effects of the CAP. The 'domestic effects' are the welfare gains and losses of producers, consumers and taxpayers, the effects on other sectors and the deadweight costs to the economy as a whole. The 'international effects' are the effects on world commodity prices, the volume and pattern of international agricultural trade and the welfare of the rest of the world. The impact the CAP has on the stability of world commodity prices is also included in this category.

In order to compare and evaluate the empirical evidence, section 1 discusses the development of the conceptual framework for the welfare analysis of price support and its limitations. Section 2 presents the evidence in five categories: domestic welfare, level of world prices, international trade, welfare of non-EC countries, and stability of world prices. Section 3 is a discussion of the conclusions and their relevance to the current debate about agricultural policy reforms.

I. THE THEORY

Although the structure of the CAP is complicated, for the large majority of

*Reprinted with minor modifications and with permission from *The Common Agricultural Policy of the European Community – Principles and Consequences*, Occasional Paper No. 62 (Washington, DC: International Monetary Fund, 1988). The authors are indebted to numerous colleagues and to staff members of the EC Commission for helpful comments on an earlier draft. The views expressed are those of the authors who are also responsible for the remaining errors.

114   EFFECTS OF THE COMMON AGRICULTURAL POLICY

products the basic method of implementation is through price support. This is achieved by a variety of instruments, such as intervention purchases, market withdrawals, export restitutions, minimum import prices and import levies.[1] Other price support devices (e.g. deficiency payments) and non-price support instruments (storage aids, input subsidies, voluntary export restraint (VER) agreements with non-Member States, etc.) are also used, but on a more limited scale.

The simplest way to examine the effects of price support on domestic welfare is the single-good partial equilibrium analysis.

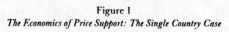

Figure 1
The Economics of Price Support: The Single Country Case

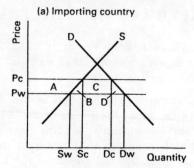

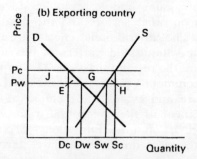

Figure 1, panel (a) illustrates the case of a small importing country. If the world price is P_w but the domestic price is maintained at P_c by a tariff, production is at S_c, consumption at D_c and the difference is imports. Reducing consumption below and increasing production above what they would be if the world price prevailed, entails a consumer loss of

[1]Some of the secondary objectives of the CAP, such as improving the quality of food consumed, improving the distribution of income within the agricultural sector, protecting small family farms and preserving rural life styles and the natural environment, create the need for a different family of instruments that generally go under the name of guidance expenditure.

DEMEKAS, BARTHOLDY, GUPTA, LIPSCHITZ AND MAYER 115

A+B+C+D, a producer gain of A and an increase in government revenue of C. The net welfare loss (or, alternatively, the net welfare gain of liberalizing) is B+D. Price support in an exporting country by means of an export subsidy is illustrated in panel (b). Here the consumer loss is J+E, the government expenditure E+G+H, and the producer gain J+E+G; by subtraction the net welfare loss is E+H.

This simple domestic welfare analysis treats the EC as a single entity. In order to examine the country-specific effects of the CAP, the previous analysis has to be modified in three ways. First, it has to allow for intra-EC commodity trade (Buckwell *et al.*, 1982, pp. 30–9). Some of the imports of an importing country will now originate in other Community members and, therefore, be priced at the CAP support level. Consequently, part of the tariff revenue C will now be forgone. Similarly, part of the government expenditure for subsidies in an exporting country will now be avoided, since the gain to producers is generated directly by sales to other Community members at the high protected prices.

Second, the analysis has to capture the function of the so-called agrimonetary system of the EC. The Monetary Compensatory Amounts (MCAs) that came into effect in the early 1970s to protect farmers from national currency fluctuations, essentially allow Member States to maintain domestic prices different from the common CAP support levels. Importers in a country with a domestic price lower than P_c can be thought of as paying P_c at the border for imports from other members and then getting a subsidy to allow these imports to compete in the domestic market. Exporters in that country must pay a tax on their exports in order not to undermine the higher prices in the rest of the Community. The situation in a member country which maintains a domestic price higher than P_c is the opposite.

Third, the principle of common financing, which means that the Community is collectively responsible for paying the subsidies for (and receiving the tariff revenue generated by) all products covered by the CAP, requires that additional transfers between the EC and members' budgets be taken into account.

Even after introducing these additional considerations to make the model capture the supranational character of the CAP, the partial equilibrium analysis still retains its simplicity. Its usefulness is limited, however, by the strong assumptions that underlie it.[2] In what follows, the main difficulties of assessing the effects of price support by means of the partial equilibrium model are outlined, and ways of dealing with these difficulties are discussed.

(1) The analysis of price support, even when amended to take into account the intra-EC transfers mentioned above, is designed to capture the effects of

[2] For a discussion of the partial equilibrium welfare analysis and its advantages, see Corden (1957); Corden (1971); Harberger (1959); Johnson (1960); Currie *et al.* (1971). For a discussion of its limitations, in particular with respect to analysing agricultural price support in the EC, see Buckwell *et al.* (1982); Valdes and Zietz (1980); Matthews (1985a); Winters (1987).

116   EFFECTS OF THE COMMON AGRICULTURAL POLICY

one specific policy. There are, however, many different CAP price support instruments, not all of which have the same effect. Deficiency payments, for example, differ from export subsidies in that, as consumers pay the world price, there are no consumer losses. Non-tariff barriers or variable import levels do not generate the same revenues as *ad valorem* tariffs. These differences are very hard to capture empirically.

(2) The analysis in Figure 1 implicitly assumes that the country is a price-taker in the world market. This 'small country' assumption means that, no matter what the level of domestic protection is, the world price remains unaffected. The welfare effects of price support can then be accurately measured with reference to that world price. It also means that these effects are limited to the home country; there is no room for international repercussions. This is clearly unsatisfactory in the case of the CAP; the EC is large enough to influence world markets.

(3) Partial equilibrium analysis assumes that the prices of all other goods remain constant. This means that substitutability and complementarity in consumption and production between the goods studied and other commodities is ignored. In order to correct this shortcoming, one has to model the interactions between markets for different goods explicitly. The choice of the relevant group of goods is, however, a difficult task, since the chain of substitution can extend from commodities very close to the one studied (e.g. different varieties of wheat) to non-agricultural goods.

(4) The preceding discussion also assumes that all demand is final. This is obviously not true for many agricultural products. The demand for those products has to be derived from the cost function of the food industry. Moreover, many commodities use other agricultural products as inputs: beef, for example, requires animal feed. The true degree of protection for beef, therefore, is captured by the effective, rather than the nominal rate.

(5) Price support policies in agriculture, especially in cases like the CAP where a wide range of commodities is covered, can have a considerable effect on total employment and the allocation of capital and labour. This, in turn, affects other sectors of the economy. The size and direction of the effects depend mainly on relative factor intensities and the policies implemented in the other sectors. Such interactions can exert a significant influence on the actual welfare gains or losses from agricultural policies.

(6) Because of the range of coverage of policies like the CAP, macro-economic considerations also enter the picture. Changes in the price support policies for many commodities can have sizeable effects on the external balance of the economy and, consequently, the exchange rate and/or the relative price of tradables and non-tradables. Either could then shift the supply and demand curves in figure 1 endogenously.

(7) Externalities and market distortions, if present, represent the greatest challenge to the welfare analysis of price support policies. Even if they are absent from the agricultural sector proper, but exist elsewhere, externalities

and distortions can affect the calculation of welfare costs and benefits in a variety of ways. Empirical work has shied away from these problems by routinely postulating perfectly competitive structures, full information and complete markets.

These shortcomings of the simple partial equilibrium model have prompted analytical efforts in several directions. First, in order to simplify the empirical question at hand and take care of the problem raised in point (1) above, most researchers convert all sorts of price-support instruments into tariff equivalents (nominal or effective, as the case may be). Alternative policy options are then described in terms of changing this notional rate of protection, without specifying how exactly this is to be done. Harling (1983) and Valdes and Zietz (1980) discuss at length the methods of calculating tariff equivalents and the ensuing problems.

Second, 'large country' effects, substitution of agricultural commodities in production and consumption, and backward and forward linkages with other sectors are incorporated in the analysis by applying partial equilibrium techniques in a multi-country multi-sector framework. This approach is used extensively in evaluating policies such as the CAP, which affect many agricultural commodities simultaneously. Trouble spots (2) to (4) from the previous list are dealt with in this way.

Multi-country multi-commodity models differ fundamentally from the simple analysis in Figure 1 in one respect: the world price loses its meaning as a reference point for the measurement of the welfare costs of protection. Since the home country is 'large', a change in domestic policies will affect the world price. The effects of the policy must be estimated with respect to what the world price would be, had the policy been absent. The calculation of that hypothetical price requires formulating demand and supply functions for the country(ies) and commodity(ies) involved, and solving the system at a notional, unobserved equilibrium. This is called counterfactual analysis.

Counterfactual analysis is necessary for the effects of domestic policies on international trade and other countries to be addresssed. Once counterfactual world equilibria have been computed, the resulting prices and trade flows can be compared with the actual ones and the distortions implied by the existing policies can be demonstrated. Moreover, the effects of the policies on the real income of other countries can also be calculated. Multi-country multi-sector partial equilibrium models that use counterfactual analysis to estimate both domestic and international effects of price support can get quite complicated.

Probably the most advanced model in this category is that of Tyers, used by the World Bank in the 1986 World Development Report.[3] It incorporates seven agricultural commodities and 30 countries or country groups. The intersectoral links are captured by cross-elasticities in both supply and

[3]See Tyers and Anderson, 1986 and also Tyers and Anderson, 1987a, 1987b; earlier versions of the same model are used in Anderson and Tyers, 1984, Chisholm and Tyers, 1985, and Tyers, 1985.

118   EFFECTS OF THE COMMON AGRICULTURAL POLICY

demand. Supply is represented by a mechanism of 'partial adjustment' of production to prices (Nerlove, 1958). It models government action explicitly by using 'transmission elasticities' which determine what proportion of a world price shock is passed through to domestic producers and consumers. It includes stockholding behaviour endogenously, and it estimates welfare effects on consumers and producers, and changes in government budgets and stockholders' profits. Finally, it is dynamic in nature, in the sense that it allows for differences in the short- and long-run effects of a shock or policy change.

Even a model of such sophistication, however, is essentially limited by the constraints of partial equilibrium methodology. Computable General Equilibrium (CGE) models make one further step and bring non-agricultural sectors, factor markets and the macroeconomy into the picture. Thus, the problems raised above in points (5) and (6) are addressed directly in CGE models.

CGE world models are essentially higher-dimensional analogues of the traditional two-sector Heckscher–Ohlin international trade model. Each region has a production function with primary and intermediate inputs and demand functions derived from utility maximization. The Armington heterogeneity assumption, which postulates that similar goods from different countries are imperfect substitutes, is usually made to account for the cross-hauling of goods observed in international trade. The countries are constrained by their total factor endowments. The balance of payments, or parts of it, is modelled explicitly and constrained by an external condition. A global general equilibrium is characterized by a set of international prices for all goods and factors such that: (i) all markets clear; (ii) the zero-profit conditions are met in all industries; and (iii) the external accounts of each country satisfy the constraints.[4]

The issues raised earlier in point (7) are not dealt with successfully in either advanced partial equilibrium or general equilibrium analysis. Externalities, in particular, are hard to handle because market prices do not reflect the true social valuations of different activities.

The discussion so far had focused on different ways of measuring the effects that price support policies have on domestic welfare, international trade and the welfare of other countries. Such policies in large countries or regions, however, have other effects as well. One that has attracted a considerable amount of attention is the effect on the stability of international commodity prices.

Price instability, especially in agricultural markets, has long been an issue of concern. The conventional view is that policies that insulate domestic markets from international price movements tend to increase world price

[4]The basic structure of CGE models is discussed in detail in Whalley (1984), Whalley (1985a) ch. 3 and Winters (1987). Whalley (1985b) outlines some of the methodological problems that applied general equilibrium analysis still faces.

DEMEKAS, BARTHOLDY, GUPTA, LIPSCHITZ AND MAYER 119

instability. This happens because, if a country does not let its domestic consumption accommodate, for example, a world production shortfall, the consumption of everybody else must fall disproportionately. To ration the reduced world output, world prices must rise by more. This, in turn, causes farmers' incomes to fluctuate. Farmers with utility functions with the usual convexity properties react with aversion to risk in their supply decisions and, in this way, affect the economy as a whole. Moreover, the poorer the country whose commodities are affected, the more undesirable these fluctuations are, for two reasons: first, because farmers there tend to be relatively more numerous and impoverished; second because owing to the reduced access to insurance markets, they are more vulnerable to income fluctuations.

This view is not completely accurate for two reasons. First, it is unclear whether all price support measures increase instability, or whether they increase it to the same extent. Bale and Lutz (1978 and 1979b) show that some policy instruments have no impact on world price stability, while others transfer different degrees of instability from one country to another.[5] Second, world prices in theory can be stabilized even if most countries insulate their markets, as long as countries or private individuals operating in the free market hold big enough stocks. The issue is, ultimately, an empirical one.

In order to measure empirically how much the insulation of particular domestic markets adds to price instability in the world, the partial or general equilibrium models used need to be modified to take into account price fluctuations. This is done by introducing stochastic supply and demand shocks in the models (see, for example, Tyers and Anderson, 1986) and observing how the specific policies change the variance of prices.

A final methodological point that ought to be mentioned has to do with the scope of counterfactual equilibrium analysis. There is no hard and fast rule for the choice of the appropriate counterfactual. 'base case'; it depends on what the specific question addressed is. If the focus is on a cost–benefit analysis of the CAP, then the free trade competitive equilibrium is the obvious choice. If, on the other hand, the objective is an evaluation of an alternative policy package (such as maintaining unchanged nominal support prices for a certain period of time, reducing protection of some communities or across the board, etc.), then this is the appropriate counterfactual. The first option has the additional advantage of being conceptually simple and familiar. The second is obviously more interesting from a policy-maker's point of view, but requires a detailed spelling out of the components of the alternative policy package.[6]

---

[5]The effect of domestic policies on international price stability is also analysed in Bale and Lutz (1979b), Blandford (1983) and Berck and Schmitz (1984). Koester (1982) compares alternative price support policy packages *vis-à-vis* their (de)stabilizing properties.

[6]Buckwell *et al.* (1982) ch. 3, Bureau of Agricultural Economics (1985) ch. 6 and Whalley (1985a) ch. 3, offer a brief discussion of the problems of counterfactual equilibrium analysis.

Table 1

Welfare Effects of the CAP on the EC Members
(1980 US$b per year)

Source	Commodity (ies)	Country (ies)	Model structure[a]	Year	Effects on				
					Consumers (a)	Tax-payers (b)	Producers (c)	Total Absolute	Total Relative (d)
Koester and Schmitz (1982)	Sugar	EC–9	PE	1978–79				–0.40	
Morris (1980)	Main CAP commodities	EC–9	PE	1978	–43.5	–10.7	38.6	–15.6	–0.53% of EC–9 GDP transfer ratio of 1.40[c]
Thomson and Harvey (1981)	All CAP commodities	EC–9	PE	1980[b]					Transfer ratio of 1.77[c]
Australia Bureau of Agricultural Economics (1985)	All CAP commodities	EC–9	PE	1978	–35.4	–18.1	44.1	–9.4	–0.48% of EC–9 GDP transfer ratio of 1.21[c]
		EC–10	PE	1983	–25.6	–20.8	39.7	–6.7	–0.32% of EC–10 GDP transfer ratio of 1.17[c]
Buckwell et al. (1982)	All CAP commodities	EC–9	PE	1980	–34.6	–11.5	30.7	–15.4	–0.55% of EC–9 GDP transfer ratio of 1.5[c]

Study	Commodities	Type	Year				(a)+(b)/(c)	
Tyers (1985)	Rice, wheat, coarse grains, ruminant and non-ruminant meat	PE	1980	-44.0	-0.9	13.9	-31.0[e]	-1.1% of EC-9 GDP transfer ratio 3.23
		EC-9						
Tyers and Anderson (1986a)	Rice, wheat coarse grains ruminant and non-ruminant meat, dairy, sugar	PE	1985[c]	-49.0	-2.2	27.2	-24.1[d]	-1.3% of EC-10 GDP or transfer ratio of 1.88[c]
		EC-10						
Spencer (1985)	All CAP commodities	GE	1980					Approx. -0.9% of EC-9 GDP
		EC-9						
Burniaux and Waelbroeck (1985)	All CAP commodities	GE	1995					-2.7% of EC-10 GDP
		EC-10						
Tyers and Anderson (1987a, b)	Rice, wheat coarse grains, ruminant and non-ruminant meat, dairy, sugar	PE	1980-82	-42.3	-0.9	36.4	-6.8[e]	-0.27% of EC-12 GDP transfer ratio of 1.19
		EC-12						
OECD (1987)	All CAP commodities	PE	1979-81	-27.8				
		EC-9						

[a] PE – Partial equilibrium (single- or multi-sector); GE: General equilibrium.

[b] The Thomson and Harvey (1981) results are for 1980 but their model used data from 1975 for calibration.

[c] The transfer ratio is defined as the cost to the economy of increasing farmers' income by 1 unit; in other words columns (a)+(b)/(c)

[d] Results are for 1985, but the model is calibrated to data from 1980–82.

[e] Includes change in net government revenue and profits from storage.

EC–9 comprises Belgium, Denmark, France, the Federal Republic of Germany, Ireland, Italy, Luxembourg, the Netherlands and the United Kingdom.

For all these studies except OECD (1987) the free-trade equilibrium is the basis of measurement.

2. THE EVIDENCE

Effects of the CAP on EC Members

This section presents a survey of recent empirical literature on the domestic effects of the CAP. Most studies treat the Community as one entity, although some provide estimates of the effects on a country-by-country basis. Most also provide a breakdown of the total welfare cost into consumer and taxpayer (or government) loss and producer benefit. Table 1 summarizes the evidence from all the existing studies that report results in a comparable form. Also presented and discussed are studies that focus on different aspects of the domestic effects of the CAP or that formulate their questions in a different way. The cost estimates in columns (a) to (d) are all converted into 1980 US dollars.

All but one of the studies presented are multi-sector models, covering all or most of the CAP commodities. Koester and Schmitz (1982) is the only exception. They examine the effects of the EC Sugar Protocol (a mixed system of price support and quotas) on LDCs, intra-EC transfers and Community welfare. The welfare costs are calculated with a free trade counterfactual world price as the reference point, which was taken to be equal to 38 per cent of the EC support price. This counterfactual world price was arrived at by a series of computations of free trade counterfactual equilibria under different assumptions about demand and supply elasticities in the Community and the rest of the world. However, no exact information about the elasticities was available and, in addition, the computed counterfactual equilibria were very sensitive to the elasticity values (*op. cit.*, p. 189). The welfare calculations, therefore, do not seem very reliable.

Morris (1980) estimates the effects of price support for the main CAP commodities (the exceptions being wine, tobacco, fruit and vegetables). A serious drawback of this study is that the counterfactual free trade prices do not come out of a demand and supply system, but are instead postulated *ad hoc*. Since these counterfactual prices are not listed in the study, it is impossible to tell *a priori* whether the paper tends to over- or underestimate the welfare costs.

Thomson and Harvey's (1981) paper models the markets for 16 groups of agricultural commodities. Their interaction is captured by a set of cross-elasticities. The study evaluates the CAP with respect to its stated objectives and does not address the wider social costs. The closest one which could come to a measure of overall efficiency is the transfer ratio of 1.77. The transfer ratio is the cost to the economy of an increase in farmers' income by one unit.

DEMEKAS, BARTHOLDY, GUPTA, LIPSCHITZ AND MAYER 123

A very comprehensive study of agricultural protection in the EC is that by the Australian Bureau of Agricultural Economics (Bureau of Agricultural Economics, 1985). They treat the Community as one country, but distinguish between different commodities, as do Thomson and Harvey (1981), and make adjustments to account for their interaction. They consider the CAP together with national price support policies and provide yearly estimates of the costs for the 1971–83 period. In table 1 estimates are reported for 1978, when, according to the study, the costs of agricultural support peaked, and 1983. Their results imply significant costs from the operation of price support mechanisms: around 0.3 per cent of total EC-10 GDP, equivalent to roughly one-third of Greece's GDP, was wasted in 1983. In per capita terms, this means approximately US$25.

Probably the most often quoted study of the effects of the CAP is the monograph by Buckwell *et al.* (1982). As with the previous two studies, they model explicitly many countries and markets, with the interaction between commodities captured by cross-elasticities. An important advantage of this paper is that it takes into account intra-EC transfers resulting from Community preference schemes, the common financing of the CAP and MCAs. Their estimate of the consumers' loss is comparable to that of the Bureau of Agricultural Economics, but that of the taxpayers' is smaller, possibly because of the inclusion of the intra-EC transfers mentioned above. The total cost estimate, however, is larger than that of the Bureau. The reason for this is probably the fact that Buckwell *et al.* model the structure of the agricultural sector in greater detail and, therefore, are more accurate in their estimation of the producers' benefit.

Tyers (1985) and Tyers and Anderson (1986, 1987a, 1987b) use different versions of the same model to estimate the costs of the CAP alone and of the CAP plus domestic policies respectively. The basic model is discussed in Section 1 of this article. In comparison to the previous studies, there seem to be several advantages in the analytical framework used by Tyers and Anderson. First, the international policy interactions are better captured, because the degree of disaggregation is higher (24 countries and country groups in the 1985 Tyers paper and 30 in the 1986 Tyers and Anderson paper). Second, government behaviour is incorporated in the model and assumed to be different in the short and the long run. Third, stockholding behaviour is modelled explicitly.

The estimates presented in the studies are for different years (1980 for the Tyers, 1980–82 and 1985 for the Tyers and Anderson studies)[7] and different country groups (EC–9 to EC–12) and for varying degrees of disaggregation of the rest of the world. In the two earlier studies, the total cost estimate is significantly higher than in any other partial equilibrium study: it is 1.1 per

[7]Note, however, that both in the 1986 and 1987 studies the base period for the estimates was 1980–82. The results reported for 1985 are merely 'scaled up' results for 1980–82 and do not take into account the major macroeconomic and supply shocks which occurred between 1980 and 1985.

124   EFFECTS OF THE COMMON AGRICULTURAL POLICY

cent of EC–9 GDP in 1980 in the Tyers study and 1.3 per cent of EC–10 GDP in 1985 in the Tyers and Anderson paper. The implied transfer ratio in the latter study is 1.88. In their 1987 study, however, the authors estimate total costs at only 0.3 per cent of EC–12 GNP and the transfer ratio at 1.2. The discrepancy with the earlier studies seems to reflect in part a change in the measurement of the welfare effects. While the model used in this and earlier studies by the same authors is non-linear, in the earlier studies linear approximations to supply and compensated demand curves were used to measure the welfare effects. The areas which emerge from such approximations are accurate only for small changes in domestic prices — in the case of the EC, however, the price changes were in fact very large. In the 1987 studies the areas under non-linear curves were measured, which resulted in some cases in substantially smaller welfare effects. In addition, the 1987 study assumes a much lower degree of transmission of world market price changes to domestic price changes.

The long-run transmission elasticities for the EC, for example, range between 0 and 0.76 depending on the particular commodity.[8] As a consequence of the higher degree of insulation of prices in the EC and other countries and geographical regions, trade liberalization in the EC has a larger impact on world market prices. This is reflected in the significantly larger increases in agricultural world market prices as a result of trade liberalization in industrial countries in the 1987 study as compared with the earlier studies (see below). Consequently, the gains from liberalization, which depend on the counterfactual world market prices, are much smaller.

The studies by Spencer (1985) and Burniaux and Waelbroeck (1985) are general equilibrium models. Spencer (1985) has a very simple CGE model with nine countries (eight in the EC, with Belgium and Luxembourg lumped together, and the rest of the world) and two goods (agriculture and non-agriculture) produced with two factors of production. He calculates that 0.9 per cent of EC-9 GDP is lost as a result of the CAP.

Burniaux and Waelbroeck (1985) use a more sophisticated CGE framework, which includes nine regions and separately models production and consumption in the urban and rural areas of each (see Burniaux and Waelbroeck, 1985, Appendix). As in the Tyers and Anderson (1986) model, different degrees of insulation of the domestic market are captured by price transmission equations. The paper distinguishes between more and less 'flexible' regions; the US and Latin America, for example, are assumed to insulate their domestic markets less than oil-exporting countries and Europe.

The Burniaux and Waelbroeck model calculates the long-run effects of a policy change today, subject to growth rate forecasts for the regions under consideration. Dismantling the CAP in 1985, according to the model,

---

[8]A value of 0 implies no pass through of changes in the world prices to the domestic prices; a value of 1 implies complete pass through.

generates a gain in real income equal to 2.7 per cent of EC GDP in 1995. This result is somewhat surprising, compared with the other studies presented here, but can be explained by the assumptions fed into the model. Burniaux and Waelbroeck, unlike other studies, assume that international commodity prices, even if nothing else changes, will be decreasing continuously until 1995. Agricultural protection in the EC with variable import levies, which maintain domestic commodity prices unchanged, is obviously bound to look increasingly expensive against this background. Nevertheless, this scenario is not unreasonable, especially if the commodity price trends of the last 30 years continue in the future.

Finally, the results from a recently released OECD study (1987a) can be construed to be based on a simple 'partial' equilibrium approach, which implicitly assumes inelastic demand for agricultural products in the EC for estimating costs to the consumers. The expenditures incurred by both the national and the EC authorities on agriculture, on the other hand, are taken in the study to represent the costs to the taxpayer. The OECD study estimates the cost of agricultural policy in the EC to the consumers at about US$28 billion in 1980 prices (or about 1.8 per cent of EC–9 GDP). The total cost (to the consumers and taxpayers) of this policy is estimated at 2.8 per cent of GDP; the annual average costs are estimated at ecu 11,437 per holding and ecu 7, 465 per agricultural worker during the period 1979–81.[9]

The diversity of the methodologies used makes it difficult to summarize the evidence presented in table 1. In general, though, the estimates of the welfare costs of the CAP seem to fall into two zones: a 'low' one, with net losses ranging from 0.32 per cent to 0.55 per cent of EC GDP (Morris, 1980; Bureau of Agricultural Economics, 1985; Buckwell *et al.*, 1982, Tyers and Anderson, 1987a, b), and a 'high' one, with net losses at around 1 per cent or more of EC GDP (Tyers, 1985; Tyers and Anderson, 1986; Spencer, 1985, Burniaux and Waelbroeck, 1985). The Thompson and Harvey study also belongs to the latter group by virtue of their estimate of the transfer ratio, which is comparable to that of Tyers and Anderson (1986).

Although it is impossible to judge the validity of these figures without some idea of the 'true' costs, it is worth noting that the studies that produce estimates in the 'high' zone use generally superior methodology and a higher level of disaggregation. To the extent that this is a valid criterion for evaluating empirical work, it can be concluded that these studies are probably more accurate in estimating the welfare costs of the CAP.

The remaining part of this section discusses briefly a few studies that focus on different, distributional or country-specific, effects of the CAP and are not included in table 1. Harling and Thompson (1985) use a partial equilibrium model to estimate the costs of intervention in the poultry industry for, among other countries, Germany and the United Kingdom. They find that in

[9]These are the 'gross' costs of the CAP and not comparable with the 'net' costs, or deadweight losses, reported in table 1.

126   EFFECTS OF THE COMMON AGRICULTURAL POLICY

1975–77 the resulting deadweight losses were of the order of US$10.5 million for these two countries together.

Bale and Lutz (1979a and 1981) calculate the costs of price support for wheat, maize, sugar and beef in selected countries. They use a very simple partial equilibrium model and report a net welfare loss of US$737.3 million for France, US$1,112.4 million for Germany and US$112.4 million for the United Kingdom.

The paper by Buckwell *et al.* provides estimates of the welfare costs by country. They are summarized in Table 2. The transfer ratio, which can be thought of as a broad measure of policy efficiency, is 1.50 for the Community as a whole. It is highest in the UK (2.07), Italy (1.87) and Germany (1.8). It is less than unity in the Netherlands, Ireland and Denmark, indicating that these countries benefit from the inter-country redistribution of income caused by the CAP (see Buckwell *et al.*, 1982, pp. 90–134; and Koester and Tangermann, 1986, p. 63).

Table 2

Welfare Effects of the CAP by Country in 1980 (US$m)

Country	Consumers	Taxpayers	Producers	Net	Transfer ratio
EC–9	–34,580	–11,494	30,686	–15,388	1.50
Germany	–12,555	–3,769	9,045	–7,279	1,80
France	–7,482	–2,836	7,237	–3,081	1.42
Italy	–5,379	–1,253	3,539	–3,093	1.87
Netherlands	–1,597	–697	3,081	787	0.74
Belgium/Luxembourg	–1,440	–544	1,624	–320	1.22
United Kingdom	–5,174	–1,995	3,461	–3,708	2.07
Ireland	–320	–99	965	546	0.43
Denmark	–635	–302	1,736	799	0.54

Sources: Buckwell *et al.* (1982), pp. 90–134, and staff calculations

This ranking of the gainers from the CAP is similar to the one in Spencer (1986). He uses a general equilibrium model to evaluate which countries would do better outside the CAP, and by how much. It turns out that Ireland would be the only clear loser, with Denmark gaining the least. The only notable difference between Buckwell *et al.* and Spencer is the Netherlands: in the former study the less than unity transfer ratio indicates that the country is benefiting, whereas in the latter the Netherlands appears to be losing from the operation of the CAP.

Greece also appears to gain a very small amount, around 5–10 million ECU per year, from participating in the CAP (see Georgakopoulos, 1986;

Georgakopoulos and Paschos, 1985). This result, however, should be interpreted with care, since it is not derived from a full counterfactual analysis.

Breckling *et al.* (1987) use a simple general equilibrium model to appraise the economy-wide effects of the CAP for four EC members: Germany, France, Italy and the United Kingdom. They conclude that the costs of agricultural price support extend beyond the traditional welfare losses. Specifically, for all countries taken together, manufacturing industries (excluding food processing) lose between 1.1 and 2.5 per cent of potential gross output and between 4.4 and 6.2 per cent of exports and total employment is reduced by around 1 per cent (or 860,000 jobs). Unemployment increases universally in these countries as non-agricultural sectors are relatively intensive employers of labour. The job loss is more in the United Kingdom and Germany followed by Italy and France. This is the result of slower growth of labour-intensive non-agricultural sectors in the former countries. However, the results suggest that despite the emerging unemployment, France is a net beneficiary of the CAP in view of its large rural sector and EC transfers under the applicable common policy. These results are broadly confirmed in a later study by Stoeckel and Breckling (1988), which uses the same model. The authors find that national and supranational protection of the agricultural sector in the four countries under investigation, reduce real aggregate income by 1.5 per cent and cause a loss of about four million jobs.

Despite the budgetary and welfare burden of the CAP, the agricultural lobby has resisted attempts to liberalize and is, instead, stepping up pressure to reinforce the CAP (Koester, 1985; Gerken, 1986; von Witzke, 1986). This movement away from liberalization is apparently accelerated by demands for more equal distribution of the CAP benefits between Member States. Josling (1979) discusses the CAP in the light of the expansion of the EC in Southern Europe and concludes that the wider range of commodities and the shifting political balance within the Community will increase the domestic costs, exacerbate the budgetary problems and amplify the international effects of agricultural protection. In the same vein, Koester (1977) argues that as long as it is possible for member countries to supra-nationalize costs of national agricultural support, the prospects for a CAP reform are poor. This argument may be questionable at a time of acute budgetary crisis.

Effects of the CAP on International Trade

This section discusses the evidence on the effects the CAP has on the level of prices and the volume and pattern of world trade in agricultural commodities. Since the policies that apply to different products vary widely, the estimated effects for each of the most important commodities covered by the CAP are presented separately. These commodities are: wheat, coarse grains

128   EFFECTS OF THE COMMON AGRICULTURAL POLICY

(barley, maize, rye, oats, millet and sorghum), rice, ruminant meat (beef and veal), non-ruminant meat (pork, poultry, etc.) sugar and dairy products. Table 3 presents the estimated effects of a hypothetical abolition of the CAP on the international prices of the above commodities. Each of the studies reviewed calculates a counterfactual world trade equilibrium with a completely liberalized EC market for the commodities in question and then compares the resulting counterfactual prices with the actual world prices.

The estimates show that abolition of the CAP would significantly increase the world prices of all the commodities examined. In other words, the CAP exerts a powerful downward pressure on the actual price level. Roughly speaking, the effect is stronger on dairy products, grains and ruminant meat and weaker on sugar and rice. This result is to be expected, since the former category of products is afforded greater effective protection than the latter (see Sampson and Yeats, 1977; Koester and Tangermann, 1986, p. 71).

All the estimates reported in Table 3 come from partial equilibrium models. There are considerable differences between the estimated price effects for each commodity, which can be, to a large extent, traced back to the differences in the methodology and the data used in each study. First of all, models that cover only a few commodities and/or do not take into account market interaction, tend to predict higher counterfactual prices and, therefore, overestimate the effects on world markets of price support in the CAP. If only a few isolated markets are liberalized, then the pressure from the other, still protected, markets will spill over via commodity substitution and the observed effects will be amplified. The first four studies listed in table 3 share this characteristic. The Koester and Valdes paper in particular, although it examines many products, does not take into account cross-effects and uses, essentially, a single-commodity approach.[10]

A second element that accounts for differences between estimated effects, even if the methodology is similar, is the data used. This explains partially why the results of the four other papers (Anderson and Tyers, 1984; Tyers and Anderson, 1986, 1987b, and Matthews, 1985a), which are all multi-commodity models and examine the effects of a generalized liberalization on individual commodity prices, are so diverse. Anderson and Tyers (1984) probably overestimate the degree of protection in the Community by using the official intervention prices as the appropriate domestic market prices (Koester and Tangermann, 1986, p. 74). Due to the existing surplus stocks, however, EC market prices are generally lower than the intervention prices (see the information provided in Commission of the European Communities, 1986, Statistical Appendix). Matthews, on the other hand, underes-

[10]Tyers (1985) and Matthews (1985a) estimate the effects of liberalization in a multi-commodity model with and without cross-effects. In both studies the models without cross-effects produce estimates 20-100 per cent higher than the models with cross-effects. This difference is most noticeable in coarse grains, wheat and non-ruminant meat, where the removal of channels for market interaction roughly doubles the calculated effects of liberalization.

DEMEKAS, BARTHOLDY, GUPTA, LIPSCHITZ AND MAYER   129

Table 3

Effects of the CAP on International Prices (% change in world market prices following complete liberalization)

Source[a]	EC-concept	Base year	Wheat	Coarse grains	Rice	Ruminant meat	Non-ruminant meat	Sugar	Dairy
Koester and Schmitz (1982)	EC-9	1979	9.6					12.0	
Koester (1982)	EC-9	1975–77		14.3[b]					
Koester and Valdes (1984)	EC-9	1980	4.6			10.5[c]	5.9[d]	9.7	28.3[c]
Sarris and Freebairn (1983)	EC-9	1978–80	9.2						
Anderson and Tyers (1984)[f]	EC-9	1980	13.0	16.0	5.0	17.0	1.0		
Tyers and Anderson (1986)	EC-10	1985[g]	0.7	2.5	0.7	9.5	1.7	2.6	11.8
Matthews (1985a)	EC-10	1978–82	0.7	2.9[h]	0.1	4.5[h]	3.6[d]	6.0	10.5[c]
Tyers and Anderson (1987b)	EC-12	1980–82	6.0	5.0	3.0	18.0	4.0	7.0	25.0

[a] All studies cited base their results on partial equilibrium analysis.
[b] Reported figure refers to barley only.
[c] Reported figure refers to beef only.
[d] Average of estimated effect on the prices of pork and poultry.
[e] Reported figure refers to butter only.
[f] Same results also reported in Tyers (1985).
[g] Results for 1985, but the model is calibrated to data from 1980–82.
[h] Average of estimated effect on the prices of beef and mutton.

130   EFFECTS OF THE COMMON AGRICULTURAL POLICY

timates the degree of protection in the Community, because he uses the EC cif price as the appropriate world price. As the Community is a net exporter of many of these commodities, however, the fob price or the price in major foreign parts should be used.

A third factor that affects crucially the outcome of counterfactual experiments is the values of the parameters used. For example, the higher the domestic demand elasticity, the stronger the domestic reaction to liberalization and the larger the final effect on the world price will be. Tyers (1985) and Anderson and Tyers (1984) use EC demand elasticities between –0.5 and –0.7 (Tyers, 1985, Appendix), whereas Matthews postulates a value of –0.4 for all commodities (Matthews, 1985a, p. 115). The former range of values is based on a more detailed survey of the relevant empirical literature. Also, as mentioned above, the difference in 'transmission elasticities' between the more recent Tyers and Anderson studies influences the results.

Finally, the last significant cause of deviations between the estimates of different models is the varying degree of country and commodity coverage and differences in the base period. The Tyers and Anderson papers (1986, 1987b) are by far the most detailed in that respect, modelling seven commodity and 30 country groups. Unfortunately it is impossible to tell *a priori* whether a greater degree of disaggregation tends to generate larger or smaller effects.

The OECD has produced a comprehensive partial equilibrium study on the effects of agricultural protection in the world (OECD, 1987). Although the emphasis is on multilateral liberalization, they report some estimates of the effect on world prices of a unilateral liberalization in the Community. Their counterfactual, however, is not the free trade equilibrium, but a 10 per cent across-the-board reduction in nominal protection of all commodities. They calculate that this partial liberalization in the EC increases the world prices of most commodities from 0.55 per cent, in the case of sugar, to 2.81 per cent in the case of milk. In the case of grains, however, prices actually fall a little following the hypothetical CAP reform, owing to decreased demand for grains by livestock producers.

The calculated counterfactual prices are important, first, because they give some idea of the degree of distortion in world agricultural markets that is due to the CAP and, second, because they provide the basis for the estimation of the effects of liberalization on the pattern and volume of world trade. Changes in the pattern and volume of trade, of course, have little importance in and of themselves. Calculating them, however, is a necessary step in assessing the effects the CAP had on the real income of Europe's trading partners. For that reason we present and discuss some of the empirical work on this issue very briefly.

Table 4 highlights the main results. Abolition of the CAP increases total commodity trade by a considerable amount. This is caused basically by a large increase in EC net imports, prompted by lower consumer and higher producer prices. The effect is stronger in the most heavily protected sectors,

Table 4

Effects of the CAP on World Trade[a] (change in volume following complete liberalization, in millions of tons)

	EC-concept	Base year	Net imports to the EC	Net imports to developed countries (including EC)	Net imports to less developed countries	Total volume traded
Wheat						
Koester (1982)	EC-9	1975–77	14.7	-8.5	-3.4	18.6
Anderson and Tyers (1984)	EC-9	1980	14.7			12.3
Tyers (1985)	EC-9	1980				0.0
Tyers and Anderson (1986)	EC-10	1985[b]	-2.4	0.2	0.2	0.0
Tyers and Anderson, (1987b)	EC-12	1980–82		4.5	-4.9	-4.0
Coarse grains						
Koester (1982)	EC-9	1975–77	26.0	-10.0[c]	-5.3[c]	68.5[c]
Anderson & Tyers (1984)	EC-9	1980	26.0			23.2
Tyers (1985)	EC-9	1980				4.0
Tyers and Anderson (1986)	EC-10	1985[b]	5.9	3.0	-3.3	0.0
Tyers and Anderson (1987b)	EC-12	1980–82		4.0	2.3	
Rice						
Anderson & Tyers (1984)	EC-9	1980	-0.2			
Tyers (1985)	EC-9	1980	-0.2			
Tyers and Anderson (1986)	EC-10	1985[b]	0.1	0.1	-0.1	0.0
Tyers and Anderson (1987b)	EC-12	1980–82		3.8	-4.0	-1.0
Ruminant meat						
Anderson and Tyers (1984)	EC-9	1980	3.0			2.7
Tyers (1985)	EC-9	1980	3.0			
Tyers and Anderson (1986)	EC-10	1985[b]	5.3	3.2	-2.6	107.0
Tyers and Anderson (1987b)	EC-12	1980–82		5.6	-2.9	58.0
Non-ruminant meat						
Anderson and Tyers (1984)	EC-9	1980	-2.0			2.0
Tyers (1985)	EC-9	1980	-2.0			
Tyers and Anderson (1986)	EC-10	1985[b]	-0.5	0.0	-0.0	3.0
Tyers and Anderson (1987b)	EC-12	1980–82		1.7	-0.7	-6.0
Sugar						
Tyers and Anderson (1986)	EC-10	1985[b]	3.0	2.8	-2.6	-5.0
Tyers and Anderson (1987b)	EC-12	1980–82		2.3	-2.9	0.0
Dairy						
Tyers and Anderson (1986)	EC-10	1985[b]	38.8	29.7	-19.6	34.0
Tyers and Anderson (1987b)	EC-12	1980–82		14.0	-22.0	17.0

[a] All studies cited base their results on partial equilibrium analysis.
[b] Results for 1985, but the model is calibrated to data from 1980–82.
[c] Reported figure refers to barley and maize only.

132   EFFECTS OF THE COMMON AGRICULTURAL POLICY

such as wheat, grains and dairy products. The reported effects would be much larger if they were expressed in value, rather than volume, terms.

The results of studies cited in Table 4 are influenced by the estimated post-liberalization counterfactual prices and the coverage and grouping of countries. Koester (1982), for example, includes in the Developed Countries group all the centrally planned economies, which form a separate group in Tyers and Anderson (1986). The only surprising result, which cannot be explained by these factors, is the negative change in EC net imports of wheat that Tyers and Anderson (1986) report. Given that the Community is a net exporter of wheat, this means that abolishing the CAP will lead to an increase in net wheat exports. Unfortunately the authors do not comment on this counterintuitive conclusion.

The net trade effects of the CAP on other trading partners are also discussed in other studies, which are not comparable to the ones reported in table 4 because in those, authors conduct a different counterfactual experiment, or use a different taxonomy for reporting their quantitative results, or do not provide quantitative results at all. Sarris (1983) calculates the effects of EC enlargement in Southern Europe on international trade in fruit and vegetables. He estimates that including Greece, Spain and Portugal under the CAP umbrella increases the value of net imports (or reduces the value of net exports) of the other major producing countries by approximately US$116.6 million (in 1980 prices). Tangermann (1978 and 1981) discusses the possible effects of reforming the CAP on the trade flows between developed and less developed countries. He concludes that, since the CAP protects mostly temperate products, the EC imports from other temperate/developed countries will increase as a result of reducing price support. The effect on trade with LDCs, however, is ambiguous. The producers of such commodities there will have an incentive to increase their production but, on the other hand, they will also have to compete with other exporters. The final outcome depends crucially on the supply elasticities. Finally, Mackel *et al.* (1984) focus on, among other things, the effect of the CAP on trade in commodities that are not protected in the EC. They argue that the CAP has increased imports of substitute products to the EC, like manioc and soya and that, therefore, a liberalization will harm producers of such commodities.

Empirical research on the impact of the CAP on international commodity trade, far from being in unequivocal agreement, has reached some common conclusions regarding at least the direction of the effects. First, the CAP has a significant depressing effect on world prices. Second, as a result of this, trade flows are severely distorted: EC exports are artificially boosted at the expense of net exports of other countries. Third, this distortion keeps the volume of world trade at a lower level than it would otherwise be. Fourth, these effects are generally more significant for the products that are heavily protected in the Community, such as wheat, coarse grains, ruminant meat and dairy products.

Effects of the CAP on the Welfare of Non-EC Countries

The influence the CAP exerts on international trade means that the real incomes of all trading partners are eventually affected. The conventional view, popular with Community officials, is that a unilateral liberalization in the EC will benefit the exporters and harm the importers of temperate zone products by increasing their prices. Consequently, given that most LDCs import temperate zone commodities, the CAP actually constitutes a transfer of income from EC consumers and taxpayers to poor countries via cheaper international food prices. Furthermore, the concessionary character of the Lomé Convention means that a liberalization, which would imply an abolition of those agreements as well, would be even more detrimental to the LDC group. The data in Table 5 seem to support this view. The table presents the effects that a hypothetical liberalization has on the welfare of two broad groups: the non-EC developed countries and the less developed countries.

The models reviewed in Table 5 are all partial equilibrium and the degree of commodity and country coverage varies, but two facts stand out. First, the size of the total effect on each of the two country groups is not large compared to GDP or total export earnings. Second, less developed countries as a group stand to lose from an abolition of the CAP, while the effect on developed countries is ambiguous.

Differences in the estimated size of the effects can be generally traced back to commodity coverage or the data used. The figures reported by Koester (1982) and Koester and Schmitz (1982) are expectedly lower than the rest, since these studies cover only cereals and sugar respectively. Therefore, although the estimated effect on the world price of the individual commodities may be higher, as discussed in the previous section, the total welfare effect is small. Matthews (1985a) also reports a small estimate of LDC loss for two reasons: (1), mentioned earlier, because he underestimates the degree of protection in the Community; (2) because he uses smaller domestic supply elasticities than other studies. The higher the LDC supply elasticity assumed, the stronger the supply response to increasing world prices and the more likely the realization of gains from increased exports. Matthews uses a supply elasticity of 0.4 for all countries (Matthews, 1985a, p. 115), whereas Koester (1982), Anderson and Tyers (1984) and Tyers (1985) use elasticities in the neighbourhood of unity (Koester, 1982, p. 27; Tyers, 1985, Appendix). Extensive empirical research has shown that long-run supply elasticities in LDCs vary widely according to the specific product, but are generally rather low, fluctuating between 0.1 and 0.3 for grains and 0.2 and 0.5 for rice (see Bale and Lutz, 1979b; Scandizzo and Bruce, 1980; and the references therein).

Anderson and Tyers (1984) conduct a different counterfactual experiment. They calculate the impact of a 2 per cent annual reduction in EC

Table 5

Effects of the CAP on the Welfare of Non-EC Countries (change in real income following liberalization (US$b)

Source	Commodity (ies)	EC-concept	Model structure	Base year	Non-EC developed countries[a]	Less developed countries
Koester (1982)	Wheat, coarse grains	EC-9	PE	1979	0.9[b]	-0.5
Koester and Schmitz (1982)	Sugar	EC-9	PE	1979		-2.3
Anderson and Tyers (1984)	Wheat, rice, coarse grains, ruminant and non-ruminant meat	EC-9	PE	1981[c]	-1.5	-3.7
Tyers (1985)	Wheat, rice, coarse grains, ruminant and non-ruminant meat	EC-9	PE	1980	0.4	-1.8
Matthews (1985b)	Wheat, rice, coarse grains, ruminant and non-ruminant meat, sugar, oil, seeds, dairy	EC-10	PE	1978-82		-0.5
Tyers and Anderson (1986a)	Wheat, rice, coarse grains, ruminant and non-ruminant meat, sugar, dairy	EC-10	PE	1985[d]	-4.1	-5.9
Tyers and Anderson (1987)	Wheat, rice, coarse grains, ruminant and non-ruminant meat, sugar, dairy	EC-12	PE	1980-82	0.1	-10.5

[a] Australia, Canada, Japan, New Zealand, and the United States.
[b] Koester's developed countries group also includes Austria, Switzerland and the Nordic countries.
[c] Anderson and Tyers estimate the final effects in 1990 of a 2 per cent per year reduction in CAP support prices from 1981 to 1990.
[d] Results for 1985, but the model is calibrated to data from 1980-82.

support prices from 1981 to 1990. Their results are difficult to interpret because, although the final effect of the phased reduction of the support prices will be significant, it is unclear how close it will be to that of a complete liberalization.

Tyers and Anderson (1986, 1987a) have the highest degree of disaggregation, and the most detailed model among the ones in the table, and report in both studies the highest welfare loss for less developed countries from abolishing the CAP.[11] In their 1986 study, Tyers and Anderson found that even non-EC developed countries lose because the increase in grain prices as a result of liberalization diminishes the welfare of producers of livestock as they have to pay higher input prices.

Table 5 may lead one to believe that, no matter what the sign is for each group, the effect of the CAP is essentially small. Reporting only net effects for two large country groups, however, conceals the distribution of gains or losses among individual countries. The information that can be pieced together about this is quite interesting. First of all, the small net gain (or the net loss) in the developed countries group is entirely due to the heavy losses of Japan. The rest of the countries in the group all register gains or very small losses (see Tyers, 1985; Tyers and Anderson, 1986). Second, the distribution of the effect within the LDC group is also very varied, depending basically on whether the country is a net exporter or importer of temperate zone commodities. For some of the countries the gains or losses are significant. Argentina, for example, appears to gain around US$200 million per year, while Korea and Pakistan each lose US$300 million (Tyers and Anderson, 1986, p. 59) from a liberalization of EC agriculture. Moreover, if liberalization implies abolition of the Lomé Conventions, it is possible that the LDC signatories will lose even more than the rest of the group. Given, however, that agricultural commodities and, in particular, temperate zone products are a very small portion of the goods that receive preferential treatment under the Conventions, the effects of abolishing the Lomé agreements is likely to be small compared to the effect of a CAP liberalization.

The evidence supporting the conventional view that most LDCs actually benefit from the operation of the CAP tends to be discounted by some researchers. They argue that the fact that LDCs are net importers of temperate zone commodities is due to protectionist policies such as the CAP in developed countries, which depress international prices and make agricultural exports unprofitable. Abolishing such policies, therefore, may imply costs for LDCs in the short run, but in the long run increased prices will stimulate agricultural production and exports, the pattern of trade will change and LDCs will realize important gains. Counterfactual analysis, which uses econometrically estimated supply elasticities, fails to capture this potential 'switching' effect and, consequently, measures only the short-run

[11] In line with the estimated larger price effects of liberalization, the authors report a higher loss to LDCs in their more recent study.

136   EFFECTS OF THE COMMON AGRICULTURAL POLICY

losses. This argument is very appealing to the proponents of unilateral
liberalization, who also point out that it is only under the CAP regime that
the Community has turned into a net exporter of many temperate
commodities (Bureau of Agricultural Economics, 1985, p. 129). It has,
however, two important drawbacks. First, the lack of reliable long-run
supply elasticity estimates makes it impossible to measure the potential
'switching' effect accurately. Second, it is not supported by the existing
evidence on agricultural policies in developing countries. If they actually
believed in the harmful effects of the present low level of international prices
and in their dynamic comparative advantage as commodity producers, they
would subsidize agriculture to stimulate domestic production. Many LDCs,
however, especially in Africa, actually tax agriculture (Koester and
Tangermann, 1986, p. 78).

Another argument that has been voiced against the estimates in Table 5
has to do with the limitations of the partial equilibrium methodology. A
unilateral liberalization in the Community will affect non-agricultural
sectors and factor markets and have repercussions on commodity trade. In
order to capture these secondary effects, a general equilibrium model must
be used.

Burniaux and Waelbroeck (1985) use a CGE to calculate how a
liberalization of trade in agricultural commodities in the Community in 1985
would affect the welfare of LDCs in 1995; the results are quite striking. They
estimate that total LDC real income would be higher by 2.9 per cent if the
CAP were abolished. This is explained by the strong assumption that, even
with no change in the CAP, foreign exchange shortages in LDCs will oblige
them to rely more and more on agricultural exports. Thus the 'switching'
occurs even with no policy change in the Community. It is obvious then that
an abolition of the CAP, which raises world prices, benefits the LDCs.

Loo and Tower (1988) use a four-sector general equilibrium model, which
they calibrate for six 'typical' developing countries, to investigate the effects
of a 10 per cent increase in agricultural prices on world markets assumed to
result from trade liberalization in industrial countries. They find that LDCs
would gain about US$26 billion in 1985 prices as a result of the assumed
increase in world market prices for agricultural commodities.[12] This gain
could be split between the developing and industrial countries in various
ways. With developing country real income unchanged, the benefit to the
industrial countries from agricultural liberalization in terms of a reduction
in the amount of aid they need to supply would amount to a real income gain
of over US$16 billion. Alternatively, the developing countries could reduce
their external public debt by 2.8 per cent on average, with reductions for the
poorest countries of up to 4.8 per cent.

[12] In order to assess the effects of the CAP alone, the results reported by Loo and Tower (1988) could be
scaled using estimates of the effects of the CAP on agricultural world market prices provided in table 3.

These results basically reflect three effects of higher agricultural world market prices on developing countries. First, there is a change in the terms of trade which affects real incomes. This effect is positive for countries which are net exporters of agricultural products, but negative for others which are net importers. Second, there is a gain in efficiency for most developing countries as resources are shifted from relatively inefficient non-agricultural sectors to agriculture. Third, as a result of resource allocation in favour of agriculture, there is an increase in government tax revenue (which allows a reduction in average tax rates) since many developing countries tax agriculture and subsidize certain non-agricultural sectors. The paper by Loo and Tower suggests that the second and third effects may well dominate any terms of trade losses that developing countries may incur as a result of a liberalization of agricultural trade in industrial countries.

Matthews (1985b) makes an additional argument in favour of substantial gains by LDCs from a unilateral liberalization in the EC. If, for example, EC real income rose as a result of a more efficient allocation of resources after liberalization, the LDCs would gain indirectly from the increased demand for their exports by the Community and by other developed countries whose agricultural export earnings would also have risen. This argument is convincing in qualitative terms. Many past studies do not take account of these secondary effects on global welfare and, therefore, probably underestimate the gains from liberalization. It is far from clear, however, that these secondary effects would be quantitatively significant.

To summarize, the empirical literature surveyed in this section seems to point to a few unambiguous conclusions. First, agricultural price support in the Community is not necessarily harmful to all, or even most, non-EC countries. A unilateral liberalization would benefit some of Europe's trading partners and harm others. In particular, current net importers of temperate zone commodities would lose, whereas current or potential net exporters would gain. Since most LDCs are current net importers, they stand to lose as a group from an abolition of the CAP, at least in the short run. The important issue is, who will be able to adjust domestic production and consumption patterns so as to take advantage of the higher world prices in the longer run?

Second, although the size of the effect on broad groups of countries is small, the distribution of gains and losses is far from uniform. Countries that are heavily dependent on temperate commodity imports because of climate and geography (e.g. Japan) or because they are poor, appear to benefit significantly from the operation of the CAP.

Finally, the above results should be interpreted with some caution. It is important to keep in mind that the gains from unilateral liberalization predicted with partial equilibrium models probably have some degree of downward bias built in, because they do not take into account secondary repercussions in non-agricultural sectors.

138   EFFECTS OF THE COMMON AGRICULTURAL POLICY

Effects of the CAP on International Price Stability

Conventional wisdom holds that countries or regions that insulate their domestic markets increase world price instability. As was discussed in section 1 of this article, this is not necessarily true. The question is essentially an empirical one. Empirical research on the effects of the CAP on price stability has given an affirmative answer: all the studies reviewed here agree that the CAP exerts a significant destabilizing influence on world commodity prices. Table 6 summarizes some of the evidence.

The impact of policies on price stability is estimated with the help of counterfactual analysis. A measure of variability is defined first, and then the price variability at the counterfactual non-CAP equilibrium is calculated and compared to actual price variability. Most studies introduce random supply and demand shocks, calculate the corresponding counterfactual equilibria and then use either the standard deviation or the coefficient of variation of the resulting distribution of prices to measure variability.[13] Table 6 presents the calculated share of world price variability due to the CAP; in other words, the decrease in variability that would obtain if the CAP were abolished. The destabilizing effect is strongest in the wheat, coarse grains and dairy products sectors.

Comparing the EC agricultural policies with price support schemes in other countries reveals that the CAP is the most important destabilizing factor in the world markets. Sarris and Freebairn (1983) estimate that the CAP alone accounts for more than half of the excess variability of the price of wheat over its global free trade level. Blandford (1983) calculates 'transmission coefficients' that show the extent to which changes in trade rather than in domestic consumption are used to stabilize the domestic market, and concludes that the Community transmits a larger absolute amount of domestic variability in grain to the world market than any other group of countries. Of all the ways in which price support can affect world price stability mentioned earlier, two are most important for the destabilizing effect of the CAP. First, the CAP relies heavily on variable tariffs, which not only protect the domestic agricultural sector, but also insulate domestic consumers from world price variations (Matthews, 1985a, p. 211). Second, protection reduces the incentive for private stock-building, which implies wider price fluctuations. The latter effect could be avoided by government-sponsored stockpiling. Koester, however, finds evidence that in some years EC stocks increased when world market prices were extremely high, thereby actually amplifying world price variability (Koester, 1982, pp. 53–65).

[13]The choice of the measure is important: the standard deviation, for example, depends on the level of the mean (in this case the price level) and, therefore, even if prices remain equally stable after liberalization, the standard deviation will be different. Koester (1982), pp. 53–4, discusses at length the different measures of variability. It turns out that even the coefficient of variation is not unbiased. Koester suggests correcting the coefficient of variation by the explanatory power of the trend regression to obtain a better measure of variability.

Table 6

Effects of the CAP on International Price Stability (% share of variability of the world price due to the CAP)

Source[a]	EC-concept	Base year	Measure of variation used[b]	Wheat	Coarse grains	Rice	Ruminant meat	Non-ruminant products	Dairy products	sugar
Svedberg (1981)	EC–6	1967–72	D		7.0[c]					
Sarris and Freebairn (1983)	EC–9	1978–80	SD	19.8						
Schmitz and Koester (1984)	EC–10	1982	CV							8.5
Anderson and Tyers (1984)	EC–9	1980	CV	50.0	33.0	12.1	25.0	0.0		
Tyers (1985)	EC–9	1980	SD	44.0	24.0	6.0	11.0	7.0		
Tyers and Anderson (1986)	EC–10	1985	CV	24.0	5.0	9.6	16.7	22.0	60.0	5.0
Tyers and Anderson (1987a)	EC–12	1980–82	CV	32.8	15.1	15.8	37.4	0.0	50.0	22.2

[a] All the studies cited base their results on partial equilibrium analysis.
[b] D: Change in the price level following a 5 per cent production shortfall; SD: standard deviation; CV: coefficient of variation.
[c] The reported figure applies to a price index for wheat and coarse grains.

140   EFFECTS OF THE COMMON AGRICULTURAL POLICY

Section 2 discussed briefly why price stability is considered important from a welfare point of view, especially for developing countries. Unfortunately, there are no empirical estimates of the welfare losses caused by the destabilizing effects of the CAP. Given the size of the effects, though, it may well be the case that a liberalization would benefit Europe's trading partners significantly by reducing world price variability.

3. CONCLUDING REMARKS

The article has been concerned with two different but related aspects of the Common Agricultural Policy of the EC: the domestic effects on the welfare of EC members, and the effects on international commodity trade and, consequently, on the welfare of the rest of the world.

Recent empirical literature that has been surveyed addresses these two issues by means of various tools, ranging from single-sector partial equilibrium models to general equilibrium models of the global economy. The differences in methodology, data used, country and commodity coverage and degree of disaggregation are considerable, and so are the differences in the quantitative estimates. A good understanding of the theoretical premises and the modelling details of each study is, therefore, necessary in order to put the reported results in perspective and compare them.

Each approach has its relative merits. The attraction of partial equilibrium models is their simplicity, which means that greater effort can be devoted to collecting data and capturing the pecularities of the sector(s) represented. On the other hand, inter-sectoral links are ignored, which in turn means that not all of the effects of agricultural policies are covered. General equilibrium models are more comprehensive in that sense, but they are more demanding both analytically and in terms of data requirements. Overall, however, general equilibrium models are preferable in that they reveal the effects of agricultural price support on other sectors and on the macroeconomy. These effects are both important for policy purposes and, in the case of the CAP, significant in size. Without a general equilibrium model it is difficult to capture the secondary repercussions that liberalization has on the world economy via factor and other product markets. Ignoring these effects may cause systematic underestimation of the gains from liberalization.

Empirical research on the domestic effects of the CAP has reached some unequivocal conclusions. First, the CAP redistributes large amounts of income to farmers, primarily from consumers and secondarily from taxpayers. This transfer is economically inefficient, in that it incurs a deadweight loss. The mean estimate of this loss is around 1 per cent of the Community's GDP.

Second, the distribution of this loss between countries is not uniform. Most countries, however, stand to lose. The heaviest loser appears to be the United Kingdom, followed by Italy and Germany. France probably also registers small losses. The clear gainer is Ireland, while the evidence on Denmark and the Netherlands is ambiguous.

Third, other than the deadweight loss that the whole economy suffers, other sectors incur costs because of the CAP as well. In particular, subsidizing agricultural production means discriminating against industry and services, diverting resources away from them and reducing their exports. This kind of cost has not attracted enough attention, mainly because it requires general equilibrium modelling. Quantification of inter-sectoral effects is, therefore, an important area for future research.

The economy-wide and sectoral losses are by no means the only costs of the CAP. Agricultural price support, especially of such magnitude, generates wasteful rent-seeking and lobbying and distorts investment. These costs are difficult to estimate, but they mean that the traditional welfare calculations, even if they include inter-sectoral repercussions, underestimate the true social costs of operating the CAP.

With regard to the international effects of the CAP, empirical research has come to some interesting conclusions. By encouraging domestic production and raising consumer prices, especially in products with low income elasticity, the CAP has artificially reduced EC consumption and boosted production, turning Europe into a net exporter of most temperate zone commodities. This increase in the EC commodity surplus depresses and destabilizes world prices and makes production in other countries less profitable. The pattern of world trade is, in this way, severely distorted. This effect is more evident in the sectors that are relatively more heavily protected, like wheat, coarse grains, ruminant meat and dairy products.

The distortionary effects of the CAP affect the welfare of the Community's trading partners. Generally speaking, net exporters of temperate zone commodities lose, while net importers gain. Since most LDCs are net importers, less developed countries as a group appear to benefit from the operation of the CAP, at least in the short run, through an improvement in their terms of trade.

This result, although it is confirmed by most existing studies, should be treated with caution. First of all, it conceals the distribution of losses and gains across countries, which is far from uniform. Second, it is derived mostly from partial equilibrium models, which ignore secondary repercussions on welfare via the non-agricultural markets; the available general equilibrium studies show that ignoring these repercussions leads to systematic underestimation of the costs of the distortion. Third, it may be relevant only in the short run; if many developing countries were able to take advantage of higher commodity prices and switch from being net importers to net exporters, the result would prove incorrect over the longer run.

142   EFFECTS OF THE COMMON AGRICULTURAL POLICY

Fourth, it ignores the cost of increased price instability, which is probably more detrimental to poor than to rich countries.

It is hard to express these qualifications quantitatively. However, even if the majority of LDCs actually gained from the CAP, this gain would be very small compared with the welfare losses in the EC. It would be easy for the Community to compensate the losers from a unilateral liberalization and still realize substantial benefits.[14] From a world welfare point of view, of course, there is an even better alternative than a unilateral liberalization-cum-compensation scheme: that of a multilateral reduction of protection in agricultural markets. All existing evidence strongly suggests that moves towards freer trade that involve more, rather than fewer, trading partners would spread the benefits more uniformly. In other words, the optimal response of the losers from a unilateral liberalization is to liberalize their markets as well.[15]

REFERENCES

Anderson, K. and Tyers, R. (1984) 'European Community Grain and Meat Policies: Effects on International Prices, Trade and Welfare', *European Review of Agricultural Economics* (Amsterdam) 11, pp. 367–94.

Bale, M. D. and Lutz, E. (1978) *Trade Restrictions and International Price Instability*, (Washington DC: International Bank for Reconstruction and Development) Staff Working Paper No. 303.

Bale, M. D. and Lutz, E. (1979a), *Price Distortions in Agriculture and their Effects: An International Comparison*, (Washington DC: International Bank for Reconstruction and Development) Staff Working Paper No. 359.

Bale, M. D. and Lutz, E. (1979b) 'The Effects of Trade Intervention on International Price Instability', *American Journal of Agricultural Economics*, 61, 4, pp. 512–16.

Bale, M. D. and Lutz, E. (1981) 'Price Distortions in Agriculture and Their Effects: An International Comparison', *American Journal of Agricultural Economics*, 63, 1, pp. 8–22.

Berck, P. and Schmitz, A. (1984) 'Price Supports in the Context of International Trade', in C. G. Storey, A. Schmitz and A. H. Sarris, *International Agricultural Trade*, (Boulder, Colorado: Westview Press).

Blandford, D. (1983) 'Instability in World Grain Markets', *Journal of Agricultural Economics*, 34, 3, pp. 379–95.

Breckling, J., Thorpe, S. and Stoeckel, A. (1987) *Effects of EC Agricultural Policies, A General Equilibrium Approach: Initial Results* (Canberra, Australia: Bureau of Agricultural Economics and Centre for International Economics).

Buckwell, A. E., Harvey, D. R., Thompson, K. J. and Parton, K. A. (1982) *The Costs of the Common Agricultural Policy*, (London: Croom Helm).

Bureau of Agricultural Economics (1985) *Agricultural Policies in the European Community*, (Canberra, Australia: Bureau of Agricultural Economics). Policy Monograph 2.

[14] It is worth noting that, even by the most pessimistic estimate, the LDC losses from a unilateral liberalization in the EC are only around 70 per cent of the official development assistance actually disbursed in 1985 by the seven largest EC members, excluding Greece, Ireland and Luxembourg (in 1980 US$; see IBRD, 1986, Statistical Appendix).

[15] OECD (1982) discusses the issue of multilateral liberalization in detail. There is also a large body of empirical evidence on this: Chisholm & Tyers (1985); Tyers & Anderson (1986); Whalley (1984); Whalley (1985a); IBRD (1986) and the references therein.

Burniaux, J.-M. and Waelbroeck, J. (1985) 'The Impact of the CAP on Developing Countries: A General Equilibrium Analysis', in C. Stevens, and J. Verloren van Themaat, eds., *Pressure Groups, Policies and Development*, (London: Hodder & Stoughton).

Chisholm, T. and Tyers, R. (1985) 'Agricultural Protection and Market Insulation Policies: Applications of a Dynamic Multisectoral Model', in J. Piggot, and J. Whalley, eds., *New Developments in Applied General Equilibrium Analysis*, (Cambridge: Cambridge University Press).

Commission of the European Communities (1986) *The Situation on the Agricultural Markets – 1986 Report* (Report from the Commission to the Council), COM(86) 700 final, (Brussels: Commission of the European Communities).

Commission of the European Communities (1987), *Proposals on the Prices for Agricultural Products and on Related Measures (1978/88)*, 1, March 4, (Brussels: Commission of the European Communities).

Commission des Communautés Européennes (1984) *Dépense publiques en faveur de l'agriculture*. Etude p. 229 (Brussels: Commission of the European Communities). November.

Corden, W. M. (1957) 'The Calculation of the Cost of Protection', *Economic Record*, Melbourne, 33, pp. 29–51.

Corden, W. M. (1971), *The Theory of Protection*, (Oxford: Clarendon Press).

Currie, J. M., Martin, J. A. and Schmitz, A. (1971) 'The Concept of Economic Surplus and its Use in Economic Analysis', *Economic Journal*, (London: Cambridge University Press) 81, pp. 741–99).

Georgakopoulos, T. A. (1986) 'Greece in the European Communities: A View of the Economic Impact of Accession', *Royal Bank of Scotland Review* (Edinburgh) 150, pp. 29–40.

Georgakopoulos, T. A. and Paschos, P. G. (1985) 'Greek Agriculture and the CAP', *European Review of Agricultural Economics* (Amsterdam) 12, pp. 247–62.

Gerken, E., (1986) *The Determinants of European Agricultural Trade Interference* (Kiel: Kiel Institute of World Economics). Working Paper No. 254.

Harberger, A. C. (1959) 'Using the Resources at Hand More Efficiently', *American Economic Review*, (Nashville) 49, pp. 134–46.

Harling, K.F. (1983) 'Agricultural Protectionism in Developed Countries: Analysis of Systems of Intervention', *European Review of Agricultural Economics* (Amsterdam) 10, pp. 223–47.

Harling, K.F. and Thompson, R. L. (1985) 'Government Intervention in Poultry Industries: A Cross-Country Comparison', *American Journal of Agricultural Economics*, 67, 3, pp. 243–9.

Harris, S., Swinbank, A. and Wilkinson, G., (1983) *The Food and Farm Policies of the European Community* (Chichester: Wiley).

International Bank for Reconstruction and Development (1986) *World Development Report 1986* (Oxford University Press and World Bank, Washington DC).

Johnson, H. G. (1960) 'The Cost of Protection and the Scientific Tariff', *Journal of Political Economy*, (Chicago: University of Chicago Press), 68, pp. 327–45.

Josling, T. E. (1979) 'Questions for Farm Policy in an Enlarged European Community', *The World Economy*, (Washington, DC: World Bank) 2, 3, pp. 343–62.

Koester, U. (1977) 'The Redistributional Effects of the Common Agricultural Financial System', *European Review of Agricultural Economics* (Amsterdam) 4, pp. 321–45.

Koester, U. (1982), *Policy Options for the Grain Economy of the European Community: Implications for Developing Countries* (Washington DC: International Food Policy Research Institute), Research Report 35.

Koester, U. (1985) 'Agricultural Market Intervention and International Trade', *European Review of Agricultural Economics*, (Amsterdam) 12, pp. 87–103.

Koester, U. and Bale, M. D. (1984) *The Common Agricultural Policy of the European Community* (Washington DC: International Bank for Reconstruction and Development) Staff Working Paper No. 630.

Koester, U. and Schmitz, P. M. (1982) 'The EC Sugar Market Policy and Developing

Countries', *European Review of Agricultural Economics* (Amsterdam) 9, pp. 183–204.

Koester, U. and Tangermann, S. (1986) *European Agricultural Policies and International Agriculture* (Washington DC: International Bank for Reconstruction and Development) background paper for the International Bank for Reconstruction and Development, World Development Report 1986.

Koester, U. and Valdes, A., (1984) 'Reform of the CAP – Impact on the Third World', *Food Policy*, 9, 20, pp. 94–8.

Loo, T. and Tower, E. (1988) 'Agricultural Protectionism and the Less Developed Countries: The Relationship between Agricultural Prices, Debt Servicing Capacities and the Need for Development Air' (Washington, DC) paper presented at the Conference on Agricultural Policies and the Non-farm Economy, 26–27 May.

Mackel, C., Marsh, J. and Revell, B. (1984) 'The Common Agricultural Policy', *Third World Quarterly*, 6, 1, pp. 131–44.

Matthews, A. (1985a) *The Common Agricultural Policy and the Less Developed Countries* (Dublin: Gill and Macmillan).

Matthews, A. (1985b), 'The CAP and Developing Countries: A Review of the Evidence', in C. Stevens and J. Verloren van Themaat, eds., *Pressure Groups, Policies and Development* (London: Hodder & Stoughton).

Morris, C. N. (1980) 'The Common Agricultural Policy', *Fiscal Studies*, 1, 2, pp. 15–35.

Nerlove, M. (1958) *The Dynamics of Supply: Estimation of Farmers' Response to Price*, (Baltimore: Johns Hopkins University Press).

Organization for Economic Cooperation and Development (1982) *Problems of Agricultural Trade* (Paris: OECD).

Organization for Economic Cooperation and Development (1987) *National Policies and Agricultural Trade* (Paris: OECD).

Sampson, G. P. and Yeats, A. J. (1977) 'An Evaluation of the Common Agricultural Policy as a Barrier Facing Agricultural Exports to the European Economic Community', *American Journal of Agricultural Economics*, 59, 1, pp. 99–106.

Sarris, A. H. (1983) 'European Community Enlargement and World Trade in Fruits and Vegetables', *American Journal of Agricultural Economics*, 65, 2, pp. 235–46.

Sarris, A. H. and Freebairn, J. (1983) 'Endogenous Price Policies and International Wheat Prices', *American Journal of Agricultural Economics*, 65, 2, pp. 214–24.

Scandizzo, P. and Bruce, P. (1980) *Methodologies for Measuring Agricultural Price Intervention Effects*, (Washington, DC: World Bank) International Bank for Reconstruction and Development. Staff Working Paper No. 394.

Schmitz, P. M. and Koester, U. (1984) 'The Sugar Market Policy of the European Community and the Stability of World Market Prices for Sugar', in C. G. Storey, A. Schmitz and A. H. Sarris. *International Agricultural Trade* (Boulder, Colorado: Westview Press.

Spencer, J., (1985) 'The European Economic Community: General Equilibrium Computations and the Economic Implications of Membership', in J. Piggot and J. Whalley, eds. *New Developments in Applied General Equilibrium Analysis* (Cambridge: Cambridge University Press).

Spencer, J. (1986) 'Trade Liberalization through Tariff Cuts and the European Economic Community: A General Equilibrium Evaluation, in T. N. Srinivasan and J. Whalley, eds., *General Equilibrium Trade Policy Modeling*, (Cambridge, MA: MIT Press).

Stoeckel, A. and Breckling, J. (1988) 'Some Economy-wide Effects of Agricultural Policies in the European Community: A General Equilibrium Study', paper presented at the Conference on Agricultural Policies and the Non-farm Economy (Washington, DC) 26–27 May.

Svedberg, P. (1981) 'EEC Variable Import Levies and the Stability of International Grain Markets', *Indian Journal of Agricultural Economics* (Bombay) 36, 1, pp. 58–66.

Tangermann, S. (1978) 'Agricultural Trade Relations between the EC and Temperate Food Exporting Countries', *European Review of Agricultural Economics* (Amsterdam) 5, pp. 201–19.

DEMEKAS, BARTHOLDY, GUPTA, LIPSCHITZ AND MAYER 145

Tangermann, S. (1981) 'Policies of the European Community and Agricultural Trade with Developing Countries', in G. Johnson and A, Maunder, eds., *Rural Change, Proceedings of the Seventeenth International Conference of Agricultural Economists* (Aldershot: Gower).

Thomson, K. J. and Harvey, D. R. (1981) 'The Efficiency of the Common Agricultural Policy', *European Review of Agricultural Economics* (Amsterdam) 8, pp. 57–83.

Traill, B., (1982) 'The Effect of Price Support Policies on Agricultural Investment, Employment, Farm Incomes and Land Values in the U. K.', *Journal of Agricultural Economics*, 33, 3, pp. 369–85.

Tyers, R. (1985) 'International Impacts of Protection: Model Structure and Results for EC Agricultural Policy', *Journal of Policy Modeling*, 7, 2, pp. 219–52.

Tyers, R. and Anderson, K. (1986) *Distortions in World Food Markets: A Quantitative Assessment* background paper for the World Bank World Development Report 1986, (Washington DC: World Bank).

Tyers, R. and Anderson, K. (1987a) *Liberalizing OECD Agricultural Policies in the Uruguay Round: Effects on Trade and Welfare* (Canberra: Australian National University) Working Paper in Trade and Development No. 87/10.

Tyers, R. and Anderson, K. (1987b), 'Global Interactions and Trade Liberalization in Agriculture', *Economic Policies and World Agriculture*.

Valdes, A. and Zietz, J. (1980) *Agricultural Protection in OECD Countries: Its Cost to Less-Developed Countries* (Washington, DC: International Food Policy Research Institute) Research Report 21, (1980).

Whalley, J. (1984) 'The North–South Debate and the Terms of Trade: An Applied General Equilibrium Approach', *Review of Economics and Statistics* (Amsterdam) 66, pp. 224–34.

Whalley, J. (1985a) *Trade Liberalization Among Major World Trading Areas* (Cambridge, MA: MIT Press).

Whalley, J. (1985b), 'Hidden Challenges in Recent Applied General Equilibrium Exercises', in J. Piggot and J. Whalley, eds., *New Developments in Applied General Equilibrium Analysis* (Cambridge: Cambridge University Press).

Winters, A., (1987) 'The Economic Consequences of Agricultural Support: a Survey', *OECD Economic Studies*, 9, pp. 7–54.

Witzke, H., von (1986) 'Endogenous Supranational Policy Decisions: The Common Agricultural Policy of the European Community', *Public Choice*, 48, pp. 157–74.

[15]

THE REFORM OF THE CAP

Lionel Hubbard and Christopher Ritson

INTRODUCTION

Virtually since its inception. the Common Agricultural Policy has been subject to proposals for reform. Among the academic community anyway. the debate rapidly achieved something of a consensus and subsequently has evolved remarkably little. Academics and other CAP specialists. either as individuals or in groups. have produced numerous reform proposals. Notable in this context have been the Wageningen Memorandum of 1973 and the Sienna Memorandum of 1984 (Ritson 1984) - because of the number of academics from various European Community member states who were willing to add their signatures to the documents. Reading these documents one is struck by how little seemed to have changed - even some of the people are the same! A typical form of this kind of argument is outlined in the next section.

THE ACADEMIC REFORM ARGUMENT

The argument would begin as follows. When the Agricultural Ministers of the original six Common Market countries launched the CAP. they made a fatal mistake. Partly because of a failure to appreciate the potential growth in production. and partly because of the overriding necessity to achieve a political agreement in agriculture to cement the establishment of the European Economic Community, they set support prices for cereals at too high a level (more than 50 per cent in excess of. what was then. a very stable world market price). As a consequence. because most other agricultural products are related to cereals, either as competitive arable crops or as users of cereal-based feeding stuffs. most other agricultural product prices had similarly to be set at relatively high levels.

From this single set of decisions there followed, so it was argued, a number of undesirable consequences - undesirable. that is, when viewed against a set of criteria. widely accepted (though often implicitly) among academics, concerning agricultural policies. This approach judges the success of agricultural policies relative to certain fundamental goals in society. such as

The Common Agricultural Policy and the World Economy

the efficient use of resources and equity in income distribution (in each case, both within agriculture and between agriculture and other sectors) and good international relations. Because support prices were so high, it was argued that the CAP encouraged inefficient, high-cost production; impeded structural adjustment; disadvantaged low-income consumers (because of high food prices); benefited large farmers greatly and small farmers very little (because the benefit was distributed pro rata to the amount produced); and damaged trading relations with both rich and poor countries alike. All would be well, however, if agriculture product support prices were reduced - and the debate, as such, was really about how to achieve this.

The problem, of course, was the damage to farm incomes that would result from lower prices. The key, in most reform proposals, was the introduction of some form of direct income supplementation for low-income farmers. Such a switch, from price support to direct income support for agriculture, seemed highly desirable when judged by the criteria listed above. Greater equity could be achieved, on account of the benefit to low-income consumers of lower food prices and the ability to target support to those farmers most in need; efficiency could be improved, in that the Policy would no longer underwrite high cost marginal output; and international relations and the prospects for developing country exports of one or two key products would be improved. Such a development seemed to favour the prospects of the low-income country exporters to the EC, and so the cause of reform of the CAP has typically been embraced by the development lobby - though, as pointed out in Chapters 12 and 13, the issue is far from clear-cut.

THE FORMAL APPROACH

Most of the literature on CAP reform, although written by academics, was directed towards a more general audience with the aim of influencing policy-makers. Underpinning it, however, was other more professional analytical work which, with the benefit of hindsight, can be seen to originate with the publication in 1969 of Josling's article 'A Formal Approach to Agricultural Policy'. It is a peculiar feature of post-war agricultural economics that, whereas an analytical approach to farm production economics was well advanced by 1969, agricultural policy had tended to be the preserve of a more 'literary' type of agricultural economist. Josling applied public choice theory to agricultural policy - attempting to analyse the appropriate choice of policy in terms of objectives, constraints and instruments.

In Figure 16.1 we illustrate, first, the idea of instruments and complementary objectives - that is where the instruments all have a positive relationship with the objectives - which are here, by way of example, to raise farm output (perhaps for balance of payments reasons) and to raise farm incomes. For the sake of argument, the instruments might be product subsidies, import controls and investment subsidies - and instrument 3, to illustrate the various possibilities, is drawn so that, past a certain level, the objectives are no longer complementary.

Figure 16.1:   Policy Instruments and Objectives

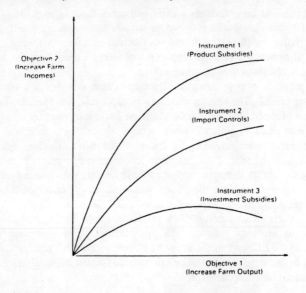

Now the important message from the diagram, and to quote the Josling (1969) article, is that: '...a necessary (though not sufficient) condition for the reaching of a number of quantitative objectives is that one employs a similar number of policy instruments'. In other words it is extremely unlikely that the choice of any one of the instruments in Figure 16.1 would allow the achievement of target levels of both objectives.

Thus, the more 'academic' version of the argument conveyed in the previous section was that 'the CAP is unsuccessful because it is attempting to use one instrument (raising market prices) in order to fulfil a number of objectives'.

OFFICIAL REFORM PLANS

Meanwhile, it was not just academics who were calling for the reform of the CAP - but also successive European Commissions. Indeed, perhaps the most famous reform plan of all - the Mansholt Plan - came from the Commission of the EC (1968), and was in general consistent with (and indeed largely pre-dated) the academic work. It advocated reduced prices for surplus commodities, but linked various forms of financial compensation to structural reform. It was either 'get out or get bigger', whereas other reform proposals were willing

The Common Agricultural Policy and the World Economy

to contemplate 'stay small - here is a bit extra to supplement your income from farming'. [1]

The Mansholt Plan was far from popular with the agricultural interests in Western Europe, but subsequently there have been a succession of Commission documents proposing change to the CAP - though after Mansholt the term 'reform' became *infra dig* - euphemisms such as 'adjustment', 'development', 'guidelines' and 'improvements' have been used. [2] Gradually, however, as we moved into the 1980s, the preoccupations of the European Commission, and some other CAP commentators, diverged from those of what one might call 'academic orthodoxy' - and a parallel debate developed. This is now the real debate, in the sense that its preoccupations are those which are driving change.

For an academic, it is somewhat sobering to realise that the arguments involved in the consensus over CAP reform mentioned earlier are almost wholly irrelevant to the actual reform of the CAP. Herein lies a paradox, for it was the peculiarity of having to forge a common agricultural policy for six countries which was partly responsible for the original mistakes with respect to the CAP; and it has been the fact that the Policy has had to meet six (and then nine, and now twelve) member state interests which has partly been responsible for the failure of the Policy to reform in the way advocated by many; but it is another peculiarity of the Common Policy which has driven change. This is the failure of the Community's automatic system of generating revenue (its 'own resources') to match the budgetary cost of its policies - mainly the cost of the agricultural policy.

REAL CAP REFORM AND PUBLIC CHOICE THEORY

Does this mean that the theory of public choice is of no relevance in practice to understanding the development of the CAP? We think not; rather it has been a failure of the academic work to catch up with the changed policy environment.

First, the 1980s have seen a proliferation of policy instruments under the CAP, which can be viewed as coming to terms with the need for more than one instrument to attain more than one objective. Second, the priority of objectives and the relation between objectives and constraints are largely a political issue. Figure 16.2 considers the second case, where the instruments are associated with conflict between the objectives. We have chosen to insert a new objective 'economic efficiency', but could also have introduced a new instrument (say quotas) to Figure 16.2. Product subsidies and import controls both adversely affect efficiency (but import controls more so, because they raise consumer prices).

1   For a full discussion of the Mansholt Plan, see Marsh and Ritson (1971).

2   The 'evolution' of Commission reform proposals is traced in a paper (Ritson and Fearne 1984) prepared for the Sienna meeting, which led to the 'Sienna Memorandum' as mentioned earlier.

Figure 16.2:   Policy Objectives : Trade-offs

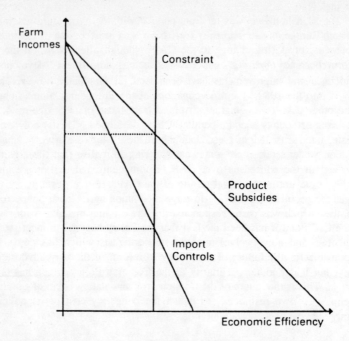

In these circumstances choosing an optimum policy is best seen as maximising one objective subject to viewing the other objective as a constraint. One then chooses the instrument which achieves the highest value of the objective (say farm incomes) subject to the constraint (efficiency). In this example product subsidies would be chosen.

In the 1970s farm incomes were usually taken as the prime objective, with equity, import saving and efficiency as subsidiary objectives. Public expenditure was seen, if at all, as a constraint. What seems to have happened to the CAP is that what was once best viewed as a constraint is now a major objective. Why this should have become so is now discussed.

THE BUDGET PROBLEM

During the past fifteen years the European Community moved from net importer to a net exporter in the case of several major agricultural commodities (see Figures 16.3-16.6). To the academic CAP specialist, at the time, the point at which the EC moves from 100 per cent to, say, 105 per cent self-sufficiency in a commodity was seen as of no greater significance than when it moves from 95 per cent to 100 per cent. High-cost, inefficient output is still

The Common Agricultural Policy and the World Economy

just that, whether or not the cost is expressed as an export subsidy or as a levy which displaces cheaper imported produce; high prices are still high prices to consumers and producers; and the world trading system is affected in much the same way by the elimination of a previous import requirement, as it is by the addition of a new export availability. But, from the point of view of the administration of the Common Agricultural Policy, the movement into export surplus matters a great deal.

This is because it represents the point at which the Community budget begins to have to 'top up' the contribution of food consumers to enhancing the revenue of farming. When the Community is less than 100 per cent self-sufficient, market prices can be supported solely by taxing imports. When EC production exceeds EC consumption, however, prices can only continue to be supported if the Community finances the purchase and disposal of surplus production; and, as surpluses grow, so does the budgetary cost of their disposal. By the early 1980s, the cost of surplus disposal had taken EC expenditure to the ceiling imposed by 'own resources', and the Community was forced to resort to various devices to balance the books. The most significant of these was to allow stocks to accumulate.

Member states bear the cost of intervention until stocks are disposed of. By manipulating the level of export refunds, the Commission is able to control the timing of exports and effectively transfer intervention expenditure forward into the next financial year. Stocks have also accumulated for two further reasons. First, in the case of dairy products, there are very few export outlets even for subsidised produce (a consignment delivered to Russia went at 13 per cent of the intervention price). Second, in the case of cereals, the fear of retaliation by the United States has limited somewhat the willingness of the Community to subsidise exports to the traditional markets for North American produce. But accumulation of stocks only delays the time at which the EC budget must bear the cost of surpluses. The consequence is that, to understand the reform of the CAP, it is necessary to appreciate that there is really only one criterion at work, epitomised by the question 'Does the change make a positive contribution to the Community budget?'; and, in attempting to classify the various policy changes under way or under discussion, it is most helpful to categorise them according to the main way in which they might be expected to contribute positively to the EC budget. This is done in Table 16.1.

In choosing between alternative policies which have similar budgetary implications, a second criterion will be apparent. This is that the reform will be favoured which involves least change in the current balance of benefit for the interest groups affected by the CAP - particularly when one interest group is biased towards some member states - which is nearly always the case.

The reform measures listed in Table 16.1 are categorised according to budgetary effect. Broadly, there are two groupings - those which seek to reduce expenditure and those which seek to increase revenue. These will be dealt with in turn.

Figure 16.3: EC Cereals Balance

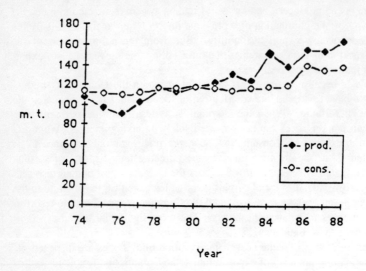

Figure 16.4: EC Sugar Balance

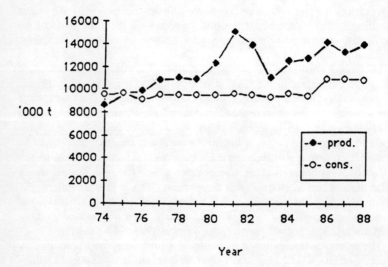

301

The Common Agricultural Policy and the World Economy

Figure 16.5: EC Butter Balance

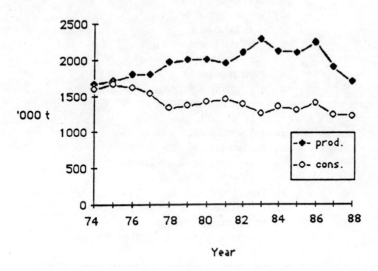

Figure 16.6: EC Beef and Veal Balance

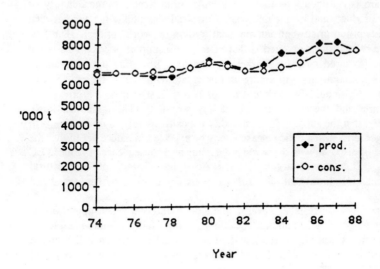

The Reform of the CAP

Table 16.1: CAP Reform Classified According to Budgetary Effect

---

Expenditure-Reducing
- 1) reduce support prices
  - a) price cuts
  - b) stabilisers
  - c) intervention criteria
- 2) limit production
  - a) marketing quotas
  - b) production quotas
  - c) 'set-aside'

Revenue-Increasing
- 1) product taxes
  - a) co-responsibility levies
  - b) vegetable oil tax
- 2) input taxes
- 3) national financing of CAP policies
- 4) new sources of revenue
  - a) related to agricultural production
  - b) related to GNP

EXPENDITURE-REDUCING MEASURES

There are two dimensions to this particular objective: a) the quantity of surplus produce, and b) the unit cost of disposal (essentially the gap between EC intervention prices and international trading or 'world' prices). The first possible reform measure cited is that of reducing support prices. This is the measure favoured most by 'market economists'. Lowering the intervention price for a commodity will secure an immediate reduction in the unit cost of disposal. Subsequently, it should reduce (or at least impede the growth in) production and therefore the size of any surplus. (This assumes, fairly rationally, that the supply of a commodity is positively related to its price.) In the longer term such a policy measure may be expected to reduce yet further the unit cost of disposal, with the world price rising as a consequence of reduced EC exports. It has been argued by the Australian Bureau of Agricultural Economics [3] (1985) that the CAP depresses world prices by between 9 and 28 per cent.

Experience suggests, however, that although in recent years support prices have been 'frozen' (in common ECU terms) and have fallen a little in real terms in recent times (see Figure 16.7), and, although the Commission will continue to put pressure on the Council of Ministers to moderate prices, it is simply not

---

3   Since renamed the Australian Bureau of Agricultural and Resource Economics.

The Common Agricultural Policy and the World Economy

possible from a political point of view to cut prices sufficiently to constrain the cost of the CAP. Whilst straightforward price cuts are the economist's solution to the problem, they are widely accepted as being politically all but impossible, as evidenced by the extreme difficulties that the Agricultural Council had in 1990 in agreeing even the modest price cuts implied by the Commission's proposal to reduce the 'Aggregate Level of Support' by 30 per cent over a ten-year period, as the EC's offer under the Uruguay round.

Since straightforward price-cutting has proved so difficult a task for the Council of Ministers, price reductions are now embodied in the agricultural 'stabilisers'. These exist for the major commodities and are designed to stabilise markets. Each stabilisation mechanism is tailored to the specific features of the relevant product, but the basic idea is always the same: whenever production breaks through a ceiling set in advance, support is automatically reduced for that product. (Commission of the European Communities, 1987). The production ceiling for a commodity is referred to as the 'maximum guaranteed quantity', and when this is exceeded a price reduction follows automatically in the subsequent season. In principle, the system has an advantage over earlier attempts at price-cutting, in that its effects are automatic and do not require approval from the Council each year. In practice, its major shortcoming is that, whilst price cuts are automatic, there is no such restraint on the setting of 'gross' prices. Thus, the price cut relates to a price which still requires the agreement of the Council of Ministers. If there is to be any significant impact on curtailing supply, these 'gross' prices will need to be kept in check. Thus, to date, the system of price determination is still open-ended. Nevertheless, there were some large reductions in prices for certain commodities in the late 1980s as a result of the stabiliser mechanism (for example, oilseeds), and the recent agreement on a 30 per cent cut in support to agriculture may signal a move to lower levels of 'gross' prices.

Over recent years a number of changes have been made in the rules governing intervention buying. Minimum quality standards have been raised, the times of the year when intervention buying is undertaken have been shortened, and the prices at which commodities are purchased by intervention agencies have been reduced, that is, the 'buying-in' price and the intervention price have become separated. In bringing about these changes the Commission has sought to persuade farmers to produce for market rather than for intervention, and to restore the intervention agencies to their original role of 'buyer of last resort'. With intervention now a less attractive option, further budgetary savings have been created.

The second group of expenditure-reducing measures is that which physically limits production. Viewed from the narrow criteria of budgetary effects and damage limitation to the existing balance of interests, quotas have considerable attractions. Production can be reduced very quickly to whatever level is regarded as manageable, and since prices do not need to be reduced as well (indeed they are likely to be increased in compensation, for most producers) the impact on net income is likely to be only marginal. In the case of milk quotas, introduced in great haste in April 1984, production has been reduced significantly. Deliveries of milk to dairies in 1988 were some 10 per cent below the peak reached in 1983, immediately prior to the introduction of quotas. Butter production was down by 26 per cent over the same period, and production of skim-milk powder down by 47 per cent. As a consequence, intervention stocks of these dairy products have fallen, although, with milk production in the Community still exceeding domestic consumption, the sector remains the most expensive within FEOGA. Quotas create innumerable problems and inequity but, perhaps somewhat surprisingly, have been integrated into Community agriculture more easily than had been originally envisaged. In part this is because, faced with a choice between quotas or a price cut equivalent, most producers will be better off opting for quotas. But there are administration problems for the authorities.

Figure 16.7: Gross FEOGA Expenditure and Annual Price Changes

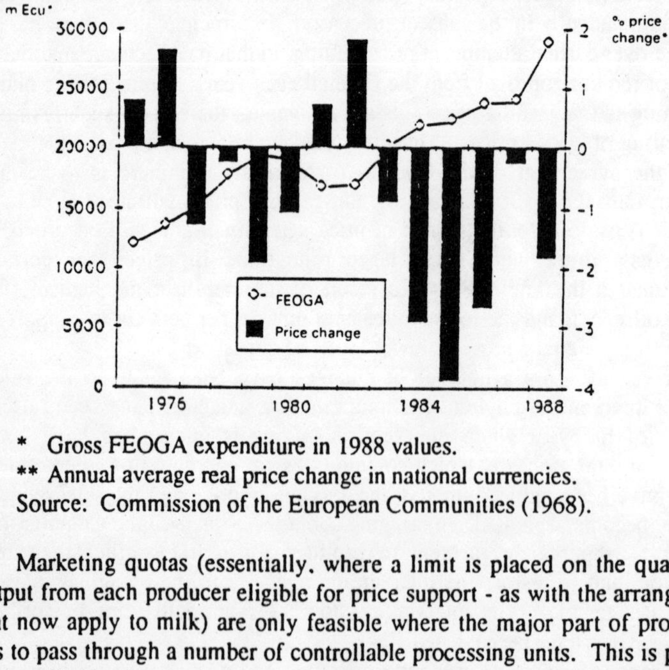

* Gross FEOGA expenditure in 1988 values.
** Annual average real price change in national currencies.
Source: Commission of the European Communities (1968).

Marketing quotas (essentially, where a limit is placed on the quantity of output from each producer eligible for price support - as with the arrangements that now apply to milk) are only feasible where the major part of production has to pass through a number of controllable processing units. This is possible with milk (and sugar), but more difficult with many other products, in particular cereals. Thus, there have appeared proposals for restricting what is produced, rather than what is marketed - though of course the response to a marketing quota is probably to reduce production. The most obvious method of directly limiting production is to control the amount of land that can be devoted to certain crops - or 'set-aside' as it is commonly known.

The Common Agricultural Policy and the World Economy

Experience of set-aside in the United States, where it has been employed intermittently since the 1930s, is not encouraging. For a number of reasons, the impact on production is not as great as might be imagined, and any reduction that does occur tends only to be short-lived, as advancing technology continues to improve yields. Indeed, this last point is particularly pertinent in the case of the EC, where a voluntary set-aside policy for cereals has now been introduced, since production over the last 20 years has risen almost entirely as a result of better yields from virtually the same land area. Work undertaken to ascertain the impact of set-aside suggests, therefore, that it needs to be combined with longer-term policies, such as price reductions. [4] Set-aside has many critics, and from the economist's viewpoint is perhaps most appropriately seen as an attempt on the part of the authorities to meddle with one of the inputs, albeit a rather special one, in the production process. In this respect, set-aside has some similarities with input taxes (see below). From a purely budgetary angle, the important question to be answered is whether the cost of the set-aside policy, in terms of the payments that have to be offered to farmers to induce them to idle part of their land, will be less than the cost of surplus grain disposal. If the former outweighs the latter, as some critics claim, set-aside offers no solution to the budgetary problem.

REVENUE-INCREASING MEASURES

Policy measures aimed at increasing the Community's budgetary revenue can seek to raise additional funds from various sources. With product taxes the intention may be to shift part of the financial burden of surplus disposal on to producers. This is the idea behind the co-responsibility levy, a measure based on the so-called 'self-financing' production levies operated in the sugar sector. Introduced for milk in 1977 and for cereals in 1986, the co-responsibility levy is a flat-rate tax on all (or most) of a product passing through marketing channels. Essentially, it means that part of what the consumer pays for the product is diverted from its previous path to the producer, and into the Community budget. Whether the levy acts also as a producer price cut (and thus discourages production) depends on what the ministers do to support prices. Provided the levy is high enough, it is quite possible to make a particular CAP commodity regime 'self-financing', with the tax revenue used to finance surplus disposal. This is the direction in which the sugar regime has gone; the milk and cereal co-responsibility levies are very small in comparison.

Co-responsibility has long been a favourite with the Commission and in fact dates back to the earliest days of the EC. The principle - to make producers bear at least part of the cost of surplus disposal - seems eminently sensible. In practice, co-responsibility has had a chequered history. The main problem is

---

4   See, for example, MAFF (1986), Buckwell (1986) and Hope and Lingard (1988)

essentially the same as that outlined above for the 'stabilisers', in that, whilst the co-responsibility levy reduces the price received by the producer, no formal restraint operates on the setting of the 'gross' support price by the Council of Ministers. Thus, it is not difficult for the levy to be transformed into a consumer tax, thereby avoiding any real hardship to producers (Hubbard 1986). Even so, it remains a fairly unpopular measure with farmers.

Included in the 1987 annual policy package from the Commission was a proposal for a tax on vegetable oils (strictly speaking, a 'consumer price stabilisation mechanism') which would operate in a similar way to a co-responsibility levy. The difference with oilseeds is that, because import tariffs are bound in GATT, EC support has taken the form of deficiency payments, and the oilseeds policy has become increasingly expensive. Domestic production has expanded and low market prices have required substantial budgetary payments. The effect of the tax would be to reduce the deficiency payments on domestically grown oils, and to raise revenue from oils based on imported oilseeds. The Commission claims that consumption and imports would not be affected - this is doubtful. In the event, the proposal was not accepted, which was probably just as well if American threats of a trade war were to be taken seriously. However, the proposal may surface again at some future date.

An alternative measure of raising revenue, and one which has the added attraction of reducing production at the same time, is that of an input tax. This will raise the price of an input, and discourage producers from using it. Recently, interest has centred on the possible use of a tax on nitrogen fertiliser. This has yet another attraction - that of lowering what are becoming dangerously high levels of nitrate in ground water. Rickard (1986) has argued that reduced nitrogen usage would inflict least harm on the smaller farms - a feature which the Commission may find particularly appealing. However, there is considerable debate about the extent to which production is really sensitive to fertiliser use and, more particularly, the extent to which the fertiliser use would be sensitive to rises in its price. So whether such a tax would have a marked impact on production is unknown but it would, of course, raise revenue. Its main attraction lies in the unusual coincidence of the preoccupation of CAP reform, as discussed here, and environmental concern.

Another area of reform, which, in part, is already under way, is that of national financing of the CAP. Member states have been responsible for partial financing of some regimes - for example, butter disposal measures and various production premiums in the beef sector. However, the main area where a major degree of national financing could prove significant is if price cuts are eventually shown to be the only way of meeting the budgetary objective (or prove unavoidable if the world trading system is not to collapse because of a failure to reach agreement for agricultural products under the GATT Uruguay round). In this case farmers may have to be compensated by national governments (*Agra-Europe* 1987a). The main concern here is that a move to national financing of agricultural policies on a significant level would be seen

The Common Agricultural Policy and the World Economy

as a regressive step and a departure from the principle of the single market. A similar but more acceptable development might be to link the financing of surplus production to those member states judged (by some criteria) to be most responsible, or to base member states' budgetary contributions on their shares of total Community agricultural production, rather than on value added tax and GNP, as at present (Buckwell *et al.* 1981).

Traditionally, the EC has obtained revenue from its 'own resources', comprising customs duties, agricultural levies and the VAT-based contributions of member states. Recently, a fourth own resource, related to member states' GNP, has been added to these original three. Whilst GNP-based contributions will alter the distribution of net costs (costs minus benefits) between member states on to a more equitable basis, it is unlikely to make it any easier in the future for the Commission to increase the total amount of revenue available. In fact, the 'budgetary discipline' now imposed by the Council of Ministers restricts the annual rate of growth in the Guarantee Section of FEOGA to 74 per cent of the annual growth rate of the Community's GNP. Whilst this has put a ceiling on the level of agricultural expenditure for any given year, it is unlikely to bring to an end the quest to reduce the budgetary burden and the need for further reform of the CAP.

THE FUTURE OF REFORM

This chapter has traced the development of the CAP reform debate from its origins within the academic community to a discussion of the forces which have motivated reform during the 1980s and into the 1990s. The reform of CAP in practice has been characterised, in the academic language of formal analysis of agricultural policies, as 'what was once best viewed as a constraint [finance] is now a major objective'. There seems no reason to believe that this interpretation of CAP reform will not remain valid as we move towards the year 2000.

Newcastle University has published a report on a Delphi survey of the future of the Common Agricultural Policy (Fearne and Ritson 1987) carried out among about 100 CAP experts throughout the Community. Among the conclusions of the experts concerning the 'CAP in 1995' were:

a) The CAP will remain (albeit somewhat more nationalised) in a Community of Twelve until 1995.

b) The Policy will, however, become increasingly dominated by budgetary pressures, which will result in stricter limitations of intervention and an increase in the general application of producer co-responsibility.

c) Budgetary resources will be increased, but the CAP (Guarantee Section) will continue to take the lion's share.

d) Average farm incomes across the Community will remain at current levels, although disparities between member states will remain.

e) The level of price support over the next 10 years will fall (in real terms) by around 10 per cent.

f) Dairy quotas are expected to remain beyond 1990, with the likelihood of further reductions in member state allocations.

Table 16.2 lists the responses to the question 'In which way is the method of support under the CAP likely to change by 1995?'

Overall, perhaps the most important message of the survey is to counteract the sensational 'CAP on the brink of collapse' view, which so often appears in the media. To characterise the contents of the Newcastle Report (as did *Agra-Europe* 1987b) as 'experts foresee no change CAP in 1995' is an over-reaction to the contrast with what normally appears in the press when reporting the future prospects for the CAP. But the considered view of experts throughout the Community does seem to be that the Policy will continue to bump along from one crisis to the next, adapting slowly and in a piecemeal fashion. There will be no dramatic radical reform; nor will the Policy 'collapse'.

Table 16.2:   Future of the CAP

Policy Change	% of Responses
Limited Intervention	17.9
Extended Co-responsibility	16.1
Direct Income Aids	15.6
Structural Aids	13.8
Extended Guarantee Thresholds	11.6
Less Border Protection	8.1
Set-Aside Schemes	7.3
More Quotas	5.6
Other	3.9

Source: Fearne and Ritson (1987).

REFERENCES

Agra-Europe No. 1225, March (1987a).

Agra-Europe No. 1238, June (1987b).

Australian Bureau of Agricultural Economics (1985) *Agricultural Policies in the European Community - Their Origins, Nature and Effects on Production and Trade*, Policy Monograph No. 2, Canberra.

Buckwell, A.E. (1986) *Cereals Set-aside in the European Community*, Paper presented at the Agricultural Economics Society Conference, Reading University, October 1986.

The Common Agricultural Policy and the World Economy

Buckwell, A.E., Harvey, D.R., Parton, K.A. and Thomson, K.J. (1981) Some Development Options for the Common Agricultural Policy, *Journal of Agricultural Economics*, Vol.32 No.3.

Commission of the European Communities (1968) *Memorandum on the Reform of Agriculture in the European Community* (the Mansholt Plan), COM (68) 1000, Brussels.

Commission of the European Communities (1987) *Implementation of Agricultural Stabilizers*, Vol. 1, COM (87) 452, Brussels.

Fearne, A. and Ritson, C. (1987) *The CAP in 1995*, Report No. 30, Department of Agricultural Economics and Food Marketing, University of Newcastle upon Tyne.

Hope, J. and Lingard, J. (1988) *Set-aside - a Linear Programming Analysis of its Farm Level Effects*, DP8/88, Department of Agricultural Economics and Food Marketing, University of Newcastle upon Tyne.

Hubbard, L.J. (1986) The Co-responsibility Levy - A Misnomer? *Food Policy*, Vol. 11, No. 3.

Josling, T. (1969) A Formal Approach to Agricultural Policy, *Journal of Agricultural Economics*, Vol. 20, No. 2, pp 175-191.

Marsh, J. and Ritson, C. (1971) *Agricultural Policy and the Common Market*, PEP, London

MAFF (Ministry of Agriculture, Fisheries and Food) (1986) *Diverting Land from Cereals (Note by the UK)*, Paper presented at the Agricultural Economics Society Conference, Reading University, October 1986.

Rickard S., (1986) *Nitrogen Limitations: a Way Forward?*, Paper presented at Agricultural Economics Society Conference, Reading University.

Ritson, C. (Rapporteur) (1984) Sienna Memorandum, The Reform of the Common Agricultural Policy, *European Review of Agricultural Economics*, Vol. 11, No. 2.

Ritson, C. and Fearne, A. (1984) Long Term Goals for the CAP, *European Review of Agricultural Economics*, Vol. 11, No. 2.

Wageningen Memorandum (1973) Reform of the European Community's Common Agricultural Policy, *European Review of Agricultural Economics*, Vol. 1, No. 2.

[16]

Internal market policy

Andrew Scott

Introduction

After almost two decades of EC membership, it is still the case that many
people in Britain, possibly even a majority, are of the view that joining the
European Community was a costly error of judgement. The progressive
deterioration in Britain's balance of trade with her Community partners in
the period since membership, along with the contemporaneous increase in
the numbers unemployed, typically are invoked as prima-facie evidence of
the costs of membership. And while all Community countries experienced
the combination of slow growth and ever increasing joblessness that, in the
early 1980s, gave rise to the term 'Euro-sclerosis', it was in Britain that the
fall in output and the associated rise in unemployment was most pronounced. Occuring as it did during a period of intense anti-EC sentiment in
Britain — fuelled by, amongst other things, the clear excesses of the CAP —
this served to reinforce the notion that Community membership was at least
part of the explanation for the secular decline in Britain's comparative
economic performance.

In this chapter we consider the view that membership of the free internal
market that lies at the very heart of the European Community (EC) has
imposed an excessive cost upon British industry.

The economic debate over EC membership

The core argument deployed by those in Britain advocating entry to the
European Communities in the 1960s, and this included successive Labour
and Conservative administrations, was that EC membership would, over the
medium term, greatly enhance our economic performance. Despite the fact
that the average annual rate of economic growth in Britain reached
historically unprecedented levels during the 1950s and 1960s, it was still the
case that our major competitor countries were doing better. In particular,
France and Germany were returning rates of economic growth considerably
above that recorded in Britain. At least part of this difference was explained
in terms of the economic benefits that accrued to members of the large and

dynamic European 'common market' — the principal one being the export opportunities which EC membership offered to the participating countries. Britain, on the other hand, continued to rely on export markets which, in the case of the Commonwealth, were continually shrinking as these countries moved to devlop their import-competing industries, or, in the case of the European Free Trade Association, were significantly smaller and less dynamic than the Community market. Simply, Britain's comparatively poor economic record was partially explained as a consequence of the inability of British firms to enjoy unrestricted free access for their products in the Community market.

The economic underpinnings of the British claim derives from the distinction which conventional international trade theory makes between the static and dynamic effects of customs union membership. The argument is conducted in terms of the change to consumer welfare that a country experiences — both immediately on accession (the static effects) and gradually over time (the dynamic effects) — as a consequence of dismantling the various import and export controls that presently distort trade between that country and the countries that comprise the customs union.

The static, or impact, effects are readily identifiable and, in the case of Britain, were generally acknowledged in the 1970 White Paper (HMSO, 1970) to be negative. The removal of formal barriers to trade will instantaneously raise economic welfare in the new member-state (the home country) if, as a result, its consumers have access to lower-cost sources of supply elsewhere in the union (the partner countries). This is called trade creation. On the other hand, where membership of a customs union results in consumers in the home country having to switch from a low-cost supplier outside the union to a higher-cost partner state supplier, the level of economic welfare will fall. This is trade diversion, and it occurs when the average level of external protection of the union as a whole is above that which the home country imposed prior to membership. In the case of Britain, it was clear from the outset that EC membership would be accompanied by an element of trade diversion as the preferential arrangements governing UK imports of agricultural produce from the Commonwealth were incompatible with the Community's agricultural policy. However, successive governments maintained that any net static losses from membership would be more than offset by dynamic gains.

It was around these dynamic effects of customs union membership that the real debate in Britain revolved. Labour's 1970 White Paper, which presented the economic case for EC membership, argued that dynamic gains would arise from:

the opportunites for greater economies of scale, increased specialisation, a sharper competitive climate and faster growth.

These dynamic gains flow directly from two sources. The first is the intensified competitive pressures that membership of a 'common market' forces upon hitherto protected home producers. Consequently, Community membership would act as a spur to British industry, shaking it out of the mood of complacency that a partial insulation from competitive pressures had engendered. Secondly, access to a large and growing market enables firms in a member-state both to reap the competitive benefits from specialization, and to exploit the cost advantages associated with larger-scale production. Once again, the White Paper was bullish on the likelihood of British industry benefiting from this dynamic gain. Of course, just as EC membership made it easier for British firms to export, so too would firms in partner states find it easier to export to Britain. The White Paper acknowledged that an increase in the rate of growth of imports was bound to follow the removal of trade barriers, but insisted that, provided British industry responded 'vigorously' to the challenge, the rate of growth of exports would rise even faster. And:

with such a response, the growth of industrial productivity would be accelerated as a result of increased competition and the advantages derived from specialisation and larger scale production. This faster rate of growth of productivity would, in turn, accelerate the rate of growth of national production and real income.

In short, a virtuous circle of export-led growth is set in motion. Exports increase as the realization of scale economies and the release of latent industrial competitiveness drive unit costs downwards. The initial rise in productivity contains the seeds of future gains as the subsequent growth in the volume of exports generates yet further opportunities for exploiting cost-reducing economies of large-scale production. Clearly, the long-term economic benefits that would accrue to the British economy from membership of a Community characterized by such a dynamic growth process would be considerable.

Before examining the empirical record, it is worth noting that at least four credible reasons can be found for doubting the robustness of the export-led growth model that successive British governments invoked, at least implicitly, in support of the case for Community membership.

The first is that conventional trade theory in general, and customs union theory in particular, assumes away certain practical adjustment difficulties that may arise as a direct consequence of removing trade barriers. Although it is certainly the case that membership of a customs union will bestow welfare gains if consumers are thereafter able to procure goods and services from a cheaper source, if these trade creating gains are exploited, then, by definition, domestic production will be displaced by imports. Consequently, output and employment in uncompetitive import-competing industries will contract. Of course, membership of the customs union will have opened up new opportunities for the export industries in the economy. However, if there is a time-lag before the capital and labour released by the import-competing sector is absorbed by these export industries, or if the mobility of factors between different industries in the economy is less than perfect, then entry to a customs union may create new — or exacerbate existing — problems of short-term unemployment. Whilst the principle which states that trade creation will always enhance economic welfare remains unchallenged, it does not follow that these gains can be appropriated costlessly.

Secondly, an important part of the dynamic gains from customs unions requires that technical economies of scale in production are exploited. The underlying assumption is that the existing market size is insufficient to allow producers to operate at what is known as the minimum efficient technical scale, i.e. at that level of output at which long-run average costs are being minimized. And some empirical estimates at the time did support the view that the domestic market *per se* was too small to allow British firms to produce at that scale which minimized average costs of production. However, it is difficult to sustain the argument that domestic market size was a limit to growth for British firms during the 1960s as these firms also had duty-free access both to markets in the EFTA countries and the countries of the Commonwealth. Focusing on market size might well have served to divert attention away from the real causes of Britain's comparatively poor economic record.

Thirdly, where economic activity is characterized by economies of scale, and this is widely held to be true for both the manufacturing and the service sectors, then the initial distribution of international competitiveness will exert a strong — possibly decisive — influence over the final international distribution of activities. This is because the mechanics of the virtuous circle which we described earlier are precisely reversed and form a vicious circle with an equally compelling logic. Higher costs of production mean that the uncompetitive firm will experience a loss in market share as barriers to trade fall. Output will decline and the firm will move up its long-run average cost curve. Unit costs therefore rise, worsening even further the firm's competitive position. And so on. In such a world, it is clear that the initial distribution of competitive advantages and disadvantages are continually reinforced, leading to cumulative gains and losses respectively. Formally, we can argue that in the presence of scale economies, the Ricardian doctrine of comparative advantage ceases to be an appropriate framework within which to appraise the economic costs and benefits of free trade.

Finally, by their very nature, whether the dynamic gains will accrue to an individual country depends entirely on the reaction of the private sector. How speedily will exporting companies adjust to new market opportunities? Confronted with intensified competition, how quickly will firms move to rid themselves of the practices that constituted the basis of their initial inefficiencies? A slow response on either count would have adverse consequences.

Reservations along these lines constituted the thrust of the anti-Common Market lobby in Britain. Kaldor, in a series of papers in the early 1970s (Kaldor, 1978), argued that rather than assisting Britain to catch up with the more prosperous economies of Europe, EC membership would expose manufacturing industry to a wave of intense competition which it would be powerless to resist. While Kaldor concurred that Britain's economic problem of low growth could be resolved by an increase in the rate of growth of exports, he maintained that his could only be achieved by a substantial rise in the competitiveness of British industry. In turn, this required either a

20   ECONOMIC POLICY

Table 3.1 *UK current account balance, selected years 1973–89 (£ million)*

	1973		1979		1985		1989	
	Total	EC	Total	EC	Total	EC	Total	EC
Visible trade	−2,586	−1,399	−3,344	−2,683	−3,132	−2,450	−20,826	−13,453
Current account	−996	1,260	−550	−3,163	3,203	−3,157	−14,617	−16,339

Source: Pink Book, HMSO

sustained fall in money wages, or a sterling devaluation. Otherwise, the cumulative unit cost advantages derived from economies of scale in production would accrue to those Community countries which presently enjoyed a competitive advantage over British industry. In this case, entry to the EC would produce economy-wide dynamic losses rather than dynamic gains, as the immediate deterioration in the balance of payments forced the government to tighten domestic fiscal and monetary policies.

The economic record

In retrospect, the claims of successive British governments that dynamic benefits would accrue to the economy as a direct consequence of membership of the European Community were quickly shown to be hopelessly optimistic. For the remainder of the 1970s Britain continued to languish near the foot of the EC economic growth league. At the same time, UK inflation for the period 1973–9 averaged 15.6 per cent annually, well above the Community average of 4.7 per cent, although UK unemployment which averaged 4.2 per cent annually was slightly below the EC average. Although British economic performance improved between 1982 and 1988, the onset of a severe recession in 1989, coupled with rising inflation and a substantial deficit on the external account, suggested that the ailments which had typified the previous two decades had not, in fact, been resolved.

More significant in terms of the economic effects of EC membership, was the deterioration on the current account of the balance of payments which set in soon after entry. The relevent data is given in Table 3.1.

It is quite clear from this data that Britain's external weakness is comparatively greater with respect to the European Community than to the rest of the world. The major part of Britain's visible trade deficit, i.e. the excess of imports over exports of goods, is accounted for by trade with the rest of the European Community (EC). The seemingly adverse impact that Community membership has had on Britain's external balance is even more pronounced when we look at the overall current account balance — the visible balance plus the balance on trade in invisibles and private net financial flows from abroad. Not only has the UK deficit on current account with the EC increased over the years, evidently it is the principal source of Britain's total current account deficit.

The post-1973 changes in Britain's external trade balance have provided the basis of many economic studies into the dynamic effect that EC membership has had on the British economy. Critics of entry maintain that not only did Community membership produce a dramatic rise in imports, particularly of manufactured goods, to the detriment of domestic output and employment, it also prevented the government from introducing formal restrictions on imports from EC countries in response to a balance-of-payments crisis. For these (Keynesian) critics, this restraint on national economic policy-making was especially harmful given that it was imports from other EC countries that seemed to account for a significant part of the balance-of-payments deficit. Fetherston *et al.* (1979), for example, argue that the restrictive macroeconomic policy in Britain during the 1970s was a direct result of the worsening balance-of-payments position that followed EC membership. The net effect was that Britain's national income was 6 per cent on average lower than it otherwise would have been. In another study, however, Morgan (1980) came to the opposite conclusion, finding that EC membership had produced an improvement in Britain's net exports worth around £1 billion over the period 1972–7.

In a review of this literature, Winters (1987) concluded that imports of manufactures to Britain from EC countries had, in fact, significantly risen as a result of EC entry. Moreover, this had produced a fall of anything between £8–12 billion in the total value of home sales accounted for by domestic manufacturing firms by 1979. At the same time, Winters finds evidence that British exports of manufactured goods to EC markets has risen by approximately £4.5 billion over the same period, although this has to be set against a fall (which he estimated to be worth £1.7 billion) in UK exports of manufactures to non-EC countries, particularly the USA and Japan. Winters concluded that:

British accession to the EC worsened her trade balance in, and reduced her gross output of, manufactures quite substantially. Even on the most conservative estimate it reduced output by at least £3 billion, about 1.5 per cent of GNP, and the effect could easily have been twice that.

However, Winters later notes, the 'cost' of EC membership in terms of lost markets for manufactured products has to be set against the welfare gains deriving from the greater choice that consumers enjoy due to the availability of foreign manufactures.

In a major study of Britain's international trade performance, Rowthorn and Wells (1987) argue persuasively that the impact of EC entry on the UK's international trade balance in manufactured goods has to be set in the context of longer-term developments which were fundamentally altering the structure of UK external trade. And while EC entry might have influenced the geographical distribution of British trade, by diverting imports away from non-Community sources to EC partner countries, they find no evidence that the deterioration in the current account of the balance of payments itself can be directly attributed to easier access of imports from EC countries. They state:

22   ECONOMIC POLICY

In many appraisals of the effect of Britain's membership of the EEC on the British economy, considerable attention has been focused on the deterioration in the UK's manufacturing balance with the EEC in the years subsequent to entry. The UK went into deficit in manufacturing trade with the EEC in 1974 and by 1984 this deficit amounted to −2.2 per cent of GDP. Can these adverse trends be ascribed to the effects of EC entry? The answer to this question is, for the most part, no.

An important factor in the secular deterioration of Britain's balance of manufacturing trade was the discovery and exploitation of North Sea oil. As the international value of sterling increased, reflecting the new status of the UK as an important oil producer, this was bound to have adverse consequences for UK exports of manufactured goods. This not only reduced the competitiveness of British products in foreign markets but, at the same time, it also increased the cost advantage that import-competing goods enjoyed in the British market.

Other authors have similarly concluded that the deterioration in Britain's trading position is best explained by the failure of British industry collectively to take advantage of the opportunities to increase their presence in EC markets that arose after 1973. Shepherd (1983) examined the extent to which EC membership increased the degree of specialization on the part of UK firms. Greater specialization would indicate that British industry was responding to the challenge of Community membership, concentrating its efforts around activities in which it had a comparative advantage. The results of the study led Shepherd to conclude that British manufacturing firms were 'at best late in following the specialisation lead of other countries and, at worst, unable to follow this lead'. Three explanations were offered. First, even after EC entry, the plethora of non-tariff barriers to trade within the Community hindered UK access to partner country markets thereby reducing the scope for specialization on the part of British industry. Second, there was evidence that British firms had failed to adjust their commercial horizons to the new markets now open to them' after EC membership. Third, in crucial instances Government policy was oriented towards non-Community solutions to specific industrial problems — such as encouraging Anglo-Japanese joint ventures — at the expense of exploiting the dynamic gains from intra-Community specialization.

The view that Britain's economic problems — including the deficit on manufactured goods trade — can best be explained by domestic failure rather than external competition, whether from the Community or elsewhere, is further reinforced by the results of studies that have examined the performance of British producers in the high-growth, high-technology industries. Britain has persistently lagged behind her major competitors in terms of the share of GDP applied to commercial research and development activity, a trend that is manifested both in a relatively low level of international patenting activity on the part of British firms, and by a deteriorating balance of trade in high-technology products. It is difficult to escape the conclusion that British industry has persistently failed to respond sufficiently quickly to changing demand and supply conditions in global markets.

There is one area in which EC membership has almost certainly benefited the British economy, namely inward investment from non-EC countries. As a member of the EC, Britain has been an attractive outlet for American and Japanese multinational companies wanting to consolidate their position in the Community market. Establishing a 'European' presence via direct investment enables non-Community firms to circumvent the various import restrictions that have come to characterize EC external trade policy. Of course, some of this foreign direct investment would have occurred had Britain not been an EC member, the substantial investment in North Sea oil being the most obvious example. However, where inward investment is for the production or assembly of consumer products, unfettered access to the large Community market has been a key factor in attracting this investment to Britain. It is, of course, easy to overstate the benefits from inward investment. For example, many commentators have expressed concern that the element of technology transfer that was assumed to be part of the process failed to materialise to any significant extent. Similarly, a large share of overseas finance is invested in operations where the element of value added is relatively low, such as component assembly lines. Local labour market distortions along with what is sometimes seen as excessive state assistance with set-up costs are other controversial aspects to inward investment. None-the-less, inward investment has been seen as a short-cut to creating jobs, and often in those areas most acutely suffering from the consequences of industrial restructuring such as the North-East of England and Central Scotland. It is most unlikely that either of these areas would have been able to attract foreign investment on the scale they have had Britain remained outside the European Community.

It is, in the final instance, difficult to maintain that membership of the European Communities of itself created new economic problems for the British economy. By the time of accession, the British economy had been displaying symptoms of a deep-seated economic malaise for almost a decade. And whilst it is true that the much vaunted dynamic gains from membership were not forthcoming, while the anticipated static costs were, this was almost certainly at least as attributable to basic deficiencies in the competitive processes operating inside the British economy as it was a consequence of membership. On the other hand, it is probably true that EC membership exposed these deficiencies more quickly than would otherwise have been the case. It is in this much more restrictive sense that there may be some truth in the often voiced view that EC membership contributed to the rise in unemployment in Britain that has occurred since 1973. However, as we have already noted, the costs of these job losses must be set against the not inconsiderable welfare gains that have accrued to Britain as a direct result of domestic consumers having access to cheaper sources of supply from elsewhere in the Community.

Britain and the completed internal market

It is somewhat ironic that Britain, arguably the country that has gained least in concrete economic terms from EC membership, should have been in the vanguard of those petitioning for action to be taken to remove the

24   ECONOMIC POLICY

remaining intra-Community barriers to the free movement of goods, services, capital and persons between member-states. The British position was spelled out in a communication presented by the Prime Minister to the European Council held at Fontainebleau in June 1984 (UK,1984). In this communication, Mrs Thatcher echoed a widely held view that the economic crisis afflicting Europe's economies, manifest by slow economic growth and high unemployment, was the direct result of a fragmented internal market. The problem of 'Euro-sclerosis', as the economic crisis was dubbed, could only be resolved by the speedy removal of the remaining barriers to free internal trade, these being responsible for inhibiting an economic recovery led by supply-side forces. The British communication maintained that: 'Only by a sustained effort to remove remaining obstacles to intra-Community trade can we enable the citizens of Europe to benefit from the dynamic effects of a fully integrated common market with immense purchasing power'.

Of course, the idea of creating a common market lay at the very heart of the Treaty of Rome. However, during the recession-torn 1970s, EC member-states had both deliberately slowed down the pace of product and factor market integration, and erected a range of new non-tariff barriers to trade explicitly designed to insulate national suppliers from external competition, even though this originated within an EC partner country. But the resulting fragmented nature of the Community market carried with it a cost that was measured in efficiency losses in production. Because of the barriers to internal trade, many EC firms were unable to exploit the economies of large-scale production that access to a single Community market would have permitted. Not only did this impose a higher production cost structure on Community firms, which led to higher prices for consumers, it also meant that many firms, particularly those operating at the high-technology end of the product spectrum, found themselves unable to compete globally with their Japanese and American rivals who were able to exploit the various economies associated with supplying a large domestic market. In this view, economic recovery in the Community could be secured only by the complete removal of all barriers to internal trade and factor movement.

The upshot was the presentation, in June 1985, of the Commission's White Paper entitled *Completing the Internal Market* (European Commission, 1985) which listed 300 or so specific measures that would have to be introduced before the Community could be considered to constitute a truly single market. Moreover, the White Paper incorporated a firm timetable for the implementation of the various directives and regulations necessary, with 31 December 1992 being set as the date by which all measures must have been implemented. These measures fall into one of three categories;

a. the removal of physical barriers to trade in the form of border checks and customs formalities;
b. the removal of technical barriers to the free flow of goods, services and capital, including different national product regulations, standards, and certification procedures; public procurement policies hitherto used by member-states to champion national firms; controls on capital move-

ments; and legal and technical obstacles to a common market in all
financial services including banking and insurance;
c. removal of fiscal barriers, in particular differential VAT rates.

The British enthusiasm for the internal market venture echoed the two
considerations that characterized the Conservative administration during
the early 1980s. In the first place, it reflected the deep hostility which the
administration felt towards state intervention of whatever sort, including all
forms of economic protectionism. For Mrs Thatcher and many of her
closest advisors, it had been state incompetence and economic mismanagement that had led the British economy to the lowly international position
that it now occupied. Economic recovery could only come about by freeing
the supply side of the economy from the host of restrictions and administrative requirements which previous governments — of both political
persuasions — had imposed upon it. The real problem for the British
economy was not excessive exposure to the forces of competition, but the
inability of our producers to exploit their comparative advantage because of
the existing barriers to intra-Community product and factor mobility.
Secondly, completing the internal market was essentially about liberalizing,
or deregulating, markets. Consequently, attention would be switched away
from any notion of moving towards a federal Europe and all that this
implied for the sovereignty of member-state governments. It would be an
error to interpret this solely as an ideological stance on the part of the
Thatcher Government. There was also a pragmatic aspect to their position
which was, broadly, that institutional reforms should not take place ahead
of events determined by market forces. Otherwise, there would be a real
danger that institutional reform would effectively stifle these forces. None
the less, as Mrs Thatcher confirmed in her 1988 address to the College of
Europe at Bruges, there remained a profound ideological void between her
position and those other EC Heads of Government.

Estimating the economic benefits from completing the internal market
formed the subject of a major research effort by the EC Commission. The
results of this 'Costs of Non-Europe' study, directed by Paolo Cecchini
(Cecchini, 1988), were presented in 1988. The Cecchini Report estimated
that substantial economic benefits would accrue to the Community as a
whole as the remaining barriers to the free internal movement of goods,
services, capital and labour were dismantled. These gains would derive from
four sources: removal of physical barriers to trade, such as border delays,
the removal of technical barriers that restrict market entry or competition
between member-states, such as preferential public purchasing; cost savings
that result from the ability of producers to exploit economies of large-scale
production; and the so-called X-efficiency gains from improved managerial
practices that are necessary as a consequence of intensified competition. The
estimates of the macroeconomic effect produced by these cost savings made
impressive reading indeed. It was predicted that completing the internal
market would add some 4.5 per cent to Community GDP; reduce consumer
prices by up to 6.1 per cent; create some 1.8 million new jobs; and improve
the external trade balance of the Community as a whole.

The publication of the Commission study has, however, raised particular
fears concerning the spatial consequences that might flow from a single
internal market. If much publicized gains to Europe's industry are to be
derived by increasing the scale of production units inside the Community,
including an improvement in their competitive position in global markets,
this necessarily implies a reduction in the number of operating units. This
raises significant questions concerning winners and losers. To the extent
that industrial competitiveness differs across the Community, and there is
little doubt that this is the case, then countries whose industry is most
competitive stand to gain considerably from the removal of intra-Community trade barriers. The obverse of this, of course, is that countries which
display an uncompetitive industrial structure stand to lose as the internal
market programme unfolds. Should regional problems worsen as a direct
consequence of the internal market, the Community's commitment to
regional policy will need to increase commensurately. Otherwise, the
political cohesion of the Community will be threatened. In its 1990 Annual
Economic Report, the Commission acknowledged that in the short term,
liberalization of the internal market would impose adjustment costs on
individual countries as industrial activity concentrates in the most efficient
location. As yet no estimate as to the particular geographical incidence of
these costs has been presented, although many commentators have
expressed concern that the peripheral regions within the Community may
well be most severely affected.

It is, of course, much too soon to say how the completed internal market
will impact on the UK economy. In the light of what appears to have been a
failure on the part of British industry to take advantage of the opportunities
that arose upon membership of the Community, there are some who
consider that completing the internal market will serve only to undermine
further British manufacturing activity. On the other hand, there is general
agreement that in the service sector, particularly financial services, British
producers stand to make considerable gains. Not only did deregulation of
British financial markets occur sooner than elsewhere in the Community,
giving domestic firms a cost advantage over foreign rivals, but the product
on offer from the City of London is of a relatively high quality (see
Pelkmans and Winters (1988) for a full discussion of the likely impact of the
internal market on the UK economy).

There are three final points to be noted. The first is that the internal
market programme has implications for other aspects of economic policy
management. In particular, the commitment to the free internal movement
of capital will profoundly affect national macroeconomic policies, although
the experience of the EMS to date suggests that most economies are willing
to accept this constraint. Secondly, the Commision must ensure that the
cost reducing gains of 1992 are not appropriated in the form of higher
profits rather than lower prices. Where scale economies result in an increase
in the degree of industrial concentration in the Community, there is an
argument for strengthened anti-trust powers to be given to the Commission.
Finally the Commission must resist pressures to increase the effective rate of
protection with respect to trade with the rest of the world upon completion

of the internal market. Should protection increase, trade diversion will occur, thereby offsetting part of the welfare gains accruing to EC consumers. Each of these issues is addressed elsewhere in this volume.

Conclusion

The benefit of hindsight notwithstanding, it is difficult to establish with any certainty the direct economic effects on the British economy that have resulted from membership of the European Community. Undoubtedly the early predictions that EC entry would be a cure to Britain's economic ills proved to be quite wrong. Britain remained one of the weaker economies inside the European Communities throughout the first decade following accession, although in recent years the UK rate of economic growth and productivity levels have compared favourably with the traditionally stronger German and French economies. However, at the time of writing the British economy seems once more to be suffering from the type of induced violent swings between boom and slump that was a hallmark of the 1960s.

But whilst it is clear that the hopes that EC membership would unleash a range of dynamic gains to the economy have been proved false, it is far from clear whether membership *per se* was to blame. Certainly the argument that membership exacerbated the endemic problems of the UK economy cannot lightly be dismissed. But it is equally difficult to argue that Britain's economic performance would have been substantially better as a non-member of the Community. Almost certainly the huge inflow of foreign investment that continues to benefit the British economy, with this rising again as a consequence of fears that Community protection against imports will increase as the single European market is completed, would not have occurred had Britain not joined the Community. In turn, this would have made more difficult the already painful process of structural adjustment in the British economy. There is nothing flawed about the argument that membership of a large internal market offers the opportunity for firms to specialise in production and reap the rewards of scale as a result. In the final instance the question that must be addressed is why the British economy failed to take advantage of those opportunities. Given that we are embarked upon a course of action that will remove the final remaining vestiges of national protectionism, it would seem appropriate that this matter is once more on the agenda.

Bibliography

Cecchini, P. (1988), *The European Challenge 1992, The Benefits of a Single Market*, Aldershot:Wildwood House Limited.
European Commission (1985), *Completing the Internal Market: White Paper from the Commission to the European Council*, Luxembourg:Commission of the European Communities.

28   ECONOMIC POLICY

Fetherston, M., Moore, B. and Rhodes, J. (1979), 'EC Membership and UK trade in manufactures', *Cambridge Journal of Economics*, Vol. 3, pp. 399-407.

HMSO (1970), *Britain and the European Communities; An Economic Assessment*, Cmnd. 4289, London: HMSO.

Holmes, P. (1983), 'The EEC and British trade' in C.D. Cohen (ed.), *The Common Market: 10 Years After*, Oxford: Philip Allan, pp. 16-38.

Kaldor, N. (1978), *Further Essays on Applied Economics*, London: Duckworth.

Morgan, A.D. (1980), 'The balance of payments and British membership of the European Community' in W. Wallace (ed.), *Britain in Europe*, London: Heinemann, pp. 57-71.

Pelkmans, J. and Winters, A. (1988), *Europe's Domestic Market*, London: Routledge.

Rowthorn, R.E. and Wells, J.R. (1987), *De-Industrialization and Foreign Trade*, Cambridge: CUP, pp. 202-3.

Shepherd, G. (1983), 'British manufacturing industry and the EEC' in C.D. Cohen (ed.), *The Common Market: 10 Years After*, Oxford: Philip Allan, pp. 39-68.

UK (1984), 'Europe — the future', *Journal of Common Market Studies*, Volume XXIII, No. 1, September, pp. 73-81.

Winters, L.A. (1987), 'Britain in Europe: a survey of quantitative trade studies', *Journal of Common Market Studies*, Volume XXV, No. 4, June, pp. 315-35.

[17]

The United Kingdom and the Community Budget

by Wynne Godley*

Mechanics and Magnitudes

Payments into the budget

Gross contributions to the Community budget are based on a principle known as 'own resources', which, in this context, means the *Community's* independent revenue: member countries under this convention are paying over to the Community what in some sense already belongs to it. Thus proceeds from common external tariffs and levies on agricultural imports from non-member countries, since their structure is determined by the Community in its supposed common interest, are considered to belong to the Community. In addition, the Community may precept up to the yield of one per cent of member countries' VAT, formally part of own resources though actually derived from national taxes.

It is important to note that the yield of VAT up to one per cent is part of the Community's own resources, as defined by the Council Decision of 21 April 1970 (on the basis of Article 201 of the Treaty of Rome). Anything beyond one per cent requires further legislation, which would have to be approved and ratified by all the member states.

As levies are chargeable on imports of food from non-member countries the gross contribution of food importers such as the UK is (other things being equal) a larger proportion of their GDP than for

* I am extremely grateful to Richard Bacon of the University of Cambridge Department of Land Economy for very extensive help in the preparation of this paper.

The United Kingdom and the Community Budget   73

countries that are self-sufficient or are net exporters. In addition, non-agricultural imports by the UK from external sources are above average and generate a relatively large yield from customs duties. For these reasons the UK will – under existing arrangements – be contributing in 1980 about 20 per cent of total budget receipts while its GDP will be about only 16 per cent of the Community's total GDP.

Table 4.1 shows the estimated gross contributions of all Community members in 1980, the share of each contribution in the total, and the share of each country in the total GDP of the Community.

Table 4.1   National contributions to the Community budget

	Gross contribution in 1980		% share of each member in Community GDP in 1977	
	£mn[a]	% share	at current exchange rates	at current purchasing power parities
Belgium–Luxembourg	617	6.1	5.1	4.3
Denmark	244	2.4	2.9	2.3
France	2016	20.0	24.1	23.2
Germany	3039	30.1	32.7	28.1
Ireland	91	0.9	0.6	0.8
Italy	1162	11.5	12.4	15.7
Netherlands	843	8.4	6.7	5.8
United Kingdom	2067	20.5	15.5	19.8

[a] Figures have been calculated from Commission figures at an exchange rate of 1 EUA = £0.664.
Sources: For contributions, Commission of the European Communities' 'Reference Paper on Budgetary Questions', COM (79) 462 Final, 12 Sept. 1979; for GDP shares, Eurostat, *National Accounts ESA*.

The revenue of the Community budget comes 14 per cent from agricultural levies, 32 per cent from industrial tariffs, and 54 per cent from VAT. Table 4.2 shows for 1980 the proportion of each of the three sources of revenue provided by each country.

Receipts from the budget
About three-quarters of the expenditure of the Community budget

74 *Britain in Europe*

Table 4.2   National contributions by sources of revenue 1980 (percentage)

	Agricultural levies	Industrial tariffs	VAT
Belgium–Luxembourg	11	7	5
Denmark	2	2	3
France	13	15	24
Germany	20	30	31
Ireland	0.5	1	1
Italy	20.5	9	14
Netherlands	15	9	6
United Kingdom	19	27	16
Total	100	100	100

Sources: as Table 4.1

is accounted for by agriculture, predominantly to support farm prices; the rest goes mainly to social and regional fund projects and to administration.

It is important to note that under Article 203 of the Treaty of Rome, as modified in April 1970 by the Treaty Amending Certain Budgetary Provisions, expenditure on agriculture is regarded as compulsory but expenditure from the social and regional funds is not. If the budget came up against a revenue ceiling, agricultural spending might under present arrangements necessitate a reduction in other areas.

Expenditure on agriculture being preponderant, receipts by member countries depend largely on the extent to which their agricultural production exceeds what can be sold at home or to other Community countries.

Estimated gross receipts by each member country in 1980 are shown in Table 4.3.

Receipts by Belgium in this table are swollen by the fact that the EEC administration is mainly situated in Brussels. This means that the foreign exchange gain to Belgium should be considered to be slightly abated by remittances home from non-Belgian employees, while the direct gain in income to Belgian nationals is overstated by all the income received by non-Belgian employees. Similar considerations of course apply to Luxembourg as well.

Economic Development of the EEC

The United Kingdom and the Community Budget   75

Table 4.3   *Gross national receipts estimated for 1980*

	Gross receipts* (£mn)	% of total
Belgium–Luxembourg	1169	11.9
Denmark	432	4.4
France	1968	20.0
Germany	2315	23.5
Ireland	380	3.8
Italy	1653	16.8
Netherlands	1036	10.5
United Kingdom	864	8.7

* Monetary Compensatory Amounts paid to exporters.
Sources: as Table 4.1.

Net budgetary contributions and excess food costs

The concept of a net budgetary contribution is less clear than is
sometimes supposed. Considered as a net financial contribution by a
member state, the concept is clear enough. But whether it is appropriate
to treat the net contribution as being what its *government* pays is highly
questionable. In the case of Britain, payments *out of* the Community
budget are not in any direct sense payments to the British government: they are payments to British farmers, warehousemen, and so on,
over which the government has only limited control. The fact that
these payments pass through the UK government accounts does not
mean they should be netted off in the presentation of its public expenditure estimates, because there have to be counterpart entries in
(positive) public expenditure on agriculture and on regional and social
programmes. In other words, the total public expenditure cost of the
EEC is the gross contribution, not the net contribution as the White
Papers on public expenditure would have us believe. This must be
emphasized, for it is not at all clear that, if the UK were not a
member of the Community, there would be a public expenditure cost
for the support of agriculture on the scale at present undertaken by
the EEC.

Now, contributions less receipts must sum to nil across all countries;
therefore some countries receive more than they pay, others pay more
than they receive. (The statement that contributions less receipts must
sum to nil across all countries is not strictly accurate because there has

76   Britain in Europe

been a small but significant increase in cash balances held by the Community which exercises a small disinflationary effect on the system as a whole.) The estimated net budgetary contributions or receipts of all member countries for 1980, derived directly from the first column of Tables 4.1 and 4.3, are shown in the first column of Table 4.4.

Table 4.4   Net national receipts estimated for 1980 (£ million)

	(1) Net budgetary receipt	(2) Excess food gain	(3) Total net cash receipt (1) + (2)
Belgium– Luxembourg	+ 557	− 60	+ 497
Denmark	+ 188	+ 244	+ 432
France	− 48	+ 528	+ 480
Germany	− 724	− 358	− 1082
Ireland	+ 289	+ 173	+ 462
Italy	+ 491	− 515	− 24
Netherlands	+ 193	+ 694	+ 887
United Kingdom	− 1203	− 127	− 1330

Sources: Col. (1), see text immediately above. The figures in col. (2) are taken from J. M. C. Rollo and K. S. Warwick, *The CAP and Resource Flows among EEC Member States*, London, MAFF, 1979; they are for 1978 trade volumes and are a 'central' estimate from the 'net effect on the trade account' presented in their Table VII.

The net contributions shown in column (1) of Table 4.4 relate solely to sums of money paid into and out of the Community budget. Although these accurately represent the results of the Community system of budgetary transfers they are seriously misleading if taken as a representation of the whole transfer system between member countries, which arises from the CAP and the budget combined. This is because, when trade takes place between member countries, the exporting country's farmer receives his EEC price directly from the consumer in the importing country, not from intervention purchasing (or subsidization of exports to non-member countries) paid for ultimately out of the Community budget. I am assuming for the time being that the green currencies of each country have the same relationship to 'par'. For a brief explanation of the green currency system the reader is directed to Appendix 1 at the end of this paper.

The United Kingdom and the Community Budget   77

One way to bring this point home is to imagine two member countries which are identical to each other except that one exports its butter surplus to the USSR, the other to a member of the Community. The position of each exporting country in respect of internal prices, total foreign exchange receipts, and farmers' incomes is the same – but only the exporter to the USSR receives cash from the Community budget for this trade. That member gets EEC prices less disposal prices in the form of an export restitution, whereas the exporter to another Community member receives the whole price directly from the importing member. Another way of illustrating this point is to consider how much would be lost by the rest of the Community if the UK ceased to be a member. Clearly our net budgetary contribution of £1, 203 million odd would be lost, but even if it could be assumed that the volume of our food imports from the Community continued the same, export restitutions would have to be made to Community farmers to bring the 'world price' we would then be paying up to the Community price – the level at which we now pay. Thus while (what we have called) 'excess food costs' are at present non-budgetary transfers, *they must be included in any estimate of the additional net charge that would fall on the budget if we were not members.*

There are serious difficulties in estimating the precise scale of excess food costs. In particular it is difficult to know what is the appropriate 'world price' that should be compared with the EEC price.

Fortunately some official estimates of excess food costs have recently been published by Rollo and Warwick. On the one hand they are based on the actual rates of levy which importers had to pay when importing from non-member countries, on the other hand on the actual rates of export restitution which exporters received when exporting. The results of this calculation (taking an average of the two estimates) are shown in column (2) of Table 4.4 above. (A suggestion was made at the conference that transfer payments arising on trade in industrial products should also be taken into account. For a note on this topic see Appendix 2 at the end of this paper.)

Each country's total net cash transfer (the sum of budgetary contributions and excess food costs) is shown in column (3) of Table 4.4. Now, the figures in column (3) can indicate how much each country gains or loses through the transfer system only if we assume that, if the Community did not exist, each country paid for the support of its own agriculture at the same level and used essentially the same method

78   Britain in Europe

as the Community does (and that implies the same level of food prices and, therefore, of domestic production and consumption); second it must be assumed that the scale and pattern of trade in food would be as at present. The first of these assumptions seems quite appropriate; for instance we are showing, for France, how much extra (£480 million) the French taxpayer would have to find if French farmers continued to be supported at existing levels. The second assumption is more questionable. Importing countries (notably Britain) would almost certainly obtain a higher proportion of their supplies from sources outside the Community. This would not, taken by itself (assuming an external levy at the present rate), make Britain better off, but it would damage the Community's exporting countries by reducing their exports and therefore give rise to more intervention buying.

Here I would like to emphasize two points in relation to the figures in Table 4.4, bearing particularly in mind the confused public discussion in Britain of all these issues.

The first point is that it is absolutely essential to count *both* the net budgetary transfers *and* the excess food costs. This drastically alters not only the scale but also the ranking of the inter-country transfers. For instance, the transfer cost to Britain is not going to be £1,200 million in 1980 as the public generally supposes, but (according to present estimates) about £1,300 million. Italy, which appears a substantial net beneficiary if the budget alone is considered, roughly breaks even when both figures are taken into account. France's net contribution is about nil, but when trade gains are included she becomes the second largest beneficiary of the whole system.

The second point is to recall that we are showing, in column (3) of the table, net payments which must sum to nil across countries. As the figures show, there are only two net payers of any magnitude, Britain and Germany; all other countries (except Italy) are substantial net recipients.

Assessment

Consider first how a budget works within a unitary state or an established federation. On the one hand services (for example, education and defence) are generally provided to a common standard and to the benefit of all component areas; on the other hand taxes are

The United Kingdom and the Community Budget   79

raised according to the component areas' ability to pay. Such a budget achieves objectives common to all areas through public expenditure but at the same time there exists a redistributive cash transfer system from the relatively rich to the relatively poor areas.

In sharp contrast, outlays from the Community budget do not in any real sense achieve common standards of any service throughout the Community and the contributions are incoherently related to members' ability to pay.

The beneficiaries are mainly the agricultural industries of major producer countries which are protected *vis-à-vis* world markets and indeed are being supported on a scale that is excessive, judged by the criterion that stockpiling and dumping or destruction of produce are occurring. And the cost of all this is spread through the Community according to no principles of equity. The arbitrary and often perverse nature of the pattern of EEC transfers may be demonstrated by expressing the total net cash receipt or payment of each member country on a *per capita* basis and setting the result alongside figures indicating relative levels of national income per head.

Table 4.5   Per capita net receipts compared with per capita income

	Estimated receipts per capita 1980 (£ per annum)	National income per capita (% unweighted mean at market exchange rates 1977)	National income per capita (% of unweighted mean at purchasing power parities 1977)
Belgium–Luxembourg	+ 49	129	109
Denmark	+ 86	136	119
France	+ 9	113	113.5
Germany	− 18	130	118.5
Ireland	+ 154	48	62
Italy	− 1	55	72
Netherlands	+ 63	120	108
United Kingdom	− 24	69	92

Sources: as Table 4.1

Table 4.5 shows once again only two net contributors apart from Germany, of which the larger is the UK, while Ireland and Denmark

80   Britain in Europe

are by a very long way the largest *per capita* beneficiaries. The UK
and Italy, among the three member countries that came off worst from
the EEC transfer system, are among the three with the lowest national
income per head. A notably anomalous gainer is Denmark, which
receives over £86 a year per head (equal to about two per cent of
its GNP), although Denmark's income per head is the highest in
Europe – just over double that of the UK. The one 'good' aspect of
the system is that Ireland, still by far the poorest member of the
Community, also receives the largest *per capita* benefit; Ireland has
been gaining rapidly in prosperity, both absolutely and relative to
other member countries.

Although this transfer system is arbitrary, perverse, and wholly
disadvantageous to Britain, no Briton should be surprised at it or
newly indignant about it. The White Paper *Britain and the European
Communities*, Cmnd 4289, which was published in 1970 and formed
the official prospectus for UK entry, states in paragraph 44 that 'the
trade effects and the financial charges' consequent on adopting the
Common Agricultural Policy would be likely to lie in a range exceeding £175–£250 million. As prices have risen more than threefold
since 1970, the forecast then made appears to be in the correct parish.

Future Prospects under Existing Policies

I believe it to be the case that if existing or similar policies are continued, that is, if farm prices on average through the Community rise
a few percentage points each year, the cost of the CAP will still rise
much faster than the growth rates of nominal GNP. By implication the
pattern of net transfers will remain the same as at present but all the
magnitudes will grow both absolutely and relative to GNP. What can
check or reverse the process?

If the growth of expenditure is unchecked the whole tax potential
of the 'own resources' system (that is, the total of levies and customs
duties and the yield of one per cent from VAT) will quite soon be
exhausted. The Community will be incapable of financing further
increases in expenditure without further increases in VAT, which the
net payers (Britain in particular) could impregnably refuse to pay.
If there were a ceiling on revenue there would presumably first be a
cut in expenditure from the social and regional funds, implying a
further increase in Britain's net contribution. But before long, because

the commitment to maintain farm prices is open ended, the CAP would surely collapse.

Short of this outcome a severe limitation in the growth of, or a freeze in, farm prices (in nominal terms) could be imposed. But it is very doubtful whether any feasible farm-price policy would actually prevent budget expenditure from continuing to rise.

Even if total expenditure *were* checked or reduced that would not alter the pattern of net contributors and recipients. The UK would still be a net contributor even if not on quite the present scale.

But there is another reason why a stringent policy towards farm prices may not be a satisfactory, let alone sufficient, policy for Britain. As long as sterling was weak it was possible for the UK government successfully to oppose a general increase in farm prices within the Community and simultaneously to obtain an increase in prices for British farmers by devaluing the green pound. And this is indeed what happened in the first half of 1979. The general increase in farm prices throughout the Community between April and September 1979 averaged about five per cent but because of green pound devaluations British farm prices, both to producers and consumers, rose about 12 per cent in this period.

However, strong sterling would make it impossible for the UK to have it both ways. Green currencies may only be devalued or revalued towards par, never away from it. Sterling recently reached a level which brought our green pound to within one or two per cent of par, and therefore no significant further devaluation of the green pound would then have been possible under the existing rules of the CAP. In other words, British farm prices could then rise only at about the same rate as European prices in general, except to the extent that sterling depreciated.

The foreign exchange market is so volatile that any prediction must be conditional. Should sterling remain strong a deep conflict will emerge. If EEC farm prices are raised significantly, net transfers from the UK to the Community will rise even faster than is at present foreseen and the mountains will grow. If EEC prices are not raised, British farmers will have their real income substantially and progressively squeezed between the stability of the prices they will receive and the increase in the cost of labour, fuel, and other materials, which looks like being about 15 per cent during this financial year alone.

On a longer time scale, unless spot sterling is devalued almost to

82 Britain in Europe

the full extent of the UK inflation rate (its absolute rate, *not* its rate relative to that of other countries) a progressive squeeze of British farm incomes is the inevitable consequence of preventing any significant growth of prices throughout the Community. Britain would then be in the astonishing position of having to pay out vast sums of foreign exchange every year mainly to support the incomes of Community farmers, while simultaneously being deprived of the power to protect the incomes of her own farmers.

More radical possibilities

Consideration of more radical possibilities for reform of the budget and CAP mechanisms cannot sensibly be considered in isolation from the major alternative ways in which the Community might now develop, many of which have been ably summarized by William Wallace in his introductory chapter. I mention three such possibilities below.

The simplest and least disruptive way in which the transfer system could be reformed would be explicitly to separate the CAP (defined as a particular level of support and protection for agriculture) from the way in which it is financed. It is very commonly supposed that reform of the transfer system necessarily requires reform of the CAP itself. In my opinion that is an incorrect judgement, just as it would be incorrect to suppose that the structure and incidence of taxation within a country could not be reformed without altering the structure and scale of public expenditure on defence, health, or education.

The CAP is indeed in need of reform, if only because of the enormous waste of resources that is daily being incurred. However, if the Community, for political or other reasons, wishes to preserve the CAP in its present form, there is nothing to stop it from doing so and at the same time radically altering the pattern of net transfers. The way in which that was done should of course reflect the objectives of the Community. It is sometimes pointed out (see, for example, Carsten Thoroe's contribution) that redistributive policies are not part of the Treaty of Rome. *But redistribution of resources is precisely what the Treaty of Rome is generating!* If it is no part of Community policy to redistribute resources, the financial reform is in principle simple to devise: let all net recipients shown in my Table 4.4 pay out of their own exchequers, to the Community, the sums of money shown in column (3) and let these be paid back to the net payers. It is easy to see possible ways of varying this theme. For instance, if it was considered inappropriate that Ireland, still the poorest Community member, should receive less than at present, Ireland alone could be spared the requirement to refund her net positive transfers.

Any or all such solutions to the manifest inequity of the existing transfer system may well encounter insuperable objections of a political nature from those countries which stand to lose. My sole concern here is to point out that there is no reason in logistics why a pattern of transfers acceptable to Britain should not be implemented without delay. Above all it is not necessary to wait for a major and probably painful restructuring of the CAP, which would certainly take many years.

Another possibility is that the scope of the Community budget could be greatly enlarged so as to make it something like a genuinely federal budget. Such budgets normally have equalizing properties since they aim to provide a uniform standard of service, say education, health or roads, in every region of the whole area.

However, to change the ranking of net payers and recipients in such a way as to make it correspond in any degree with the ranking of GDP per head would require a very large increase in total expenditure and a correspondingly large increase in total gross contributions.

On the one hand the contributions, both gross and net, of the richer countries would have to be very much increased, which they might find unacceptable. But in addition individual governments would have to hand over to Brussels very substantial powers to spend money on a new range of services. The political institutions to which such important powers would be delegated do not at present exist. It would thus be a risky, cumbersome, and expensive way of achieving an equitable transfer system. It would certainly take several years.

A third possibility, which the conference discussed at some length, is that substantially larger sums might be paid out to assist the development of poorer, or declining, regions or even whole countries. Such expenditure would have a fundamentally different character from the refund mechanisms adumbrated in the first of the three suggestions discussed in this section. Instead of consisting of un-hypothecated transfers of foreign exchange, such regional or quasi-regional expenditure might, for instance, generate investment that would otherwise not be undertaken; it could even directly subsidize

84 Britain in Europe

employment in the less successful and competitive areas, following the pattern of the Regional Employment Premium which was operated in Britain with some limited success during the 1960s.

Appendix 1: The Green Currency System

The original intention to institute uniform food prices throughout the Community was abandoned because of major changes in the exchange rates between the currencies of member countries, which greatly exceeded the differences in their inflation rates. These exchange rate changes have been governed by factors – notably performance in world markets for manufactured products and the conduct of monetary and fiscal policy – which have little to do with trade in agriculture. Had agricultural trade continued to take place at common prices calculated at actual exchange rates, the farmers in those member countries which have been most successful in world markets – particularly Germany – would have suffered a disastrous fall in their incomes; consumers in the relatively unsuccessful manufacturing countries would have had to face extremely sharp increases in food prices, and their farmers would have made extremely large profits. It was principally for these reasons that, when exchange rate parities flew apart, the 'green currency' system was invented. In form this system introduces a new *numéraire* in terms of which agricultural prices are denominated. But the simple way to think of it is as a device whereby agricultural prices in individual countries are partly or wholly insulated from the process of exchange rate adjustment; in other words, internal prices do not necessarily change at all when currencies are adjusted. In consequence, prices differ from country to country when measured at actual exchange rates, and when trade takes place between countries this difference has to be made up by a cash levy or subsidy. If Germany exports butter to be sold in the UK at a price in sterling which is only 60 per cent of the price received by the German farmer (and 60 per cent of that paid by the German consumer), the difference is made up by a 'monetary compensatory amount' (MCA) paid out of the Community budget.

Now MCAs are sometimes paid out of the budget directly to the exporting country, in which case the importing country is paying a price equal to the Community price expressed at par *minus* the MCA; but sometimes the importing country pays the full Community price

and itself receives the MCA. The difference between these two ways
of arranging things is one solely of administrative convenience; the
position of neither importing nor exporting country is in any significant way altered by the method chosen.

In 1976 the arrangements for the UK were changed. Until then
MCAs were paid to the UK as an offset to the high prices being paid
to exporters; since 1976 MCAs have been paid direct to the exporter
and the UK has paid a correspondingly lower price. Again, no
significant difference was made to anything important but the UK's
net contribution to the budget was increased to be precisely offset by
a reduction in the amount paid as 'excess food costs'.

This example underlines the importance of always including both
excess food costs and net budgetary contributions when measuring the
total scale and pattern of the transfer system; so long as both kinds
of transfer are included no difference is made to the presentation (in
accordance with the realities), regardless of whether MCAs are
credited to exporters or importers.

Unfortunately this matter has given rise to much misunderstanding,
largely because budget figures are habitually presented on their own.
And confusion has been positively invited by the double presentation
of net contributions, with MCAs credited on the one hand to exporters
and on the other to importers.

Appendix 2: Transfers Arising from Trade in Industrial Products

Trade in industrial products between member countries gives rise to
transfers between them which are in principle the same as the transfers arising from trade in food (see Appendix 1 above). The existence
of a common external tariff implies that, as in the case of food, there
is a world price for competitive industrial products which (ex tax)
is lower than the price at which trade takes place inside the
Community.

The scale of these transfers cannot, however, be very large. Not all
imports from outside countries are subject to the common external
tariff, and the 'world price' (an even more difficult concept for manufactures than for food) is probably lower than the Community price
by something less than the tariff. Suppose the world price to be on
average six or seven per cent lower than the Community price, the

net transfer could be estimated by applying this percentage to the deficit or surplus in the balance of trade in manufactures of any member country with the rest of the Community. As the UK is now in heavy deficit in its manufacturing trade with the rest of the Community its total net transfers would be somewhat increased (conceivably by £100–£200 million) compared with the figures shown in Table 4.4. Net transfers by Germany, on the same principle, would be somewhat reduced.

Comment
by Stephen Milligan

I fully share the general thesis advanced by Godley – that Britain's share of budget costs added to the cost of trade transfers is absurdly high. I also agree that reform of the system is going to be extremely difficult, but I am not quite as pessimistic as he is about possible solutions.

At the beginning of his paper he refers briefly to the concept of own resources, the Community's independent revenue. The Community's own resources are, by formal agreement among member states, the property of the Community and therefore escape the control of national parliaments. When the Community instituted the principle of own resources in the early 1970s the Dutch insisted that, as a counterpart, the European Parliament should be given some control of the budget. The French reluctantly accepted this extension of the Parliament's role, because they believed that the introduction of own resources would prevent national parliaments from interfering each year with the budget for agriculture. Thus VAT is in this sense very much an 'own resource', derived from a harmonized base of assessment, even though VAT rates and coverage are not fully harmonized throughout the Community.

The system agreed has two important consequences for the present debate. First, the European Parliament has the right to alter the Community's annual budget. In 1979, for the first time, the newly elected

Parliament attempted to cut the amount of cash devoted to the CAP (the Dankert amendment) and then rejected the budget altogether, with the aim of obliging member governments to accept its proposals. The notion that the Parliament has no power over farm spending is wrong: it can significantly alter the CAP budget – although it needs the support in the Council of a blocking minority of governments to achieve success, for example Britain and Italy.

Second, the present ceiling on own resources will be hit by 1982. At that point the Community will run short of cash – and no more will be available until *all* nine national parliaments agree to a new *tranche*. Thus each country will have a veto over additional resources (Britain, Germany, and France have already said that they are opposed to increasing revenue). Germany and France may well change their minds when they come to terms with the threat that the ceiling represents to the CAP. Britain is left with an irresistible bargaining counter in the right to withhold agreement on new own resources until the CAP and/or its budget contribution is reformed. The Parliament is unlikely to change the shape of the Community budget radically from one year to the next, but it could have an important impact over a period. The fact that the Parliament more accurately represents the urban citizens of Europe than does the pro-farmer Council of Ministers will be a continuing force for a better balanced budget.

Godley argues that, if a ceiling was imposed on EEC spending, agriculture might simply swallow up more and more cash at the expense of, for example, the regional fund. Theoretically, he is quite right. But in practice, I do not think that would happen. The combination of a majority in the European Parliament and the votes of Britain and Italy in the Council would be enough to stop it (even if, for example, the Dutch and the Irish agreed to support 'swallowing up' – which I doubt). 'Compulsory' expenditure means that it is obligatory for the EEC to provide price support for, say, milk – but the level of support, which is the crucial question, is not specified. I therefore believe that the crisis presented by the exhaustion of own resources will offer a most promising way to reshape the EEC's spending. And such a crisis might also help the reformers within the German and French governments (including Helmut Schmidt), who have long sought a means to tackle the excesses of their own farm ministers.

88   Britain in Europe

On the question of what reform should be introduced there are various options. The immediate problem of Britain's excess budget bill can be tackled by a reform of the corrective mechanism established during the renegotiation of 1974–5. This mechanism has so far proved useless, partly because it is linked only to Britain's gross contribution, and partly because it is hedged about with conditions – for example, that Britain can claim a refund only when running a trade deficit. If the mechanism was linked to net contributions and the hedging conditions removed, most of Britain's 'excess' bill could be eliminated. If Britain's problem was resolved the Community budget overall would not be quite as regressive as Godley suggests. This is because his figures are partly based on 1978, which was an erratically bad year for Italy. The Commission's projections for 1980 (Table 4.6) show that Italy will become the biggest beneficiary from the EEC. A variety of new EEC policies, for example interest-rate relief grants for EMS membership, the Mediterranean aid programme, and the increase in the regional fund, have all helped.

The apparent high benefits for rich Belgium and Luxembourg are based on the assumption that *all* cash paid for the EEC institutions in those countries is a transfer to those countries. This is obviously an exaggeration. (British Eurocrats, for instance, transfer some of their

Table 4.6 Forecast net transfers 1980 (£ million)

United Kingdom	– 1161
Germany	– 671
France	– 12
Luxembourg	+ 187
Denmark	+ 237
Netherlands	+ 271
Ireland	+ 328
Belgium	+ 352
Italy	+ 470

Note: Monetary Compensatory Amounts are attributed as a subsidy to exporting countries. The orders of magnitude are not greatly changed if they are attributed to importers, because MCAs in 1980 are likely to be much smaller than in recent years.

Source: based on Commission of the European Communities paper COM (79) 620, 31 October 1979.

salaries back to Britain – and much of the cash they spend in Belgium is in exchange for resources supplied by Belgium and is thus not simple profit for Belgium.)

Godley's Table 4.5 also exaggerates the spread of income within the Community by comparing countries at market exchange rates. Table 4.7 shows that the dispersion at purchasing power parities is considerably less and slightly alters the ranking. However, it should be pointed out that budget payments are of course made at market exchange rates not at purchasing power parities.

In the long run two reforms are needed to make the budget system fairer. First, as and when an agreement is reached on new own resources, revenue should be raised on a progressive basis. The Commission has already proposed that the next *tranche* should be raised from a further one per cent on VAT – but at a variable rate linked to relative GNP. (In any case, the higher the fraction of Community revenue raised from VAT – as opposed to tariffs and levies – the fairer the system will be. Part of Britain's unfair gross contribution stems from the fact that it pays an unfair share of tariffs because of its high share of non-Community trade.) A progressive key could even be extended to cover all VAT payments – including the existing one per cent *tranche* paid to the Community.

Second, part of the financial cost of the CAP must be transferred to national governments, as Godley suggests, and the level of price support must be cut. The problem for Ireland would indeed be

Table 4.7 Estimated dispersion of GDP at purchasing power parities 1979
(EEC = 100)

Germany	118
Denmark	116
France	112
Luxembourg	111
Belgium	108
Netherlands	105
United Kingdom	91
Italy	77
Ireland	61

Source: Commission of the European Communities, *Annual Economic Review*, November 1979.

90   Britain in Europe

serious – but Ireland would remain a net beneficiary under any hypothesis and it would be easy to adjust other spending policies to compensate.

I disagree with Godley's argument that a low farm price policy would not suit Britain. It is true that once British farm prices are aligned on Community prices, there is no scope for giving British farmers 'real' price increases while at the same time freezing Community prices. But why should Britain want to give its farmers real price rises? Britain's farm prices, like those in the rest of the Community, are now well above world prices – with a corresponding burden on consumers. Traditionally, real farm prices have fallen by some one per cent a year to reflect rising productivity. An illusory argument is that rising British real farm prices would benefit the British trade balance. This ignores the welfare cost of transferring resources towards farming from other sectors of the economy.

Surely there is a confusion here. British farmers are worried that, without the possibility of regular green-pound devaluations, they will not even be able to obtain nominal price rises. But either British inflation will be low – in which case farmers will not need large nominal price rises – or British inflation will be high, in which case the real pound will fall again and there will once more be scope for nominal price rises via devaluation of the green pound. The only risk for British farmers is if the real pound is valued at an exaggerated level.

[18]

Changing patterns of monetary interdependence
Elke Thiel

Patterns of market interaction have changed considerably during the course of the 1970s and 1980s. The dynamics of market integration have moved from foreign trade to foreign investments. Cross-border production and sales of subsidiaries located abroad have gained weight against foreign trade. The tendency may become even more marked with the deregulation of services and settlement rights. Competition among countries has shifted from trade to overall foreign economic activities, for which the exchange rate is a less important value.[1]

Macro-economic policy conceptions and views on exchange rates have altered as well. When macro-economic policies turned from Keynesianism to monetarism at the end of the 1970s, currency appreciation became a forceful tool in the pursuit of domestic price stability goals. Financial flows are now a major source for the financing of current account deficits. Movements in exchange rates are dominated by capital flows rather than by trade flows. Shifts of capital from one country to another may push exchange rates in a direction unfavourable to the adjustment of trade imbalances.

Monetary interdependence is a worldwide phenomenon. What makes a difference is how countries react to market interdependence. The search for more distinctive patterns of monetary interactions brings into focus the formal or semi-formal framework of institutions, rules and procedures that cause adjustment to external disturbances. Globalization of financial markets has passed Europe by. In the European Community, however, a regional sub-system of formal monetary rules was established in 1979. It is the European Monetary System of pegged exchange rates that distinguishes European cooperation from cooperation pursued within the global monetary system by the Group of Seven.

Rules and procedures provide the formal framework within which market transactions are performed. In this respect, they have an impact on informal flows. Markets have been very ingenious, however, in circumventing formal restrictions, with the present globalization of capital markets as an obvious example. Market forces can also destroy monetary rules when handled inadequately, as happened with the monetary system of Bretton Woods. The

European monetary sub-system has turned out to be more stable than had been anticipated. Adherence to the rules has increasingly shaped domestic policies. As confidence in the system has grown, it has also influenced market expectations and capital flows. Western Europe now looks like an area of closer coherence within a less stable, global monetary system.

The background

Until 1971, monetary interactions among European countries were framed by the global monetary order of Bretton Woods, launched by an Anglo-Saxon initiative in 1944. It was a system of pegged exchange rates, the dollar being the key international currency. The pound sterling was used as a currency of reserve for the sterling area, though the United Kingdom had great difficulty in maintaining that situation.

In the immediate postwar period, European cooperation was aimed at reconstructing the economies and reintegrating them into an open world economy. When the OEEC was founded in 1948, the overall emphasis was on promoting trade liberalization among European countries as a precondition for their integration into the global system of the GATT. In 1950, the European Payment Union (EPU) was established as a multilateral clearing facility for OEEC members' claims and liabilities in foreign transactions. The objective was to facilitate multilateral trade and gradually to implement currency convertibility. This goal was achieved at the end of 1958 by the European Monetary Agreement (EMA), replacing the European Payment Union. With the introduction of convertibility, West European currencies became fully integrated into the dollar area.

Monetary cooperation of the 1960s was global. The IMF was a major actor in promoting credit assistance and also had to approve changes in par values. Because the dollar was the numeraire for all other currencies, it could not change value unilaterally. Adjustment had to come from the other currencies of the dollar-centred system, and realignments thus immediately concerned the US as well.

Cooperation focused particularly on the backing of the reserve currencies of the system, the pound sterling and the dollar. The most important grouping in bringing about rescue operations was the 'Group of Ten. It was established in 1962, when central bank governors met at the Bank for International Settlements (BIS) in Basle to agree upon actions to stabilize sterling balances (the Basle Agreement). Group of Ten membership formally includes the United States, Canada, the United Kingdom, France, West Germany, Italy, Belgium, the Netherlands, Sweden and Japan. Switzerland also participated before it became a formal member of the Group of Ten in 1984. The BIS provided assistance and the gnomes of Zurich also became important actors in the financing of rescue packages.

The pound sterling was devalued in 1967. In 1971, the United States suspended dollar-gold convertibility and enforced a dollar depreciation. The D-mark emerged as a strong currency and became the currency of reserve second to the dollar when markets built up D-mark balances to diversify dollar reserves, starting in the final years of the Bretton Woods System.

The rules and institutions of the Bretton Woods System provided the monetary order for the Common Market, founded in 1958. The Treaty of Rome leaves macro-economic policy in the domain of national authorities. According to Articles 103–105, however, Member States are obliged to reduce external imbalances, to consider short-term economic and monetary policy with respect to the business cycle and exchange rates a matter of common concern, and to pursue policy coordination. The treaty explicitly provides for the establishment of a consulting Monetary Committee, already in existence in 1958.

In March 1961, the D-mark and the Dutch guilder were revalued upwards. When the Community established a common agricultural policy in the following years, however, currency realignments were to split the Community-wide system of farm prices. A closer coordination of policies thus became even more desirable. In 1964, the Committee of Central Bank Governors was introduced. This came as a belated effort to activate consultations when a rescue operation for the Italian lira had been mounted primarily by American credits and with IMF support, but with no advance notice in Brussels.[2] When the Community later attempted to approach Economic and Monetary Union with the Werner Plan, the institutional equipment for policy coordination was further enlarged by the Economic Policy Committee, introduced in 1974.

In November 1968, the European Community of the Six experienced a major currency crisis, involving the French franc and the D-mark. Both countries declined to adjust parities at this time. The crisis was finally settled by a franc depreciation in August 1969, followed by a D-mark appreciation in October. In the course of events, the Commission launched a new initiative aimed at promoting currency coherence within the Common Market. The Barre Memorandum of February 1969 recommended measures to strengthen and extend economic and monetary policy coordination, including the creation of a mechanism of mutual credit assistance for members experiencing balance-of-payments difficulties. In the same year in December, the Hague summit initiated the Werner Plan for Economic and Monetary Union, submitted in October 1970.

The Werner Plan originally assumed that EMU would be established within the global framework of fixed exchange rates, as provided by the order of Bretton Woods. At the first stage of EMU, margins for currency fluctuations were to be narrowed so that deviation among EC currencies would not exceed currencies' deviation vis-à-vis the dollar, still the numeraire for all other currencies.

The first approach to EMU failed at a time when the end of Bretton Woods made a closer European monetary coherence even more desirable. In March 1971, the Council of Ministers decided to begin with the first stage of EMU. The moment could not have been less auspicious. The global monetary order was about to collapse. The D-mark was subject to large capital flights from the dollar area and was floated freely in May. In August, the dollar-gold convertibility was suspended. In December, the Smithsonian agreement made a last effort to rescue the system. In March 1973, the global system turned to managed floating.

Stage one of the Werner Plan had to be postponed, but started in March 1972 and then involved all members of the Community of Nine. The transition to floating exchange rates in March 1973, however, revealed the differences in economic performances among EC members. While the D-mark was appreciating, other currencies came under downward pressure, in particular the lira and the pound sterling. The United Kingdon, Ireland and Italy left the snake at the very beginning. France tried at first to remain in the system but stepped out later. When the D-mark pulled the snake upwards vis-à-vis the dollar appreciation of the franc was held to be detrimental to French international competitiveness. Countries staying out of the snake also believed that managed floating would give more leeway for domestic demand expansion. The rapid increase of the oil bill, starting in the autumn of 1973, further deepened diversities in economic policies between EC members.

The European snake contracted into a D-mark bloc, formally including the Benelux countries and Denmark as well as Norway and Sweden. Austria and Switzerland informally followed a monetary course that kept their currencies in line with the snake. In 1979, the snake was replaced by the European Monetary System and was thus brought back into the European Community. It then included all members of the Community of Nine, except the United Kingdom, while the Nordic countries left the system.

The European Monetary System can be considered as the European response to the instabilities of the international monetary system. It was triggered by disillusionment with managed floating and the US policy of benign neglect. The overall emphasis was on achieving a zone of monetary stability for Common Market transactions with a view towards making European currencies less vulnerable to disturbances emanating from the dollar. Yet, given large differences in inflation, the reintroduction of pegged exchange rates was widely considered an inadequate response to global interdependence, in particular by German critics. Capital markets would test the system and could easily demolish it. That the system would render European currencies more coherent was scarcely believed at the time.

The EMS-EC relationships

The EMS initiative

The creation of the EMS goes back to the political initiative of the French president, Valery Giscard d'Estaing, and the West German Chancellor, Helmut Schmidt. For France, the emphasis was on restablizing the franc. Bringing the franc back into a system of pegged exchange rates could help to cut past vicious cycles of currency depreciation and high domestic inflation. Italy finally decided to participate for similar reasons, as did Ireland.

At the end of the 1970s, most industrial countries adopted policies to fight high rates of inflation. Accordingly, a strong exchange rate was favoured to support domestic price stability goals. Yet only those countries joining the EMS as a system of pegged exchange rates with the D-mark as the strong currency then committed their anti-inflationary course to formal rules. The

United Kingdom followed an independent track. Like the United States, it looked for gains in price stability from its currency's upwards floating, caused by high interest rate levels and capital imports.

The introduction of the EMS was feasible and the system has been sustainable because economic concepts have become more convergent, starting in the late 1970s. The initial drive to engage in the EMS, however, came from the political sphere. Economic performances in member countries differed enormously when the EMS started. France and Italy were affected by high levels of inflation. Both countries had to fear that their currencies would come under strong downward pressures when pegged with the D-mark. In order to stay in the EMS, they would have to follow a more restrictive monetary course and this could cause too much strain in their inflation-minded domestic economies.

In West Germany, French interest in participating in the European currency system was seen as an opportunity to strengthen the Franco-German relationship and to give new impetus to the European Community. Yet, pegging the D-mark to the French franc and the Italian lira could have put German monetary policy at risk. The commitment of the Bundesbank to support the weaker currencies of the system by intervening in exchange markets would make it more difficult to keep inflation under control. From an economic standpoint, there were thus strong reasons on all sides not to participate in the EMS.

In retrospect, the EMS has worked much better than was anticipated. In the early years, the weakness of the D-mark vis-à-vis the dollar kept EMS currencies together. In France and Italy, EMS membership helped to calm inflation mentalities and could also be used as a scapegoat for unpopular austerity policies.[3] For the Germans, the EMS did not endanger price stability. On the contrary, while strongly supporting the EMS, the Bundesbank also shaped its rules in a way that made the system more resistant to inflation.

The creation of the EMS included elements of bargaining. France had stepped out of the snake twice in the 1970s. By replacing the snake with the EMS, the country could come into the system again without losing face. EMS instruments were framed differently from the snake in order to make participation more acceptable to France. The European Currency Unit (Ecu) was introduced, suggesting a common European currency. The Ecu was also to be used as an indicator for currency divergencies, that should trigger early consultations and adjustment measures. Credit mechanisms were enlarged, and, at the second stage of the EMS, national monetary reserves were to be transferred to the European Monetary Fund. Most of these measures were designed to provide assistance for the weaker currencies in the system. For Italy and Ireland the bargain also included regional compensation.

Yet these specific elements of bargain only played a minor role in the performance of the EMS. What made the EMS a success was a continuous process of learning and common understanding. The watershed year was 1983, when the Mitterrand government turned policy from economic expansion towards a more restrictive course in order to keep the French franc within the EMS. Inflation rates were brought down in the following years and current French price stability is very close to German figures.

Drawing others into the system

The EMS started as a 'two-speed' community. The United Kingdom did not participate in the exchange rate mechanism that pegs currencies together. The whole framework was, however, designed to include all EC members. The EMS works within the institutional framework of the European Community. Regular consultations on economic and monetary issues among all EC members take place at the meetings of the Council of Ministers for Economics and Finance, the Monetary Committee, the Economic Policy Committee and the Committee of Central Bank Governors. The last regularly meets in Basle at the Bank for International Settlements, which also acts as an agent for the settlement of EMS central banks' balances.

Short- and medium-term credit facilities provided by the European Fund for Monetary Cooperation are available to all EC members. These funds were already created in 1971 at the time of the European currency snake and they were expanded in 1979, when the EMS was established. The objective was to provide assistance for members facing balance-of-payment problems, but these funds have never been employed in the more than ten years of the EMS. The Ecu, a basket of EC currencies, included the pound sterling since its creation and the drachma since Greece entered the Community in 1981. The peseta and escudo came into the basket in 1989. All EC members can draw Ecus from the European Fund for Monetary Cooperation by delivering part of their monetary reserves to the Fund.

When the European Summit in Hanover in June 1988 launched a new initiative for an Economic and Monetary Union, all EC members were drawn into the project, although the British were reluctant. All EC central bank governors were members of the Delors Committee, established by the Hanover mandate in order to examine and propose concrete stages leading towards economic and monetary unification. In June 1989, the European Summit in Madrid agreed to start with the first stage of Economic and Monetary Union in July 1990, the date when capital liberalization has to be fully achieved by most EC countries, and all members of the Community are supposed to embark on the process.

Spain had joined the common exchange rate mechanism at the end of the Spanish presidency in the EC. Great Britain, Greece and Portugal are to take part in the course of stage one, although the date for their entry has been left open. The intergovernmental conference, scheduled to convene in December 1990, will bring all EC members together in negotiating a treaty for the subsequent stages of EMU.

EMS rules

The European Monetary System is a system of pegged, but adjustable, exchange rates as opposed to a managed floating system. Currency deviations from the official margins are generally limited to a range of 2.25% in either direction. For Italy, an extended margin of 6% was applied, but the lira was brought into the narrow margin in January 1990, which can also be considered part of the drawing-in process. Since Italy joined the inner circle of the EMS, the 6% margin applies only to Spain.

The system provides a very short-term credit mechanism for the financing of central bank balances occurring from exchange market interventions at the official margins. These interventions are obligatory for all members. The EMS internal exchange rate management has, however, been achieved more frequently by intra-marginal interventions on the part of weak currency countries. Regarding the external exchange rate management, the Bundesbank intervenes primarily in the dollar market, while intra-marginal interventions within the EMS exchange rate combine to keep EMS currencies within the pegged margins.

The accords of Basle and Nyborg in August and September 1987 have therefore extended the use of the very short-term credit mechanism to include intra-marginal interventions as well, although certain restrictions apply regarding the obligation of creditor central banks to accept balance settlements in Ecus. There is, furthermore, no obligation for strong currency central banks to intervene within the margins. This brings about what is called the asymmetry of the system. It implies that the stability-oriented monetary policy of the German Bundesbank has a strong influence in the EMS, and this has sometimes caused other members to complain. Asymmetry is, however, held to be an indispensable element of a monetary system aimed at achieving price stability.[4] As the system now functions, it works towards strengthening the stability-oriented course of the members with the weaker currencies.

Coordination among EMS Central Banks evolved in a rather pragmatic way.[5] Short- and medium-term credit facilities were never used. The EMS functioned more smoothly and private capital flows became a source for the financing of current-account deficits. Since currencies have recently become more coherent, this has also enlarged prospects for a sound 'domestic' European monetary policy instead of having frequent adjustments to currency fluctuations involving the dollar. Although closely linked with global markets, the EMS now seems better prepared to absorb shocks coming from the outside.

Coherence of economic policies

If anything makes the EMS the inner core of West European monetary integration, it has to do with the adherence to the rules of pegged exchange rates. A system of pegged exchange rates is not sustainable unless there is a certain coherence in macro-economic policies and economic fundamentals, namely, monetary policy and inflation, fiscal policy and external balances. The extent to which coherence in these fields has been achieved tells more about the intensity of monetary integration, the sustainability of the system and its strains.

In the early 1970s, the first attempt to achieve a European Economic and Monetary Union failed because national policies of adjustment to international monetary disturbances and rising oil prices had become incompatible. When the EMS was introduced in 1979, conceptions of economic policy had become more congruent. Concern to avoid inflation and currency depreciation similar to the concern which marked the beginning of the EMS was, and still is, however, not confined to the EC Member States which participated in the EMS exchange rate mechanism from the beginning. How do economic performances of the initial EMS 8, therefore, compare with non-EMS 4 countries?

Monetary and fiscal policy

In a system of pegged exchange rates, the scope for an independent domestic monetary policy is very limited. Exchange market interventions and official balance settlements automatically bring about converging monetary policies and inflation rates. In the case of the EMS, coherence of monetary policy has grown, as can be expected in a system of pegged exchange rates. Moreover, inflation rates have converged towards lower levels, indicating a sustained preference for price stability on the part of EMS members. Adjustment to the D-mark as a strong currency has supported or forced this tendency. Inflation rates differed enormously during the first years of the EMS. The difference between the lowest and highest inflation rate was 13.6% in 1980 but then declined to about 4% for 1987–8.

Inflation rates peaked in the years 1980 to 1982 in all EC Member States and steadily decreased from 1983–4 onwards for most countries. In Greece, Portugal and Spain inflation rates moved down only more recently. On a weighted average, the EMS 8 inflation rate was 2.5% in 1987, only half the rate of the non-EMS 4 average, i.e. 5.2%.[6] This was, however, due to the still high (although declining) levels of inflation in Greece and Portugal. For the United Kingdom and for Spain, inflation rates were more or less within the range set by the lowest and highest inflation rates of the EMS currencies in 1987.

Inflationary pressures have increased in all EC countries in 1988–9. For the inner circle of the EMS, i.e. members pegging the exchange rate within the smaller margin, inflation rates were, however, kept on lower levels than in other EC countries. Moreover, those countries' performances in price stability do not differ very much from each other. In the United Kingdom, and also in Italy and Spain, rates of inflation have risen above the EC average.

In a system of pegged exchange rates, the immediate impact of rules is greater on monetary policy than on fiscal policy. If the rules of the system keep monetary policies on a restrictive path, however, this will also restrict options for the financing of public deficits and debts in the medium run.

Most EMS members have made an effort to reduce public deficits and debts in the 1980s, but have not yet reached the same coherence in fiscal policy as in monetary policy. Public deficits are currently highest for Italy (10%), followed by Belgium (6%). Corresponding figures for non-EMS participants are 20% for Greece and 6% for Portugal. Public debts are also high in these countries. Huge fiscal deficits and public debts make it more difficult for countries to pursue a monetary course that keeps their currencies pegged. They are thus a potential source of instability in the EMS exchange rates. Similar progress in budgetary consolidation was achieved by Denmark, France and West Germany, in particular, as well as by the United Kingdom and to a lesser extent by Spain.

Comparing EMS 8 and non-EMS 4 countries, the main difference lies in the way by which adjustment to price stability goals has been brought about. While EMS 8 members have pursued price stability by linking their currencies to a strong D-mark, the United Kingdom and Spain have independently followed a rather similar course. For Spain, the main impetus had been to prepare for its forthcoming full EC membership and subsequent participation in the EMS.

On the part of the United Kingdom, reining in fiscal deficits and inflation has been an essential goal of the Thatcher government. Yet, as it looks now, maintaining economic stability may have become more burdensome under conditions of managed floating. The country is presently more exposed to inflation and rising interest rates than are EMS participants, and it also faces a major current-account deficit.

Current account imbalances and capital flows

The EMS is a system of pegged exchange rates, but does not rule out parity adjustment as a means of correcting external imbalances. In the first years of the EMS, some of its members experienced large current-account deficits, and parity adjustments took place more frequently. With respect to frequency and size of currency realignments, the bulk of parity adjustments took place between October 1981 and March 1983. Since then, realignments have become rarer and the margins of adjustment have narrowed.

Starting in 1983, balances of current account have improved for most EMS countries. This particularly applies to countries such as Belgium, France, Ireland and Italy which had formerly had a deficit and which experienced a downward correction of their currencies in previous EMS realignments. Current-account imbalances have widened in intra-EMS transactions, however, as West Germany's trade surpluses with other EC members have increased during the last four years. Yet, with the exception of a slight depreciation of the lira when it was brought into the inner margin of the EMS exchange rate mechanism in January 1990, the EMS saw its last currency realignment as long ago as January 1987. Since them, EMS members have not considered a new currency realignment to be a suitable means of correcting external imbalances and neither have currency markets expected a realignment to occur.

Regarding the role of the exchange rate in the overall process of bringing about economic adjustment, the EMS now functions in a completely different way than the exchange rate management of the Group of Seven which evolved from the Plaza and Louvre accords. With respect to the latter, the particular emphasis is on bringing exchange rates into line with the requirements of reducing current-account imbalances. The external value of the dollar is a key variable in this process. Accordingly, in view of the persistent US trade deficit, the question of how far the dollar should decline in relation to the currencies of the major surplus countries in order to support the restructuring of the US economy is a major issue in the current domestic discussion in the United States.[7]

On the contrary, EMS members presently tend to consider the exchange rate as a standard to which the domestic economy has to perform rather than as an instrument to bring about easier adjustment of the current account. The overall emphasis now seems to be on restructuring the domestic economy with a view towards dealing with the challenges of 1992. As competition among countries has generally shifted from foreign trade to all kinds of foreign economic activities, where the exchange rate matters less, this applies even more to the internal market. Furthermore, regarding 1992, the attractiveness of a country for European investments depends on the overall performance of the domestic economy, and currency depreciation is considered detrimental in this context. With an eye to 1992, the French emphasis with respect to the EMS, for instance, is now on making the French franc as strong as the D-mark.

Also, as long as currency markets do not expect large realignments in the EMS, capital movement works for exchange-rate stability rather than to destabilize the EMS. While France and Italy have been removing foreign exchange restrictions – a process which started in 1986 – this has not destroyed the system, as some observers feared, but actually bolstered confidence in these respective currencies. As realignments have diminished in frequency and size, private capital flows have functioned as a means for the financing of current-account deficits and for exchange-rate stabilization. The system has become more like a monetary area in which external imbalances between regions are compensated for by financial transfers rather than corrected by exchange-rate adjustments. This can be looked at as an indicator for intensified monetary integration.

Nevertheless, in view of present current-account imbalances (with a German surplus of more than 5 per cent of GNP in 1989), some parities may have to be adjusted. Such a decision is, however, not visible on the political horizon in early 1990. Moreover, within the inner core of the EMS, currencies have become very coherent and their adjustment is not regarded as necessary.

To secure capital imports, countries with weaker currencies have to keep interest rates at higher levels. Compared with West Germany or the Netherlands, domestic nominal interest rates have been very high in some EMS countries, largely reflecting differences in the rate of inflation. Moreover, interest rates have been higher in all EC countries except West Germany and the Netherlands than in the United States. This illustrates the force of capital drains from Western Europe and other parts of the world into the US in the 1980s.

For France, Belgium and Denmark, from 1985 onwards interest rates were on lower levels than in the United Kingdom. Real interest rates were below UK levels in some EMS countries as well. Obviously, exchange markets no longer expected major EMS realignments at that time. As confidence in the system strengthened, it shaped conditions for capital inflows which were more favourable for members belonging to the inner core of the EMS. UK policy was to keep the pound sterling in a sound relationship between the dollar and the D-mark in those years. Yet, as the currency was not anchored, interest rates probably had to be higher to cover the risk of currency fluctuation.[8] This experience may also suggest that managed floating is not a sound option, even for a country the size of the United Kingdom, and that autonomy in monetary policy is, in fact, rather limited.

Solidarity: regional compensations

The fundamentals on which an economic and monetary union could be built up are the Common Market, including capital liberalization, the EC insitutions and the EC Structural Funds. The last of these could be considered as a nucleus for regional financial compensations. Such compensations are indispensable if economic coherence is to be achieved between centres and peripheries as laid down in the Single European Act.

Disparities in regional income and levels of economic development can be a major obstacle to economic and monetary integration. Mutual assistance of central banks in exchange-market interventions and credit mechanisms for the financing of balance-of-payments deficits are common instruments in all systems of pegged exchange rates. They were (for instance) employed in the monetary system of Bretton Woods.

When the EMS was introduced in 1979, special credits for regional compensation were temporarily granted to Italy and Ireland to secure EMS membership for these countries. Leaving these short-term relief measures aside, the EMS does not possess the means to allow for specific regional compensation for countries participating in the pegged exchange rate combine. The European Community, however, is in a position to take such measures.

Compensations are aimed at strengthening the economic and social coherence among regions within the Common Market. In 1975, the European Fund for Regional Cooperation was established as a part of the bargain on the implementation of the second stage of the European currency snake. In 1986, the Integrated Mediterranean Programme was concluded in support of structural adjustment in the Mediterranean regions of France and Italy, as well as in Greece. At that time, emphasis was placed on providing compensation for the detrimental effects of the southern enlargement of the Community. The largest payments at that time went to Italy, followed by the United Kingdom and France.

With the southern enlargement of the EC, regional disparities within the Community have increased. The least developed regions now are on the new periphery, primarily Ireland, Greece, Portugal and Spain. In accordance with the decisions of the European Council in February 1988, the financial assets of the EC Structural Funds will almost double by 1993. Compensation will be provided in particular for the fringe regions. If there is a European identity, it cannot be confined to monetary rules and intensified market transactions. Identity is also associated with solidarity, and the overall framework for achieving solidarity is not the EMS but the EC.

The European space

The global dimension of monetary cooperation

More than international trade, the globalization of capital markets has linked national economies more closely than ever. Financial transactions are now 25 times larger than trade in goods and services, and capital flows know no

Table 4.1 Share of national currencies in total identified official holdings of foreign exchange

	1979	1988
US dollar	73.2	63.3
Yen	3.6	7.2
D-mark	12.0	16.2
Pound sterling	1.8	3.1
French franc	1.3	1.7
Guilder	1.0	1.1
Swiss franc	2.4	1.5

Source: International Monetary Fund, *Annual Report*, 1988 and 1989.

boundaries. Western Europe is closely integrated into this highly inter-dependent international economic system. The United States is still the key currency country in the global system, although it may have ceased to be the super-core. The dollar ranks first in the composition of official reserves and international financial transactions. The D-mark and the yen are the main counterparts to the dollar because these currencies are mostly used as altern-atives for currency diversification (Table 4.1).

The US has accumulated huge current-account deficits and external debts in the course of the 1980s. Japan emerged as the main and most visible individual creditor of the United States in these years. Yet the West European net creditor position with the US amounted to $437 bn at the end of 1988, more than three times what it was for Japan ($128 bn).[9] Moreover, Western Europe has been in a creditor stance towards the United States since at least the early 1970s. Due to its own adjustment problems and its external indebtedness, the US itself now has to rely on international cooperation. The main partners are Japan, Canada and the major European industrial countries – the UK, France, West Germany, Italy – as well as the European Community regarding trade policy.

Starting with the Plaza Accord in September 1985, global monetary coopera-tion has been revitalized. It currently centres on managing the dollar rate within sound margins. Rapid shifts in capital flows from one country to another cause large fluctuations in exchange rates. In order to calm currency fluctuation, central banks work together in the management of floating exchange rates on a global basis. There are inner and outer circles in the pursuit of monetary policy coordination, namely the informal G2 or G3 (the United States and Japan plus West Germany) and regular meetings of the G7 (which is the G3 plus Canada, the United Kingdom, France and Italy). The next circle is the G10, already established in 1962.

The most important currency relationship in the global system at present is the G3. Shifts in the exchange rate of the dollar almost immediately push the D-mark or the yen in the opposite direction. As the D-mark is the key currency in the EMS, it also serves as a link between the dollar and other EMS currencies.

Table 4.2   International claims of banks located in main financial centres ($ bn)

	1984	1987	1988
Britain	489.3	875.6	883.6
Japan	126.9	576.9	733.7
USA	409.6	508.9	555.8
Offshore centres:			
Asia			598.3
Caribbean			421.4
Other EC 12:			
France	141.5	266.4	275.9
Germany	64.2	206.0	206.0
Luxembourg	85.6	182.3	188.6
Belgium	68.3	164.8	142.8
Netherlands	56.5	115.3	122.3
Italy	36.7	63.4	62.8
Spain		25.5	24.3
Denmark		17.1	19.8
Other W. European:			
Switzerland	52.8	130.2	117.0
Austria		54.9	50.3
Sweden		17.1	14.9

Source: Bank for International Settlements, 55th/58th/59th *Annual Reports* (German edition).

The Werner Plan failed when the depreciation of the dollar moved European currencies apart. In the early years of the EMS, large fluctuations of the D-mark with respect to the dollar were most likely to cause strains in EMS exchange rates. Yet, when the dollar was brought down (starting in 1985), EMS currencies had already become more converging.

Moreover, in the case of dollar disturbances, a close coordination of exchange-market interventions and interest rates has been achieved on the part of all West European central banks concerned. Coordination has been particularly strong between the Bundesbank and its counterparts in Switzerland, Austria, the United Kingdom and in the EMS. In comparison with the 1970s, Western Europe has become a more stable and coherent monetary area.

Centres and periphery: the financial network

Financial Europe is not on the fringe of the global system. The Euromarket for money and capital functions as a switchboard for private capital flows all over the world. European financial centres serve as a platform for the global activities of international banks. London is a pre-eminent international banking place. In regard to the dimension of foreign activities of financial institutions

Table 4.3   Composition of international claims by the national origin of banks ($ bn)

	1985	1988
USA	590.2	675.2
Japan	706.2	1756.4
Britain	192.8	238.6
France	244.0	384.1
Germany	191.2	353.8
Others	789.1	1190.1

Source: Bank for International Settlements, 59th *Annual Report* (German edition).

located there, London ranks far above financial centres in the US or continental Europe. Yet, foreign activities of banks located in Japan came very close to those of London banks in 1988 (Table 4.2). Offshore centres in East Asia and the Caribbean have also gained in importance recently.

Moreover, competition between London and the financial centres of the continent increases in view of 1992. The British financial community is now urging the Thatcher government to join the inner circle of the EMS because this would give London a stronger foothold in the internal financial market. Also, when international claims are examined with respect to the national origin of financial institutions, British banks rank below French and German banks (Table 4.3). Regarding the currency composition of international bank positions, the pound sterling is behind the Swiss franc. The D-mark is the most used European currency in this field, comparable with the yen, but far behind the dollar (Table 4.4).

In continental Europe, financial centres are roughly equivalent in size. France holds the first rank, followed by West Germany, Luxembourg, Belgium and the Netherlands. Each of them ranks above or is comparable to Switzerland, which can be viewed as the main European financial centre outside the EC. Total international activities of EC continental financial centres exceed the international activities of banks located in the United States or Japan.

These figures indicate, first of all, that Western Europe and the European Community certainly play more than a peripheral role in the global dimension of financial interactions. Although London is the main banking centre in Europe, the dimension of international activities of banks with origins in other EC Member States or in Switzerland, and the currency composition of financial transactions, suggest that intra-West European financial relations are shaped more by mutual interdependence than by unilateral dependence on one single financial centre.

The financial cores are on a north-south axis, within an area stretching from the United Kingdom over the Benelux countries, France and Germany to Switzerland. Smaller West European banking places, ranking second to the major centres (and whether located within the EC or not), can hardly be considered as belonging to the fringe, however, due to their own involvement in the Euromarket.

Table 4.4 International claims of banks by currency composition ($ bn)[a]

	1988
US dollar	1818.0
Other currencies	1647.5
of which:	
Yen	503.7
D-mark	438.4
Pound sterling	146.1
Ecu	86.0
Swiss franc	168.9

[a] Euromarket positions and external positions in domestic currencies.

Source: Bank for International Settlements, 59th *Annual Report* (German edition).

Europe as a financial space has no clear-cut boundary lines. Capital flows have a global orientation and are rather volatile. Capital flows tend to follow short-term incentives in money and security markets. They can change direction quite rapidly. Germany has recently experienced net capital exports with respect to all Western industrial countries. The destination of German capital outflows may thus be looked on as an indicator of financial interactions. German short-term capital flows went mainly to the financial centres of the Euromarket, where they may have been recycled to other destinations inside and outside the EC or Western Europe, The main destinations were the UK and Luxembourg, and to a lesser extent France, the Netherlands, Switzerland and Austria. In 1987, a large portion of German short-term capital export directly went into the US as well (Table 4.5). Looking at German direct investment abroad, a major part went to the United States and a steady stream to West European countries (Table 4.6). These figures also demonstrate recent capital drain from Europe to the US. Yet financial flows may become more favourable for Europe when the internal market offers more attractive opportunities for investment.

Dynamics of monetary integration

When the Werner Plan failed in the early 1970s, the snake became the framework for a closer monetary cooperation of West European countries within the global system. The snake was a fairly stable monetary system centred on the D-mark. It was, however, not aimed at achieving more ambitious goals of economic and monetary integration among its members.

As the EMS replaced the snake in 1979, the immediate emphasis was not on economic and monetary unification but on re-establishing exchange rate stability in support of domestic price stability. Yet, the smooth functioning of

Table 4.5 German balance of capital account, short-term (bn DM)

	1985	1986	1987	1988
All industrial countries	−37.7	−108.0	−18.0	−25.4
EC-12	−28.2	−100.0	−6.1	−16.4
Britain	−9.8	−44.9	−1.4	−5.0
Bel/Lux	−13.7	−39.5	−3.4	−8.0
France	−4.5	−5.8	−0.6	−2.4
Italy	−1.3	−2.4	−1.5	−0.9
Netherlands	1.7	−6.7	0.3	1.4
Spain	−0.7	0.7	0.3	−1.5
Other W. European				
Switzerland	−4.6	−3.7	1.6	−2.0
Austria	−4.2	−4.2	−1.0	−2.0
Sweden	2.0	−1.0	−1.1	−0.4
Norway	0.4	−0.5	−0.8	0.4
USA	1.6	0.8	−7.6	−0.5
Japan	−2.7	0.7	−2.0	−5.3

Source: Deutsche Bundesbank, *Statistische Beihefte (Beilage)*, Series 3, No. 7, July 1989 (for 1985 EC-10).

the system enlarged prospects for further steps in West European integration. It is hard to imagine that the 1992 initiative would have been feasible at a time when the main EC currencies largely diverged from each other. The perspective of the internal market has now revitalized the objective of Economic and Monetary Union. When the Community achieves a single market, going ahead with Economic and Monetary Union seems to be a logical step within the overall economic and political destination of West European integration. However, when EC members agreed at the summits in Hanover and Madrid to advance economic and monetary integration, this only became feasible by virtue of past EMS success.

So far, monetary integration in Western Europe has centred on the D-mark, which was the leading currency in the snake and has become a key currency in the EMS. Austria and Switzerland did not officially participate in the European currency snake but followed, and still pursue, a stability-oriented monetary course that keeps their currencies close to the D-mark. The D-mark has gained such a pre-eminent role because it offers a strong currency option favoured by other countries in accordance with their own price stability goals. This is particularly so in the case of smaller West European countries. Furthermore, since the introduction of the EMS, the number of countries pursuing a course oriented towards price stability has increased. Thus, when the core of strong EMS currencies strengthens further, relations between members may become more balanced rather than being dominated by one single strong-currency country.

Table 4.6   German balance of capital account, direct investments (bn DM)

	1985	1986	1987	1988
All industrial countries	−11.7	−18.2	−11.0	−16.3
EC-12	−2.4	−5.3	−3.5	−4.2
Other W. European	−0.9	−0.7	−0.0	0.2
USA	−8.5	−11.5	−7.3	−11.5

Source: Deutsche Bundesbank, *Statistische Beihefte (Beilage)*, Series 3, No. 7, July 1989 (for 1985 EC-10).

Moreover, the success of the EMS would not have been possible if the EMS partners had not pledged themselves to a strong currency position.[10] The Bundesbank cannot swim against the stream, but can only achieve price stability in the EMS when other participants are also committed to this goal. With the mandate from the Hanover and Madrid meetings, the issue now is to ensure a common understanding on the principles and goals of a European monetary policy over the long term. As the EMS functions continuously as a zone of monetary stability, it will also provide an anchor for monetary policy of other West European countries following similar goals.

When the EMS replaced the snake, participation in the exchange rate mechanism was not ruled out in principle for third European countries that are closely linked economically and financially with the European Community.[11] The countries most closely connected with the EC are the EFTA states. A large portion of their foreign trade is destined for the EC. It thus goes without saying that the external value of EFTA currencies with respect to EC currencies is most significant. Yet, although some EFTA members (Norway and Sweden) were formal members of the snake, no EFTA member has so far applied for formal participation in the EMS.

Norway and Sweden dissociated from the D-mark when they assumed a more expansionary monetary course in order to counter unemployment in the early 1980s. They now peg their exchange rate to a currency basket representing a composite of the main currencies used in foreign trade. The same holds for Finland. Switzerland has renounced formal links with the EMS for reasons of autonomy. Austria is now considering EMS participation in line with its application for EC membership. As the EFTA states and the EC aim to deepen economic relations in accordance with the elimination of boundaries within the internal market, market integration may also work for an intensifying monetary relationship.

In summary, the evolution of the EMS can be considered as an illustration of the dynamics of West European integration. In 1979, the introduction of the EMS was a response to monetary disturbances in the international system. The emphasis was on creating a European zone of monetary stability and on making European currencies less vulnerable to external shocks. Yet, private capital flows can easily destroy a system of pegged exchange rates if diverging economic policies erode confidence in the system. The most remarkable aspect of the EMS is thus that the common understanding on price stability goals was strong enough to make the system sustainable.

The European business community pushed the 1992 project because a unified market offers gains in economic growth and international competitiveness. It now favours a single European currency because this would further rationalize Common Market transactions. Moreover, as an inner circle of EC countries has moved ahead by reconciling economic policies, prospects for West European economic and monetary unification have improved. There are still considerable obstacles to overcome. Yet, as the core of EMS members now aim at Economic and Monetary Union, the worst policy for other EC countries would probably be to keep apart. Starting from an inner circle, the dynamics of economic and monetary integration thus draw all EC members into the process and may eventually also spread beyond EC boundaries, if the project succeeds.

Notes

1. See also DeAnne Julius, *Global Companies and Public Policy: the Challenge of the New Economic Linkages* (London, RIIA, 1990).
2. The rescue package also included a smaller credit from the German Bundesbank and the Bank of England. See Susan Strange, *International Monetary Relations* (London, Oxford University Press, 1976), p. 133 and Andrew Shonfield, (ed.), *International Economic Relations of the Western World 1959–1971*, Vol. 2 (Oxford: Oxford University Press/RIIA, 1976).
3. See also John B. Goodman, *The Domestic Impact of International Regimes: France, Italy and the European Monetary System*, paper delivered at the Joint Annual Convention of the British International Studies Association and the International Studies Association, London, 28 March–1 April 1989.
4. See also Daniel Gros and Niels Thygesen, *The EMS: Achievements, Current Issues and Directions for the Future* (Brussels: Centre for European Policy Studies, 1988), CEPS-Paper No. 35.
5. Elke Thiel, 'From the Internal Market to an Economic and Monetary Union', *Außenpolitik*, Vol. 40, No. 1 (1989), pp. 66–75.
6. EC Commission, Annual Economic Report 1988–9, Com (88) 591 endg.; vol. 1, p. 15.
7. See e.g. 'All Exports Aren't Created Equal', *The Wall Street Journal*, 3 July 1989, p. 1.
8. See also Andrew Scott, 'Britain and the EMS: an Appraisal of the Report of the Treasury and Civil Service Committee', *Journal of Common Market Studies*, Vol. 24, No. 3 (March 1986), pp. 187–201.
9. *Survey of Current Business*, Vol. 69, No. 6 (June 1989), p. 42.
10. The Delors Report attributes the success of the EMS to the following three achievements: 'the participants' willingness to opt for a strong currency stance'; 'the flexible and pragmatic way in which the system has been managed'; and 'the role played by the D-mark as an anchor for participants' monetary and economic policy': Committee for the Study of Economic and Monetary Union, *Report on Economic and Monetary Union in the European Community*, 12 April 1989, p. 2.
11. Conclusion of the European Council on 5 December 1978 in Brussels on the establishment of the European Monetary System, cipher 5.2.

[19]
Regional Policies and Redistribution

Traditional economic theory concentrates on questions of efficiency and the maximization of global welfare, while considerations about equity and the distribution of the economic pie are usually left to more 'normative' disciplines; alternatively, they are simply assumed away as problems. The theory of customs unions is a good example of this eclectic approach. But everyday politics is largely about the distribution of gains and losses among participants in any system. Depending on the nature of the latter, the relevant participants can be countries, regions, different social groups and classes, or even individuals.

A relatively equitable distribution of the gains and losses, or at least the perception of such an equitable distribution, can be a determining factor for the continuation of the integration process. Regional integration schemes in other parts of the world have often foundered precisely because of the failure to deal effectively with this problem. It would have been surprising if distributional politics had not entered the European scene. Indeed, its absence could have been interpreted as an unmistakable sign of the irrelevance of the EC as an economic and political system. But there should be no cause for alarm among 'Euro-enthusiasts'. The distributional impact of integration has been paramount in the minds of national politicians and representatives of various pressure groups; and it has strongly influenced negotiations within the common institutions from a very early stage. This was evident in the first package deals on which the Paris and Rome treaties were based. Yet those package deals made few provisions for explicitly redistributive instruments. This is a more recent development brought about through the international economic recession of the 1970s, the increased

internal divergence of the EC, caused mainly by successive
rounds of enlargement, and, last but not least, the progressive
deepening of the process of integration.

Redistribution is one of the central elements of the European
mixed economy at the national level; and this has become
increasingly true of the EC as well, although still to a limited
extent. Redistribution can also be considered as an index of the
political and social cohesion of a new system; large transfers of
funds across national frontiers not being a normal feature of
international organizations. The objective of the EC extends, in
fact, beyond a balanced distribution of gains and losses associated
with integration. The explicit objective enshrined in the treaty is
the reduction of existing disparities between regions, not only
countries. This chapter will examine the nature and size of
the regional problem inside the Community, the link between
integration and regional disparities, and the development of
redistributive instruments at the European level. The role of the
EC budget will be discussed mainly with respect to its redistributive function. The relaunching of integration in the second half of
the 1980s was partly based on the agreement reached on the
broad outlines of the budget for the period 1988–92. The same
remains true for the future. The proposed establishment of EMU
will be closely linked with public finance issues at the Community
level.

Regional Policy: In Search of Effectiveness

'Regional problems are difficult to define but easy to recognise'
(Robson, 1987: 168). Perhaps the main difficulty does not lie so
much with the identification and definition of those problems as
with their explanation and even more so with the ways of solving
them. Regional problems refer to the persistence of large disparities among different regions of the same country in terms of
income, productivity, and levels of employment, to mention only
some of the most representative economic indicators. To understand the nature of these problems, one usually needs to go
beyond neoclassical economic theory and the host of simplifying
assumptions on which it is founded, including perfect competition, full employment, constant returns to scale, and perfect
mobility of factors of production. The literature on regional

230   Regional Policies and Redistribution

economics concentrates, precisely, on various forms of market
failure which constitute a radical departure from the strong
assumptions of neoclassical models. It stresses the existence of
economies of scale and learning curves for individual firms. It
points to external economies such as location advantages associated with easy access to large markets, centres of administration
and finance, and sources of skilled labour and technological
knowledge. It argues that the imperfect nature of labour markets
can lead to situations in which money wages in different regions
do not necessarily reflect differences in productivity rates. This is
referred to in the literature as differences in 'efficiency wages',
defined as money wages over productivity. Furthermore, interregional mobility of labour, which is certainly far from perfect,
can have perverse effects in terms of regional disparities to the
extent that migration to fast developing areas is usually led by the
most dynamic and highly skilled members of the labour force in
the lagging regions (Myrdal, 1957; Robson, 1987; Begg, 1989).

Under these conditions, initial differences in productivity and
economic development or simply an autonomous shift in demand
for the goods produced by a particular region can lead to 'circular
and cumulative causation' and thus growing polarization between
different regions; hence the creation and perpetuation of regional
problems. This is what Myrdal calls the 'backwash' effects. On
the other hand, the growth of dynamic regions will also have
'spread' effects arising from an increased demand for imports and
the diffusion of technology from those regions, and eventually
also from diseconomies of location associated with over-congestion
in the rapidly growing centres. The relative importance of
'backwash' and 'spread' effects will determine the development
of regional disparities within a country.

The main message from regional economic theories is that
there are no strong reasons to expect the elimination of regional
problems through the free interplay of market forces. On the
contrary, such problems could be aggravated without the countervailing influence of government intervention. Interestingly
enough, there is a close similarity between the literature on
regional economics and the new theories of international trade
which also place the emphasis on the role of economies of scale,
imperfect competition, differentiated products, and innovation.
Comparative advantage is no longer seen as the result of different
factor endowments. Instead, the reasons for the large intra-

Regional Policies and Redistribution **231**

industry trade which characterizes relations among industrialized countries, including members of the EC, seem to lie 'in the advantages of large-scale production, which lead to an essentially random division of labour among countries, in the cumulative advantages of experience which sometimes perpetuate accidental initial advantages, in the temporary advantages conveyed by innovation' (Krugman, 1986: 8). Although the new theories do not reject completely the old Ricardian premise regarding the welfare improving effects of free trade, associated in those theories mainly with economies of scale and increased competition, this conclusion is now hedged with many 'ifs' and 'buts'. Tariffs, subsidies and strategic trade policies can make perfect economic sense from the point of view of an individual country, although they can be disastrous when pursued by all countries concerned. On the other hand, gains and losses from trade liberalization are unlikely to be distributed evenly among different countries and regions.

The dividing line between regional and international economics becomes blurred as economic interdependence among different countries increases. After all, what basically distinguishes an intra-country from an inter-country problem in terms of economic disparities is the higher degree of labour mobility within a country and the automatic transfer of resources through the central budget, factors which are meant to compensate for the lack of independent trade, monetary, and exchange rate policies for a region. It is those factors which differentiate the problem of the Mezzogiorno inside Italy from that of Portugal or Greece in the EC.

However, with the progressive deepening of European integration, and especially with the establishment of the internal market and later EMU, this distinction will become increasingly less obvious, particularly with respect to policy instruments aimed at influencing relative prices and, ultimately, the inter-country allocation of resources. Independent trade policies have long since been merged in the context of the common commercial policy of the EC. Monetary policy and the exchange rate will also need to be sacrificed at the altar of monetary union in which case intra-EC trade will be determined by absolute and not comparative advantage; thus effectively turning inter-country disparities in the EC into regional problems. On the other hand, linguistic and cultural frontiers are likely to remain for long a major barrier

232   Regional Policies and Redistribution

to labour mobility inside the EC. In fact, it would not even be
politically desirable for labour mobility to act as an important
adjustment mechanism among member countries. Thus the
avoidance of serious regional problems inside an increasingly
integrated Community would have to depend essentially on two
factors, namely the flexibility of product and factor markets and
compensating measures, most notably in the form of regional
policy.

The Community of Twelve is characterized by large economic
disparities among countries and regions, which greatly exceed
those inside the United States (Boltho, 1989). There are various
reasons why international comparisons of income levels should be
treated with considerable caution. They include the distortions
created by exchange rates which do not adequately reflect relative purchasing power over goods and services, a problem which
is only partially dealt with by attempts to establish purchasing
power standards (PPSs), and the large differences in the size of
the unrecorded sector of the economy. Cross-country regional
data are even less reliable given the non-comparability of some
administrative regions in EC member countries (the *Land* of
Hamburg is, for example, hardly comparable to the autonomous
region of Andalucia). Yet available data can be treated as a
rough indicator of income disparities inside the EC. On the basis
of PPSs, per capita income levels in Greece and Portugal are less
than half those enjoyed in Germany and Luxembourg (Table
8.1). Interregional disparities are much more pronounced. Thus
the difference between Hamburg and Groningen on the one
hand, and the poorest regions of Greece and Portugal on the
other is more than 4:1 (Commission of the EC data). It should
come as no surprise to anybody at all familiar with the European
economic scene that income disparities have a strong centre–
periphery dimension, the poorest regions of the EC of Twelve
being concentrated in the southern and western periphery (Map
8.1; the incorporation of the new German *Länder* has now added
an eastern dimension to the periphery of less developed regions
of the EC).

With respect to regional policy, three main phases can be
distinguished since the establishment of the EEC in 1958. The
first phase, which lasted until 1975, was characterized by the lack
of any common regional policy worth the name. The second was
marked by the creation of new instruments, the strengthening of

Regional Policies and Redistribution **233**

Table 8.1. Divergence of GDP per capita, 1960–1990

	1960	1970	1975	1980	1985	1990
Belgium	95.4	98.9	103.1	104.1	101.6	102.6
Denmark	118.3	115.2	110.5	107.8	115.8	108.2
Germany	117.9	113.2	109.9	113.6	114.2	112.8
Greece	38.6	51.6	57.3	58.1	56.7	52.6
Spain	60.3	74.7	81.9	74.2	72.5	77.8
France	105.8	110.4	111.8	111.6	110.6	108.6
Ireland	60.8	59.5	62.7	64.0	65.2	69.0
Italy	86.5	95.4	94.6	102.5	103.1	103.1
Luxembourg	158.5	141.4	126.7	118.5	122.4	125.6
Netherlands	118.6	115.8	115.5	110.9	107.0	103.1
Portugal	38.7	48.9	52.2	55.0	52.0	55.7
United Kingdom	128.6	108.5	105.9	101.1	104.2	105.1
EC-12	100.0	100.0	100.0	100.0	100.0	100.0

Note: Per capita GDP is given at current market prices and purchasing power parities.
Source: Commission of the EC (1991*a*).

the regional policy dimension of others already available, and the steady increase in the amounts of money spent. The third phase is connected with the reform of the so-called Structural Funds in 1988. It constitutes a turning-point in the search for greater effectiveness of common instruments, coupled with a substantial further increase in EC expenditure with a regional bias.

The original six members of the EC constituted a relatively homogeneous economic group, with the exception of the south of Italy; a problem which was, in fact, recognized in the protocol for the Mezzogiorno, attached to the Treaty of Rome. Article 2 of the treaty referred to the objective of a 'harmonious development of economic activities, a continuous and balanced expansion', while in the preamble the contracting parties went even further by calling for a reduction of 'the differences existing between the various regions and the backwardness of the less favoured regions'.

There were only a few provisions made in the treaty for the creation of instruments which could contribute towards this 'harmonious development' and the reduction of regional disparities. The European Investment Bank (EIB) was intended as a source of relatively cheap interest loans and guarantees for the less developed regions of the Community. Provisions for the free

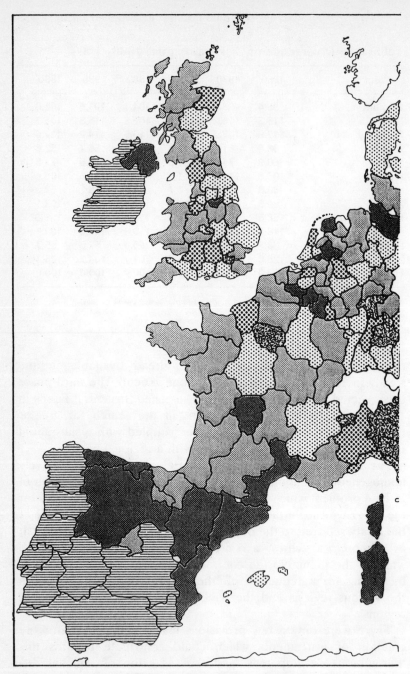

Map 8.1. Regional GDP per Inhabitant, 1988
Source: Commission of the EC, 1991*c*.

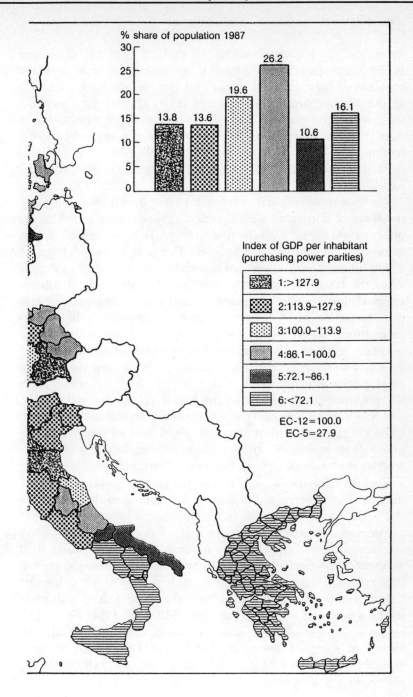

% share of population 1987

Index of GDP per inhabitant
(purchasing power parities)

1: >127.9

2: 113.9–127.9

3: 100.0–113.9

4: 86.1–100.0

5: 72.1–86.1

6: <72.1

EC-12 = 100.0
EC-5 = 27.9

236 Regional Policies and Redistribution

movement of labour also had an indirect regional dimension
in the sense that labour mobility would help to deal with the
problem of high unemployment in a less developed region such
as the Mezzogiorno. Last but not least, the setting up of the
CAP should be expected to contribute towards the reduction of
disparities, since farm incomes were generally much below the
national or EC-6 average, while economic backwardness was
most often identified with a heavy regional concentration on
agriculture.

There was no explicit reference to regional policy, albeit in
the form of derogations from general provisions in the different
policy areas dealt with by the treaty. This is true of social,
transport, and agricultural policies. The best known derogation
which bears upon the regional dimension can be found in Article
92 of the treaty. It indirectly accepts state aids for intra-country
regional development purposes, thus making a big exception to
the application of the common competition policy. The various
derogations, together with the lack of any separate chapter on a
common regional policy, suggest that the authors of the Treaty of
Rome, while recognizing the regional problem and the need to
employ special instruments to deal with it, had decided to leave
the responsibility basically to the hands of national authorities.
The role of the Community would remain marginal in this respect,
while the relevant institutions were asked to show some flexibility
in the development of other common policies in order to accommodate the regional policy objectives of national authorities.

Regional disparities were not as yet generally recognized as a
major policy concern at the time of the signing of the treaty. On
the other hand, large transfers of money across frontiers were
considered as politically impossible. Since the redistributive
mechanisms could only be very modest, the six signatories tried
to 'control and distribute the gains and losses which might arise in
the particular sectors involved in such a way as to determine
beforehand the extent to which the national interest of each party
to the agreement would be satisfied' (Milward, 1984: 498).[1] This
explains the complicated and perhaps economically 'irrational'
nature of some of the treaty provisions. On the other hand,
equitable distribution of gains and losses basically referred to the
distribution among countries.

[1] This comment by Milward was in fact made with reference to the Paris Treaty of 1951. It
can equally well apply to the EEC treaty signed 6 years later.

Regional Policies and Redistribution   **237**

Although regional policy had its heyday in most Western European countries during the 1960s and the early 1970s, with large sums of money spent in this direction (Nicol and Yuill, 1982), very little happened at the EC level. The EIB did, as originally envisaged, orient its lending activities mainly towards the less developed regions of the Six, and the south of Italy in particular. However, the sums of money involved were relatively small and the attraction of EIB loans consisted entirely of the preferential rates charged on loans. The EIB could not, according to its statutes, offer any capital grants or subsidies to inputs. The ESF and, to a lesser extent, the EAGGF (European Agricultural Guidance and Guarantee Fund) also played a modest redistributive role during this period. On the other hand, the first serious attempt towards the co-ordination of national regional policies was made as late as 1971, with the aim of preventing an 'overbidding' between regions, which would normally be at the expense of the poorer ones.

Distributional issues in general did not become a serious political problem in the early years of European economic integration. But this was the golden age of the Western European economies, characterized by rapid economic growth, high employment rates, and relative monetary stability. The overall size of the cake grew constantly bigger and European integration continued to be perceived as a positive-sum game in which there were gains to be made by all the countries involved. The reduction of inter-country income disparities among the Six during the same period helped to allay earlier fears about the effects of trade liberalization on the weaker economies (Perroux, 1959; Vanhove and Klaassen, 1987; see also below for further discussion of intra-EC disparities).

On the other hand, national governments pursued active regional and redistributive policies inside their borders aiming at a reduction of income disparities. At the time of prosperity and the rise of social democracy, equality became a widely respected political objective, while the rise of autonomist movements in several European countries surely strengthened the political will for an effective reduction of regional inequalities.

Interest at the Community level grew as a result of the first enlargement of the EC and the rapid deterioration in the international economic environment, both coinciding in the early 1970s. The accession of three new members brought countries

238 Regional Policies and Redistribution

with serious regional problems inside the EC. On the other hand, clearly dissatisfied with the overall economic package which had taken shape prior to the UK's accession to the Community, the Government in London searched for other mechanisms which would partly compensate for the budgetary loss arising from the operation of the CAP. The creation of the European Regional Development Fund (ERDF) soon became the spearhead of this effort (H. Wallace, 1983). Regional policy and redistribution have been used almost interchangeably ever since.

The ERDF was set up in 1975. Its birth signalled the growing concern with intra-EC disparities. Strangely enough, this growth of interest in EC regional policy has almost coincided with the noticeable decline in the popularity of regional policies at the national level. Is this contradiction simply another of the peculiarities of the contemporary European scene? What is beyond doubt is that different developments at the two levels do not indicate any conscious transfer of powers and responsibilities to the emerging European centre.

The ERDF started with small sums of money which were initially distributed among member countries on the basis of quota allocations determined by the Council of Ministers. This meant a dispersal of funds among countries where the regional problem of one was the dream of economic development of another. A 5 per cent, non–quota element, allocated at the discretion of the Commission, was first introduced in 1979, while, with the 1984 reform of the ERDF, quotas were replaced with indicative ranges for each country's allocation of funds. Intermediate changes in terms of country allocations were introduced in 1981 and 1986 as a result of the second and third enlargement of the EC.

Funds available through the ERDF grew steadily over the years. Disbursements were in the form of matching grants for the financing of investment projects, with almost exclusive emphasis on infrastructural investment (approximately 85 per cent of total expenditure for projects for the period 1975–88; see Table 8.2). There was also a clear redistributive bias in favour of countries with more severe regional problems and an increasing concentration of resources on the least developed regions. However, the total sums of money remained small, when compared with expenditures in terms of regional policy at the national level. In 1988, the year before the implementation of the latest reform,

Table 8.2. ERDF Commitments, 1975–1988
(Mio ECU)

	Programmes	Projects				Studies	Total Commitments
		Industry and Services	Infrastructure	Other	Total		
Belgium	26.70	41.67	131.97	1.35	174.99	2.00	203.69
Denmark	10.26	25.35	140.42	0.57	166.34	6.14	182.74
Germany	77.01	502.96	347.39	–	850.34	0.19	927.55
Greece	263.38	34.51	2149.65	–	2184.16	0.24	2447.78
Spain	75.59	11.20	1945.23	2.29	1958.72	0.09	2034.40
France	261.90	370.42	2156.66	13.11	2540.19	12.04	2814.13
Ireland	144.01	311.27	841.94	3.67	1156.88	0.99	1301.88
Italy	136.19	975.72	6777.60	0.58	7753.90	21.95	7912.04
Luxembourg	1.94	–	14.69	–	14.69	–	16.63
Netherlands	14.18	32.42	200.85	0.01	233.28	0.19	247.65
Portugal	117.20	–	1080.56	1.48	1082.04	0.58	1199.82
United Kingdom	465.17	1000.02	3620.97	6.43	4627.42	10.66	5103.25
EC-12	1593.53	3305.54	19407.93	29.49	22742.42	55.07	24391.56

Notes: ERDF funds have been available to Greece, Portugal, and Spain for a shorter period than for the other member countries because of more recent dates of accession. Country figures are therefore not strictly comparable.

Sources: Commission of the EC. 1990f.

240   Regional Policies and Redistribution

ERDF assistance amounted to only 0.09 per cent of EC GDP
and 0.46 per cent of gross fixed capital formation (GFCF)
(Commission of the EC, 1990*f*).

On the other hand, while EC regional expenditure increased,
there was little evidence until the 1988 reform to suggest that the
money spent by the ERDF was in addition to regional aid which
would have been given by national governments in its absence.
This is again the so-called problem of additionality to which
reference has been made earlier with respect to ESF expenditure.
On the contrary, many governments seemed to consider EC
money as a means of replacing national expenditure for regional
development. The strict quota system in terms of national allocations in the beginning and the limited powers of discretion enjoyed
by the EC Commission in the selection of projects did not help to
solve this problem. It is highly indicative that for years the overwhelming majority of projects receiving ERDF assistance had
begun before application for funds was made by the national
governments. In the attempt to achieve high absorption rates
of funds allocated by the Commission, national and regional
administrations were often tempted to sacrifice economic efficiency. Regional aid by the EC was generally viewed by national
governments as a means of redistribution across national boundaries, with little effect on actual regional policies or the total
sums of money involved. This led a member of the European
Parliament from Northern Ireland to argue that 'there never
was a regional policy at all, it was a Regional Fund operated
on a Red Cross basis, with handouts here and there' (quoted in
Shackleton, 1990: 44). Nor was there any serious co-ordination
with other instruments of EC policy, and this further reduced the
effectiveness of ERDF assistance as a means of tackling regional
problems in the Community.

While the ERDF operated on the basis of grants, the EIB
continued its lending activities, drawing from national contributions and its high credit rating in international capital markets,
which in turn enabled it to raise money at attractive rates of
interest. With the setting up of the EMS in 1979, the so-called
New Community Instrument (NCI) was created in order to
provide through the EIB subsidized loans to the less prosperous
members, namely Ireland and Italy. Although, traditionally, the
bank has favoured large loans, attention has also been paid
to small and medium enterprises (SMEs) which have received

Regional Policies and Redistribution **241**

Table 8.3. EIB Financing within the EC, 1986–1990
(Mio ECU)

	Sector			Total
	Industry, services, agriculture	Energy	Infrastructure	
Belgium	218.7	—	16.4	235.1
Denmark	191.3	949.1	984.4	2124.9
Germany	1124.9	729.2	851.7	2705.7
Greece	366.9	283.4	372.4	1022.7
Spain	1562.7	460.0	3036.7	5059.4
France	1985.8	252.0	2758.5	4996.3
Ireland	49.4	220.0	706.5	975.9
Italy	7042.6	4118.6	6134.4	17295.6
Luxembourg	11.8	—	19.8	31.6
Netherlands	497.9	3.2	367.3	868.4
Portugal	911.3	603.9	988.5	2503.7
United Kingdom	1401.3	1885.8	3610.4	6897.6
Other (Article 18)[a]	—	198.5	660.8	859.3
Total	15364.5	9703.7	20507.8	45576.0

[a] Article 18 of the Statute of the EIB allows for the provision of loans for investment projects in the non-European territories of member countries.
Sources: EIB (1991).

assistance from the bank through the system of global loans. These are large lump sums lent to a financial institution in a member country, which in turn lends out the money to SMEs locally (Pinder, 1986). This indirect form of lending has been considered necessary in view of the limited administrative resources of the EIB.

Table 8.3 gives a breakdown of EIB lending between 1986 and 1990 by country and sector. There is a clearly discernible bias in favour of the poorer countries, with Italy far ahead of the rest. After all, it was with Italy, and the Mezzogiorno in particular, in mind that the EIB had been originally set up. As with ERDF expenditure, the figures show a strong bias in favour of energy and infrastructural investment. In 1989 EIB lending accounted for 6.17 per cent of GFCF for Portugal; the corresponding figures for Ireland and Greece were 3.61 per cent and 2.76 per cent respectively.

A new approach to regional policy was introduced in 1985 with the Integrated Mediterranean Programmes (IMPs), intended for

242   Regional Policies and Redistribution

the Mediterranean regions of France, Italy, and the whole of Greece. The creation of IMPs was in recognition of the special development problems of these regions and the relative bias of the CAP against southern agricultural products. The Iberian enlargement, which was generally expected to accentuate these problems, acted as the catalyst, strengthening the need for policy adjustment measures (Yannopoulos, 1989). Each IMP would last for three to seven years and a combined total of 6.6 billion ECUs was to be allocated to them, coming partly from the various EC Funds and the EIB and partly from the creation of additional resources through the budget. The main innovation of IMPs was that finance would be based on medium-term development programmes, instead of individual project submission, and on a close co-ordination of different EC instruments. They were the precursor of more general reforms to be introduced later with respect to the various Community Funds. The new Iberian entrants have not benefited from IMPs, although special programmes were designed for Portugal in order to assist the adjustment of the Portuguese economy to the requirements of EC membership.

The ground was gradually prepared for a major qualitative change in the use of policy instruments coupled with a major shift in the scale of EC intervention. The decision to establish the internal market and the dramatic improvement in the economic and political environment in Western Europe provided the catalyst. This eventually led to the reform of Structural Funds in 1988. But the legal foundations had been laid earlier with the SEA. The latter introduced Title V to the Treaty of Rome under the heading 'economic and social cohesion'. It was a formal recognition of the greater political importance of the redistributive function, while also constituting an integral part of the overall package deal behind the SEA and the relaunching of European integration. The new Articles 130a to 130e were the first attempt to link the objective of 'harmonious development' and the reduction of regional disparities, previously mentioned only in a very general way in the preamble and Article 2 of the original text of the treaty, with specific EC instruments, namely the ERDF, the ESF, the EAGGF-Guidance Section (all three referred to now as Structural Funds), and the EIB. The ERDF was entrusted with the principal task of redressing intra-EC regional imbalances. The new articles called for the effective co-

Regional Policies and Redistribution **243**

ordination and rationalization of the activities of Structural Funds and the Commission was invited to submit proposals in this direction. This eventually ushered the Community into a new phase in terms of regional policy.

The reform of the Structural Funds started with the agreement reached at the European Council meeting in Brussels in February 1988, when a decision was also taken for the doubling, in real terms, of the resources of the three Funds between 1987 and 1993. The doubling of the resources of the Structural Funds, undoubtedly the most important decision taken until then by the Community in terms of internal redistribution, was part of a package of measures, including the reform of the CAP and the EC budget. The so-called Delors package was presented as a necessary precondition for the successful implementation of the internal market programme. Interestingly enough, the link established between the internal market and the doubling of resources through the Structural Funds also meant an implicit recognition of the danger that the weaker regions of the Community could end up as net losers from further market integration. The creation of new resources was the necessary side-payment for the political acceptance of the internal market programme and a means of preparing weaker regions for the new cold winds of competition.

The doubling of resources went hand in hand with an effort to improve the effectiveness of EC action through the adoption of clearer objectives, an improved co-ordination of different financial instruments, and a close monitoring of jointly financed programmes. The main outlines were agreed upon by the Council of Ministers through the adoption of several regulations in June and December 1988. Five priority objectives were assigned to the Funds, and the EIB was also expected to contribute to those objectives. The latter related to:

1. The less developed regions
2. Areas of industrial decline
3. The long-term unemployed
4. Employment of young people
5a. Adjustment of agricultural structures
5b. Development of rural areas.

The first objective is intended to deal with regions where income falls below 75 per cent of the EC average, and which are

244 Regional Policies and Redistribution

characterized by a relatively high percentage of the labour force engaged in agriculture. The list approved by the Council of Ministers includes the whole of Greece, the Republic of Ireland, Northern Ireland, Portugal, the greater part of Spain, the Mezzogiorno, and the overseas departments of France and Corsica. A few regions which are slightly above the 75 per cent rule have been included; after 1993, the list will also be extended formally to the new German *Länder*. The areas under the first objective represent approximately 21 per cent of EC population and they are expected to receive 80 per cent of ERDF expenditure and in excess of 60 per cent of the total expenditure of the Structural Funds by 1993. The areas under the second objective represent approximately 16 per cent of the population of the Community. They are situated mainly in central and north-western Europe, with a high concentration in the UK. The first two objectives require co-ordinated action by two or more Funds. The third and fourth objectives are the exclusive domain of the ESF, following on the steps of the policy established earlier for the Social Fund. As regards objectives 5a and 5b, the funds allocated are significantly smaller (Van Ginderachter, 1989).

Another feature of the 1988 reform was the emphasis on multi-annual programming as a means of identifying and quantifying economic priorities over a period of five years. It may be interesting that at a time when liberal economic ideas seemed to prevail, the notion of economic planning, even in a mild form, was still very much alive in Brussels and in other places where policy-makers were trying to tackle problems of regional development. For those countries and regions which came under Objective One, regional development programmes were submitted to Brussels, and these in turn provided the basis for the adoption of Community Support Frameworks. The latter set the main guidelines for expenditure through the Structural Funds in each region for the period 1989–93. The switch from the financing of individual projects, which had been the main characteristic of EC action in the past, to medium-term 'operational' programmes and global grants has now been generalized. Programming had been introduced, in a modest fashion, with the 1984 reform of the ERDF and the Integrated Mediterranean Programmes. Strong emphasis has also been placed on the close monitoring of different programmes in an attempt to deal with earlier criticism regarding the wastage of resources and widespread malpractices. The other important feature of the 1988 reform was the concept of partnership which was intended to lead to close co-operation between EC, national and regional authorities both at the planning and implementation stage, thus also establishing direct lines of communication between regional authorities and the EC Commission.

The 1988 reform has led to a remarkable increase in overall expenditure. For the five-year period 1989–93, a total of 60.3 billion ECUs (in 1989 prices) has been committed to be spent through the three Structural Funds; and another three billion ECUs were added at the end of 1990 for the new German *Länder*. By 1992, expenditure through the Structural Funds had risen to 27 per cent of overall EC expenditure, as compared with 17 per cent in 1987. The redistributive impact has been further strengthened through the greater concentration of resources. Thus, by 1992 annual transfers through the Structural Funds represented 3.5, 2.9, and 2.3 per cent of GDP for Portugal, Greece, and Ireland respectively (EC Commission figures). The main emphasis remained, as before, on infrastructural investment which accounted for 29 per cent of overall expenditure for Objective One regions. Naturally, the corresponding figure in terms of GFCF was much higher (exceeding 10 per cent in the case of Greece). Since the outlays through the Structural Funds are in the form of matching grants, ranging from 75 per cent to 25 per cent of total expenditure, the implication is that a very substantial part of public investment in the main beneficiary countries and regions has been tied to EC-approved programmes.

The experience until 1992 points to a high absorption rate of the financial resources committed through the Structural Funds, although high absorption is not always directly related to the most efficient use of resources. The operation of the Structural Funds has, in fact, raised some general questions which can be summarized under the following four headings: subsidiarity, transparency, efficiency, and additionality. Several trade-offs have appeared between those objectives. For example, the division of competences between Brussels and national or regional authorities has always been a moot point. Why should Brussels know better than national capitals and regional authorities about their own development needs and priorities? This is not only a question of principle; it is also linked to the very serious administrative limitations of the EC executive. The small staff and the internal

246 Regional Policies and Redistribution

organization of the Commission do not match the ever growing sums of money which it has been asked to administer; and this has become increasingly clear in recent years. The problem of efficiency in the use of financial resources is added to that of limited transparency in the Community system of decision-making, not to mention the problem of accountability.

There are, however, powerful counter-arguments which can be used. First of all, the objective of additionality, namely that EC expenditure should represent a net increase in the amounts spent on development and not on consumption, militates in favour of some central control. This point has been very clearly expressed in the Delors report on EMU (Committee for the Study of Economic and Monetary Union, 1989: 22–3):

The principal objective of regional policies should not be to subsidize incomes and simply offset inequalities in standards of living, but to help to equalize production conditions through investment programmes in such areas as physical infrastructure, communications, transportation and education so that large scale movements of labour do not become the major adjustment factor.

The experience of the ERDF and the other Structural Funds suggests that the efficiency of some regional and even national administrations leaves much to be desired, thus making the EC Commission look like a model of efficiency. After all, low levels of development are not only manifested in income statistics. Administrative inefficiency is often compounded by short-term political considerations which are not always consistent with long-term development needs. Thus, the Commission has often been forced to navigate dangerously between the Scylla of national sovereignty and the Charybdis of administrative inefficiency and political short-termism (or corruption). How much of the responsibility for the planning and the implementation stages, including the monitoring of programmes, could be left to outside experts? This will remain an awkward question for the future.

The 1988 reform has acted in some cases as a catalyst for decentralization within member countries and the strengthening of regional administrations in order to be able to cope with the demands made in Brussels. On the other hand, it represents an important step in the development of genuinely common policies and a shift of power towards the centre. In this respect, national

Regional Policies and Redistribution **247**

capitals seem to be increasingly squeezed between the other two competing levels of authority.

The discussion about the role of Structural Funds in the post-1993 period has already started; and it is inevitably linked to EMU. The Maastricht treaty has made two new additions to the institutional set-up of the EC, namely the Committee of the Regions and, more importantly, the Cohesion Fund which should come into operation before the end of 1993. This new Fund will make financial contributions to projects in the fields of environment and trans-European networks and only to those member countries with a per capita GNP below 90 per cent of the EC average. Thus, the list of beneficiaries will be limited to Greece, Ireland, Portugal, and Spain; with Italy being, for the first time, left out of an EC regional development scheme. There is also a new element of conditionality introduced with respect to the Cohesion Fund: the countries benefiting from it will need to have a programme of economic convergence approved by ECOFIN in the context of multilateral surveillance. Thus, the link with EMU has been directly established. The Cohesion Fund, which will be added to the already existing Structural Funds, has been mainly a concession to Spain, as part of the overall package deal of Maastricht. It has a distinct Spanish flavour both in terms of the priorities adopted and the GNP ceiling for the beneficiary countries, and this is very likely to be translated into a large Spanish share of total expenditure.

Following on the steps of the Delors package of 1988 which had contributed so much to the budgetary peace and successful implementation of the internal market programme during the intervening years, the EC Commission submitted the so-called second Delors package in February 1992. The aim was to agree on the main budgetary guidelines for the next five years (1993–7). As regards the operation of the Structural Funds, the Commission did not propose any major changes. It did, however, call for more flexibility in the planning and implementation stages; more decentralization towards the regional level; more money to be spent on the so-called Community initiatives (programmes operated by the Commission and not specifically linked to any country or region); higher EC participation rates, especially in cases of budgetary constraints linked to the convergence effort undertaken by member countries; and the extension of EC action into new areas, such as health and education. Even more

248   Regional Policies and Redistribution

importantly, the Commission called for a further substantial
increase in the overall resources of the Structural Funds, which
should raise expenditure to approximately 33.5 per cent of the
EC budget in 1997 (compared with 27 per cent in 1992). For the
less developed countries and regions, which would also benefit
from the new Cohesion Fund, the aim would be for a further
doubling of resources in real terms. At the time of writing, the
negotiation on the second Delors package is still in its early
stages; but it promises to be a tough negotiation taking place in
times of economic recession and financial stringency.

Until now, the private sector has benefited directly from only
a relatively small share of the expenditure undertaken by the
Structural Funds. This may be changed in the future, although
such a change will require new and more flexible forms of EC
intervention. An important aspect of regional policy is the coordination and control of regional aids at the national level.
Commission policy has been in the direction of greater transparency of aid systems, the imposition of ceilings on aid intensity,
and the shift from general to regionally and sectorally specific
aids. Commission control in this area has become more effective
over the years in the context of the progressive strengthening of
its competition policy; but there are still too many holes and *ad
hoc* exceptions. Supervision over national aids is very important
for the poorer regions of the Community which stand little
chance of winning in a free-for-all subsidy game for the attraction
of investment, especially if there is further progress towards
EMU. The Community may in the future consider the use of
regionally differentiated aids and incentives, with more EC
money being directed in the form of matching grants towards
private investment in the less developed regions.

Country Profiles: Ireland, Greece and Spain

Intra-EC income disparities are very large, and they have become
wider with each successive enlargement. The figures in Table 8.1,
which are based on estimates of purchasing power parities, point
to a considerable stability in the rank order of EC countries in
the GDP league over a period of thirty years. But they also
highlight the remarkable performance of the three southern
European NICs (Greece, Portugal, and Spain) between 1960 and

Regional Policies and Redistribution **249**

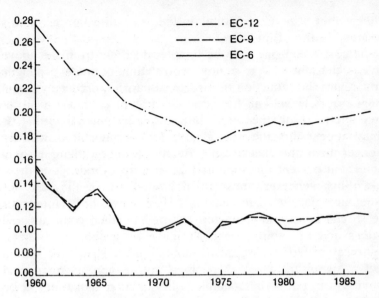

Fig. 8.1. Evolution of Income Disparities between Member
Countries, 1960–1987
(Standard deviation of real GDP per capita as a ratio of the
Community average in percentage terms)
Source: Padoa-Schioppa *et al.*, 1987: 163.

1975, when they also enjoyed the fruits of limited reciprocity in
terms of trade liberalization with the two main European trade
blocs, the steady rise of Italy, and the decline, with some ups and
downs, of Denmark, Luxembourg, the Netherlands, and the UK.

On the other hand, there is little evidence to suggest that
economic integration has itself contributed to the widening of
disparities, although it is virtually impossible to isolate the effect
statistically. Broadly speaking, it appears that inter-country disparities in the EC were reduced during the 1960s and early 1970s.
The trend was reversed during the long recession and this continued to be true until the mid-1980s when growth rates in most
of the less developed members of the Community picked up
again, leading to another reduction of disparities which coincided
with the economic boom of recent years (Table 8.1 and Fig. 8.1;
see also Vanhove and Klaasen, 1987; Molle, 1990; Commission
of the EC, 1991*a*, 1991*c*). As far as interregional disparities are
concerned, the evidence is less clear and also, certainly, less

250   Regional Policies and Redistribution

reliable; but it generally points in the same direction as indices for inter-country disparities.

The conclusion one may be tempted to draw from the above data is that there is a positive correlation between economic growth and the reduction of income disparities, especially at the inter-country level. This has also been true of the latest phase of integration. Using the terms introduced by Myrdal (1957), it would appear that the 'spread' effects of economic growth are stronger than the 'backwash' effects. However, there is only insufficient evidence to support a general hypothesis along these lines. Such generalizations are of limited use, if they are not sometimes positively misleading. They leave little room for the special economic characteristics of individual countries and regions and the political choices made by each one of them. Historical experience suggests that although structural factors play a significant role, there is always a certain margin of manœuvre in terms of economic policy. This proposition will be illustrated below with a brief summary of the experience of three among the poorest members of the Community.

The Republic of Ireland joined the Community in 1973, together with Britain and Denmark. It brought with it a large agricultural sector, heavy dependence on the British economy, and a model of industrialization which heavily relied on the attraction of foreign investment through generous grants and tax incentives. The Special Protocol, signed together with the Treaty of Accession, enabled Ireland to continue acting as a gateway to Europe for foreign, and especially US, multinationals.

Between 1973 and 1980, the Irish economy fared better than the EC average in terms of growth and employment creation. Exactly the opposite happened in subsequent years and until 1987 when economic activity started picking up again. During the period of EC membership, Ireland's position in the income league has improved considerably, and especially in more recent years when the country has experienced exceptionally high rates of growth (see also Table 8.1). The large and continuous inflow of funds from the Community (Ireland being the biggest net beneficiary of EC transfers per capita) has, of course, contributed to this improvement in living standards. Participation in the CAP has had positive budgetary and trade effects for Irish farmers, which has meant large transfers of funds through EC intervention and higher prices for agricultural exports. This cornucopia did

Regional Policies and Redistribution   **251**

not, however, last for very long as the gradual alignment of Irish
farm prices to the higher EC prices more or less coincided
with more determined efforts to bring CAP expenditure under
control.

In the manufacturing sector, the increased exposure of the
domestic economy to international competition has strengthened
its dualistic character, with modern, capital-intensive and high
technology-oriented sectors dominated by subsidiaries of multinational firms, while traditional, more labour-intensive sectors
have remained the privileged domain for Irish entrepreneurs.
The National Economic and Social Council of Ireland (1989: 208)
refers to a 'continuous output and employment decline in a long
list of exposed industries, and their replacement by foreign firms
in a narrow range of manufacturing activities'. This dualism is
also manifested in Ireland's foreign trade: the internationalization
and diversification of market outlets has relied mainly on foreign
firms, while indigenous entrepreneurs have remained more
domestically and UK-oriented (McAleese and Matthews, 1987).

In 1989, exports of foreign-owned firms accounted for approximately 30 per cent of GDP and for a very large part of output
and employment in the manufacturing sector (OECD, 1991).
Cross-linkages with the domestic economy have remained limited,
and this explains the large dependence on imported inputs which
reduces the contribution of those firms in terms of the balance of
payments. Furthermore, capital inflows for productive investment
have been followed by a large repatriation of profits. In 1989
repatriated profits reached almost 14 per cent of GDP. On the
other hand, the capital-intensive nature of foreign investment
in Ireland has not helped much to alleviate the very serious
problem of unemployment; and industrial policy has been partly
responsible for distorting the relative price between capital and
labour.

Membership of the EC has contributed to the further opening
of the Irish economy. In fact, the change has been quite dramatic:
exports of goods and services rose from 38 per cent to 67 per cent
of GDP between 1973 and 1989 (Eurostat data). The internationalization of the economy has gone hand in hand with an increasing
concentration on European markets and a corresponding reduction of the old, virtually exclusive, dependence on the UK. The
constraints of a small and very open economy were not, however,
immediately realized by Irish policy-makers. Expansionary fiscal

252   Regional Policies and Redistribution

policies and accommodating monetary policies sustained, during
the second half of the 1970s, rates of economic growth and
employment creation which were substantially higher than the
EC average. This survived the second oil shock and the decision
to join the ERM in 1979. The result was an explosion of the
public sector deficit coupled with a large increase in inflation and
the current account deficit.

Thus, the change of gear became inevitable. The stabilization
policies pursued in the 1980s have produced impressive results,
especially since 1987. They have been based on a broad consensus of the main political parties and the social partners,
which took a concrete form through the Programme for National
Recovery. Participation in the ERM has provided the anchor and
the external discipline for anti-inflationary monetary policy.
Fiscal consolidation has led to a reduction in the public debt/
GDP ratio, although the latter still remains at much higher
levels than those permitted by the convergence criteria established at Maastricht (Fig. 7.7). On the inflation front, the progress has been absolutely remarkable: between 1981 and 1987,
Irish inflation had dropped by more than fifteen percentage
points, reaching close to the average of the narrow band countries
of the ERM (Fig. 7.1). With such progress on the inflation front,
interest rate differentials were bound to follow, as domestic
stabilization policies became more credible.

The combination of macroeconomic stability, declining unit
labour costs and the favourable external environment of the late
1980s enabled Ireland to achieve a sustained recovery in recent
years, thus reversing the miserable performance of the first half
of the previous decade. High growth went hand in hand with a
considerable increase in investment and also a big improvement
in the current account. The same is not, however, true of unemployment. Despite the creation of new jobs during the boom and
the continued exodus of Irish people in search of employment
abroad, the rate of unemployment has remained around 16 per
cent, with the prospect of a further worsening due to the more
recent downturn in economic activity. High unemployment has
been the price for stabilization, and it has been a very heavy price
indeed (see also Dornbusch, 1989).

Ireland's economic experience as a member of the Community
points to some of the unequal effects of integration between
countries which start from different levels of development, tech-

nology, and scale of production. The opening of frontiers has led
to the elimination or contraction of many indigenous firms in the
manufacturing sector, while the 'gateway' policy towards foreign
multinationals has been at best a mixed blessing. Large transfers
from EC Funds had been until recently directed mainly towards
consumption and an internal redistribution of income in favour of
the farming community. Serious errors in macroeconomic policy
and the attempt to postpone economic adjustment have increased
the cost of the latter. Although there has been considerable
improvement of the macroeconomic scene since 1987, Ireland is
still faced with major structural problems and difficult policy
dilemmas. The accumulated public debt can act as a serious
constraint on economic growth (not to mention the continuation
of generous grants and tax concessions to foreign firms), and this
constraint will become tighter as Ireland tries to meet the conditions for entering the final stage of EMU. Rigidities in the
labour market and the large excess in the supply of labour,
compounded by the highest birth rates in the Community, present
a formidable economic and social problem. Large emigration
could once again in Irish history act as the safety valve, although
this would further weaken the demographic structure by increasing
an already large percentage of non-active population (both young
and old), while also depriving the economy of much local talent.
The search for jobs abroad is nowadays led by graduates and
skilled workers who have received an expensive and high quality
education at the expense of Irish taxpayers.

Greece's accession to the Community in 1981 was in some
respects the next logical step after a long period of association
with the EEC (the Treaty of Athens being the first association
agreement signed by the EEC in 1961), which had contributed to
the gradual opening of the Greek economy, despite the limited
reciprocity as regards trade liberalization between the two sides
(Tsoukalis, 1981). Yet one of the most successful European NICs
of the 1960s ended up as the biggest problem case of the EC
during the 1980s. Membership of the Community coincided with
a steady deterioration of Greece's position in the European
income league (Table 8.1). In the diplomatic words of an international organization, 'the performance of the Greek economy
has been one of the least good in the OECD area' (OECD, 1990:
88). It has been, in fact, disastrous. Although it may be tempting
to link Greece's membership of the EC with negative develop-

254   Regional Policies and Redistribution

ments in the domestic economy in a cause and effect relationship,
relatively few economists have succumbed to this temptation.

The problems of the Greek economy started much earlier. The
oil shock of 1973 was almost immediately followed by the fall
of the military dictatorship; and democratic consolidation took,
perhaps naturally, precedence over economic adjustment. There
was, in fact, a very strong similarity to political reactions in both
Spain and Portugal to the rapid deterioration in the international
economic environment (Diamantouros, 1986). While in other
Western European countries measures of economic adjustment
were taken, in southern Europe government expenditure was
growing rapidly, and so too were wages and salaries, leading
to a wage–price spiral and a deterioration of international
competitiveness.

The resistance to economic adjustment proved to be particularly stubborn in Greece. The second oil shock coincided with the
intensification of the domestic political struggle on the eve of the
1981 elections which brought the Socialists to power. The new
Government put the emphasis on rapid structural adjustment and
internal redistribution, with the State expected to act as the main
driving force of economic development. But in the pursuit of its
economic policies, the new Government took little notice of the
external constraints imposed on a small and open economy and
the gross inefficiency of the Greek public sector (see also the
relevant chapters in Tsoukalis, 1992).

While the rest of Western Europe quickly shifted into a deflationary gear, which brought unemployment to unprecedented
levels, Greece continued strolling happily down the road of
expansionary policies; and the latter succeeded only in financing
a consumption boom. Rapidly widening public sector deficits,
partly financed abroad, and high rates of inflation were combined
with extremely low rates of growth and investment. The balance
of payments constraint forced the Government to adopt a stabilization programme at the end of 1985, aided by an EC balance of
payments loan and following a devaluation of the drachma. But
political considerations soon put an end to economic stabilization:
the electoral cycle came back in full swing, and the story was
repeated once again in 1989–90 when public sector deficits and
inflation rates reached new peaks in a period of political instability. Thus the divergence of Greek macroeconomic policies

Regional Policies and Redistribution 255

from those pursued in the rest of the EC became even more pronounced.

Although statistics are not very reliable, unemployment in Greece appears to have remained consistently below the EC average, thus offering the only bright spot on an otherwise dark economic horizon. But this has been achieved through the continuous expansion of the public sector, characterized by excessive overmanning and the operation of political patronage, and the artificial survival of many debt-ridden firms which have been kept alive through state subsidies. This policy was hardly sustainable, as public sector deficits reached record levels (exceeding 20 per cent of GDP in 1990).

Import penetration of the Greek market by EC suppliers has grown rapidly, especially in more traditional sectors which had enjoyed in the past high rates of protection, mainly of the non-tariff kind. There has been both a trade creation and a trade diversion effect. On the other hand, Greek exporters have proved unable to secure higher export shares of European markets. The inevitable result has been the steady worsening of the trade deficit and a depressing effect on domestic industrial production. The opening of the economy also seems to have contributed to the gradual shift of Greek entrepreneurs back to traditional sectors such as food, beverages, textiles, and clothing, thus further strengthening the inter-industry division of labour between Greece and the rest of the Community (Giannitsis, 1988; see also Neven, 1990). Greece's main competitors in the manufacturing sector are Third World NICs which operate on very low wage costs; a factor which will continue to act as a major constraint on the further expansion of Greek exports.

Similarly to Ireland, Greece has benefited from large transfers from EC Funds which have contributed to the financing of the large trade deficit. The bulk has gone to the agricultural sector in the form of price intervention, and it has been translated into higher consumption levels. This has, however, changed following the 1988 reform of the Structural Funds. Unlike Ireland, the positive budgetary effects of Greece's participation in the CAP have been partly compensated by negative trade effects due to a different product distribution and the fact that Greece has become a net importer of food products. Unlike also the experience of other new members of the EC, foreign investment

256 Regional Policies and Redistribution

inflows into Greece during this period were hardly influenced by accession. Presumably, this needs to be interpreted as a vote of no confidence by foreign investors.

The structural weaknesses of the Greek economy have been, undoubtedly, an important factor behind the difficulties in adjusting to strong European competition. Low levels of development and technology, small size, poor infrastructure, and a long history of external protection have created serious handicaps for Greek industrialists. This also explains the continued reference to infant industry arguments and the appeals for greater flexibility in the application of EC rules made by some Greek economists (Giannitsis, 1988). Such arguments were repeatedly used in the past by the Socialist Government as a justification for the lengthening of the transitional period, following Greece's accession, and the granting of derogations from EC rules which, while causing serious friction with the Commission, were used, almost invariably, as a means of postponing adjustment (Mitsos, 1989).

Structural weaknesses are, however, only one part of the explanation for Greece's difficulties in adjusting to the new European and international environment. The struggle for international competitiveness has been strongly undermined by persistent resistance to modernization, especially of the public sector, structural rigidities and macroeconomic mismanagement. The latter has also led to the overvaluation of the currency since the exchange rate has been used as an anti-inflationary instrument (see also the experience of some of the more inflation prone countries of the ERM), while large public deficits continued to work in the opposite direction. Economics is intimately linked to politics: a polarized society and a predominantly inward-looking political class acted as important constraints on economic adjustment.

Under a conservative government since April 1990, based on a small parliamentary majority, Greece has started a major stabilization effort aiming at the correction of both domestic and external financial imbalances. This stabilization effort will require a substantial shift of resources away from consumption and towards exports and investment; and it will need to continue well into the 1990s, if Greece wants to join the other EC countries into the final stage of EMU. In February 1991 a new loan was given by the Community in order to assist the stabilization pro-

Regional Policies and Redistribution 257

gramme, although with tighter conditions this time. The required drastic reduction in budget deficits, which started in 1991, promises to be a very painful exercise, because of the large cost of servicing the accumulated debt. Ireland's earlier experience is quite indicative. Macroeconomic stabilization has been accompanied by policies aiming at deregulation and privatization, although those policies have so far proceeded at a relatively slow pace. Thus, Greece has started, with considerable delay and much hesitation, to catch up with economic changes in the rest of Europe.

Because of major structural and macroeconomic problems, Greece has not been able to benefit much from the '1992 effect'. The opening of Eastern Europe, and the Balkan countries in particular, should provide Greece with a valuable economic 'hinterland' and improved prospects for trade and co-operation. But this is more of a medium- and long-term prospect. The serious political instability which has followed the collapse of communist regimes in Greece's neighbouring countries has produced an additional economic burden. This is particularly true in the case of Yugoslavia: reduced bilateral trade has been combined with higher transport costs for a good part of Greece's exports and imports from its EC partners as well as the loss of receipts from tourism. The problem of large numbers of economic refugees from Albania has been added to the misery list, thus making the early 1990s a very difficult period for Greece.

On the basis of the early years of EC membership, which is still too short a period to draw any firm conclusions, Spain's experience contrasts sharply with that of Greece. Spain became a member of the Community in 1986, together with Portugal. The signing of the treaty of accession constituted a major turning-point in a long and sometimes tumultuous phase of relations with Brussels, which had started back in 1962 with an unsuccessful application for association with the EEC.

Spain is, undoubtedly, one of Europe's most successful NICs. The stabilization plan of 1959 marked the beginning of a more outward-looking phase of industrialization, characterized by high rates of growth and rapid structural adjustment, which gradually produced a relatively diversified industrial base and the progressive internationalization of the economy through external trade, labour migration, and foreign investment. Yet high external protection remained for a long time one of the dis-

258   Regional Policies and Redistribution

tinguishing features. The two successive oil shocks of the 1970s and the world economic recession fundamentally changed the external economic parameters, while the domestic political scene was also radically transformed after the death of the Francoist dictatorship. For approximately ten years (1975–85) the Spanish economy stagnated. Growth rates lagged behind even the depressingly low EC average. Unemployment reached record levels for Europe (21.8 per cent in 1985), while inflation remained above the EC average. Public expenditure and deficits grew rapidly, although Spain never approached the levels of indebtedness reached by countries such as Belgium, Greece, Ireland, and Italy (Fig. 7.7). Furthermore, unlike some of the weaker European economies during this period, Spain did not experience a severe balance of payments crisis.

The first half of the 1980s was characterized by a major stabilization effort and a substantial restructuring of the domestic economy. Stabilization relied mainly on monetary policy instruments and wage restraint. An extensive programme for the reconversion of the industrial sector, including large capacity cuts, financial restructuring, and technological modernization, was launched in 1984; public firms under the aegis of the Instituto Nacional de Industria strongly felt the pinch (OECD, 1989*b*). Measures aiming at a greater flexibility of the labour-market were introduced, and the first steps were taken towards the liberalization and deregulation of the financial sector. The impending accession to the EC acted both as a convenient excuse and a catalyst for a basically unpopular package of measures. Some of the results were quickly evident: inflation fell rapidly (it picked up again in 1989), profits rose steadily, and this eventually had a positive effect on investment. However, the price paid in terms of job losses was very heavy indeed. Restrictive macroeconomic policies and industrial restructuring, combined with rigidities in the labour market, the continuous exodus from land, and the termination of traditional patterns of emigration led to levels of unemployment which had been literally unheard of in Europe for some decades; even when some allowance is made for jobs in the black market.

The reward came soon in the form of a big economic boom coinciding with the first years of EC membership. Between 1986 and 1990, Spain registered the highest rate of economic growth among the Twelve. Investment grew at spectacular rates and unemployment began to fall (close to 16 per cent in 1990). With domestic demand growing faster than the demand for exports and the investment boom drawing ever increasing imports of capital equipment, the trade deficit widened rapidly. The progressive overvaluation of the peseta and the EC effect also worked in the same direction. Trade creation and trade diversion, as a result of EC membership, mainly benefited EC exporters to Spain. There was a significant shift in the geographical distribution of Spain's external trade, especially imports, in a very short period of time. Manufacturing imports from the EC more than doubled in real terms between 1985 and 1988. On the other hand, there are strong elements of both intra-industry and inter-industry trade between Spain and the rest of the Community, itself a sign of the more developed state of the Spanish economy as compared with that of Greece and Portugal (Hine, 1989; Neven, 1990; Commission of the EC, 1990c).

Trade and current account deficits were more than compensated by large inflows of capital which, in turn, produced a substantial increase in official reserves and the appreciation of the peseta in foreign exchange markets. Foreign capital was attracted to Spain for two main reasons; that is, in addition to the attraction of a sunbelt country which has been traditionally translated into purchases of real estate. On the one hand, high nominal and real interest rates, the product of a restrictive monetary policy, attracted short-term capital; and this was reinforced by the entry of the peseta into the ERM. On the other, the favourable business climate and the improved export prospects to the rest of the EC (accession plus the '1992 effect') acted as a big incentive for foreign direct investment and the buying of participation in Spanish firms. Political stability, surplus skilled labour, low wages by European standards, attractive living conditions for foreign managers, a booming economy, and the prospect of free access to the large European market helped to turn Spain into one of Europe's last frontiers in the eyes of foreign investors. There was an explosion of foreign direct investment in Spain (and also Portugal) during the last years of the 1980s; and, unlike Ireland, this investment came mostly from European countries. Foreign direct investment accounted for approximately 35 per cent of total investment in the manufacturing sector in the period betwen 1986 and 1988. For the so-called strong demand sectors, the corresponding figure was as high as 88 per cent (Viñals, 1990).

260   Regional Policies and Redistribution

Foreign investment also seemed to reinforce internal regional disparities, with the bulk going to Madrid and Catalonia.

Net budgetary transfers from the EC have played a minor role, although rising in more recent years because of the gradual incorporation of Spanish agriculture into the CAP and the doubling of the resources of Structural Funds, of which Spain is a net beneficiary. Yet, in relative terms, Spain cannot look forward to the size of net transfers directed to Ireland, Greece, and, increasingly, Portugal. In the case of Spain, the market is likely to continue playing a much more important role than inter-country transfers of funds.

Why has Spain's experience from the early years of EC membership been so different from that of Greece and, to a lesser extent, also Ireland? One explanation must surely be that stabilization and restructuring in Spain had preceded EC accession and thus had created the appropriate environment for the positive effects of integration to materialize. This may in turn point to the wisdom of the Socialist Government which introduced the necessary and unpopular measures in time; a wisdom coupled with the strong ambition of Spain's young political leadership to turn the country into one of the big industrial (and political) powers of Europe.[2] Wisdom being rarely a sufficient condition for political success, the Government of Mr Gonzalez also took advantage of its virtually unchallenged position in the domestic political system. A heavy price for stabilization and industrial restructuring has been paid in terms of unemployment, and the subsequent benefits of economic recovery have been unequally distributed. Thus the continuation of the new 'economic miracle' in the future should largely depend on political stability and the development of industrial relations.

There are also other factors which have played a significant part in the positive experience of the early years of EC membership. The large size of the economy, its geographical location, a reasonable infrastructure, and a relatively diversified industrial base clearly distinguish Spain (and, particularly, the most prosperous northeastern part, together with Madrid) from the other less developed and more peripheral countries and regions of the

---

[2] In an interview to the *Financial Times* (20 Nov. 1991), the Spanish Minister of Economics and Finance, Mr Solchaga, declared: 'We are a province of Europe, and that is the best thing that has ever happened to us.' Although, perhaps, uncharacteristically Spanish for its modesty, this statement reflects the importance attached to Europe, and the EC in particular, in post-Franco Spain.

Community. Last but not least, accession to the EC coincided with economic recovery all over Europe and the fall in oil prices. The time was, therefore, highly propitious. On the other hand, a large part of the economic adjustment to EC membership and the creation of the internal market still remains to be done, and this is likely to take place under a less favourable macroeconomic environment. Domestic economic policies will also have to be geared increasingly towards meeting the convergence criteria agreed at Maastricht. But this seems to be well understood by the Spanish political class.

The EC Budget: A Reluctant Acceptance of Redistribution

An easy extrapolation of 'invisible hand' ideas to the real world of regional economics in the presence of market-opening measures would be unwarranted in the light of economic history and theory (Padoa-Schioppa, 1987: 93).

Historical experience suggests, however, that in the absence of counter vailing policies, the overall impact [of EMU] on peripheral regions could be negative (Committee for the Study of Economic and Monetary Union, 1989: 22).

Redistribution constitutes an important function of national budgets in all advanced industrialized countries. Through taxation and government expenditure, resources are transferred automatically to the poorer regions and lower income groups, thus bringing about a reduction of disparities within a country. Federal grants in existing federations within the OECD group of countries constitute between 15 per cent and 30 per cent of regional revenue (Commission of the EC, 1990e). According to an earlier study (MacDougall report: Commission of the EC, 1977), primary income differentials between regions in those federations are reduced by 30 per cent to 40 per cent through the workings of central public finance. A strong redistributive role of the federal budget is a function of political cohesion and a developed sense of *Gemeinschaft*. In this respect, the European Community is still in its early stages. The gradual acceptance of the redistributive function of the EC budget and hence the link between economic integration and solidarity across national frontiers makes the

262   Regional Policies and Redistribution

Community very different from traditional international organizations, and can be interpreted as a sign of the EC slowly acquiring the traits of a proper political system.

The distributional impact of integration does not, of course, operate only through the budget. Trade effects through the establishment of the customs union and the CAP have been much more important than any explicit redistribution through the budgetary mechanism of the EC. Yet the latter has attracted a great deal of public attention which is disproportionate to its real economic significance; and this explains the prominence given to budgetary disputes in the more recent history of the EC. Gains and losses through the budget are much more easily identifiable than, for example, the welfare effects of intervention prices in the agricultural sector, thus leading to the unavoidable trench warfare in Council meetings.

In the early years of European integration, the common budget remained completely in the background. Unlike national budgets, which represent the main economic policy statement of the government, EC budgets were the end-product of decisions taken almost independently and in a non-co-ordinated fashion by different Councils of Ministers in Brussels in the context of EC action in separate policy areas. The overall expenditure, arising from these decisions, was then financed through national contributions, and the keys for those contributions had been established by the treaty. As explained earlier, the common budget was not seen as an instrument of redistributing resources across national frontiers, since equity in terms of the distribution of benefits from integration was to be achieved essentially through the package of different policies which had been agreed upon in advance.

The creation of own resources for the Community and the extension of the powers of the European Parliament in this area were major items in the Commission's proposals of 1965 which led to the first serious constitutional crisis inside the Community. But the real dispute, provoked by General de Gaulle, was about questions of national sovereignty and the division of power between Brussels and the national institutions. The budgetary questions were only of secondary importance. In fact, both proposals were to be adopted some years later, with the Luxembourg agreement of April 1970.

The financial independence of the Community has had in fact a

Regional Policies and Redistribution 263

much longer history. The Paris Treaty of 1951 gave the High Authority of the ECSC the right to raise levies on coal and steel production. The creation of own resources was envisaged in Article 201 of the Treaty of Rome. This has always been a very important subject for the EC Commission and European federalists more generally for both practical and symbolic reasons. The financial independence of EC policies and institutions has been considered as a source of political power and an unmistakable sign of the qualitative difference of the Community from other international organizations (Strasser, 1990).

The 1973 enlargement, the economic recession, and the plans for the creation of an EMU combined to usher budgetary issues to the forefront of Community politics. The efforts of the UK to reduce its own net budgetary contribution opened the Pandora's box by turning net national contributions to the budget for the first time into an important, and also explosive, political issue, and thus raising alarm in Brussels about the negative consequences on further integration of a possible entrenchment of the *juste retour* principle (meaning that each country would strive for at least a zero balance in its net budgetary contribution and thus risk the transformation of the integration process into a zero-sum game). With the gradual swing to the right in European politics in the early 1980s and the strong emphasis on budgetary consolidation, an ideological factor was later added to the intra-EC debates about the budget.

The bargaining position of the UK was progressively strengthened as the EC budget approached the limits imposed by the 1970 treaty revision in terms of own resources, because of the rapid increase in agricultural expenditure. A new revision required a unanimous decision by the Council and the subsequent ratification by all national parliaments. It thus provided an excellent opportunity to strive for a more wide-ranging restructuring of the EC budget as part of the general reform exercise of common policies in which the Community became gradually engaged. The new political climate was also more propitious to such an attempt.

The first important step was taken at the Fontainebleau summit of June 1984. The package agreed then included new measures to control the growth of agricultural surpluses, an increase of the VAT rate (as part of the Community's own resources), and the introduction of a permanent mechanism for the partial com-

264	Regional Policies and Redistribution

pensation of the UK based on the difference between its VAT contribution and its overall receipts from the budget. Special provision was also made for the reduction of the net contribution of the Federal Republic. Thus the objective of a certain degree of equity (not the same as redistribution) in terms of net national contributions to the EC budget was in the end officially recognized (Denton, 1984). It had taken a great deal of pressure on other members by the then British Prime Minister, Mrs Thatcher, for this principle to become finally, and reluctantly, accepted. But it was a very important turning point.

The Fontainebleau agreement did not, however, succeed in imposing an effective control over agricultural expenditure. Thus the new own resources were exhausted even before the increase in the VAT rate could be implemented; and this led to the opening of new negotiations on a subject which had deeply divided EC countries for years. But this time, the negotiations took place in a much more favourable political environment in the aftermath of the signing of the SEA and the adoption of the internal market goal. Furthermore, the new budget negotiations could build on earlier agreements, especially as regards the UK compensation.

Then came the agreement reached by the European Council in Brussels in February 1988. It covered the creation of new budgetary resources, much tougher measures with respect to CAP expenditure, and a considerable strengthening of redistributive policies. The agreement also incorporated provisions for the UK compensation basically along the lines established earlier at Fontainebleau. The European Council decision was followed in June of the same year by an inter-institutional agreement on the budget. This meant that member countries and EC institutions had reached an agreement both on the overall size of the budget as well as on the main items of expenditure for the period extending to 1992. It was unprecedented, and the ensuing budgetary peace has contributed significantly to the new momentum of integration.

Two basic characteristics of the EC budget are its very small size, compared with national budgets, and the legal requirement for zero balance between revenue and expenditure. Thus its role in terms of the traditional functions of allocation, stabilization, and redistribution can only be extremely limited. In 1992, EC expenditure was expected to reach 1.15 per cent of Community GNP. Since 1973, total expenditure had more than doubled as a percentage of GNP. However, this rapid upward trend, admittedly starting from a low base, has slowed down in recent years in view of the ceiling imposed by the agreement reached at the Brussels summit of 1988 (1.2 per cent of EC GNP for payments until 1992). On the other hand, important financial operations are outside the EC budget. They include the borrowing and lending activities of EC institutions, such as those of the EIB, and aid to developing countries through the European Development Fund (EDF). There is also a separate budget for the operations of the ECSC.

As shown in Fig. 8.2, EC revenue consists of customs duties on imports from outside the Community, agricultural levies (variable taxes on imports plus sugar and isoglucose levies on production), VAT contributions calculated on a harmonized base, and GNP-related national contributions since 1988. The item 'miscellaneous' includes national contributions of new members during the transitional period and intergovernmental advances for the years 1984–6 when *ad hoc* measures were needed in order to balance the books. Due to the progressive lowering of the common external tariff, as a result of GATT negotiations (the latest being the Tokyo Round), the relative importance of customs duties was bound to decline over time, and this also is evident in Fig. 8.2. The rapid increase in EC self-sufficiency in agricultural products largely explains the declining trend in agricultural levies as a source of revenue; declining but also variable, since those levies depend on the difference between world and EC prices for agricultural goods, and thus also on the exchange rate of the dollar in which most farm products are still quoted. Only the revenue from sugar levies has remained fairly steady over time.

Customs duties and agricultural levies constitute the traditional own resources of the Community. Their declining importance will be accelerated by a future agreement for further trade liberalization in the context of the Uruguay Round and CAP reform which should reduce the difference between EC and world prices.

The structural weakness of the above sources of revenue forced the Community to rely on a constantly growing share of VAT contributions in order to finance expenditure. The upper ceiling of VAT contributions had been set in 1970 at 1 per cent of a theoretical harmonized base, while waiting for the harmonization of indirect taxation, which may prove to be like waiting for Godot. As growing expenditure hit against the VAT ceiling, the

266 Regional Policies and Redistribution

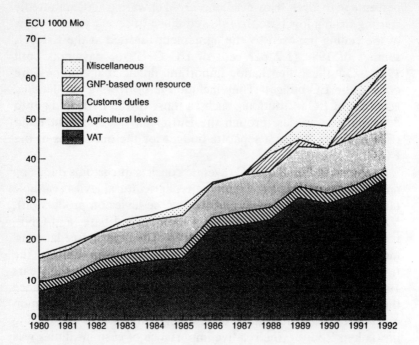

Fig. 8.2. Structure of EC Budget Revenue, 1980–1992

Source: Commission of the EC, 1991*a*; for 1992: 'final budget as adopted by the European Parliament', O.J. L 26 of 3 Feb. 1992.

latter was raised to 1.4 per cent at Fontainebleau, with effect from 1986. In fact, the VAT rates actually payable differ between countries because of the operation of the compensation mechanism for the UK and the various complicated provisions which have accompanied it. The so-called fourth resource was introduced in 1988. It consists of national financial contributions, based on a GNP key, which cover the difference between total expenditure, within the limits defined by the 1988 agreement extending to 1992, and the revenue raised by traditional own resources and the 1.4 per cent VAT contribution (Fig. 8.2).

Before the introduction of the fourth resource, any redistributive impact of the EC system of revenue had been totally haphazard: the distribution of tax revenue among countries depending on their propensity to import from third countries (customs duties and agricultural levies), their propensity to consume (there is no VAT on investment), and the efficiency of their tax collection systems (southern countries in particular suffer from widespread tax evasion). An important step towards the application of the ability to pay principle, which still does not contain any form of progressivity in terms of the tax burden, was made with the 1988 decisions. The fourth resource is more closely related to the ability to pay than any other source of EC revenue. It also has the advantage of flexibility in order to meet further increases in expenditure. Furthermore, the European Council in Brussels also decided to limit the VAT base, in terms of which VAT contributions are calculated, to a maximum of 55 per cent of GNP in order to avoid an excessive penalization of countries with a high propensity to consume.

On the expenditure side, the predominance of the EAGGF Guarantee Section has continued all along, although steadily declining in relative terms after 1988 (Table 8.4). The CAP has not met earlier expectations regarding its redistributive role. Not only have income differentials in the agricultural sector remained large, but the CAP has, in fact, contributed through its operation to the worsening of regional and income inequalities inside the Community (Buckwell *et al.*, 1982; Rosenblatt *et al.*, 1988). This was the unavoidable result of a policy which relied for years almost exclusively on price support for unlimited quantities, thus favouring the large and efficient producers. Structural measures through the EAGGF Guidance Section have always accounted for only a small percentage of total agricultural expenditure.

Expenditure per farmer has been a function of farm size, productivity, and product specialization. Thus the subsidy received by the average Dutch farmer is a multiple of the amount paid to his less fortunate colleagues in southern Europe. As a consequence, the overall receipts of the Netherlands from the EAGGF have always exceeded those of Greece, despite the much larger number of farmers in the latter country (Table 8.5). The figures for Spain and Portugal are not comparable, because of transitional arrangements still being in operation. Despite the relative bias of the CAP, among the poorer countries both Ireland and Greece are important net beneficiaries of expenditures through the EAGGF Guarantee Section, precisely because of the

268   Regional Policies and Redistribution

Table 8.4. Structure of EC Budget Expenditure, 1980–1990 (in Mio ECU and as % of total budgetary expenditure)

Sector	1980		1983		1985		1988		1990	
	Mio ECU	%	Mio ECU	%	Mio ECU	%	Mio ECU	%	Mio ECU	%
EAGGF Guarantee	11485.5	71.0	15811.0	63.1	19955.0	70.2	27500.0	62.8	26431.0	56.3
Agricultural structures	328.7	2.0	653.4	2.6	687.7	2.4	1222.0	2.8	2073.5	4.4
Fisheries	64.1	0.4	84.4	0.3	111.7	0.4	281.0	0.6	358.6	0.8
Regional policy	722.7	4.5	2383.0	9.5	1697.8	6.0	3201.4	7.3	5209.7	11.1
Social policy	768.8	4.8	1495.1	6.0	1626.2	5.7	2845.3	6.5	3667.0	7.8
Research, energy	379.5	2.3	1386.5	5.5	706.8	2.5	1153.6	2.6	1733.4	3.7
Development co-operation	641.6	4.0	992.2	4.0	1043.7	3.7	870.5	2.0	1489.6	3.2
Administration	938.8	5.8	1161.6	4.6	1332.6	4.7	1967.2	4.5	2381.3	5.1
Miscellaneous	852.8	5.3	1093.8	4.4	1271.8	4.4	4779.4	10.9	3584.3	7.6
Total budget	16182.5	100.0	25061.1	100.0	28433.2	100.0	43820.4	100.0	46928.4	100.0

Sources: Commission of the EC, 'The Community Budget: The Facts in Figures', various issues. For 1990 budget: Court of Auditors Annual Report, O.J. C 324. 13.12. 1991.

Regional Policies and Redistribution **269**

Table 8.5. EAGGF Payments to Member Countries, 1980–1990

(in Mio ECU)

	1980	1983	1985	1988	1990
Belgium	596.3	630.0	928.7	732.8	877.9
Denmark	639.0	701.2	842.3	1183.8	1110.6
Germany	2593.5	3183.5	3706.6	4638.6	4100.9
Greece	—	1029.3	1276.3	1452.0	2174.4
Spain	—	—	—	1870.7	2292.0
France	2960.6	3748.6	4755.6	6294.1	5388.4
Ireland	603.4	703.5	1239.9	1072.7	1676.9
Italy	1921.0	2923.5	3586.2	4314.1	4170.8
Luxembourg	12.6	4.8	6.6	5.1	10.7
Netherlands	1565.2	1740.0	2065.5	3774.7	2648.8
Portugal	—	—	—	256.9	459.4
United Kingdom	984.4	1840.6	2004.1	1929.5	1886.8
EC-12	11876.0	16505.0	20411.8	27525.0	26804.8

Notes: EAGGF payments consist of guarantee and guidance expenditures. Outlays on a number of specific structural measures have not been included. The figures for Spain, Portugal, and Greece should be interpreted with caution. Transitional arrangements after accession mean that receipts from EAGGF during this period are significantly lower than under conditions of full participation.

Sources: Court of Auditors annual reports.

sheer size of their farming sector. But so also are Denmark and the Netherlands, which are at the top of the EC income league.

According to the 1988 decision, the rate of growth of EC expenditure on agriculture under the Guarantee Section of the Fund should not exceed 74 per cent of the annual rate of growth of EC GDP. Special provisions were made for exchange rate fluctuations and the running down of accumulated stocks. The aim was to bring the figure down to approximately 55 per cent of total expenditure by 1992, which is very likely to be met. The attempt to control agricultural expenditure was helped in the beginning by the strengthening of the dollar and the more favourable conditions applying in world agricultural markets. Thus collective political will in Europe was given a welcome boost by US monetary policy and climatic conditions in North America (a possible sign that God was in favour of European integration); but, alas, not for very long. As supply started growing again in international markets, so did EC surpluses and the overall cost of the CAP.

270   Regional Policies and Redistribution

With still more than half of total EC expenditure going to
agriculture, there is a limit on how much can be spent on other
policies. Clearly, there is an enormous difference from national
budgets where a large bulk of total expenditure goes to defence
and social security. Expenditure through what is now called the
Structural Funds covers a major part of the rest; and this is very
likely to continue increasing further beyond 1992. This is, in fact,
the only item of the EC budget with a clear redistributive bias.
According to Table 8.4, other policies, including industry, energy
and research account for only a small percentage of total agricultural expenditure.

The EC Court of Auditors undertakes a painstaking work
every year in an attempt to trace receipts and payments through
the budget. This in turn makes possible the calculation of net
national contributions based on approximately 90 per cent of
total expenditure, that is excluding administrative costs and
development aid. Those calculations are subject to the usual
qualifications about accuracy, including the so-called Rotterdam–
Antwerp effect.[3] Table 8.6 shows that in absolute figures, the
Federal Republic has remained all along the biggest net contributor to the budget, thus justifying the popular image of
Germany as the paymaster of Europe. But the overall sums are
clearly very small. It is followed, at some distance, by the UK,
despite the operation of the compensation mechanism. In relative
terms, Belgium and Luxembourg are also important net contributors, although those two countries receive other pecuniary
and non-pecuniary benefits, not incorporated in those figures, by
having the seat of EC institutions. The net contribution of France
has risen significantly in recent years, and Italy has also become a
net contributor. Those developments are not unrelated to the
entry of poorer countries into the EC, while, in the case of Italy,
it is also connected with the upward revision of income statistics
in recent years to take account of the large underground economy
in that country. Thus, the prestige of a higher position in the
European income league has been paid for by the Italians in hard
cash.

---

[3] This refers to the general problem created by large transit trade in calculating net
national contributions to the EC budget. Should the revenue raised from imports through a
Dutch port, with Germany as the final destination, be attributed to the Netherlands or the
Federal Republic? A substantial amount of trade in northern Europe goes through the ports
of Antwerp and Rotterdam.

Table 8.6. Net Transfers from EC Budget, 1980–1990
(Receipts minus contributions expressed in Mio ECU and as % of national GDP)

	1980 Mio ECU	%	1982 Mio ECU	%	1984 Mio ECU	%	1986 Mio ECU	%	1988 Mio ECU	%	1990 Mio ECU	%
Belgium	-273.4	-0.32	-499.0	-0.57	-398.2	-0.41	-283.9	-0.25	-995.0	-0.79	-773.9	-0.54
Denmark	333.9	0.70	228.3	0.40	487.2	0.70	421.1	0.50	350.9	0.38	422.5	0.42
Germany	-1670.0	-0.28	-3171.7	-0.47	-3033.1	-0.39	-3741.8	-0.41	-6107.1	-0.60	-5550.4	-0.49
Greece	–	–	604.3	1.53	1008.2	2.34	1272.7	3.10	1491.6	3.30	2470.2	4.90
Spain	–	–	–	–	–	–	94.9	0.04	1334.3	0.46	1711.3	0.47
France	380.4	0.08	-827.3	-0.15	-459.8	-0.07	-561.5	-0.07	-1780.9	-0.22	-1804.9	-0.20
Ireland	687.2	5.00	671.5	3.50	924.1	4.01	1230.3	4.90	1159.3	4.30	1892.5	6.19
Italy	681.2	0.21	911.4	0.22	1519.0	0.29	-130.3	-0.02	124.2	0.02	-416.7	-0.05
Luxembourg	-5.1	-0.15	-24.3	-0.67	-40.1	-0.93	-59.3	-1.20	-67.4	-1.20	-60.0	-0.97
Netherlands	394.5	0.32	86.9	0.06	434.8	0.27	167.5	0.10	1150.0	0.60	368.4	0.17
Portugal	–	–	–	–	–	–	219.0	0.73	514.9	1.45	600.8	1.44
United Kingdom	-1364.6	-0.35	-1193.6	-0.24	-1337.0	-0.24	-1438.4	-0.26	-2070.0	-0.30	-3386.9	-0.45

Notes: Approximately 10% of all expenditure is absorbed by administrative costs or is used for development aid. These outlays cannot be apportioned among the member states and consequently the aggregate of member states contributions to the EC budget exceeds the total for receipts.

Sources: Court of Auditors annual reports.

272 Regional Policies and Redistribution

Ireland and Greece have been the only important net beneficiaries, with net inflows from the EC, excluding loans, accounting
now for 5–6 per cent of GDP. Ireland's relatively high net
inflow, which in absolute per capita terms is the highest in
the Community, is evidence of the advantage of being a small
member of the Community. Those figures will be even higher in
1992 and 1993, thus making the EC contribution to economic
welfare in these two countries far from insignificant. On the other
hand, the overall effect of these transfers in terms of economic
development is reduced by the very fact that a large bulk is
still devoted to agricultural price support and not to structural
measures.

Portugal is also expected to join gradually the group of important net beneficiaries, as it approaches the end of its transitional
period following accession to the EC. Thus the three poorest
members among the Twelve will end up as beneficiaries of sizeable
transfers of resources through the budget. The corresponding
figures for Spain, the fourth poorest country of the EC, are not
expected to reach similar levels as a percentage of GDP, partly
because of the considerably higher level of economic development of that country and also partly because of its relatively large
size.

In this respect, the redistributive function of the budget is
already a reality; certainly limited, when compared with the
size of interregional redistribution of resources inside member
countries and federal systems outside the EC, but no longer
negligible. Important anomalies, however, still remain, being
basically the product of financial arrangements in the agricultural
sector which still play a dominant role in the EC budget. Given
the size of the budget, the net contribution of Germany and
the UK is disproportionately large, both countries being big net
importers of agricultural products. Exactly the opposite is true
of prosperous countries such as Denmark and the Netherlands
which continue as net beneficiaries from the EC budget, because
of their large agricultural production which is concentrated mainly
in products characterized by heavy intervention.

The battles waged by the UK for many years helped to bring
budgetary issues to the forefront of public attention. UK representatives waved the flag of equity which for some Europeans
was almost indistinguishable from the banner of *juste retour*,
associated with infidels. In more recent years, the battleline has

shifted considerably: the poorer countries of the Community have been fighting for ever bigger budgets, waving the flag of redistribution. The European Parliament has been a valuable ally in this respect in its effort to make the best possible use of its limited budgetary powers set by the treaty revision of 1975. Through its sustained attempts to increase the so-called non-compulsory expenditure, defined as expenditure other than that necessarily resulting from the treaty, on which it has greater powers *vis-à-vis* the Council of Ministers, the European Parliament has been in effect pushing consistently for more money for regional and social policy, thus acting as an important lobby in favour of redistribution and bigger budgets (Shackleton, 1990).

Back in 1977, the MacDougall group (Commission of the EC, 1977) had stressed the redistributive role of the central budget in existing federations such as the United States and West Germany, which accounted for a substantial reduction of inter-state income disparities. This was due to the differential impact of taxation and expenditure policies and the specific and general purpose grants from the federation to the states. The German system of fiscal equalization (*Finanzausgleich*) is a good example of how relatively small amounts of transfers can have a large effect in terms of the tax revenue of each individual *Land* and the reduction of disparities. This is due to the importance of tax sharing arrangements and horizontal transfers between the *Länder*, which bring the 'fiscal capacity' of the poorer *Länder* to a minimum of 95 per cent of the federal average, the general aim being to achieve a homogeneous supply of public services across the country (see also Biehl, 1988c).

Aware of the political constraints in what it called the pre-federal state of European integration, the MacDougall study group had proposed a relatively small and high-powered budget. An EC budget accounting for 2–2.5 per cent of GDP, with heavy concentration on structural, cyclical, unemployment, and regional policies as well as external aid coupled with progressive taxation, could result in a 10 per cent reduction of interregional disparities inside the Community, while also providing an effective insurance policy against short-term economic fluctuations. True enough, the MacDougall group had written about the EC of Nine; the task would be much bigger for the EC of Twelve. In any case, those proposals stood little chance of being adopted in the political climate of the late 1970s and early 1980s.

274 Regional Policies and Redistribution

This issue was later taken up by the Padoa-Schioppa group which argued in favour of a long-term social contract between the Community and its member states based on competitive markets, monetary stability, redistribution, and growth. According to this group, redistribution through the budget should become virtually automatic. Thus net national contributions should be progressively (and of course inversely) related to national income per capita. The need for stronger redistribution in the context of EMU was again reiterated in the Delors report and, in a somewhat milder form, in the Commission's study on the costs and benefits of EMU. Meanwhile, Brussels was getting increasingly worried that the intergovernmental conference on EMU could become tied up with demands from the weaker countries for large transfers (Commission of the EC, 1990e).

As with the earlier package deal, which led to the adoption of the SEA and the internal market programme, redistribution is an integral part of the new package of which the other most important part is EMU. Following again the example of the SEA, the Maastricht treaty does not attach any specific price tags. It does, however, include Title XIV on 'economic and social cohesion' and, more importantly, a separate protocol on the subject, which refers among other things to the correction of regressive elements in the own resources system, the setting up of the Cohesion Fund and to several changes in the operation of the existing Structural Funds aiming at greater flexibility in financing and higher levels of Community participation.

The second Delors package, submitted to the Council of Ministers in February 1992, constitutes a first attempt by the Commission to translate those general objectives into concrete proposals with figures attached to them. The Commission has proposed a further increase in the budget which would raise the ceiling to 1.37 per cent of Community GNP by 1997, implying an increase of 5 per cent *per annum* in real terms. Although this would certainly not alter substantially the distribution of financial power between Community and national institutions, it would, nonetheless, lead to a significant further strengthening of EC intervention in certain areas.

Although their distributional impact is largely haphazard, customs duties and agricultural levies (including sugar levies) naturally belong to the EC system of own resources; hence being

called natural or traditional own resources. They are the end
product of common policies in the fields of agriculture and
external trade. On the contrary, there is little economic logic in
the Community's reliance on a small percentage of total receipts
from VAT, calculated on a notional common base, because of
the lack of harmonization of national tax systems; unless it is
meant as a reminder of the role of the EC in the introduction of
VAT itself. In the previous budgetary reform and in search for a
more equitable system, the EC had partly gone back to national
contributions based on a GNP key. The EC Commission is now
ready to move further in this direction, by reducing the VAT
element in the budget and thus relying even more on national
contributions. This may be regarded with some apprehension
by traditional federalists, although perhaps misguidedly, since
European integration has gone much beyond the stage where
reliance on national contributions may endanger its financial
independence and the development of common policies. A
stronger redistributive bias on the revenue side could be, of
course, achieved through progressive taxation related to GNP.
This would simply mean transposing to the EC level principles
which have long guided taxation policies within the European
nation-state. But the Community does not seem ready as yet to
take such a step; nor does it appear ready to introduce a proper
EC tax.

On the expenditure side, the Commission has proposed substantial increases in three main areas, namely structural policy,
industrial policy, and external aid. More than half of the total
increase would go to the Structural Funds, including the new
Cohesion Fund. This would, therefore, further strengthen the
redistributive impact of the budget. For the least developed
countries and regions of the Community (Objective One), the
Commission wants to go as far as doubling again in real terms the
resources available. Since the Commission has not proposed any
radical changes in the priorities of the Structural Funds, the
emphasis should remain on investment rather than the compensation of losers, although some element of the latter can be found
in existing policies and especially in some of the actions undertaken by the Social Fund. However, the choice between the two
may become more pressing and, indeed, difficult in the future, if
unemployment rises again. Should the compensation of losers be

276   Regional Policies and Redistribution

left entirely to national governments, especially in view of the
limitations to be imposed on national budgets by the convergence
criteria?

There is another difficult choice to be made in the next few
years, with the prospect of a limited increase in overall EC
resources, namely between intra-EC redistribution and economic
aid in favour of third countries, and most notably countries in
Eastern Europe and the southern part of the Mediterranean (see
also Chapter 9). Implicit in the Commission's proposals is
a strong choice in favour of intra-EC redistribution—a sign,
perhaps, of political realism—even though a considerable increase
in external aid is also being proposed. The third area singled out
for a major increase in EC expenditure for the next few years is
that related to the competitiveness of EC industry. But the EC
Commission does not have any ambitions for an active industrial
policy. Instead, the emphasis has been on R & D and the development of infrastructure networks.

Agricultural policy will remain, for some time at least, the
biggest item of EC expenditure, although continuing to decline
in relative importance. In the second Delors package, CAP expenditure would fall below the 50 per cent line by 1997. At
the time of writing, the chances for a radical reform of the
CAP, leading to a substantial shift from price support to income
subsidies, appear to be very high indeed. But since there will be
an attempt to preserve existing income levels for all farmers, this
reform is unlikely to change much the redistributive dimension of
the CAP, at least in the short- and medium-term.

An agreement on the main budgetary guidelines for the next
few years should contribute a great deal to the successful implementation of the Maastricht package and the smooth functioning of the Community in general. It will not be, however,
an easy agreement to reach in times of economic recession and
also given the budgetary difficulties of the biggest net contributor,
namely Germany. The budgetary constraints imposed by the convergence criteria will further temper the enthusiasm of other net
contributors to accept a new substantial increase in expenditure;
and any re-opening of the question of the UK rebate would make
matters worse. Furthermore, as EC policies acquire a stronger
redistributive dimension and the number of net beneficiaries (in
terms of countries) becomes more limited, agreements for further
increases in EC expenditure may also prove more difficult to

Regional Policies and Redistribution **277**

reach. For all these reasons, the Commission's proposals in the second Delors package may be very close to the maximum in terms of political feasibility. On the other hand, one of the main arguments against a rapid transition to irrevocably fixed exchange rates has been based on the large adjustment costs for the weaker economies, with higher propensities to inflation and also greater reliance on the inflation tax as a partial substitute for a weak tax base. Would the Community budget be able to help much those countries faced with a huge task of fiscal consolidation? And where are the automatic stabilizers to be found in order to deal with asymmetric external shocks in an EMU?

On the other hand, the strengthening of the EC budget and its redistributive function raise more general questions regarding the efficiency in the use of scarce resources, transparency and democratic accountability. On all these questions, the Community's record until now has not been impressive. The deficiencies of the system will become more glaring as more power and money are transferred to the centre; and this will automatically lead to further discussion about the powers of the Commission and the European Parliament. These are the inevitable questions faced by a fledgeling political system, which have not been answered adequately by the last intergovernmental conference. Not surprisingly, they are centred on public finance.

References

Begg, Iain (1989), 'European integration and regional policy', *Oxford Review of Economic Policy*, Summer.

Boltho, Andrea (1989), 'European and United States regional differentials: a note', *Oxford Review of Economic Policy*, Summer.

Buckwell, Alan, *et al.* (1982), *The Costs of the Common Agricultural Policy*. London: Croom Helm.

Commission of the EC (1977), *The Role of Public Finance in European Economic Integration* (MacDougall report), i and ii. Brussels.

— (1990c), 'The impact of the internal market by industrial sector: the challenged for the Member States', *European Economy*, Special Edition.

— (1990e), 'One market, one money', *European Economy*, 44, October.

— (1990f), *European Regional Development Fund. Fourteenth* Annual Report (1988). Luxembourg: Office for Official Publications of the European Communities.

— (1991a), 'Annual economic report 1991–92', *European Economy*, 50, December.

— (1991c), *Panorama of EC Industries 1991–92*. Luxembourg: Office for Official Publications of the European Communities.

Committee for the Study of Economic and Monetary Union (Delors report) (1989), *Report on Economic and Monetary Union in the European Community*. Luxembourg: Office for Official Publications of the European Communities.

Denton, Geoffrey (1984), 'Restructuring the EC budget: implications of the Fontainebleau agreement', *Journal of Common Market Studies*, December.

Diamantouros, Nikiforos (1986), 'The southern European NICs', *International Organization*, Spring.

Dornbusch, Rudiger (1989), 'Credibility, debt and unemployment: Ireland's failed stabilization', *Economic Policy*, 8, April.

European Investment Bank (1991), *Annual Report 1990*. Luxembourg.

Giannitsis, Tassos (1988), *I Entaxi stin Evropaiki Koinotita kai Epiptoseis sti Viomihania kai sto Exoteriko Emporio* [Accession to the European Community and Effects on Industry and External Trade]. Athens: Institute for Mediterranean Studies.

Hine, R. C. (1989), 'Customs union and enlargement: Spain's accession to the European Community', *Journal of Common Market Studies*, September

Krugman, Paul (1986), 'Introduction: new thinking about trade policy'. In id. (ed.), *Strategic Trade Policy and the New International Economics*. Cambridge, Mass.: MIT Press.

McAleese, Dermot, and Matthews, Alan (1987), 'The Single European Act and Ireland: implications for a small member state', *Journal of Common Market Studies*, September.

Milward, Alan S. (1984), *The Reconstruction of Western Europe 1945–51*. London: Methuen.

Mitsos, Achilleas (1989), *I Elliniki Viomichania sti Diethni Agora* [Greek Industry in the International Market]. Athens: Themelio.

Molle, Willem (1990), *The Economics of European Integration*. Aldershot: Dartmouth.

Myrdal, Gunnar (1957), *Economic Theory and Underdeveloped Regions*. London: Duckworth.

National Economic and Social Council (1989), *Ireland in the European Community: Performance, Prospects and Strategy*. Dublin: NESC.

Neven, Damien (1990), 'EEC integration towards 1992: some distributional aspects', *Economic Policy*, 10, April.

Nicol, William, and Yuill, Douglas (1982), 'Regional problems and policy'. In A. Boltho (ed.), *The European Economy*. Oxford: Oxford University Press.

OECD (1989), *OECD Economic Surveys: Spain*. Paris: OECD.

— (1990), *OECD Economic Surveys: Greece*. Paris: OECD.

— (1991), *OECD Economic Surveys: Ireland*. Paris: OECD.

Padoa-Schioppa, T. *et al.* (1987), *Efficiency, Stability and Equity*. Oxford: Oxford University Press.

Perroux, François (1959), 'Les formes de concurrence dans le marché commun', *Revue d'économie politique*, 1.

Pinder, David (1986), 'Small firms, regional development and the European Investment Bank', *Journal of Common Market Studies*, March.

Robson, Peter (1987), *The Economics of International Integration*, 3rd edn. London: Allen and Unwin.

Rosenblatt, Julius, *et al.* (1988), *The Common Agricultural Policy of the European Community*, International Monetary Fund, Occasional Paper No. 62, November.

Shackleton, Michael (1990), *Financing the European Community*. London: Pinter for The Royal Institute of International Affairs.

Strasser, Daniel (1990), *Les Finances de l'Europe: Le Droit budgetaire et financier des Communautés Européennes*, 6th edn. Paris.

Tsoukalis, Loukas (1981), *The European Community and its Mediterranean Enlargement*. London: Allen and Unwin.

— (ed.) (1992), *I Ellada kai i Evropaiki Koinotita: I Proklisi tis Prosarmogis* [Greece and the European Community: The Challenge of Adjustment]. Athens: Papazissis for the Hellenic Centre for European Studies.

Van Ginderachter, J. (1989), 'La réforme des fonds structurels', *Revue du Marché Commun*, May.

Vanhove, Norbert, and Klaassen, Leo (1987), *Regional Policy: A European Approach*, 2nd edn. Aldershot: Avebury.

Viñals, José, *et al.* (1990), 'Spain and the "EEC cum 1992" shock'. In C. Bliss and J. Braga de Macedo (eds.), *Unity With Diversity in the European Economy*. Cambridge: Cambridge University Press/Centre for Economic Policy Research.

Wallace, Helen (1983), 'Distributional politics: dividing up the Community cake'. In H. Wallace, W. Wallace, and C. Webb (eds.), *Policy Making in the European Community*, 2nd edn. Chichester: John Wiley.

Yannopoulos, George (1989). 'The management of trade-induced structural adjustment: an evaluation of the EC's Integrated Mediterranean Programmes', *Journal of Common Market Studies*, June.

[20]

Technology and the dynamics of integration
Margaret Sharp

The purpose of this chapter is to examine the role of technology as an integrative factor within Western Europe, broadly throughout the postwar period, but primarily within the last decade. It begins with a discussion of general trends in technology world wide, then focuses on developments in Europe, asking whether these are in any respect different from developments elsewhere. The formal mechanisms being established to encourage technological collaboration within Europe are then discussed, followed by consideration of the informal structures. The concluding section comes back to the central issue – the role of technology within the dynamics of integration.

Global trends

Throughout the history of the industrialized world, technology has advanced by a series of fits and starts, with periods of intense technological activity succeeded by periods of seemingly near stagnation. Part of this pattern reflects broader macro-economic factors, not least the advent of war and its aftermath, and also fashions in the management, or mismanagement, of economic policy. A period of rapid growth usually coincides with an upturn in investment ratios which in turn brings the rapid diffusion of new technologies prevalent at that time. The antithesis is that a period of economic stagnation – the 1920s in Britain, for example – means low investment and little perceived technological advance.

If economic factors influence the pace of technological change, the reverse is also true. Technology itself is observed to have strong cyclical characteristics. There have been periods, such as that of the industrial revolution, when intense technological activity has brought major changes affecting not just what was made and how it was made, but how people lived and worked. Indeed, since the industrial revolution a series of long, 50-year cycles has been observed, associated with major technological changes such as the introduction of the railways, electricity, and the developments in petroleum chemistry in the 1930s. In the wake of the major changes has come a further clustering of associated innovations – better ways of doing things – and this in turn encourages investment and reinforces the cyclical nature of events. When this clustering effect ceases and the new technologies are mature and diffused through the economy, the pace of change slows, growth rates fall, unemployment increases and competitive pressures intensify.

The 50-year periodicity of the long cycle was first measured and noted by the Russian statistician, Kondratieff. The technological explanation for the cycle, however, derives from the work of Joseph Schumpeter, who emphasized the importance of technical change and innovation as a source of dynamism in the capitalist economy.[1] Like other classical economists (Smith, Mill, Ricardo, Marx), Schumpeter developed a unified theory of economic development which, while giving a central role to technology and innovation, linked together organizational, social and managerial changes with the technological. Radical changes in technology, for example the development of the railway engine, had major impact on all aspects of life over a long period.

The resurgence of interest in Schumpeter's ideas came with the slowdown of growth in the world economy in the 1970s and 1980s, and the simultaneous emergence of important new technologies, in particular micro-electronics and information technology.[2] The long boom of the 1950s and 1960s represented, on the one hand, the flowering of the new technologies of that time, particularly those associated with the petrochemical industry – plastics, man-made fibres, detergents, fertilizers – and, on the other, a catching-up on ownership of consumer durables, above all the motor car, which had expanded so fast in America in the 1920s and 1930s. The backlog of investment, created first by the economic mismanagement of the European economies in the interwar period and subsequently by war and its immediate aftermath, helped sustain the long boom through the 1960s and into the 1970s. Its demise coincided, symbolically, with the ending of the period of cheap oil on which both the petrochemical revolution and the motor car were predicated. But the difficulties economic policy-makers encountered in trying to handle simultaneously the inflationary and deflationary impact of the two oil crises did little to smooth the path of technological change. As in the 1930s, the immediate reaction was to attempt to restore the status quo: only in retrospect was it recognized that things would never be quite the same again.

It is difficult to judge how important today's technological changes will be 50 years on. There are those who speak of a second industrial revolution; others who see them as no more, and no less, revolutionary than the petrochemical developments of the 1930s and 1940s. Freeman likens current developments in micro-electronics and information technology to the advent of electricity which over time meant major changes not only in the range of new products available but also in the way in which people worked and their whole lifestyle.[3] Both Freeman and writers such as Piore and Sabel go further and see in current developments a new industrial divide which puts behind us the old Fordist principles of mass production and looks towards a new logic of flexible specialization.[4]

Whatever the view taken about the long-term impact of today's new technologies, few would deny that we are experiencing a period of major technological change. Today's new technologies – micro-electronics, information technology, automation, biotechnology, new materials – are pervasive. All industries are affected, and there is the reinvigoration of the old as well as the development of the new. This has two implications worth noting. First, the growth opportunities are very substantial as a result both of cost reduction and the opening of new markets. Given sound economic management, the inflationary threat of the 1970s is also alleviated because there is an inherent bias in the new technologies towards savings in energy, raw materials and labour which relieves pressures on scarce resources.[5] Secondly, the discontinuity implicit in the technological changes – above all the need for wholesale renewal of equipment and skills – destroys established positions of power and offers opportunities for new entrants. This leads to an active jockeying for position, not only among firms but also in the new geopolitical power structure which is emerging, and in turn to intense competition between old and new players.

In previous cycles, three phases can be identified: the first, when the new technologies emerge but do not diffuse or combine thoroughly; the second, when there is widespread diffusion accompanied by major institutional innovation both to help assimilate new technologies and to mitigate their negative distributional effects; and the third, mature, phase when there is considerable growth but along established trajectories. We appear to be in the second phase. The institutional changes are occurring at various levels. First, in production and distribution, with new approaches, particularly following the Japanese, in the organization of productive activities, such as R&D collaborations, just-in-time techniques, and quality circles. Secondly, in the very processes of technological change as new techniques cut across established boundaries of production organization. 'Cadcam', for example, integrates design with production; biotechnology requires project teams which combine chemists and biologists with information scientists and engineers. Thirdly, changes are taking place in intra- and inter-industry structures where new technologies require industries to redefine core activities and diversify outside traditional areas. Finally, new technologies are demanding changes in regulatory structures with new industries requiring new regulations (for instance, on the use of genetic engineering) and where new technology is making nonsense of existing regulations (as in telecommunications).

Some of these institutional changes are explored in Chapter 2. In essence its authors, like Piore and Sabel, argue that the old Fordist industrial paradigm of mass production and mass competition has now been replaced by a new industrial paradigm of collaboration and cooperation – networking. They see the driving force for integration as the need to work together in networks. The view taken in this chapter will be somewhat different. While acknowledging the existence and growing importance of such collaborative networks, it argues that the driving force behind West European integration has come from fears of technological dependency (and with it, loss of competitiveness) on Japan and the US. The result has been both to foster collaboration within Europe (with some prodding from the Commission) and also to encourage the rationalization and restructuring of European industry to create groupings of a size capable of matching the US and Japanese multinationals.

European trends

Concern about Europe's technological dependence came to the fore in the 1960s with Servan-Schreiber's *Le Défi americain*.[6] At that time the fear was of domination by the US multinationals, particularly IBM. The issue resurfaced in the late 1970s when the very fast advances made by US and Japanese firms in micro-electronics and associated technologies began to impinge upon their European counterparts. By the early 1980s it was widely accepted that a new and more important 'technology gap' existed between Europe and both the US and Japan.

It is worth looking in more detail at this question of the technology gap. Tables 3.1–3.4 derive from work at the Science Policy Research Unit, University of Sussex, by Pari Patel and Keith Pavitt[7] and present a set of statistics which summarize Europe's relative position in technological activities. Tables 3.1 and 3.2 look at R&D statistics, which, although an input rather than an output in relation to technological activities, are the most widely used indicator of such activity. Table 3.1 takes R&D as a proportion of industrial output, looking at both total industrial R&D expenditures and industry-financed expenditures. In Table 3.1 a very different picture emerges if, rather than looking at Western Europe as a whole, the statistics are disaggregated between countries. Two countries, West Germany and Sweden, show a

Table 3.1 Industrial R&D as a proportion of industrial output in some OECD countries, 1967–1985

	Total			Industry financed[a]		
	1967	*1975*	*1985*	*1967*	*1975*	*1985*
Japan	0.92	1.28	2.11	0.90	1.26	2.07
USA	2.35	1.84	2.32	1.15	1.18	1.54
France	1.36	1.36	1.78	0.75	0.87	1.24
FRG	1.31	1.65	2.42	1.07	1.30	1.99
Italy	0.43	0.61	0.92	0.41	0.55	0.71
Netherlands	1.45	1.45	1.50	1.31	1.30	1.22
Sweden	1.29	1.64	3.03	0.94	1.48	2.64
UK	2.01	1.72	2.01	1.34	1.08	1.32
W. Europe[b]	1.27	1.35	1.81	0.92	1.00	1.37

[a] Industry-financed R&D excludes that funded by governments which is very important in some defence fields. As a figure it is generally taken to give an indication of industry's commitment to R&D.

[b] Western Europe is defined as the six European countries listed above, plus Belgium, Denmark and Ireland. Total R&D and industrial output for Europe have been calculated by first transforming each country's data into US dollars on the basis of purchasing power parities and then aggregating.

Source: K. Pavitt and P. Patel 'The International Distribution and Determinants of Technological Activity', *Oxford Review of Economic Policy*, vol. 4, No. 4, December 1988. Their figures are based on OECD data.

Table 3.2 Growth rates of industrial R&D compared with growth rates in output, 1967–85 (calculated using 1980 GDP deflator for each country)

	R&D	Output	R&D/Output
Japan	10.0	5.4	5.6
USA	4.6	3.0	1.6
France	5.6	2.8	2.8
FRG	5.8	2.4	3.4
Italy	5.8	2.7	3.1
Netherlands	2.3	2.7	−0.4
Sweden	7.3	1.6	5.7
UK	1.8	1.9	−0.1

Source: OECD.

commitment to R&D which matches the Japanese commitment. France, Italy and the UK are the weaker players. This finding is reinforced by Table 3.2 which looks at growth rates of R&D and output over the period 1967–83. Japan's outstandingly good performance on both scores shows clearly. In Europe, Sweden, West Germany, France and Italy all record major increases in the growth of industrial R&D, and usually also in output. Surprisingly, Sweden (which had topped the R&D league) does not score highly on output growth. Again the poor performance of the UK is notable.

Table 3.3 turns from an input to an output measure of technological activity and looks at patenting in the United States, a good proxy for involvement in mainstream technological activities since any major innovation tends to be patented in the US as well as the home market. There are major differences between industries in the use of patents – they are far more important, for example, in chemicals than in engineering – but these differences tend to hold between countries, and hence patenting does provide a reasonable indication of technological activities both overall and within broad industrial sectors. Table 3.3 looks at the differences in per capita patenting between countries over two five-year periods, 1963–8 and 1980–5. Again the substantial improvement in the Japanese position is noteworthy, as is the significant fall in the US position as leader. As with Tables 3.1 and 3.2, the increasing strength of West Germany and Sweden also stands out.

Table 3.4 breaks down the patent data by industrial sector and looks at the relative position of different countries in different sectors by using an indicator of relative technological advantage, and comparing 1963–8 this time with 1981–6. A number of interesting features emerge from this table:

(1) Western Europe as a whole has a comparative advantage in the chemical and engineering sectors, and does least well in the electrical and electronics sectors;
(2) within Western Europe, West Germany, Sweden and Switzerland have tended to gain advantage in mechanical and electrical engineering sectors

Table 3.3 Trends in per capita patenting in the United States by major OECD countries

	Patents per million population	
	1963–8	1980–5
Japan	10.40	78.98
USA	236.13	157.88[a]
France	26.64	38.79
FRG	55.32	97.01
Italy	8.15	14.03
Netherlands	36.61	46.89
Sweden	65.30	89.12
Switzerland	140.74	182.34[b]
UK	44.38	40.51
W. Europe[c]	36.71	51.15

[a] The differences in magnitude of per capita patenting between the USA and the other countries are an exaggeration of the differences in innovative activity, as the propensity of US firms to patent in their home country is higher than that of firms from other countries.
[b] Switzerland's high rate of patenting is explained by the concentration of the chemical and pharmaceutical industry in that country.
[c] Western Europe is defined as the seven European countries listed above, plus Belgium, Denmark and Ireland.

Source: As Table 3.1.

(but not electronics) and to lose advantage (though retaining overall comparative advantage) in the chemical sectors. The UK, by contrast, has tended to gain advantage in chemicals but to lose advantage in the mechanical engineering sector and in electronics. Both the UK and France show increasing advantage in the defence sector;
(3) the US has lost advantage in electronics but is still considerably 'better' in this sector than Western Europe. In other sectors its relative position has remained surprisingly stable.

All four tables confirm the considerable and growing technological strength of Japan. Generalization about the position of Western Europe is more difficult, given the variety of trend and pattern of sectoral experience. Two features, however, stand out. First, the dominant position of West Germany: not only does its performance in some sectors match, or even go beyond, that of the Japanese, but it now accounts for more than 40% of all European patenting in the US.[8] Secondly, there is across-the-board weakness among the Europeans in electronics. Both of these factors play an important part in the processes of integration which are discussed next.

Table 3.4 Sectoral patterns of relative advantage in total US patenting for some OECD countries: Revealed Technology Advantage Index[a]

| | Chemicals | | Mecha nical | Motor veh. | Raw mater. | Defence | Elec. mach. | Electronics[b] | |
	Fine	Other						Cons. goods	Capital
Japan									
1963–8	3.01	1.38	0.77	0.65	0.51	0.35	1.10	1.37	1.80
1981–6	0.87	0.96	0.81	2.08	0.40	0.11	1.11	1.71	1.86
USA									
1963–8	0.89	0.94	1.01	0.95	1.08	0.99	1.01	0.99	1.01
1981–6	0.86	0.98	1.01	0.68	1.21	1.16	1.00	0.92	0.94
France									
1963–8	1.95	0.96	1.02	1.89	0.54	1.10	1.12	1.04	0.80
1981–6	1.45	0.94	0.99	0.80	0.84	1.66	1.08	1.10	0.86
FRG									
1963–8	1.11	1.41	0.96	1.37	0.61	1.03	0.82	1.25	0.88
1981–6	1.17	1.24	1.12	1.48	0.67	1.14	0.90	0.60	0.54
Italy									
1963–8	1.21	1.66	0.95	1.01	0.76	0.78	0.68	0.64	0.36
1981–6	2.23	1.02	1.16	1.15	1.07	0.95	0.69	0.64	0.40
Netherl.									
1963–8	1.72	1.40	0.70	0.17	1.00	0.15	1.16	1.36	2.22
1981–6	0.63	1.05	0.75	0.36	1.69	0.30	1.10	1.44	1.59
Sweden									
1963–8	0.92	0.60	1.20	1.05	1.03	2.35	0.97	0.90	0.57
1981–6	0.59	0.61	1.47	0.75	1.38	2.07	0.95	0.55	0.24
Switzerl.									
1963–8	2.18	1.72	0.89	0.45	0.51	1.44	0.90	0.43	0.48
1981–6	2.02	1.30	1.00	0.44	0.73	1.01	0.98	0.55	0.32
UK									
1963–8	0.88	1.00	1.06	1.55	0.65	1.28	1.04	1.06	1.09
1981–6	2.00	1.00	1.01	0.97	0.86	1.02	0.97	0.89	0.68
W. Europe									
1963–8	1.30	1.24	0.99	1.29	0.66	1.15	0.94	1.05	0.91
1981–6	1.44	1.11	1.08	1.07	0.86	1.18	0.94	0.76	0.62

[a] Revealed Technology Advantage Index is defined as a particular country's share of US patents within a sector divided by that country's share of total US patents. Thus a value of greater than one shows relative strength of a country in a sector and vice versa.

[b] The definition of the sectors is based on an aggregation of three-digit US patent clauses, the precise correspondence being available from the authors.

Source: As Table 3.1

Euro-pessimism and the moves towards integration

The early 1980s, therefore, saw Western Europe confronted, on the one hand, by a foundering of the economic and technological regime which had carried the momentum of growth throughout the postwar period, and, on the other, by the rise of Japan and major changes in the geopolitics of the global economy. Both worked to rekindle a European consciousness and hence to provide a new momentum for West European integration.

As we have seen, Europe's technological performance was in general terms moderately good in relation to the performance of the US and Japan. This was not, however, the perception within Western Europe itself. In particular, the failures in electronics were given high profile. On 31 January 1984, the *Wall Street Journal* carried an article analysing a survey of West European business-men assessing Europe's competence in new technologies and summed up by the headline 'Europe's Technological Erosion Leaves Huge Competitive Gap'.

Europe's businessmen at that time were, indeed, obsessed by developments in electronics. They (rightly) perceived that micro-electronics and its applications in manufacturing and information technology were vital to competitiveness in all industries, but they were deeply pessimistic as to whether Europe was capable of responding to the competitive pressures building up in that industry. Most of the European firms had already pulled out of mainstream semi-conductor production, even with the general recognition that this sector provided the leading edge to the industry.[9] Moreover, in spite of substantial subsidies over many years, neither ICL nor Bull could hold its own against IBM in computers. In telecommunications, long considered a sector where European firms had an edge on other competitors, the Siemens EWS-A fiasco in 1978 had shaken confidence,[10] and it was increasingly clear that, with the next generation of digital switches requiring an R&D expenditure of upwards of $1 billion for a life of uncertain length, Europe could no longer afford the luxury of seven different manufacturers geared largely to national markets. Meanwhile, in consumer electronics, the Japanese, thwarted from exporting by the rapid proliferation of bilateral voluntary export restraints, were steadily increasing their market presence through inward investment, mainly into Britain and West Germany; and in both those countries the indigenous manufacturers were in difficulties.[11]

As if these troubles were not enough, there was a new threat on the horizon. With deregulation in the United States, AT&T had been released from its commitment not to participate in foreign markets, and IBM similarly given the go-ahead to diversify into telecommunications markets. Pressure from US multinationals in the IT sectors, therefore, looked set to increase rather than decrease.

Formal mechanisms for integration

This was the background against which Vicomte Davignon, EC Commissioner for Industry and (after 1982) also for Research and Technology, established his Round Table of Industrialists,[12] gathering together the managing directors of the 12 largest electronics firms in Europe and confronting them with the state of their industry and the imminent competitive threat from the US and Japanese multinationals. Fragmentation of the market among national champions, he told them, was depriving the industry of the one major advantage it had over its US and Japanese rivals, namely the European market of 320 million people; moreover the absolute protection offered by public purchasing in such important areas as defence and telecommunications meant too much concentration on lucrative home contracts and insufficient attention to competitiveness in world markets. With the increasing importance of civilian markets in electronics, and the advent of satellite and cellular telecommunications, their markets were far from inviolate. Unless they improved performance they were in great danger of finding themselves 'rolled over' by their American and Japanese competitors.

Davignon's aim was to establish a Japanese-type consensus programme of collaborative R&D to be called 'Esprit' (European Strategic Programme for Research in Information Technology). The Commission had actually been trying to get such a programme off the ground since the mid-1970s but, until Davignon's initiative in 1980–81, their pleas had fallen upon deaf ears.[13] His initial proposals were modest – a pilot scheme in which the 12 companies could participate for one year to see whether they thought it worthwhile. The response was favourable and by December 1982 the Commission had the go-ahead for the pilot phase costing 11.5 million Ecus timed to last through 1983. This in turn led to the first phase of the full 'Esprit' programme for the years 1984–8 with Community expenditure of 750 million Ecus; this has now been succeeded by the second phase (1988–92) with expenditure of 1.6 billion Ecus.

Symbolically 'Esprit' has been of far greater importance than either its expenditure or the specific projects it promoted would imply. There are four main reasons for this:

(1) It marked a new departure in style for Commission programmes based on demand-led projects, where teams of companies and research groups bid by project in broadly defined programme areas;
(2) it provided a model for future programmes such as 'Race' (Research in Advanced Communications for Europe) and 'Brite' (Basic Research in Industrial Technologies for Europe). With 'Esprit' these represent the three most important (and most expensive) projects, and all are company-led programmes, with tight timetables and monitored schedules;
(3) it has proved to be a turning point in confidence and has helped to bring about a reshaping of European industry to meet the challenge coming from US and Japanese firms. On the one hand, 'Esprit' has provided a channel for cooperation between its European participants that had until now been noticeably absent. It has also served as a mechanism for creating convergent expectations.[14] For the first time Europe's fragmented electronics industry confronted the threat of competition together, and came to recognize that in a world of tougher competition, protection and/or national champion status had diminishing value. To compete successfully, even *within* Europe, they needed to set their sights on global markets and global competitiveness;

(4) it has created an important constituency in big business, pressing for the completion of the internal market and the abolition of all remaining internal barriers to trade, such as divergent standards and regulations. Once these firms had discarded their national champion role it was logical that they should begin to look to Europe as their home base and to see the divergent European standards, for example on data transmission, as a major hindrance to effective operation in those markets.

In addition to 'Esprit' and the EC programmes of sponsored collaboration, 'Eureka' has played an important part in helping Western Europen revitalize its technological efforts. 'Eureka' was originally the French alternative to President Reagan's Strategic Defence Initiative (SDI or Star Wars) launched in April 1985. The French government was worried that British and German partici- pation in SDI programmes would further weaken Europe's technological position and suggested 'Eureka' as a civilian alternative to Star Wars, focusing on a number of major civilian technology projects. The British opposed the big project orientation of the French proposals and under their influence 'Eureka' became a much looser collaborative mechanism, aimed at encouraging European firms to collaborate at the near-market end of the R&D spectrum, thus complementing the (initial) emphasis in 'Esprit' on pre-competitive research. From the beginning, 'Eureka' has sought to encourage participation by firms in European countries outside the Community; indeed the British deliberately projected 'Eurcka' as an alternative to involvement in the Commission's programme. Unlike the Commission programmes, 'Eureka' offers no direct EC subsidies; instead, any project deemed by the 'Eureka' secretariat to meet 'Eureka' requirements (that is, to be a collaborative R&D project involving firms from at least two participating countries) is eligible for innovation support from the national governments of the countries concerned. 'Eureka's' slim-line secretariat (eight) in Brussels – their task is really to act as registrar of marriages, although on occasion they also play a marriage-broking role – contrasts with the 200-strong DG XIII – the Directorate General responsible for Information and Telecommunications and the present-day successor to the 'Esprit' Task Force.

By mid 1986, the champion of European cooperation, present in one out of every six projects, was the British General Electric Company (GEC), which was one of 'Esprit' 's original 12 Round Table firms (but otherwise better known for its liking of subsidies than for its commitment to European causes). Other firms with high participation in European programmes are Phillips, IRI- Stet, Daimler-AEG, and Thomson, all with involvement in more than 40 projects, while Siemens, CGE, Olivetti, Bull, ICL/STC and the pre-merger ITT are all in the second layer with between 30 and 40 participations. Although some US-based multinationals are involved in various programmes, their presence is seen as token and has been a source of some contention with European-based competitors.[15]

In considering the origin of participants, the dominance of French companies in all programmes stands out. In most programmes, French participants are involved in at least two-thirds of the projects; British and German participation in the 'Esprit' and 'Brite' projects is at a similar level, but considerably lower in

'Eureka'.[16] In 'Eureka', firms and instituitions from smaller European countries have a more marginal role than in the other programmes. In the programmes coordinated by the European Commission the principle of 'juste retour' has had some effect on the degree to which smaller countries participate. In particular, the 'Brite' programme, aimed at helping existing industries to use new technologies, has been more successful in some of the smaller EC countries, but the position of Portugal and Greece is still very weak, largely because of a lack of firms with competence to cooperate. In the case of Greece, the University of Athens is almost the sole participant. Outside the European Community, Sweden and Switzerland have both taken advantage of 'Eureka' to involve themselves in the network of European R&D collaboration, and Austria and Finland also show relatively high participation rates. 'Eureka' has also been an important mechanism for helping to bring companies from the EFTA countries into the fold of other European programmes and has encouraged the Commission to open its programmes to non-EC companies. Note the involvement now of companies such as ASEA, Brown-Boveri and Ericsson in the EC-sponsored programmes.

Firm-to-firm collaborative agreements

The formal mechanisms encouraging collaboration within Europe may have helped to stimulate a network of collaboration, but this has been added to greatly by private collaboration between firms. While the motives underlying 'Esprit' and 'Eureka' have been, at least in part, mercantilist – to promote European technological competence and competitiveness – the motives which have underlain the flowering of firm-to-firm collaboration in the 1980s are more complex and reflect both the underlying uncertainties about technology and the intensification of competition.

Taking a somewhat cynical view, it could be observed that whenever the world economy has encountered a period of great uncertainty associated with the emergence of major new technologies, the gut reaction of industry has been to seek security in the company of others. Hence the trusts of the latter part of the nineteenth century and the cartels of the 1930s. The pressures that impinge on today's world are associated, on the one hand, with the emergence of three major new and pervasive technologies – information technology, biotechnology and new materials technologies – and, on the other, with the expansion of the world trading system to accommodate a large number of new players. These trends combine to create, in almost all markets, intense competition at a global level, which in turn leads the older industrialized countries to seek new markets in which they are insulated from new entrants – hence the push up-market towards higher value-added goods, and the increasing emphasis on research- and technology-intensive activities. The more effort is put into R&D, the faster the pace of technological change, and the higher the cost of keeping up. The intensity of international competition means that new ideas are rapidly picked up and exploited: this is good in so far as it means the rapid diffusion of new ideas, but bad for business in that technological advantage, once gained, is quickly eroded.

These pressures are all interlinked, and they combine, as far as the individual firm is concerned, to make collaboration an obvious route. Collaboration gives the firm:

(1) *access to markets* through cross-licensing and distribution agreements;

(2) *access to technological skills and competences* which they may not have in-house. The pace of change is such that there is often not time to build up in-house teams of experts, particularly since so much knowledge is a matter of learning by doing. The tendency for new technologies to cut across traditional disciplines and to require teams with a wide range of competences also militates in favour of cooperation;

(3) *a means of sharing costs and risks* associated with developing new technologies. Firms are often able to meet the costs, but cannot justify the expenditure because of the very real uncertainties about whether the new technologies will prove feasible either technically or in marketing terms. Sharing costs with others means these risks are spread.

At this juncture it is worth taking a closer look at precisely what is meant by collaboration and at some figures which put developments into perspective. A number of databases of collaborative agreements have been developed.[17] All depend upon combing the press and other published sources for information on agreements and are obviously deficient in so far as many agreements, particularly those involving comparatively little commitment, such as cross-licensing, are not publicized. Nor is publicity given to the dissolution of agreements, or the extent to which agreements or joint ventures culminate in a takeover or merger (which has happened quite frequently). Nevertheless, the figures do provide something of a snapshot of what is happening on collaboration, and for this reason it is worth considering their findings.

The database considered here is that developed at TNO in the Netherlands and has the advantage of covering most of the 1980s but it is concerned

Table 3.5 Number of technological cooperation agreements in information technology and biotechnology

	Before 1970	1970 –75	1976 –79	1980	1981	1982	1983	1984	1985	1986	1987	Total (%)
Biotechnology	3	5	63	48	55	68	43	55	123	124	108	695 (30.5)
Information technology	12	34	122	68	110	128	161	206	242	252	249	1584 (69.5)
Total	15	39	185	116	165	196	204	261	365	376	357	2279 (100)
(%)	(0.6)	(1.8)	(8.2)	(5.1)	(7.2)	(8.6)	(9.0)	(11.4)	(16.0)	(16.4)	(15.7)	(100)

Source: J. Hagedoorn and J. Schot, *Cooperation between companies and technological development* (Studiecentrum voor Technologie en Belied, TNO, Delft, 1988).

Table 3.6 Regional distribution of technological cooperation agreements

Regions	Total	Biotechnology	Information technology
W. Europe	352	82	270
	15.4%	11.8%	17.0%
W. Europe-USA	481	117	364
	21.1%	16.8%	23.0%
W. Europe-Japan	104	19	85
	4.6%	2.7%	5.4%
USA	729	316	413
	32.0%	45.5%	26.1%
USA-Japan	388	94	294
	17.0%	13.5%	18.6%
Japan	95	41	54
	4.2%	5.9%	3.4%
Other combinations	130	26	104
	5.7%	3.8%	6.5%
Total	2,279	695	1,584
	100%	100%	100%

Source: J. Hagedoorn and J. Schakenraad, *Strategic Partnering and Technological Cooperation* (MERIT, University of Limburg, 1988).

specifically with information technology and biotechnology.[18] The data relate only to technological cooperation agreements and exclude, therefore, agreements that concern marketing or distribution (but not, of course, agreements that trade market access for technological know-how). The database covers a total of 2,279 agreements, divided approximately one-third/two-thirds between biotechnology and information technology. Table 3.5 sets out the time dimension of agreements. A few date back to the 1970s, but the majority are grouped in the period 1983–7. Table 3.6 sets out the regional distribution of the agreements. The largest number (729, or 32%) are agreements concluded between US firms, the next largest category being agreements concluded between West European firms and the US. To date, agreements between West European firms and Japan lag behind similar agreements between US firms and Japanese firms, but agreements within Western Europe were a not insignificant proportion of the total (15.4%). Unfortunately the regional data are not broken down by time dimension – if they were they would show (as does Table 3.5) a strong push towards intra-European agreements from 1983 onwards.

These figures describe two distinct developments. The first relates to technology. One of the rational reactions to perceptions of the technology gap in the early 1980s has been for European firms to buy-in the process technology they lacked, primarily from outside the Community. Collaborations within the Community have tended to be concerned with new product development. Hence, for example, in 1982–3 Siemens and Phillips combined in what is known as the mega-project to develop, first, a one-megabit chip and subsequently a four-megabit semi-conductor chip. At the same time Siemens

Table 3.7 Community and international mergers (including acquisitions of majority holdings) by companies in the EC

Sector	Community				International			
	1983–4	*1984–5*	*1985–6*	*1986–7*	*1983–4*	*1984–5*	*1985–6*	*1986–7*
Food	2	1	7	11	2	1	2	2
Chem.	13	23	28	27	11	5	6	6
Elec.	2	5	0	6	2	4	3	2
Mech.	3	4	3	8	4	3	7	2
Comp.	0	0	0	0	0	1	0	0
Meta.	0	3	1	4	0	1	2	0
Trans.	3	2	0	6	2	0	4	0
Pap.	1	5	4	7	1	3	5	1
Extra	2	0	3	1	2	0	0	0
Text.	0	0	1	2	0	0	1	0
Cons.	3	1	2	3	1	0	0	3
Other	0	0	3	0	0	0	0	1
Total	29	44	52	75	25	18	30	17

KEY
Food	Food and drink
Chem.	Chemicals, fibres, glass, ceramic wares, rubber
Elec.	Electrical and electronic engineering, office machinery
Mech.	Mechanical and instrument engineering, machine tools
Comp.	Computers and data-processing equipment (in 1983–4 included under mechanical engineering)
Meta.	Production and preliminary processing of metals, metal goods
Trans.	Vehicles and transport equipment
Pap.	Wood, furniture and paper
Extra	Extractive industries
Text.	Textiles, clothing, leather and footwear
Cons.	Construction
Other	Other manufacturing industry

Source: Commission of the European Communities, *Seventeenth Report on Competition* (Luxembourg 1988).

teamed up with Toshiba in order to 'import' the production technology for the project, and admit that without Toshiba's help they would not have achieved their target. The second development has been political. As noted earlier, 'Esprit' broke the ice in respect of collaboration with European partners. The formal collaboration programmes of the Community have led to many more links, formal and informal, being forged between European partners.

There is one further dimension, however, that needs to be explored – that of mergers. Table 3.7 summarizes merger activity in the Community over the course of the period 1983–7. It includes only mergers taking place across country boundaries and excludes the majority of mergers which are with firms within the same country. The two most active areas for both collaborations and mergers have been chemicals and electronics, but the chemicals sector has been far and away the most active in mergers, mainly because companies such as ICI have been seeking to consolidate their position in the speciality chemicals sector. Looking at the table as a whole, perhaps the most interesting feature is the sharp rise in Community mergers in 1986–7 and the relative drop in other international merger activity that year. Again there are a number of factors at work. First, as indicated earlier, collaboration often precedes merger. Hence one of the fruits of more intra-European collaboration is likely to be more intra-European mergers. Secondly, it is reasonable to speculate that the commitment to 1992, which came to the fore in 1985–6 with the Single European Act and the White Paper, also had some effect on this merger activity. Many European companies, unlike the US and Japanese multinational companies, were nationally based and are now hastily seeking to widen their activities across the whole of Europe.

These figures accord well with what we know to be happening on the ground. A number of major mergers have hit the headlines – ASEA-Brown Boveri; Electrolux-Indesit; Nestlé-Rowntree; CGE-ITT; Siemens/GEC-Plessey. In nearly every sector – semiconductors, consumer electronics, telecommunications, heavy electrical equipment, chemicals, pharmaceuticals – we are seeing, both within Europe and within the global framework, a coalescence of activity around large multinational companies. Within Europe, the national champions of yesteryear – Thomson, Olivetti, Siemens, CGE, even GEC – are transforming themselves by a process of collaboration and merger into global players, with research, production and marketing capabilities on a worldwide basis. This, in turn, has resulted in a major rationalization and restructuring of European industry and the creation of firms which are European (or global) rather than national in allegiance. Whether Europe, or the world, has the mechanisms to contain or control the activities of such firms is an important question, but not one for consideration here. Suffice it to register that the processes of cooperation, collaboration and merger have, in the last seven years, brought a marked shift in the degree of integration and concentration in the West European economies.

Conclusions

The previous section has demonstrated how rapidly the fabric of the West European economies is now being woven together through the process of collaboration and merger. 'Being woven together' in fact means being integrated, and the developments discussed in the last section are some of the more obvious and visible signs of the integration that is taking place. However, as William Wallace notes in his introduction, the process of integration is not smooth and continuous, but has proceeded throughout the postwar history of Europe in a series of spurts, followed, it would seem, by a period of adjustment and assimilation – a lull – before another push forward. Another way of looking at it would be to suggest that the process of integration has proceeded through various stages. The first stage involved only aspects of the periphery – the Council of Europe, the Court of Human Rights, the Coal and Steel Community. With the Treaty of Rome it shifted towards the centre, and the rapid growth of internal trade – first among the Six and subsequently among the Twelve of the enlarged Community – bears witness to the degree to which the economies of Member States are becoming interdependent. But trade is about flows of goods and services (primarily goods). One of the notable features of the Community throughout its first 25 years was the vitality of its trade flows and the almost complete absence of movement among factors of production. The Colonna report, for example, lamented the absence of cross-border mergers, regarding these as the sign of a truly consummated union, and this was to be a theme of regret on the part of committed Europeans throughout the 1970s.[19] It was little comfort that the relatively few cross-border mergers that did take place (Dunlop-Pirelli, for example, in tyres, or Hoesch-Hoogovens in steel), proved to be unsuccessful and were unravelled as soon as was feasible.

The new spurt towards integration that is now taking place is marked by the fact that, for the first time, it involves not just trade flows, but substantial movements among factors of production, both capital and labour.[20] This constitutes a significant shift in the process of integration. The question to be answered is what caused this shift. The contention of this chapter is that the main impetus came – and still comes – from technology.

Briefly, the argument is as follows. The 1970s saw the end of the long postwar boom and the beginnings of a period of turbulence from which, by the 1980s, it was clear that the new technologies deriving from micro-electronics – automation, robotics, the information technologies – would rapidly be replacing the technologies of the electro-mechanical era. This technological discontinuity has had major repercussions. Essentially it means that all existing equipment and existing skills are rapidly becoming obsolete and need to be replaced and/or updated. But it has also provided the opportunity for the major Japanese electronics firms to break the established hegemony of the US and enter the world market as major players. This, in turn, has impinged on Europe. First, this entry of Japanese firms enormously intensifies competition. Secondly, Japanese success in breaking US dominance in a number of sectors, including electronics, had led to renewed pressures for protection in the US, and protection not only for manufactured products but also for intellectual property. In other words, whereas throughout the postwar period Europe (and Japan) has had open access to US technology (and it is partly on the basis of this that Europe was able so readily to 'catch up' with the US during this period), Europe was now faced by the possibility of the US closing its doors on this ready source of know-how.

Meanwhile, the relatively slow progress of reequipment and retraining in European firms raised questions over the degree to which they were themselves competitive. There seemed a great danger of being squeezed at both ends of the spectrum of production – at the labour-intensive end by the entry of newly industrialized countries such as South Korea and Taiwan; at the higher value-added end by the escalating R&D costs and the shortening product life of new products. Hence in the early 1980s the era of Euro-pessimism. As we have seen, there was no real need for pessimism. Europe had some sectors of considerable strength (such as chemicals and pharmaceuticals), and some economies, notably West Germany and Sweden, whose performance was in many areas as good as that of Japan. But Euro-pessimism reflected the general feelings of uncertainty and insecurity prevalent at that time.

The 'Esprit' programme was a deliberate attempt to respond to this sense of insecurity. It reflected, it is true, the mood of the moment – joint ventures and other collaborative projects were the fashionable answer to many corporate problems. But there is little doubt that 'Esprit' itself acted as a catalyst to other actions and to encouraging firms to self-help solutions – among them collaborations – as well as government-led action. These moves in turn have paved the way to merger and the wholesale restructuring of European industry that is currently under way. In the process, many European firms have found a new confidence in their own capabilities, and it is this new spirit of confidence that has carried the Single European Act and the commitments for 1992. In other words, 'Esprit' marks not only a new period in technological collaboration, but a new period in European integration.

1990 finds many European firms facing in at least two directions. As the figures on collaborations quoted in the previous section made clear, although intra-European links have been established as never before, so too have what might be called the Triad linkages across the Atlantic and with Japan.[21] To operate successfully as global players, Europe's multinationals must do as other multinationals and establish production and research capabilities around the globe, but particularly in the US and Japan. These remain the countries with the greatest competence in electronics. But the increasing protectionism of the United States (as well as the continuing difficulties of operating in the Japanese market) raises a marker for the future, and provides the rationale for an element of European mercantilism. It is not inconceivable that European firms may, in the future, find that they are 'on their own' – cut off from both Japanese and US sources of technology. It is worth, therefore, hedging bets and backing the European as well as the Triad option.

Notes

1. Schumpeter's theories were expounded in his mammoth work on business cycles (J.A. Schumpeter; *Business Cycles: A Theoretical, Historical and Statistical Analysis of the Capitalist Process* (New York, McGraw Hill, 1939). See also his *Capitalism, Socialism and Democracy* (New York, Harper and Row, 1943).
2. See, in particular, C. Freeman, J. Clark and L.L.G. Soete, *Unemployment and Technical Innovation: A Study of Long Waves in Economic Development* (London, Frances Pinter, 1982) and J.E. Elliot, 'Schumpeter's Theory of Economic Development and Social Change: Exposition and Assessment', *International Journal of Social Economics*, vol. 12, 1984, parts 6 and 7, pp. 6–33.
3. See C. Freeman, 'The Third Kondratieff Wave: Age of Steel, Electrification and Imperialism', paper prepared for international colloquium on 'The Long Waves of the Economic Conjuncture – the Present State of the International Discussion', Vrije Universiteit, Brussels, 12–14 January 1989 (Maastricht: MERIT/Brighton: SPRU, September 1988).
4. M. Piore and C. Sabel, *The Second Industrial Divide: Possibilities of Prosperity* (New York, Basic Books, 1985). See also C. Freeman, *Technology Policy and Performance: Lessons from Japan* (London, Frances Pinter, 1987).
5. The UK is, of course, currently experiencing substantial inflationary pressures, but these derive entirely from internal imbalances and macro-economic mismanagement. For the rest of the world, as a recent GATT report spelled out, the

prospects for growth are good, and forecasts of inflation low. See *Financial Times*, 15 September 1989, 'World markets set for continued rapid expansion'.

6. Jean-Jacques Servan-Schreiber, *Le Défi americain* (London, Hamish Hamilton, 1968).

7. K. Pavitt and P. Patel, 'The International Distribution and Determinants of Technological Activities', *Oxford Review of Economic Policy*, vol. 4, no. 4, December 1988.

8. P. Patel and K. Pavitt, 'Technological Activities in FR Germany and the UK: Differences and Determinants', *National Westminster Quarterly Review*, May 1989, pp. 27–42.

9. M. Sharp, 'European Technology: Does 1992 Matter?', Papers in Science, Technology and Public Policy, No. 19 (Science Policy Research Unit, University of Sussex, 1989).

10. The EWS-A fiasco refers to the first Siemens experiment with a digital telecommunications switching system in 1977–8. The first model it developed for the Bundespost retained an analogue voice transmission system (hence EWS-A) which, by the time it was made public, had been superseded by fully digital systems being developed elsewhere. Siemens rapidly back-tracked and threw resources into developing a fully digital system (EWS-D) which is the backbone of their current very successful range of switching systems. Nevertheless, the Siemens failure to recognize that the product did not match state-of-the-art technology shook West German confidence in their national champion. See G. Dang Nguyen, 'Telecommunications: A Challenge in the Old Order', Chapter 4 in M. Sharp, (ed.), *Europe and the New Technologies* (London, Pinter, 1985).

11. See A. Cawson, P. Holmes, K. Morgan, A. Stevens and D. Webber, *Hostile Brothers: Competition and Closure in the European Electronics Industry* (Oxford, Oxford University Press, forthcoming 1990).

12. Davignon's Round Table consisted of the chief executives of Europe's 12 largest electronic firms: ICL, GEC, Plessey, AEG, Nixdorf, Siemens, Thomson, Bull, CGE, Olivetti, STET and Phillips. Together their output constituted 85% of the output of the European electronics industry. They have continued to play a central role both within Community projects and in the wider collaborations being developed in Europe. Davignon's Round Table of 12 is not to be confused with the wider Gyllenhammer Group of 27, also sometimes known as the Round Table of European Industrialists, which at that time attempted to raise governments' awareness of the need for extensive infrastructure investment in Europe. See M. Sharp and C. Shearman, *European Technological Collaboration*, Chatham House Paper No. 36 (London; Routledge & Kegan Paul, 1987), pp. 49–50.

13. See C. Layton, 'The High Tech Triangle', in Roger Morgan and Caroline Bray, (eds), *Partners and Rivals in Western Europe: Britain, France and Germany* (Aldershot, Gower for the Policy Studies Institute, 1986).

14. The importance of convergent expectations should not be minimized. It is, *par excellence*, the role that MITI performs with Japanese industry, bringing industrialists together, providing them with well-researched information about market trends and technological advances, and encouraging the development of a consensus view as to how best to meet new challenges. Such a process helps to dispel some of the uncertainties that inevitably surround major decisions on new technologies.

15. R. Van Tulde and G. Junne, *European Multinationals in Core Technologies* (Chichester, John Wiley, 1988), p. 277.

16. The high French participation is explained partly by the high level of subsidy offered to firms joining 'Eureka' projects.

17. See, in particular, C.S. Hacklisch, 'International Technical Cooperation in the Semi-conductor Industry: Private Sector Linkages', in H.I. Fusfeld and

R.R. Nelson, (eds), *Technical Cooperation and International Competitiveness* (Proceedings of an International Conference, Lucca, Italy, Centre for Science and Technology Policy, Rensselaer Polytechnic Institute, New York, 1986); J. Hagedoorn and J. Schot, *Cooperation between Companies and Technological Development*, Studiecentrum voor Technologie en Belied, TNO, Delft, 1988; and J. Hagedoorn and J. Schakenraad, *Strategic Partnering and Technological Cooperation* (MERIT, University of Limburg, 1988).

18. See J. Hagedoorn and J. Schot, op. cit. (above, n. 17).
19. See, La Politique Industrielle de la Communauté, (Colonna Report), Commission Memorandum to Council. Com(70)100 Final Commission to the European Community, Brussels, 1970. Also Michael Hodges, 'Industrial Policy: Hard Times or Great Expectations?' in Helen Wallace *et al.*, *Policy-making in the European Community* (Chichester and New York, Wiley, 1983).
20. There is now increasing recruitment of labour, particularly skilled labour and people with professional qualifications, across national boundaries. See *Sunday Times* Business World, 29 October 1989, 'The Rise of the Executive Nomad', pp. 22–3.
21. The concept of the US, Japan and Europe as the Triad, and of the need for multinationals to collaborate between Triad partners rather than within regions was developed by a McKinsey consultant, K. Ohmae, in his book, *Triad Power: The Coming Shape of Global Competition* (London & Basingstoke, Macmillan, 1985).

[21]

The Best Example of Industrial Policy: The Single Market

The single market is what domestic industries have been demanding for years: a domestic market of high purchasing power, unified technical standards and a lack of border controls which waste time and money. Following 1992, every product legally produced in the European Community may be marketed in all 12 member states at the same time. In the European Community national standards are either recognized or unified. European industry must no longer produce in line with various national standards and laws. This reduces production costs and increases the marketing range of products. The European consumer wins as well, having a larger range of products from which to buy and often at lower prices. The single market not only has the advantage of size but of increased competition as well. Initially, those interested solely in the larger market did not realize that competition would also increase. Now, however, even these last few have started their intensive preparations for 1992. The wailing of lobbyists and interest groups has lost its weight. There have been too many rapid changes for national governments to be easily interested in the egoistic goals of these groups. National slowdowns are increasingly less successful now that economic questions are decided in Brussels by a qualified majority.

THE SINGLE MARKET IS JUST THE BEGINNING

The single market is frequently just the beginning for further steps
in deregulation and liberalization. Free trade forces national governments to review their own domestic regulations in order for their
own countries to avoid losing appeal as business locations. One of
the most regulated markets of the European Community is, for
example, the pharmaceutical market. The price of medicine varies
drastically due to the different social insurance systems within the
Community. Prices are lower in countries where patients pay for a
larger amount of their medicine themselves and higher in others.
This will change when medicine is sold in the whole European
Community. Wholesalers and retailers will buy where medicine is
the cheapest. Health insurances will most probably not refund more
than a medicine costs in another European country if this medicine
can be imported with few problems. This will result in medicines
produced in Germany being reimported via Greece or Portugal in
order to benefit from the various profit ranges. Similar or identical
medicines, or other products, will tend to have the same price in the
whole Community. This will lead to substantial price reductions for
medications in many EC countries. But this is not the end of it. The
social insurance systems will be forced to adapt as well when the
pharmaceutical industry starts pricing on an economic basis. One
step of liberalization almost automatically leads to the next. These
dynamics will make the single market the largest deregulation
programme ever started in the European Community.

However, there is still a lot to do before the single market is
completed. Although there have been no duty fees within the
Community for a long time and the European Community's
founding Treaty of Rome requires the abolition of non-tariff trade
barriers, trade within the Community is still not pure free trade.
When exporting goods to other countries of the Community,
businesses must still, 30 years after the founding of the European
Community, expect difficulties, albeit illegal difficulties, if their
products do not fulfil national requirements exactly. The individual
member states of the European Community have proven very
innovative in creating new trade barriers. Foreign companies are
currently only rarely discriminated against openly. EC law is now
abided by, at least in this respect, in all countries of the Community.
Nevertheless, governments try time and time again to give domestic
industries unfair advantages by placing special demands on the
production, marketing and labelling of products. The single market
will alleviate this problem by the multilateral recognition or unification of these standards. This will allow traders and manufacturers to

38 / Meeting the Global Challenge

conduct transactions freely in the whole European Community. The resulting increased competition will be an advantage for the businesses themselves. Although they will no longer be able to hide behind national regulations, the competition in the single market will be a good preparation for the much harder competition in the world market.

The single market is exactly what European businesses need in order to practise for international markets. 'Go European' is the first step to global thinking. Businesses which succeed in the European single market have passed the acid test for the world market. Many European businesses would not have expanded beyond their cosy domestic markets if left to themselves. The single market is forcing them, sometimes quite brutally, to rethink. In the European Community, it is no longer possible to avoid confrontations with foreign competitors. This will get people used to new and different markets, resulting in increased willingness to conduct international activities. Several European companies have only just realized that they can supply (and could have supplied) foreign customers, despite significant difficulties, and that they can even create sales and production facilities in other countries. As such, the single market has given free tutoring to those companies which previously did not look beyond their domestic markets.

COMPETITION BETWEEN SYSTEMS AS AN IMPETUS FOR INDUSTRIAL POLICIES

It cannot be said often enough: the single market is the new, relevant market for European companies and will decide the success or failure of business transactions. This does not mean that the domestic basis has become unimportant. Quite the opposite: nowhere are customers more demanding than at home. The best example for this is German car production. German drivers are well known for being very demanding about rust protection and the paintwork of their cars. These demands are an advantage for the German car manufacturers. 'Made in Germany' stands for high quality and a long service life. This is primarily a result of demanding domestic customers. Creating competitive advantages always starts in one's own country. The performance of suppliers and the quality of the employees is closely linked to the local conditions of a facility. Globalization of business strategies cannot replace maintenance of the home base. Global competition is the expansion of domestic advantages by creating foreign sales facilities and moving certain functions to other countries to take advantage of lower wages, lower costs for materials or more favourable research conditions. It must not be forgotten when globalizing markets that decisive competitive advantages are the result of unique local conditions which must not be given up, even for the single market.

In terms of European industrial policy, this means that we cannot completely do without the incentive of national or even regional competition. Member countries and their regions must maintain enough freedom to develop an unambiguous image with which they can aggressively advertise, ie, low taxation or wages or by a special quality of work. For purposes of industrial policy, a levelling of location factors within the Community is totally undesirable. Even within a unified single market, incentives for differentiation and improvement are required. This is the real secret of the single market's success.

Many advantages of a location are linked to regional conditions which are based on traditions and centuries of experience. The strict, local concentration of successful industries is a good example. It is not a coincidence that flowers come from Holland, cars come from Germany and movies come from Hollywood. It is always a result of know-how acquired over a long period of time and special production and sales methods which cannot be easily copied. It is relatively easy to sell something for a reduced price – sooner or later, someone will come along who sells for less. Long-term competitive advantages must be based on more than just a price. Long-term success is based on competitive advantages which are part of a society and which enable an economy to make products and to develop production and sales methods faster than others, time and time again. This system-linked capability of innovation is itself linked to national location conditions.

RIVALRY STRENGTHENS COMPETITIVENESS

Strong domestic rivals are even more effective as an incentive for innovation than international competitors. With domestic competition, a lack of success cannot be excused with some mystifying explanation. Competitive chances are the same for both. Consequently, success or failure is a result of the company's own ability or inability. There are some elements of chance but they leave little room for excuses. Successful domestic rivals are, consequently, an even larger stimulus than international competitors. The domestic market is very prestigious and is something nobody likes to lose. Accordingly, it is fought over. BMW has indirectly had a great influence in the newly developed S-class series of Daimler-Benz. In

40 / Meeting the Global Challenge

the same way, Renault and Peugeot both won from their battle over French market shares for middle-class cars. Domestic rivalry must not be sacrificed to some mistaken megalomania in the single market. As important as large production series may be, rivalry between companies over the number one position in their home country is almost more important.

More so, as the proximity of a direct competitor makes demands for protectionism even less likely to be heard by one's government than in the case of a solitary domestic supplier. If number one competes successfully in the international market, it is rather difficult to believe number two when it laments over unfair dumping or trade transactions by foreign companies. If there were only a single European supplier for important sectors of the single market, internal competitive pressure would be reduced considerably. Consequently, size is not everything. The presence and strength of local competition is also an important factor in the development of competitive advantages. This is something which we cannot do without in the single market.

THE PRINCIPLE OF MUTUAL RECOGNITION SOLVES MANY PROBLEMS

The principle of mutual recognition within the European Community is a solution to the problem of increasing markets for enterprises without sacrificing the advantages of regional products and production methods. Differing technical standards concerning product safety, health, the environment and consumer regulations are frequently a basis for many types of trade barrier. For a long time the attempt to solve this problem was to unify regulations for individual products. The Commission has basically stopped this approach now. Harmonization of Community law has simply proven too slow and inefficient. Total technical harmonization has been replaced by the principle of mutual recognition. Every product which has been legally produced within one of the member countries can, principally, be sold within the entire European Community. Enforcing this principle is not as simple as it seems. Not everything is accepted just because it is sensible.

... BUT SOME PROBLEMS CAN ONLY BE SOLVED POLITICALLY

Academic circles consider systems competition to be the most unregulated realization of the single market. The reality is often slightly different. The member countries of the European Community are not always willing to let foreign products into their country without a fight. Reasons can always be found, especially in the food sector – one of the most difficult in the single market. Are French consumers being cheated if synthetic vinegar is sold in France as *vinaigre*? Can heat-treated yoghurt be sold as yoghurt? Is 'caviar ersatz' promising more than it can deliver? These daily issues regularly result in national import prohibitions and frequently lead to legal action against the respective country because of its breach of treaties.

We do not want to define a unified product quality. For example, every brewery can brew beer according to their own recipe; they can even advertise the method. The customer must know what type of beer he is drinking. Labelling, again, can lead to new trade conflicts. For example, the decision on the maximum alcohol concentration a beer may have and still be called 'free of alcohol' or even 'alcohol reduced'. The effort in these day-to-day decisions is largely ignored by the populace. The single market will just not work without any rules at all. The member countries are simply not willing to recognize every document and every label without an argument. Besides, these arguments are frequently based on fundamental differences in opinion on health and consumer protection. As a result, the countries continue to require that national regulations are met. The single market cannot survive without a minimum of unified regulations and controls to produce a certain amount of trust in foreign products. Critics who often hastily accuse us of centralism and pedantry should realize that it is the sectarian regulations of the individual countries that create these problems – problems which must then be resolved at Community level.

Such trade disputes are frequently only conducted about technical details. However, sometimes disputes are based on fundamental differences which must be solved jointly. Should the irradiation of foodstuffs be permitted or not? Which sweeteners, colouring agents, and preservatives should be permitted or forbidden? Should all pieces of furniture have low flammability? In licit cases such as these, we must either accept a segmentation of the market or define minimal requirements for technical and consumer safety for the whole Community. This is the only way to achieve a single market. There are over 100,000 different national regulations for food additives, most of which contradict each other. There is hardly one sweetener permitted for use in all member countries, and then only with differing maximum concentrations in the various products. A

42 / *Meeting the Global Challenge*

similar confusion exists concerning colouring agents and preservatives. We are far from a unified market for foodstuffs, or for almost
any sector of special public interest.

The method used to destroy unity in the single market is almost
always the same: a member state discovers a health or safety risk, for
example in hazardous substances. This country releases a national
directive, limiting or even forbidding production and use of this
questionable substance. As long as there is no contradicting EC rule,
the Commission usually accepts such a national solo. However, it
cannot accept it if free trade is restricted in an excessive or
discriminating manner or the Commission is already working on a
harmonized regulation. A solo by one government usually encourages others to follow, albeit with slight differences and new and
special exceptions to the rules. This subdivides the single market
until the Commission can only suggest a harmonization which, at
best, removes the trade barriers resulting from the different
regulations, or, in the worst case, transfers the most restrictive
solution to the whole Community, as done in the case of tobacco
advertisement. The blessing and curse of Community harmonization are often close neighbours but they are always the result of an
attempt to avoid something worse. This is sometimes highly
frustrating.

THE SINGLE MARKET IMPROVES ENVIRONMENTAL PROTECTION

The European Unification Treaty, in which the goal of a single
market is defined, requires the Commission to conduct harmonization at as high a level as possible. This is to prevent companies of one
country from obtaining unfair competitive advantages over other
countries with higher legal standards by using hazardous additives
in food, by not using safety devices in machines or vehicles, or by
circumventing environmental safety measures. Industrial policy
requires common standards which are as high and as ambitious as
possible, for only this will guarantee that European products can be
sold all over the world. Environmental protection is proof of this
thesis. It is extremely difficult to regain the lead in environmental
protection. This is especially true in comparison with foreign
competitors, who may procrastinate investing in environmental
protection and thus achieve a competitive advantage. Such an
advantage, however, is mostly deceptive and temporary. Sooner or
later, these companies will be forced to invest in environmental
protection as well. However, they will not have the experience and

know-how of those pioneering companies. The need for environmental protection will create new markets. The fight against the greenhouse effect, against polluted water and the dying forests can only be won with great technological feats. Industry will only develop new measuring and control technologies, solar collectors or biotechnological methods for sewage treatment, if the government forces them, by law, or persuades them, by tax benefits, to do so.

... AND ENVIRONMENTAL PROTECTION CREATES NEW JOBS

The Overseas Economic Committee for Development (OECD) estimates the current global market for environmental products to be DM 130 to 180 billion annually of which DM 80 billion are spent in the European Community. This market is said to have extremely high growth rates. Ambitious environmental goals and high environmental standards will ensure that European suppliers of products for environmental protection will be forced to accomplish even greater technological feats. It will also ensure that they will be able to capture the lead in the global market. Lax laws would only let this chance escape unused, leaving this growing market open to others. High environmental standards are not damaging, at least not if they are defined responsibly and flexibly and do not demand the impossible. This again requires that industry and politics are fair to each other; something which frequently must still be learned. The need to distinguish oneself on the one hand and the tendency towards pretense on the other are, unfortunately, still widespread. However, slogans and 'green' sales tags do not constitute a responsible environmental policy. Decisiveness is the sole environmental effect of a policy – something many seem not to care much about.

If what the experts say is true, that the carbon dioxide emissions are responsible for the hole in the ozone layer, then the price for fossil fuels should actually be increased in order to reduce consumption. I would agree completely with this reasoning on industrial policy grounds even if it would result in large, additional costs for energy-intensive industries. It would be almost impossible to pass such consumption-related carbon dioxide taxation for political reasons because it would not burden nuclear energy as well. This would not fit into the simplistic picture that many have of environmental policy. The principle of causation cannot be divided indefinitely, as it would then lose its credibility and intrinsic persuasiveness. Sensible, just solutions in environmental policy cannot be found when beliefs start to replace facts.

44 / Meeting the Global Challenge

CHEATING DOES NOT PAY OFF

I can still remember the 'battle of the catalytic converter'. A substantial portion of the blame belongs to industry because it fought far too long against introducing the catalytic converter. Initially rejected as technically impossible or too expensive, it suddenly belonged to the car's standard equipment. Industrial policy must ensure the predictability and credibility of the environmental policy. Nevertheless, the industry must stop dissembling to procrastinate stricter environmental standards. This trick only works once. Next time around, excuses are no longer credible and environmental politicians feel it necessary to go beyond what the industry admits to be barely technologically feasible.

Cheating does not pay off in environmental policy nor anywhere else. The environment will not profit from strict environmental standards in a few countries of the Community if, as a result, others lag even further behind. We must also ensure that environmental protection does not harm the goal of a single market. As mentioned earlier, environmental solos are becoming increasingly 'in vogue'. The best answer to this would be high and legally binding environmental standards for the whole Community. However, sometimes this can only be achieved with a certain delay. Consequently, such measures should be conducted gradually wherever possible. Two different norms should be defined: the first, a legally binding limit which is based on currently available technology and which can be met immediately by even the poorer countries; the second, a long-term target, should be based on the highest level which is currently defined by scientific and technological research. Tax benefits could be arranged for such measures. This guarantees a certain amount of environmental equality in the Community and creates a strong incentive for technological innovation. In this way, industrial and environmental policy can pull on the same side of the rope. Hazardous substances could be treated similarly: dangerous substances must be forbidden. If a substance is only suspected of being dangerous, general interdiction is hardly justifiable. It would, however, be possible to allow individual countries to pass stricter standards if a less hazardous substitute is available. The unity of the single market remains intact and health protection is not neglected. I will attempt to use this concept of Community adaptation for the first time for asbestos.

FAREWELL TO THE CONCEPT OF DETAILED HARMONIZATION

These examples have shown the enormous implications of the

single market on industrial policy. Depending on the strictness of consumer and health protection, different economic structures appear. In the past, technical standards were to be defined in detail by the legislative. Now, however, following the German example, industrial self-administration is called for. Only basic safety and health requirements which a product must meet to be legally eligible for sale will be defined by law. National standardization experts then decide which technical standards will fulfil the legal minimal requirements. The national experts consult with each other on a European level so that differing national standards do not – purposely or accidentally – result in trade barriers. The Commission is not interested in becoming a bureau of standards: it has neither the manpower nor the expertise for such a task. In any case, the regulations of the European Community could not be changed as rapidly as technology changes.

Legislative work has been greatly simplified by foregoing detailed technical regulations. The European Community must no longer establish the maximum decibel level for lawn mowers, for example, nor define the shape of a tractor seat that would qualify them for sale in the whole Community. This can be done by national standardization experts, reducing the work load of the Commission and freeing it from the false charge of wanting to control every last detail. This love of detail was only necessary because the individual members of the Community were so pedantic themselves that they would not allow a product in their markets which did not exactly fulfil their standards and sizes. The principle of mutual recognition is thus one of the most sensational achievements of the single market, as it shatters national arbitrariness and the standardization monopoly of individual organizations.

... AND WELCOME TO INCREASED SELF-ADMINISTRATION

Standards do not require legal definition if the industry can agree on them by themselves. Standards have always been a matter of private agreement and, as such, this new principle has a deregulating effect. Nevertheless, the efficiency of the European standardization procedure must be improved. Currently, almost 1,000 European technical standards have yet to be defined for the legal minimum requirements for the single market. Consequently, international standards should be used directly wherever possible. This will not only save time and effort, but also reduce difficulties with our trading partners. American and Japanese companies tend to assume

46 / Meeting the Global Challenge

that competition will make their technical standards the industrial standards and, as a result, show little interest in collaborating with international standardization bureaux. This, also, must change if the world is not to split into various trading blocs with differing technical standards.

This is not a danger in the European Community. Products made according to European standards are assured of meeting legal requirements whether produced in Germany, Spain, the US, or Korea. European industry could also do with a similar transparency of regulations concerning foreign markets. Before a refrigerator can be sold in Japan, for instance, the supplier must prove that it meets the special Japanese regulations in all details. Such a procedure can take years. This special proof of conformity is now only rarely required in the European Community. Normally the manufacturer's certificate which states that the product has been produced in accordance with EC regulations suffices. An official test certificate is not required. Even products manufactured according to a different standard are not barred from the single market. The manufacturers must only prove that their products take into account the concerns of public safety in the same manner as assumed in the European standards.

Our trading partners are not as generous. European suppliers would love to be able to say the same of the American and Japanese markets. The 'CE-stamp' – CE is the French abbreviation for European Community – which certifies conformity with EC laws for critical products, can even be used by any manufacturer in the world, and usually by self-certification only. Toys from Korea or China carry this stamp of approval as do toys from Germany or Great Britain. Nor shall this be changed in the future. However, the CE-stamp should not be mistaken to mean 'made in Europe'. The European Community needs a unique and unmistakable sign of European origin. The importance of European symbols for the single market is often underestimated. The frequent use of the European flag shows that manufacturers have now recognized the advertising value of such symbols. The flag is a proprietary symbol of the European Council; the European Community only borrows it. This makes it all the more important that European manufacturers have a symbol under which they can sell their products all over the world.

POSSESSION OF STANDARDS IS OFTEN POSSESSION OF THE MARKET

Limiting legal definitions to basic requirements does not mean that the goal of unified technical standards has been totally abandoned. We have only stopped attempting this by legal means: the industry will have to agree on common standards by itself. The majority of European standardization is already conducted in this unregulated manner, ie, without being forced to define the technical details of EC regulations. For example, standardization experts have discussed intensively the definition of the 'Europlug', a plug which should fit all European sockets. However, due to the differing installation regulations of the various countries, the attempt at harmonization was aborted. The only result of this effort is a pamphlet with the bland title 'Plugs and sockets: living with differences'. For reasons of industrial policy, the unification of technical standards is still very important. For many industrial sectors standardization is the key to European competitiveness. An old and true saying of standardization experts is: possession of standards is often possession of the market.

New technologies offer the unique chance to start with common European standards. However, this requires that standards are introduced immediately. If not, one company will create its own standards which can no longer be changed, and so capture a leading position in the market. The case of VCRs and PC software, for example, demonstrates how single suppliers can force their standards, which are not necessarily the best, onto a whole market. Quality for consumers stagnates and the competition is forced to pay high licence fees. This is an important field for the collaboration of European industrial policies. It is, however, primarily a responsibility of industry itself.

For the single market it is sufficient that all electrical devices which meet the basic technical requirements can be sold freely. It is nonsense, for industrial policy reasons, to produce a different type of plug for each segment of the European market. Changing this, however, is the responsibility of industry itself, which must agree on a European standard. The uneconomical suggestion that the consumer buys himself an adapter cannot be the solution. This is not the customer's idea of a single market. Nor does it help industry to be forced to produce 18 different plugs just for a place in the whole Community market. Not one of these plugs has a chance of international success. If Europeans cannot agree on a single plug, they can hardly expect others to be willing to accept it either.

THE SINGLE MARKET ALSO EXISTS FOR GOVERNMENT CONTRACTS

Another focus of the single market programme on which the

48 / Meeting the Global Challenge

Commission has been working for a long time is the liberalization of the process of awarding government contracts. In the 1970s regulations were already drawn up that required requests for bids on government supply and construction contracts to be advertised in the whole Community. However, large sections, such as power and water utilities, transportation, telecommunications and public services, were exempt. Only about 4 per cent of government contracts in the European Community are currently awarded to foreign companies. If the private sector is included, about a fifth of all supply and construction contracts are imported. This reveals the amount of protectionism which still exists for government contracts in the European Community. It will not be easy to change as government contracts are almost always a matter of politics and frequently an election issue. Advertising the request for bids on government contracts in the whole Community would, in many cases, require a severe change in political structures which will only be hinted at here but not discussed.

Government construction and supply contracts are limited to a few industrial branches where, however, they often constitute more than half of the total demand. Governments or public enterprises buy 90 per cent of all locomotives, railway cars and telecommunication equipment. The relationship of these industries with the government is correspondingly close. The result is an extreme loyalty to these companies. Government demand is also important in space technology, computers and power stations. Governments have a very large direct and, via state-owned companies, indirect influence on which trains will be bought, which cellular telephone may be installed, or whether new nuclear power plants are built or not. The awarding of government contracts is pure industrial policy, even if nobody likes to call it that.

As of 1993, it will become mandatory to advertise for bids on government contracts in the whole Community, even for those areas which were previously exempt, for example, power and water utilities, transportation and telecommunications. It is suggested that public services should also be included. Public or semi-public contracts exceeding a certain value will have to be advertised in the whole Community. As with the restriction of government subsidies, this will possibly lead to a new surge in privatization of publicly-owned enterprises. Community-wide advertising of contracts will make it very difficult to follow egoistic, national goals. The Commission will keep a close eye on advertising to ensure that these laws are upheld. The laws improve the right of companies to a fair hearing and their ability to sue for damages. The improvements are the only way to ensure that government contracts are awarded according to law.

The mandatory opening of markets will completely change the situation for many companies which are very dependent upon government contracts. They will no longer receive a predetermined contract volume from 'their' government or municipal administrations but will have to compete with companies from all over Europe. They will be forced to look for innovations and lower production costs. As such, the free market will be finally forced upon those companies whose principal customer has been the government. On the other hand, it will no longer be possible to conduct politics by making the awarding of large contracts dependent upon conformity or using large contracts for regional job policies. This will have a profound impact upon the relationship between industry and government administrations.

EUROPEAN LAWS WILL ALSO BE REFORMED

Advertising for bids on government contracts in the whole European Community is also an important part of the single market. Businesses are beginning to adapt to these changes by forming multinational cooperations and creating branches in foreign countries. An increasing number of European companies no longer have a certain nationality but are, in the best sense of the word, multinational. Good examples are the American multinational companies in Europe, such as IBM, Ford, General Motors and Exxon. Several Swiss and Scandinavian companies are also developing an international character. These companies all own production facilities in several countries, including the European Community, and none of these facilities rules over the others. The employees are international from the top to the bottom level. Enterprises of this type, with Europe-wide networks of subsidiaries, research, development and sales facilities are increasing. Although national locations will not lose their importance, new types of European cooperation are developing for which the legal framework must be created.

Company law has not kept up with the Europeanization of companies. In cases of multinational mergers or subsidiaries, at least one partner is forced to conduct business under foreign company laws. This can also lead to tax disadvantages. Several European cooperations were never completed because the partners could not agree upon a common legal structure or on the location of the joint venture's headquarters. Companies wanting to do business throughout Europe should no longer be limited by national

50 / *Meeting the Global Challenge*

legal structures which result in uncoordinated taxation. A first step was taken in 1989 with the introduction of a European economic interest association. This has given bidder communities and non-commercial organizations a legal European status of their own. It is a beginning. The real breakthrough will come with the introduction of the independent legal structure: the European limited company, or Europe Ltd. This will supplement, and not replace, legal structures in national company laws. Europe Ltd, is only a suggestion. The future will decide whether this suggestion is accepted or not.

IS CO-DETERMINATION THE PROBLEM?

The goal is to enable companies from various member countries to merge or conduct joint ventures according to European law and not be hampered by national laws. I am positive that this simplification would greatly increase the willingness for such multinational cooperations. The ability to choose national or European law would lead to healthy competition between the various legal structures. Europe Ltd, would be forced to compete as well. Consequently, there is really no reason not to permit it.

Co-determination creates a problem for this type of legal structure. For some member countries co-determination is a 'sacred cow' and, for others, a provocation. Even the various trade unions in the European Community have two different minds about co-determination by law. As a result, the Commission did not even suggest unified co-determination. The various member states are able to choose between different models which are roughly equivalent in substance but differ in detail. I, personally, believe that co-determination is a very sound principle, not only for reasons of social policy but also of industrial policy. However, national characteristics must be taken into account and, therefore, the proposition is a sensible compromise.

My positive opinion of co-determination may come as a surprise to those who do not believe that co-determination and liberalism fit together. I am of the opinion, however, that only an economy which is based on a social understanding has the flexibility and adaptability necessary to survive the ever faster changes in economic structure. Communication, the subject of this book, must start in one's own company. The employees must be convinced of their own products, products which are going to be sold. Creativity cannot be compelled and, for this reason, I do not consider co-determination to be the competitive disadvantage it is occasionally said to be. I do not know of a single case where a large company left Germany because of co-determination.

SOCIAL DUMPING IS NOT A GOOD INDUSTRIAL POLICY

Occasional conflicts may be quite fertile and stimulating, but a successful economy needs a stable social basis, a basis which can only be created by the government, industry and its employees. There is a social side of the single market which must guarantee that basic social rights are given in the whole Community and which must prevent social dumping. High wages, ambitious environmental goals, or high-level social security are not competitive disadvantages, they are social goals which must be pursued aggressively. People must know what they are working for. Low wages, a polluted environment and social dependency will not inspire them to work. On the other hand, a society can only afford what it earns by competition. The social wealth of a society is primarily a result of its productivity. Therefore, the main goal of industrial policy must be the growth of productivity, thus creating the best conditions for sensible environmental and social policies.

It is not possible to unify social services dependent on productivity in the whole Community. It would remove the only competitive advantage of the poorer countries, their low costs, and financially overtax the more productive countries. The social gap between the individual countries of the Community must be closed by an increased economic growth in the poorer countries and not by an increased social transfer. This also means, however, that the wealthier countries cannot expect their higher social level to become the Community standard. He who wants to earn more but work less must be more productive. Each company will have to live with its own mistakes in the single market and these mistakes will be uncovered much more quickly due to international competition. This is the main reason for the economic dynamics which no member state can escape currently radiating from Europe. Not even the German shop closing law will remain unchanged in the single market. That, however, is not a reason to worry but a ray of hope. It shows that modern politics originate more and more in Brussels.

[22]

THE ECONOMIC IMPLICATIONS OF '1992'

Early in 1988 the Commission published its own estimates of the likely benefits to be accrued as a result of the implementation of the internal market programme. Such research was potentially a crucial aid to its campaign to see the internal market programme through to its completion. Lord Cockfield, then one of the Commission's vice-presidents, with special responsibility for the internal market programme, appointed Paolo Cecchini in 1986 to head a European-wide team of economists to undertake research on the current costs of 'non-Europe' and the probable gains to be made as a result of a single European market. The nature of the research task Cecchini faced was unprecedented: first for the sheer size of its scope, but also because of the novelty of the subject matter and the methodological difficulties that were encountered in making the analysis and calculations based on it.(1) Much of the subsequent publicity given to the result of the Cecchini research neglected the qualifications that were built into it: "Any estimates of the effects of a complex action like completing the internal market", the Cecchini team said, "can only be regarded as very approximate".(2) They were concerned to produce "some rough order of magnitude",(3) but quantitative estimates "are extremely difficult to evaluate at all precisely".(4)

The Cecchini team first identified the barriers which segment the EC market. Tariffs and quantitative restrictions on trade have been mostly eliminated inside the Community, but four categories of obstacles which continue to block free trade were identified:

> (i)   delays at national frontiers for customs purposes and related administrative tasks;

European Internal Market Policy

(ii)   differences in technical regulations between member states;

(iii)   restrictions on competition for public purchases through excluding bids from other Community suppliers;

(iv)   restrictions on freedom to engage in certain service transactions or to become established in certain service activities in other EC countries.

Taken together, Cecchini <u>et al</u>. argued, these restrictions imposed high costs on companies wishing to participate in intra-Community trade, and they were reflected in the substantial differences in consumer prices existing in member states. This categorization of the barriers of 'non-Europe' followed the Commission's own White Paper listing of <u>physical, technical and fiscal</u> obstacles: a three-part division which underscores the rationale of the internal market programme as a whole.

The completion of the internal market is seen as directly lifting certain barriers to trade and as fostering greater competition within the EC market. Four principal types of benefit were identified by the Cecchini study as resulting from a single EC market:

(i)   a significant reduction in costs due to a better exploitation of economies of scale;

(ii)   an improved efficiency, a rationalisation of industrial structures, and a setting of prices closer to costs of production, as a result of more competitive markets;

(iii)   adjustment between industries on the basis of a fuller play of comparative advantages;

(iv)   a flow of innovations, new processes and new products, stimulated by the dynamics of the internal market. (5)

24

European Internal Market Policy

In short, both consumption and investment would increase.

The Cecchini study sought to estimate the benefits of a single market using two distinct methods: a micro-economic and a macro-economic approach. Their micro-economic calculation of 'welfare gains' is summarized in Table 1. It is based on gains accruing from four steps in creating a single market. The estimate of gains is spread around a mid-point of ECU 216 billion, which would represent a benefit of 5.3% to the Community's gross domestic product in 1988. (6) Cecchini argued that further benefits could be expected as a result of market dynamics and technological progress.

The macro-economic analysis sought to place the (micro-economic) 'supply-side shock' of the removal of the barriers referred to above in the wider perspective of the overall effects on the main indicators of the EC's economy: GDP, inflation, employment, public budgets, and the external position. The analysis uses two main models - one from the EC and the other from the OECD - to simulate the main macro-economic mechanisms. The study bases its estimate of the macro-economic effects on an analysis of four major aspects:

    (i)   the removal of border controls (customs barriers);

    (ii)   the opening up of public procurement markets;

    (iii)   the liberalisation of financial services;

    (iv)   business strategies reacting to market integration and tougher competition (the supply-side effects).

The result of these calculations are summarised in Table 2. On average, the removal of the barriers and restrictions, is estimated to add 4.5% to Community GDP, to lower consumer prices by 6.1%, and to create 1.8 million jobs. These gains would accrue in a situation where macro-economic policy remained unchanged. They

25

Table 1 Potential gains in economic welfare for the EC resulting from completion of the internal market: Cecchini Report

	Billions ECU	% of GDP
Step 1 Gains from removal of barriers affecting trade (e.g. customs formalities)	8-9	0.2-0.3
Step 2 Gains from removal of barriers which hinder market-entry and which affect overall production (e.g. protective public procurement, standards, restrictions on services)	57-71	2.0-2.4
Gains from removing barriers (sub-total)	65-80	2.2-2.7
Step 3 Gains from exploiting economies of scale more fully	61	2.1
Step 4 Gains from intensified competition reducing business inefficiencies and monopoly profits (e.g. reduction of over-manning, admin. costs)	46	1.6

Continued overleaf

Table 1 (continued)

	Billions ECU	% of GDP
Gains from market integration	62*-107	2.1*-3.7
Total		
– for 7 Member States at 1985 prices	127-187	4.3-6.4
– for 12 Member States at 1988 prices	174-258	4.3-6.4
– mid-point of above	216	5.3

*   The alternative estimate of the sum of step 3 and 4 cannot be broken down between the two steps.

Source: Commission of EC, study of Directorate-General for Economic and Financial Affairs, published in P.Cecchini *et al*., op.cit.   The table here has been adapted to give more clarity

Notes:
The ranges for certain lines represent the result of using alternative sources of information and methodologies.   The seven Member States (Germany, France, Italy, United Kingdom, Benelux) account for 88% of the GDP of the EC twelve.   Extrapolation of the results in terms of the same share of GDP for the seven and twelve Member States is not likely to over-estimate the total for the twelve.   The detailed figures in the table relate only to the seven Member States because the underlying studies mainly covered those countries.

Table 2 Macroeconomic consequences of EC market integration for the Community in the medium term: Cecchini Report

	Customs formal- ities	Public procure- ment	Finan- cial services	Supply side effects (1)	Average value	Total spread
Relative changes(%)						
GDP	0.4	0.5	1.5	2.1	4.5	(3.2-5.7)
Consumer prices	-1.0	-1.4	-1.4	-2.3	-6.1	(-4.5--7.7)
Absolute changes						
Employment (millions)	200	350	400	850	1800	(1300-2300)
Budgetary balance (% point of GDP)	0.2	0.3	1.1	0.6	2.2	(1.5-3.0)
External balance (% point of GDP)	0.2	0.1	0.3	0.4	1.0	(0.7-1.3)

Source: HERMES (EC Commission and national teams) and INTERLINK (OECD) economic models, published in P.Cecchini *et al*., op.cit.

Note:
Based on a scenario which includes the supply-side effect estimated by the consultants, economies of scale in manufacturing industry and competition effects (monopoly rent, inefficiency).

Table 3   Macro-economic consequences of EC market integration accompanied by economic policy measures (medium-term): Cecchini Report

Name of economic policy	Margin for manoeuvre exploited	Economic consequences				
		GDP (in %)	Consumer prices (in %)	Employ-ment (in millions)	Public budget balance (in % point GDP)	External balance (in % point GDP)
Without ac-companying measures (see Table 2)		4.5	−6.1	1.8	2.2	1.0
With ac-companying measures (1)						
- Public budget balance		7.5	−4.3	5.7	0	−0.5
- External balance		6.5	−4.9	4.4	0.7	0

Name of economic policy	Margin for manoeuvre exploited	Economic consequences				
		GDP (in%)	Consumer prices (in %)	Employment (in millions)	Public budget balance (in % point GDP)	External balance (in GDP% point)
- Price reductions(2)		7.0	-4.5	5.0	0.4	-0.2

Margin of accuracy	+/-30%

Source: HERMES (EC Commission and national teams) and INTERLINK (OECD) economic models, published in P.Cecchini et al., op.cit.

Notes:
1. Accompanying economic policy measures (increased public investment, income tax reductions) are calibrated so that all the room for manoeuvre created by market integration for alternatively public balances, external balances and price reductions is fully used.

2. In this case, accompanying economic policy was calibrated so as to use 25% of the deflationary reservoir created by consumer price reductions. Full use of the margin for manoeuvre created by price reductions could have led to a totally unrealistic outcome (including, in particular, massive deterioration in the EC's external position).

European Internal Market Policy

"thus represent the raw, unaccompanied benefits to the
Community economy of EC market integration".(7)
   Beyond these raw benefits the Cecchini team estimated
the gains that would result if EC governments pursued
well co-ordinated, growth-oriented macro-economic
policies. The easing of the major economic constraints
- inflation, unemployment, public and trade deficits -
open up, they argued, a further potential for growth in
the medium and longer term. For example, even if a
member government sought to use the benefit to the
public deficit to balance its budget, even such a
stringent policy would offer greater room in the longer
run for consideration of more expansionist policy
options. In other words "the positive impact of market
integration on public finances (estimated at 2.2% of
GDP) will play a key role in whatever economic policy is
chosen".(8) The main effects of three distinct policy
scenarios are indicated in Table 3; each of them, to a
greater or lesser extent, uses the budgetary surplus
generated by the internal market programme. The first
scenario involves the full conversion of the budgetary
gain into economic growth; it achieves maximum benefits
in GDP growth and in jobs, but has a parallel worsening
of the external trade balance. The second scenario is
more cautious; it uses only part of the budgetary gains,
has no effect in the external balance, but still
produces growth (6.5%) and jobs (4.4m). The Cecchini
team regards the third scenario as the most plausible;
it is a mid-way economic policy response, partially
exploiting the benefits of price deflation and budgetary
gains, though it involves a slight deterioration in the
external balance. The gains under this third scenario
are impressive: a medium term increase in GDP of 7%, the
creation of 5 million new jobs, and still a significant
budgetary gain for governments to alleviate their
concerns as to financial orthodoxy.
   The optimism underlying such forecasts is qualified,
as has already been noted, by the fact that the authors
themselves regard them as only "very approximate"
estimates. Some of the gains will have a short-term
impact (e.g. removing border controls) whilst others
will be felt in the longer term (e.g. industrial

31

European Internal Market Policy

restructuring and innovation). Similarly, whilst the medium-term forecast is for significant gains in employment, there are risks of short-term losses. The Cecchini team recognises that their forecasts of economic gains are to be regarded as having a margin of accuracy of +/-30% (see Table 3). This is a salutory warning to those who debate the advantages and disadvantages of the single market. The team did find some reassurance, though, in the fact that their micro and macro-economic estimates "converge on broadly similar - and economically very substantial - levels of gain for the European economy."(9)

Whilst the overall economic gains are difficult to forecast, the Cecchini team points out that "this task is relatively manageable compared to that of forecasting (their) distribution by country or region".(10) Indeed, "neither economic theory nor relevant economic history can point to any clear cut pattern of likely distributional advantages or disadvantage".(11) The Cecchini study thus made no attempt to measure the impact of the single market programme on particular countries or regions. A complicating factor here is the impact of future EC policies to maintain "economic and social cohesion" and of the recently increased EC structural funds.

After the optimism, even euphoria, of these forecasts, it was inevitable that they would be subjected to wider economic scrutiny and that some would prove more doubtful and sceptical. A detailed discussion is beyond the scope of this volume, but the range of interpretations and opinions can be indicated.

A study by Jacques Pelkmans and Alan Winters, published in 1988, avoided giving estimates of the costs and gains involved in the internal market programme, but it did clarify the economic options available. The complete fulfillment of a unified market was "a very optimistic scenario": the Community might end up with something much less grand.(12) The authors regret the absence of any provision for monetary union in the Single European Act - a neglect which would probably not be tenable in the long-run - and they question the durability of an internal market with "such minuscule

32

European Internal Market Policy

central expenditures" when the EC's revenues are
expected to involve only about 1.5% of the overall tax
revenue of member-states by 1993.(13)   Three stylized
scenarios are outlined as variants of '1992': the first
involving full market integration (though not for
labour), with complementary policies (e.g. vigorous
competition policy, low external protection, and
acceptance of the policies on 'cohesion'), removing
virtually all distortions of competition, would produce
the greatest economic gains.   The second scenario based
on the removal of barriers to free movement of goods,
capital and perhaps labour, but with distortions
remaining, (especially for services) would produce
important, though fewer, economic benefits.   The
pressures generated by the second scenario might
ultimately result in something like scenario 1.   The
third scenario is the one that the authors argue ought
to be avoided: 1992 à la carte.   This results from
clear failures to agree on some crucial issues (e.g.
fiscal harmonization, public procurement, financial
services, exchange controls and trade policy).   Here
much rhetoric would produce unimpressive economic gains
and would have an uncertain impact on markets.
   A report produced by the British UBS-Phillips & Drew
research group accepted that the bulk of the '1992'
proposals will be implemented.(14)   Given the enormity
of the task, "some modest slippage hardly matters".   The
report believed the Commission and the Cecchini team
have been overly optimistic: the Commission's forecasts
were "at the top end of expectations".   Instead,
"Additional GDP growth over the medium term of 2-4% and
a reduction in the level of consumer prices by some 2-4%
will probably be closer to the mark".   This would barely
be enough to return to the growth rates of the 1970s,
although it would involve much lower inflation and
somewhat higher employment than the early 1980s.   In
short "the goal of moving Europe into a higher growth
path is certainly possible and the reduction of market
barriers is a start".
   The Henley Centre for Forecasting (UK) produced a
report in 1988 which sought to qualify some of the
points raised by the Commission in relation to the

33

European Internal Market Policy

internal market.(15)   The gains from '1992' were not
seen as inevitable, they would not be 'one-off' but
spread over time, nor would they necessarily come to EC
firms rather than non-EC firms.   Moreover, the wider
world economic environment (e.g. the value of the
dollar) will be as crucial as '1992' to the
competitiveness of the EC market.   In addition, as
others have noted, EC firms are vulnerable in the high-
growth, high-technology industries.   The report
considered that the '1992' programme could have one of
two possible outcomes: either it would lead to the
removal of frontier controls without the approximation
of indirect taxes or a core group of member states (the
original six in the EEC) would both abolish the controls
and harmonize indirect taxes, to the disadvantage of
those left excluded.   The differentiation of these two
scenarios may well be over-taken by events, however, and
in any case it is not yet clear which countries might
constitute an inner group.   Such analyses helped to
clarify the issues at stake and to promote a wider,
independent examination of some of the Commission's
assumptions.

A more sceptical analysis was published by the London
Business School early in 1989.(16)   The authors argued
that the benefits of '1992' had been greatly exaggerated
and in some respects trends were likely to be quite
different from those predicted.   "The fragmentation that
remains within the EC is only to a very limited extent
the result of trade barriers of a kind which it is
within the power of the European Commission to remove",
the report said.   The diversity of demand across the EC
"is mainly because of differences in preferences,
habits, language, culture, climate and incomes which
will be wholly unaffected by 1992".   Moreover, the
authors argued that the cost savings from the removal of
frontier controls and deregulation of transport are
likely to be too small to stimulate changes in the
production structure of most industries.   Indeed, the
economies of scale already available in the EC were
adequate in most industries and little extra benefit
could be expected from a more integrated market.

Further scepticism has been expressed by labour

34

European Internal Market Policy

representatives concerned about changes to the distribution of industry and employment. Increasing specialization of economic activity it is feared might lead to skill shortages in certain regions, but increasing unemployment and industrial decline in others. A British economist, Henry Neuberger, has claimed that the UK would be particularly adversely affected: losing £2,200m of industrial output a year and a total of 135,000 jobs.(17) Britain, France and Belgium (if not other countries) also faced the challenge of the completion of the Channel Tunnel, establishing a physical link between Kent and northern France. Socialist parties and trade unions have argued that the priority is for the EC to develop an industrial policy and to ensure that aid to industry helps to secure Europe's employment base. The appeal is thus for intervention, not just de-regulation, and for much more than "miniscule" central expenditure rather than a merely liberalised market place.

A wide-ranging debate on the internal effects of establishing a single European market is thus beginning to emerge. It is striking, however, that so much of the early public debate has been dominated by the data and estimates produced by the study sponsored by the EC Commission itself. For a policy programme which has the potential of changing the economic face of Europe, this neglect is surprising, if not worrying. Moreover, the estimates produced by the Cecchini team are acknowledged by their authors to be somewhat speculative and imprecise. The level of uncertainty is increased by the doubts as to how fully the internal market will be integrated: differential progress in policy implementation between sectors is likely, making forecasts yet more hazardous. It is unclear, for example, as to how far a 'European financial area' will be established: the British Government, for one, opposes harmonization of indirect taxes (VAT) and European control over monetary and fiscal policy. Yet some doubt the durability of an internal market without such responsibility being given to the centre. More generally, uncertainty is reinforced by the continuing and unresolved debate as to the degree of intervention

35

European Internal Market Policy

that should be permitted in the economy: the extent to which the dismantling of national regulatory controls should be replaced by new ones at the EC level, and how EC expenditure and policy should be adapted to meet the agreed objectives of 'economic and social cohesion'.

The macro-economic implications for the EC economy as a whole remain unclear; further research is needed before idealism and reality can be fully separated. The Community has, indeed, embarked on a 'journey to an unknown destination'.(18) For the individual company, however, it is already apparent that many in the market are currently planning on the assumption that '1992' will become a reality. A momentum has been created and it would be dangerous for an individual firm to seek to ignore it. The impact of '1992' will, of course, vary from one economic sector to another and expectations as to which sectors will experience the biggest impacts are discussed below.

Notes

(1)   P. Cecchini et al., The European Challenge 1992: The Benefits of a Single Market (Aldershot UK, Wildwood House, 1988), p.xviii.

(2)   "The Economics of 1992: an assessment of the potential economic effects of completing the internal market of the European Community", European Economy, 35, March 1988 (EC publications), p.18.

(3)   Op. cit. p.18.

(4)   Op. cit. p.19.

(5)   European Economy, op. cit. p.17.

(6)   At an average exchange rate for 1987 of 1.15, this converts as approximately $248 billion.

(7)   P. Cecchini et al., op. cit. p.99.

European Internal Market Policy

(8)   P. Cecchini *et al*., op. cit. p.99.

(9)   P. Cecchini *et al*., op. cit. p.71.

(10)   *European Economy*, op. cit. p.21.

(11)   Op. cit. p.21.

(12)   J. Pelkmans & A. Winters, *Europe's Domestic Market* (London, Royal Institute of International Affairs/Routledge, 1988), p.84.

(13)   Op. cit. p.85-6.

(14)   UBS-Phillips & Drew, "*Europe 1992: Breaking Down the Barriers: Economic and Sector Prospects*", London, June 1988.

(15)   Details available from The Henley Centre for Forecasting Ltd, Henley, UK.

(16)   The Centre for Business Strategy, London Business School, February 1989.

(17)   Report produced in January 1989 for the British Labour Group in the European Parliament.

(18)   Phrase used by A. Schonfield, *Europe: Journey to an Unknown Destination* (Penguin, Harmondsworth/ Middlesex, 1973).

37

[23]

The Road to Monetary Union

The Maastricht treaty on Economic and Monetary Union is the result of a long period of evolution. There has been very rapid progress on European integration since 1984, and the negotiations stimulated by the Delors Committee of 1989 have been complex. They have culminated in the intergovernmental conferences during 1991. However, the fundamental features of the agreement stem from ideals derived from the very earliest days of the conception of the Community after the war. To understand the Treaty, therefore, we have to go back to its postwar origins.

The postwar international economic order

The postwar economic order was dominated by the United States. The widespread destruction of the economic system in continental Europe led to heavy dependence on US funds for reconstruction. There was also widespread reliance on the US for the building up of a new security system, particularly as the polarisation between east and west became clear. The system developed readily as the US was prepared to play that role of leadership and to help generate the stability of the international financial system, with the Bretton Woods system of fixed but adjustable exchange rates.

The Organisation for European Economic Cooperation was set up in 1948 to help the recovery and, within its auspices, the European Payments Union followed in 1950, to try to alleviate the problems of the dollar shortage and, through the Bank for International Settlements, organise a system of international payments among the European countries. The use of funds for reconstruction on top of this produced a viable system even if it did not go as far as Keynes and some of its original architects envisaged, with the development of an international currency.

2   *Achieving Monetary Union in Europe*

The Bretton Woods system was not very open at its inception. Because of the dominance of domestic over international transactions after the disruption of the war and the existence of substantial controls on trade and payments, countries could exercise a measure of independence in their monetary policies in a way not true today. They were often able to sterilise their domestic currencies from the impact of fluctuations in international payments. The common link in the system came through the US dollar, to which each currency was pegged within narrow bands. The dollar in turn had a fixed parity with gold. The controls on capital flows gave the countries the scope to manage their exchange rates, provided they kept sufficient reserves to withstand short-run shocks.

For over twenty years that system dominated international transactions in Europe. It proved to be remarkably stable. There was the major realignment associated with the UK's devaluation in 1949, and two French realignments in the 1950s, but in general countries adhered to their narrow bands of fluctuations around the agreed central rates. This adherence meant that some countries, notably the UK, encountered a series of balance of payments problems, whenever they attempted to expand too rapidly.

The system therefore came under pressure, on the one hand from countries seeking a more flexible route to adjustment to external shocks, and on the other from the pressures on the United States, particularly from the Vietnam war, which meant that it found it increasingly difficult to act as the anchor for the whole system. Weaker currencies like sterling were seeking some means of trying to avoid the need to make major step devaluations, with their inflationary and other destabilising effects, while the stronger currencies sought something better than dependence on the US dollar.

One facet of the evolution of European monetary union is thus the response to the breakdown of that system at the end of the 1960s. This strand of evolution was based very much on the international financial system and concerned with the development of a stable system of foreign exchange to replace the fixed peg on the US dollar. It was a reflection of the success of the recovery of the European economies, particularly that of West Germany, and the emergence of a viable counterweight to the US, which had previously dominated both trade and payments. In 1950 US GNP per head was nearly four times that of the future EEC(6), whereas by 1969 it was only twice as large. Meanwhile the EC's share of OECD exports reached 40 per cent by 1969, double that of the US, which declined to 20 per cent.

In a sense it was the very success of the system in assisting the post war recovery which imposed the strains on it. As countries recovered and grew they developed their international trade to enter wider markets and continue to expand. This involved a reduction in the barriers between them, both through a series of multilateral reductions in tariffs and easing of quantitative restrictions under the auspices of the GATT (General

The Road to Monetary Union

Agreement on Tariffs and Trade) and through other bilateral or region
agreements, including EFTA, the EEC, Commonwealth Preference and th
Benelux union. Reductions in the barriers to trade both reduced countries
abilities to control their international payments and exposed them more
widely to shocks from outside. In general it was the smaller among the
industrialised countries which experienced this most obviously. (Although
it was developing countries which experienced the greatest fluctuations,
through variations in commodity prices, exposing them rather more harshly
as they also gained independence from the various European empires.)

Integration in Europe

A second theme leading towards monetary union was based more firmly
on the development of Europe itself. As the West European countries
emerged from the postwar chaos so the discussion of the future face of
Europe also developed. Much of that discussion involved a tighter
relationship between the countries in some sort of union. This was not just
a matter of economic concern but of much wider political interests, leading
to the formation of the European Coal and Steel Community in 1951 and
the European Economic Community in 1958, between Belgium, France,
Italy, Luxembourg, the Netherlands and West Germany. Attempts to form
a political community among these six countries failed in 1952 and the
European Defence Community foundered on French opposition in 1954.

Although questions of monetary union were on the ultimate agenda even
from the beginning they were clearly not a matter for immediate decision
and therefore did not attract more than vague consideration, the major aim
in this regard being freedom of movement of capital. The emphasis was
more on 'economic union' in the formation of the EEC, involving
cooperation and coordination among member states. Discussion of
international currency systems remained largely in the domain of
academics and a few visionaries.

Although there are substantial arguments about the ordering or
sequencing, to use a more fashionable word, of the steps in the process of
voluntary economic integration among countries, monetary union did not
come high on the list. Indeed the debate is still alive, as the Bundesbank
has been arguing recently that EMU will not work properly without closer
political union. However, it is also argued by others that monetary union
may not merely be one of the appropriate early steps but can be a major
unifying force, other aspects of economic, political and social integration
coming later on. One of the reasons for making it such an early step is the
ease of its achievement through the banking system and its importance in
the control of the economy. It is no coincidence that monetary union
came right at the beginning of German unification in 1989, a point we come
back to in subsequent chapters. However, for monetary union to adopt

4   *Achieving Monetary Union in Europe*

a leading role in integration, suitable mechanisms must exist for the automatic transfer of funds from surplus to deficit regions, which requires an open internal economy and considerable fiscal as well as monetary integration. This did not characterise the European economy of the early 1950s.

The main distinguishing feature of European integration since the war has been its voluntary nature, with countries perceiving it to be in their political and economic interests to be more closely related rather than having that requirement thrust upon them. Such processes have tended to be rather more limited in the past except as a response to a common external threat and hence there has been no obvious blueprint to follow and no neat definitions and preconceptions of what various concepts like common markets, economic, monetary and political unions might actually involve. (See Pelkmans, 1984, and El Agraa, 1985, for a discussion of these definitions.)

The European Economic Community always had high ambitions and a widely made mistake in the early economic literature was to describe it simply as a customs union, differentiating it from EFTA (the European Free Trade Association) as an organisation dedicated to the removal of tariffs on mutual trade in manufactured goods, only by virtue of the fact that it had a common external tariff, rather than allowing each member state to maintain its own tariffs on imports from third countries (Aitken, 1973, for example). Even in purely economic terms it was always envisaged that a much wider range of barriers to trade would be eliminated to establish a Common Market in which goods and services could flow freely throughout the Community. What was not clear was how that might be achieved, given the differences in tax regimes, technical rules and standards, to say nothing of the indirect restraints on trade and measures of domestic policy that favoured national producers through subsidies and other preferential agreements.

No clear distinction was made between what Kay and Posner (1989) have described as the Bismarckian and Jeffersonian routes to integration. The Jeffersonian route, based largely on the interstate arrangements in the US, is essentially liberalising in character, permitting the free movement of items approved by the local rules in their place of production or destination, with a minimum of new universal rules to govern commerce. The Bismarckian route on the other hand aims to produce a common market by agreeing common rules, that apply in all member states. This latter approach involves far more positive steps to achieve integration and is essentially a process of harmonisation. Furthermore, unlike EFTA, the EC has, with the Court, the Commission, the Parliament and the European Investment Bank, had more than the minimum of central institutions to manage a trading system.

Although the early Community was dominated in budgetary terms by the Common Agricultural Policy, which still accounts for over half the

Community's spending, there were further Community competences in social policy, regional policy, industrial policy and competition policy among others aimed at completing some form of common market. These were seen as part of the progress to the 'ever closer union', whose form was not spelt out but would involve closer economic, political and monetary union as well as some element of redistribution to assist the development of the less advantaged parts of the Community. Right from the outset, the EEC established a Monetary Committee under Article 105 to 'review the monetary and financial situation in member states and the Community as a whole and to review the system of currency payments in the Community', opening the way to greater monetary cooperation and integration.

The nature of such a union among the member states was widely interpreted, from a United States of Europe, exhibiting a federal structure with states with rather greater powers than those in the United States of America, to a union of independent states, a Europe of Nations in the phraseology of de Gaulle, where the central institutions would have relatively limited powers and the existing nation states would remain as the principal entities. (It has been very obvious during the last couple of years that, although this debate has evolved considerably, the distinction of views still exists, with the UK holding a position more towards the Europe of Nations concept than do the other member states, for whom some sort of 'federal' structure could be acceptable.) In practice, even after the intergovernmental conference on 'political union', culminating in the Maastricht agreement, the nature of any longer-run political arrangement among the member states is far more tenuously described than that of economic and monetary union. Indeed it is the monetary union proposals which are the most highly developed. Here the institutions are set out, the form of timetable laid down and the competences established, as described in Chapter 2. Economic union on the other hand is still part of an evolving process, where legislative changes are being put in place but their consequences are far from clear (see, for example, Shipman and Mayes, 1990, and the wider ESRC research initiative, The Evolution of Rules for a Single European Market, NIESR, 1992).

The process of reducing tariffs and eliminating trade restrictions proceeded very much to timetable in the early years of the Community's existence, as it involved removing restrictions rather than coming to common agreements on new harmonised systems. Indeed the last tariffs were removed in 1968, some eighteen months ahead of schedule. (EFTA, which was formed later, in 1960, and set a faster timetable for tariff removal, also found that it could implement these changes more rapidly.) Progress in establishing the CAP was also steady, coming into force in 1962. The way forward in other areas proved rather more elusive as all the member states had to agree on the detail of harmonised systems. There were considerable disagreements of some issues and even a period when France did not participate fully, leaving 'an empty chair' at meetings.

6   *Achieving Monetary Union in Europe*

This last controversy, ended by the 'Luxembourg compromise' of 1966, which established the rule of unanimity in the Council, was generated largely by the establishment of the concept of 'own resources', whereby the Community got its own funds to administer the CAP through the levies on imports from non-member states, a milestone in the process of fiscal integration.

The Commission put forward proposals in 1962 to move towards monetary union by 1971 in three stages; it is interesting to note that the idea of a three stage approach stretches back 30 years. Initially this was to involve greater consultation and cooperation over financial, economic and monetary policies among finance ministers and central bank governors. Although the proposals were not adopted, the Committee of Governors of Central Banks of the EEC was set up in 1964, along with a Budgetary Committee and a Medium-Term Economic Policy Committee.

As early as the late 1960s it was clear that further measures would have to be taken if progress towards closer union was to be advanced significantly. This, therefore, provided the second thread of an internal, European-derived, set of pressures towards closer economic and monetary union, which was occurring while the international framework was also under strain. Taken together this increased the chance that the European countries would produce 'European' solutions to the international difficulties. The balance of economic power in international trade and payments had moved strongly towards them in the previous two decades and they wished to advance joint action for its own sake. Had the EC moved forward earlier with its own ideas for European monetary cooperation and the Bretton Woods system survived longer we might have seen a very different path for European monetary history and quite possibly the international system as a whole.

The precursor to Maastricht in the 1970s

The main decisions of principle, to move towards economic and monetary union, were taken in 1969. The 'Barre Report' from the Commission set out the need for greater coordination of economic and monetary policies and the establishment of short-term and medium-term monetary support facilities. After discussions in Council, the summit of heads of state in The Hague at the end of the year called for the establishment of EMU, by three stages, based on the Barre proposals.

This pressure resulted in the Werner Report of 1970, which set out what the objectives of closer union were in much more exact terms as an economic and monetary union 'in which goods and services, people and capital will circulate freely and without competitive distortions, without thereby giving rise to structural or regional disequilibrium' (Pierre Werner was Prime Minister of Luxembourg). It would further imply 'the total and irreversible convertibility of currencies, the elimination of margins of fluctuation in exchange rates, the irrevocable fixing of parity rates'. While the Werner Committee was still meeting, the Governors of the EEC Central Banks agreed to set up a short-term monetary support mechanism and the system of own resources was extended to cover agricultural import levies and payments from VAT in the member states, up to 1 per cent of a standardised base. (The medium-term financial assistance facilities were not agreed until March of 1971.)

The immediate similarities between the Werner proposals and those which have been agreed at Maastricht are further emphasised when we recall that central controls would also be required: 'creation of liquidity ... and monetary and credit policy would be centralised; monetary policy in relation to the outside world will be within the jurisdiction of the Community; and policies as regards capital markets would have to be unified'.

The report was not clear whether there would be an actual single currency or merely a de facto one from the locked exchange rates. However, it did recommend that central banking be organised on a basis similar to that of the Federal Reserve System in the US. Fiscal policy coordination was required and a new economic policymaking body was to be set up which would be responsible to the European Parliament. The coordination was intended to increase progressively. In the first or second stages of the process a European Fund for Monetary Cooperation was to be set up, to be integrated in the final Stage 3 into the central banking system. A series of indicators was to be used of the effectiveness of the coordination of monetary and fiscal policies, particularly to highlight any potentially dangerous departures from what was expected.

Thus, with only small exceptions, the Werner proposals are very much the precursor of Maastricht. Since the differences are so small it is of paramount importance to explain why it is that the new attempt to attain economic and monetary union should succeed where the plans of 21 years ago failed.

The Bretton Woods system finally collapsed in early 1971 at the same time that the Werner proposals were being adopted. This involved the ending of fixed parities, the floating of the major currencies against the dollar and the ending of convertibility of the dollar for gold at a fixed rate. In December 1971, at what is known as the Smithsonian agreement, the ten largest trading countries agreed to try to hold their currencies around new parities but within wider 4 per cent bands.

The first step by the Community in response was to try to stabilise EC exchange rates rather more closely by having only 2 per cent bands with respect to each other within the wider bands with respect to the dollar. This arrangement was described as the 'snake' as the EC exchange rates would move together in a band relative to the dollar (within the 'tunnel' of the agreed dollar fluctuations - however it did not prove possible to

8   *Achieving Monetary Union in Europe*

constrain the dollar exchange rate as planned and by 1973 the currencies were effectively floating and the idea of the tunnel was abandoned).

The European Monetary Cooperation Fund was set up in 1973 and in 1974 requirements were agreed to set annual guidelines for policies in the member states, consistent with increasing convergence, and member states were to put in place means of altering spending, tax and debt arrangements to respond to these guidelines.

In practice these arrangements were overtaken almost immediately by the pressures of the first oil crisis and the differential impact and responses of member states to it. The Werner plan therefore really did not get as good an opportunity to succeed as it might. However, it is also argued by Baer and Padoa-Schioppa (1988) that the plan was weakly conceived in a number of respects, most of which have now been addressed in the Maastricht agreement. First of all there was no means of compelling member states to follow guidelines towards convergence. Secondly there was no clear allocation of responsibilities among the various institutions for setting and achieving the objectives of policy. There was also an exaggerated view of the ability of the member states to achieve the necessary convergence with the instruments available. Finally they argue that the process lacked dynamism to move through the stages to EMU.

However, what is far more important is the economic development of the last twenty years and the progress of other aspects of European integration over the same period. The Werner Report came at the end of a period of considerable economic success and dynamic stability. Had that stability and growth continued, then the chances of achieving monetary union would have been greatly enhanced because many of the conditions of convergence, which we discuss in the next chapter, already existed and the process of increasing coordination of policy would have had a much shorter road to travel. Exchange rates were already fixed within narrow bands, inflation rates were low, as were unemployment rates outside the South of Italy, debt ratios and public sector deficits were, in general, within the target ranges laid down at Maastricht.

However, as subsequent history has shown, this would have been an unstable equilibrium, which would probably have fallen apart had the shocks from the US or the oil crises hit after monetary union was in place. Furthermore, capital movements were heavily restricted and freeing them up might have released very considerable pressures, making the final transition to irrevocably locked exchange rates impossible. The Europe of 1970 was much less integrated than the Europe of 1992. Trade patterns were more diverse, non-tariff barriers to the free flow of goods, services and labour abounded and fiscal systems and policy responses varied widely. For a monetary union to succeed it requires not just a framework of rules for its administration but the existence of an economic area which responds to shocks in a sufficiently homogeneous manner that the inability to change relative prices in parts of the area through exchange rates is not seen to reduce the relative welfare of those regions significantly. In an integrated area such variations are automatically compensated to a large extent, through the tax and benefit system, through regional policy and through the ability of those worst affected to move to other regions where prospects are better. The EEC of 1970 was a long way from those ideals.

In the remainder of this chapter we show the extent to which these deficiences have been corrected during the ensuing years, first by considering the development of the European Monetary System, second by exploring the process of European integration and finally by examining the changes in the economic environment.

The European Monetary System

As we noted in the last section, the blueprint for the current agreement on monetary union was drawn up twenty years ago. The progressive locking of exchange rates has also been evolving over the same period, first with the snake and second with the European Monetary System, which was put into effect in March 1979. The snake has largely been regarded as a failure, as only the Benelux countries were able remain in the system throughout with West Germany and, although France, Ireland, Italy, Norway, Sweden and the UK had all participated at some stage, only Denmark was also in the system when it ended (table 1). However, it played an important role in developing the processes of cooperation between the European central banks, which are essential in bringing together the currencies in an EMU and highlighted the sorts of problems that occur and have to be dealt with if the system is to survive. Without the experience of the snake, the EMS could readily have fallen apart. Indeed had the EMS been implemented in 1971 instead of 1979 it would probably not have achieved the credibility necessary for survival.

The European Monetary system was set up in 1979 following the decision of the July 1978 European Council in Bremen to set up 'a zone of monetary stability in Europe'. In many respects it was primarily a tightening up of the previous arrangements to prevent mutual exchange rates from fluctuating outside a 2 per cent band round their central parities and an integration of a European currency, the ecu, into the system. Previously, the European Unit of Account (EUA) had been introduced in 1975 as a basket of the member states currencies to provide a common central unit, which was used as the accounting unit for the Community institutions from 1978 onwards. (For details and a good assessment of the EMS see Gros and Thygesen, 1988.) However, the EMS was also seen as a clear step towards economic and monetary union through trying to achieve economic convergence as well as monetary control. (The experience of the 1970s led to a general change in approach to macroeconomic policy, with an emphasis on monetary control primarily

10 *Achieving Monetary Union in Europe*

aimed at the control of inflation and a rejection of traditional 'Keynesian' policies of fiscal expansion to counter high unemployment. Thus an emphasis on joint monetary action had become the prime tool with fiscal cooperation as its necessary adjunct.)

During over a decade of operation the EMS has evolved very considerably and still has further to go. Portugal and Greece are still not members of the exchange rate mechanism (ERM) and Spain and the UK joined only in 1989 and 1990 and operate within a wider 6 per cent band. In the early years there were frequent realignments (see Chapter 7, table 1) seven in the first four years up to March 1983. This period saw a progressive upward realignment of the D-Mark and the Dutch guilder relative to the other currencies, particularly the lira. Since then realignments have been much more infrequent and with the exception of the Italian realignment within its bands and its simultaneous move from a 6 per cent band to the 2 per cent band there has not been a realignment since the beginning of 1987. This therefore has seen a change from something akin to a continuation of the snake to an increasingly fixed exchange rate system.

The EMS system has not evolved quite as envisaged. The idea originally was that the currencies would fluctuate relatively freely inside the intervention limits but that when the limits were reached there would be general intervention by the central banks. In practice, action has been taken earlier and there has been intervention inside the margin, largely undertaken by the banks in the countries approaching the lower edge of the band. The system has become increasingly dominated by the role of the German Bundesbank, whose policy has determined the general strategy of economic policy in the other member states, hindering the ambitions of those for whom growth is more important.

The role of the ecu as a European currency has also evolved rather differently from that which was expected. The official ecu has had rather limited uses. It has been a currency of settlement but not generally one of intervention, as it could not be used for inframarginal intervention, prior to 1985, without a market. As the role of the dollar has declined, that of the D-Mark has increased, not that of the ecu. The private ecu has, on the other hand, blossomed. This ecu, composed of the member currencies in the same weights as the official ecu, has proved useful as a hedge against exchange risk and has offered a good rate of return compared with some other strong currencies. It is the second most important currency in net bond issuance but, despite growing encouragement from the Commission and member states, its growth is slowing, aided ironically by the growing convergence of the EC currencies and their rates of return, which means there is less need to use an intermediate composite currency. This private role was not fully thought out and as a result the system lacked some of the necessary payments systems which would have turned it into a more significant means of introducing a European currency. As it is, those people outside the banking sector receiving ecu instruments in

European transactions of relatively small size have often had difficulty converting them into domestic or other currencies.

Changes have been made in the borrowing facilities as the EMS has developed, extending the roles of both the medium-term financial support (MTFS) and very short term facility (VSTF). The major changes came after the experience in 1986-7, when external changes forced realignments rather than internal disequilibria. These changes are known as the Basle/Nyborg agreements (recommended by the central bank governors meeting in Basle and endorsed by the economics and finance ministers (ECOFIN) at their Nyborg meeting). In practice, these changes, which have recognised the need for intramarginal intervention, seem to have improved the ability of the system to survive external shocks, including almost immediately the October 1987 US stock market crash and its reverberation round the world and a bout of speculative pressure in September 1988. They tried to make the responsibility for intervention more symmetric so that all central banks have a responsibility for maintaining the integrity of the system, not just those whose currencies are under threat at the lower boundary of the range.

The EMS has thus developed into a very stable system for a number of reasons. Its practitioners have improved their techniques and changes in the rules of the system have made it easier to defend parities and to get cooperative action from all the participating central banks, not just from those whose currencies are at risk. At the same time there has been considerable convergence both in policy objectives and in economic performance among the member states which makes the task of defending the rates rather easier. Together these provide many of the ingredients for the possible success of moves towards closer EMU. However, the most important ingredient has been the extensive development of the process of European integration.

Closer European integration

The most obvious changes in the EC during the 1970s and early 1980s were the three expansions which increased the Community from six to twelve countries in three stages, the UK, Denmark and the Irish Republic joining at the beginning of 1973, Greece in 1981 and Portugal and Spain in 1986. These accessions have considerably complicated the path of integration, not least because it has been necessary to get the agreement of twelve parties rather than six. Spain, Portugal, Greece and Ireland had a standard of living considerably below that of the other member states, which extended the process of convergence (an issue we return to in detail in Chapter 5). This meant that the Community needed an expanded approach to regional policy, cemented by the implementation of the European Regional Development Fund (ERDF) in 1975. The accession of

12   *Achieving Monetary Union in Europe*

the UK added a large country, which had a rather different structure and behavioural approach, that has resulted in a number of problems, the most recent of which is manifested in unique requirements for the UK in the Maastricht agreement (as set out in Chapter 2).

Perhaps the most dramatic and certainly rapid expansion of the Community is the most recent one, involving the unification of East and West Germany and the incorporation of the whole in the Community, within a space of just a few months in 1990. The small size of the addition and the dominant role that West Germany is playing in assimilating the new area has meant that, despite extensive derogations, the impact on the rest of the Community has been limited. The change-round in Germany's budgetary and trade positions has placed a strain on interest rates throughout the Community, however, and the change in the pattern of German investment has raised worries in some of the less favoured regions in other member states that the path of their relative improvement will now be more difficult.

The developments in the whole of central and eastern Europe and the potential expansion of the EC within the foreseeable future to a Community of as many as 32 states transforms the prospects for the progress not just to economic, political and monetary union but to the whole scope and nature of the integration process. This is such a large question that we consider it separately in Chapter 6.

Progress on developing the integration of the Community, in terms of implementation of new measures, proved relatively slow in the years after 1968. The relative emphasis on harmonisation meant that agreement proved elusive in many areas and laborious in others. Indeed the major progress was made by Court judgements, particularly that on the Cassis de Dijon case in 1978, which established the principle of mutual recognition, emphasising that local rules could not be used to exclude products produced according to the rules of another member state. This opened the gates to a more comprehensive attack on the non-tariff barriers to trade.

By contrast with the years before, 1985 to date has seen a whirlwind of activity in Community decision-making. This process began with the the decision to tackle the whole network of measures imposed by member states, for a variety of domestic reasons, which in practice inhibit the operation of a single internal market in goods, services, capital and labour. These were set up in a White Paper, published in June 1985, containing nearly 300 areas in which action was required if the physical, fiscal and technical barriers to completing the internal market were to be removed. Furthermore it set a target date for completing the implementation of these measures at the end of 1992.

The White Paper did not increase the scope of the Communities' ambitions, it merely spelt out what was needed to achieve some of the intentions set out in the Treaty of Rome in 1956. Its contribution came in its comprehensiveness and the speed at which it hoped to achieve the change.

Agreement on the measures of economic integration is very much a political process but that process can lead or lag the aspirations of the market. By 1985 the process of legislative integration was lagging the practical integration of the market by firms. The process of internationalisation of production and distribution had become highly developed. European companies were losing market share in traditional areas to Japanese companies and, following a period of relative success in the US, after the consequences of the major budget deficit spilled over into a trade deficit, were losing out to the American response. Fragmentation of the European market, because different rules applied in the various member states for registering products and for the standards to which they had to comply, meant that European companies tended to face a 'home' market that was smaller and higher cost than those of their US and Japanese competitors. Practices of government procurement and industrial support also meant that existing divisions were emphasised rather than being eliminated. Barriers at the frontier slowed the transit of goods and restrictions on transport made deliveries more complex, between them making adoption of Japanese style just-in-time manufacturing methods and other aspects of flexible production more difficult to achieve.

Industry was thus tending to lead the political decision makers and the European Round Table had earlier put forward a plan of its own to achieve a single market in five years (by 1990). There was, therefore, a momentum to achieve what might be described as microeconomic integration in Europe. The removal of tariff and quantitative barriers to trade was only a step in that process. Questions of macroeconomic coordination, monetary control and closer alignment of exchange rates may have helped create conditions which encouraged integration at the level of the firm and of the market players but they did not enable it. The 1992 programme is creating an integration of a far more detailed and pervasive nature, one which converts the interest in monetary union from a largely macroeconomic perspective to one of microeconomic benefit as well. The prospects for monetary union are thus very different for the period after 1992 than they were in 1970 at the time of the Werner Plan or in 1979 when the EMS was established.

The White Paper measures were only part of the process of achieving this dramatic change in the process of integration. The Single European Act, which was signed in February 1986, coming into force in July 1987, not only embodied these aspirations into a new treaty but it established mechanisms which would help break the logjam that had held up the previous piecemeal attempts to advance the process of microeconomic integration. The move towards qualified majority decision-making in most areas related to the single market, rather than unanimity, has vastly increased the pace at which decisions can be taken. Although it may appear that unanimity is often still used in many cases, the practice is that those in the minority extract what concessions they can in the bargaining stage but

14   *Achieving Monetary Union in Europe*

then agree to the final proposal when that process has been exhausted, or at any rate register only symbolic opposition.

The Single European Act goes far further than the narrow economic concerns, increasing the role of the European Parliament and setting objectives and requiring action in the fields of monetary policy, economic and social cohesion, social policy and research and technological development. The process did not stop there, as the Brussels Council in 1988 agreed a package of flanking measures, including further reform of the Common Agricultural Policy and a doubling of the structural funds to provide a substantial increase in the developmental assistance for the least favoured regions of the Community in Greece, Portugal, Ireland, parts of Spain and Southern Italy.

These measures are intended to increase the scope of convergence of the Community from integration of markets to a distribution of the gains throughout the regions. These aims are very clearly set out in Padoa-Schioppa's (1987) book on Efficiency, Stability and Equity. Macroeconomic concerns, particularly through the EMS and associated monetary measures, had focussed very much on trying to establish more stable conditions for growth. The single market measures, on the other hand, were aimed principally at increasing the efficiency of economic organisation within the Community. This left the dimension of equity which, as we suggest in Chapter 5, may be the key to the successful achievement of EMU throughout the Community. Equity is being addressed through the social dimension and through the use of the structural funds. However, budgetary equity, achieved for the UK in the 1980s by the Fontainbleau Agreement, is still to be negotiated and it is clear that many of the interests in the process of integration conflict.

While the structural funds try to ensure that the potential benefits of closer integration are achievable by all parts of the Community, the social dimension is intended to ensure that the benefits to industry are also spread to the personal sector both to people in the workplace and elsewhere - to the employed and the non-employed. To an extent this was embodied in the Social Charter (Community Charter of Basic Social Rights for Workers), published in 1987, and the Social Action programme of some 50 measures that were thought necessary to implement it. This social charter covers free movement of persons throughout the Community, fair treatment of the employed, vocational training, workplace consultation, health, safety and working conditions and the treatment of the disadvantaged.

Some of the motives for agreeing the social dimension have been rather mixed. Some of the countries with more extensive programmes of social provision have feared that there might be some form of 'social dumping', whereby those countries with lesser provision could undercut them by offering lower labour costs to mobile international producers and also that the more dependent sections of their communities would emigrate to take advantage of the better provision. These twin forces would add   to unemployment in the areas of high social provision through successful competition for the location of productive activity and increase the burden on contributors for the support of immigrants. The UK has expressed continuing doubts on the need for some aspects of the social dimension and worries about their adverse effect on competitiveness. As a result the UK did not adopt the Social Charter and, as is explained in the next chapter, has not agreed to the inclusion of the 'social chapter' in the new treaty drawn up at Maastricht.

The intention and the result of these various programmes is not of course the same thing. Although the single market measures will go a long way to reducing barriers, they will go nowhere near creating single markets in the sense that they exist in the United States, Japan and Australia. Barriers of language, custom and local preferences will take generations to break down and many may never be eliminated (nor indeed is it necessarily in the economic, let alone social or political, interests of the Community to do so). Pressures for local autonomy and the importance of 'subsidiarity' (allocation of responsibility for executing EC policy to the member states, rather than Community institutions, where this is efficient and avoids substantial spillover effects) indicate that the underlying diversity of the Community is something that it will wish to retain. In practice there has been very little migration, although the member states are very sensitive to it, and the degree of relocation in the lower labour cost regions has been rather limited, with rationalisation tending to occur among the regions of industrial strength in the more central parts of the Community. Consequently, the less advantaged appear to be facing a more severe burden of adjustment.

The European market will continue to be driven by the forces of international competition rather than its own concerns, as the market is being opened up to establishment by firms from any country not just from the member states. The fears that the single market might create some form of 'Fortress Europe', whereby external barriers to trade were made more effective and a concerted programme of European industrial support was developed, as envisaged by some members of the Round Table of Industrialists, have largely been allayed (although the strong anti-dumping policy helps maintain some of the fears). Much of the significance of the single market comes from the fact that it extends international competition from the traditional area of manufactured goods to the whole of the private sector (and some public services). By freeing up the movement of capital all firms have the potential to benefit from this and invest where they think the conditions are best. The effects of this expansion of opportunity have been seen most obviously in the field of financial services as creating the free movement of capital, which as a necessary precursor for monetary union involves Community-wide access to international financial services.

Agriculture has not been an explicit part of the process of integration of

16   *Achieving Monetary Union in Europe*

the Community in recent years but, in practice, it is playing a crucial role. The success or failure of the Uruguay Round is going to have a major impact on the conduct of international trade policy over the coming years. At present the negotiating parties have managed to manipulate the discussions so that overall success appears to   hinge   on the making of further concessions on agriculture by the EC.   The   United States is seeing the upsurge of protectionist feeling that accompanies a presidential re-election period (Woolcock, 1990).   A more acrimonious approach to commercial policy could easily destabilise the exchange rate system and set back the progress to EMU for reasons other than the success of the internal integration of the Community.   Establishing a more equitable budgetary balance within the Community itself also involves a downgrading of agricultural price support relative   to   other programmes designed to improve cohesion in a period where budgetary expansion is unlikely to be popular.

In 1988 the pressure for continuing integration moved on with the directive requiring full liberalisation of capital movements by July, 1990, being agreed in June (with some derogations) and the 'Delors Committee' of central bank governors and two experts, chaired by the President of the Commission, to study and propose concrete steps to   the achievement of EMU by stages, being set up in the same month by the Hannover Council. This and the subsequent progress to the intergovernmental conferences on economic, political and monetary   union we consider explicitly in the next chapter.

The economic transformation of the Community

The European Community of 1968 showed very considerable 'convergence' in a number of macroeconomic respects, exchange rates, inflation, debt ratios, external and internal balance, as we noted above. In the intervening years that convergence and stability was severely disturbed, first by the collapse of the Bretton Woods system and the first two oil shocks and second by the expansion of the Community itself to include six new and rather diverse member states. Those two sources of destabilisation are now being overcome.   We have already noted how exchange-rate stability has increased but this process of convergence has been much more widespread including not just nominal variables like price inflation and interest rates but real characteristics of the economy as well.

The creation of an integrated Community involves increasing 'convergence' of economic behaviour in a number of respects - policy, structure and behaviour. If the structure of the various member states is particularly different in terms of patterns of production, trade and structure of assets and liabilities, then their response to external shocks will tend to be different, particularly in terms of prices and employment. We have already cited the case of countries with oil and gas reserves, whose rates of exchange tended to rise as a result of the first and second oil crises, relative to those of their European partners, who did not have such resources. In the same way, a larger exposure to dollar imports has a greater impact on domestic prices from changes in the dollar exchange rate. In these circumstances the adjustment costs to a member state for an external shock may very well be less if it has a separate exchange rate. By varying prices it may be possible to ease the structural adjustment required and reduce the aggregate unemployment cost in the process.

The same inequity in the response may occur if the systems of economic policy are widely different, this may include the degree to which the system of taxes and benefits provides anticyclical support, through the release of investment reserve funds, for example. More important may be the differences in behavioural responses to the same shocks. Some member states are able to come to more consensual decisions about the levels of wage increases that can be afforded under conditions of inflationary pressure and hence adjust to the shock with lower unemployment costs. Each of these differences will both encourage and compel countries to break away from a permanent fixed exchange rate system to ease the costs of adjustment.

Over the 1970s and 1980s these sources of difference have been reduced by the process of integration. Trade patterns have been becoming increasingly dominated by mutual trade, reducing the importance of differences in exposure to foreign currencies. There has also been a measure of integration in the structure of production. However, the new members of the Community substantially reduced the degree of convergence in the short run. We have already noted a number of dissimilarities for the UK. Ireland, Spain, Portugal and Greece also showed clear structural differences, in particular from a greater emphasis on agriculture. The product composition of the latter three countries is of course different in character because of their Mediterranean location. Their policy and behavioural responses were also different. Social provision via the state tends to be lower.

The existence of these differences is a matter of fact but whether they are sustainable in an EMU is also a matter of political decision-making. The process of increasing integration of industry, rule systems, cooperation between governments and other authorities all tend to reduce these differences. In Chapter 4 we discuss whether these differences will be eliminated sufficiently in the run-up to EMU for it to be implemented in practice. Chapter 7 looks at the problems country by country.

However, the main focus of convergence in the popular literature and in the terms of the Maastricht agreement is on a set of nominal variables, including inflation, interest rates, internal and external balance, and public debt ratios. If countries have too high rates of inflation compared with the target level at the time of the final locking of exchange rates they will

18   *Achieving Monetary Union in Europe*

tend to find that the adjustment costs are politically unacceptable. These, however, are principally problems of the transition to EMU rather than of its sustainability or suitability. Similarly countries with high public and external debt ratios will tend to find that the service costs of these debts are difficult to sustain and that actions will need to be taken to reduce them. Here and in the case of the large budget deficit the concern is not just for the adjustment problems of these particular countries but for the burden that they will impose on the others if they fail to adjust.

One last aspect of convergence, or rather the lack of it, has also characterised the 1970s and 1980s. As is shown in chart 1, Spain, Portugal, Greece and Ireland had been steadily closing the gap between their real GDP per head and that of the rest of the Community in the 1960s. Indeed had that rate of convergence continued Spain would by now have closed the gap completely. Since the first oil crisis, however, that process of clear convergence has been absent. In recent years, assisted by the transfers within the EC, Ireland, Spain and Portugal have begun to narrow the gap again, however the gap for Greece has actually widened.

There is no reason why an integrated Community should not operate with the prevailing range of diversities in real incomes and other indicators of the real standard of living. However, integration in itself tends to imply the wish to reduce the extent of such differentials. In the context of the EC, the question at issue is whether the costs of transition for the less advantaged countries will be sufficiently offset by the increased real convergence offered by membership of the Communities. We consider this question in Chapter 5. At this stage, we can merely note, from the experience of the last twenty years, that there is no obvious conclusion that the unaided process of development will lead to a narrowing or widening of differentials. Hence the less advantaged may very well feel that they wish to see more coming from the process of integration than maintenance of the relative status quo.

The basis for Maastricht

In the case of the 'completion of the internal market' and the proposals for economic and monetary union, the political decisions to try to proceed were taken before the economic justifications were presented. Monetary union has been presented as a necessary adjunct to a properly operating single market and it is clear that it offers major microeconomic benefits in its own right, in reducing transactions costs and removing exchange-rate uncertainty between the member states, which should result in clear welfare and growth gains. There will be further macroeconomic improvements from the joint attempt to achieve the aim of monetary stability, particularly for those member states which are particularly inflation prone at present.

What the pattern of European integration since the war has shown is that monetary union has been assigned a high priority within the EC right from the early days. However, it has only been with the continuing integration of the European economies, particularly the progress to the single market and the experience with managing an orderly exchange rate system, that proceeding to EMU has become really feasible rather than a desirable sounding long-run aim. The evolution of that integration over the next few years will show whether that aim is really attainable.

The oil shocks and the long learning process to develop a new order to replace the Bretton Woods system have delayed progress towards monetary union in Europe and revealed not just its difficulty but the ability to overcome those difficulties. EMU offers two major facets in this context, the largely microeconomic extention of benefits from a further step in the process of ever closer union in Europe and the benefit to the macroeconomic policy aim of monetary stability, through the particular structure of the system that has been proposed at Maastricht. This puts the control of inflation as the main aim and is intended to provide the independence to the central banking system necessary to achieve it through the operation of monetary policy and the cooperation of the member state governments in the approriate operation of fiscal policy.

These are considerable ambitions and we consider in the next chapter how the Maastricht agreement plans they should be achieved and the way the argument developed, that resulted in them, following the decision of the Hannover Council in 1988 to set up the Delors Committee.

20   *Achieving Monetary Union in Europe*

Table 1   *History of the Snake*

Date		Change
1972	April	Snake established
	June	£ floated, sterling leaves the snake
	Dec.	Lira leaves
1973	March	Joint float agreed, D-Mark revalued by 3%
	June	D-Mark revalued by 5½%
	Sept.	Guilder revalued by 5%
	Nov.	Norwegian kroner revalued by 5%
1974	Jan.	French franc leaves
1975	July	French franc rejoins
1976	March	French franc leaves;'worm' agreement for narrower bands between Benelux currencies abandoned.
	Oct.	Realignment, D-mark up by 6% against Danish krone, 3% against Swedish krona and Norwegian krone and 2% against Benelux
1977	April	Swedish krona devalued by 6%, Danish and Norwegian kroner by 3%
	August	Swedish krona leaves
		Norwegian and Danish kroner devalued by 5%
1978	Feb.	Norwegian krone devalued by 8%
	Oct.	Realignment, mark up 4% against Danish and Norwegian kroner and by 2% against Benelux
1979	March	EMS comes into effect

Source: *Brooks (1979).*

Chart 1   *The evolution of disparities among the member states*

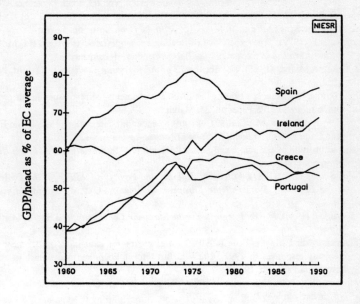

References

Aitken, N.D. (1973), 'The effect of the EEC and EFTA on European trade: temporal cross-section analysis', *American Economic Review*, vol. 63, no. 5, December.

Baer, G.D. and Padoa-Schioppa, T. (1989), 'The Werner Report revisited', in (Delors) *Report on Economic and Monetary Union in the Community*, pp. 53-60.

Brooks, S.J. (1979), 'The experience of floating exchange rates' in Major, R.L.M. (ed), *Britain's Trade and Exchange Rate Policy*, London, Heinemann.

El Agraa, A.M. (ed) (1985), *The Economics of the European Community*, Oxford, Philip Allan.

Gros, D. and Thygesen, N. (1988), 'The EMS: achievements, current issues and directions for the future', CEPS Paper no. 35, March.

Kay, J.A. and Posner, M.V. (1989), 'Routes to economic integration. 1992 in the European Community', *National Institute Economic Review*, no. 129, pp. 55-68.

National Institute of Economic and Social Research (1992), *Single Europe Market Newsletter*, no. 1, January.

Padoa-Schioppa, T. (1987), *Efficiency, Stability and Equity: a Strategy for the Evolution of the Economic System of the European Community*, Oxford, Oxford University Press.

Pelkmans, J. (1984), *Market Integration in the European Community*, The Hague, Martinus Nijhoff.

Shipman, A. and Mayes, D.G. (1990), 'A framework for examining government and company responses to 1992', National Institute of Economic and Social Research Discussion Paper no. 199.

Woolcock, S. (1990), 'US views of 1992', *National Institute Economic Review*, no. 134, November, pp. 86-92.

Name Index